Switching Between Programs with Windows Flip 35

Saving a Document 36

Creating a New Document 37

Opening a File 38

4 **Working with Folders 40**

Working with Explorers 41

Viewing the Contents of Your Computer's Drives 42

Understanding Windows Preset Folders 43

Understanding an Explorer Window 44

Navigating Folders 46

Selecting a Folder 48

Changing the View of the Window Contents 49

Sorting the Contents of a Window 50

Customizing the Explorer Window Layout 51

Grouping Content 52

Creating a New Folder 53

Copying Folders 54

Moving Folders 55

Renaming Folders 56

Deleting Folders 57

5 **Working with Files 58**

Working with Files 59

Selecting Files 60

Viewing File Details 61

Renaming a File 62

Moving a File 63

Copying a File 64

Copying a File Using the Send To Command 65

Deleting a File 66

Undeleting a File from the Recycle Bin 67

Opening a File from an Explorer 68

Setting File Associations 69

Printing a File from an Explorer 70

Using Instant Search 71

Saving Searches 72

Running a Saved Search 73

Adding a Tag to a File 74

Adding Other Properties to a File 75

6 Working with Printers 76

Viewing Available Printers 77

Adding a Printer 78

Displaying Installed Printers 82

Setting the Default Printer 83

Setting Printing Preferences 84

Viewing Printer Properties 86

Previewing a Document before Printing 87

Printing a Document 88

Viewing the Print Queue 90

Canceling a Print Job 91

Viewing Fonts 92

Installing New Fonts on Your Computer 94

7 Working with Scanners or Digital Cameras 96

The Windows Photo Gallery 97

Setting Up a Scanner or Camera Automatically 98

Transferring Images from a Digital Camera 99

Setting Up a Scanner or Digital Camera Manually 100

Using the Windows Photo Gallery to Organize Pictures ... 102

Copying Pictures to a CD or DVD 103

Fixing Photographs 104

Printing Photographs 106

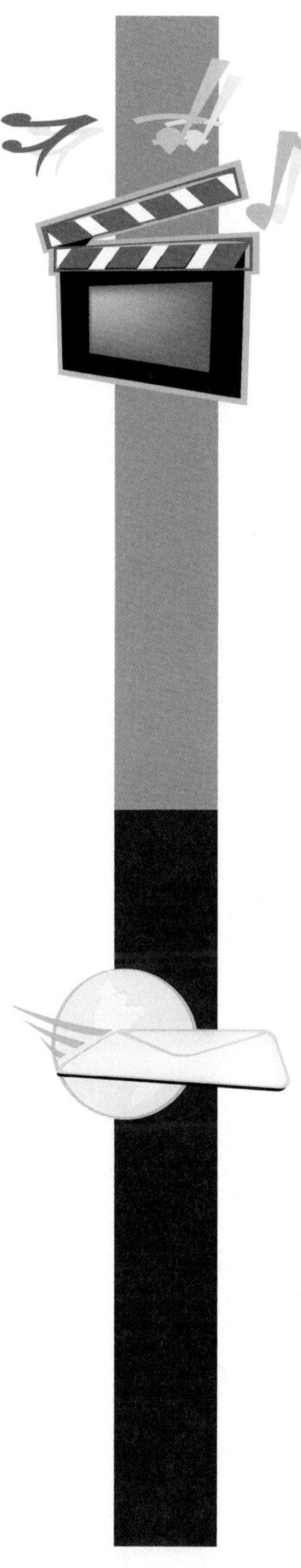

8 Entertainment 108

Windows Media Player 109

Playing an Audio CD 110

Understanding the Windows Media Player Window 111

Working with Media Player Controls 112

Playing Another Audio Track 113

Setting Volume Options for Audio Input and Output Devices 114

Changing the Visualizations 115

Using the Library 116

Searching for Music 117

Finding and Buying Music Online 118

Creating a Playlist 120

Copying (Ripping) CD Tracks 122

Burning (Creating) a CD 123

Playing a Video Clip 124

Playing Games 125

9 Sending Email 126

Windows Mail 127

Starting Windows Mail 128

Reading Mail 130

Replying to Mail 131

Forwarding a Message 132

Sorting Messages 133

Creating and Sending New Mail 134

Attaching a File 136

Opening a File Attachment 137

Deleting Messages 138

Cleaning Out the Deleted Items Folder 139

Setting Email Options 140

Adding Addresses to Your Contacts List 142

Using Your Contacts List to Enter Names 144

Creating Mail Folders 145

Moving Messages to Folders 146

Searching for a Message 147

Configuring Your Fax 148

Creating and Sending a Fax 150

Managing Junk Mail (Spam) 151

Setting Junk Mail Options in Windows Mail 152

10 Browsing the Internet 154

The Internet Explorer 7 Window 155

Starting Internet Explorer 156

Browsing with Links 158

Typing an Address 159

Viewing Tabs 160

Searching the Internet from MSN 161

Searching the Internet Using a Search Engine 162

Adding a Site to Your Favorites Center 163

Organizing Your Favorites Center 164

Going to a Site in Your Favorites Center 165

Rearranging Your Favorites Center 166

Using the History List 168

Clearing the History List 169

Setting Your Internet Explorer Home Page 170

Emailing a Page or Link 171

Previewing and Printing a Web Page 172

11 System Security and User Accounts 174

Windows Security Center 175

Checking System Security with Windows Security Center 176

Starting and Scanning with Windows Defender 177

Setting Windows Defender Options 178

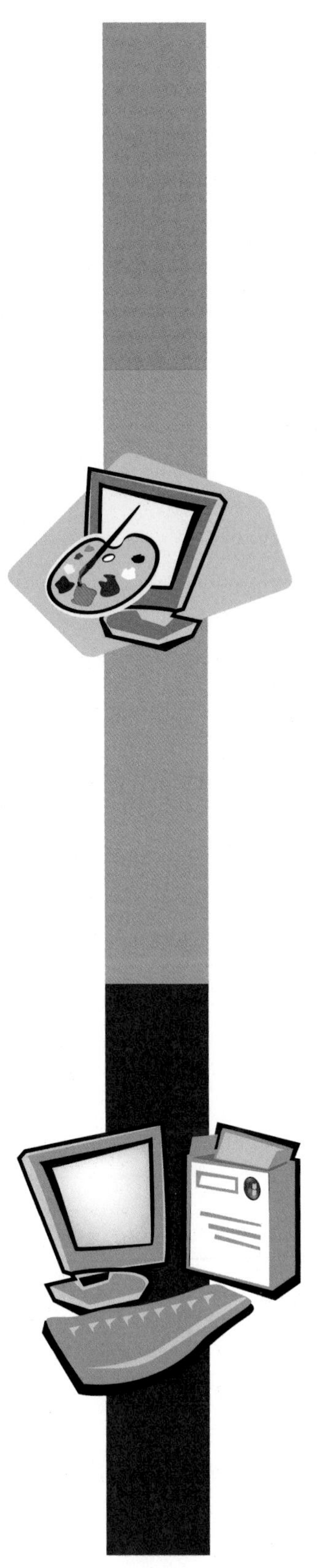

Checking the Virus Status on Your Computer 180

Turning On or Off Firewall Protection 182

Checking a Web Site for Phishing 183

Blocking Pop-Ups 184

Setting Internet Privacy Levels 185

Setting Up Windows for Multiple Users 186

Adding a Password to the User Account 188

Setting Parental Controls 190

12 Personalizing Windows 192

Personalization Control Panel 193

Selecting a Desktop Theme 194

Changing the Color Scheme 195

Applying a Background Color to the Desktop 196

Applying a Background Image to the Desktop 197

Choosing a Screen Saver 198

Setting Resolution and Color Quality 199

Changing How the Mouse Works 200

Changing the Sound Scheme 202

Changing the System Date and Time 204

Using Accessibility Options 206

13 Setting Up Programs 210

Programs and Features Control Panel 211

Installing a New Program 212

Creating a Program Shortcut Icon 213

Uninstalling Applications 214

Deleting a Shortcut Icon 216

Pinning a Program to the Start Menu 217

Customizing the Start Menu 218

Customizing the Taskbar 220

Changing the Notification Area 222

Displaying or Hiding Toolbars 223

Setting Default Programs 224

Setting AutoPlay Options 225

14 Performance and Maintenance 226

Windows Vista Control Panel's System and Maintenance Category 227

Controlling Windows Updates 228

Updating Windows Manually 230

Setting Power Options 231

Displaying System Information 232

Displaying Disk Information 234

Cleaning Up Unnecessary Files 235

Saving Space by Compressing Files 236

Using Compressed Files 238

Using the Memory Diagnostic Tool 239

Scanning Your Disk for Errors 240

Configuring the Defragment Feature 242

Scheduling Tasks 244

Installing New Hardware Manually 248

Viewing and Troubleshooting Installed Hardware 250

Protecting Your PC with System Restore 252

Backing Up Files 254

Restoring BackUp Files 256

15 Using Windows Accessories 258

Using Accessories 259

Using the Calculator 260

Adding New Contacts 261

Editing Contact Information 262

Finding a Contact 263

Grouping Contacts 264

Deleting a Contact 266

Viewing Your Calendar 267

Scheduling an Appointment 268

Changing Calendar Views 270

Entering a Task 271

Using WordPad 272

Typing Text 273

Selecting Text in a WordPad Document 274

Deleting Text 275

Copying Text 276

Moving Text 278

Formatting Text 280

Using Notepad 282

Using Paint 283

Drawing a Shape with Paint 284

Adding Text to a Drawing 285

Adding Color to a Drawing 286

Erasing Part of a Drawing 287

16 Home Networking Basics 288

Using the Network Map Feature to Create a Diagram of Your Network 289

Setting Up a Wireless Network Client 290

Setting Sharing Options 294

Viewing Network Status 296

Viewing Network Folders and Files 298

Setting Up a Network Printer 300

Selecting a Shared Printer 302

Transferring Files and Settings from Another PC 304

Glossary 312

Index 320

EASY MICROSOFT® WINDOWS VISTA™

U.S. International Standard Book Number: 0-7897-3577-6

U.K. International Standard Book Number: 0-7897-3659-4

This Book Is Safari Enabled

The Safari® Enabled icon on the cover of your favorite technology book means the book is available through Safari Bookshelf. When you buy this book, you get free access to the online edition for 45 days. Safari Bookshelf is an electronic reference library that lets you easily search thousands of technical books, find code samples, download chapters, and access technical information whenever and wherever you need it.

To gain 45-day Safari Enabled access to this book:

- Go to http://www.quepublishing.com/safarienabled
- Complete the brief registration form
- Enter the coupon code A4FD-U1UG-YY6J-SCG8-VDPG

If you have difficulty registering on Safari Bookshelf or accessing the online edition, please e-mail customer-service@safaribooksonline.com.

Library of Congress Cataloging-in-Publication Data

O'Hara, Shelley.
Easy Windows Vista / Shelley O'Hara. – 1st ed.
p. cm.
Includes index.
ISBN 0-7897-3577-6
1. Microsoft Windows (Computer file) 2. Operating systems (Computers) I. Title.
QA76.76.O63O349144 2007
005.4'46—dc22

2006031870

Printed in the United States of America

First Printing: December 2006

09 08 07 06 4 3 2 1

TRADEMARKS

All terms mentioned in this book that are known to be trademarks or service marks have been appropriately capitalized. Que Publishing cannot attest to the accuracy of this information. Use of a term in this book should not be regarded as affecting the validity of any trademark or service mark.

Microsoft is a registered trademark of Microsoft Corporation. Windows Vista is a trademark of Microsoft Corporation.

WARNING AND DISCLAIMER

Every effort has been made to make this book as complete and as accurate as possible, but no warranty or fitness is implied. The information provided is on an "as is" basis. The author and the publisher shall have neither liability nor responsibility to any person or entity with respect to any loss or damages arising from the information contained in this book.

BULK SALES

Que Publishing offers excellent discounts on this book when ordered in quantity for bulk purchases or special sales. For more information, please contact

U.S. Corporate and Government Sales
1-800-382-3419
corpsales@pearsontechgroup.com

For sales outside of the U.S., please contact

International Sales
international@pearsoned.com

Associate Publisher
Greg Wiegand

Acquisitions Editor
Michelle Newcomb

Development Editor
Laura Norman

Managing Editor
Gina Kanouse

Project Editor
George E. Nedeff

Copy Editor
Elise Walter

Indexer
Julie Bess

Proofreader
Karen A. Gill

Technical Editors
Mark Hall
Vince Averello

Publishing Coordinator
Cindy Teeters

Interior Designer
Anne Jones

Cover Designer
Anne Jones

Page Layout
Nonie Ratcliff

ABOUT THE AUTHOR

Shelley O'Hara is the author of more than 120 books, including the best-selling *Easy Windows XP* and other top-selling titles. She has published books on everything from the philosopher Nietzsche to how to buy and sell a house to a kids' book for the iPod. Her main focus is teaching beginning users how to use technology, including Windows. She has a BA in English from the University of South Carolina and an MA in English from the University of Maryland.

DEDICATION

To one of my best and life-long friends, Jerome C. Hanley. Things are on their way up, I promise.
—Shelley

ACKNOWLEDGMENTS

Thanks to Michelle Newcomb and her infinite patience in dealing with the bazillion setbacks on this project. I also appreciate the help and insight from Todd Brakke and Laura Norman, developmental editors; Georgius for his superior project management skills, his willingness to troubleshoot problems, and most important his keen wit; Elise Walter for her excellent editing; and Mark Hall, technical editor, for his review.

—Shelley O'Hara

WE WANT TO HEAR FROM YOU!

As the reader of this book, *you* are our most important critic and commentator. We value your opinion and want to know what we're doing right, what we could do better, what areas you'd like to see us publish in, and any other words of wisdom you're willing to pass our way.

As an associate publisher for Que Publishing, I welcome your comments. You can email or write me directly to let me know what you did or didn't like about this book—as well as what we can do to make our books better.

Please note that I cannot help you with technical problems related to the topic of this book. We do have a User Services group, however, where I will forward specific technical questions related to the book.

When you write, please be sure to include this book's title and author as well as your name, email address, and phone number. I will carefully review your comments and share them with the author and editors who worked on the book.

Email: feedback@quepublishing.com

Mail: Greg Wiegand
Associate Publisher
Que Publishing
800 East 96th Street
Indianapolis, IN 46240 USA

READER SERVICES

Visit our website and register this book at www.quepublishing.com/register for convenient access to any updates, downloads, or errata that might be available for this book.

IT'S AS EASY AS 1-2-3

Each part of this book is made up of a series of short, instructional lessons, designed to help you understand basic information.

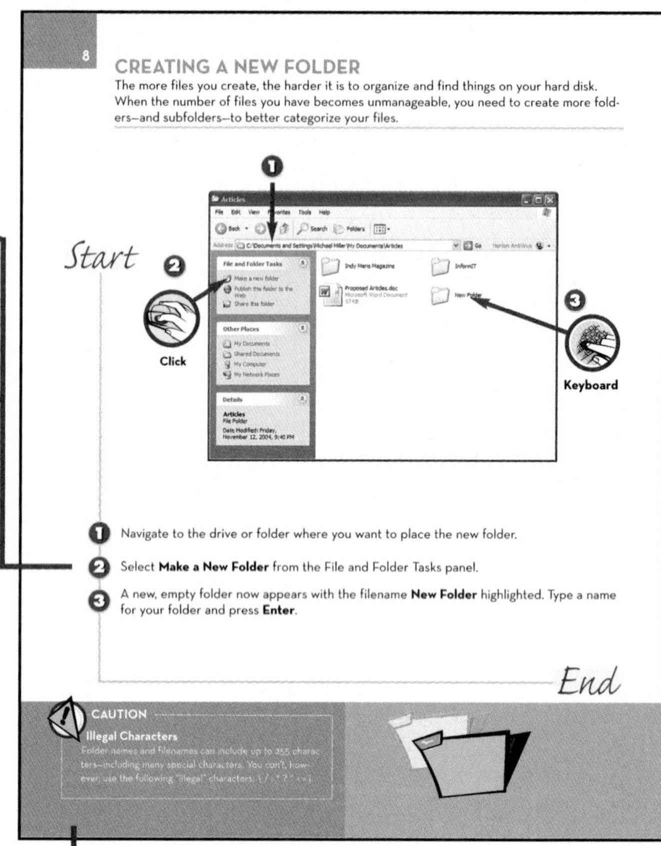
8

CREATING A NEW FOLDER

The more files you create, the harder it is to organize and find things on your hard disk. When the number of files you have becomes unmanageable, you need to create more folders—and subfolders—to better categorize your files.

1. Navigate to the drive or folder where you want to place the new folder.
2. Select **Make a New Folder** from the File and Folder Tasks panel.
3. A new, empty folder now appears with the filename **New Folder** highlighted. Type a name for your folder and press **Enter**.

End

CAUTION

Illegal Characters

Folder names and filenames can include up to 255 characters—including many special characters. You can't, however, use the following "illegal" characters: \ / : * ? " < > |.

1. Each step is fully illustrated to show you how it looks onscreen.
2. Each task includes a series of quick, easy steps designed to guide you through the procedure.
3. Items that you select or click in menus, dialog boxes, tabs, and windows are shown in **bold**.

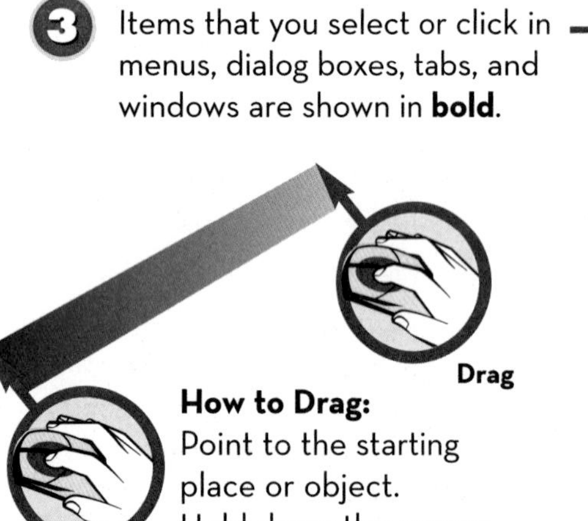

How to Drag:
Point to the starting place or object. Hold down the mouse button (right or left per instructions), move the mouse to the new location, and then release the button.

Tips, notes and cautions give you a heads-up for any extra information you may need while working through the task.

Click:
Click the left mouse button once.

Keyboard

Click & Type:
Click once where indicated and begin typing to enter your text or data.

Selection:
Highlights the area onscreen discussed in the step or task.

Double-click:
Click the left mouse button twice in rapid succession.

Right-click:
Click the right mouse button once.

Pointer Arrow:
Highlights an item on the screen you need to point to or focus on in the step or task.

INTRODUCTION TO EASY MICROSOFT WINDOWS VISTA

Becoming familiar with a new operating system, such as Windows Vista, can seem like a daunting task. There's so much to learn! And in this new version of Windows, there are so many different features; the interface looks different, commands aren't where you expect them to be, the entire way things work has seemingly been overhauled, all with the goal of making things easier. And they *will* be easier ... after you learn how Windows Vista is set up and how it works.

When you sit down to use a computer, you don't want to spend your time staring at it, hoping to figure out how to send a simple email. You want to be able to start right away; you want to take advantage of all the cool things you see advertised. Sending pictures of your children or grandchildren, listening to music and burning your own CD collection of your favorite tunes, watching movies, and so on, are all easily accomplished if you have the right foundational understanding of how to use Windows.

That's why *Easy Windows Vista* comes in so handy: it provides concise, visual, step-by-step instructions for showing you how to do the things you want to do with your computer. And while it's perfect for beginners, it's also ideal for anyone upgrading to this new version of Windows.

In this book, you'll start with a quick overview of what is new in Vista and then move straight into the basics of getting around and getting things done. You'll learn how to start programs, the main reason you have a computer. (A program is what you use to "do" things on your computer—send email, browse the Internet, write letters, edit photographs, and so on.) Plus, you'll discover so much more—how to play games, how to purchase music online and then burn it to a disk, and how to get pictures from your digital camera to your computer and then print or email them.

In addition, you'll find out how to maintain your computer to avoid problems, protect your computer from viruses and other security concerns, improve your computer's performance, personalize your computer so that it works the way you want, and expand its capabilities (like adding a printer or setting up a network).

All the skills you need to use your computer and Windows Vista are covered and in an easy-to-follow, visual format that gets you up and running with Windows Vista in no time.

As for using this book, you can read it cover to cover or use it as a reference when you encounter a problem or a feature you don't know how to use. Either way, *Easy Microsoft Windows Vista* lets you see it done and then do it yourself. Here's to happy computing!

1

part

WHAT'S NEW IN MICROSOFT WINDOWS VISTA

Vista is the newest version of Microsoft Windows. Introduced in 2007, this version includes a major overhaul to the interface from the desktop to the content windows (now called Explorers). The goal of Vista is an interface that's easier to use, more consistent, and more intuitive.

Finding files easily is also a big priority with this version. Starting with the Instant Search feature included on the Start menu and in other places, and including special Search folders, Windows seeks to make finding not only documents but all kinds of information (music, movies, email messages, and so on) easier.

Beefed up security features are another benefit in Vista. As computers have become more popular, potential security risks and the need for caution have become more important. You need to protect against viruses, phishing (when someone tries to gather personal information from you without your knowledge or consent), spyware, and more. Windows Vista includes features to address each of these security concerns; it also offers ongoing updates so that new threats are taken care of as soon as possible.

In addition to design changes and security upgrades, you'll find other fun and useful features, including the Windows Photo Gallery, a new Games folder, updated Media Center, and more.

While Vista may take some time getting used to you'll find that in no time you'll be taking advantage of all the new features, especially with the guidance of this book, which shows you how to use this new interface, step-by-step.

Part 1 gives you an overview and highlights of the new features; later Parts cover how to use these features in more detail.

THE WINDOWS VISTA INTERFACE (AERO)

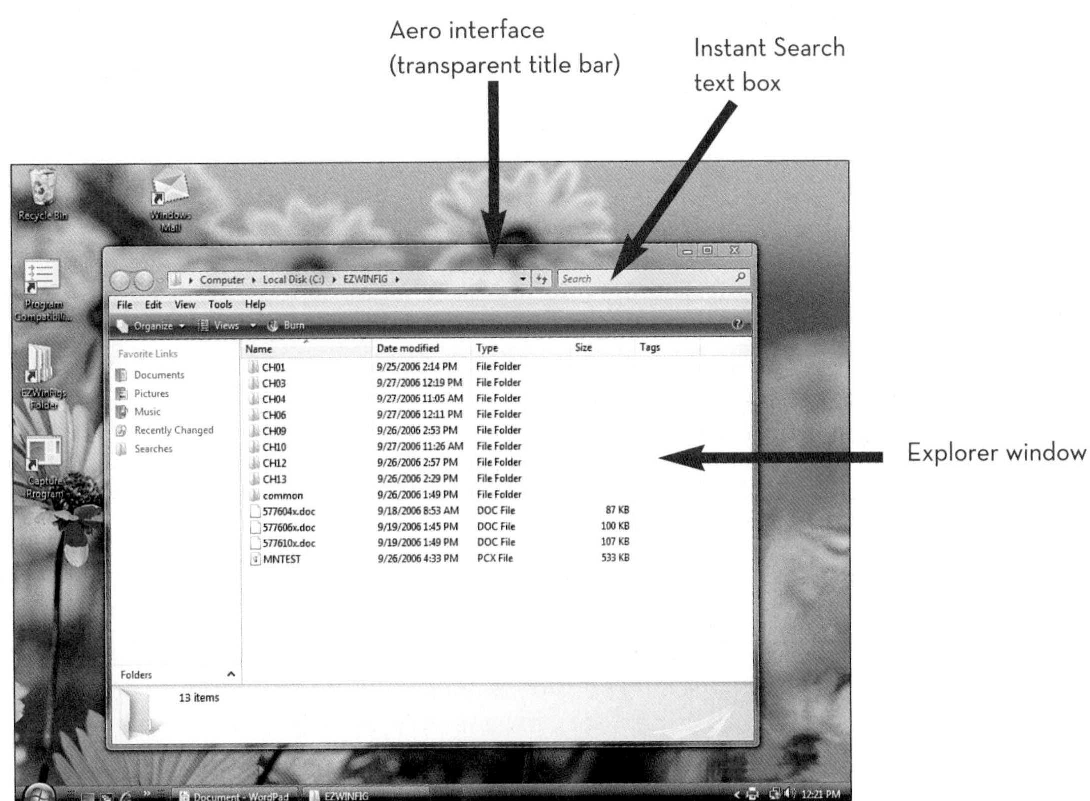

NEW INTERFACE

The updated desktop is the first thing you'll notice with Windows Vista. And if you have the Premium or Business version of Windows, you'll notice the new Aero Glass, which makes parts of windows transparent so that you can see through to other windows and the desktop. The Start menu also has been revamped.

Start

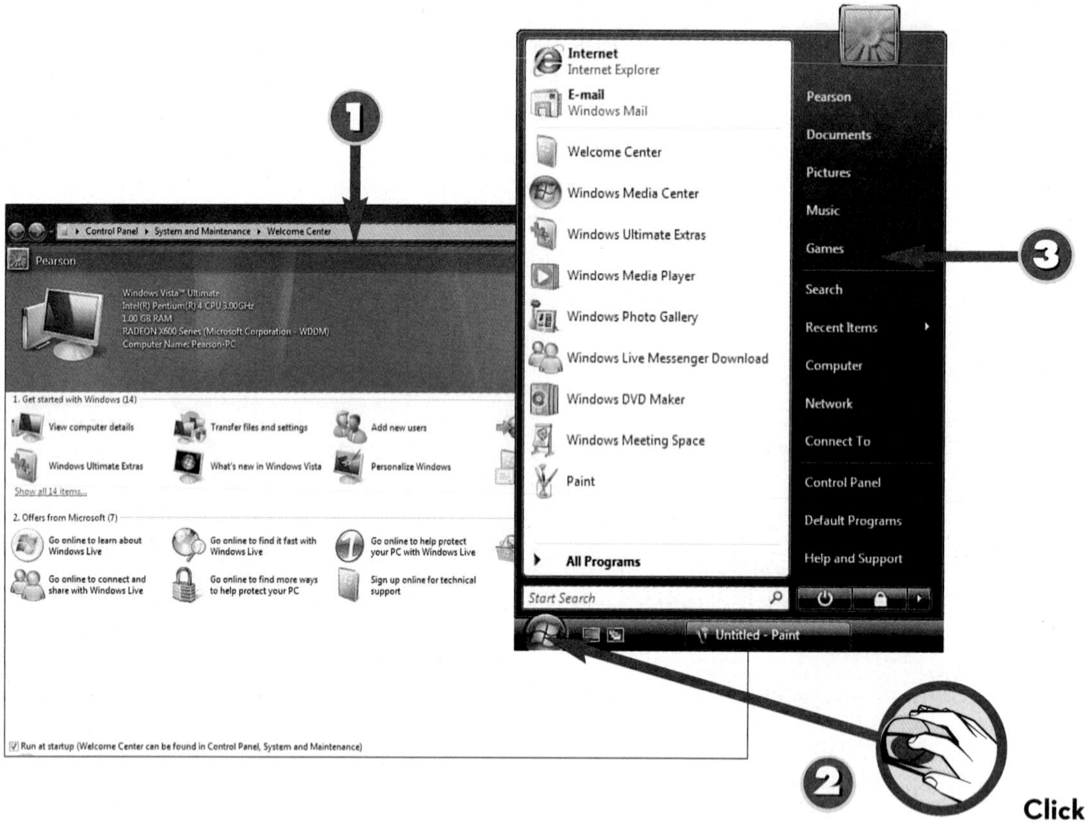

Click

1. The new Aero interface provides a streamlined cool open environment.
2. Click the **Start** button to view the Start menu. It no longer includes long cascading menus to list all installed programs. When you select a program folder, it simply updates and lists programs in the left pane. Like past versions, some programs are listed by default. You can also display all programs by clicking the **All Programs** button.
3. The right pane of the Start menu provides access to commonly used folders, as well as familiar commands such as the Control Panel.

End

TIP

Aero

If your system doesn't have the graphics required to display the Aero interface or you don't have a version of Windows that supports this interface, you'll see a simplified version of the Windows Vista interface.

REDESIGNED EXPLORERS

Windows Vista has also updated its content windows so that they are consistent. These Explorers are what you use to find, view, and manage documents, photos, and email messages. They are also used to display and manage devices and Control Panel options.

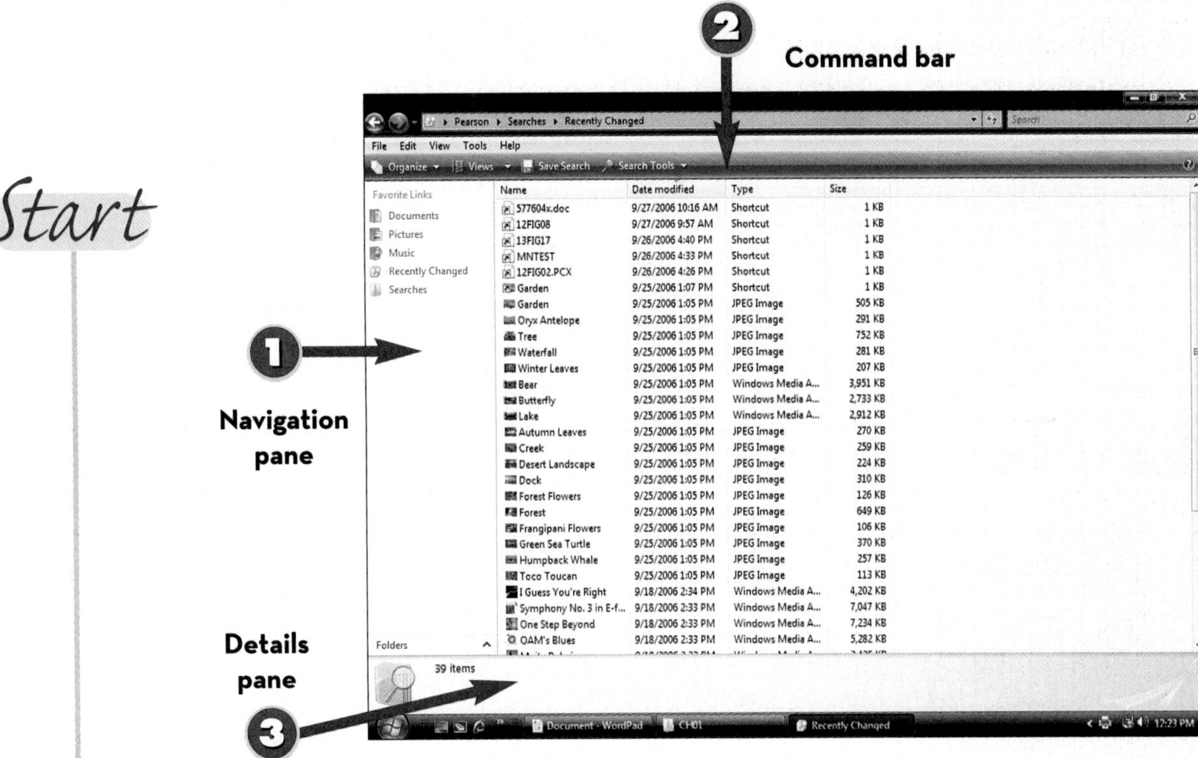

1. The Navigation pane includes commonly accessed folders so that you can switch to other folders and view their content.
2. The command bar (like task panes in previous versions of Windows) includes commands that are relevant to the content of the Explorer windows. For instance, if you are working with photos, you'll see commands and features for managing photos.
3. The Details pane appears at the bottom of the window and displays file properties (so that you no longer have to open a separate File Properties dialog box).

End

TIP

Preview Pane

Some programs and folders also include a Preview Pane so that you can preview the contents of a document without opening it.

TIP

Exploring Vista

The really nice thing about Explorer windows is that the consistent format, after you get used to it, will make using your computer much easier. No matter where you go in Vista, you'll see the same familiar window.

FINDING FILES SIMPLIFIED

Finding files is a task that many users spend a lot of time on. Where did you save that file? How could it have disappeared? Have aliens snatched it? It's frustrating because you *know* the document or email message or program is somewhere on your computer. But where is it? Windows Vista provides several new features for finding files of all types.

Start

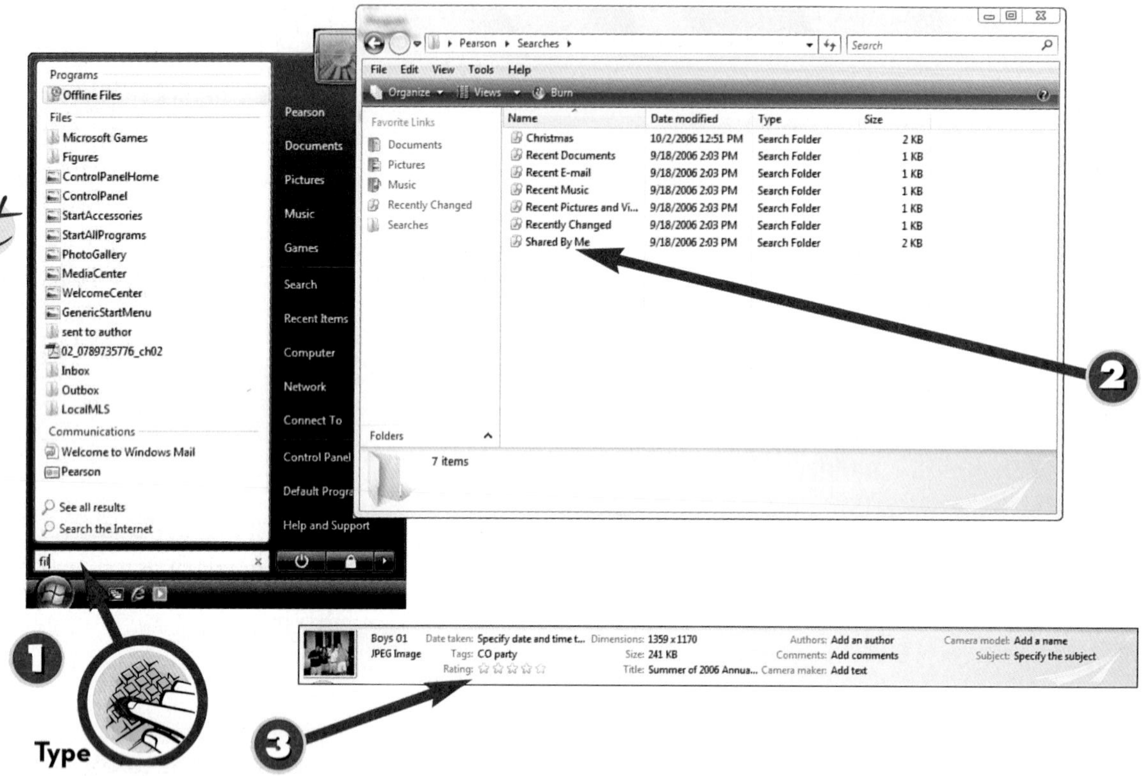

Type

1 The new **Instant Search** feature is included on the Start menu so that you can easily search from this main menu. You can search for documents, applications, email messages, music, and all other types of computer content.

2 **Search Folders** give you easy access to items stored in different locations. Rather than reorganize documents, worksheets, images, and so on so that they are stored in one place, you can keep them in their original locations but create and save a search. When you want to work with the same set of files, you simply open the folder to run this search again.

3 To help manage files and associate similar files, you can assign tags or keywords to files. Doing so provides more options for searching for and finding files as well as organizing them.

End

HINT

Instant Searches

You can find the Instant Searches feature in Explorer windows and other locations in Vista, not just the Start menu. This search feature also enables you to search for a file by file-name, keyword or tag, or text contained within a file.

TIP

Predefined Search Folders

Windows comes with some predefined search folders that you can use right away. For example, Recent Documents shows you all the documents you have recently worked on.

UPDATED ENTERTAINMENT AND MEDIA FEATURES

Windows Vista also recognizes that many people use their computers for entertainment—to play music, watch movies, manage photos, and more. Therefore, Windows includes new features and revamped elements of existing features to help organize and manage your media.

Start

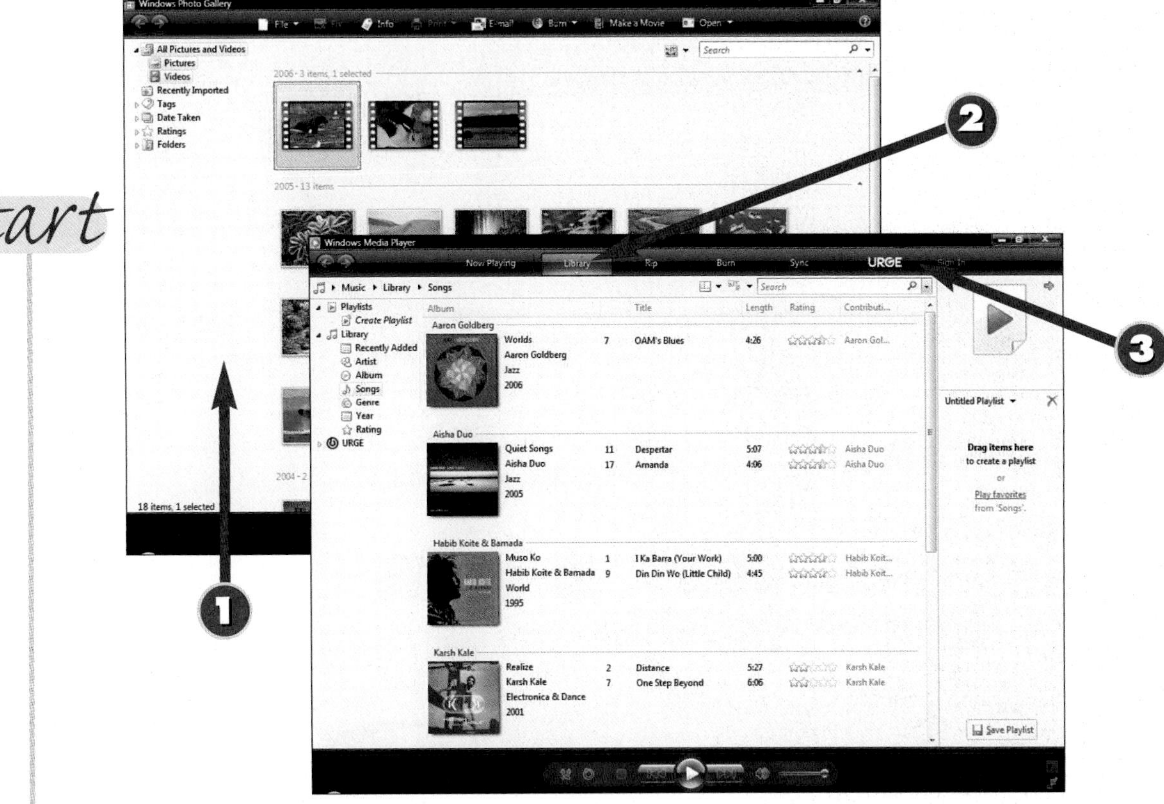

1. **Windows Photo Gallery** helps you find and organize your photos and videos. Combined with other new features, such as tags, you can help better identify (and then group) items.
2. The **Media Library** in Windows Media Player has also been enhanced, making it easy to locate media (music, videos, and so on). You can also customize album art and track artist and CD information more easily.
3. Windows has teamed up with MTV's URGE, a new digital music service; URGE is integrated with Windows Media Player and makes finding and buying music online easier (or at least gives you more options).

End

HINT

Photo Editing

Windows Photo Gallery also includes some simple photo-editing functions for cropping, rotating, removing red eye, and making color adjustments.

HINT

Games Folder

The Games folder has also been revamped, and Windows has added parental controls for keeping track of what games are allowed (or forbidden).

NEW AND IMPROVED ACCESSORIES

New accessories (and newly named accessories) are also included with Windows Vista. Calendar and Contacts should be familiar, but Gadgets is something entirely new.

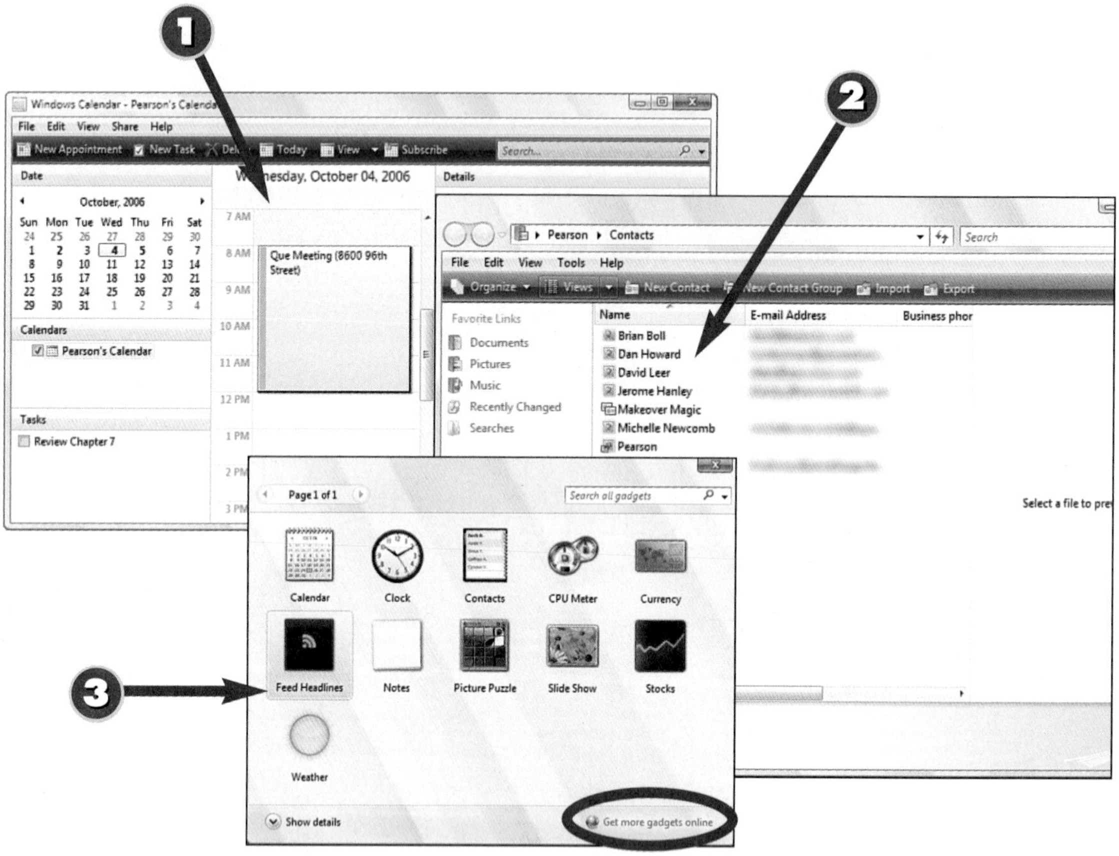

1. **Windows Calendar** lets you set up appointments and events; it also includes a task list so that you know what you need to get done by what deadline.
2. The **Contacts List** has been revamped, and entries are now simply called Contacts. You can keep as little (such as email addresses) or as much data as you want to manage (such as work information, mailing addresses, and so on).
3. **Gadgets** are new mini-applications that include a calendar, a clock, contacts, news headlines, stocks, weather, and a slide show of images that can be delivered to your desktop. Windows comes with some preset Gadgets that you can experiment with, and there are more you can download.

TIP

Sharing Calendars

You can share calendars with other family members on your home network. You can also post calendars on the Internet if you want others to have access to your plans.

ENHANCED INTERNET FEATURES

Really Simple Syndication (RSS) a new feature of the Internet, means that information feeds, like weather updates and sports scores is sent to your computer automatically on a regular basis without your having to search for it. You'll also find tabbed browsing and live previews of other new features worth exploring. Finally, Internet security has been overhauled and improved.

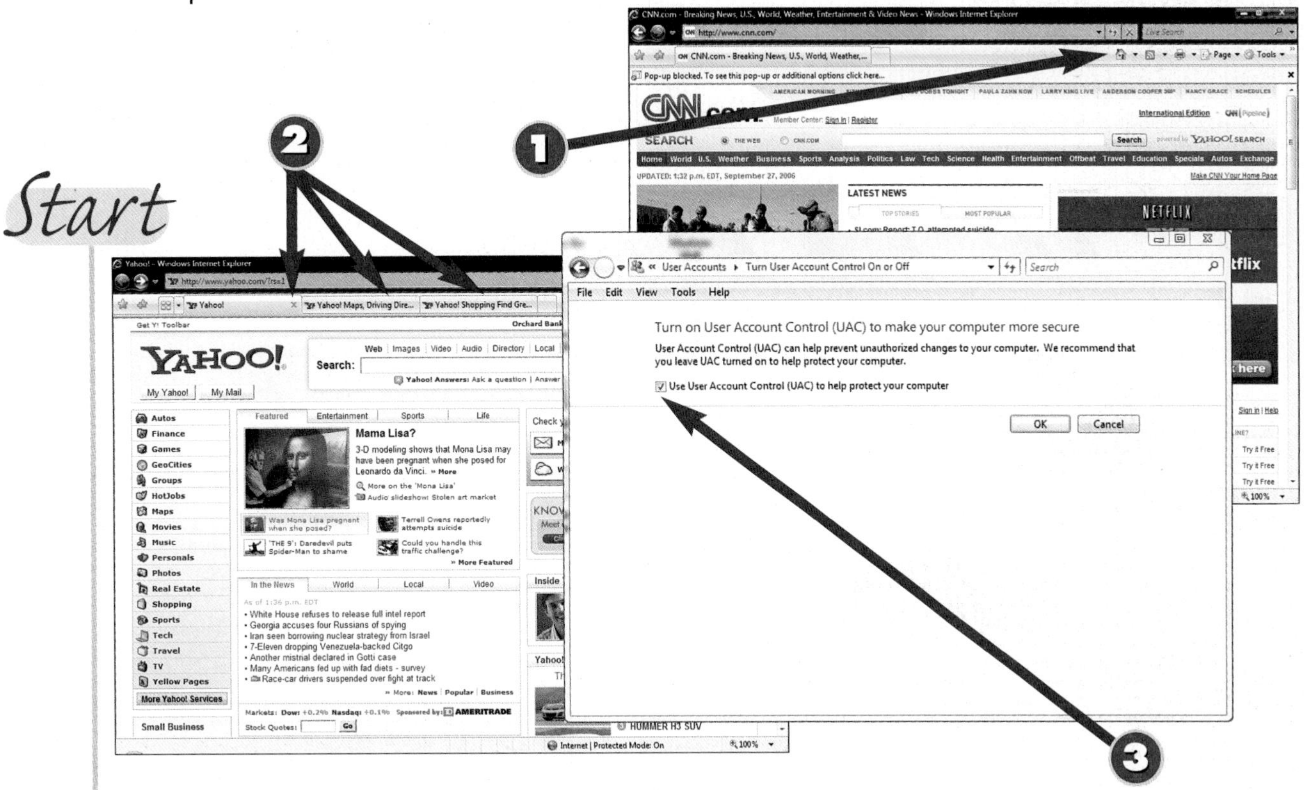

Start

1. If a Web page has live RSS feeds available, the Feeds icon appears in color, and you can click it to access feeds.
2. Tabbed browsing lets you view tabs of several links; you can switch among the tabs to view different pages or sites.
3. Internet security has also been beefed up in many ways, including User Account Control, which prevents attacks and hijacked settings.

End

TIP

User Account Control (UAC)

UAC provides protection in other areas as well, keeping programs from automatically installing without your permission.

REDESIGNED WINDOWS MAIL

The mail program in Windows Vista is no longer named Outlook Express but is now called Windows Mail. Like other elements of Windows, Windows Mail includes improved features, such as those that help you locate messages. Security features for blocking spam and handling phishing are also improved functions in Windows Mail.

Start

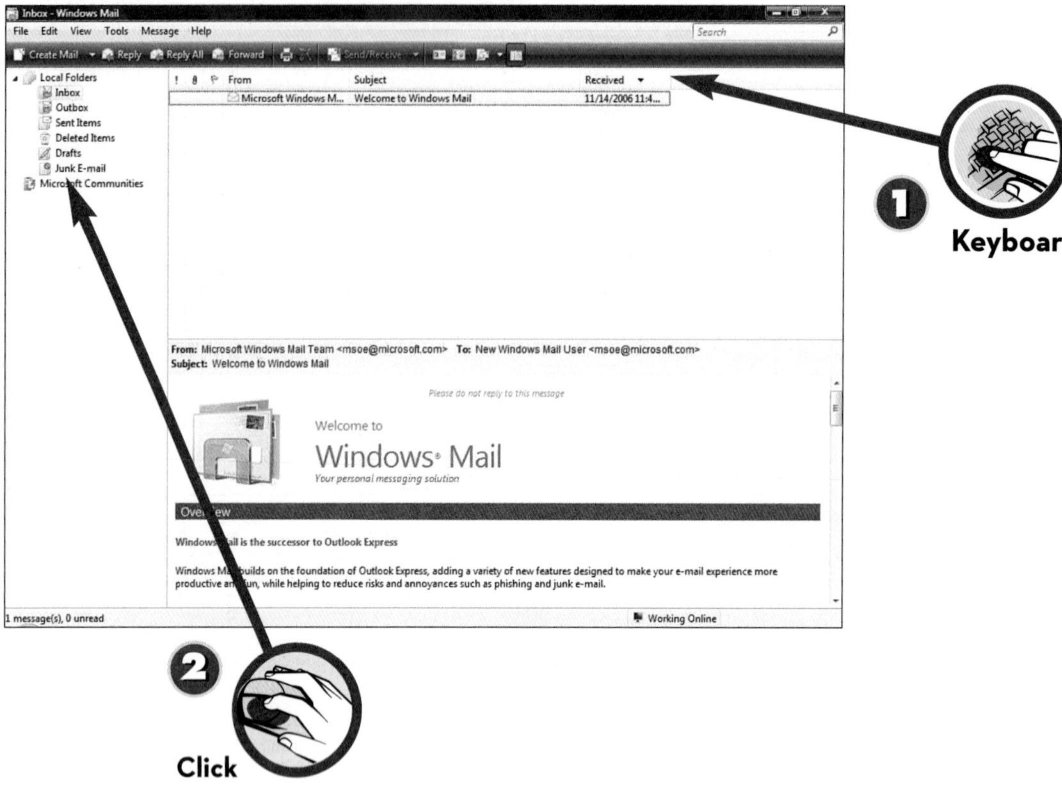

1. Type in the **Instant Search** field to search and find mail messages quickly.
2. Junk mail (spam) is not only annoying but can also include malicious programs. Windows Mail includes features for handling junk mail.
3. Phishing filters also provide security, making sure that you aren't providing personal data to persons you don't intend.

CAUTION

Phishing Defined

Phishing scams attempt to get you to give out personal information for what seems like a perfectly legitimate reason. You may get an email from a trusted financial organization or what seems like a legitimate company you've worked with (such as eBay). These messages include links that then prompt you for personal information. Windows Mail filters analyze and detect these

EXPANDED NETWORK FEATURES

More and more computer users are setting up and using networks to share data, printers, and Internet connections. Windows Vista has greatly expanded its network features for managing and securing the network.

Start

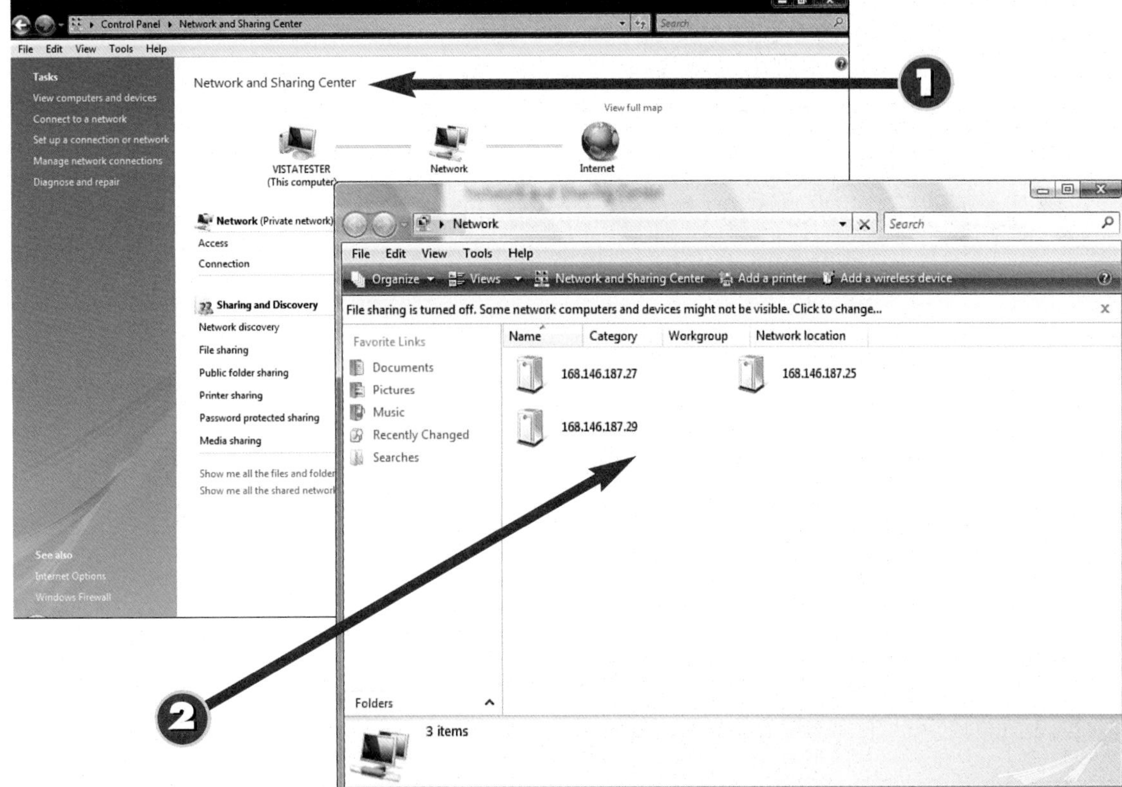

1. **Network and Sharing Center** is the central place for checking your connection status and troubleshooting any connection problems.
2. **Network Explorer**, like other Explorers, makes it easy to share files and to view all of the PCs, devices, and printers connected to the network.

End

TIP

Sharing Wizard

Windows includes a Sharing Wizard that helps you set up access to documents and devices that are shared on the network.

TIP

Network Diagnostics and Awareness

Network Diagnostics can help you troubleshoot problems with network connectivity. With Network Awareness, your computer can report to applications any changes to network connectivity and make appropriate changes.

GETTING STARTED

You don't need to do anything to start Windows Vista other than turn on your computer—Windows Vista starts automatically. You are then prompted to log on, and after logging on, you see a screen called the *desktop*. The desktop is your starting point. Here you find key tools for working with your computer. From your Windows desktop, you can use shortcut icons or the Start menu to start programs and open documents, open control panels to make changes to your setup, and more.

For customization changes, for instance, you can change the color of your desktop or use an image. See Part 12, "Personalizing Windows," for more information. You can also set up new programs, pin programs to your Start menu, and make changes to your program setup; these changes are covered in Part 13, "Setting Up Programs."

This Part describes what you see on your desktop and explains some key skills for working with Windows Vista.

THE WINDOWS VISTA DESKTOP

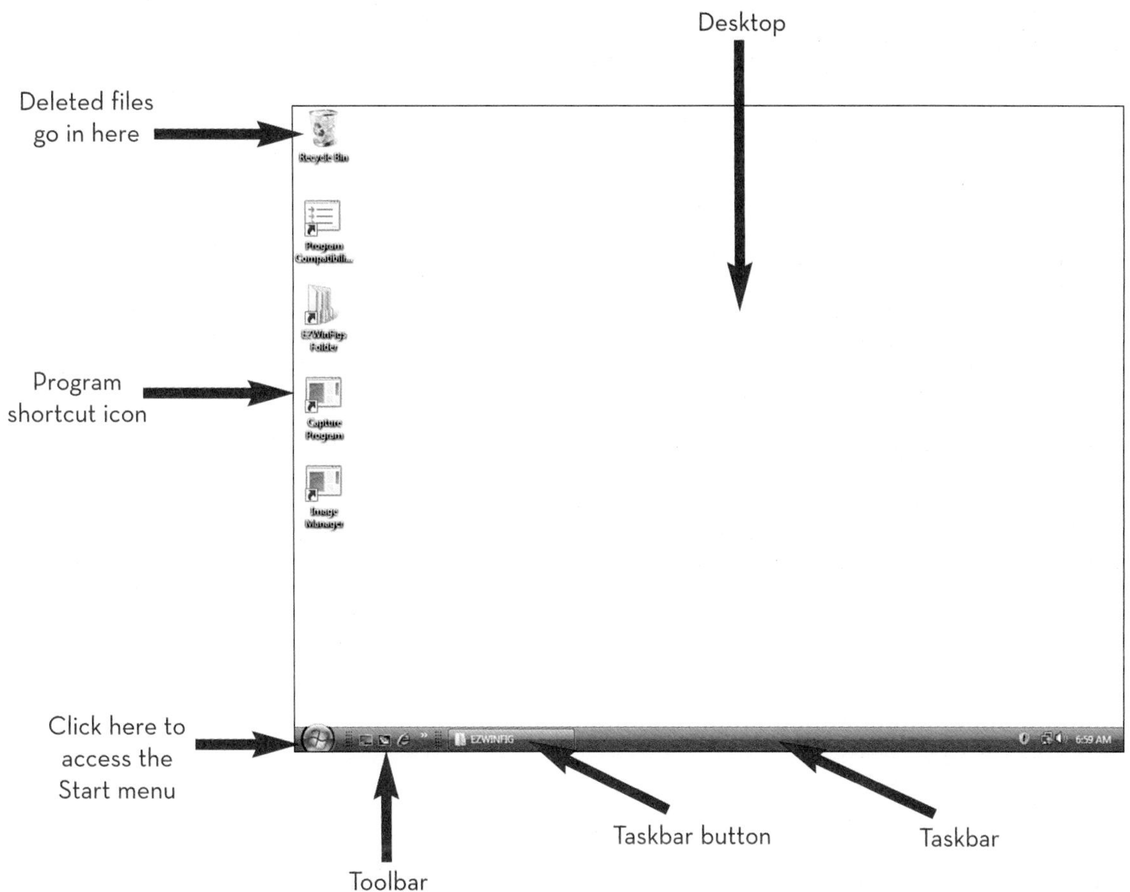

LOGGING ON TO THE COMPUTER

Windows uses accounts to keep track of the different individuals who may use a computer. If you are the only one using the computer, you'll have just one account. You can select this account to log on. If you have several accounts, you can select which account to log on with.

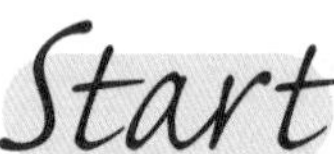

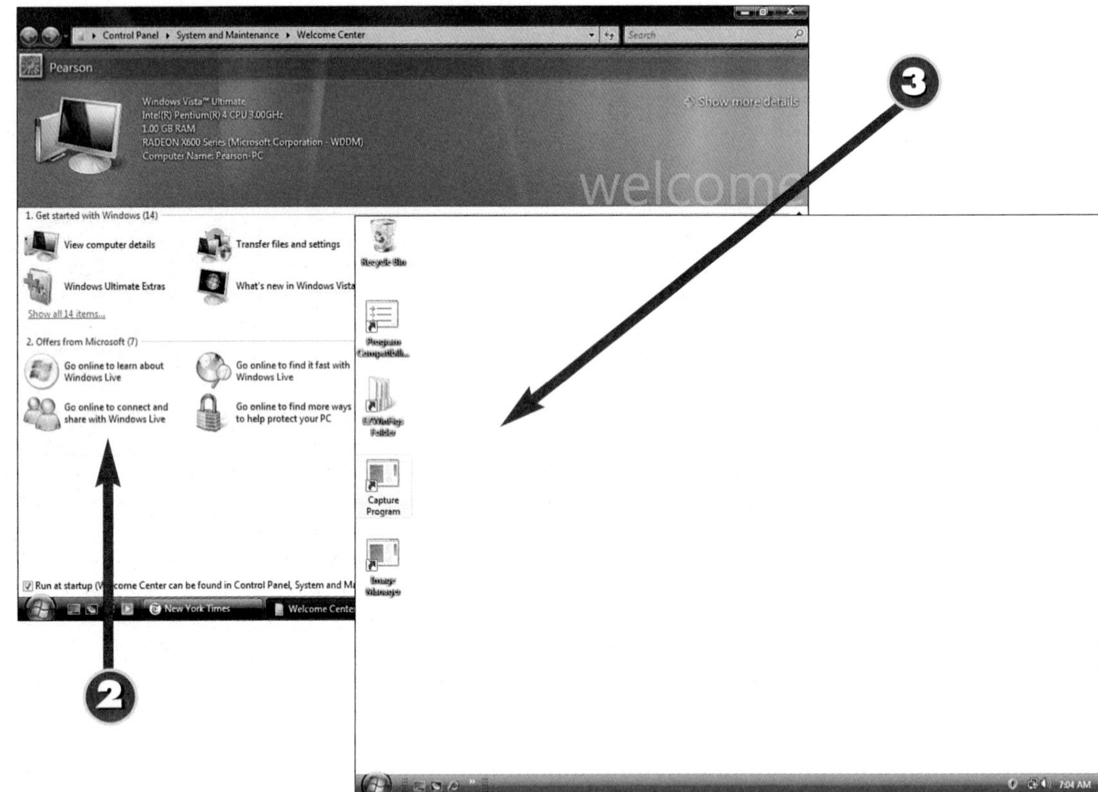

1. Turn on the computer and click the arrow next to your account (not shown).
2. You are logged on and see the Welcome Center. Choose any of these options or click its **Close** button.
3. You see your desktop.

TIP

Adding a Password

You can add a password to your account as a security measure. For more information on passwords and setting up other accounts, see Part 11, "System Security and User Accounts.",

TIP

Turning Off the Welcome Center

If you want to go directly to your desktop and skip the Welcome Center, uncheck **Run at startup** in the Welcome Center.

UNDERSTANDING THE DESKTOP

The desktop is your starting place, what you see when you first start your computer and Windows. This opening screen provides access to all the programs and files on your computer. This task introduces the main parts of your desktop.

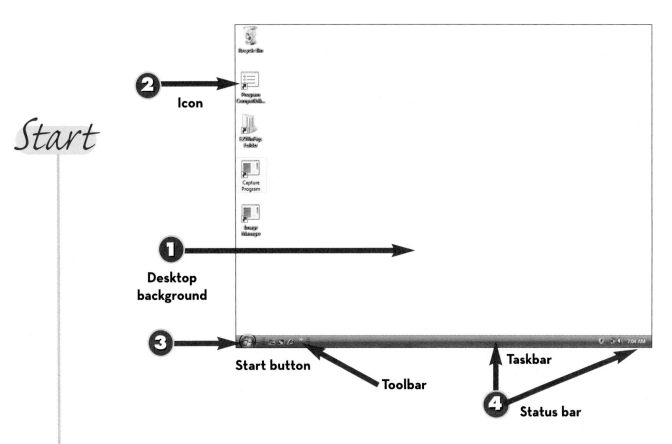

2 Icon

1 Desktop background

3 Start button

Toolbar

Taskbar

4 Status bar

Start

1. The **desktop background** is the area where icons are placed.
2. Desktop **icons** provide access to commonly used programs, folders, and files. Some icons are displayed by default. You can add other icons.
3. The **Start** button is where you access programs and open folders.
4. The **taskbar** displays buttons for open windows and programs. The status bar part of the taskbar displays the date and status icons. The toolbar part of the taskbar provides quick access to programs.

End

NOTE

Change the Desktop Background

You may see a picture for your background rather than a plain screen. You can change the picture used as well as the colors for the desktop. See Part 12 for more help on changing the appearance of the desktop.

NOTE

Add Desktop Icons

Windows usually displays only the Recycle Bin on the desktop. Your computer's manufacturer may have also added icons for accessing help or free trials to online programs. In any case, you can also display folders and program icons. Part 13 explains how to add shortcut icons.

UNDERSTANDING THE START MENU

The Start menu is the "launching pad" for using your computer. This is where you can access common programs, folders, recently used documents, settings for changing the way your computer works, and more. If you had a previous version of Windows, the Vista Start menu looks and works a little differently. If you are new to Windows, this task gives you details on what the Start menu contains.

Start

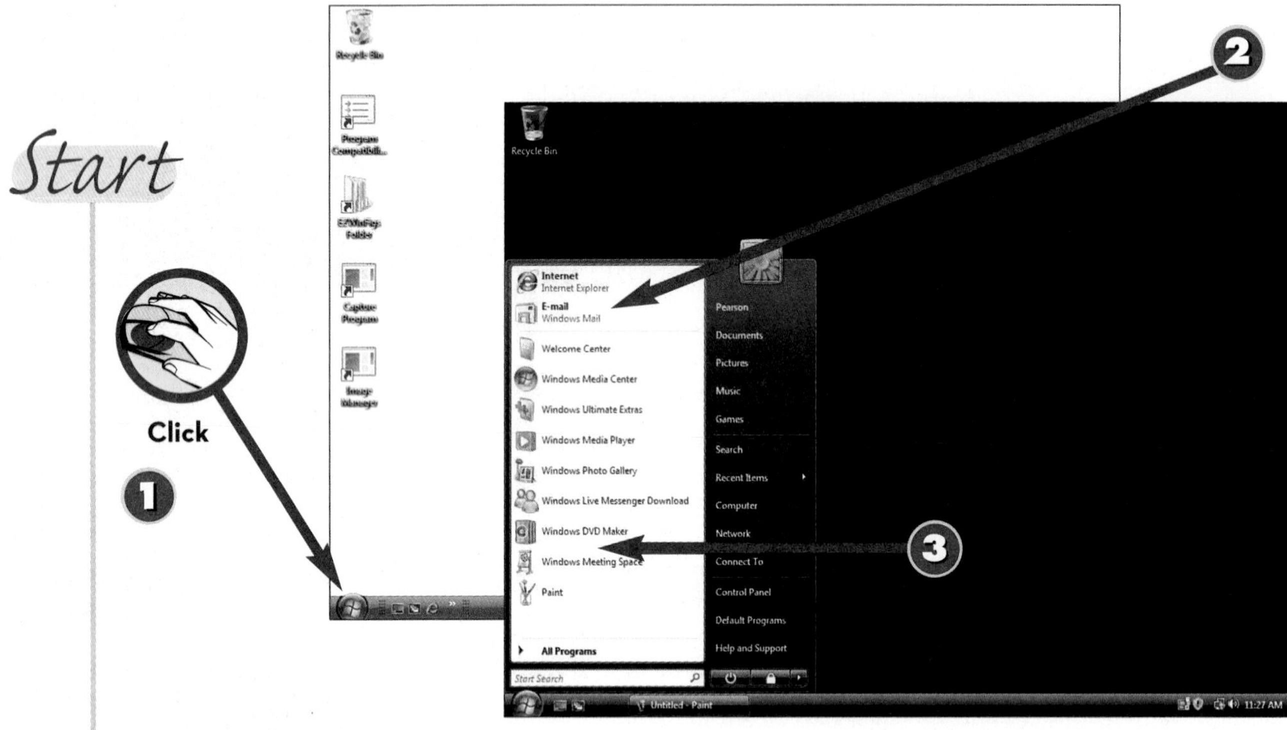

1. To open the Start menu, click the **Start** button.
2. At the top of the menu, you can list frequently used programs so that they are quickly available. You can click the program to start it.
3. Other frequently used programs are listed on the bottom-left side of the Start menu. You can click any of the listed programs to start that program.

Continued

NOTE

It's Still the Start Button

If you are familiar with other versions of Windows, one thing you'll notice right away about the Start button is that it no longer says "Start" on the button. The Vista Start button is actually the button with the Windows logo in the lower-left corner of the desktop.

4 To view all programs on your system, click **All Programs**. You learn more about starting programs in Part 3, "Working with Programs."

5 All the programs that are installed on your computer appear in the list. Some programs are contained within folders (such as Accessories). Click a folder to access the programs within it.

6 On the right side of the Start menu, you have access to commonly used folders. You can also access the Control Panel, default program, and help.

7 These buttons enable you to lock, log off, and turn off the computer.

End

NOTE

Different Menu

What you see in your Start menu will be different from what appears here. You see the programs you use frequently.

TIP

Control Panel

The Control Panel lets you customize different components of Windows Vista, such as the desktop appearance, the mouse, the printer, security, and other features. You learn more about using the Control Panel in other parts of this book.

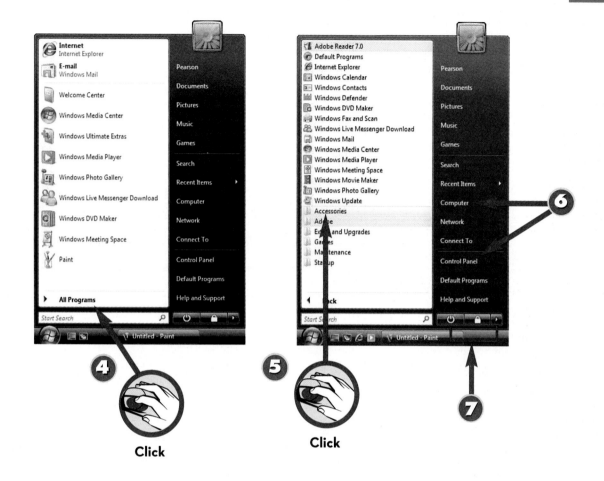

MAXIMIZING, RESTORING, AND MINIMIZING WINDOWS

You can maximize the window so that it fills the entire screen. If a window is maximized and you want to return it to its original size, you can restore it. You may also want to reduce (minimize) a window so that it is still available as a taskbar button but is not displayed on the desktop. You might want to minimize a window to temporarily move it out of your way but keep it active for later use.

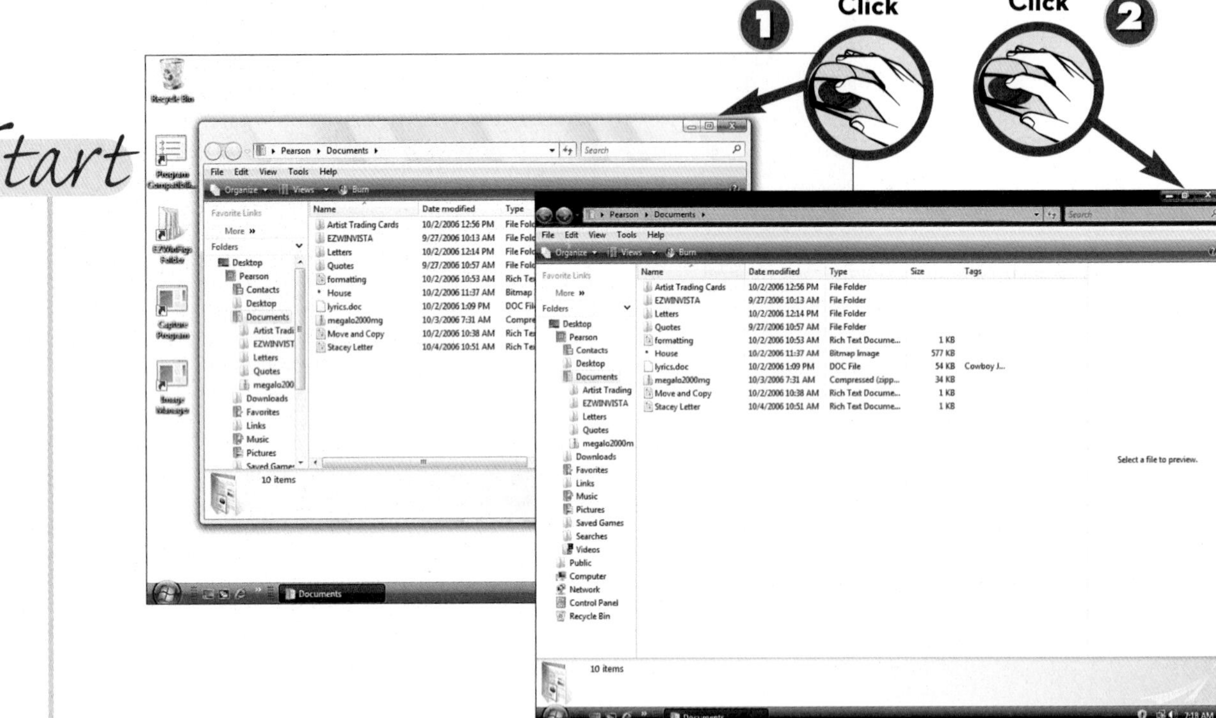

1. To maximize a window, click the **Maximize** button.
2. The window fills the screen, and the **Maximize** button turns to a Restore button. To restore the window, click the **Restore Down** button.

Continued

TIP

Moving and Resizing Windows

Note that when a window is maximized, it does not have borders, so you cannot move or resize it, as covered in the next tasks. To resize or move a window, you must restore it so that it has borders.

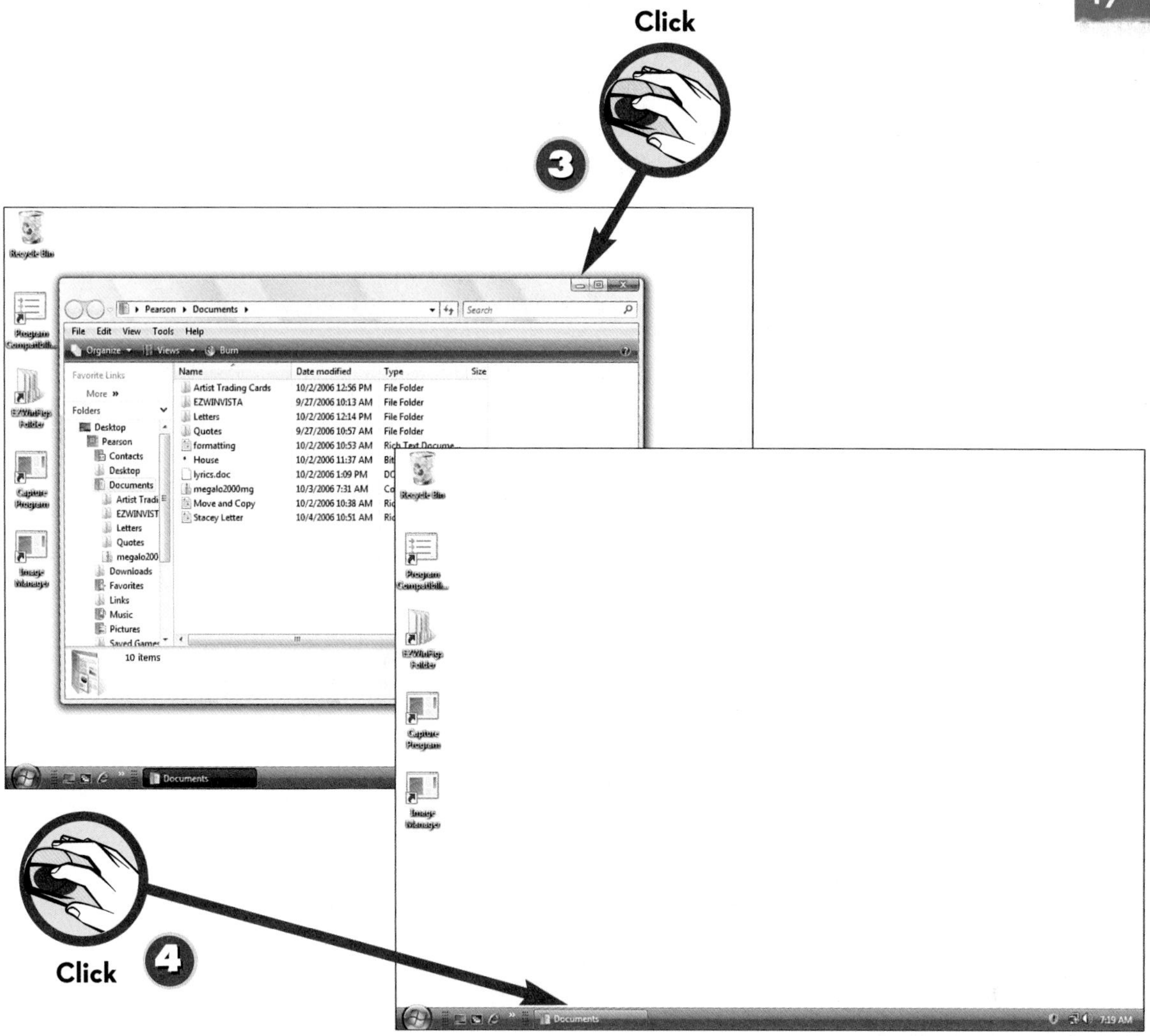

Click

3

Click 4

3 To minimize a window, click its **Minimize** button.

4 The window is still open but appears only as a taskbar button. You can click this taskbar button to display the window again.

End

TIP

Use Commands

You can also access these same features from a menu in program windows. Click the icon in the upper-left corner; the icon varies depending on the program. You see a drop-down menu. You can then select the appropriate command: Restore, Move, Size, Minimize, Maximize, or Close.

MOVING A WINDOW

As you open more applications, folders, shortcuts, and so on, you'll need more room to display these windows on the desktop. You can easily move windows around so that you can see more open windows at one time.

Click and hold

Drag

Start

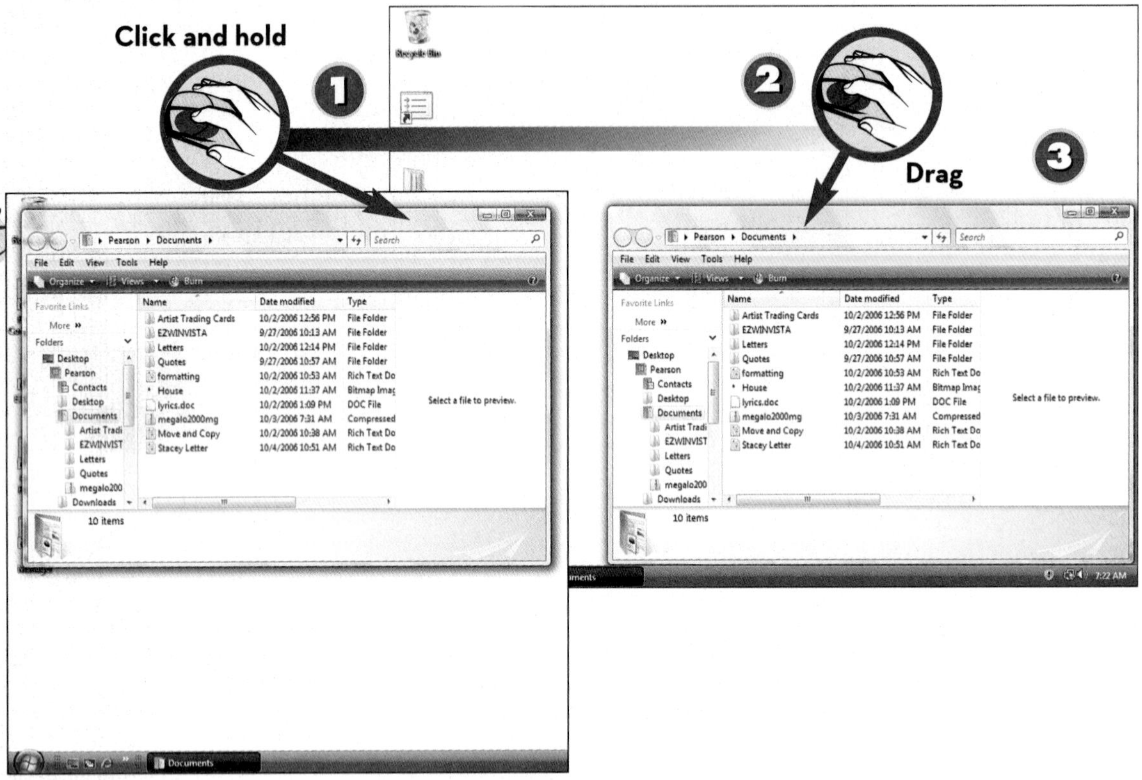

1. To move an open window, point to its title bar. Click and hold down the mouse button.
2. Drag the window to a new position.
3. Release the mouse button. The window and its contents appear in the new location.

End

TIP

The Title Bar

Be sure to point to the top row of the window, the title bar. If you point to any other area, you might resize the window instead of moving it.

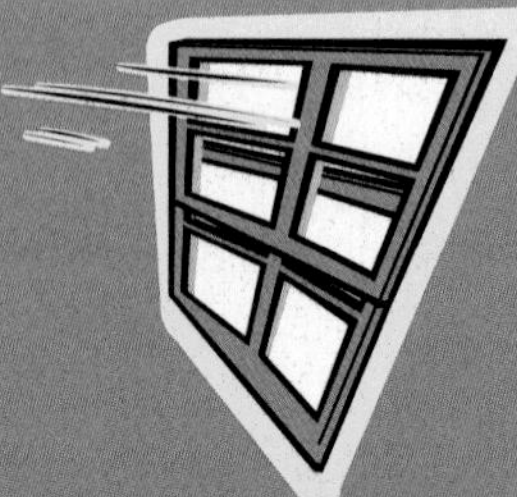

RESIZING A WINDOW

If you want to see more or less of the window, you can resize it.

Start

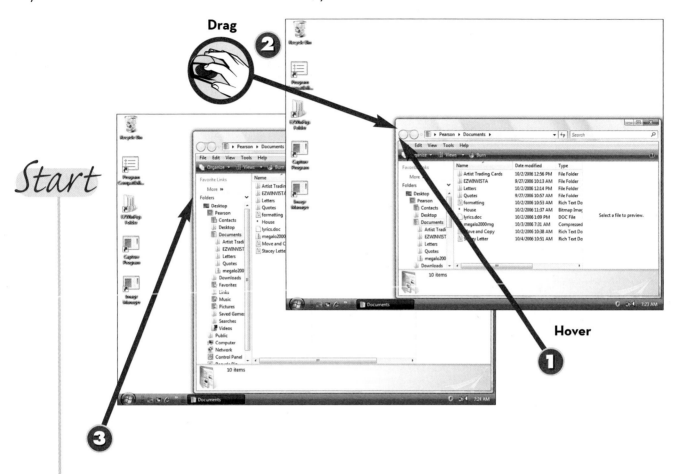

1. Make sure the window is restored (not maximized), and hover the mouse over any window border. You should see the cursor change to a double-headed arrow pointing out the directions in which you can size the window.
2. Drag the border to resize the window, and then release the mouse button.
3. The window is now resized.

End

TIP
Resize from Corner

You can drag a corner of the window to proportionally resize both dimensions (height and width) at the same time.

TIP
Scroll Through a Window

If a window is too small to show all its contents, *scrollbars* appear along the edges of the window. You can use these bars to scroll through the window and view the other window contents. You can click the scroll arrows to scroll in that direction or drag the scroll box to scroll more quickly through the contents.

CLOSING A WINDOW

When you are done working in a window, you can close it. Doing so removes it from the desktop and frees up any system resources used to display the contents.

Click

Start

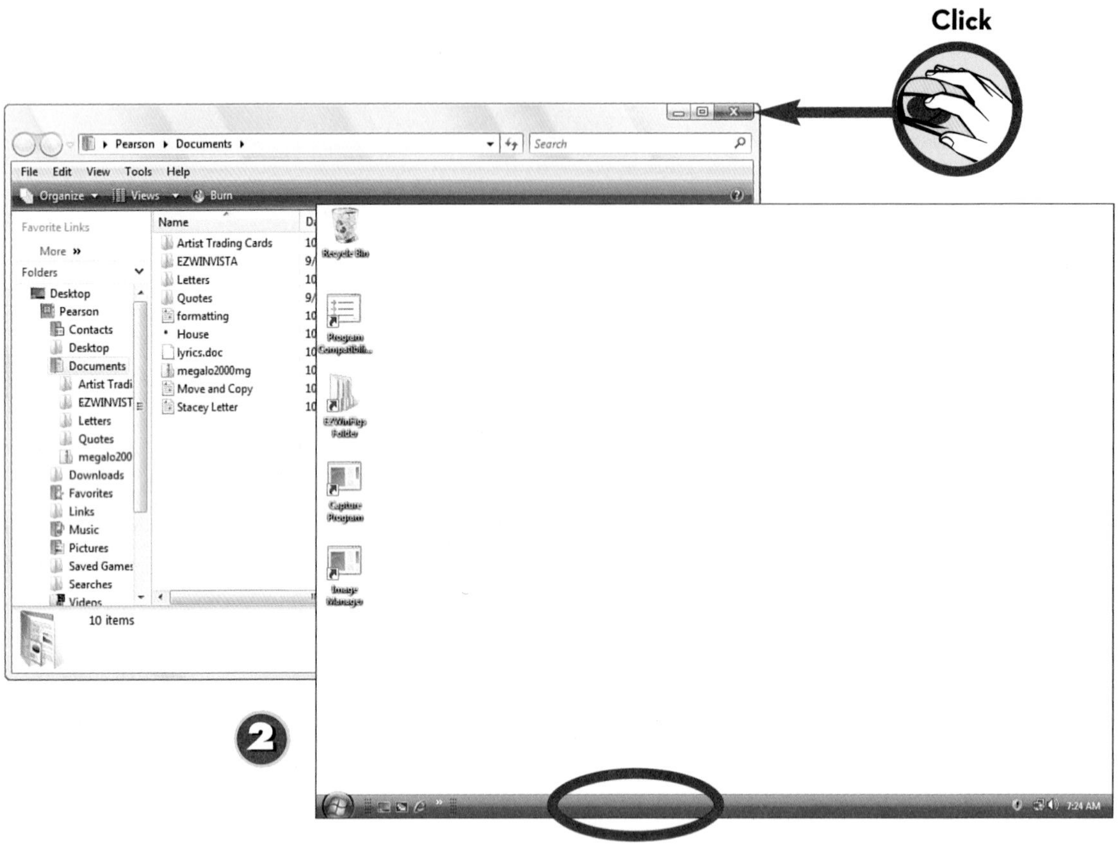

1. Click the **Close** button of an open window.
2. The window is closed. Notice also that there is no longer a button for the window in the taskbar.

End

TIP

Use the Taskbar Button

You can also use the taskbar button for the window to close, move, resize, minimize, or maximize the window. To do so, right-click on the taskbar button and then select the desired command from the shortcut menu.

ARRANGING OPEN WINDOWS

As you work, you will often have several windows open on the desktop at one time. The windows probably overlap each other, which can make it difficult to find what you want. To make your work easier and more efficient, Windows enables you to arrange the windows on the desktop in several different ways.

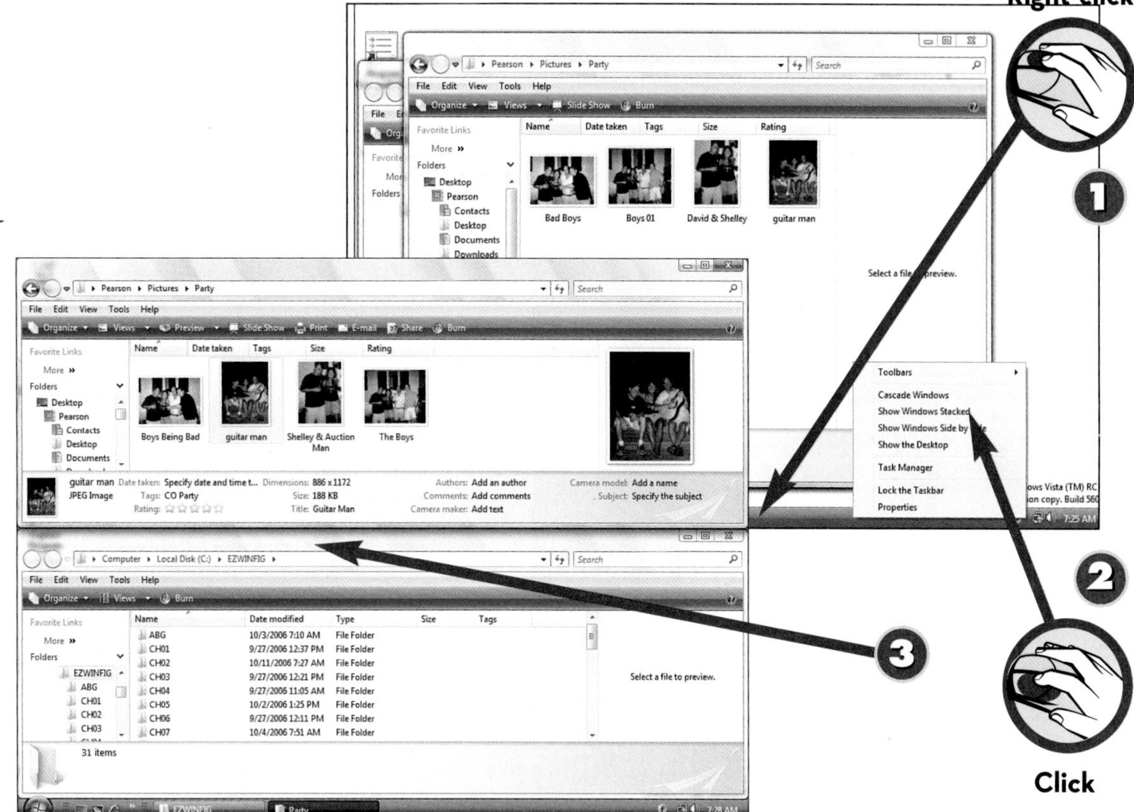

1. With multiple windows open on the desktop, right-click a blank area of the taskbar.
2. Click the arrangement you want. You can stack them, arrange them side by side, or cascade them.
3. Windows arranges the windows; here they are stacked.

End

TIP

Right-Click a Blank Part

When choosing a window arrangement, be sure to right-click a blank area of the taskbar, not a button.

TIP

Undo

Undo the arrangement by right-clicking again and choosing the **Undo** command.

GETTING HELP

You can use the Windows Help command to get help on common topics. You can click a link for Windows Basics or Troubleshooting to get specific answers on those topics, or you can click Table of Contents to view a list of the help topics that are available on the site. You can even view what's new in Windows Vista by clicking the What's new? icon. This task covers using the Table of Contents link.

Start

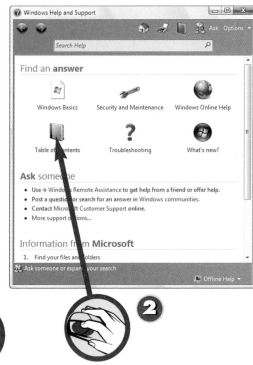

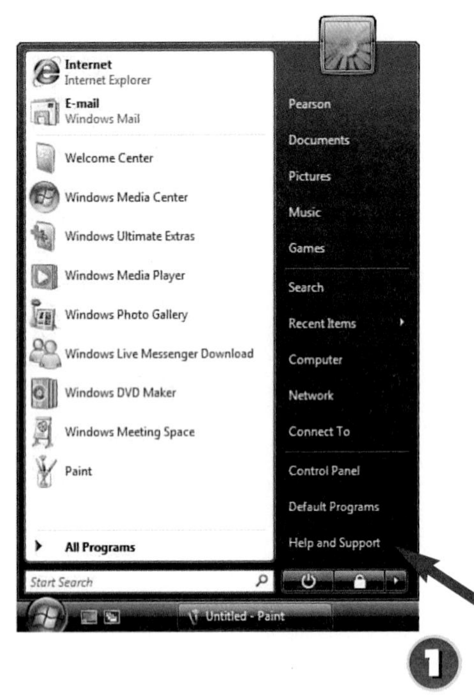

Click

Click

1. Click **Start** and then **Help and Support**.
2. Click **Table of Contents**.

Continued

TIP

Search for Help

As an alternative to browsing the contents, you can search for help. You can even search online. Type the topic in the Search box, and then click the **Search** button.

TIP

Go Back

Click the **Back** button to go back to the previous help page.

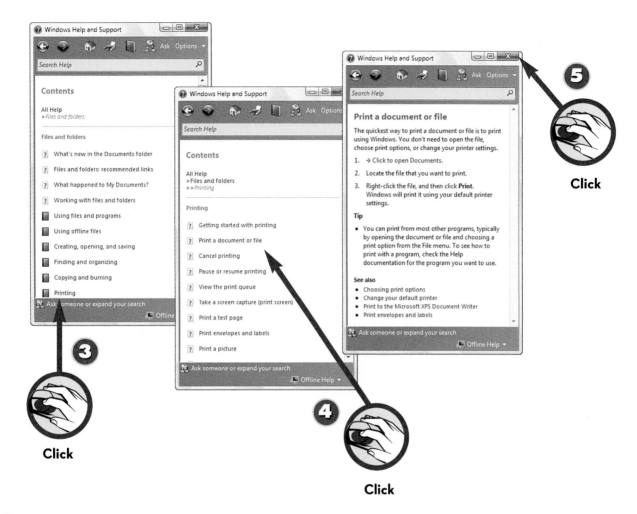

3. In the list of available topics, click the topic you want.
4. The list displays available help topics (indicated with a question mark icon) as well as other categories of additional help topics. Continue clicking categories until you see the help topic you want; then click that help topic.
5. When you have reviewed this information, click the **Close** button to close the Help window.

TIP

Return Home

If you want to go back to the beginning to start from the initial options, click the **Home** button.

TIP

Print Topic

To print the current help topic, click the **Print** button.

LOGGING OFF THE COMPUTER

If you have multiple accounts, you can log off when you are done working in one account before switching to another account. You might log off even if you are the only user as a means to protect your computer.

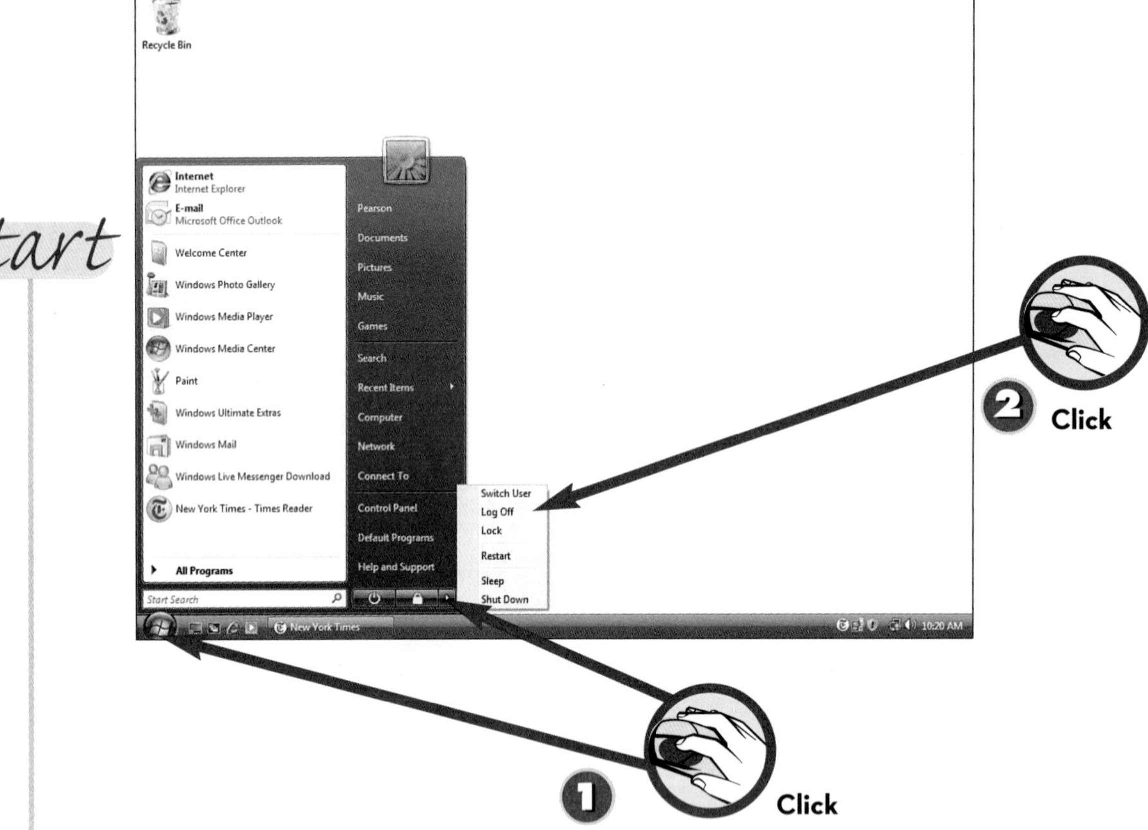

1. Click **Start** and then click the arrow next to the lock icon.

2. Click **Log Off**. You are logged off and returned to the logon screen.

TIP

Logging On and Switching Users

Another user can now log on. You can also select Switch User to keep both users logged on, but simply switch to another user account. For more information on using accounts, see Part 11.

TIP

Hibernate and Other Options

You can also choose to Hibernate (save power and put your computer "to sleep"), switch to a different user, and restart or shut down (covered next) from this menu.

RESTARTING AND SHUTTING DOWN THE COMPUTER

You should never turn your computer off by pressing its power button. Instead, use the Shut Down command so that Windows is properly shut down before the computer is off. You might also need to simply restart the computer, such as after you install a program or update. Both of these commands are found on the Start menu window. If you want to simply turn off the computer (or as Microsoft calls it, "put it to sleep"), you can use the Power Off button. This option saves your work and turns off the display but doesn't require you to close programs and files.

Start

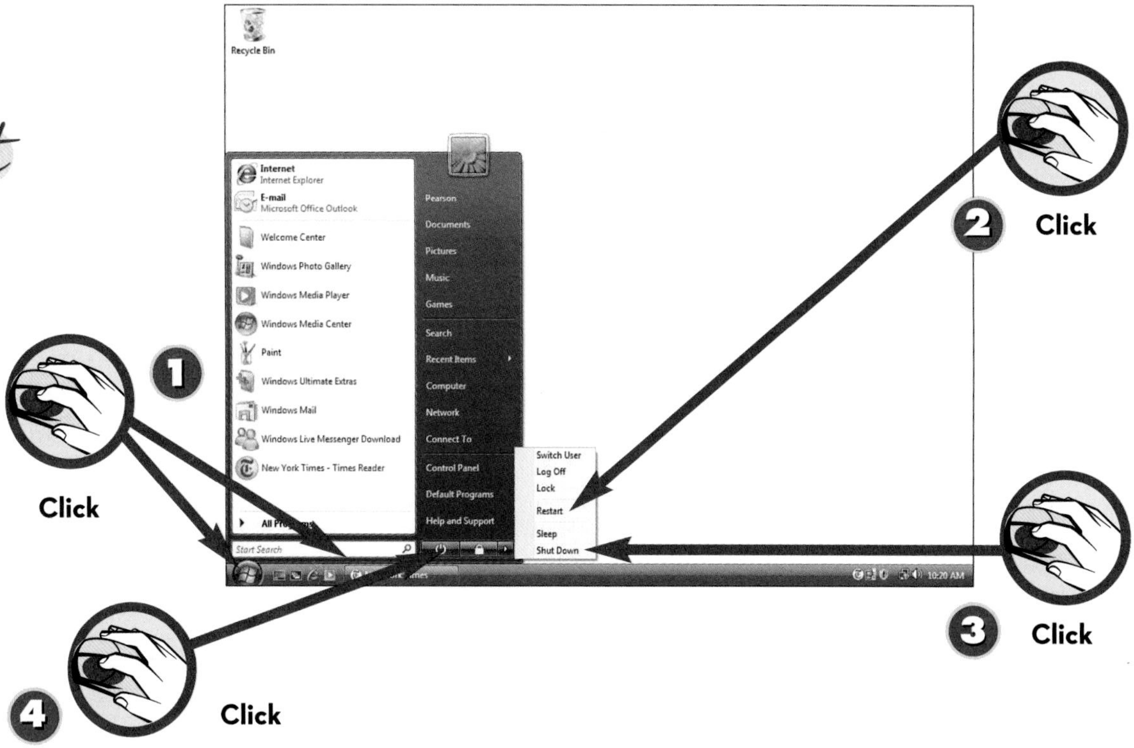

1. Click **Start**, and then click the arrow next to the lock icon.
2. Click **Restart** to restart the computer. The computer is shut down and restarted.
3. To shut down the computer, click **Shut Down**. The computer is turned off.
4. To put the computer to sleep without shutting it off entirely, click the **Power Off** button.

End

TIP

Save Documents and Close Programs

Before you shut down or restart, save any documents that you are working on and close any open programs. You can find out more about these topics in the next part, "Getting Started."

TIP

Manually Turning Off

Sometimes your computer will get stuck, and you won't be able to use the Shut Down command. If needed as a last resort, you can turn off the power to the computer. Most often you have to press and hold down the power button until the computer power shuts off.

WORKING WITH PROGRAMS

You can find an enormous number of programs that are available to use with Windows Vista. For example, a word processing program, such as Microsoft Word, enables you to create, edit, and print documents. There are Windows programs for just about anything you can possibly dream of doing on your computer, and probably a few you've never thought of. You can use word processing, database management, movie creation and editing, drawing, and other programs in Windows. This variety of programs gives you all the tools you need to perform your work, do everyday tasks, or simply have fun.

In Windows, you can use one of several different ways to start a program; none of them is necessarily better than the other. Which method you use will depend on what you happen to be doing on the computer at the time you go to start up a program.

This Part covers not only how to start and exit programs but also provides some basic information that is important to know when working with any type of program.

STARTING PROGRAMS

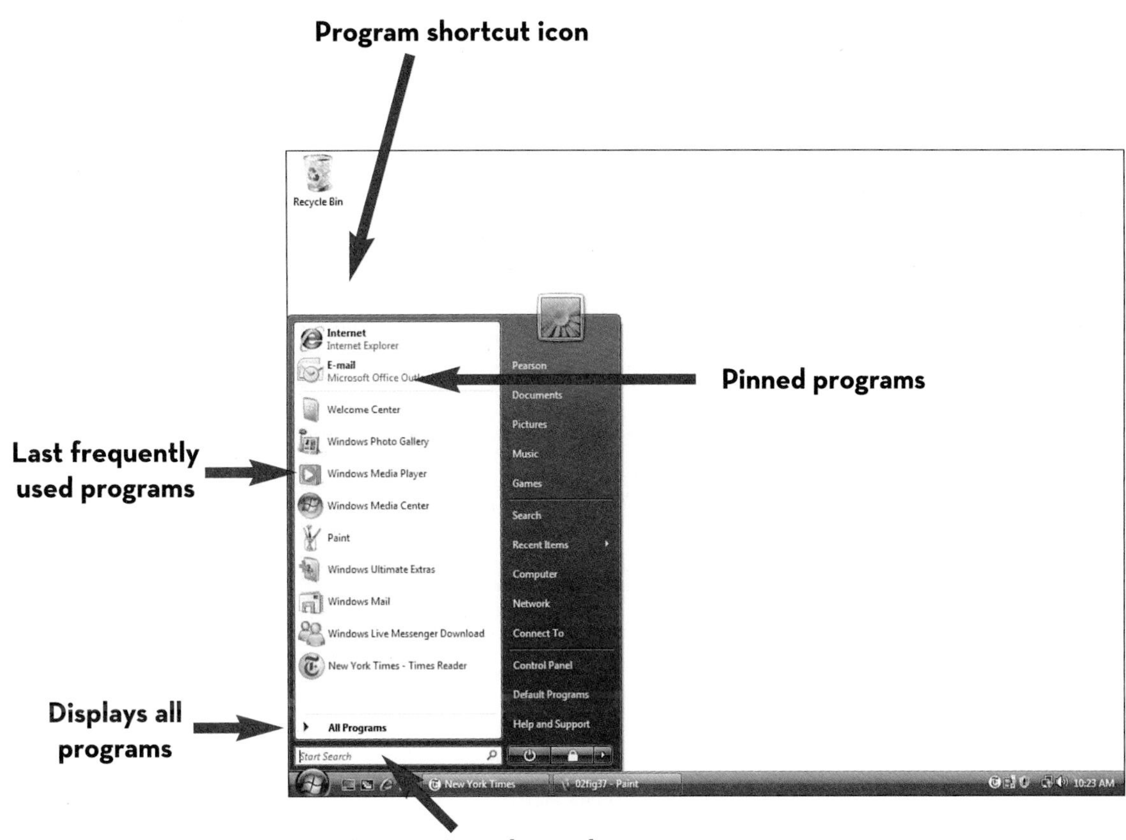

STARTING A PROGRAM FROM THE START MENU

Most of the time you spend using your computer will be spent working in some type of a program—a word processing program to type letters, a spreadsheet program to create budgets, and so on. You can start a program in many ways, including from the Start menu. When you install a new Windows program, that program's installation procedure will set up a program folder and program icon on the Start menu.

Start

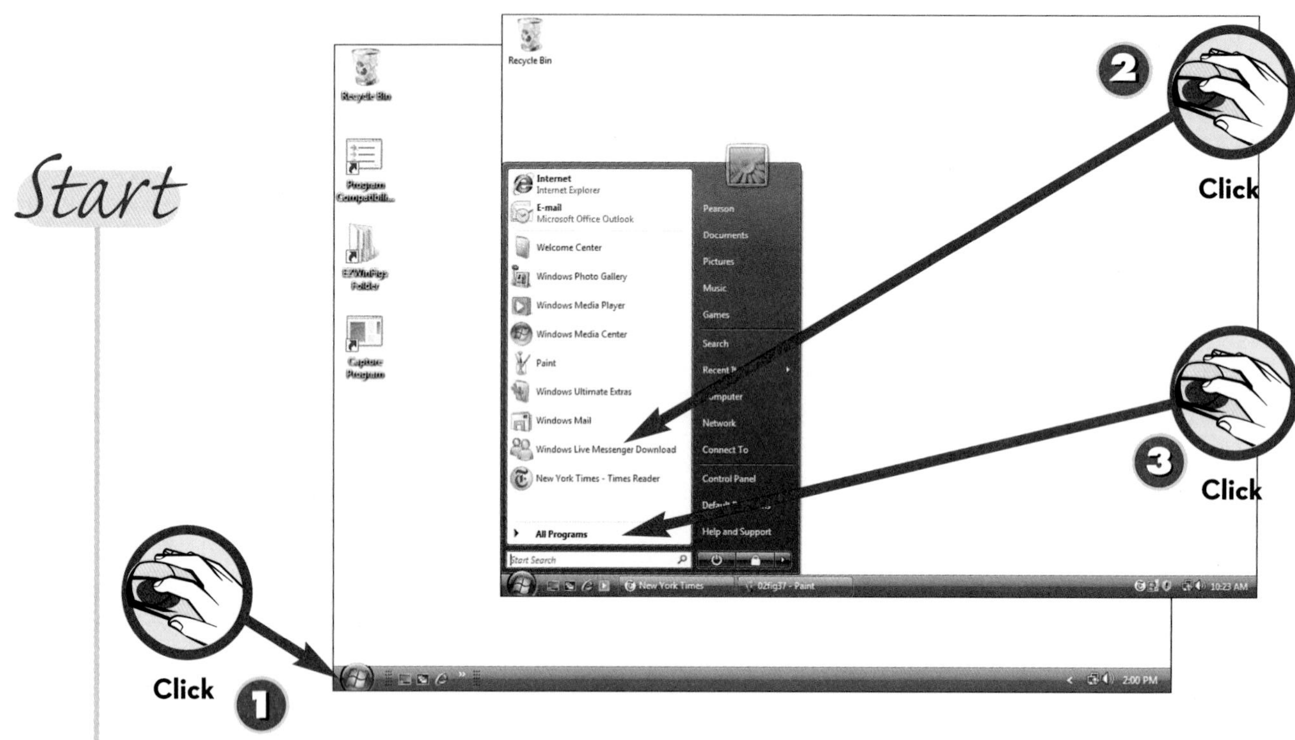

1. Click the **Start** button.
2. If you see the program listed that you want to start, click it from the opening list. Skip to step 7.
3. If the program is not listed, click **All Programs**.

Continued

TIP

Programs Listed

Windows Vista lists the programs you use most often on the opening Start menu. The programs you see listed will vary from those shown with this task.

TIP

Programs vs. Applications vs. Software

The terms program, application, and software are used interchangeably and mean the same thing. That is, if you hear about a word processing application, it's the same thing as saying word processing program.

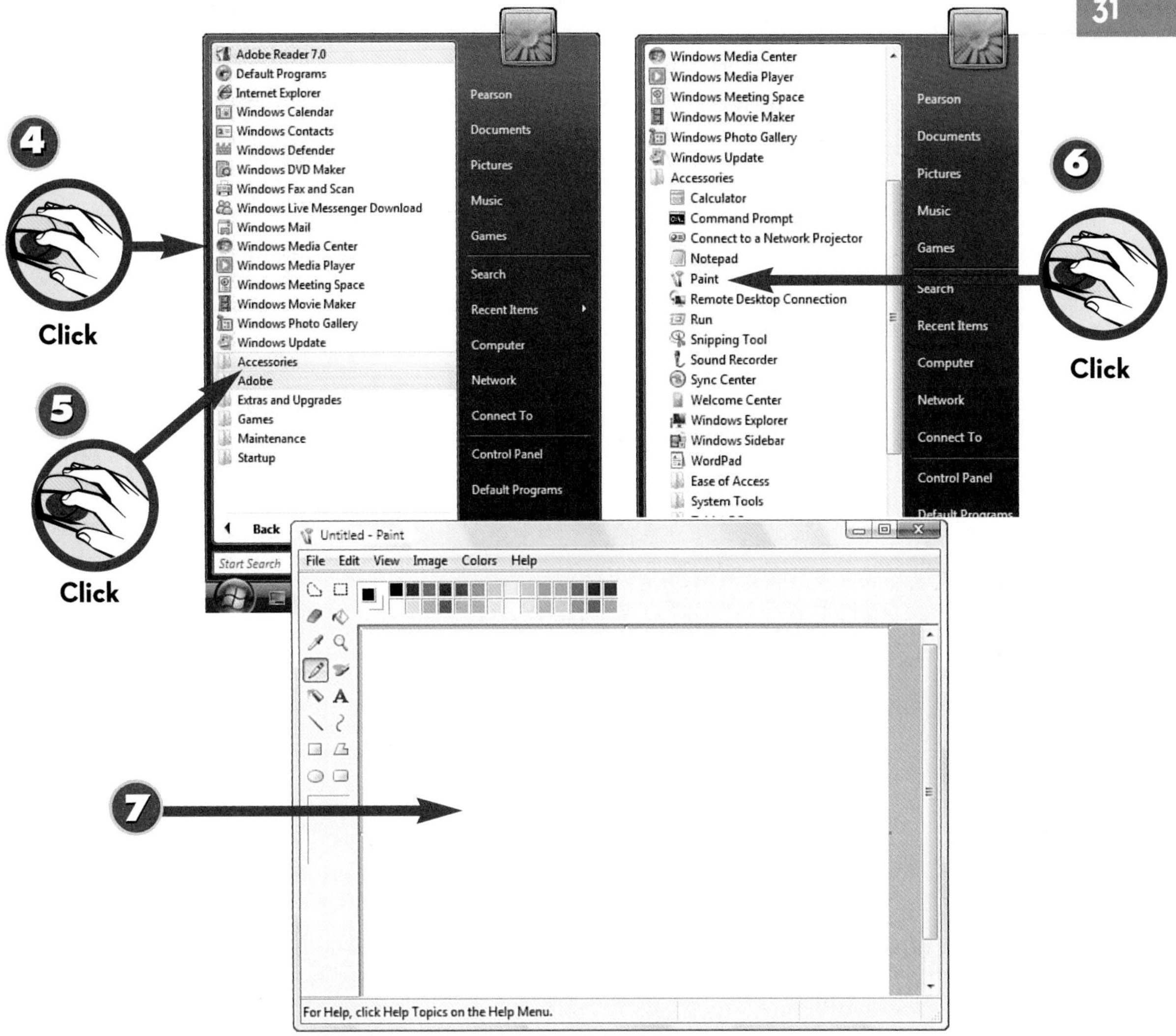

4. If you see the program you want to start, click it, and then skip to step 7.
5. If you don't see the program listed, it may be contained in a folder (for example, Accessories). Click a folder to view the programs contained in the folder.
6. Click the program you want to start.
7. The program is started. (Here you see Paint, an accessory program included with Windows that is found in the Accessories program folder.)

End

TIP

Listed Programs

Opening programs from the Start menu can be a little confusing until you become familiar with where they are stored. Windows automatically lists some programs on the main Start menu, while other programs are found in the All Programs list. Other programs are stored in folders within the All Programs list.

TIP

Setting Up Programs

You can find information about installing new programs in Part 13, "Setting Up Programs." In that same Part, you also learn how to add program shortcut icons to your desktop, making programs easier to find and start.

EXITING A PROGRAM

Close a program when you finish working in it to free system memory. Too many open programs can tax your system's memory and slow the computer's processes, such as saving, printing, switching between programs, and so on.

Start

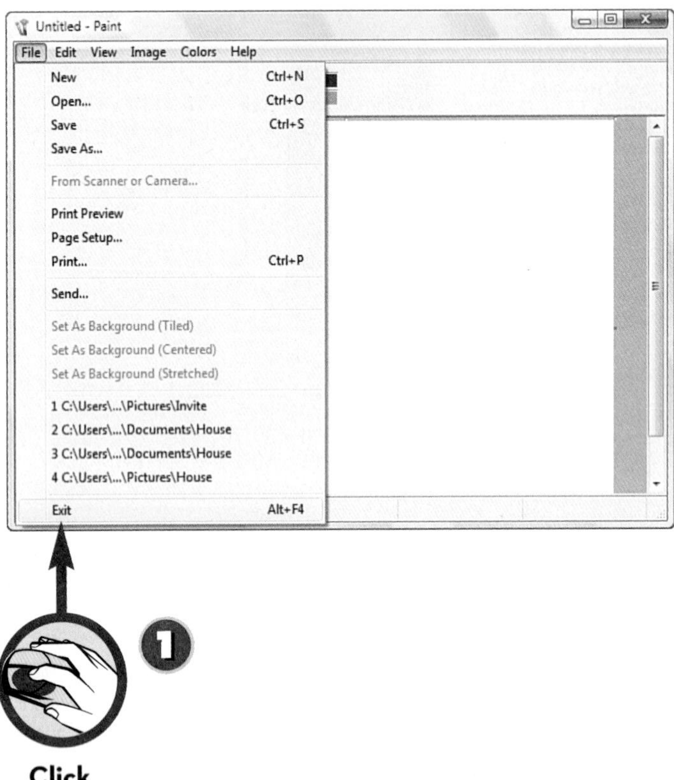

1. Click **File** and then click **Exit**.
2. The program is exited.

End

TIP

More Ways to Close

You can also press **Alt+F4** or click the **Close** button (the one with the X) in the program's title bar to close a program.

CAUTION

Save First

If you have not saved a file before closing that file's program, a message box appears asking if you want to save the file. If you do, click **Yes**; if not, click **No**. If you want to return to the document, click **Cancel**.

STARTING A PROGRAM FROM A SHORTCUT ICON

In addition to the Start menu, you can start programs from shortcut icons. Some programs automatically place shortcut icons on the desktop when the program is installed. You can also manually create shortcut icons to programs. This task covers how to start a program from a shortcut icon.

Start

Double-click

1. Double-click the shortcut icon on the desktop. (Shown here is a shortcut icon for Windows Mail.)
2. The program starts and displays in its own window. A taskbar button for the program appears in the taskbar.

End

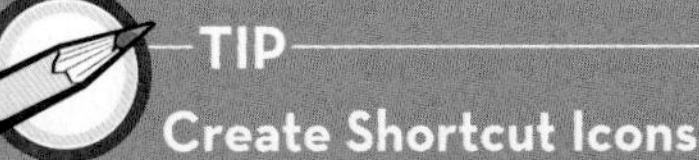

TIP

Create Shortcut Icons

You can create shortcut icons to any of your installed programs. To do so, see Part 13, "Setting Up Programs."

SWITCHING BETWEEN PROGRAMS USING TASKBAR BUTTONS

You may often work with more than one type of program at the same time. For example, you might want to compare price figures from an Excel worksheet with a price list you've set up in Word. You might want to copy text from a word processing document to a presentation program, such as PowerPoint. Switching between programs enables you not only to compare data but also to share data among programs. Windows Vista enables you to quickly switch from one program to another.

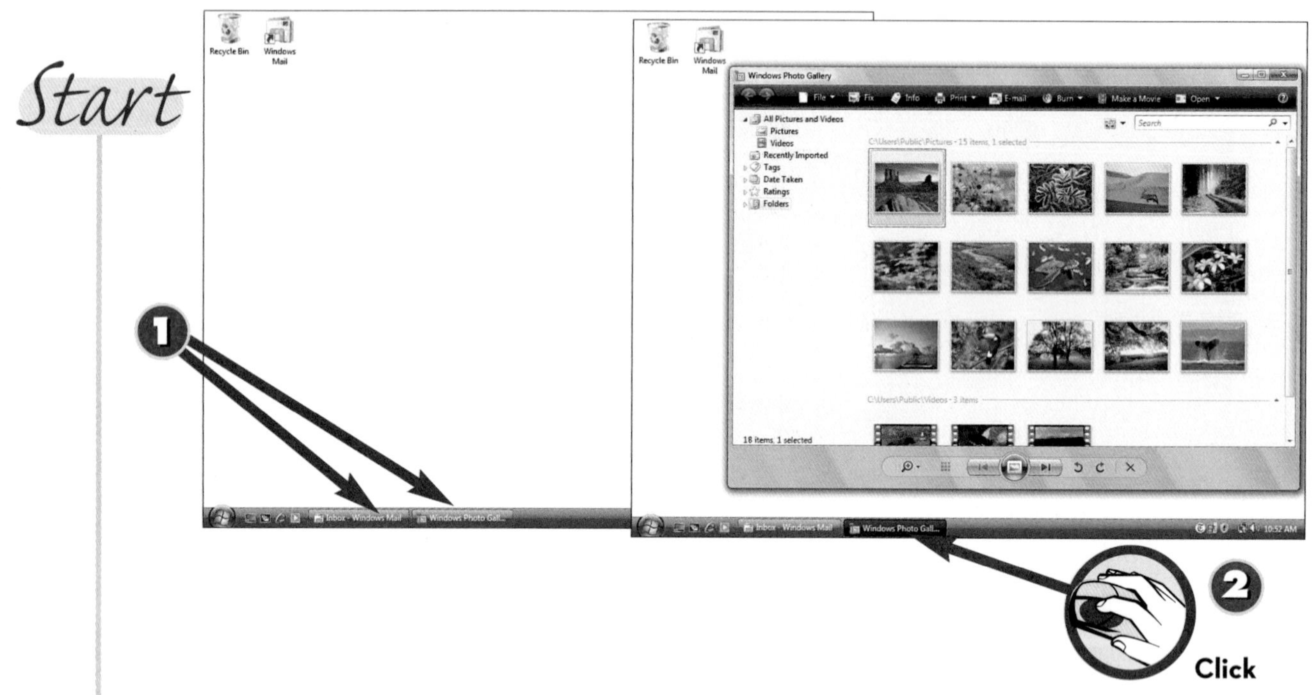

1. If you have more than one program running, you should see a taskbar button for each program.
2. Click the button for the program you want to switch to (in this case, **Windows Photo Gallery**). That program becomes the active program.

End

TIP

How Many?

The number of open programs at any one time depends on the amount of RAM (random access memory) in your computer. If you find you constantly have to close programs or the computer runs very slowly when you have several programs open, you might want to look into increasing the amount of physical RAM in your computer. Check with your computer's manufacturer or a local computer hardware store.

SWITCHING BETWEEN PROGRAMS WITH WINDOWS FLIP

In past versions of Windows, you could press Alt+Tab to see mini-pictures of the open programs. You could then scroll to the program you wanted. Windows Vista has improved on this capability. You can now see live thumbnail versions of the windows rather than stagnant icons. You can also use this feature (called Windows Flip) to switch between programs.

Start

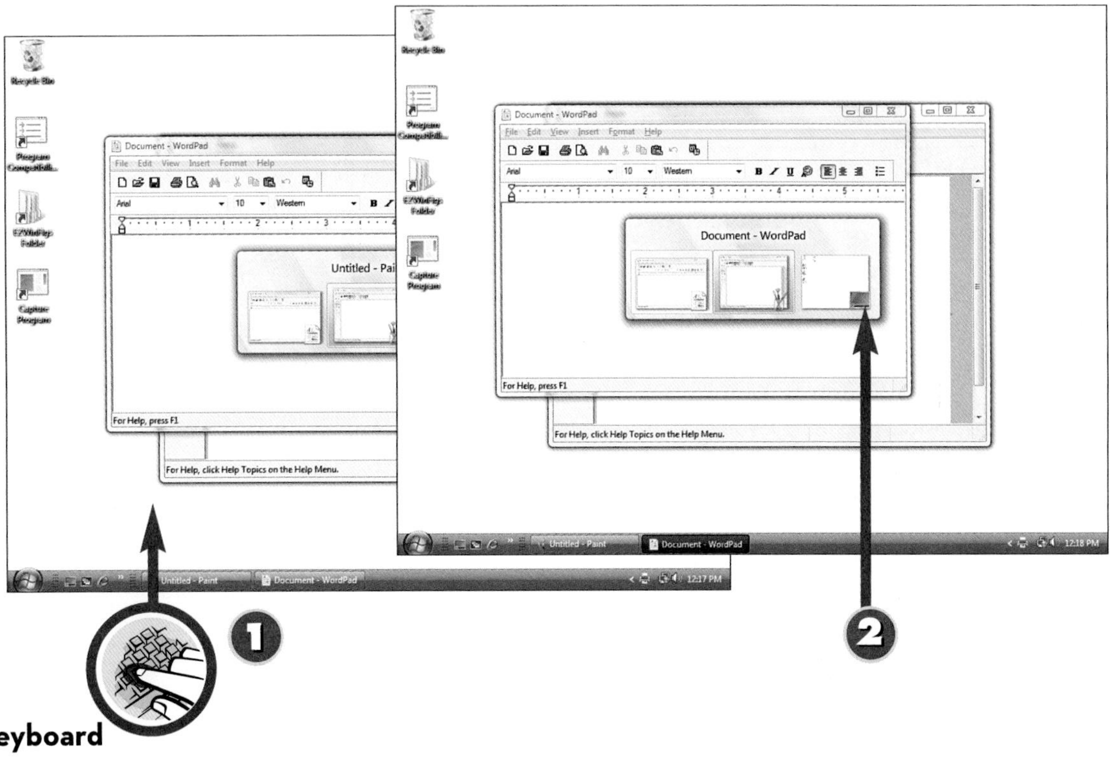

Keyboard

1. With more than one program running, press **Alt+Tab**.
2. Icons for all open programs display in the window. You can use the arrow keys to scroll to the icon to get information, such as the program name. You can also scroll to the program to select the one you want to switch to.

End

TIP

Windows Flip 3D

If your computer supports Aero (a glass-like, transparent interface), you can also use Windows Flip 3D. It works like Windows Flip only you see a three-dimensional stacked view of your open windows.

SAVING A DOCUMENT

You save documents and files so that you can open them later to print, edit, copy, and so on. The first time you save a file, you must assign that file a name and folder (or location). You save documents pretty much the same way in all Windows programs; this task shows you how to save a document in WordPad.

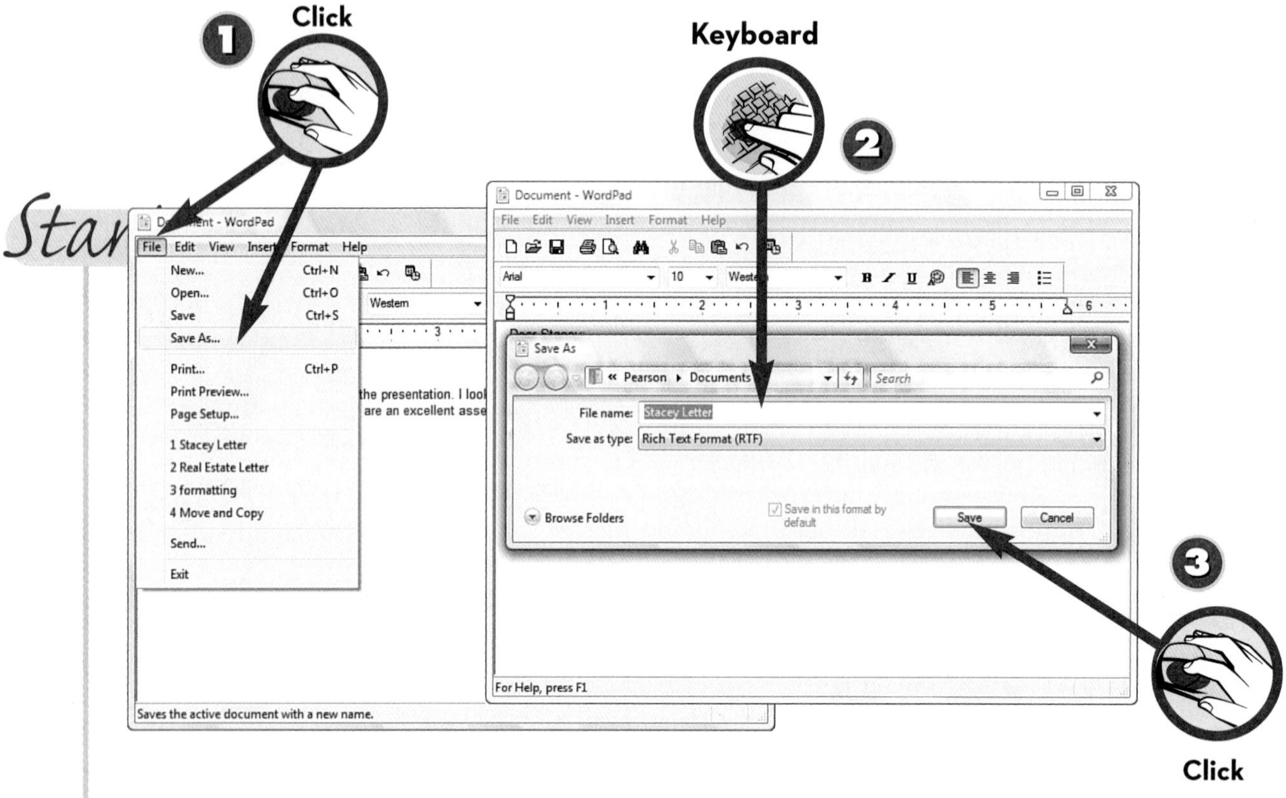

Start

1. With an unsaved file open, click **File**, **Save As** in the program.
2. In the **File name** text box, type a descriptive filename, replacing the generic name.
3. Click the **Save** button. The document is saved.

End

TIP

Save Again

After you've saved and named a file, you can simply click **File** and select **Save** to resave that file to the same location with the same name. Any changes you have made since the last save are reflected in the file. You can also use program shortcuts such as a toolbar button for saving or a shortcut key (usually Ctrl+S).

TIP

Save As

You can also save the file you are working on to another folder on your system or with a different name. This is often useful when working with photographs that you are editing so that you don't lose your original file.

CREATING A NEW DOCUMENT

When you create a new document, many programs prompt you to select a template on which to base the new document. A *template* is a predesigned document. You can select the template, if prompted, and create the new document.

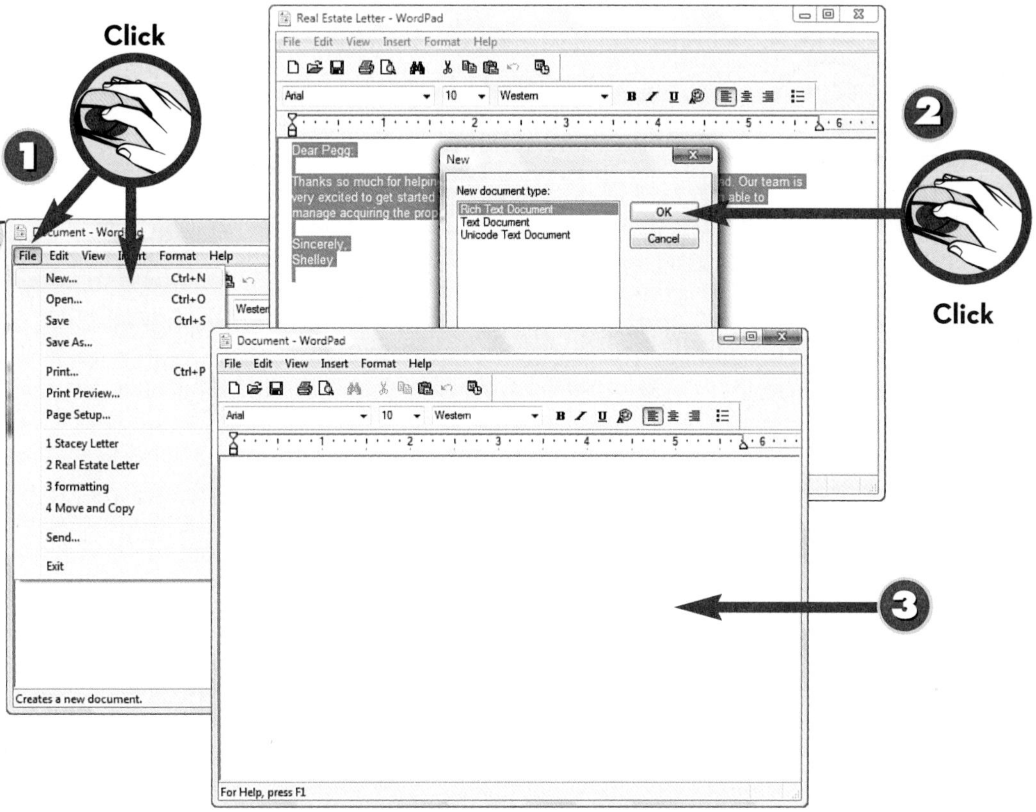

1. In the program, click **File**, **New**.
2. If you see a **New** dialog box, click the type of document you want to create and then click the **OK** button.
3. A new document is displayed.

TIP

Shortcut

As a shortcut, you can click the **New** button to create a new document based on the default template.

HINT

Exceptions

For complex programs, such as PowerPoint (a presentation program) and Access (a database program), you might be prompted to make some selections before the new document is created. Refer to your program documentation for help on creating new documents with these programs.

OPENING A FILE

When you save a document, the program saves the document information as a file with the name you entered and in the location you specified. The purpose of saving a document is to make it available for later use. You can open any of the documents you have saved. You can then make changes or print the document.

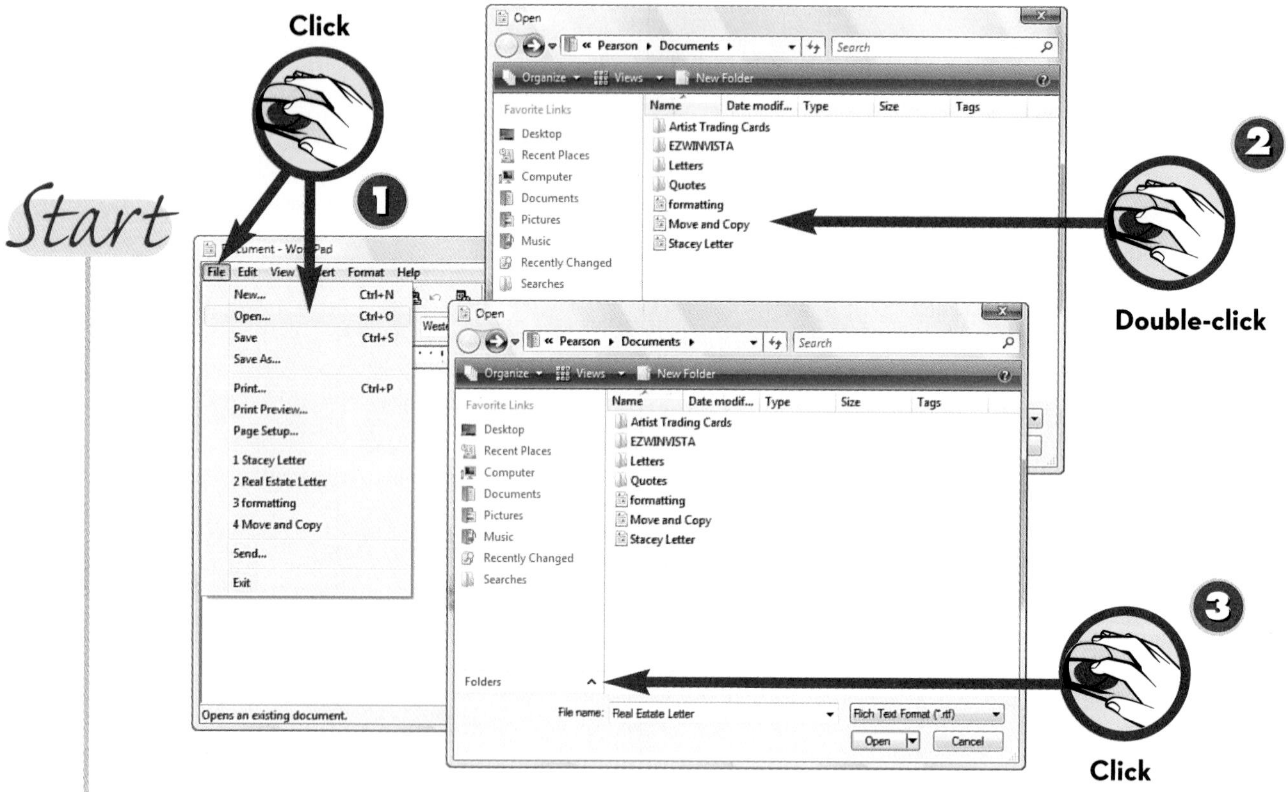

Start

Click

Double-click

Click

1. Click **File** and then click **Open**.
2. If you see the file you want to open, double-click it and skip the remaining steps. If you do not see the file you want to open, move to step 3.
3. Click the arrow next to **Folders** to expand the list of folders on your computer.

Continued

TIP

Can't Find a File?

If you can't find the file you want to work with, it could be because you did not save it where you thought you did. Try looking in a different drive or folder. If you still can't find it, try searching for the file. (For more information about searching for files, see Part 5, "Working with Files.")

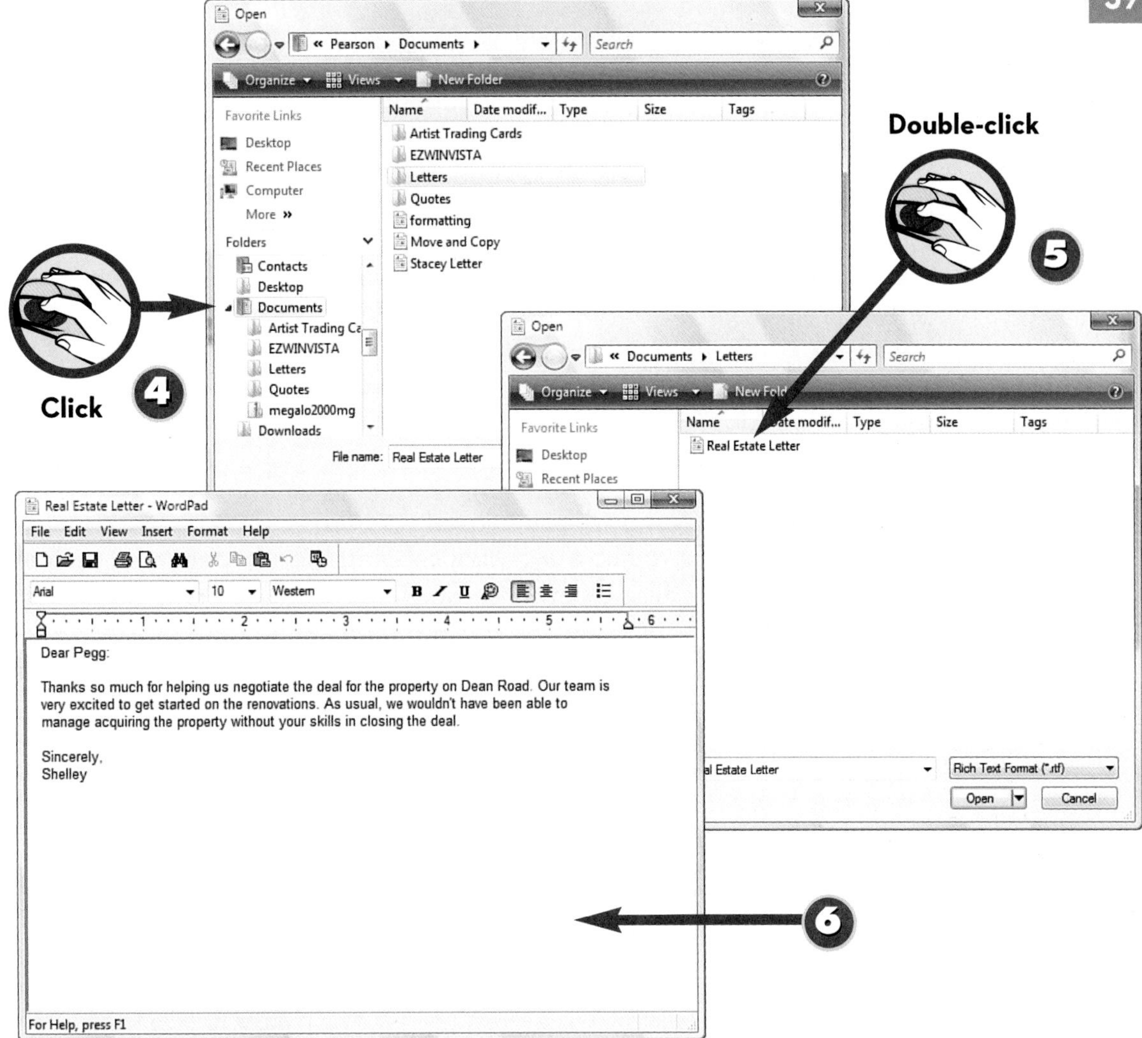

4 In the list of folders, navigate to the folder that contains the document you want, and then click the folder name to view the list of documents within the folder.

5 Double-click the document you want to open.

6 The document is opened.

End

TIP

Use Favorite Links Pane

Explorers include a pane with favorite links of commonly used folders or locations for storing documents. You can select a drive or folder from this list to find the document you want to open. See Chapter 1, "What's New in Microsoft Windows Vista," for more information on Explorers.

WORKING WITH FOLDERS

Part of working with Windows is learning how to work with the files you save and store on your system. Each time you save a file (a letter, worksheet, database, or other document), that information is saved on your hard disk with a specific name and location.

To keep your files organized, you can set up folders to store them in. If you think of your hard drive like a big filing cabinet, then folders are like drawers. Each folder can hold files or other folders. You can open and close folders, view a folder's contents, copy and move folders, and create or delete folders. This part covers how to navigate among folders as well as perform other key folder-related tasks.

WORKING WITH EXPLORERS

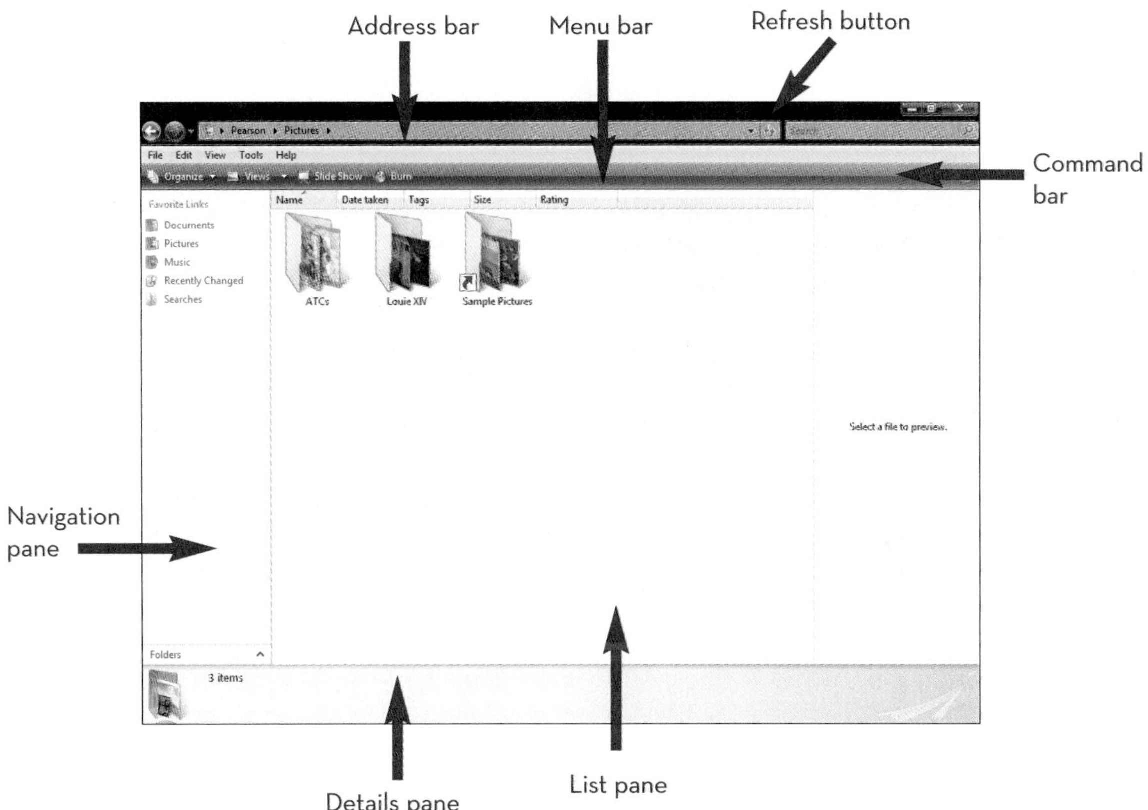

VIEWING THE CONTENTS OF YOUR COMPUTER'S DRIVES

Windows Vista includes a Computer command in the Start menu; clicking this command opens this folder, which displays all the drives on your system. You can use this folder to open and view the contents of your system. You can also use it to open a drive and navigate to folders on that drive.

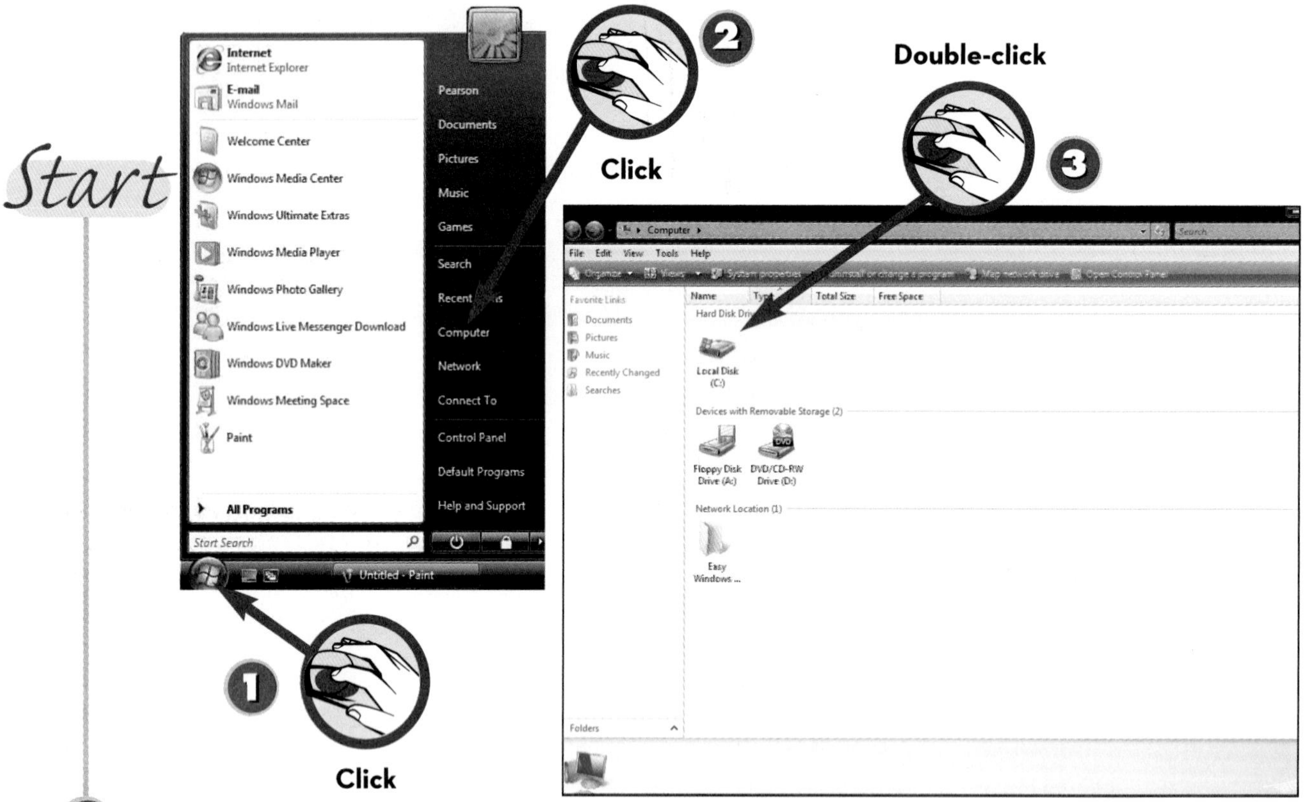

Start

Click

Click

Double-click

1. Click **Start**.
2. Click **Computer**.
3. You see the drives on your computer. You can double-click any of the drives to open and view their contents. For instance, to open your hard drive, double-click the icon for this drive.

End

TIP

Favorite Links

You can click any of the folders in the Navigation pane, under Favorite Links, to open that folder.

UNDERSTANDING WINDOWS PRESET FOLDERS

To help you keep information organized, Windows Vista has set up some standard folders. For instance, the Pictures folder is useful for storing all pictures in one location. You also can use the Music folder for storing music. These preset folders are listed on the Start menu by default.

Start

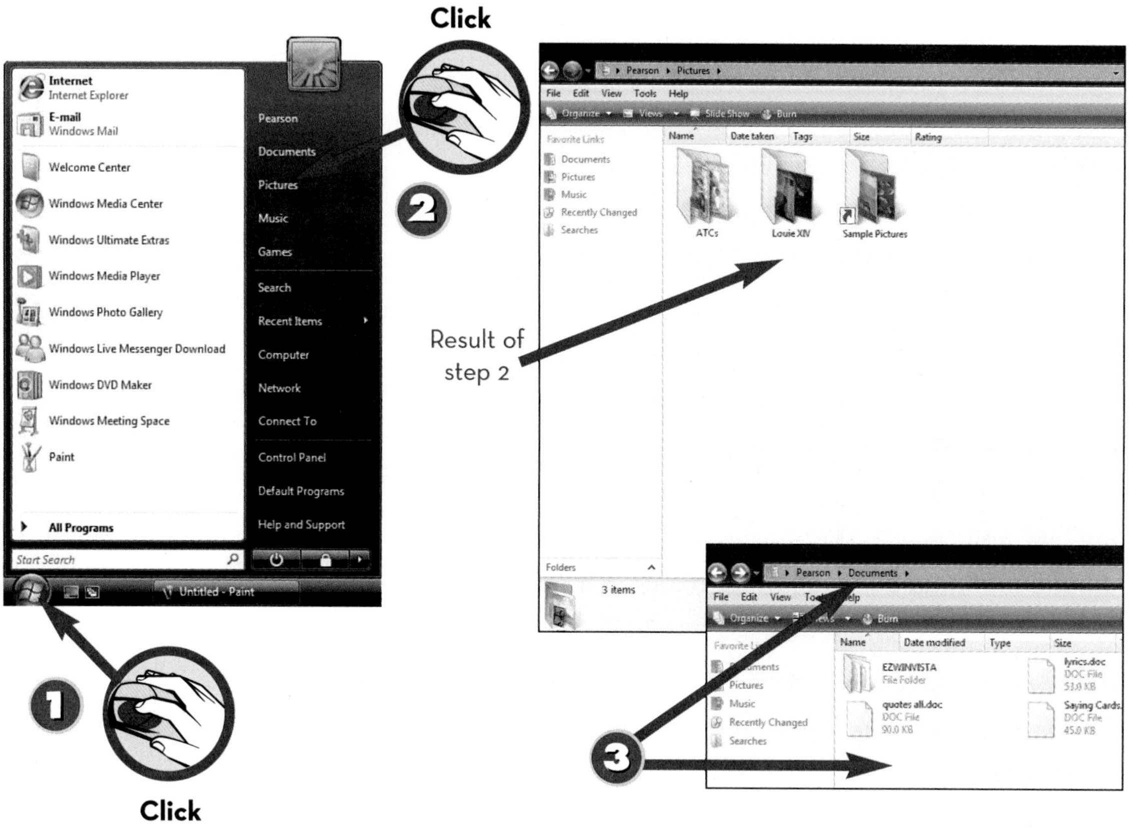

Click

Result of step 2

Click

1. Click the **Start** menu.
2. Click the folder you want to open. For instance, to view the Pictures folder, click **Pictures**. You see the contents of this folder.
3. To view the contents of another folder, follow the same steps: Click **Start** and then click the folder name. For instance, the Documents folder is a key folder.

End

NOTE

Using the Preset Folders

Using the preset folders to store your files helps you stay better organized. Windows automatically defaults to those folders when you are working with certain types of files. Image files, for example, would be expected to be stored in the Pictures folder, and documents in the Documents folder. To further organize your files, create subfolders within those preset folders. (See the task "Creating a New Folder" later in this Part.)

UNDERSTANDING AN EXPLORER WINDOW

When you open a folder or drive, you see its contents in an Explorer window. Windows Vista has made the features in this window consistent to provide one interface. Learning the various elements in an Explorer window can help you better learn how to navigate among folders and keep your folders and files organized.

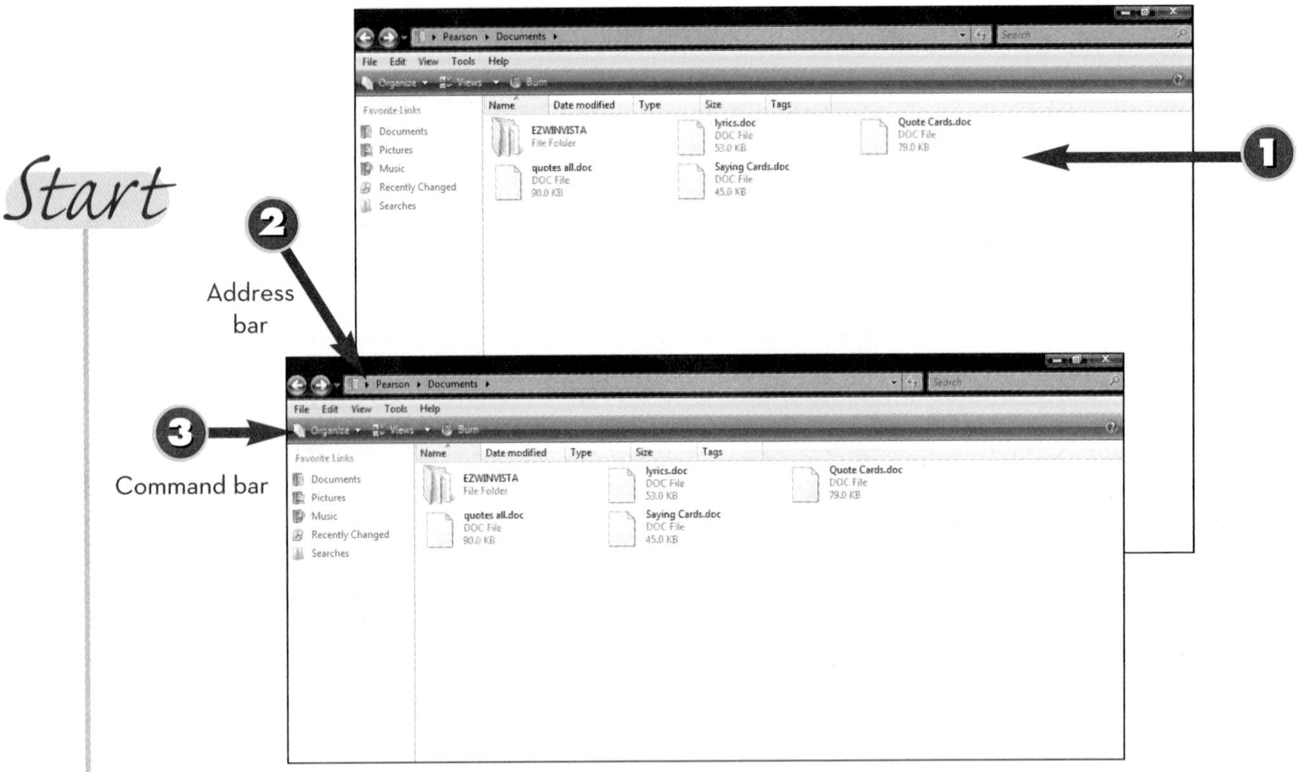

Start

Address bar

Command bar

1. Open any Explorer window. In this example, you see the contents of the Documents folder.
2. The Address bar shows you where you are in the folder structure. You can also use this list to move to another of the listed folders or drives.
3. The Command bar lists the available commands for working with the contents of this window.

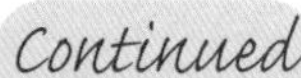

TIP

Open a Folder

To open a folder in the Navigation pane, simply double-click the link.

TIP

Command Bar Commands Vary

The commands in the Command bar will vary depending on the type of Explorer and also depending on what is selected in that Explorer.

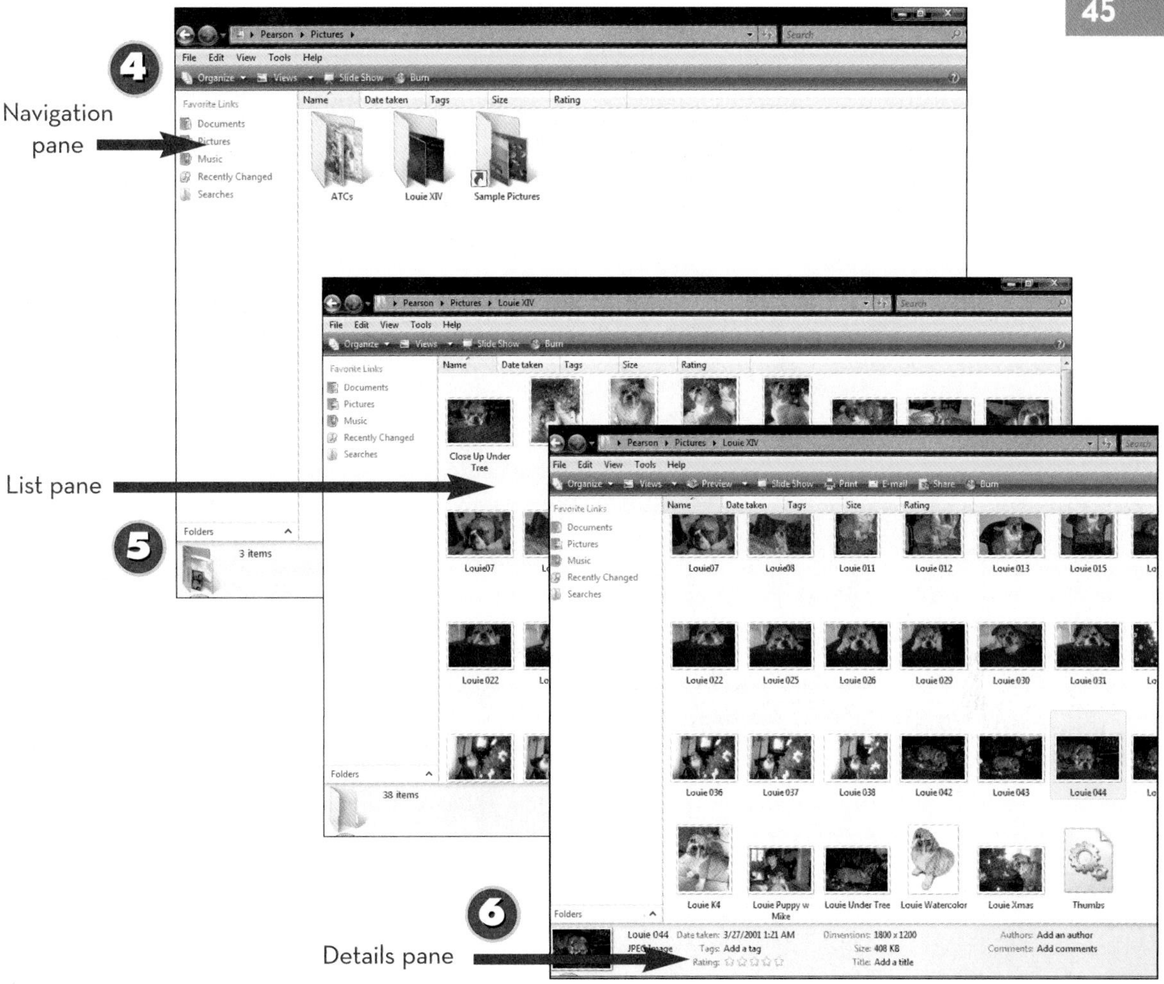

Navigation pane

List pane

Details pane

4 In this example, you can see the Favorite links in the **Navigation** pane of the Pictures folder. This pane contains commonly accessed folders.

5 The **List** pane displays the contents of the folder.

6 The **Details** pane displays information about the selected file.

End

NOTE

Preview Pane

You can find more about previewing file information in Part 5, "Working with Files."

TIP

Folders List

You can display a hierarchical list of all the folders on your system in the Navigation pane. See the next task.

NAVIGATING FOLDERS

Part of using a computer is learning to navigate among the various folders on your system. When you need to find a document, open the folder that contains that document. When you want to create a new folder, open the folder where you want to place it.

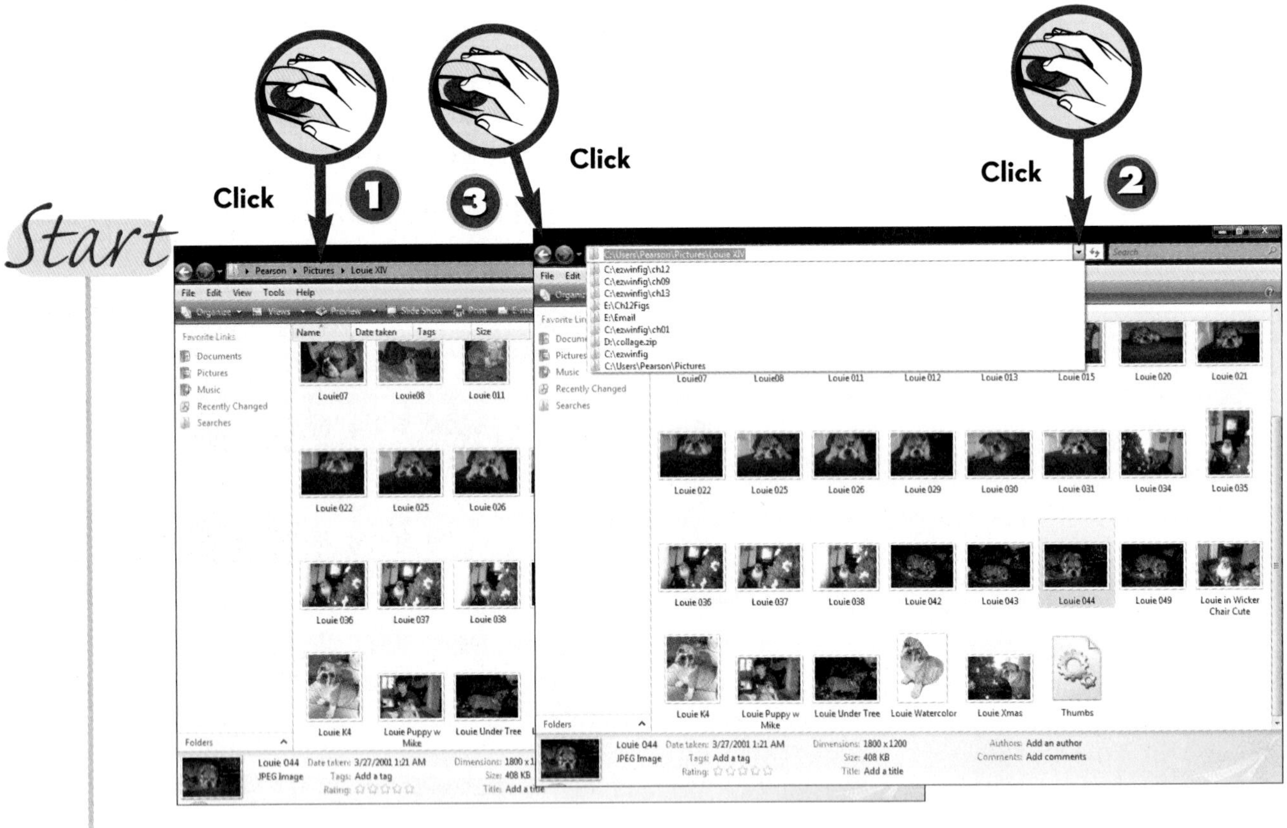

Start

Click 1

Click 3

Click 2

1. The Address bar lists the chain or path of folders that lead to the current one. You can click any of the listed folders to view that folder. For instance, you can click **Pictures** to go back to the Pictures folder.
2. Click the down arrow next to the Address bar to display a list of folders you have previously viewed. You can click any folder in that list to go to that folder.
3. If you have gone from one folder to the next, you can click the **Back** and **Forward** buttons to move back to a previous folder or forward (if you have gone back).

Continued

TIP

Refresh File List

If you have made changes to the window contents, you can update the list by clicking the **Refresh** button (next to the Address bar drop-down arrow).

TIP

Use Instant Search

Next to the Address bar, you see the Instant Search bar; you can use this text box to type a word or phrase to find a file, program, or folder. See "Using Instant Search," in Part 5 for more information.

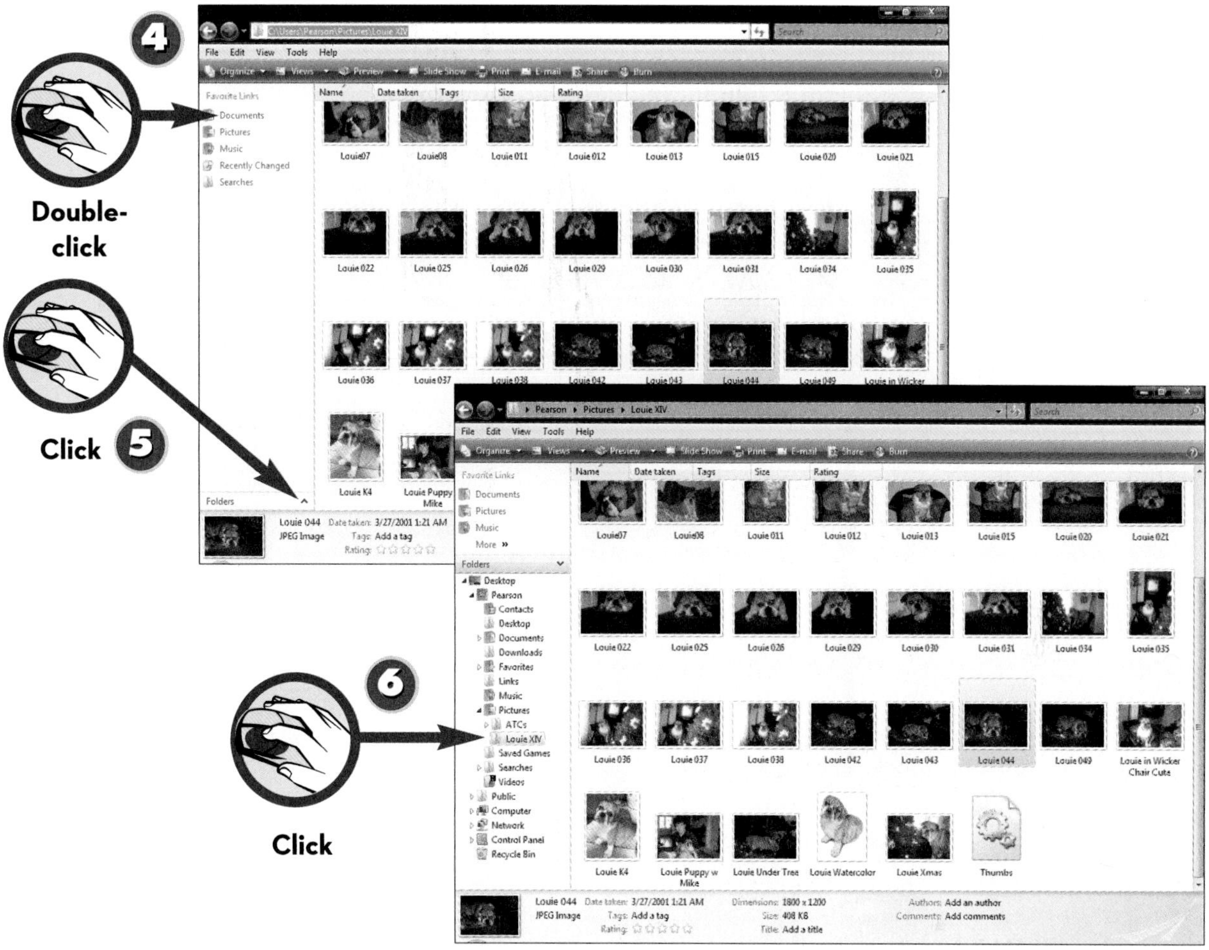

Double-click

Click 5

Click

4 To go to a folder in the Navigation pane, double-click the folder name. You see the contents of that folder.

5 To view and navigate using the Folders list, click the up arrow next to **Folders**.

6 In the Folders list, click any of the folders to display its contents.

End

TIP

Windows Explorer

Previous versions of Windows included Windows Explorer, which was basically a file window with the Folders list displayed. You can display the same Explorer window you get when clicking Start, Computer by clicking **Start**, **All Programs**, **Accessories**, and then **Windows Explorer**.

SELECTING A FOLDER

When you are working with folders, you start by selecting a folder. You can then rename, delete, copy, or move the folder. You can also view detailed information about the selected folder in the Details pane.

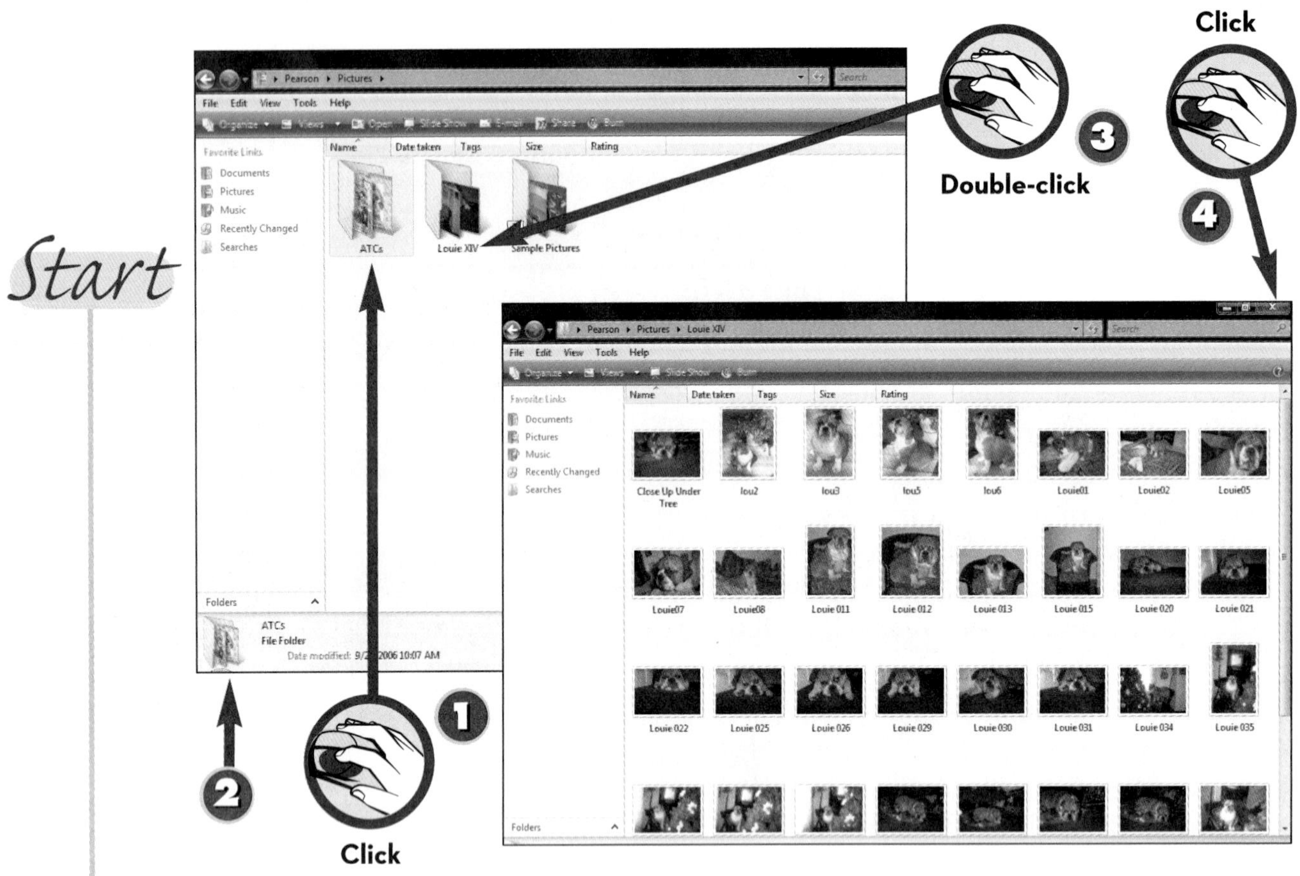

Start

1. Click the folder you want to select.
2. Look in the Details pane for details about the selected folder.
3. To open a folder, double-click it; you see the contents of that folder.
4. Click the **Close** button to close the folder window.

End

NOTE

Hide and Display Panes

You can hide or display areas of the window. See "Customizing the Explorer Window Layout" later in this Part for more information.

CHANGING THE VIEW OF THE WINDOW CONTENTS

You can change the way you view the contents of an Explorer window. If you want to see more of a window's contents at one time, change the view to List. Use the Details view to view information about the files (such as size, name, type, or modification date). You can choose to view the files using icons of different sizes. Or select Tiles, which display a small image of the file with file information.

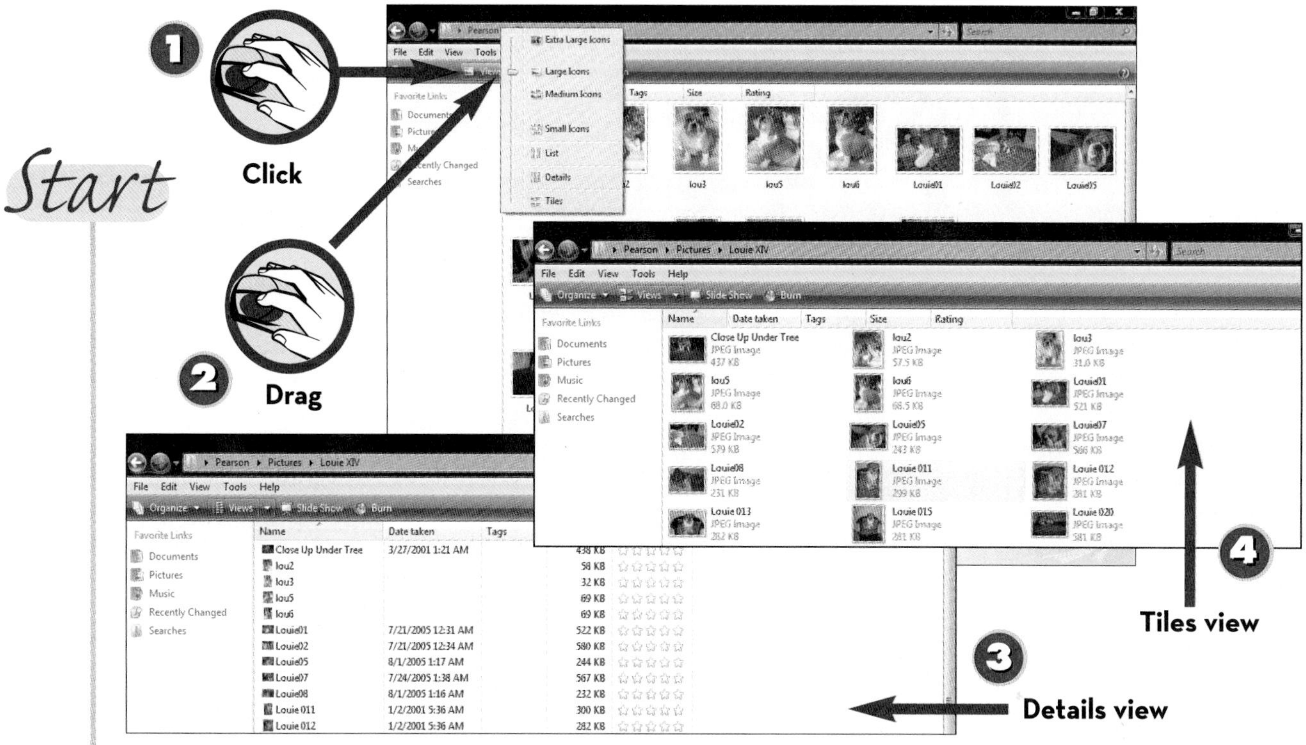

Start

1 Click

2 Drag

3 Details view

4 Tiles view

1. In the window you want to change, click the down arrow next to the **Views** button.
2. Use the slider bar to select the view you want.
3. The window displays the contents in that view (in this case, the **Details** view).
4. This figure shows **Tiles** view, another option.

End

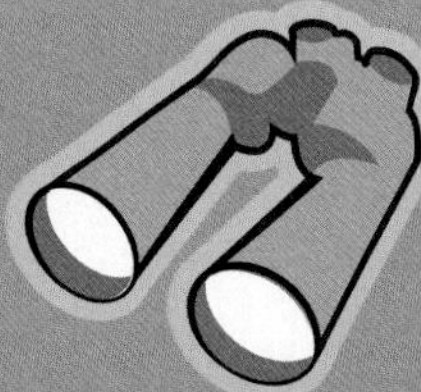

SORTING THE CONTENTS OF A WINDOW

You sort the contents of a window so that you can more easily find the folders and files you want. Windows enables you to arrange the contents of a window by name, type, date, and size. All views (see the previous task for information on the types of views) show the sort, but the change is most apparent in Details view.

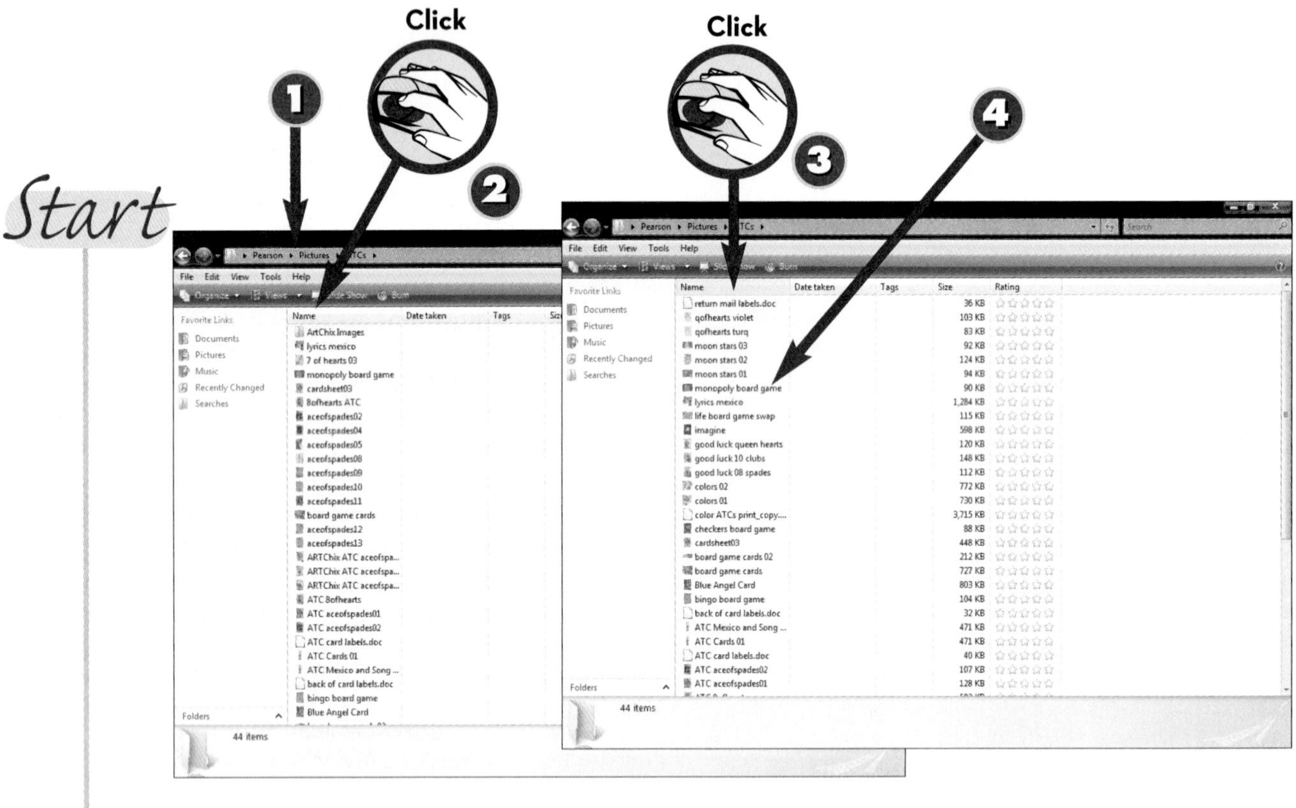

Start

1. Open the folder you want to sort.
2. Click the column heading on which you want to sort. For instance, to sort in order from A–Z by name, click the **Name** column.
3. To sort in descending order, click the column heading again.
4. The contents are sorted here in descending alphabetical order.

End

TIP

Computer Sorts

If you are working in the Computer window, you have different options for arranging the icons. You can arrange by name, type, total size, or free space.

TIP

Using a Menu Command

You can also right-click a blank part of the window and click **Sort By**. Then select a sort order.

CUSTOMIZING THE EXPLORER WINDOW LAYOUT

The redesigned Explorer window in Vista has a flexible layout with its various panes. You can choose which panes are displayed when you open an Explorer window by customizing the window to contain only the panes you find most useful.

Start

Click

1 Click the **Organize** menu, click **Layout**, and then click the pane you want to hide or display. Click an item with a check mark next to it to remove it from your view; click an item without a check mark to add it to the view.

2 That pane is then either displayed or hidden; here you see the Preview pane displayed.

End

TIP

View Menu Bar?

If you want to view or hide the menu bar (rather than the command bar) that includes menu names such as File, Edit, View, Tools, and Help, click **Organize**, **Layout**, **Menu Bar**. Checked means the menu bar appears; unchecked means the menu bar is hidden.

GROUPING CONTENT

You can group file contents so that they are easier to work with. You can choose to group by name, date modified, type, authors, tags, as well as additional options.

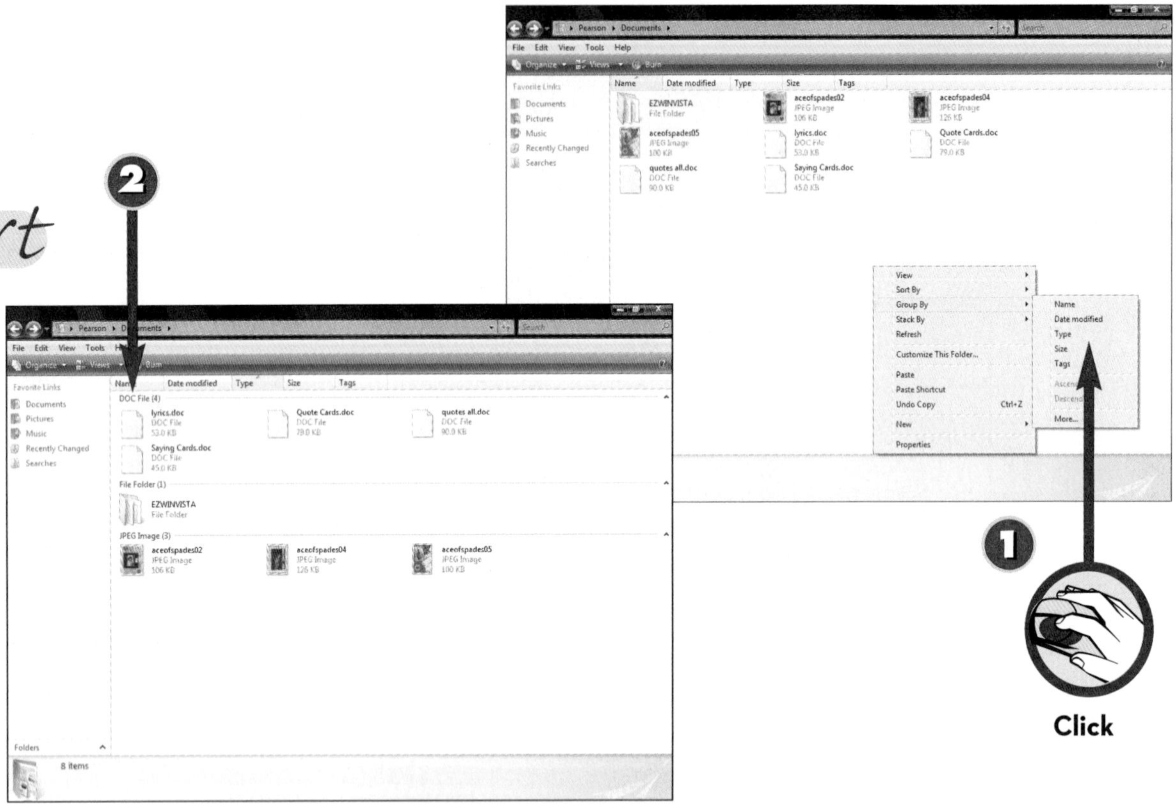

Start

Click

1. Right-click a blank part of the window, click **Group By**, and then select a grouping option.

2. The contents are grouped as selected (in this case, by type). In this example, you see three group headings for the type of files in the folder: DOC File, File Folder, and JPEG Image.

End

TIP

Undo the Groups

To undo the groups, right-click a blank part of the window and select **Sort By**. Then select a sort order.

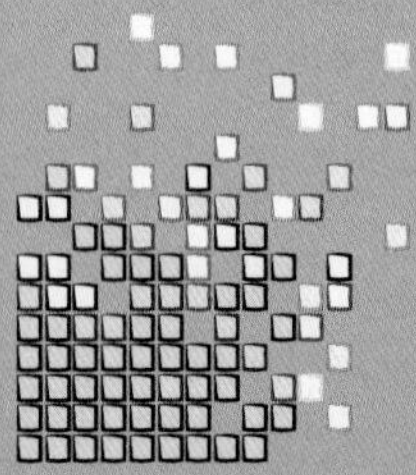

CREATING A NEW FOLDER

Finding, saving, and opening documents is easier if you group related files into folders. For example, you might want to create a folder for all your word processing documents, or you might create folders for each person who uses your computer. Creating a folder enables you to keep your documents separated from the program's files so that you can easily find your document files.

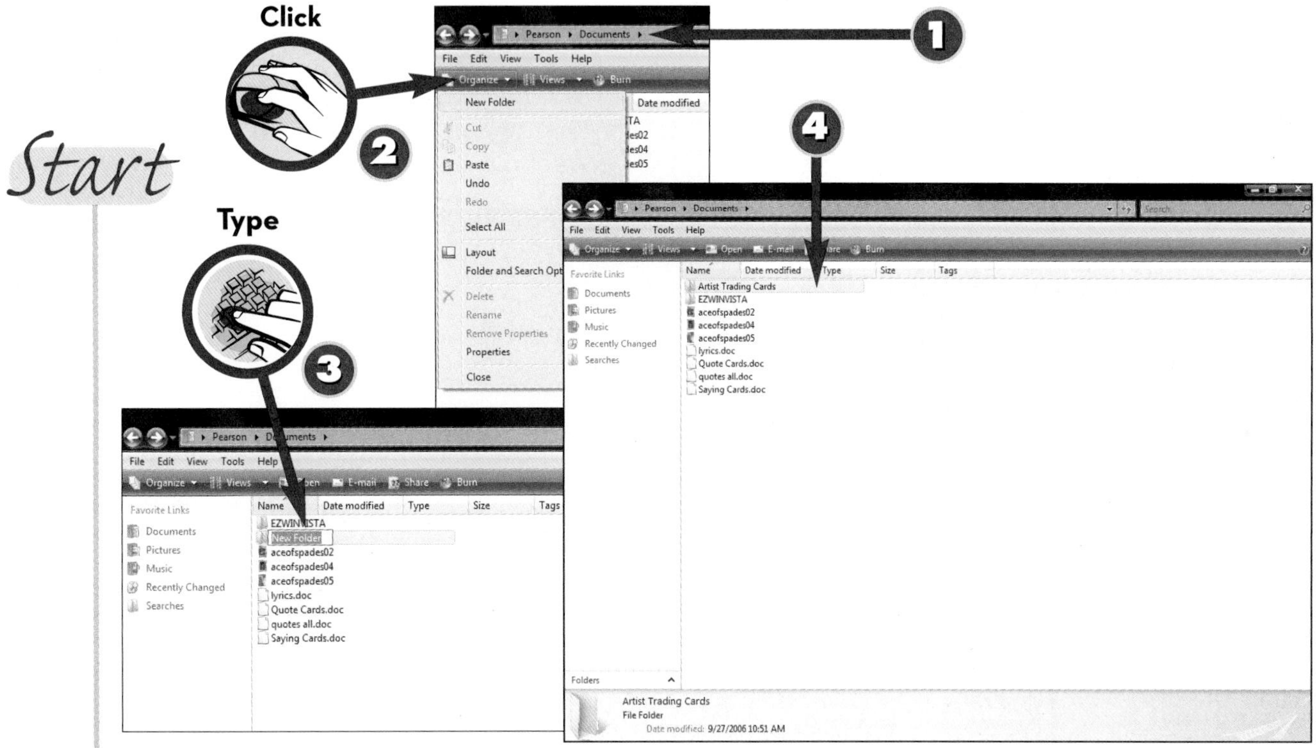

Start

Click

Type

1. Open the folder where you want to create the new folder.
2. Click **Organize**, and then click **New Folder**.
3. The new folder appears in the window, and the name is highlighted. Type a new name and press **Enter**.
4. The new folder is added to the list.

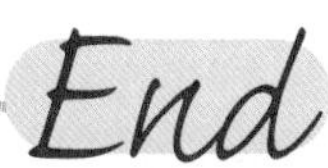

TIP

Delete a Folder

If you change your mind about the new folder, you can always delete it. To delete the folder, click on it once to select it, and then press the **Delete** key on your keyboard. Click the **Yes** button to confirm the deletion.

NOTE

Folder Name

The folder name can contain as many as 255 characters and can include spaces. You cannot include these characters: | ? / : " * < > \

COPYING FOLDERS

You can copy a folder and its contents to a new location. For example, you can copy a folder to a disk to use as a backup or to use the folder contents on another computer. In addition, you can copy a folder and its contents to another location on the hard drive if, for example, you want to revise the original files for a different use.

Start

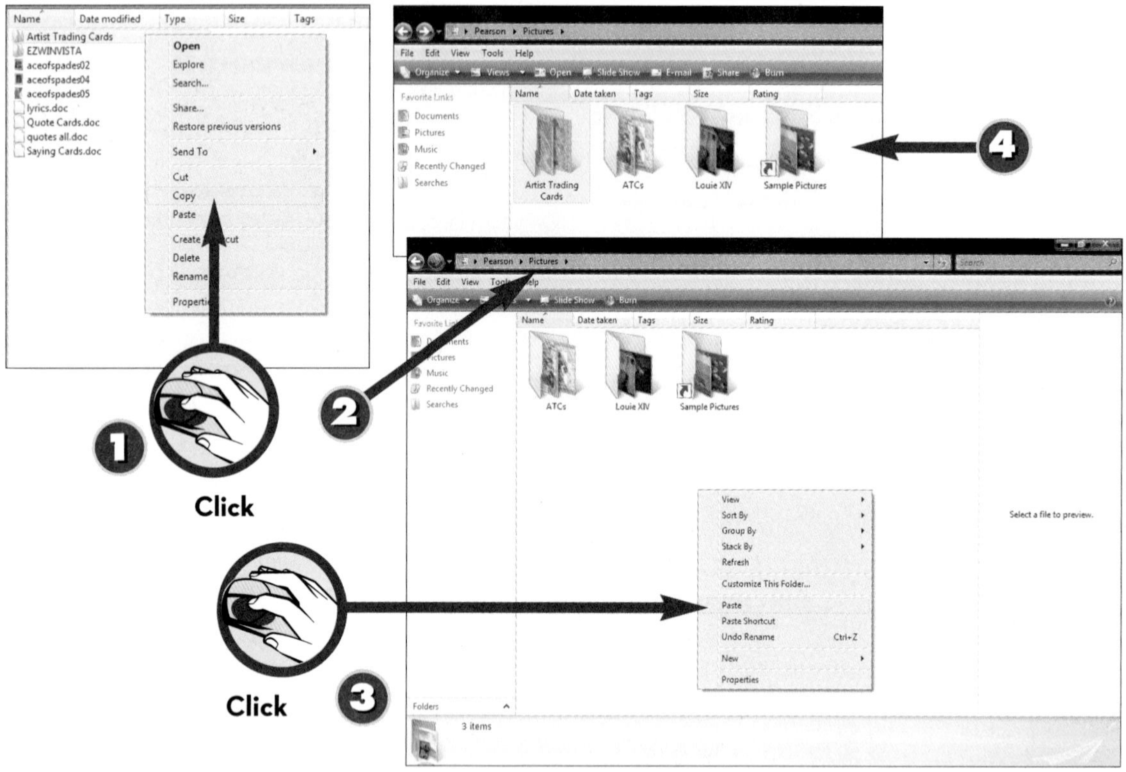

Click

Click

1. With the folder you want to copy displayed, right-click the folder you want to copy and click **Copy**.
2. Navigate to the folder where you want to place the copy.
3. Right-click a blank area of the folder's List pane and click **Paste**.
4. The folder and its contents are copied to the new location.

End

TIP

Drag-and-Drop Copying

You can also drag a folder to copy it. Hold down the **Ctrl** key and drag the folder to a folder in the Navigation pane.

TIP

Navigating to a Folder

If you need help displaying the folder you want to copy, see "Navigating Folders" earlier in this Part.

MOVING FOLDERS

You can move a folder and its contents to another folder or to a disk so that you can reorganize the folder's structure. For example, you might want to move a document folder to Documents to place all your folders within the one main Documents folder.

Start

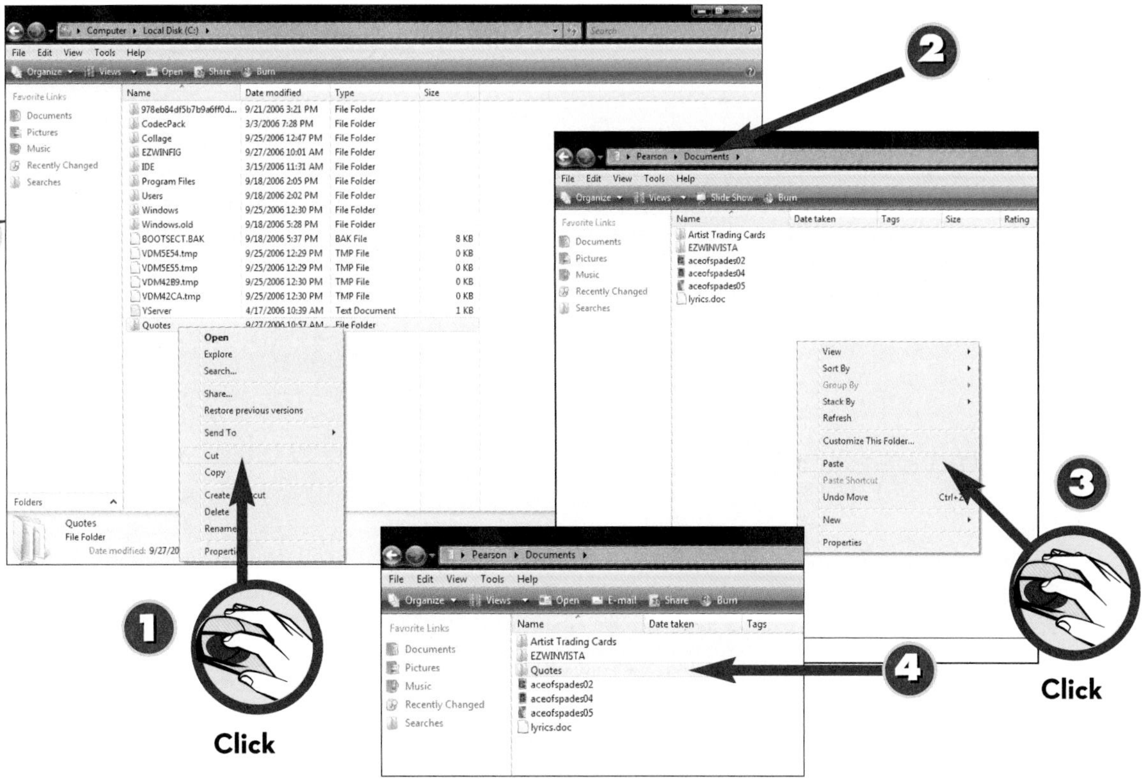

1. Right-click the file you want to move and click **Cut**.
2. Navigate to the folder where you want to move the file.
3. Right-click a blank area of the file list and click **Paste**.
4. The folder and its contents are pasted to the new location.

End

TIP

Undo Move

If you make a mistake, you can undo the move by right-clicking a blank area of the file window and then clicking **Undo Move**. (Or press Ctrl+Z on the keyboard.)

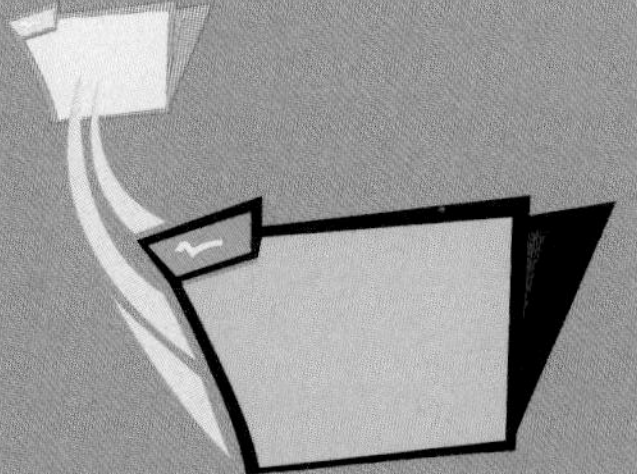

RENAMING FOLDERS

If you did not type a descriptive name for a folder, you can rename the folder to a more fitting name. Using descriptive names helps you identify at a glance the contents of a particular folder.

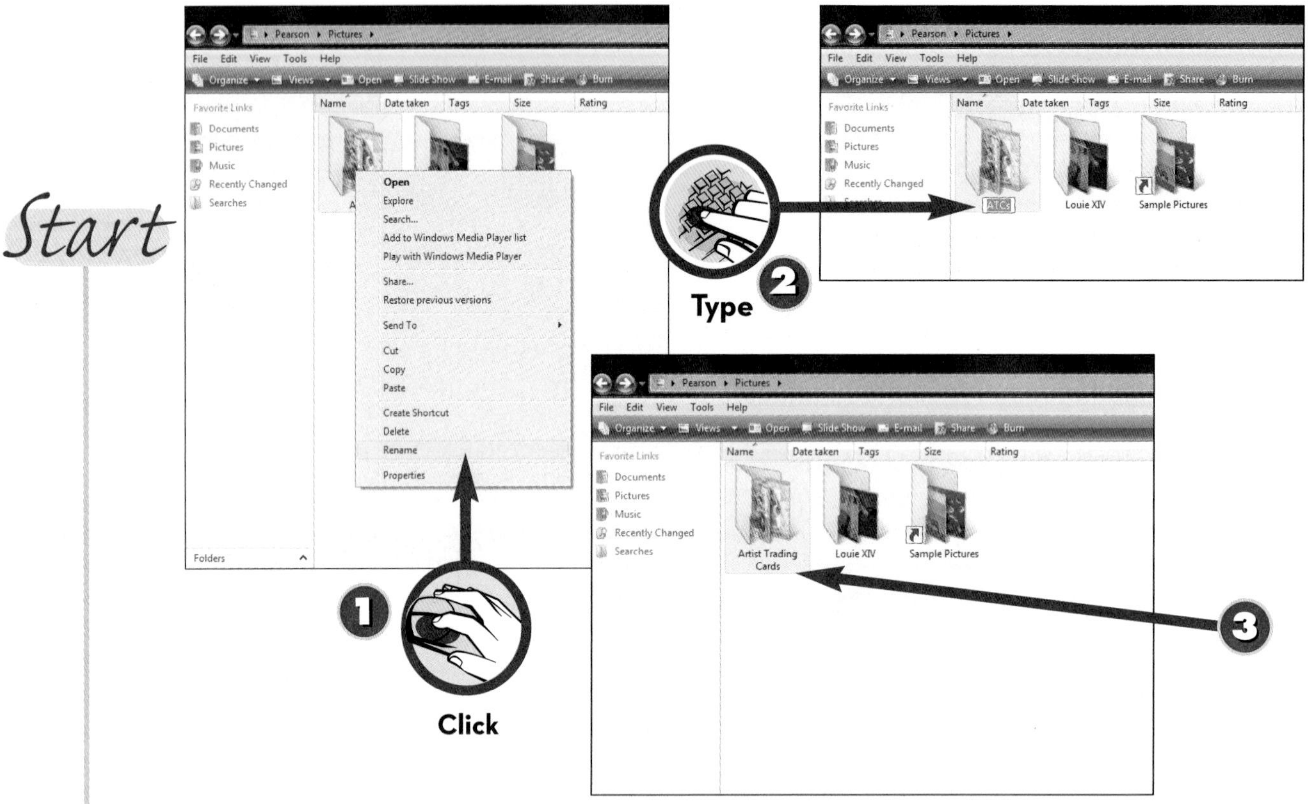

1. Right-click the folder you want to rename and click **Rename**.
2. The current name is highlighted. Type a new name and press **Enter**.
3. The folder is renamed.

NOTE

Folder Names

Folder names can contain as many as 255 characters, including spaces. You also can include letters, numbers, and other symbols, except the following: | ? / : " * < > \

DELETING FOLDERS

You can delete folders when you no longer need them. When you delete a folder, you also delete its contents. Windows Vista places deleted folders in the Recycle Bin. You can restore deleted items from the Recycle Bin if you realize you have placed items there by accident.

Start

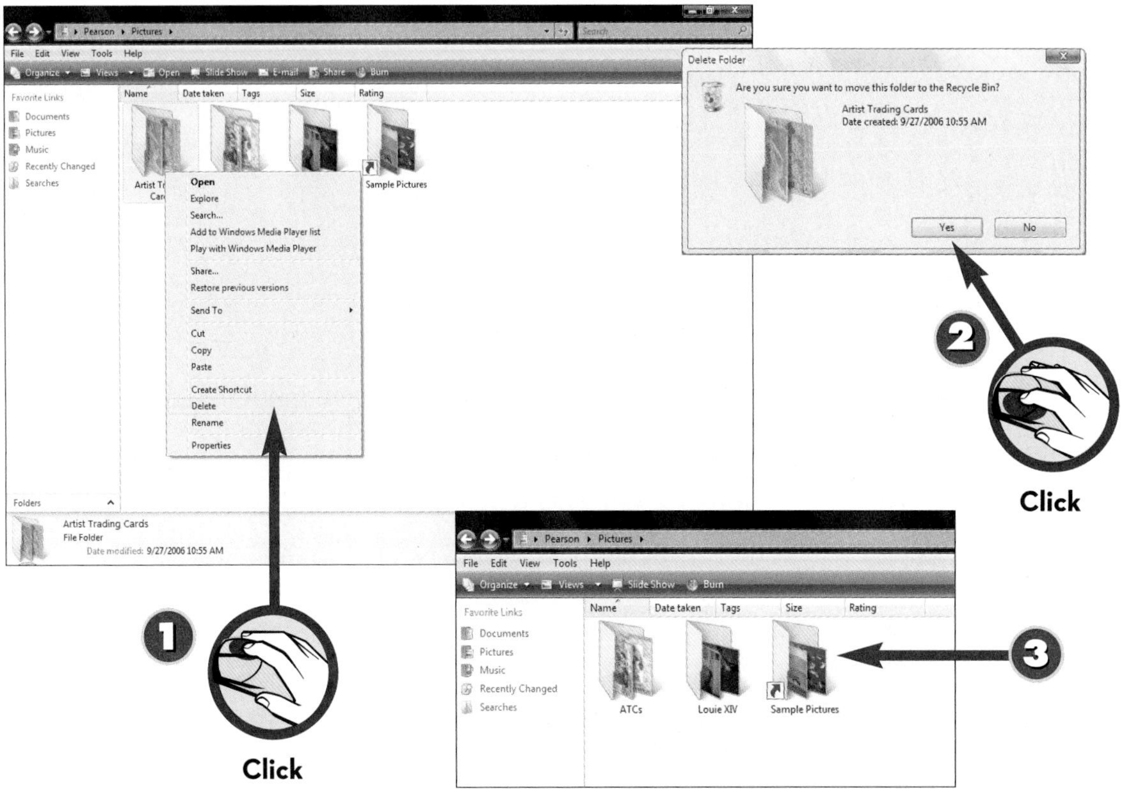

Click

Click

1. Right-click the folder you want to delete and then click **Delete**.
2. Confirm the deletion by clicking **Yes**.
3. The folder is deleted and removed from the content list; it is placed in the Recycle Bin.

End

TIP

Undo the Deletion

You can undo a deletion by right-clicking a blank part of the window and clicking **Undo**. Alternatively, you can retrieve the deleted item from the Recycle Bin. See the task "Undeleting a File from the Recycle Bin" in Part 5 for more information.

TIP

Deleting a File

Deleting a file works in the same way (only the file is deleted, not the folder and all its contents). See Part 5 for more information on working with files.

part 5

WORKING WITH FILES

Each time you save a document, its information is saved as a file on your hard disk. When you save that document, you assign both a specific place for the file (a folder) and a name.

The more you work on your computer, the more files you add. After a while, your computer will become cluttered, and you'll need a way to keep these files organized. Windows provides features that can help you find, organize, and manage your files. The first step is to learn how to select files; you can select one or several files. After files are selected, you can perform file-management tasks such as copying a file to another location or deleting a file you no longer need. If you delete a file by accident, you can recover it. You can also view file details and change the name of a file. All these tasks are covered in this Part.

WORKING WITH FILES

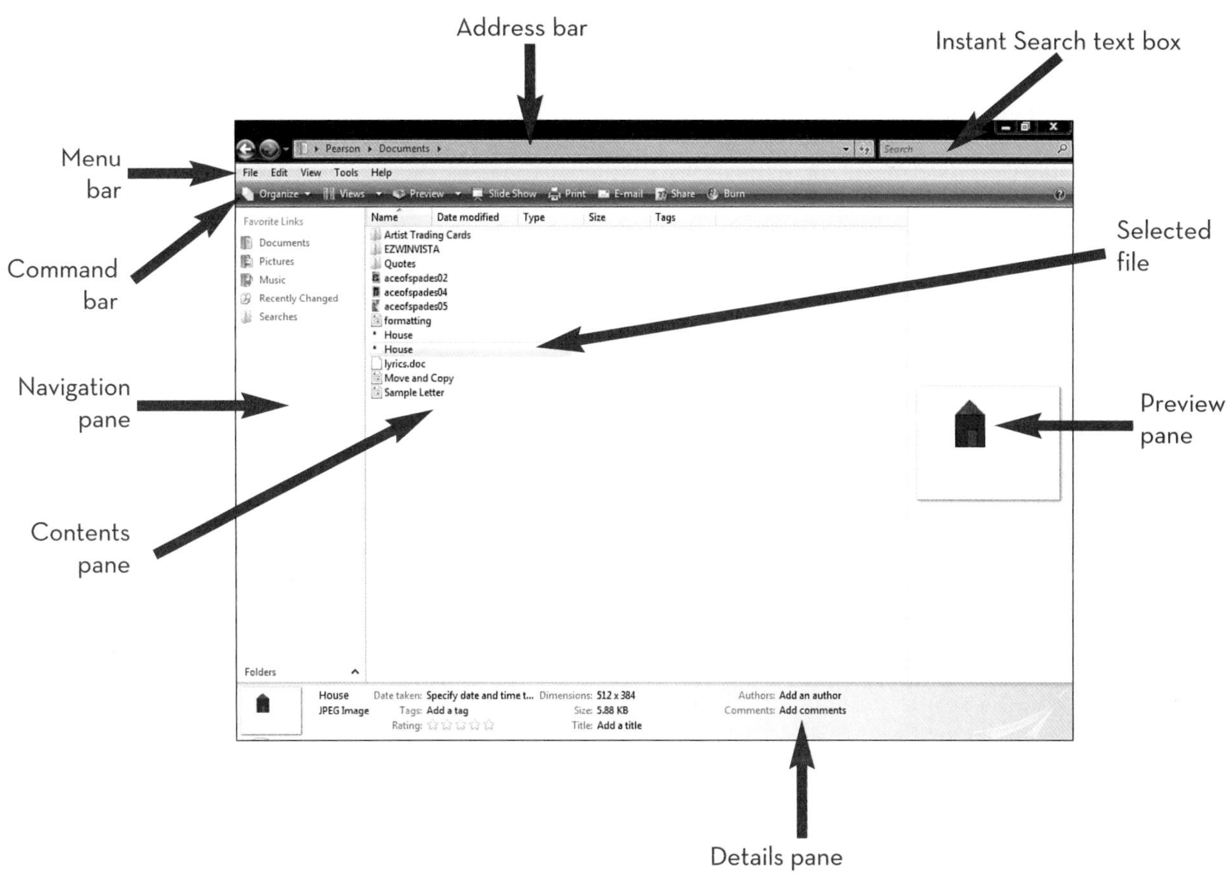

SELECTING FILES

When you want to work with files (copy, move, print, delete, and so on), start by selecting the file(s) you want. You can select a single file or several files.

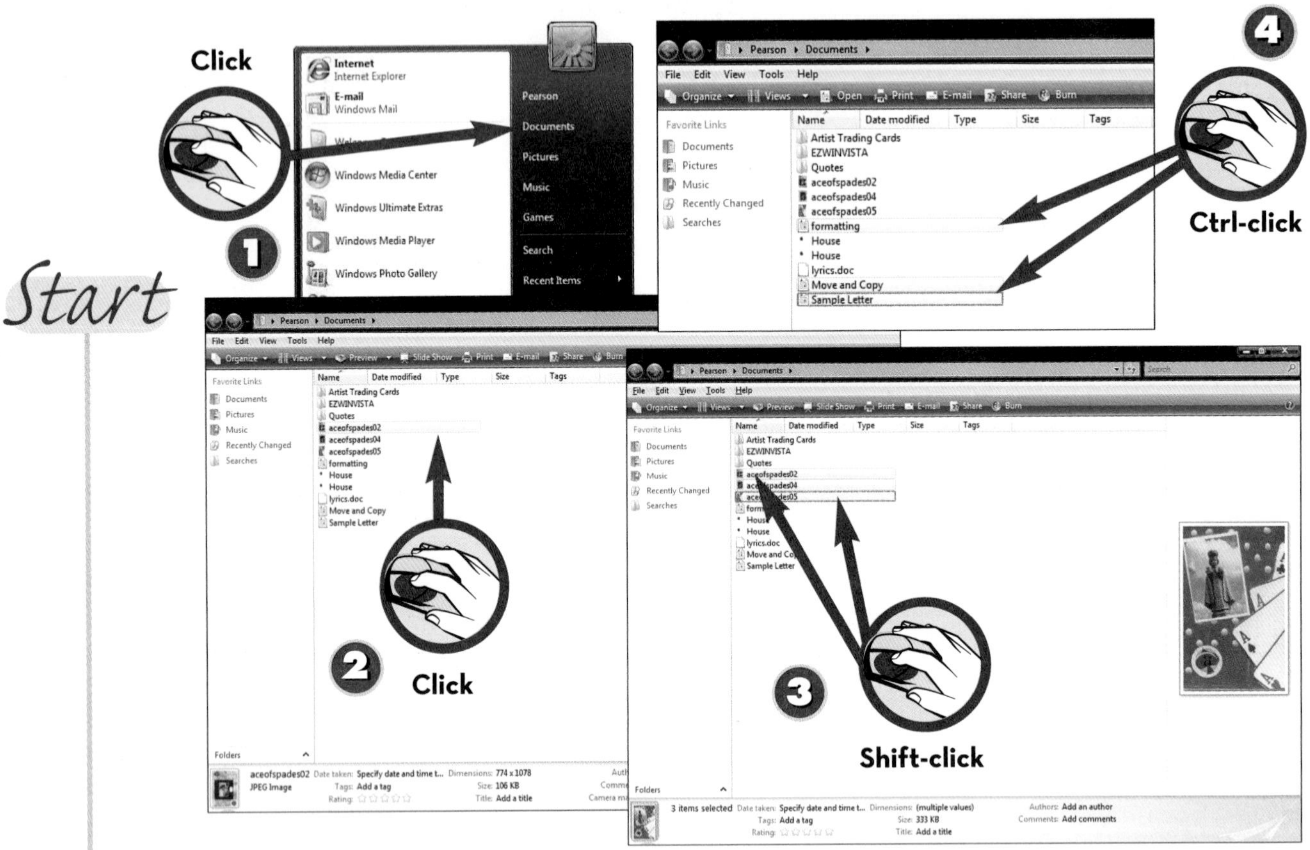

1. Open the Explorer that contains the files you want to work with. For instance, click **Start** and then **Documents** to display the Documents folder Explorer window.
2. To select a single file, click it. The file is selected.
3. To select several files next to each other, click the first file of the group that you want to select, and then hold down the **Shift** key and click the last file. The first and last files and all files in between are selected.
4. To select several files that are not next to each other, hold down the **Ctrl** key and click each file you want to select.

NOTE

Deselect a File

To deselect a file, click outside the file list.

TIP

Select All Files

To select all files, click **Organize** and then click the **Select All** command. Alternatively, press **Ctrl+A**.

VIEWING FILE DETAILS

When you are working with files, you may not be able to tell from the filename what the file contains. In that case, you can view basic file information by viewing the file properties. In past versions, you used a command in the File menu. In Windows Vista, when you select a file, the file properties are displayed in the Details pane at the bottom of the Explorer window.

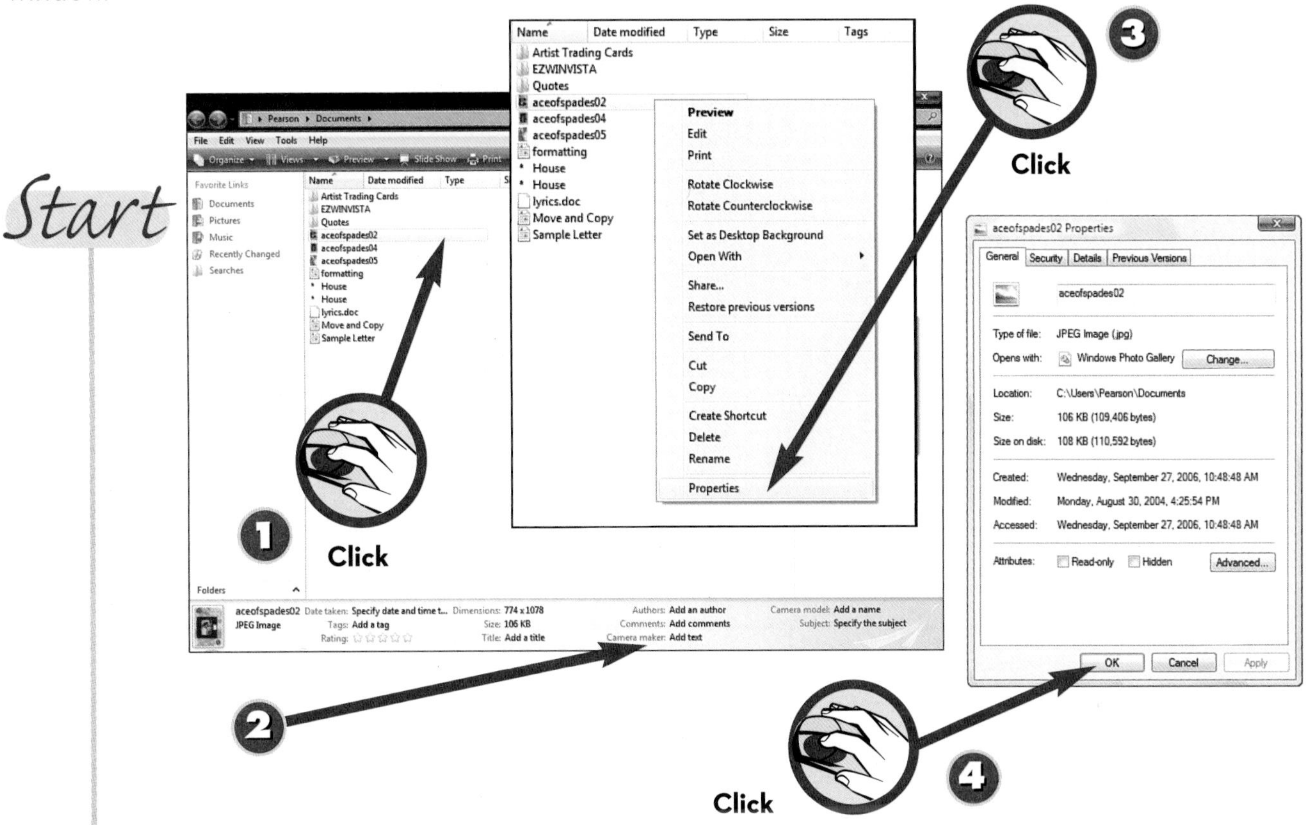

1. Select the file.
2. In the **Details** pane, you see file information on the selected file, including the file type, the key dates (modification, creation, access), and the size.
3. You can also view this and other information by right-clicking the file and clicking **Properties**.
4. You see most of the same information, but you also see the file's storage location, what program is used to open the file, and other details. Click the **OK** button to close the Properties dialog box.

NOTE

Change Views

Another way to assess the content of a file is to change how the window content is displayed. You can display a list, icons, tiles, or a detailed list. See Part 4, "Working with Folders," for information on changing the window view.

TIP

Several Files Selected

When you select more than one file, you see information in the Details pane about the total number of files selected, the total file size of the selected files, and a list of the selected files.

RENAMING A FILE

If you did not use a descriptive name when you saved the file, you can rename it. You can rename only one file at a time in an Explorer.

Start

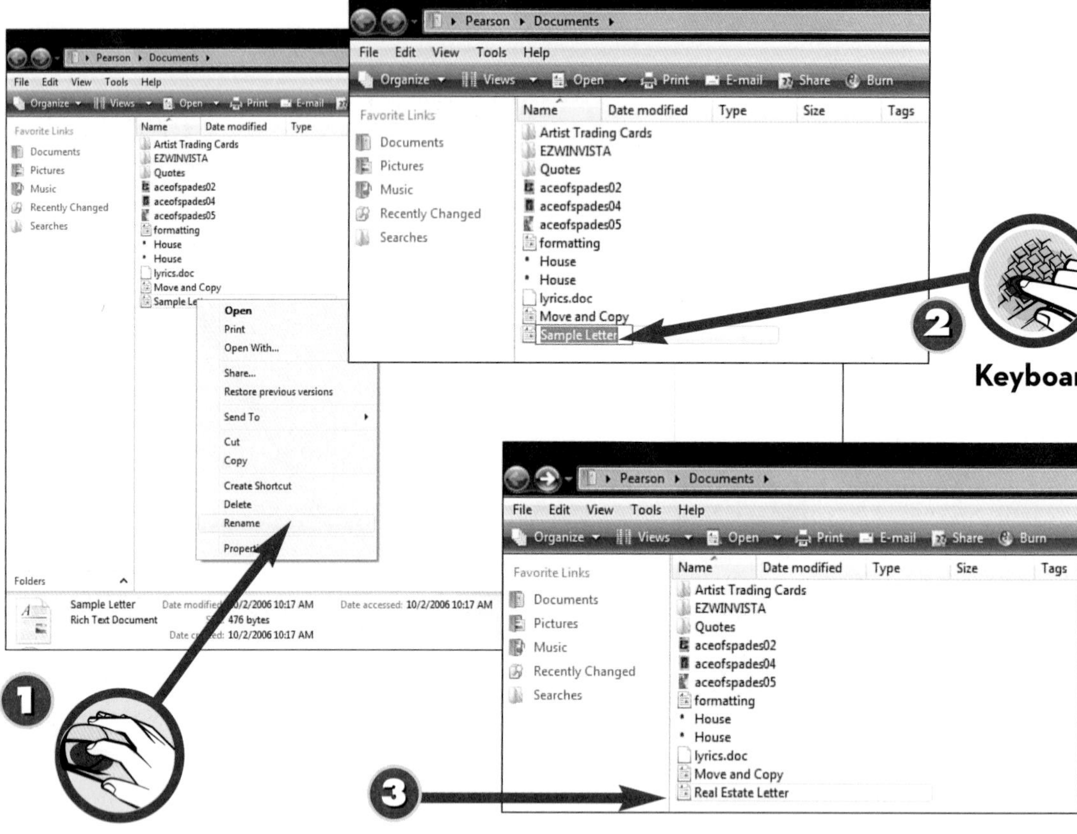

1. Right-click the file you want to rename and click **Rename**.
2. The current name is highlighted. Type a new name and press **Enter**.
3. The file is renamed.

End

TIP

Naming Rules

You can type as many as 255 characters, including spaces. You can also include letters, numbers, and other symbols, except the following: | ? / : " * < > \

MOVING A FILE

You might need to move files from one folder or drive to another (for example, to reorganize folders by putting similar files together in the same folder). You can also move a file that you accidentally saved in the wrong folder.

Start

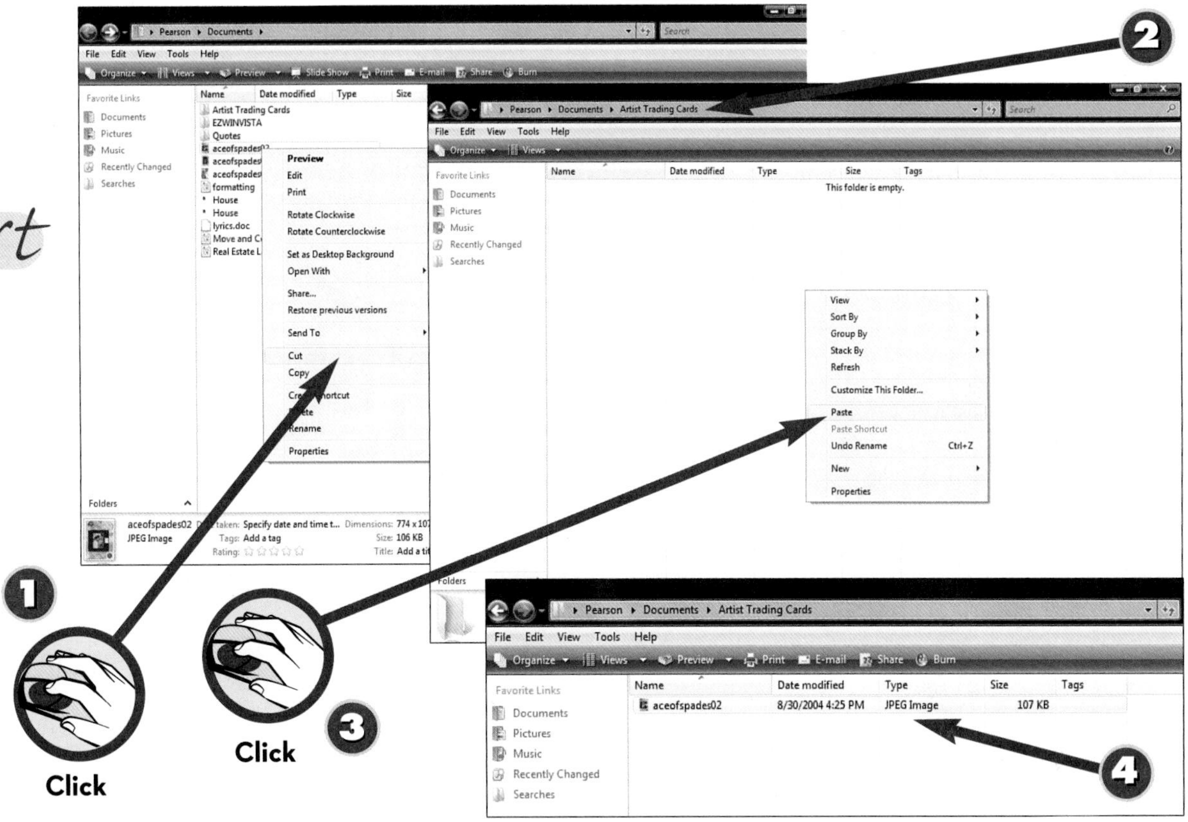

1 Click

3 Click

1. Right-click the file you want to move and click **Cut**.
2. Navigate to the folder where you want to move the file.
3. Right-click a blank area of the file list and click **Paste**.
4. The file is pasted to the new location.

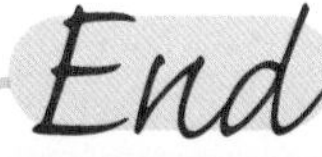

TIP

Undo Move

If you make a mistake, you can undo the move by right-clicking a blank area of the file window and then clicking **Undo Move**. (Alternatively, press the shortcut key **Ctrl+Z**.)

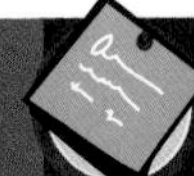

NOTE

Drag to Move

You can also drag a file or group of files in an Explorer from the file list to any of the folders in the Navigation pane to move them.

COPYING A FILE

Windows makes it easy to copy files from one folder to another and from one disk to another. You might copy files to create a backup copy or to revise one copy while keeping the original file intact. Like moving, copying a file works just like copying text: You first copy the file, and then you paste it to its additional location.

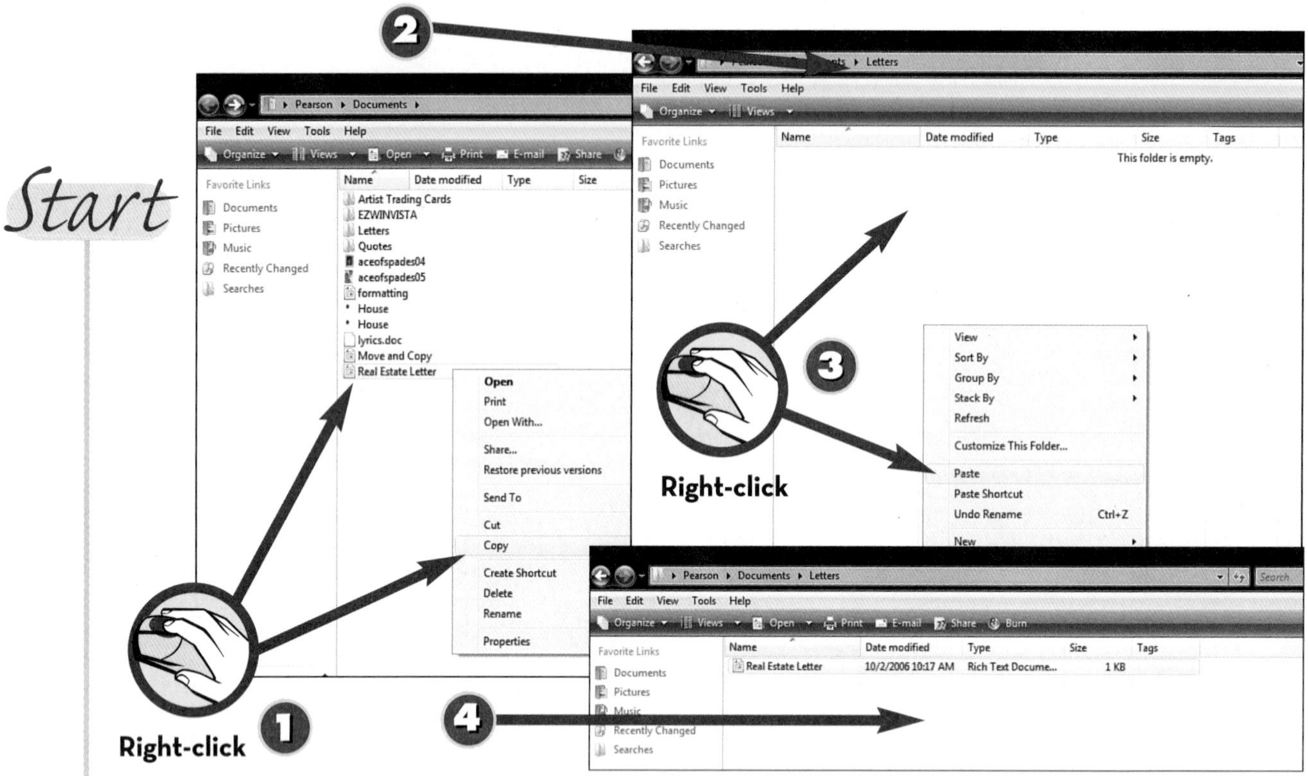

Start

Right-click

Right-click

1. Right-click the file(s) you want to copy and click **Copy**.
2. Navigate to the folder where you want to place the copy.
3. Right-click a blank area of the window and click **Paste**.
4. The file is copied to the new location.

End

TIP

Drag-and-Drop Copying

You can also drag a file to copy it. Hold down the Ctrl key and drag the file to a folder in the Navigation pane.

COPYING A FILE USING THE SEND TO COMMAND

You might want to copy a file to another disk to take the file with you or to make a backup copy. Windows provides a shortcut (the Send To command) for copying a file to a disk.

Start

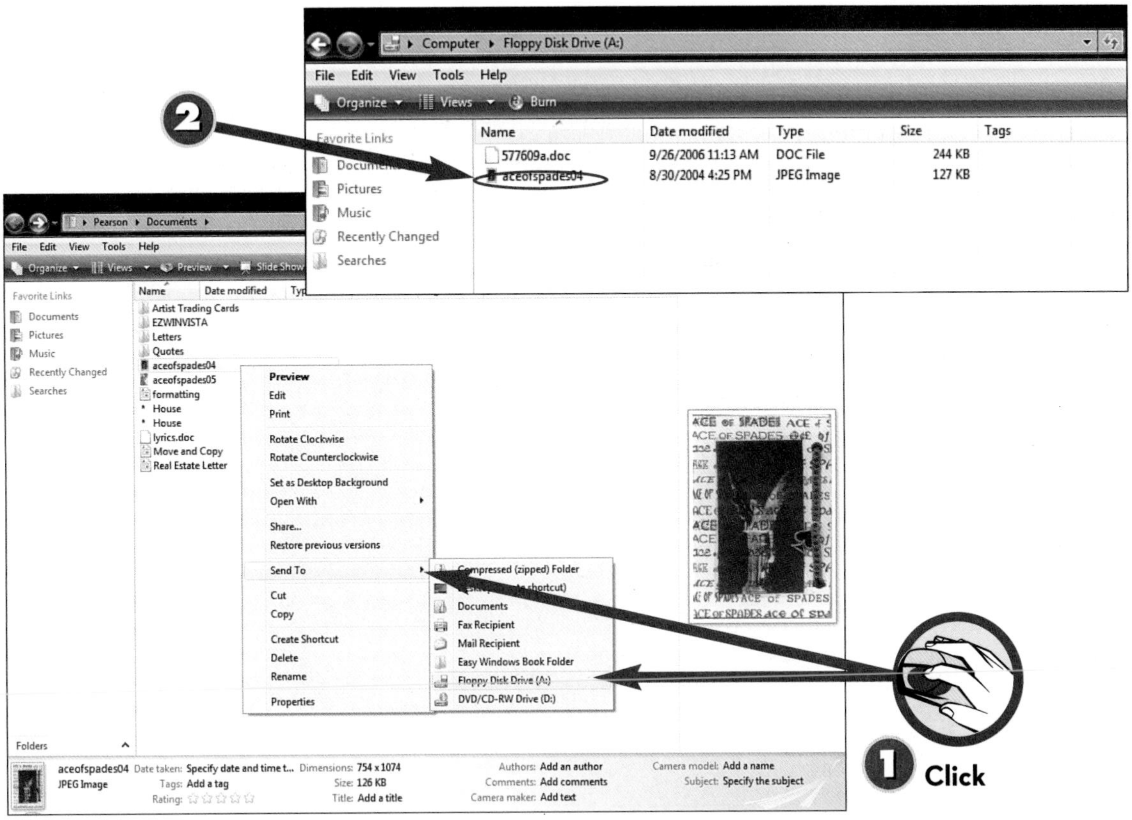

1 Click

1. Right-click the file you want to copy and click **Send To**, and then choose a location from the list. (You can also email a file to someone using this technique.)
2. The file is copied. View the contents of the disk in the Explorer window to double-check that the file has been copied.

End

TIP

Copy to CD-ROM

If you choose to copy to a CD-ROM or DVD drive, you'll be prompted to follow the steps to copy the files. Simply follow the onscreen instructions.

DELETING A FILE

Eventually, your computer will become full of files, and you'll have a hard time organizing and storing them all. You can delete any files you no longer need. Using the steps in the previous task, you can also make room by copying files you want to keep but don't need to work with again, to a disk. Then you can delete the files from your hard drive as shown in this task.

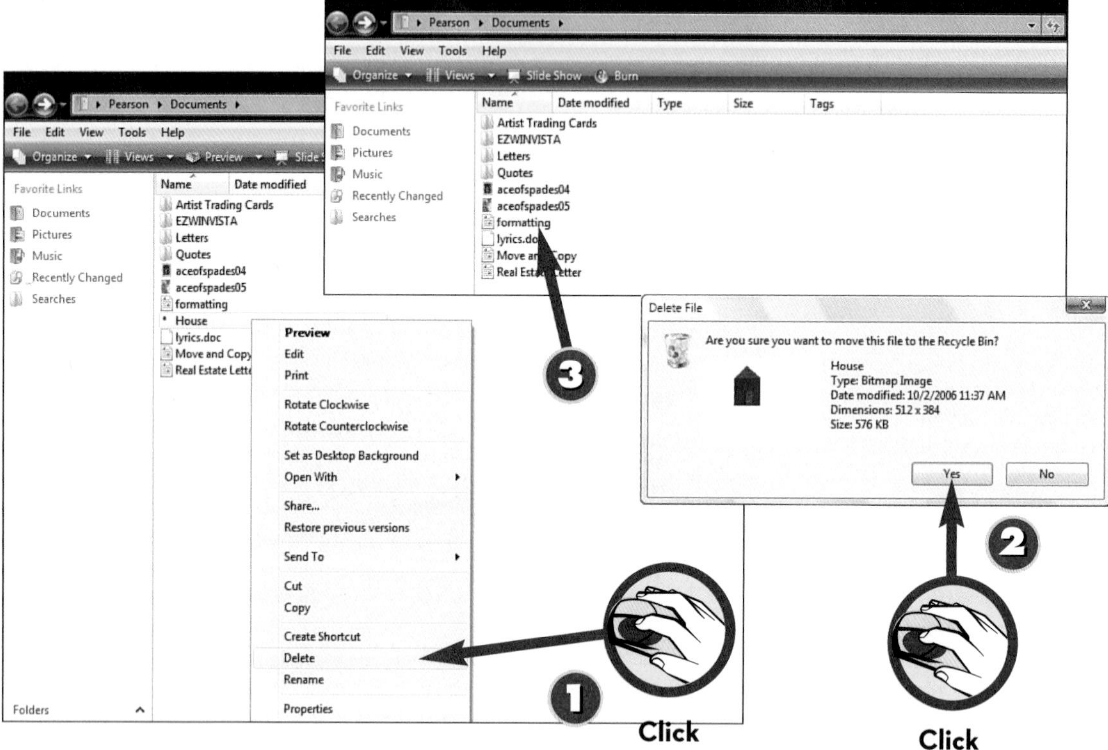

1. Right-click the file you want to delete and then click **Delete**.
2. Confirm the deletion by clicking **Yes**.
3. The file is deleted and no longer appears in the file list. (The file is actually moved to the Recycle Bin.)

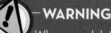

TIP

Undo the Deletion

You can undo a deletion by right-clicking a blank part of the window and clicking **Undo**. Alternatively, you can retrieve the deleted item from the Recycle Bin, as covered in the next task.

WARNING

When you delete a folder from a disk drive, that item is not placed in the Recycle Bin; it is immediately deleted from your system.

UNDELETING A FILE FROM THE RECYCLE BIN

Sometimes you will delete a file or folder by mistake. If you make a mistake, you can retrieve the file or folder from the Recycle Bin (as long as the Recycle Bin has not been emptied) and return it to its original location.

Start

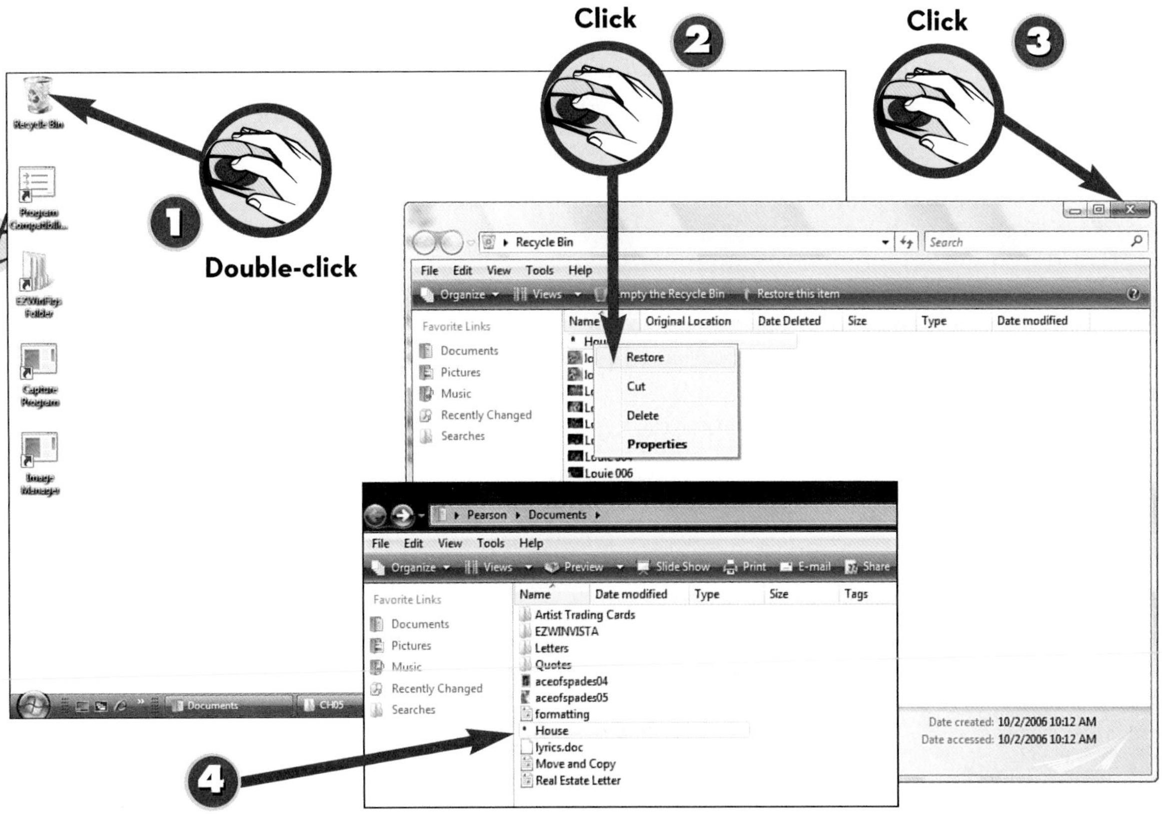

Double-click

Click

Click

1. Double-click the **Recycle Bin** icon on your desktop.
2. In the Recycle Bin window that appears, you see all the files, programs, and folders you have deleted. Right-click the file you want to undelete and click **Restore**.
3. Click the **Close** button to close the Recycle Bin.
4. You can open the original folder to confirm the file has been restored (as shown here).

End

TIP

Deleting Individual Files Permanently

If you want to permanently delete a file in the Recycle Bin, right-click the file and click **Delete**. Confirm the deletion by clicking **Yes**.

TIP

Deleting All Files in Recycle Bin

If you want to permanently delete all the files in the Recycle Bin, you can empty it. Double-click the **Recycle Bin** icon and make sure that it doesn't contain anything you need to save. Then click **Empty Recycle Bin** in the command bar. Click **Yes** to confirm that you want to permanently delete all these items.

OPENING A FILE FROM AN EXPLORER

As you are organizing your files, you may need to open a file to view its contents. You may also browse through folder windows to find a particular file and then open it, rather than open it from within the program. When you open a file, the associated program is started, and the file is opened.

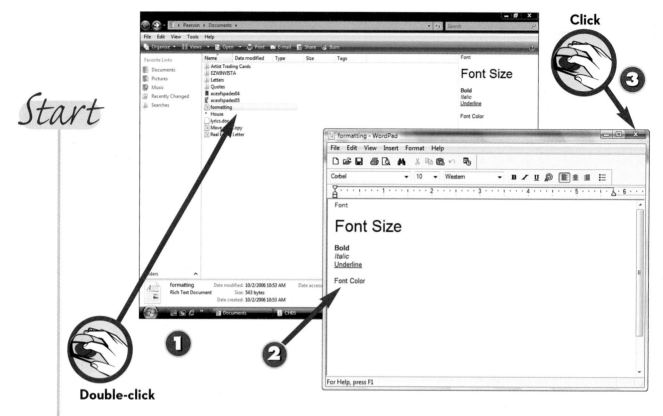

Start

Click

Double-click

1. In the Explorer, double-click the file you want to open.
2. The associated program is started, and the file is displayed.
3. When you are done viewing the file, click the **Close** button to close the document and program.

End

TIP

Error Message

If Windows Vista does not know which program to use to open the file, you get a dialog box and are prompted to use the Web service to find the correct program or to select the program from a list of installed programs. To view or set the associated programs for particular file types, see the next task.

SETTING FILE ASSOCIATIONS

When you double-click a file icon, Windows opens the program associated with that file type. If no program is associated, you are prompted to select a program. You can set and check program associations so that you don't have to continually tell Windows which program to use to open certain types of files.

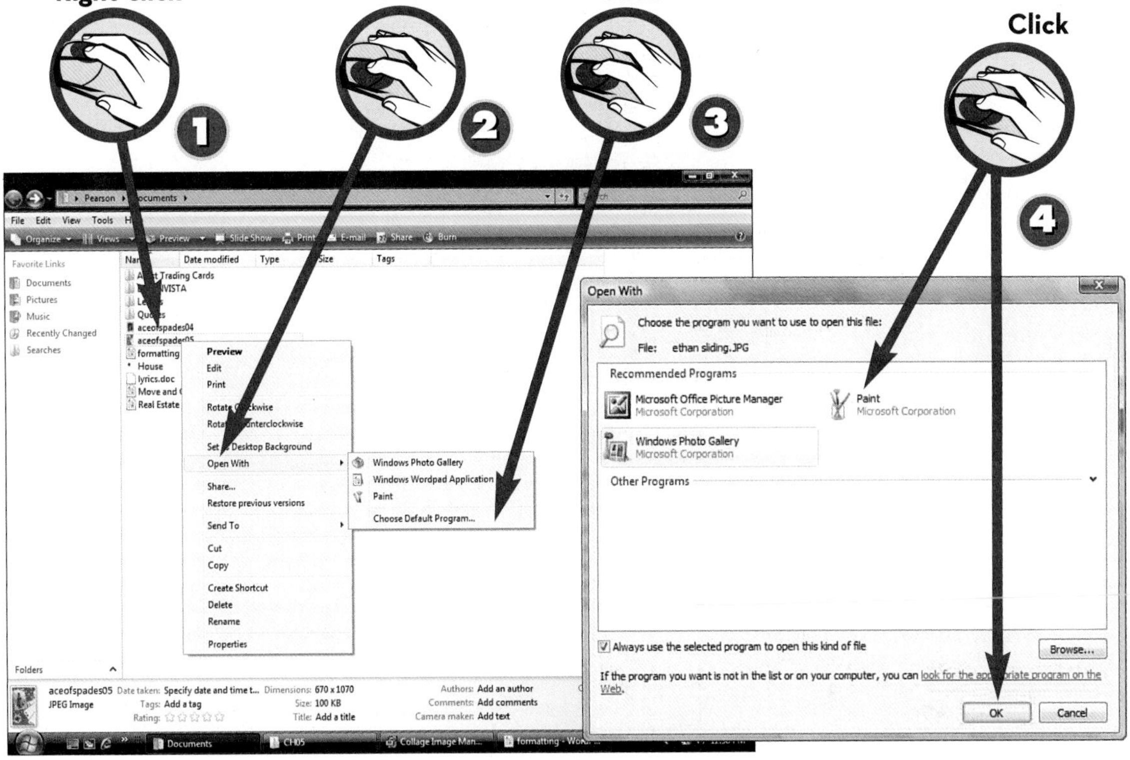

Start

1. Right-click the file icon for which you want to check or change the associated program.
2. Click **Open With**.
3. If the program you want to use is listed, select it and skip the remaining steps. To select an unlisted program, click **Choose Default Program**.
4. Select from any of the recommended or other programs listed and then click **OK**.

End

TIP

Set as Default Program

To always use the program you selected to open the file, check **Always use the selected program to open this kind of file**.

TIP

Program Not Listed?

If the program is not listed, click **Browse**, navigate to the program you want to use, and select it.

PRINTING A FILE FROM AN EXPLORER

If you do not want to open a document and then print from the program, you can print from a folder window. Printing from a folder window is helpful when you want to print several files; you can select all of the files and print them with one command.

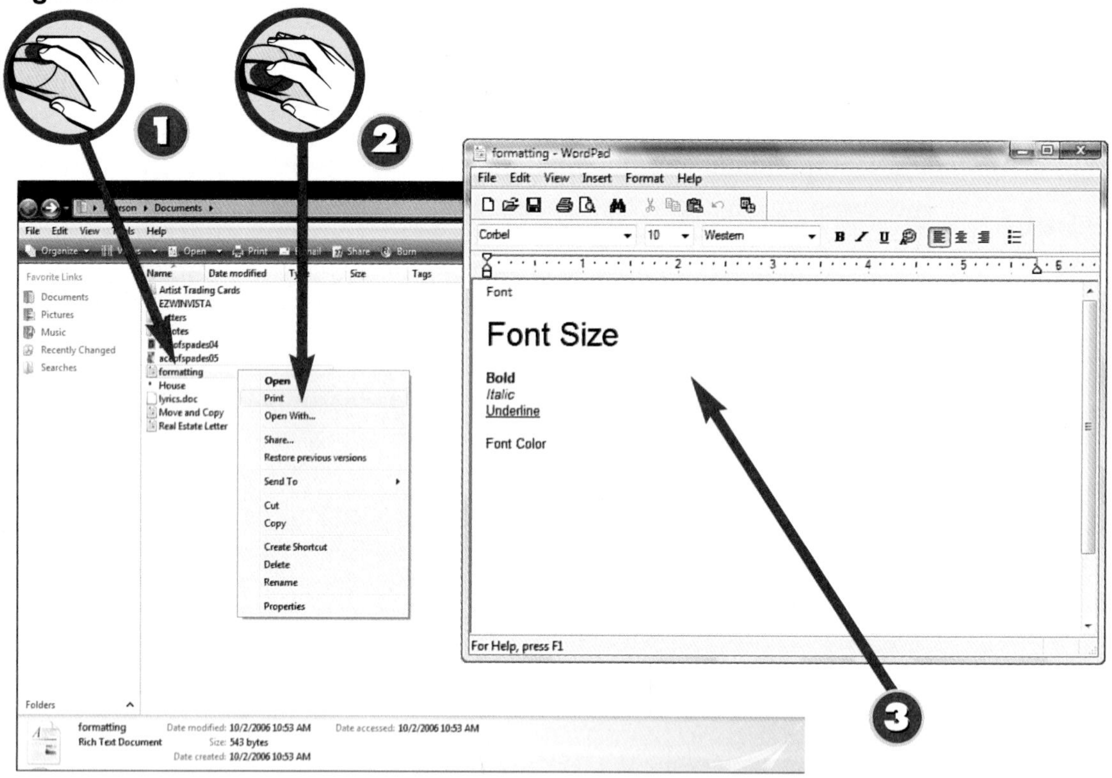

Right-click

Click

Start

1. Right-click the file you want to print.
2. Click **Print**.
3. Windows opens the associated program and prints the file(s), and the file is sent to your printer.

End

TIP

Printer Setup

When printing from folders, Windows Vista uses the default printer you have selected in the Printers control panel. For more information on setting up printers and printing, see Part 6, "Working with Printers."

TIP

Email a File

You can email a file by selecting it and clicking **E-mail** in the command bar. Click the **Attach** button, complete the email message, and click **Send**. See Part 9, "Sending Email," for more information on sending emails.

USING INSTANT SEARCH

It is easy to misplace a file by accidentally saving it in a folder other than the one you intended to use. If you have saved a document but cannot locate it by browsing through your folders, search for it. New with Windows Vista is Instant Search, and all the Explorers as well as the Start menu include a search box. You can use this search box to search for files by a variety of criteria, including name, content, file tags, and so on. Keep in mind that to search based on tags, you have to have applied a tag.

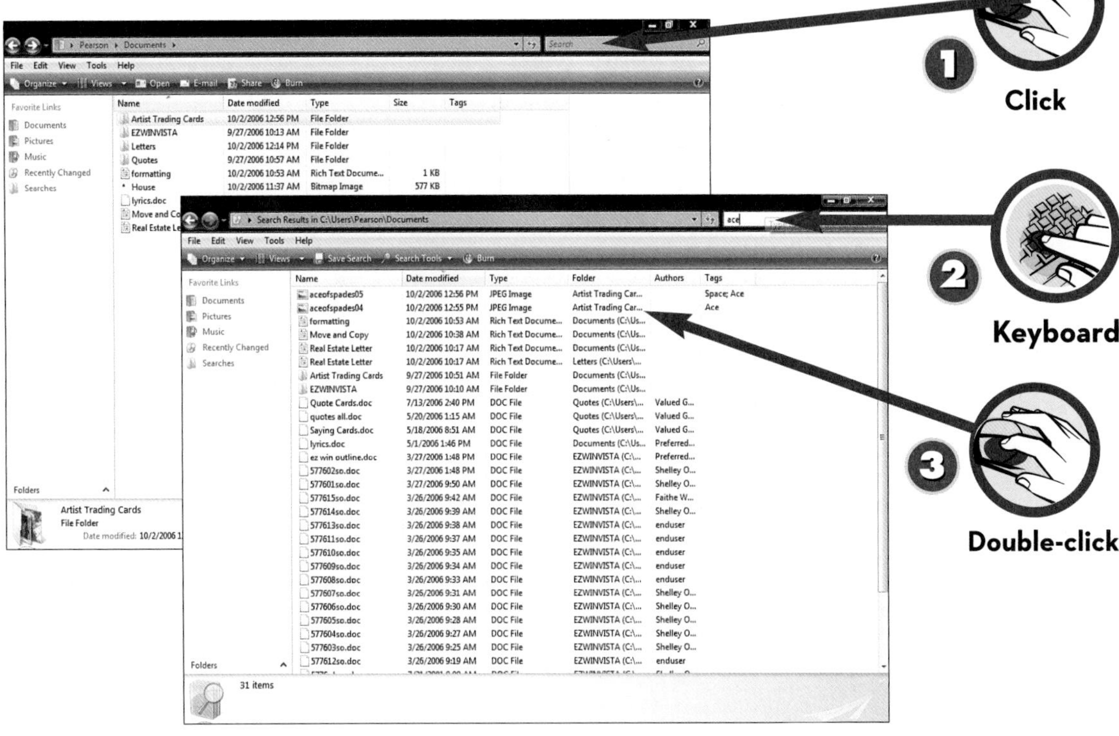

1. In an Explorer, click in the **Search** text box.
2. Type an identifying word within the file to search for.
3. Windows displays any matching files. You can double-click the file to open it or perform any other file-related tasks.

End

TIP

Search from Start Menu

You can follow this same method of searching from the Start menu. Click the **Start** button, and then in the **Start Search** box at the bottom of the Start menu, type a word or phrase to find.

TIP

No Search Results?

If you see a message that says "No items match your search." Try searching using another word or phrase to locate the file. Or use the Advanced Search options by clicking the link and completing the exact fields and criteria to search. Then click **Search**.

SAVING SEARCHES

If you frequently search for a file or set of files, you can save the search. That way you can quickly locate the file or group of files without having to perform a search each time. This task covers how to save a search.

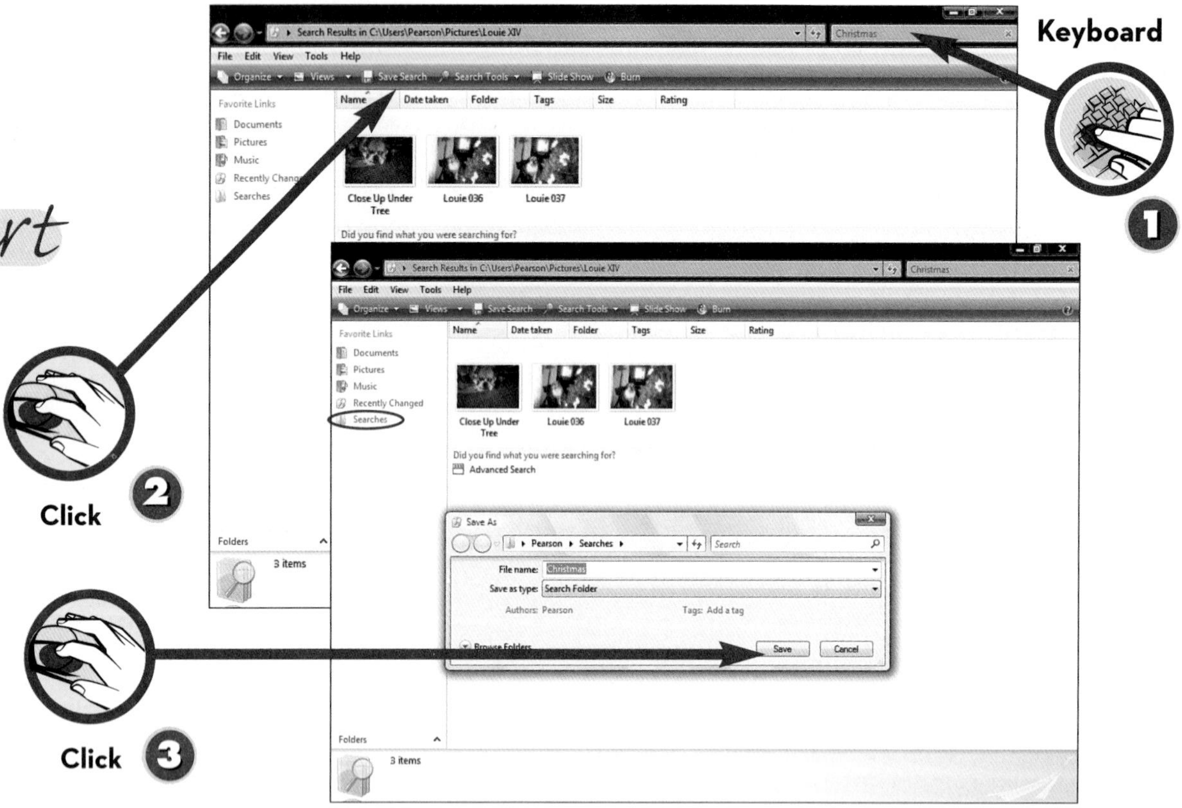

Start

Keyboard

Click 2

Click 3

1 Perform the search that you want to save.

2 In the command bar, click the **Save Search** button.

3 Type a name for this search and click **Save**. The search is saved in your Searches folder, which appears in the Navigation pane.

End

TIP

Running a Saved Search

To run a search you have saved, see the next task.

RUNNING A SAVED SEARCH

If you have saved a search that you perform frequently, you can run that same search quickly by using the Searches folder, a special folder in the Navigation pane. This is a new feature in Windows Vista that helps you quickly locate a file or group of files.

Start

Click

Double-click

1. In the Navigation pane, click the **Searches** folder. You see any searches you have saved, as well as some of the default searches that Windows Vista has created.
2. Double-click the search you want to perform.
3. You see the results of that search. You can open or perform any file- or folder-related tasks on the matches.

End

TIP

Running a Windows Search

Windows Vista sets up some default searches, which are common searches that you may want to perform. For instance, for email you have sent in the past seven days, you can search for messages with attachments and double-click any of the other listed searches to execute that search.

ADDING A TAG TO A FILE

One of the most hailed features of Windows Vista is the capability to add tags or keywords to files (and folders). Doing so gives you more options to search for the file; it also helps you group similar files. This task covers how to add a tag to a file.

Start

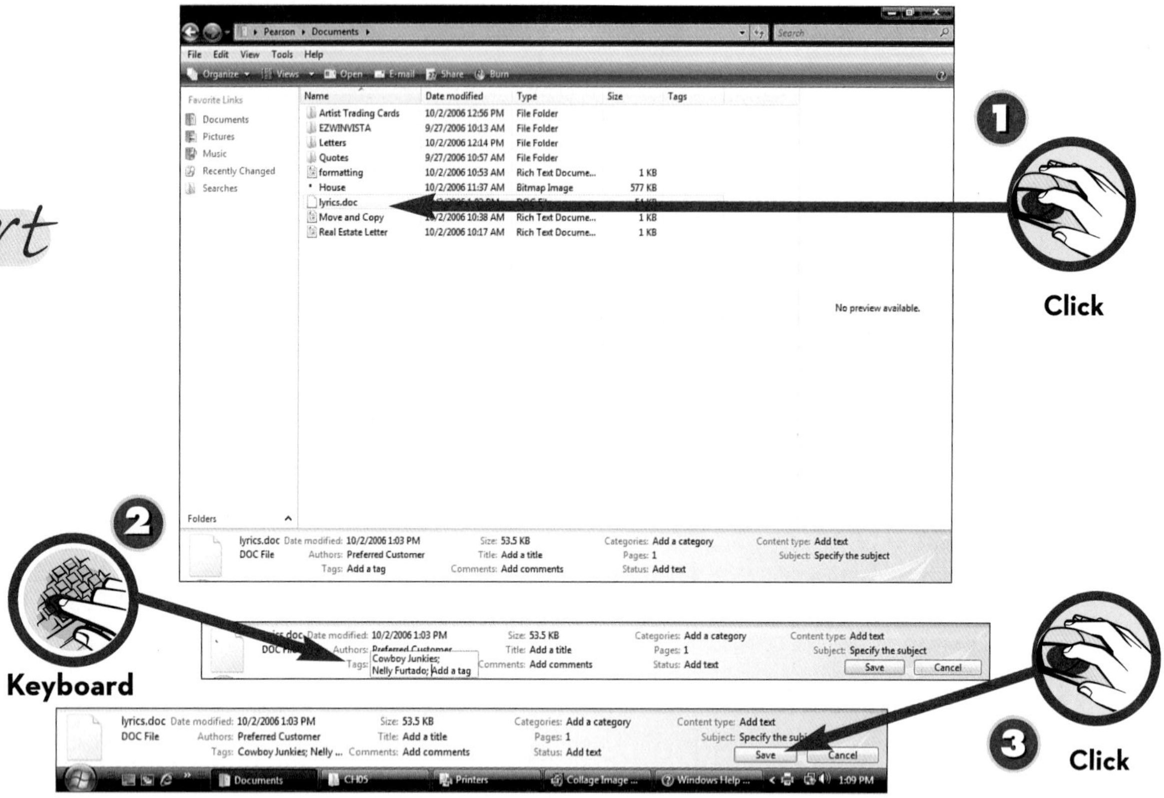

1. Select the file you want to add a tag or keyword to. In the **Details** pane, you see the available properties, including tags that you can add.
2. Click in the **Tags** field and type the tag. The reminder text for tags will still appear, and a semicolon will be added automatically in case you want to add more than one tag. Continue typing all the tags you want to include.
3. Click the **Save** button. The tags are saved to the file properties.

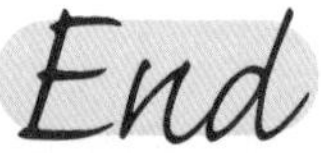

TIP

Editing or Deleting a Tag (or other property)

You can click in the Tag field to type other tags. You can also click in the field and delete any tags you don't want to include by

ADDING OTHER PROPERTIES TO A FILE

In addition to tags, you can add other identifying information to a file. Again, including this information will enable you to search based on any of the properties you add. You can add a title, comments, author, category, subject, rating, camera model, and other information. Note that the properties available for adding depend on the file type. For instance, ratings are used for pictures, but not for Word documents.

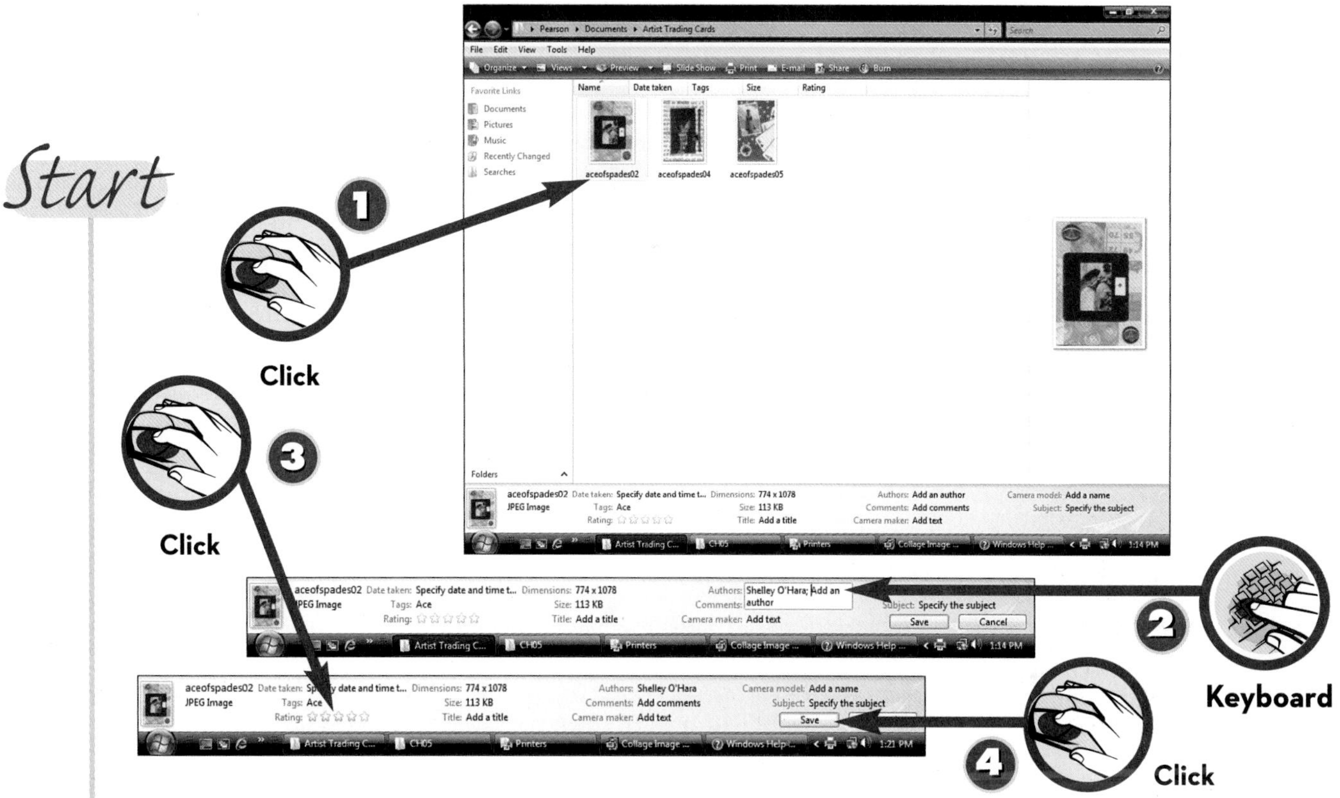

Start

Click

Click

Keyboard

Click

1. Select the file you want to add information to.
2. Click in the field and type the entry. For instance, click in the Authors field and type the author. Press **Enter** when the entry is complete.
3. Complete any other fields; for instance, for pictures, you can click the stars to rate the picture.
4. Click the **Save** button. The tags are saved to the file properties.

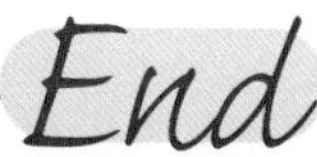

TIP

Semicolons and Reminder Text

When you type in a field, the reminder text (such as "Add an author") appears. Also, after you complete one entry, a semicolon is automatically added so that you can type additional information as needed.

WORKING WITH PRINTERS

All Windows programs use the same setup for your printer, which saves time and ensures that you can print from any Windows program without resetting for each program. When you first install Windows, it sets up your printer. If needed, you can set up more than one printer in Windows and choose the printer you want to use at any given time. In addition, you can easily manage printing for all your programs from Windows. You can pause, restart, and cancel printing, for instance, from the print queue.

You can also make customization changes to the printer, such as setting the default printer or default settings for how the printer works (for instance, landscape versus portrait orientation). You access and manage the printer through the Control Panel.

VIEWING AVAILABLE PRINTERS

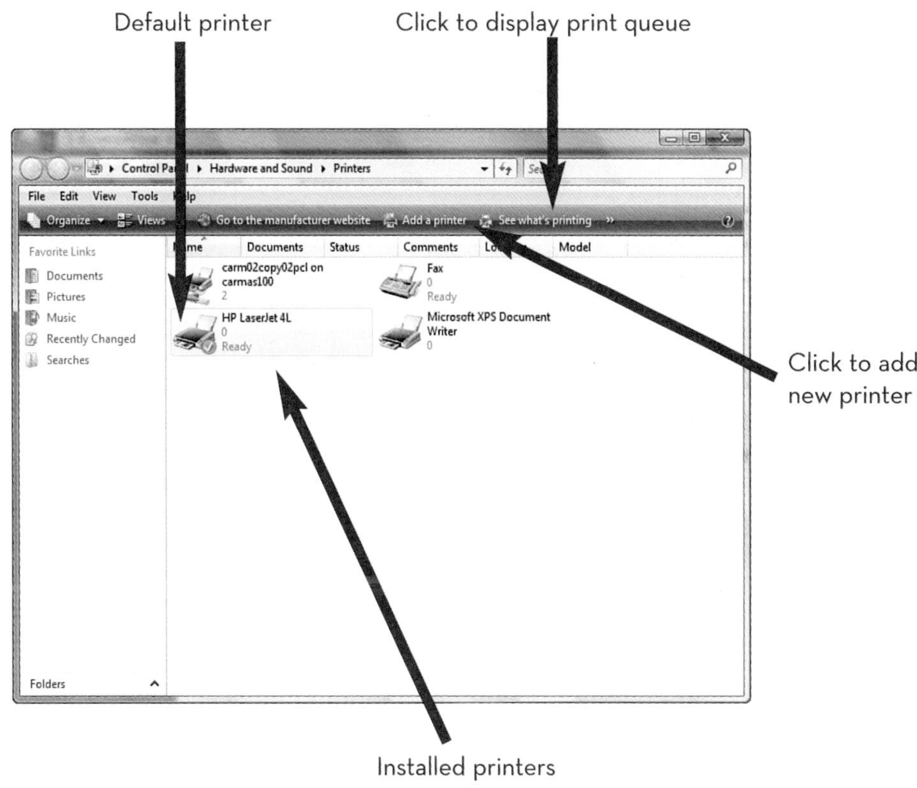

ADDING A PRINTER

You can add a new printer to your Windows setup by using a step-by-step guide called a *wizard*. In many cases, Windows can automatically set up your printer after you attach its cable to your computer. If this doesn't work for some reason, you can use the wizard to set up the printer.

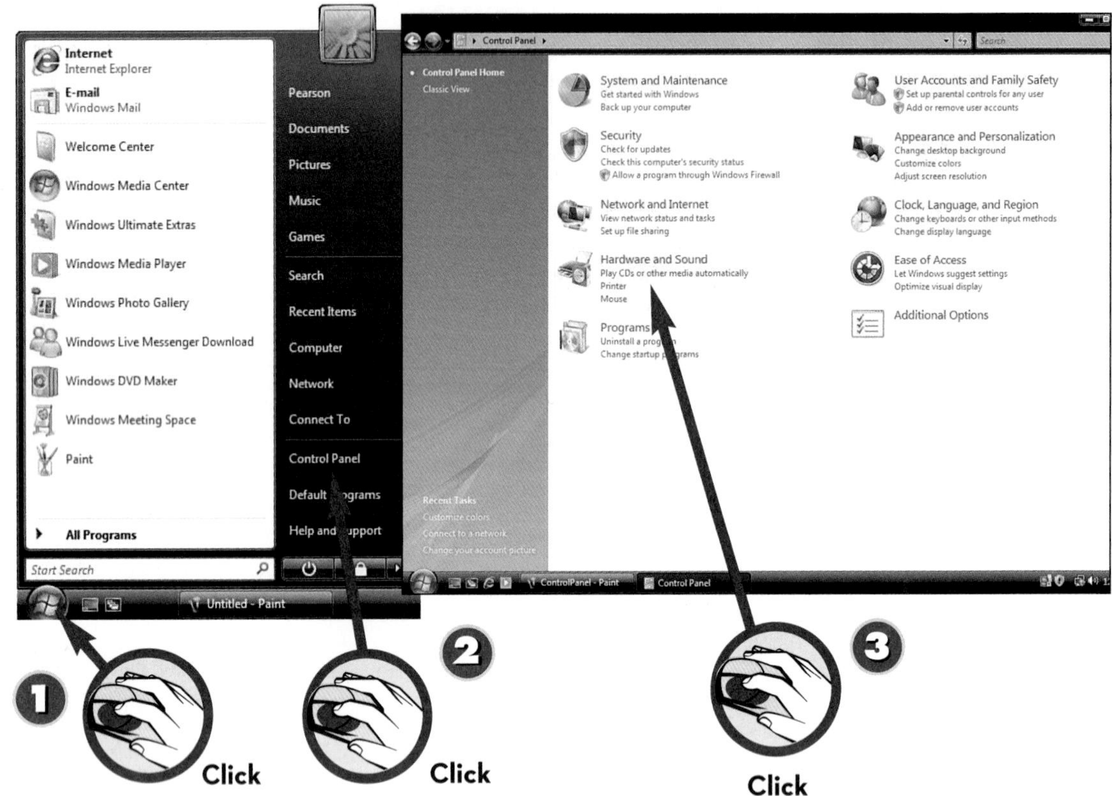

1. Click **Start**.
2. Click **Control Panel**.
3. Under **Hardware and Sound**, click **Printer**.

Continued

NOTE

Classic View

Two views are available for Control Panel icons. The default is Control Panel Home, in which the icons are organized by category. The other view is Classic View. Choosing this view displays all control panels as individual icons. You can switch between the views by clicking the View option in the left pane of the window.

TIP

Go Back a Step

In a wizard dialog box, click the **Back** button to return to the previous dialog box and review or modify your selections.

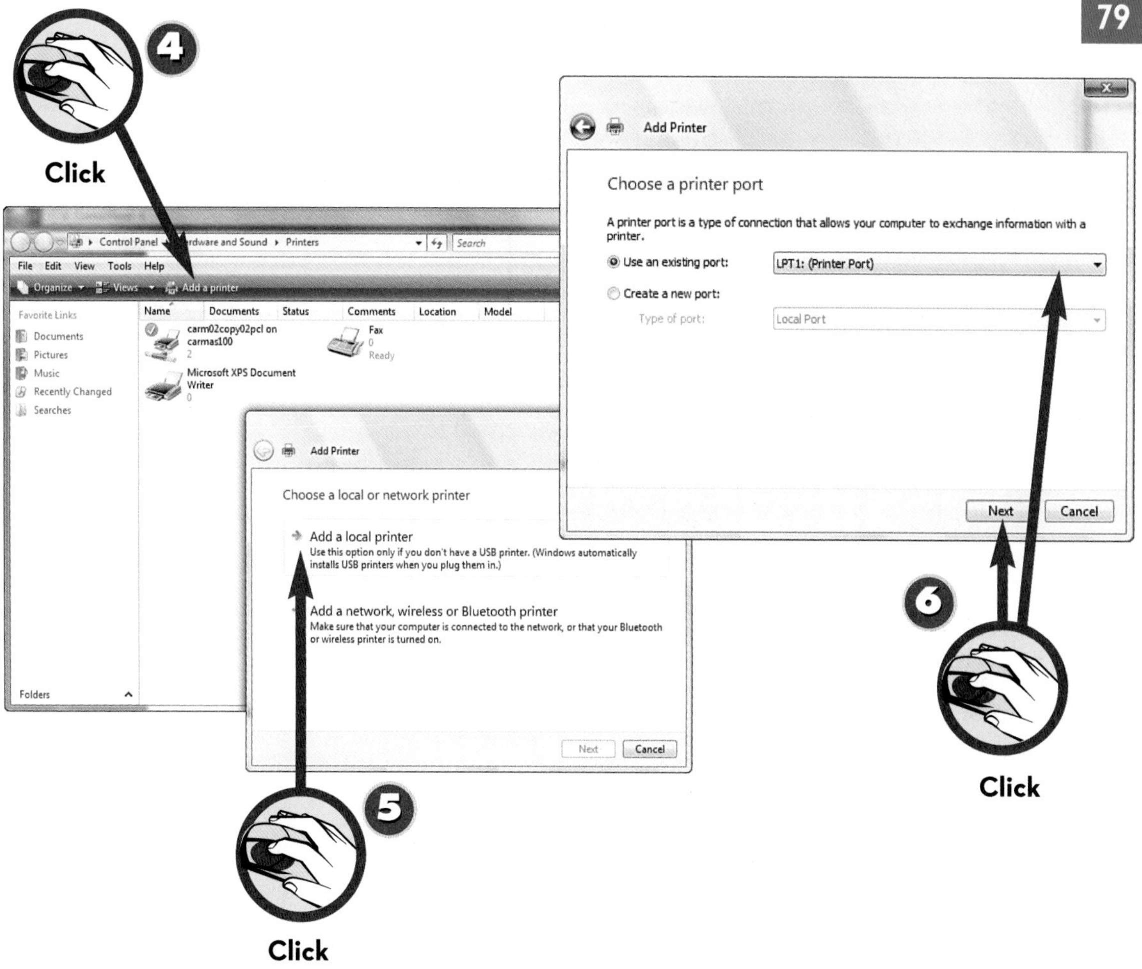

4. Click **Add a printer**.
5. Make sure your printer is connected and turned on and then click the **Add a local printer** option. (If you are using a network printer, see the "Install Network Printer" tip at the bottom of this page.)
6. Select the port to which your printer is connected (usually the default LPT1 port that is selected already). Click **Next**.

Continued

TIP

Install a Network Printer

If you are installing a network printer, see Part 16, "Home Networking Basics," for more information on how to use the Add Printer Wizard.

TIP

Defining a Port

Your printer is connected to your computer through a cable. Most often printers connect via a special printer port called an LPT port, although you can also find and connect printers through USB or serial ports. You just need to make sure that you select the appropriate port for your printer cable connection.

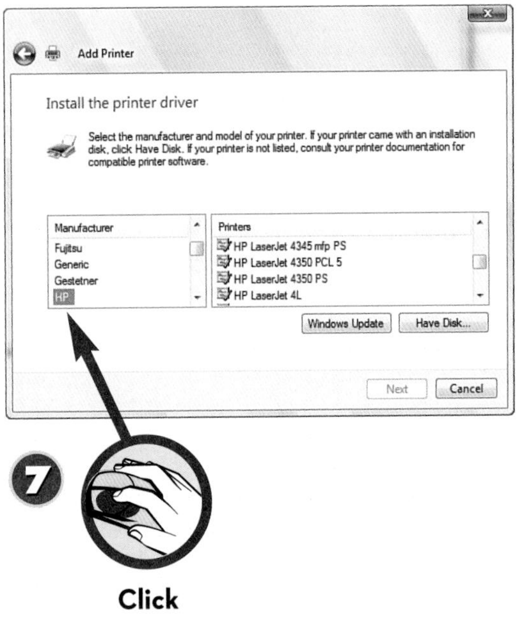

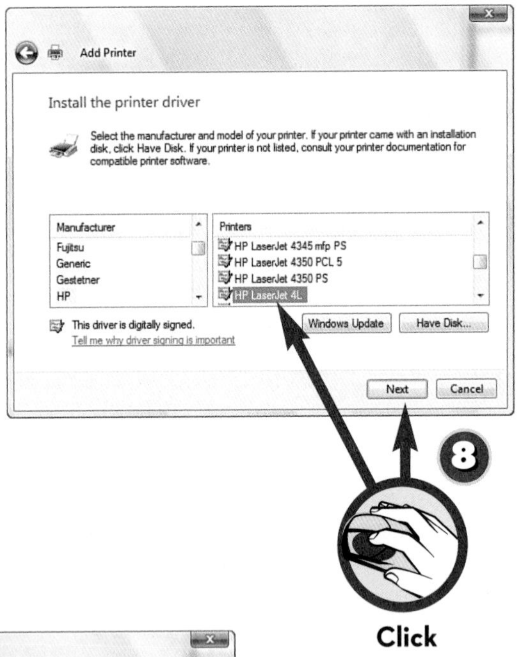

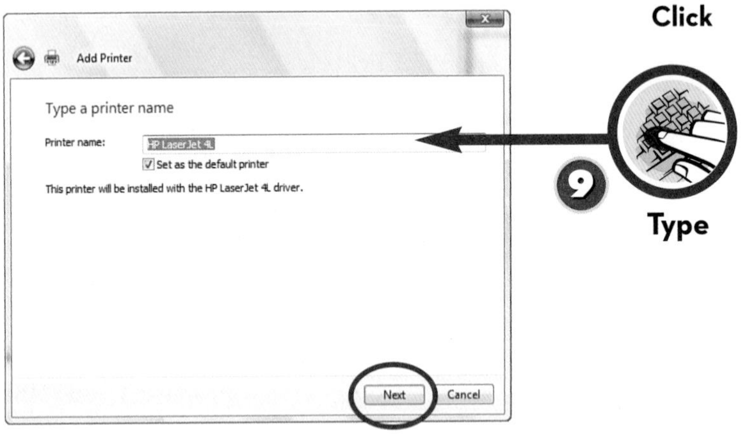

7. From the list of printer manufacturers, select the company that made your printer.

8. The Printers list is updated with available models after you select your particular manufacturer. Select your printer from the Printers list. Click **Next**.

9. Type a name to identify this printer and click **Next**.

Continued

TIP

Default Printer

Every time you print something, the program will first attempt to use the default printer. (If you have more than one printer, you can select which printer to use.) When you install a new printer, you can set it as the default printer. To do so, leave the **Set as the default printer** check box checked. (You can change your default printer at any time, covered later in this Part.)

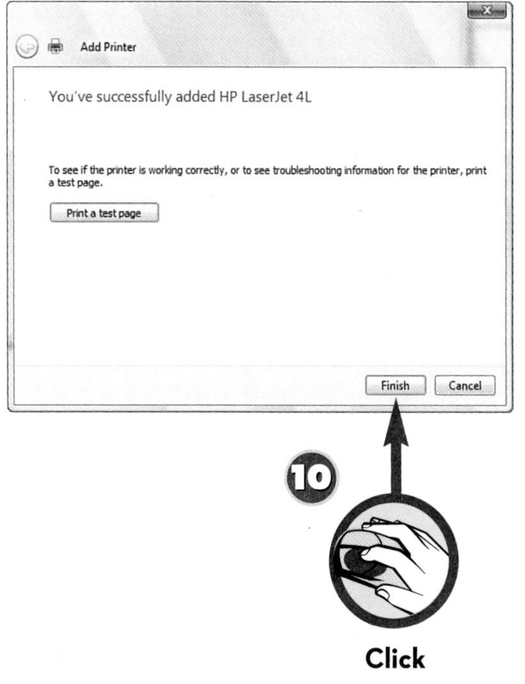

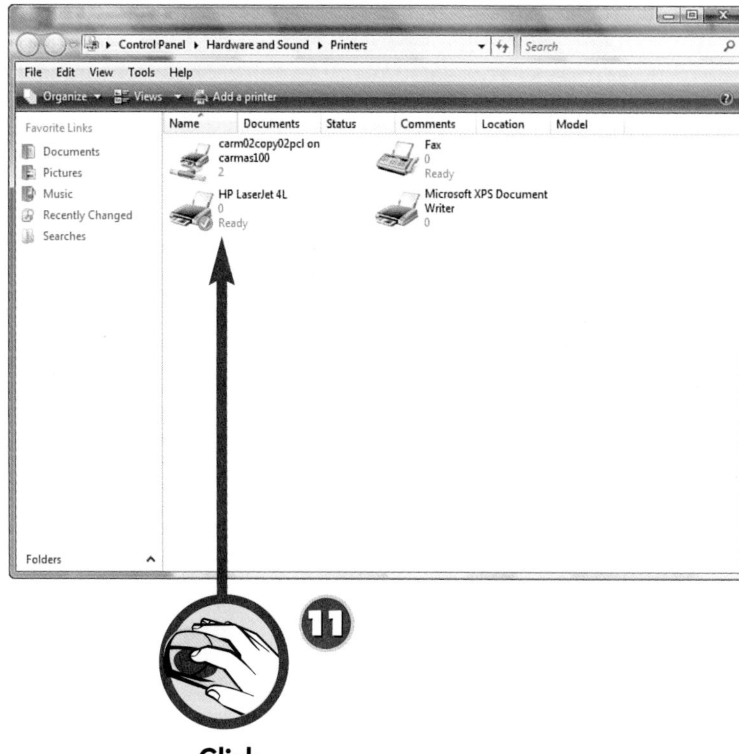

10 Click **Finish**. Your printer is installed.

11 You see your new printer listed in the Printers control panel.

End

TIP
Use the Printer Disk

If you have trouble using this method, try using the disk that came with your printer. During the installation, click **Have Disk**, insert the disk, and then select the drive to search for the file. Follow the steps to install the printer using the disk.

TIP
Printing Test Page

Before you click Finish to complete setting up the printer, you can print a test page. To do so, click the **Print a test page** button in the final dialog box.

DISPLAYING INSTALLED PRINTERS

If you want to modify a printer's settings or delete an installed printer, open the Printer Control Panel. You can then view and change the preferences and properties for any of the printers. You can also access the print queue to pause, restart, or cancel a print job.

Start

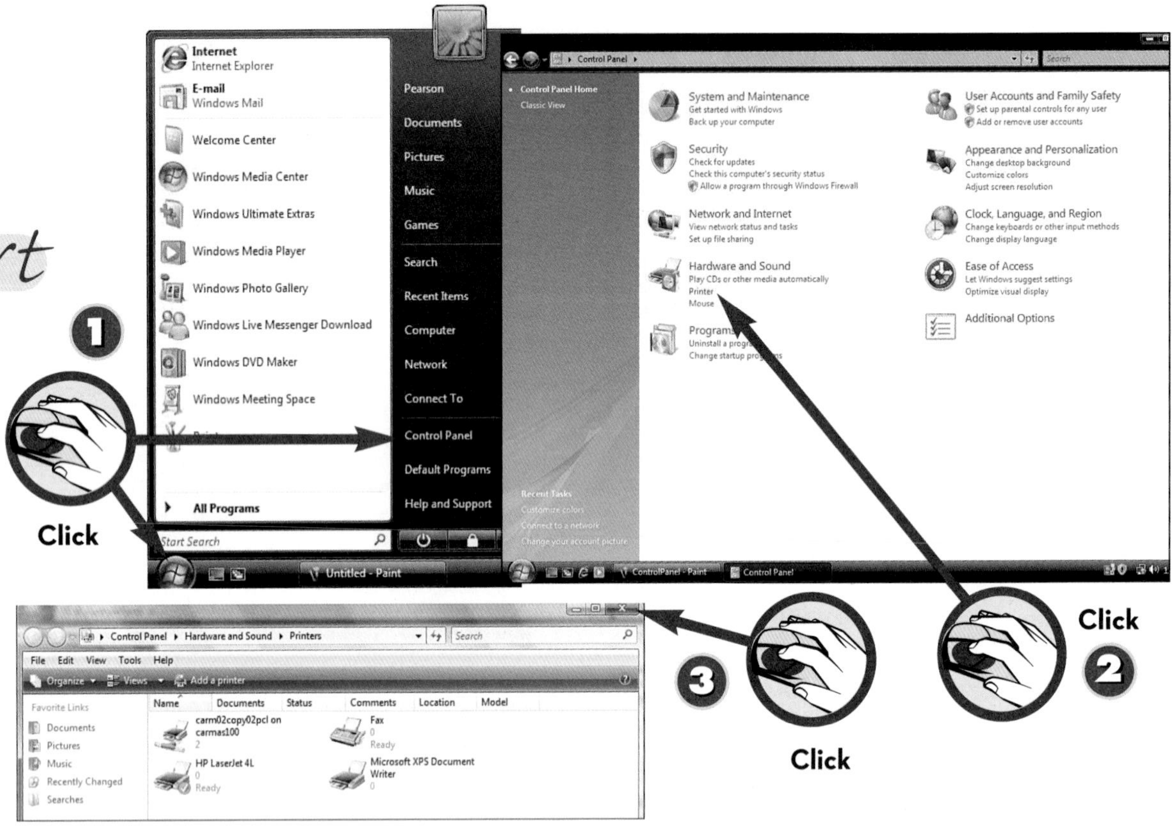

Click

Click

Click

1. Click the **Start** button and then click **Control Panel**.
2. Under **Hardware and Sound**, click **Printer**.
3. You see a list of the installed printers. To close the window, click its **Close** (X) button.

End

TIP

Classic View

The Control Panel has two views—one is by category as shown here. The other view (Classic) just shows Control Panel icons. You can switch to Classic View by clicking it in the Navigation pane.

SETTING THE DEFAULT PRINTER

When you print a document, the program will always attempt to use the default printer. So you should set the printer you use most often as the default (if you have more than one printer).

Start

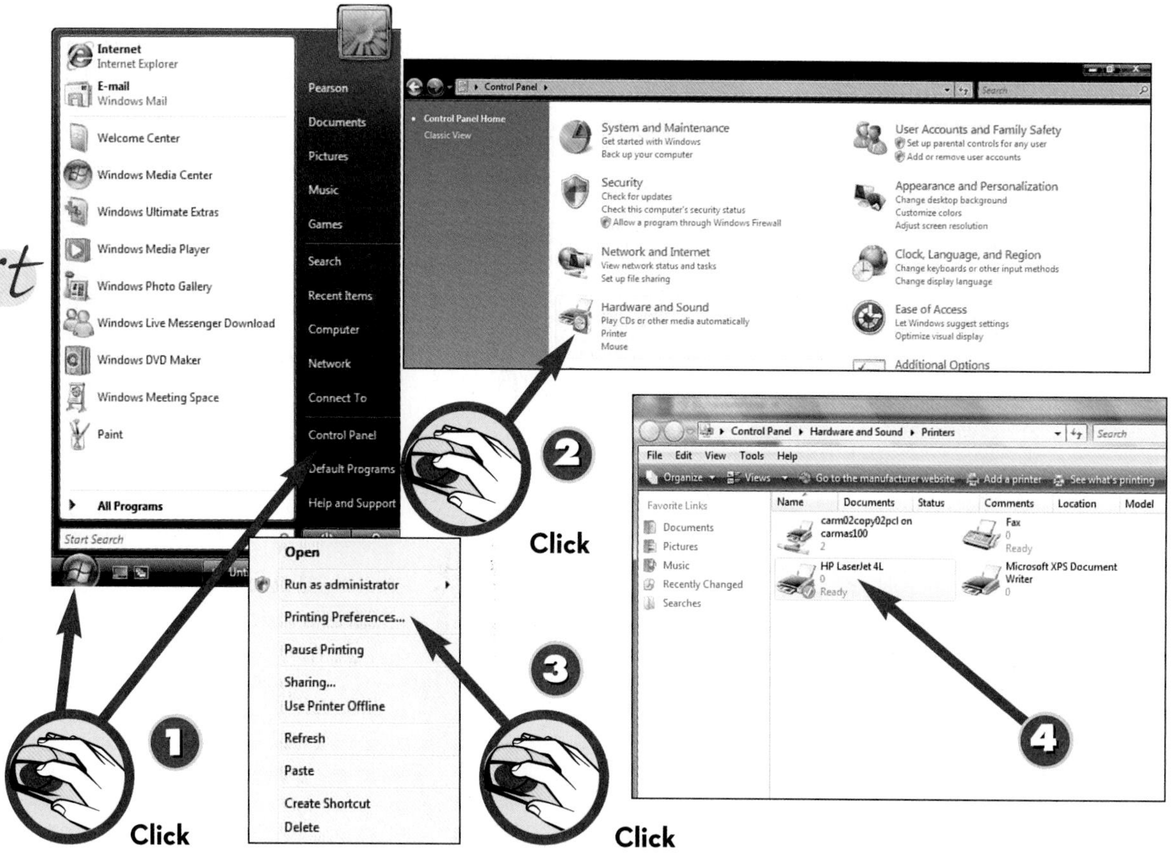

Click

Click

Click

1. Click the **Start** button and then click **Control Panel**.
2. Under **Hardware and Sound**, click **Printer**.
3. The default printer is indicated with a check mark. To select another printer as the default, right-click the icon for that printer and under **Printing Preferences...** select your default printer.
4. The printer is flagged as the default printer.

End

TIP
Delete a Printer

If you replace a printer, you can delete the icon for the old printer so that you are not confused. To delete (and uninstall) a printer, right-click the printer icon.Select **Delete** and then click **Yes** to confirm the deletion.

TIP
Select a Different Printer

You aren't stuck always using the default printer. You can select which printer to use for each print job in whatever application you are using at the time.

SETTING PRINTING PREFERENCES

Printing preferences are settings, such as the order in which pages are printed (beginning to end of document, or end to beginning), page orientation (portrait or landscape), and paper source. If you always print a certain way, you can change these settings accordingly; these settings will be used for all print jobs. If you only occasionally need to make these changes, don't change the printer's settings. Instead, you can just change them for that particular print job.

Start

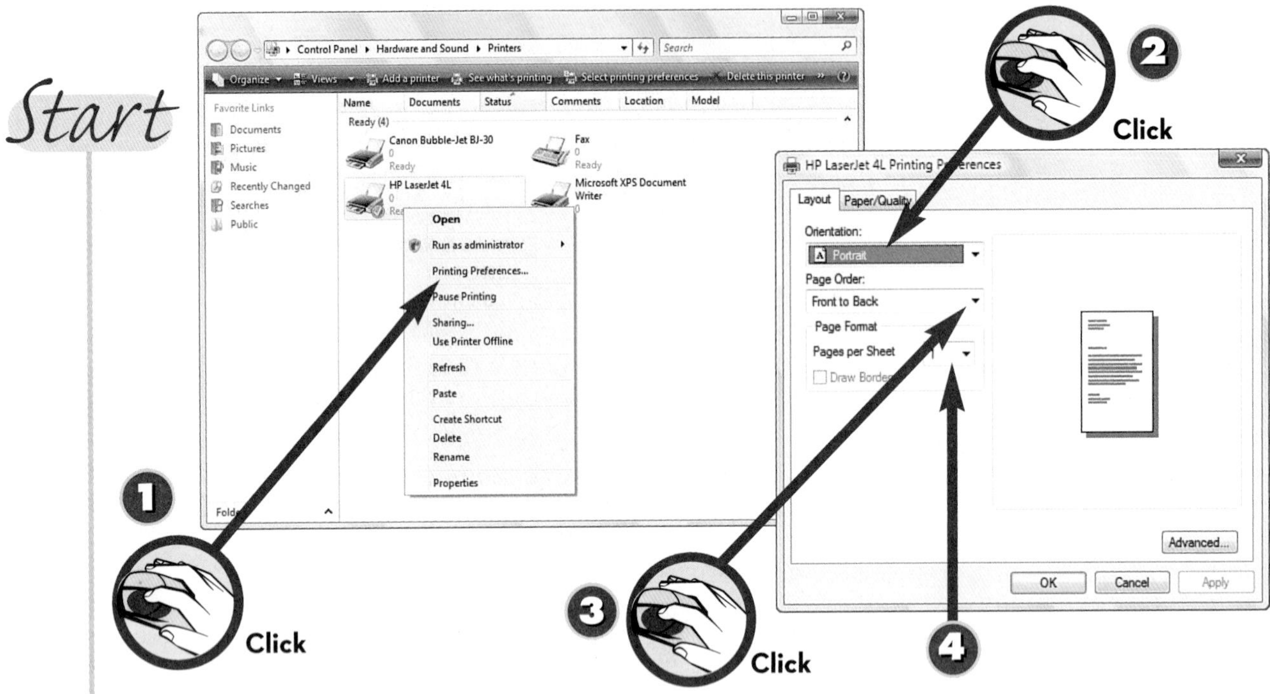

1. Open the **Printers** control panel (as shown in previous tasks) to display your installed printers. Right-click the printer you want to modify and then click **Printing Preferences**.
2. On the **Layout** tab, select a default orientation (portrait or landscape).
3. Select a page print order (front to back or back to front).
4. Select the number of pages to print per sheet. (Note that this is available only for printers that support this option.)

Continued

TIP

When to Change Preferences

Changing the printer's preferences changes them for all documents you print on this printer. If you want to change settings for just one document, change the setting for that document instead.

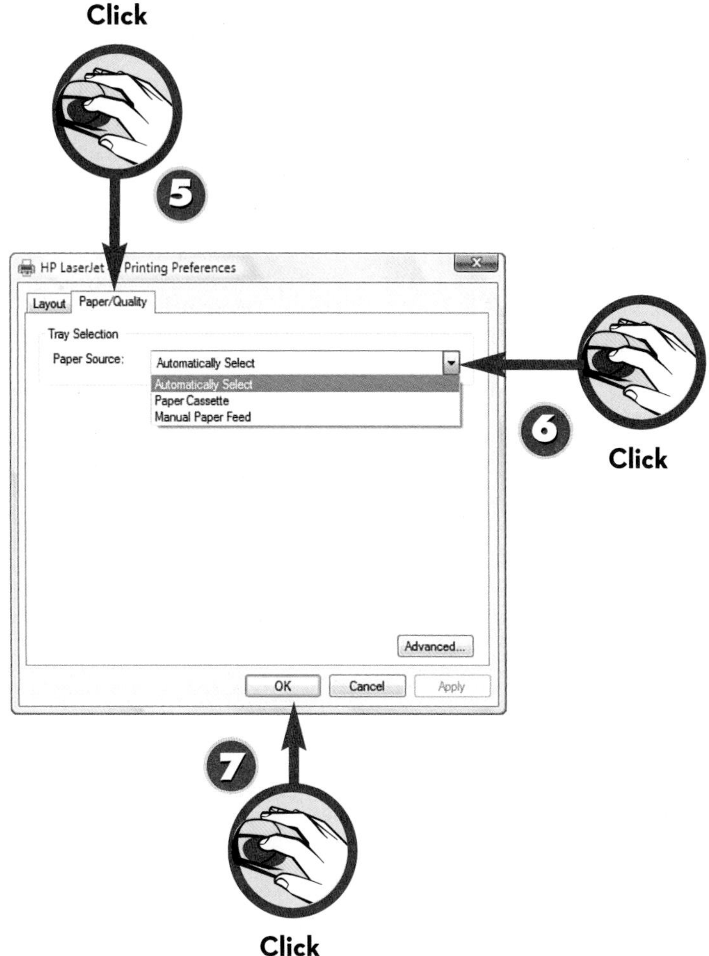

5. Click the **Paper/Quality** tab.
6. Display the **Paper Source** drop-down list and select what source you want the printer to use for paper.
7. Click **OK**.

End

NOTE

Paper Source

Your printer likely has different sources for paper. For instance, your printer may be able to pull letterhead from one tray, or you may manually feed special paper like envelopes. You can change paper sources as needed for special print jobs (rather than changing them for *all* print jobs).

TIP

Advanced Options

To change options for paper size, graphic quality, copy count, and others, click the **Advanced** tab. Make any changes and click **OK**.

VIEWING PRINTER PROPERTIES

In addition to printing preferences, you can also view and change printer properties. These are more technical details of how your printer works—for instance, when the printer is available, the port to which the printer is attached, whether printer sharing is enabled, and other options. For the most part, you don't need to make changes, but you can view these settings to see what's available.

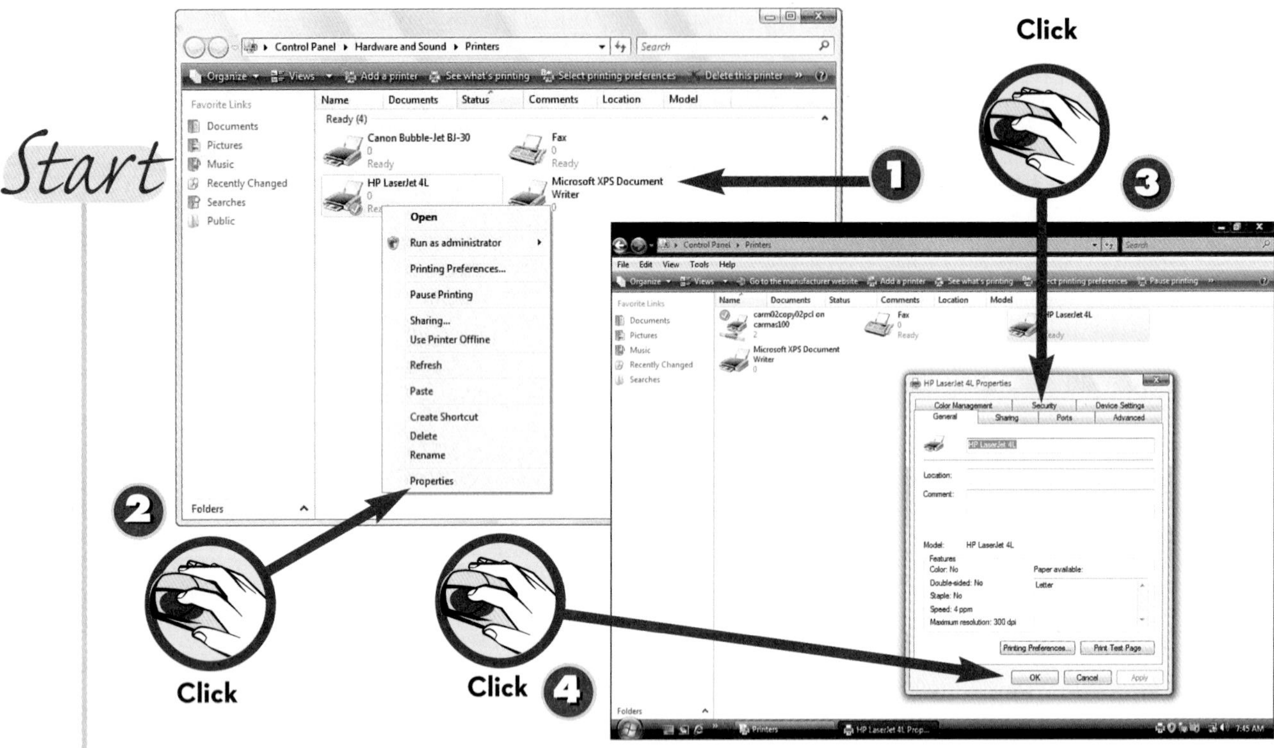

1. Display your installed printers. See the earlier task "Displaying Installed Printers" if you need help with this step.
2. Right-click the printer you want to modify and then click **Properties**.
3. Click any of the available tabs to view the various settings and options.
4. Click **OK** to save any changes, or click **Cancel** to close the dialog box without saving changes.

End

NOTE

What Is Spooling?

Spooling is the action of copying a document temporarily to the hard disk when printing. The document is then fed to the printer from the spooler. Spooling lets you get back to work within the program faster.

TIP

Other Tabs

Use the **Sharing** tab to enable printer sharing, usually a network feature. Use the **Ports** tab to change the port to which the printer is connected. For printer memory and font options, click the **Device Settings** tab.

PREVIEWING A DOCUMENT BEFORE PRINTING

After your printer is set up, you can print your documents. Most programs enable you to preview a document to check the margins, heads, graphics placement, and so on before you print. Previewing can save time and paper because you can make any needed adjustments before you print.

Start

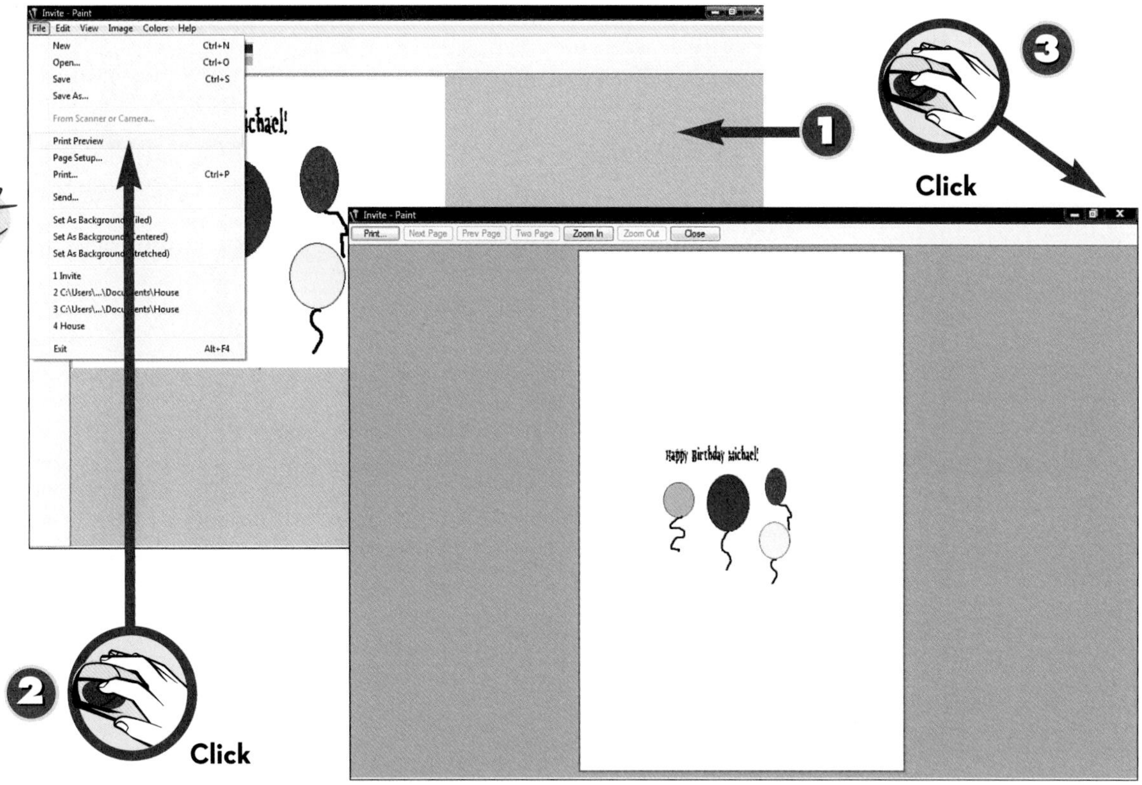

Click

Click

1. Open the document you want to preview.
2. Click **File** and then click **Print Preview**.
3. When you are done previewing the document, click the **Close** button.

End

TIP

Shortcuts

The Print Preview window usually includes a toolbar for working with the document. Using buttons in this toolbar, you can magnify the view, send the file to the printer, change the margins, and more.

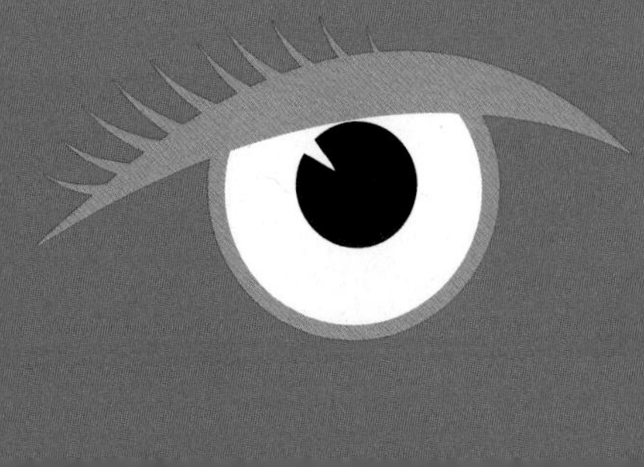

PRINTING A DOCUMENT

Printing your documents gives you a paper copy you can proofread, use in reports, give to co-workers, and so on. The options for printing vary from program to program, but the basic steps are the same.

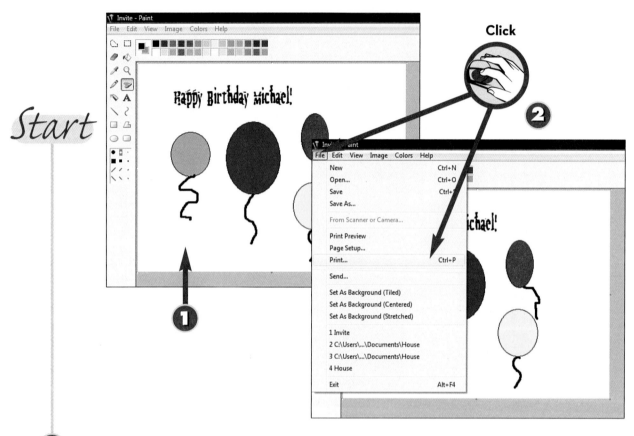

Start

1. Open the document you want to print.
2. Click **File** and then click the **Print** command.

Continued

TIP

Shortcut

As a shortcut, look for a **Print** button (the icon that looks like a little printer) in the program's toolbar (or Ribbon if you are using Office 2007). Alternatively, you can use a keyboard shortcut (usually **Ctrl+P**) to print.

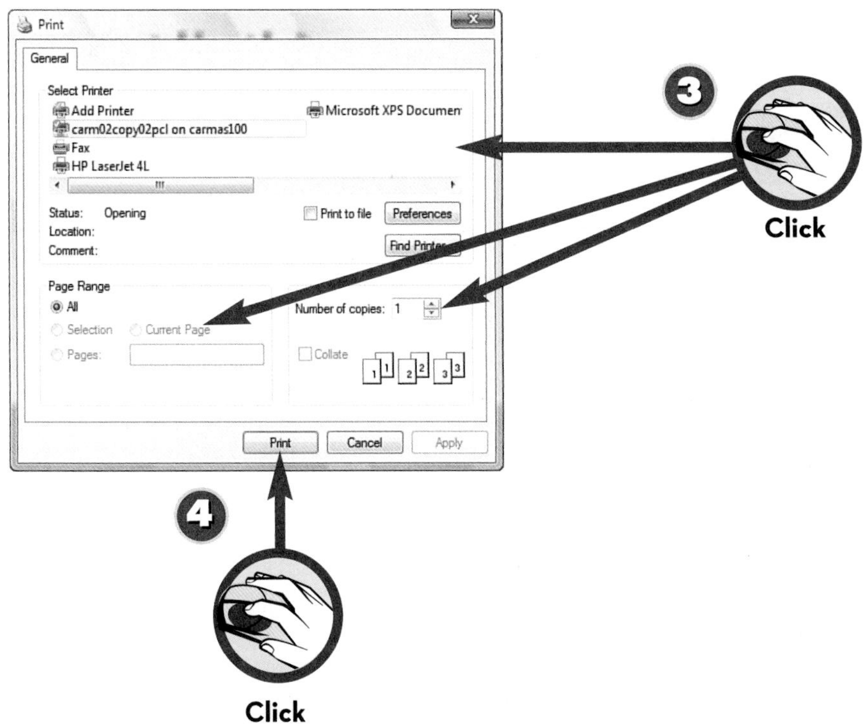

3 Make any changes to the print options. For instance, select a different printer. You can also select to print more than one copy.

4 Click the **Print** button. The document is printed.

End

NOTE

Print Multiple Copies or a Print Range

To print more than one copy, enter the number to print or use the spin boxes to select the number. For multiple-page documents, you can select all, a range, or just the current page in the Page Range area.

VIEWING THE PRINT QUEUE

The print queue lists the documents that have been sent to a printer, and it shows how far along the printing is. Using the print queue, you can pause, restart, or cancel print jobs. This task shows how to view the print queue.

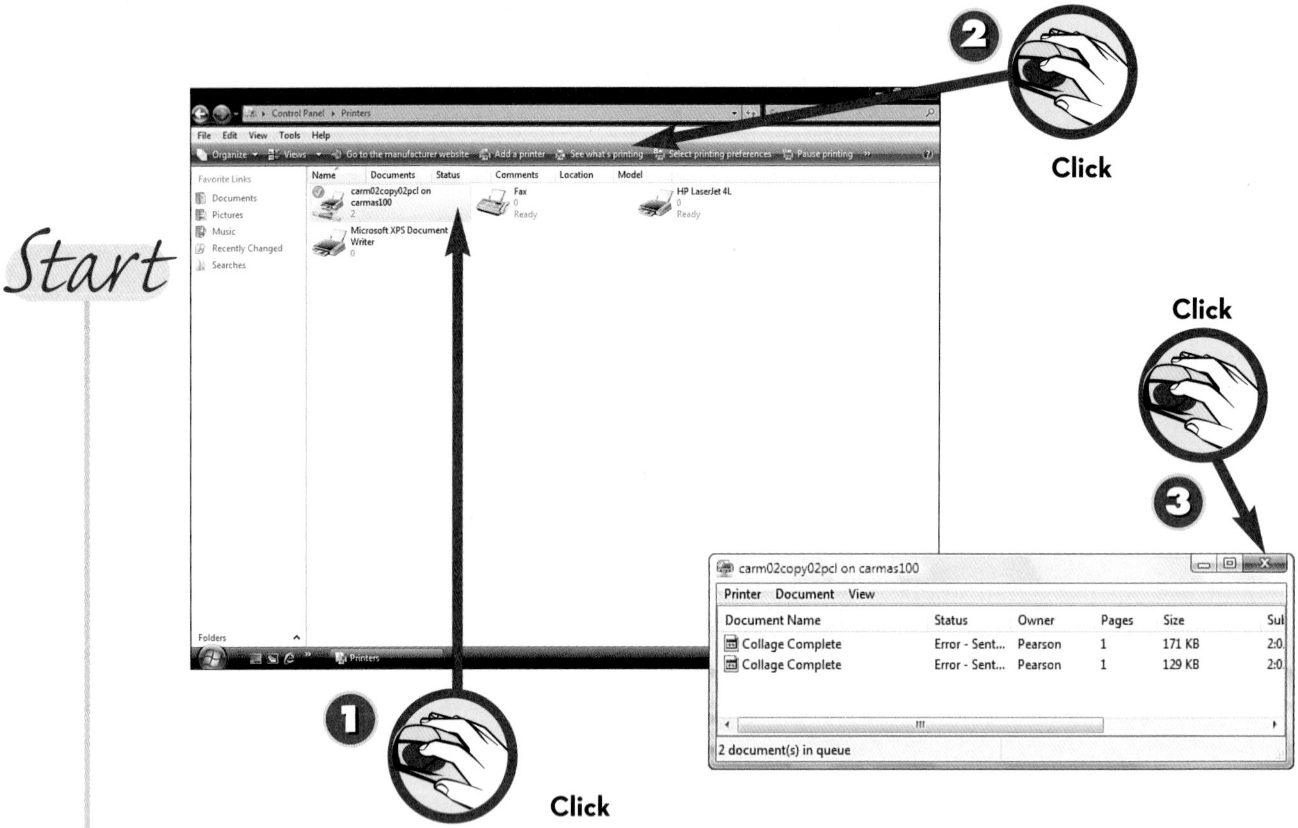

Start

Click

Click

Click

1. After printing the document, display the **Printers** control panel and select the printer.
2. Click **See what's printing**. You see the list of documents to be printed.
3. Click the **Close** button to close the print queue.

End

TIP

Double-Click the Icon

You can display the print queue by double-clicking the **Printer** icon in the notification area of the taskbar (appears on the far right side of the taskbar). The Printer icon displays whenever you are printing a document.

NOTE

Nothing Listed?

You can cancel or pause a print job; however, you must get to the print queue box quickly to stop it. If nothing appears in the print queue, it probably means that the entire print job has already been sent to the printer.

CANCELING A PRINT JOB

If you discover an error in the job you are printing, or if you decide that you need to add something to it, you can cancel it before it begins printing. Canceling printing prevents you from wasting time and paper.

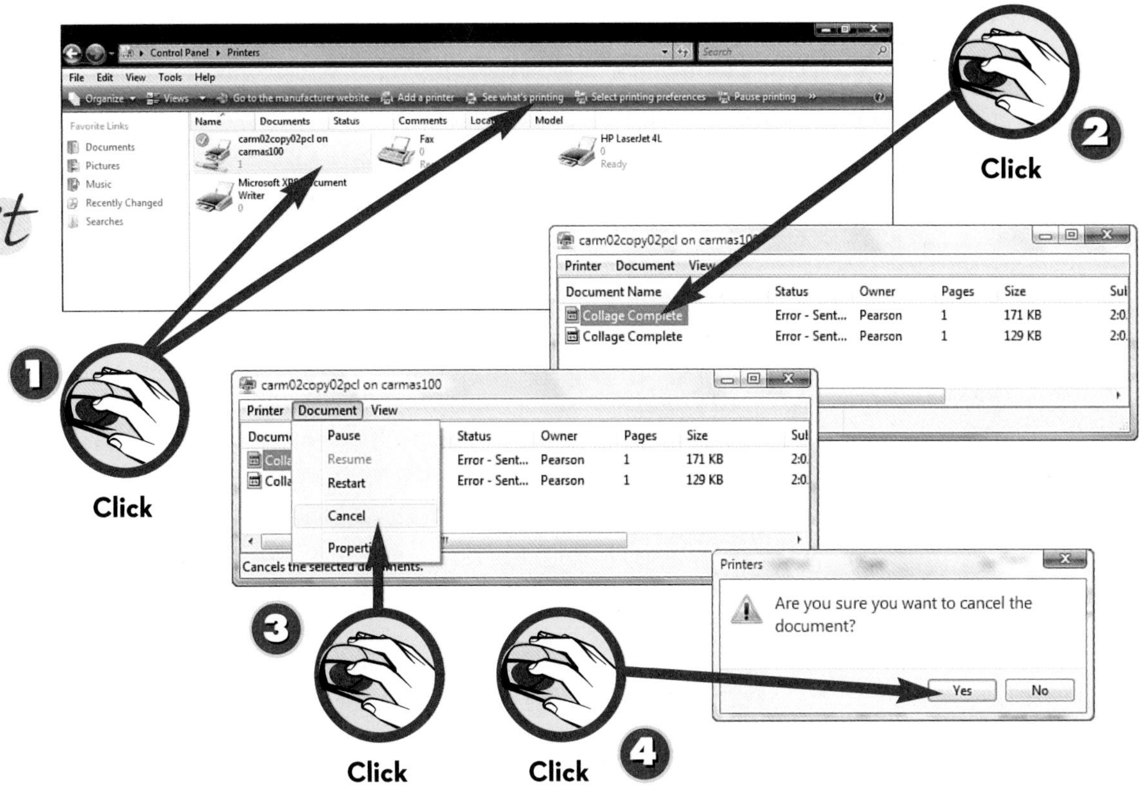

1. After printing the document, display the **Printers** control panel and select the printer you sent the file to for printing. Click **See what's printing** to display the print queue.
2. Select the print job you want to cancel.
3. Click **Document** and then click **Cancel**.
4. When asked to confirm the cancellation, click **Yes**. You can then click the **Close** button on the print queue dialog box.

TIP

Pause the Printer

You might want to pause printing when you want to load a different paper type or need to change the order or print jobs. To pause all print jobs, click **Printer** and then click **Pause Printing**. To restart the printer after you have paused it, click **Printer** and then click the **Pause Printing** command again.

TIP

Cancel All Jobs

You can also cancel all print jobs. You might do this if the printer isn't working. Click **Printer** and then **Cancel All Documents**. Click **Yes** to confirm the cancellation.

VIEWING FONTS

The fonts you can use in your documents depend on the fonts you have set up in Windows, and Windows can use two types of fonts: the fonts built in to your printer and the fonts installed on your system. You can view a list of fonts and see examples of the available fonts in the Font control panel.

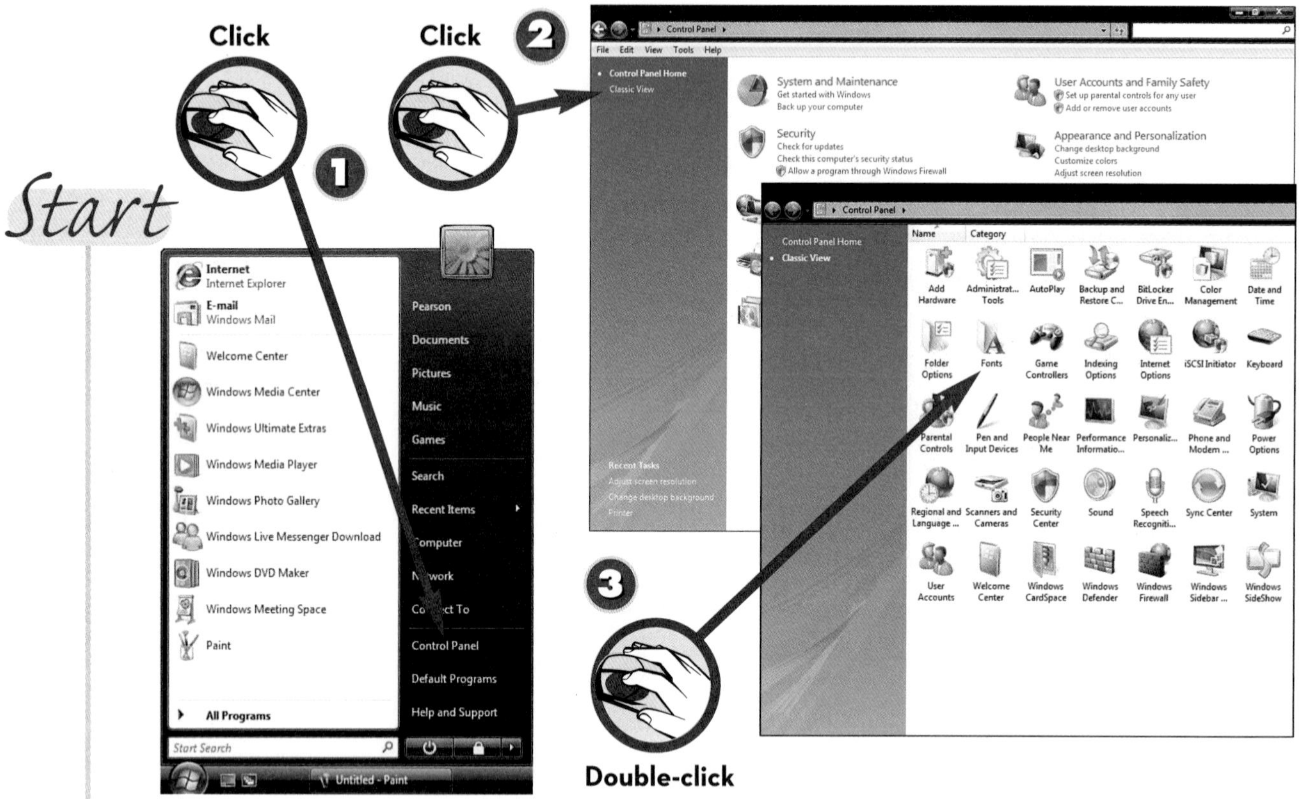

Start

Click

Click

Double-click

1. Click the **Start** button and then click **Control Panel**.
2. In the Control Panel window, click **Classic View** (on the left pane of the window).
3. Double-click the **Fonts** icon.

Continued

TIP

Font Sources

Fonts come from a variety of sources. Some are installed on your printer. Some come as part of Windows. Also, some programs include fonts that are installed when the program is installed. You can also purchase and add fonts to your system as well as download free fonts. See the next task for more information on adding fonts to your system.

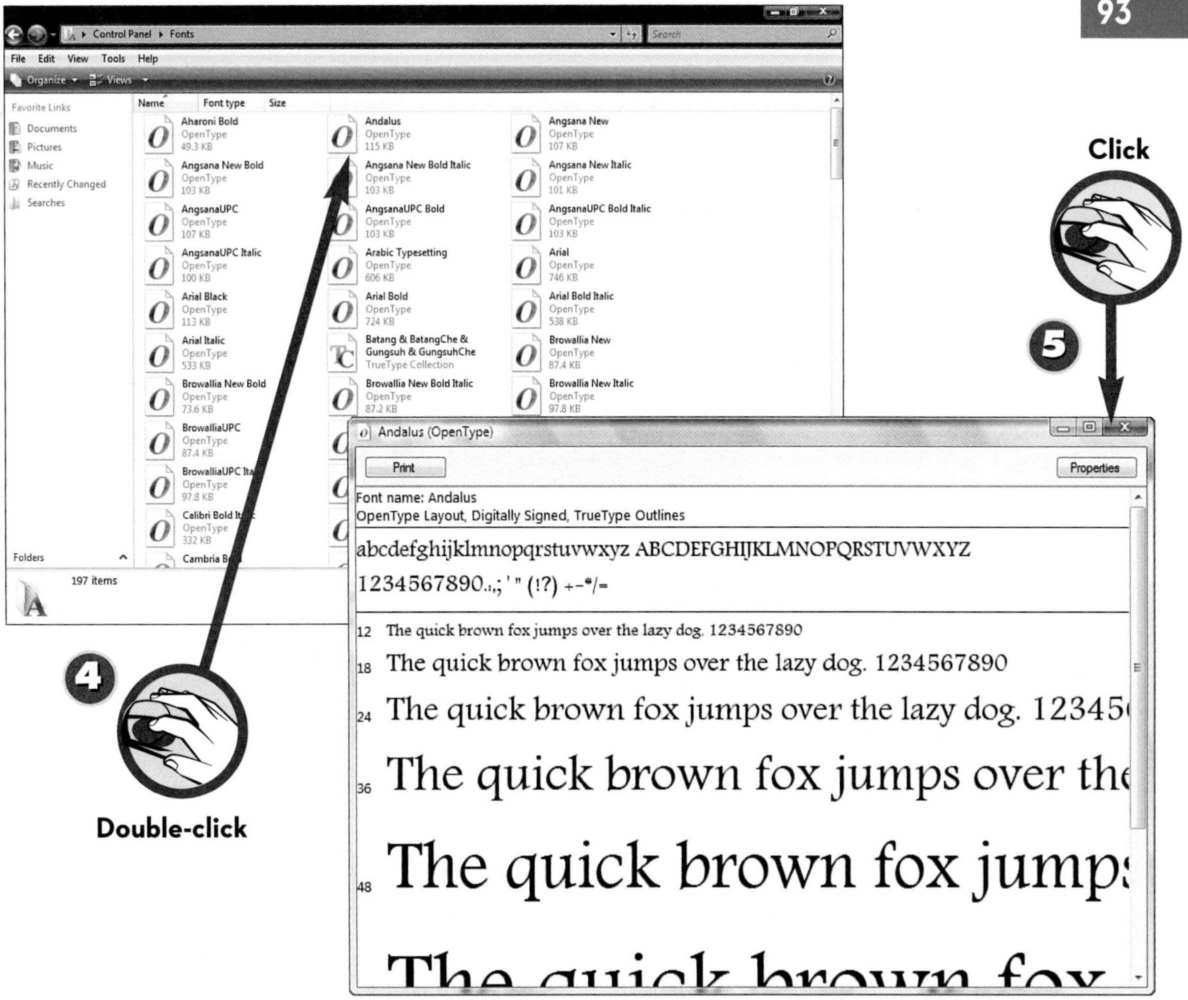

Click

Double-click

4. You see a list of fonts. To view a font, double-click its icon.

5. Click the **Close** button to close the font preview.

End

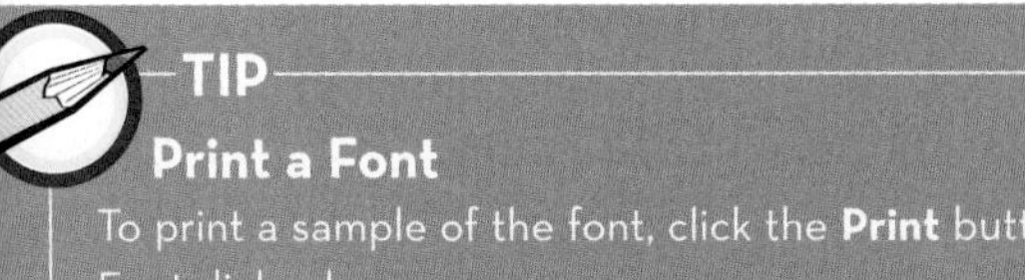

TIP

Print a Font

To print a sample of the font, click the **Print** button in the Font dialog box.

INSTALLING NEW FONTS ON YOUR COMPUTER

You can purchase additional fonts to add to your system. When you do so, you need to install them in Windows so that you can use them with any Windows programs.

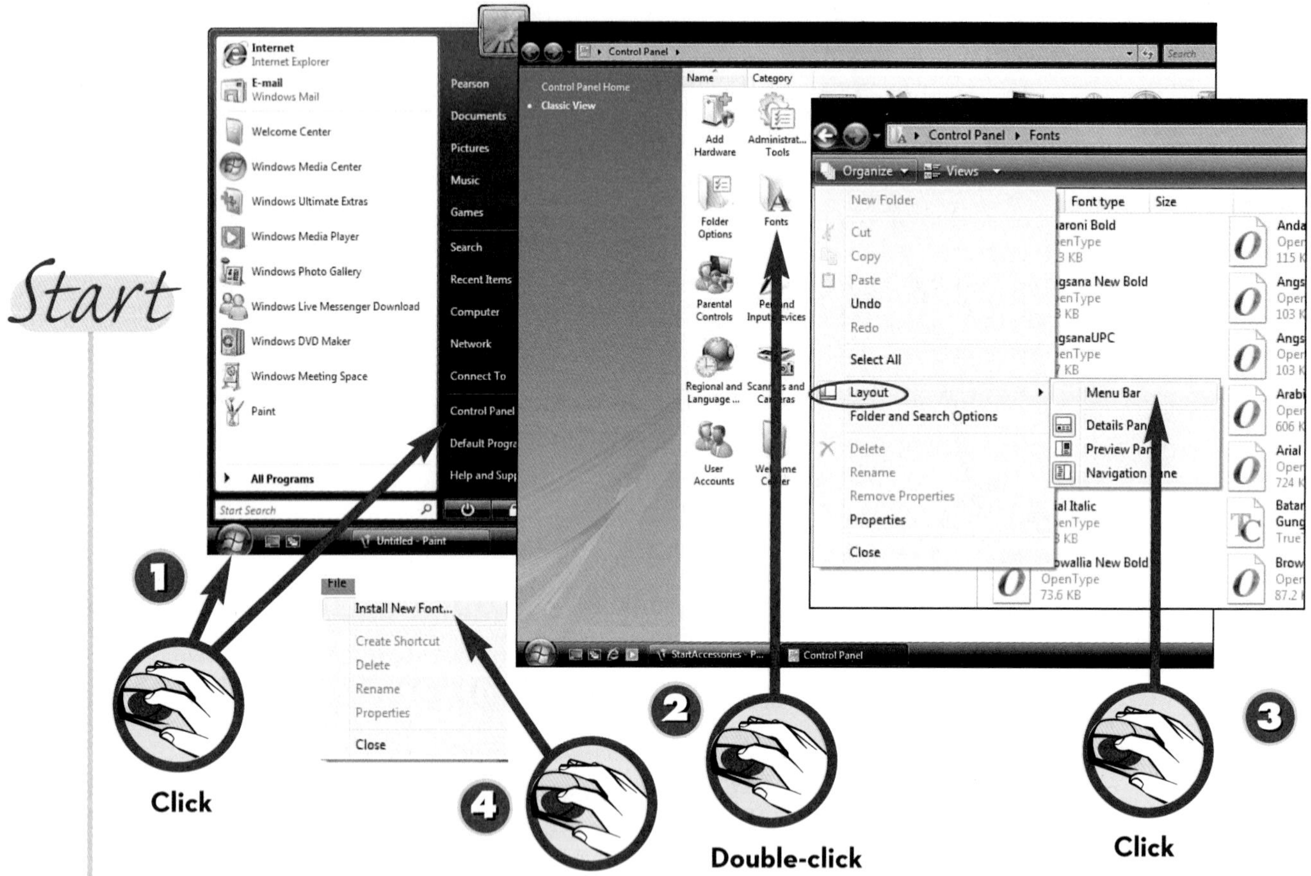

Start

Click

Double-click

Click

1. Click **Start** and then select **Control Panel**.
2. In Classic view, double-click **Fonts**.
3. You see a list of all the fonts installed. Click **Organize**, **Layout**, **Menu Bar** to display the menu bar.
4. Click **File** and then click **Install New Font**.

Continued

TIP

Uninstall a Font

Click **Start**, **Control Panel**, and then **Fonts**. Select the font(s) you want to delete. You can select more than one font by holding down the Ctrl key and clicking on each font. Click **File**, **Delete**.

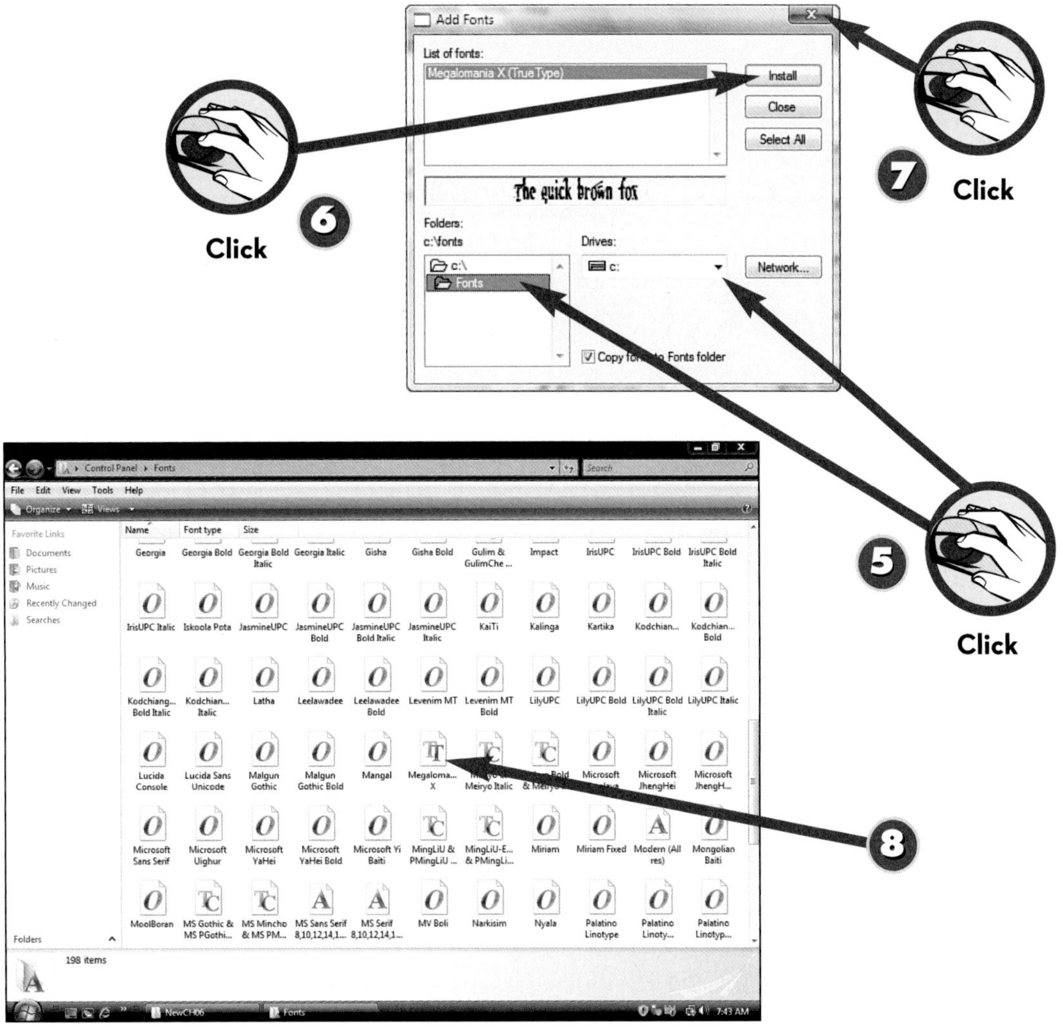

5. Select the drive and folder that contain your font files.
6. Select the font(s) you want to install and click **Install**.
7. Click **Continue**. Click the **Close** button to close the font window.
8. The fonts are installed.

End

TIP

No Fonts Listed?

If no fonts are listed, it's because no font files are in the selected folder. Be sure to select the drive and folder where the files are stored.

TIP

Select All Fonts

If you want to add all the fonts, click the **Select All** button.

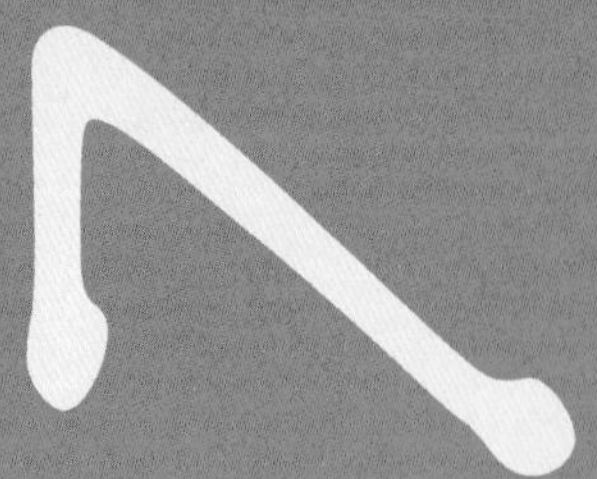

WORKING WITH SCANNERS OR DIGITAL CAMERAS

Two popular devices that enable you to work with images on your computer are scanners and digital cameras. With a scanner, you can scan documents or illustrations. With a digital camera, you can take pictures and then copy them from the camera's memory or media card to your computer. You may wonder why we would talk about scanners and digital cameras in a book on a computer operating system. These imagery tools have become so much a part of our everyday lives that the necessary software interfaces have actually become integrated into Windows. In years past, you needed special software in order to move images through your scanner into your computer or to transfer photos from your digital camera to your computer. Those software applications still exist and often come bundled with your scanner or camera when you purchase one, but the necessity of this extra layer of interaction has become extinct in recent years due to the existence of the same functionality within your Windows software. The ability to communicate directly between your scanner or digital camera and your computer began several Windows versions back, but Vista continues to include the functionality and has improved on that of previous versions.

Digital cameras have become popular and offer a lot of advantages; they are often considered a key component of computers because they provide so much versatility. If you want, you can edit, email, print, and upload photos to a private online photo album. If you have a digital camera, you can find out in this Part how to set up that camera and manage the picture files using features within Windows Vista.

Using a scanner, you can essentially "photograph" the items (documents, illustrations, or even small objects) and view them on your computer's monitor. You can then insert the scanned images into documents or use a photo/image editing program to make changes. While the specifics of using your particular scanner will be different, you can learn how to set up your scanner in this part.

THE WINDOWS PHOTO GALLERY

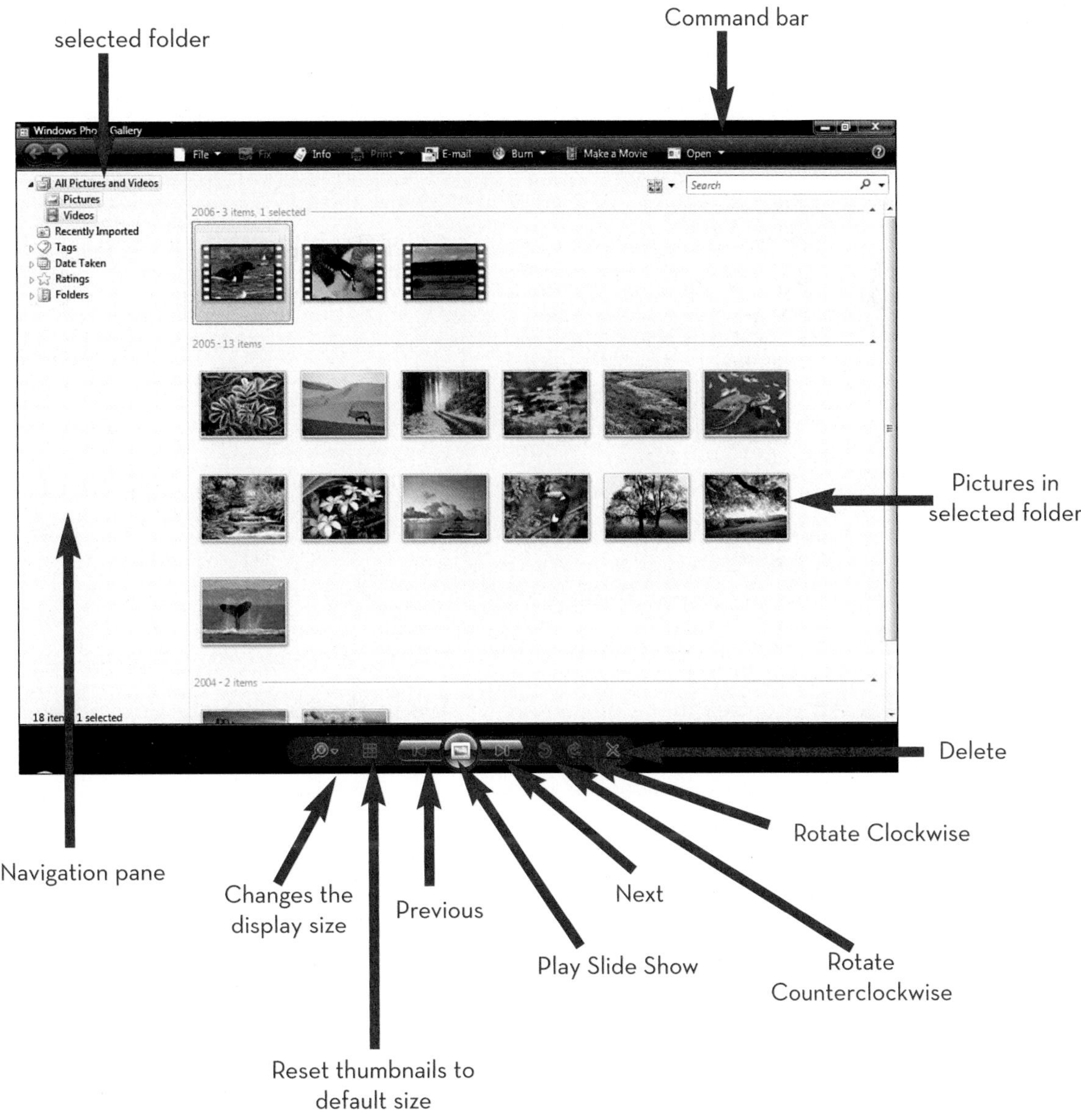

SETTING UP A SCANNER OR CAMERA AUTOMATICALLY

When you connect a scanner or camera to your computer via the appropriate connector, Windows Vista should automatically install the device. You simply see a notification icon when the device is being set up and when it is finished.

Start

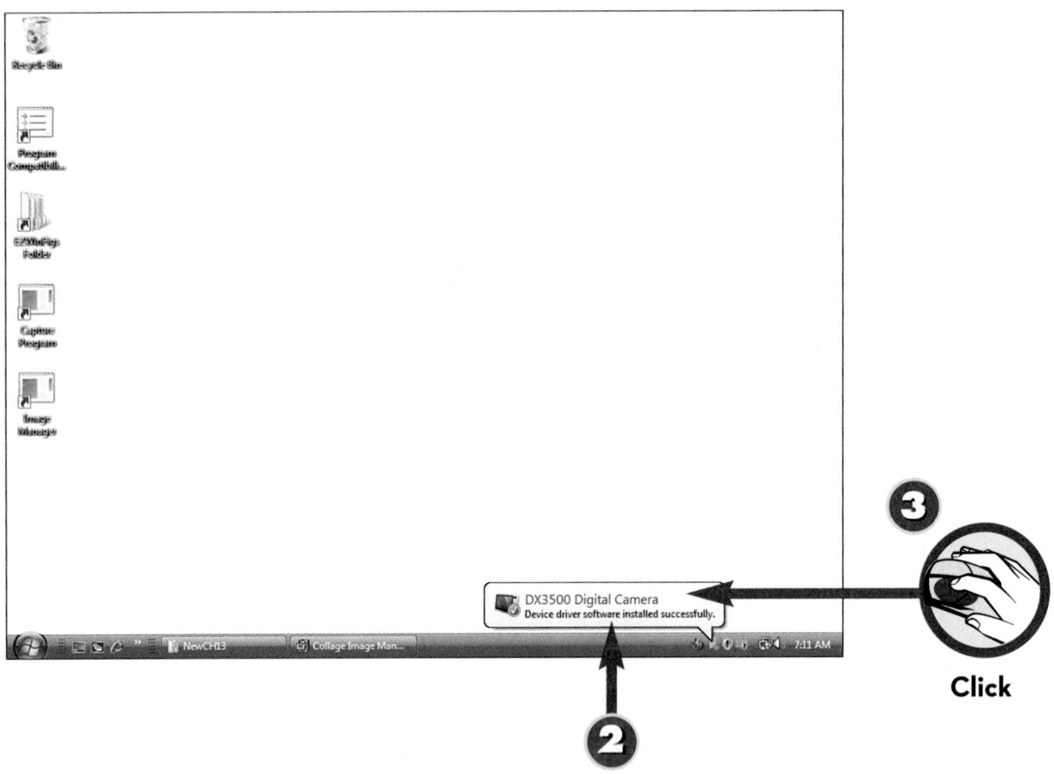

1. Connect your scanner's or camera's cable to the appropriate port on your computer.
2. When the camera or scanner is installed, you see a message in the notification area.
3. Click the **Close** button to close the message.

End

TIP

Start from Disk

If this automatic setup does not occur, you can use the Add Device Wizard to set up the scanner covered in the latter task, "Setting Up a Scanner or Digital Camera Manually."

NOTE

Device Driver Defined

A *device driver* is a software file that provides Windows with the details about the hardware device—how it works, what features it includes, and so on. The device driver is integral to setting up the device so that it works on your system.

TRANSFERRING IMAGES FROM A DIGITAL CAMERA

If your camera is set up for AutoPlay, you'll be prompted for how Vista is to handle images when you connect the camera to your computer. You can choose to import the pictures (copy from the camera to your computer) or view the pictures. If not, you can use the Windows Photo Gallery to import pictures.

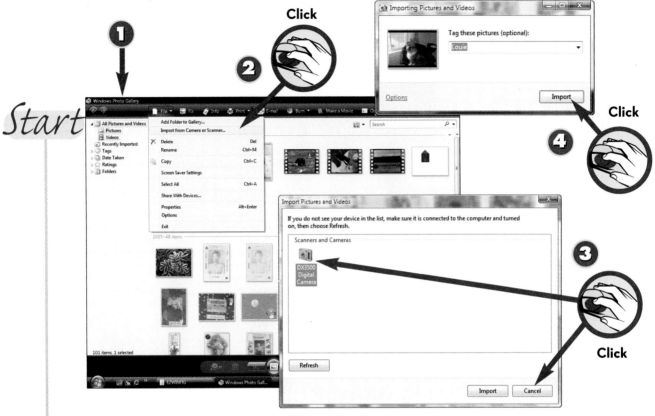

Start

1. Connect the camera and open the Windows Photo Gallery.
2. Click **File** and then **Import from Camera or Scanner**.
3. Select the camera to import from and click **Import**.
4. Type a tag for this set of pictures and click **Import**; the pictures are imported and added to the Windows Photo Gallery.

End

TIP

Delete Images from the Camera

When you import images from the camera, you usually have the option of deleting the images from the camera to free up its memory. Look for an option to select keeping or deleting images, and make the choice you want. (Your camera also has options for manually deleting images.)

SETTING UP A SCANNER OR DIGITAL CAMERA MANUALLY

If your scanner or camera does not install automatically, you can use the Scanner and Camera Installation Wizard to install a scanner (shown here) or camera. The wizard leads you through the steps until the setup is complete.

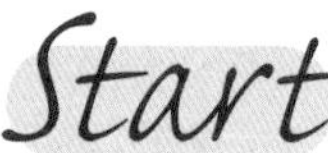

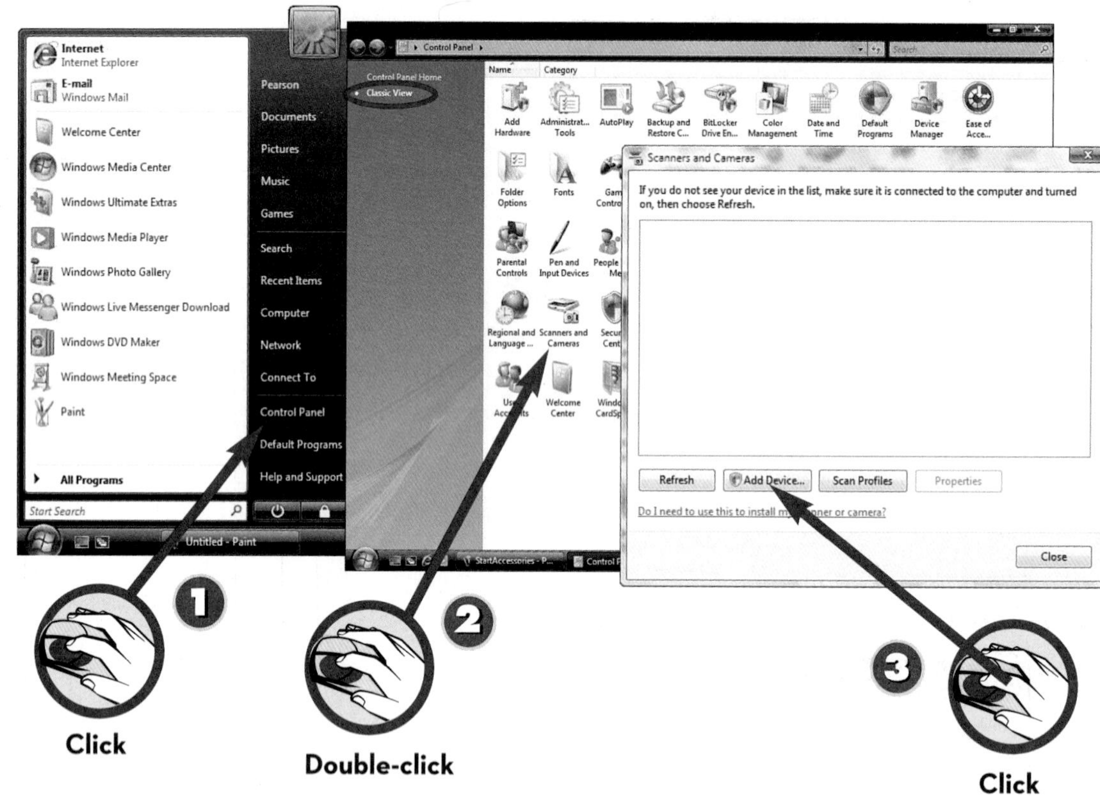

1. Click **Start** and then click **Control Panel**.
2. If necessary, switch to Classic View by clicking the option on the left side, and then double-click **Scanners and Cameras**. (You may have to scroll through the icons to locate it.)
3. Click **Add Device**. This starts the Scanner and Camera Installation Wizard.
4. If prompted to confirm permission to make this change, click **Continue** (not shown here).

Continued

TIP

Automatic Installation

Most cameras and scanners will install automatically. Simply connect them to your computer and turn them on if needed. You'll see a pop-up balloon in the notification area telling you when the device has been successfully installed.

NOTE

How Do I Scan?

The steps for actually scanning a document vary depending on the scanner and the scanner software, so you need to consult your scanner documentation for help on scanning.

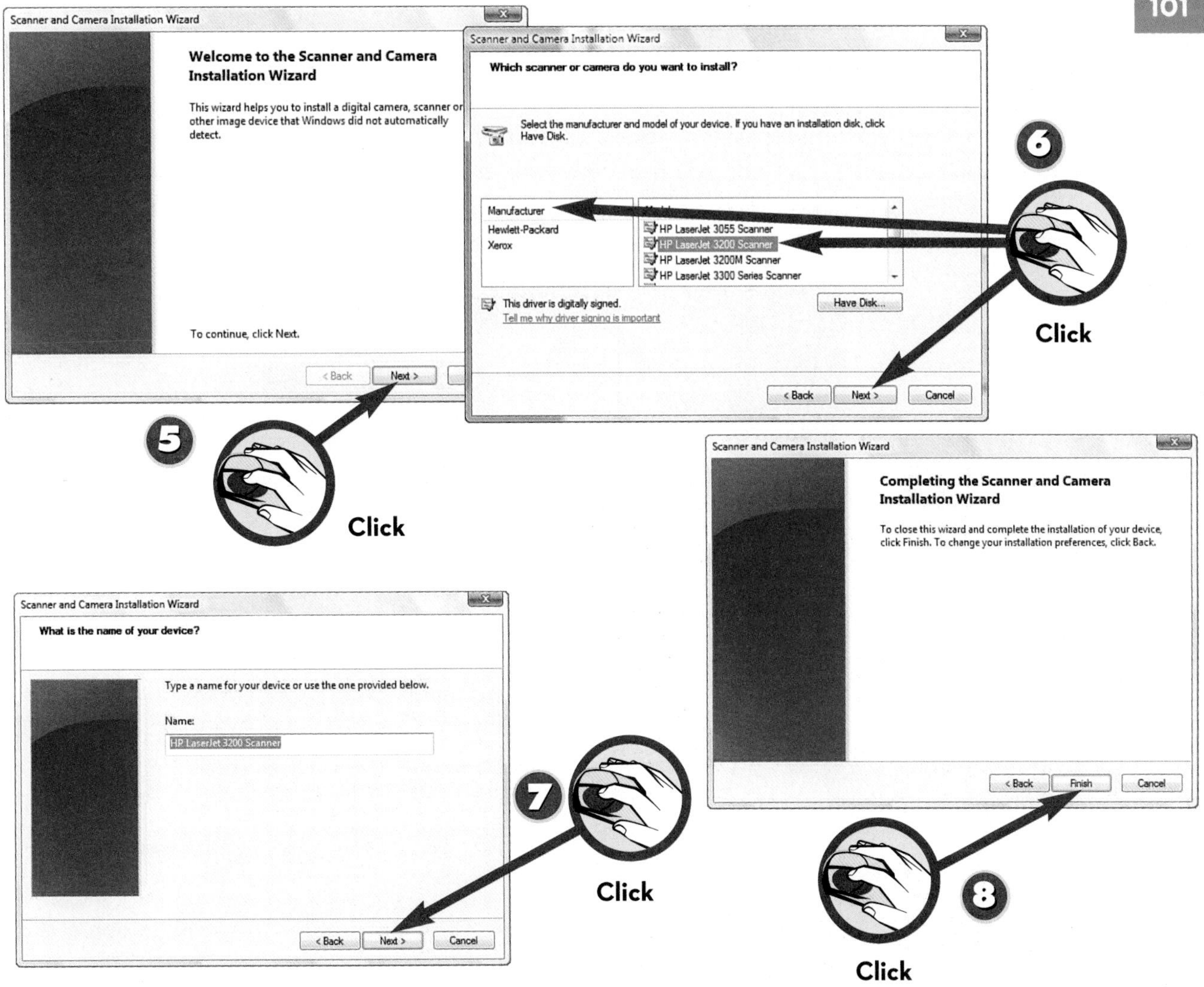

5. At the Welcome screen, click **Next**.
6. Select the manufacturer for your camera or scanner. The model list is updated; click your model from this list. Click **Next**.
7. Type a name for the camera or scanner (or keep the default) and then click **Next**.
8. Click **Finish**.

End

NOTE

Take Pictures

The features of your camera, as well as how to use it, vary from camera to camera. Check your camera's documentation to learn how to take pictures and transfer them to your PC.

TIP

Pictures Folder

Windows Vista has some preset folders, including a Pictures folder. Consider storing your pictures in this folder (or, even better, in subfolders within this main folder) to keep your pictures organized.

USING THE WINDOWS PHOTO GALLERY TO ORGANIZE PICTURES

To help you keep your pictures and videos organized, Windows Vista has added the Windows Photo Gallery. It gives you many ways to access them, including by folder, by ratings (if you have tagged them), by date taken, or by recently imported. The Photo Gallery also includes some basic options for editing your photos.

1. Click **Start**, **All Programs**, and then **Windows Photo Gallery**.
2. Use the Navigation links in the Explorer pane to select the folder that contains the images you want to view.
3. To view a close-up of a particular picture, double-click it.
4. To return to the Gallery, click **Back to Gallery**.

TIP

Slide Show

To display a slide show of the images, use the control panel at the bottom of the window. Click the **Play Slide Show** button to start the slide show. Use the **Next** and **Previous** buttons to display the next or previous pictures.

COPYING PICTURES TO A CD OR DVD

Because a CD drive can hold lots of information, it makes a good medium for making a copy of files you want to save, especially pictures. Copying files to a CD is often called "burning" a CD. You can copy your pictures to a CD or DVD.

Start

1. Insert a disc into the appropriate drive. Open the **Windows Photo Gallery** and select the pictures you want to copy to disc.
2. Click the down arrow next to the **Burn** button and then click the disc type.
3. When prompted to type a name for the disc, type a descriptive name and click **Next**.
4. The files are copied to disc. You can open that folder or drive to confirm the copy as shown here.

End

TIP

Typing a Tag Name

The tag you type is applied to all pictures, so type something that applies to all pictures. You can assign other tags to each task as well.

TIP

Share and Archive

Putting your photos on CD or DVD is a good way to share them with others (you can make it really interesting by creating a digital scrapbook or slideshow) or to make sure you have a backup of your precious memories, just in case.

FIXING PHOTOGRAPHS

Windows Photo Gallery includes some simple photo-editing features you can use to alter your photographs. You can rotate them, fix red eye, crop them, adjust the color, and more.

Start

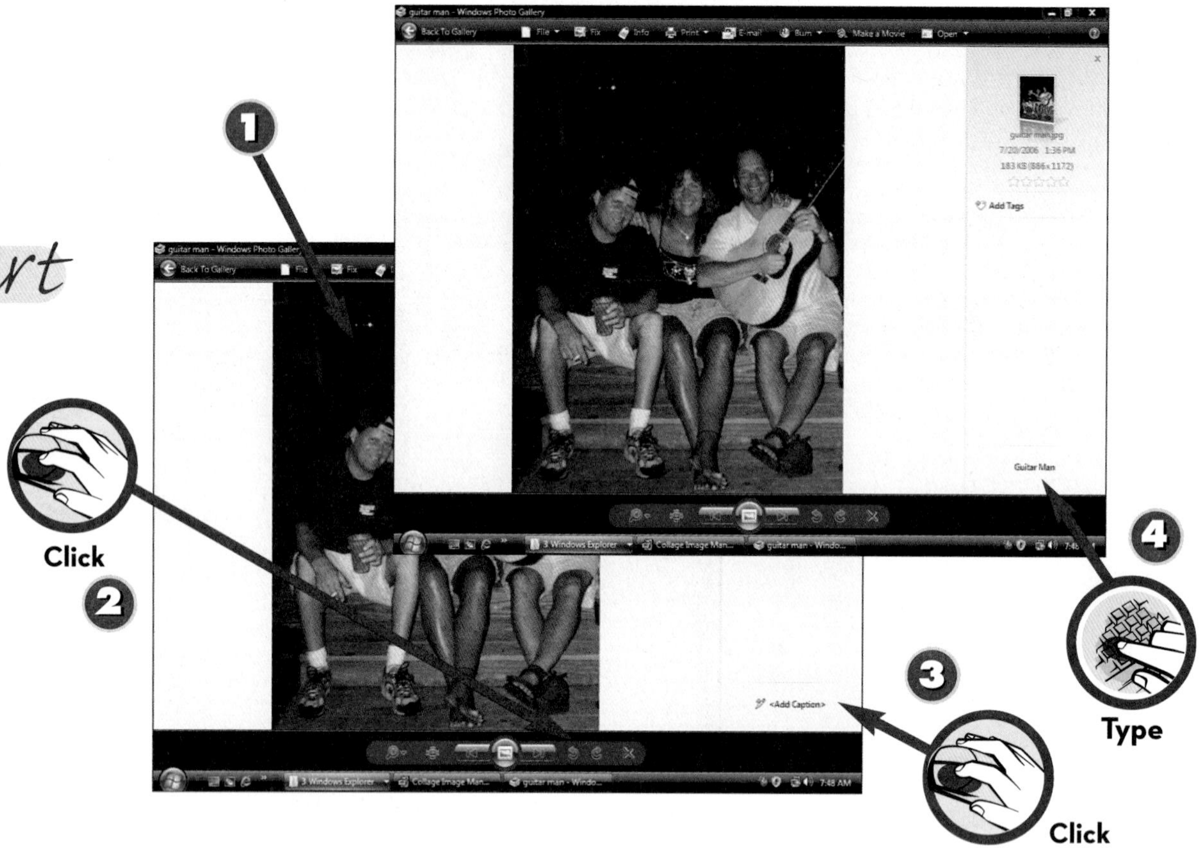

Click

Click

Type

1. Open the picture you want to edit in the Windows Photo Gallery.
2. To rotate the pictures, click one of the Rotate buttons (counterclockwise or clockwise).
3. To add a caption to the picture, click the **Add Caption** link.
4. Type a caption to be displayed with your picture.

Continued

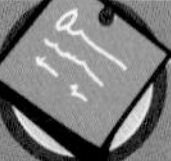

NOTE

Adding Tags

You can also add tags to help further identify pictures; this helps you not only find pictures but also group similar pictures. For more information on adding tags, see Part 5, "Working with Files."

TIP

Deleting a Picture

To delete a picture, click the **Delete** button and then click **Yes** to confirm the deletion.

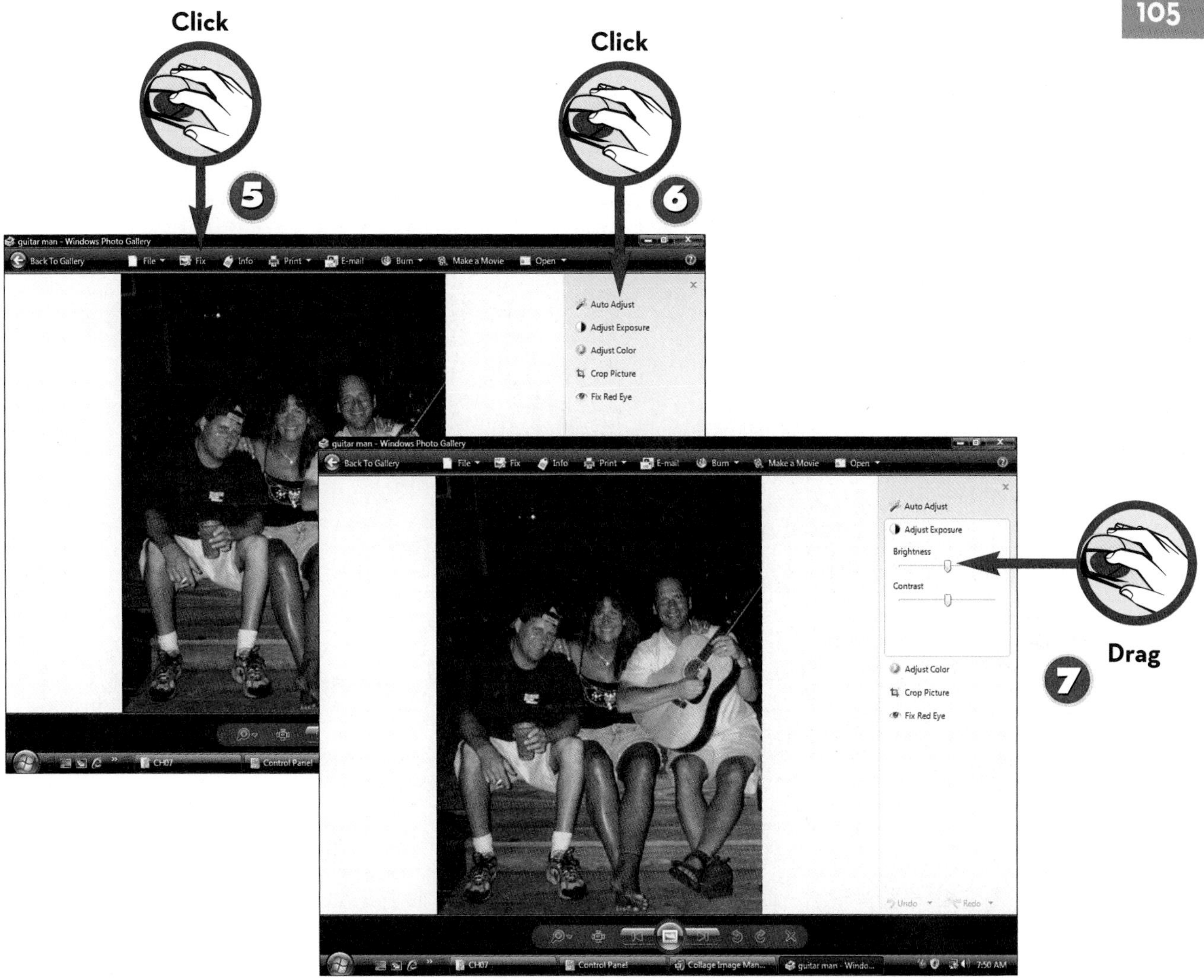

5. To make adjustments to color, clear up red-eye, or crop the picture, click the **Fix** button in the Command Bar.
6. To have Windows automatically make adjustments, click the **Auto Adjust** option. Click **Undo** if you don't like the results.
7. To adjust the exposure or color, click these options and then use the sliders to make changes. For exposure, you can adjust the brightness and contrast. For color, you can adjust the color temperature, tint, and saturation.

End

TIP

Fixing Pictures

To crop the picture, click **Crop Picture**; a box appears in the photo. Adjust the box so that it surrounds the area you want to include in the photo. Then click **Apply**. Click **Fix Red Eye** and follow the instructions.

TIP

Saving an Edited Picture

While you can't save the original file after you've edited it, you can use the **Rename** command to save the file with a new name. You then have the original and edited file.

PRINTING PHOTOGRAPHS

If you have a "regular" printer, the quality won't be great but will be acceptable for some purposes. You can also purchase and use a special photograph printer that uses special ink and glossy paper to print lab-quality photos at various sizes. This task shows you how you can print photographs from the Windows Photo Gallery.

Start

1. Click **Start**, **All Programs**, **Windows Photo Gallery**.
2. Select the pictures you want to print. Use Ctrl and click to select multiple pictures to print at one time.
3. Click the down arrow next to the **Print** button and select **Print**.
4. Click the arrow to display the drop-down list, and select the printer you want to use.

Continued

TIP

Preview Other Pages

If you have more than one page of pictures, you can use the next and previous buttons to scroll to other pages to see how these pages will look when printed.

TIP

Email Pictures

Send pictures by selecting the picture(s) you want to email and then clicking the **E-mail** button. Select a picture size and click **Attach**. Complete the email (recipient, subject, and any message) and send. See Part 9, "Sending Email ," for more information on email.

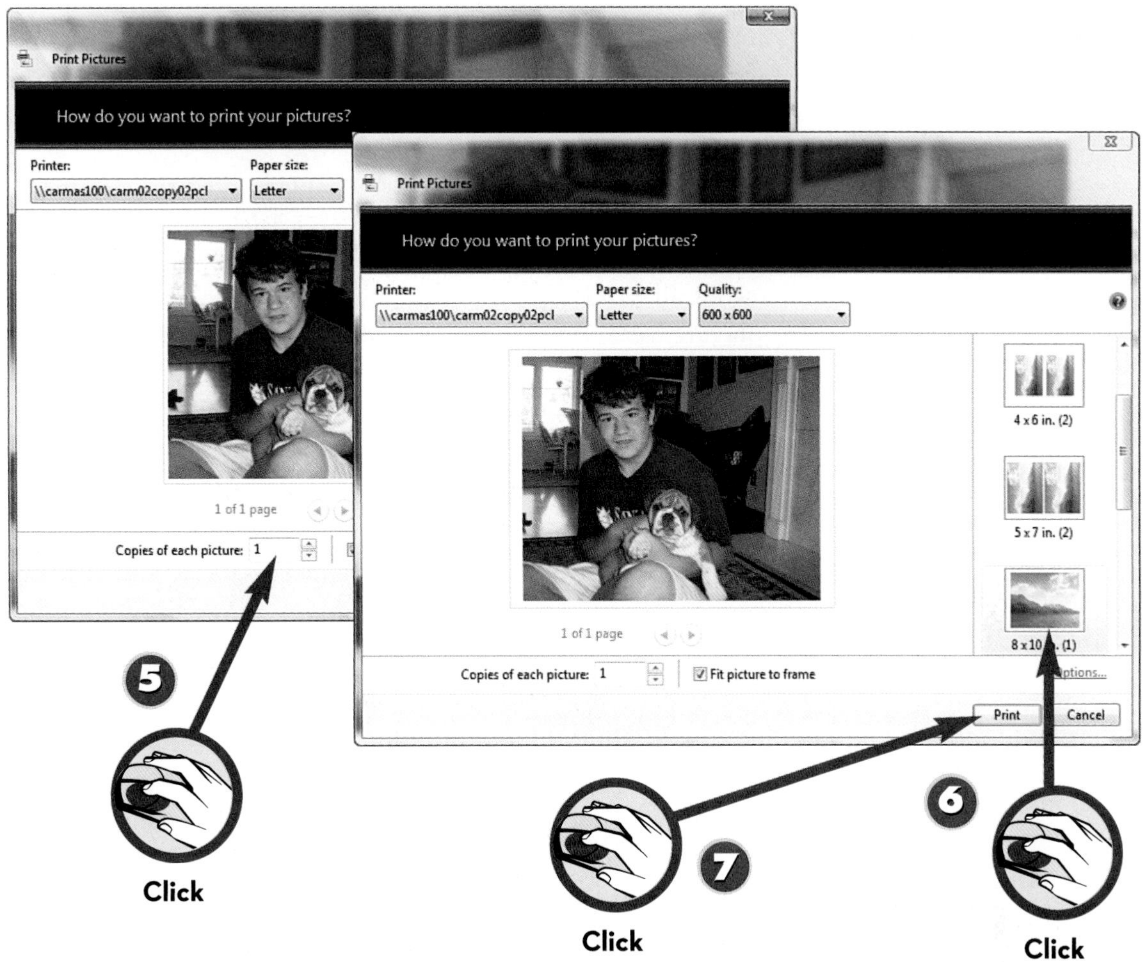

5. Select the number of copies of each picture you want to print.
6. Scroll through the list of available print layouts, and then select the one you want for your pictures.
7. Click the **Print** button. Your pictures are printed.

End

TIP

Ordering Prints Online

You can also submit your photos to an online printing service to be printed. To do so, click **Print**, **Order prints**. Then select the printing service to use, and follow the specific instructions for sending your photos, selecting options (such as picture size), paying for your pictures, and supplying other required information. The process will vary from service to service.

ENTERTAINMENT

Computers are not all work and no fun. Windows Vista includes entertainment programs for playing CDs, viewing multimedia files, and recording and playing back sounds. You can also watch DVDs, and if your computer has the capability, you can burn your own CDs and DVDs.

This chapter, for the most part, focuses on the Windows Media Player. With this program, you can listen to music, visit websites and sample music (and purchase it from MTV's URGE site), create your own customized play lists, and more. You can also burn songs from a CD to your library and then in turn burn these songs to a new audio CD. The new CD may include songs from one album or a customized playlist.

This chapter focuses the fun stuff you can do on your computer.

WINDOWS MEDIA PLAYER

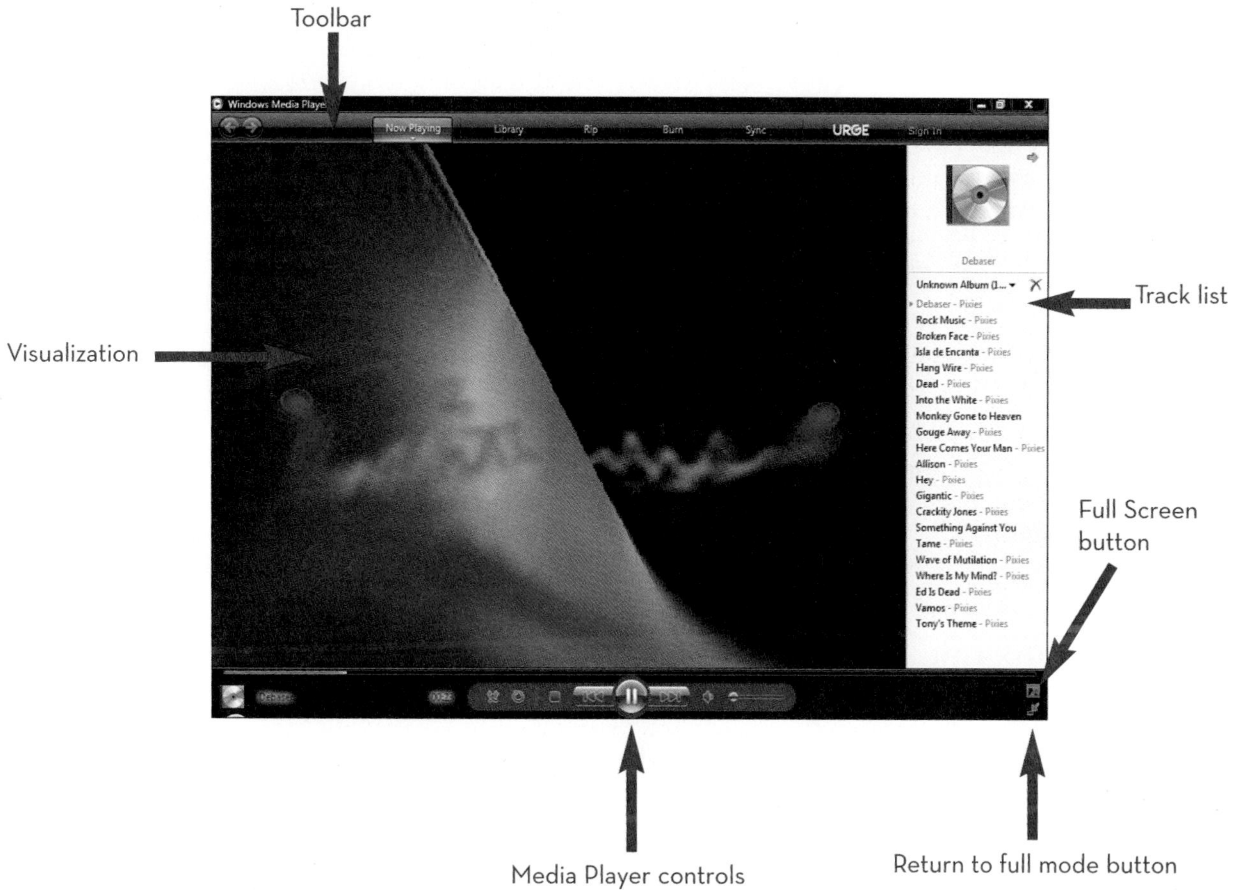

PLAYING AN AUDIO CD

To keep you entertained, you can play audio CDs using Windows Media Player. Note that the quality of the playback is determined by the quality of your speakers.

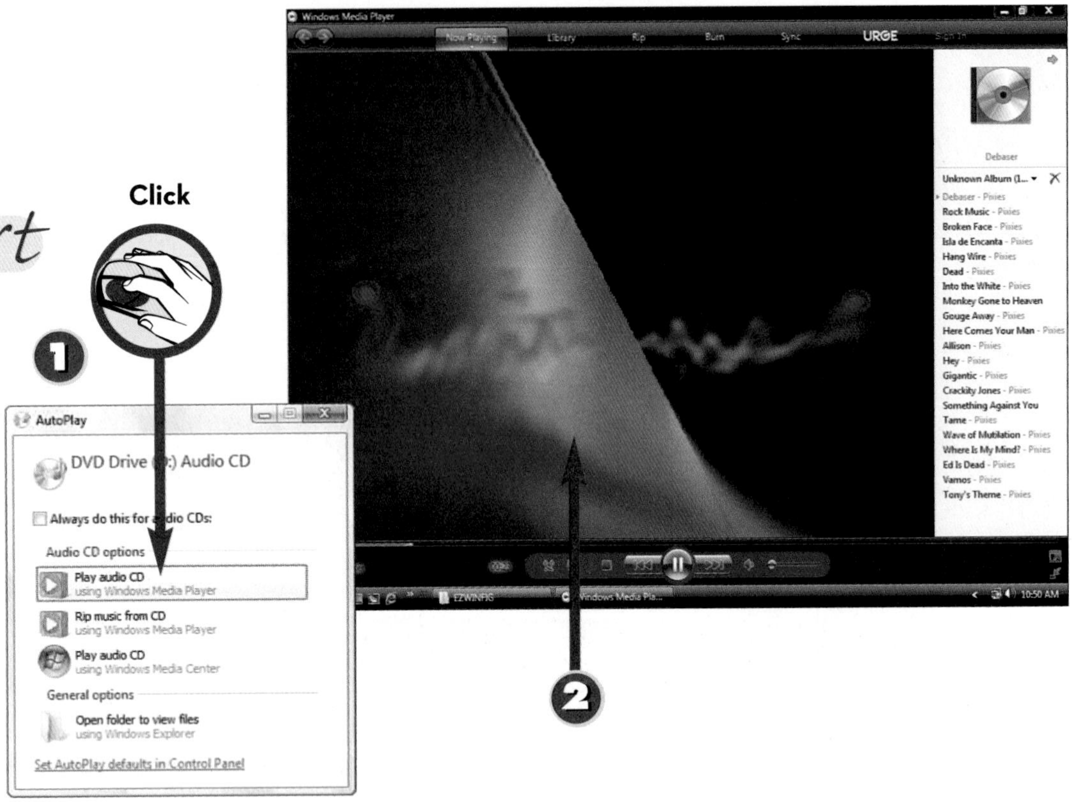

1. When you insert the CD into the drive, you may be prompted to select how to handle this CD type. If so, click **Play audio CD**.
2. The music plays in the Windows Media Player window and you see the visualization. You learn more about the Windows Media Player window and its controls in the next task.

TIP

Audio CDs Default

For audio CDs, Vista's default option is to "Play audio CD." If you want to select this option consistently in the future, leave **Always do this for audio CDs** checked in the AutoPlay dialog box. Then you won't be prompted for an action; the CD will just begin playing.

UNDERSTANDING THE WINDOWS MEDIA PLAYER WINDOW

Getting familiar with the different features and parts of the Windows Media Player window will help you learn to use its many options. This task provides an overview of the different parts of the window; see the next task for information on using the controls for adjusting the volume, stopping playback, and so on.

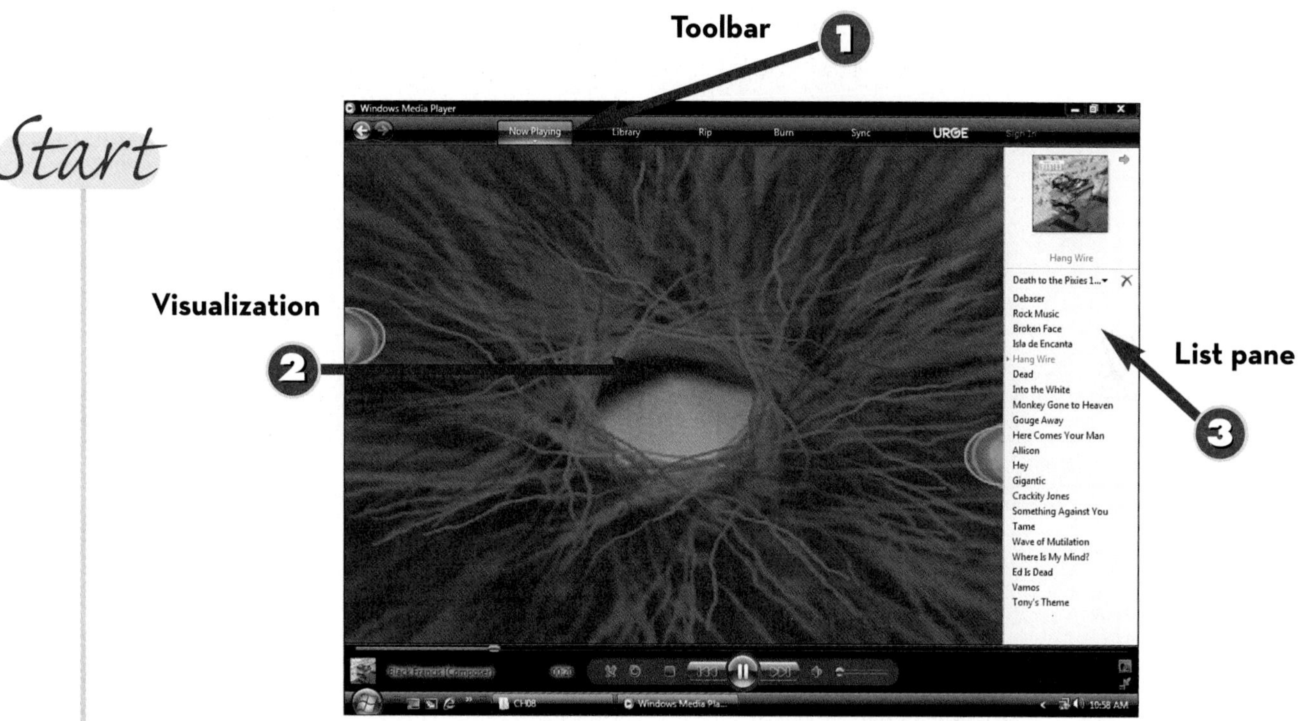

1. The toolbar displays the various options. You can use these to access other Windows Media Player features, such as the Library for organizing your media files.
2. In addition to sound, Windows Media Player displays a visualization or pictorial representation of the music.
3. Information about the CD (if available) is displayed in this pane. Here you see a list of the tracks.

End

TIP

Hide the List Pane

You can hide the List pane by clicking **Now Playing** and unchecking **Show List Pane**. To redisplay the List pane, follow the same process, this time selecting Show List Pane so that it is checked.

WORKING WITH MEDIA PLAYER CONTROLS

When you are listening to your CD, you can use any of the control buttons in the Media Player window to stop the playback, play the next or previous song, adjust the volume, or make other changes.

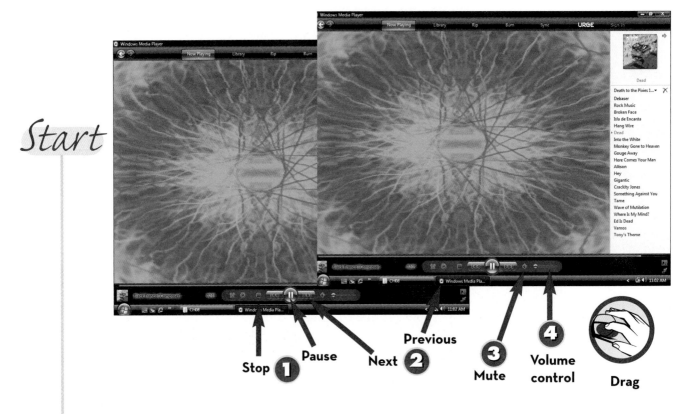

1. To stop the playback, click **Stop**. To pause the playback, click **Pause**.
2. To play the previous track, click **Previous**. To play the next track, click the **Next** button.
3. To mute the sound, click the **Mute** button.
4. To change the volume, drag the volume control slider.

TIP

Full Window or Minimized

You can click the **Full Screen** button to view the Windows Media Player in a full screen. If you don't want the window displayed but want to listen to the music, minimize the Media Player window.

PLAYING ANOTHER AUDIO TRACK

You can use the Next and Previous buttons to play another track, but you can also select a specific task, such as having Media Player shuffle through the tracks (play them in random order) and repeat the songs (from the beginning after the entire CD has been played).

Start

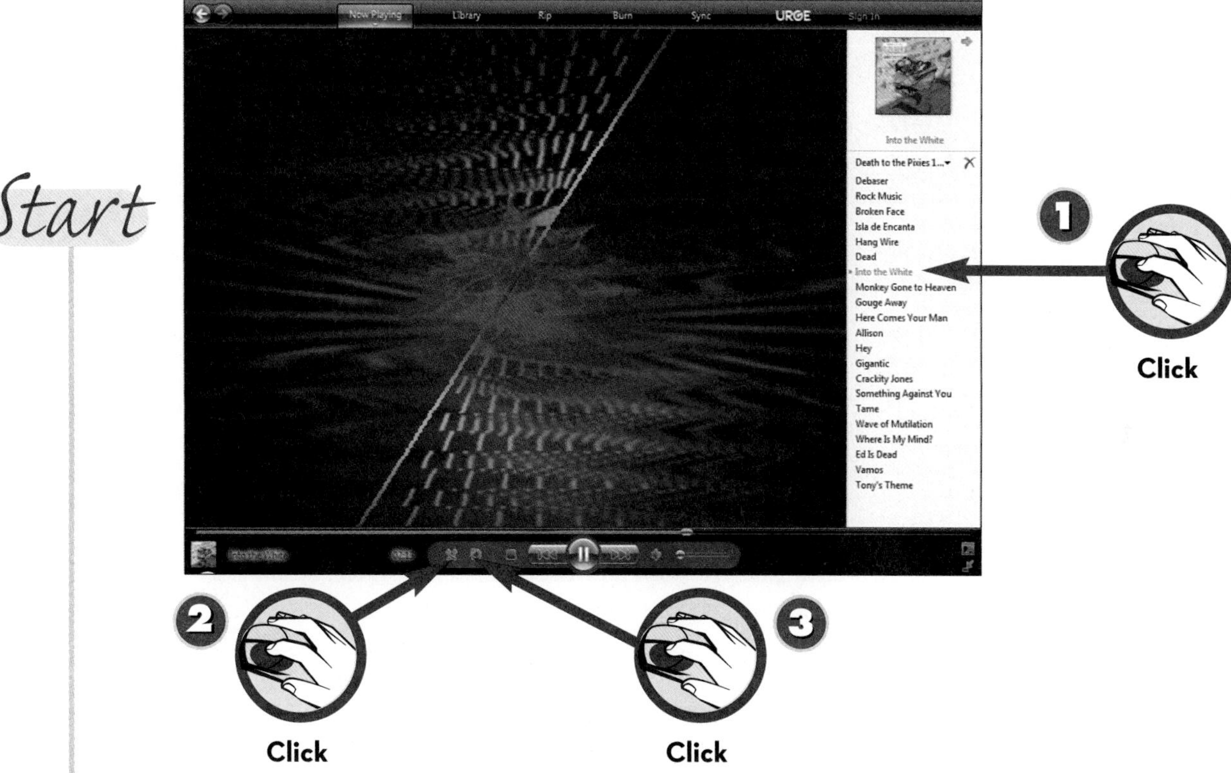

1. To play a different track, click it in the track list. The song is played.
2. To play tracks in random order, click the **Turn shuffle on** button.
3. To repeat songs, click the **Turn repeat on** button.

End

TIP

Set Music Options

To set audio CD options, such as whether songs are automatically copied to your Windows Media Player Library and whether the playlist and CD information is downloaded automatically, click **Now Playing** and then click **Options**. Make any changes on the **Player** tab, and then click **OK**.

SETTING VOLUME OPTIONS FOR AUDIO INPUT AND OUTPUT DEVICES

If the sound on your PC is too loud or too quiet, you can adjust the volume. To do so, use Volume Control. This feature enables you to set the volume for several types of audio input and output devices.

Start

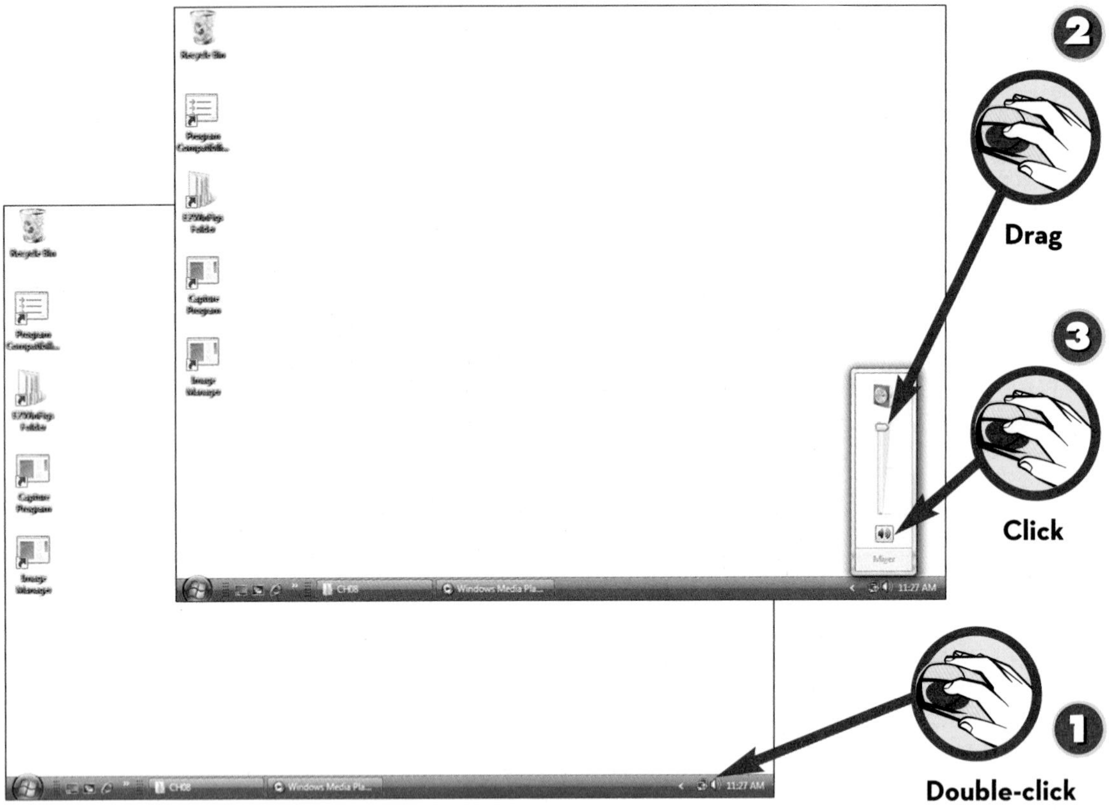

Drag

Click

Double-click

1. In the notification area of the status bar, double-click the **Volume Control** icon.
2. Drag the volume control bar to set the volume.
3. To mute sound, click the Mute button.

End

NOTE

Speaker Volume

You might also have a volume control on your speakers or on your keyboard. You can use these to adjust the sound, too.

CHANGING THE VISUALIZATIONS

If you like to view the visualizations, you can experiment, selecting from several different styles. If you don't like the visualizations, you can choose to turn them off.

Start

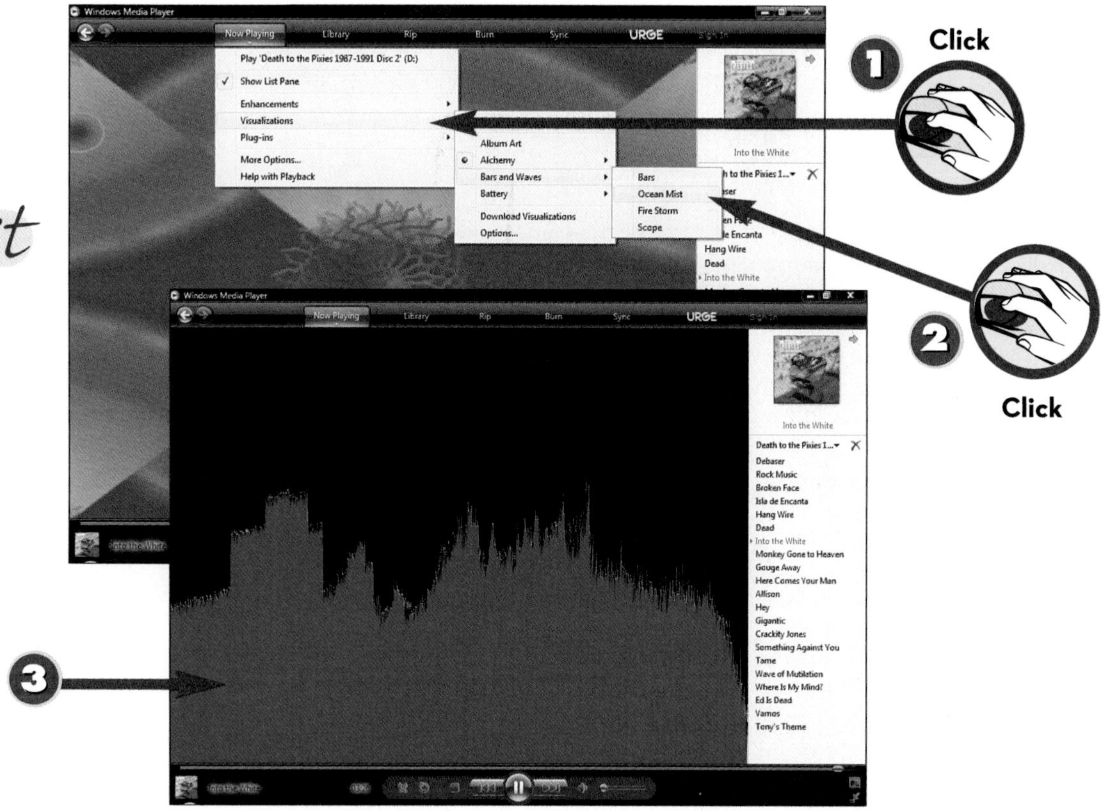

1 Click Now Playing, and then click Visualizations.

2 Click one of the visualization categories, and then click the visualization you want. (Here Ocean Mist is chosen.)

3 You see the new visualization.

- **1** Click **Now Playing**, and then click **Visualizations**.
- **2** Click one of the visualization categories, and then click the visualization you want. (Here Ocean Mist is chosen.)
- **3** You see the new visualization.

End

NOTE

View Enhancements

You can also choose to view enhancements that show Graphic Equalizer settings. Click **Now Playing**, **Enhancements**. You can then adjust the various graphics equalizer settings by dragging the slider bar for each option.

TIP

Download Visualizations

To download additional visualizations from the Internet, click **Visualizations** and then **Download Visualizations**. You see a page with visualizations from the Windows Media Player Internet page. Use the links and follow the instructions to download the visualization(s) you want.

USING THE LIBRARY

To organize all the various media on your PC, you can use the Windows Media Library. This library stores music and videos by several different methods so that you can easily find a particular file for playback. can You also use the library to create playlists (see "Creating a Playlist" later in this Part).

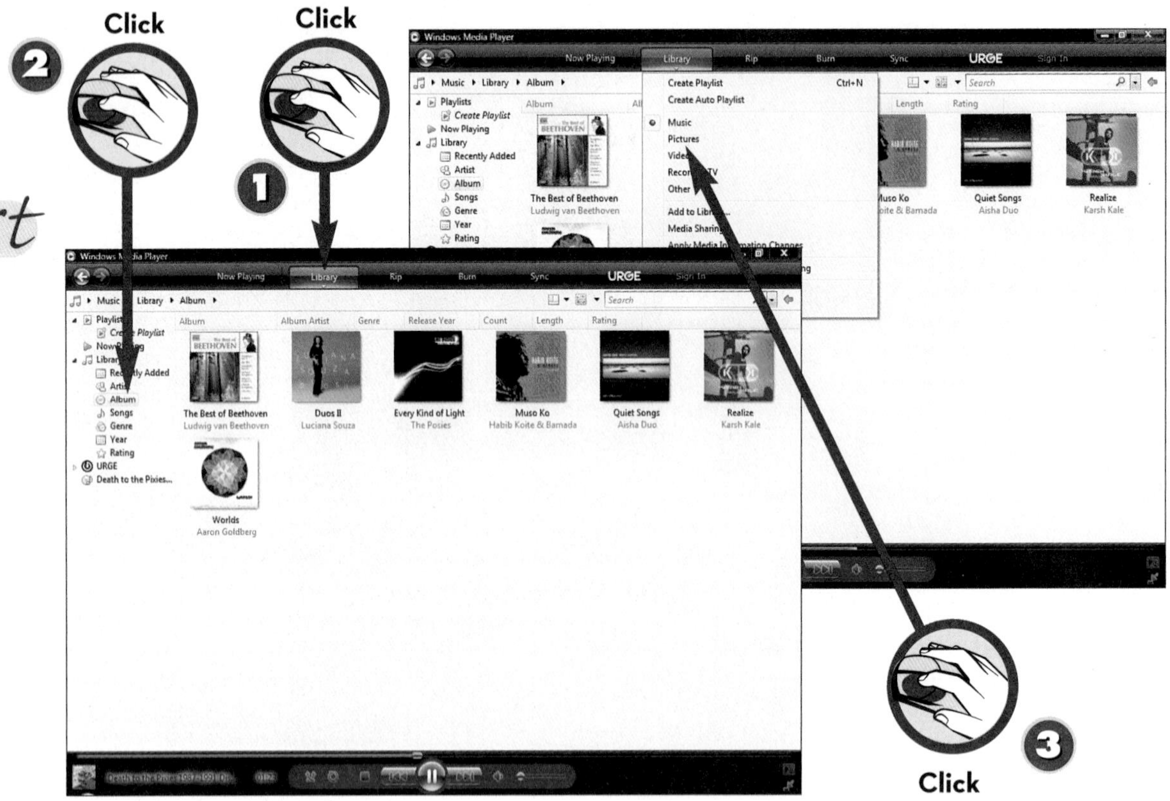

1. Click the **Library** button in Windows Media Player.
2. To view a particular category of media, click it under Library. For instance, you can view media by artist, album, genre, rating, and so on.
3. To view other types of media, such as video or pictures, click the **Library** button and then click the media. For instance, to view pictures, click **Pictures**. You can then select picture categories in the Navigation pane.

NOTE

Adding Songs to the Library

For information on adding songs to the Library, see "Copying (Ripping) CD Tracks" later in this part.

TIP

Change How Contents Are Viewed

To change how the items in the window are viewed, click the **View Options** button and select a view. You can select **Icon**, **Tile**, or **Details**.

SEARCHING FOR MUSIC

As you add more media to your Windows Media Player Library, you may find it difficult to find a song or album by navigating through the list. Instead of manually hunting for what you want, you can search the library for a song, picture, video, or other media.

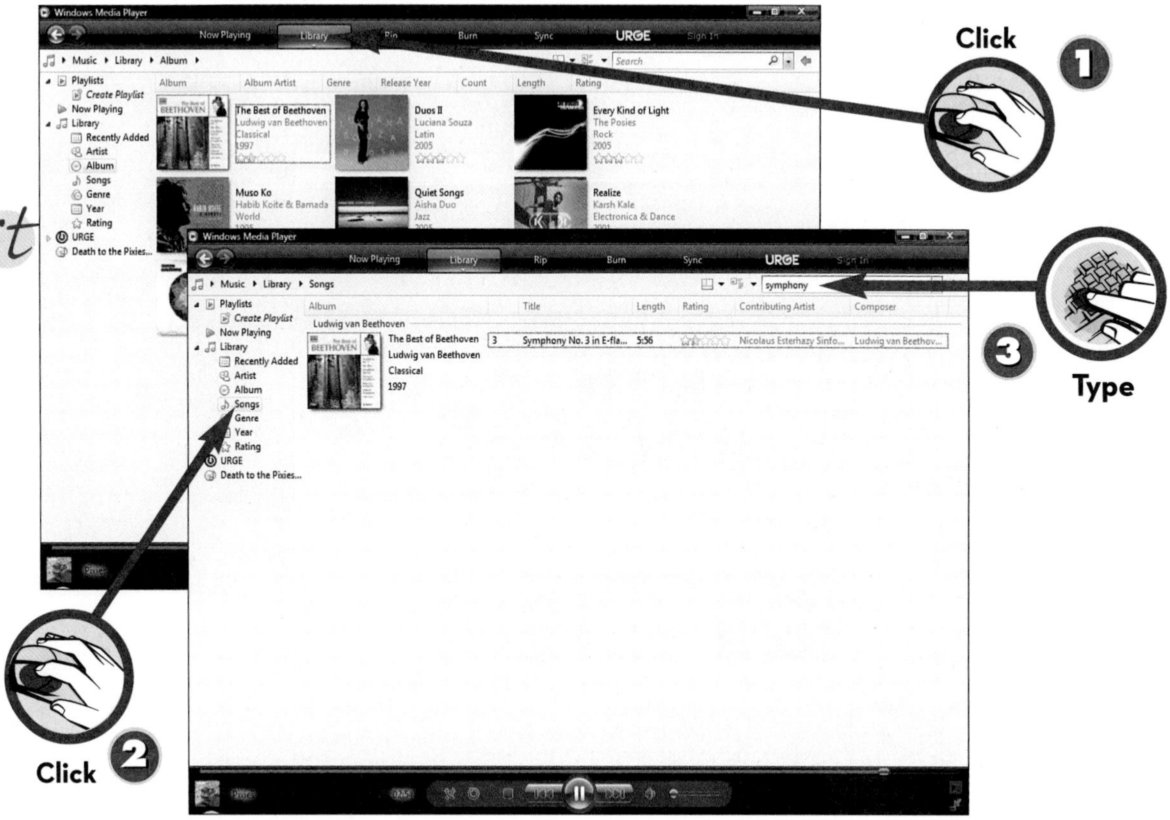

1. Click the **Library** button in Windows Media Player, and select the type of media you want to search.
2. Click how you want to search (for instance, by artist, album, song, and so on).
3. In the search box, type a word or phrase to identify the media you want to find. Windows Media Player automatically displays any matches.

FINDING AND BUYING MUSIC ONLINE

You can get information about new music, sample new tunes, and purchase music from various online sites. You can also view videos and read online news stories about the music industry. In addition, you can purchase music. This task covers using Windows Media Guide to purchase music.

1. Click the **URGE** button and select **Media Guide**.
2. From the Media Guide page, click **Music**.
3. You see the current music page listing highlighted videos and albums as well as providing access to categories such as Top 40 Radio.

Continued

TIP

Use URGE

The first time you access URGE you will be prompted to accept its user agreement. You then must download and install this feature. Follow the onscreen instructions.

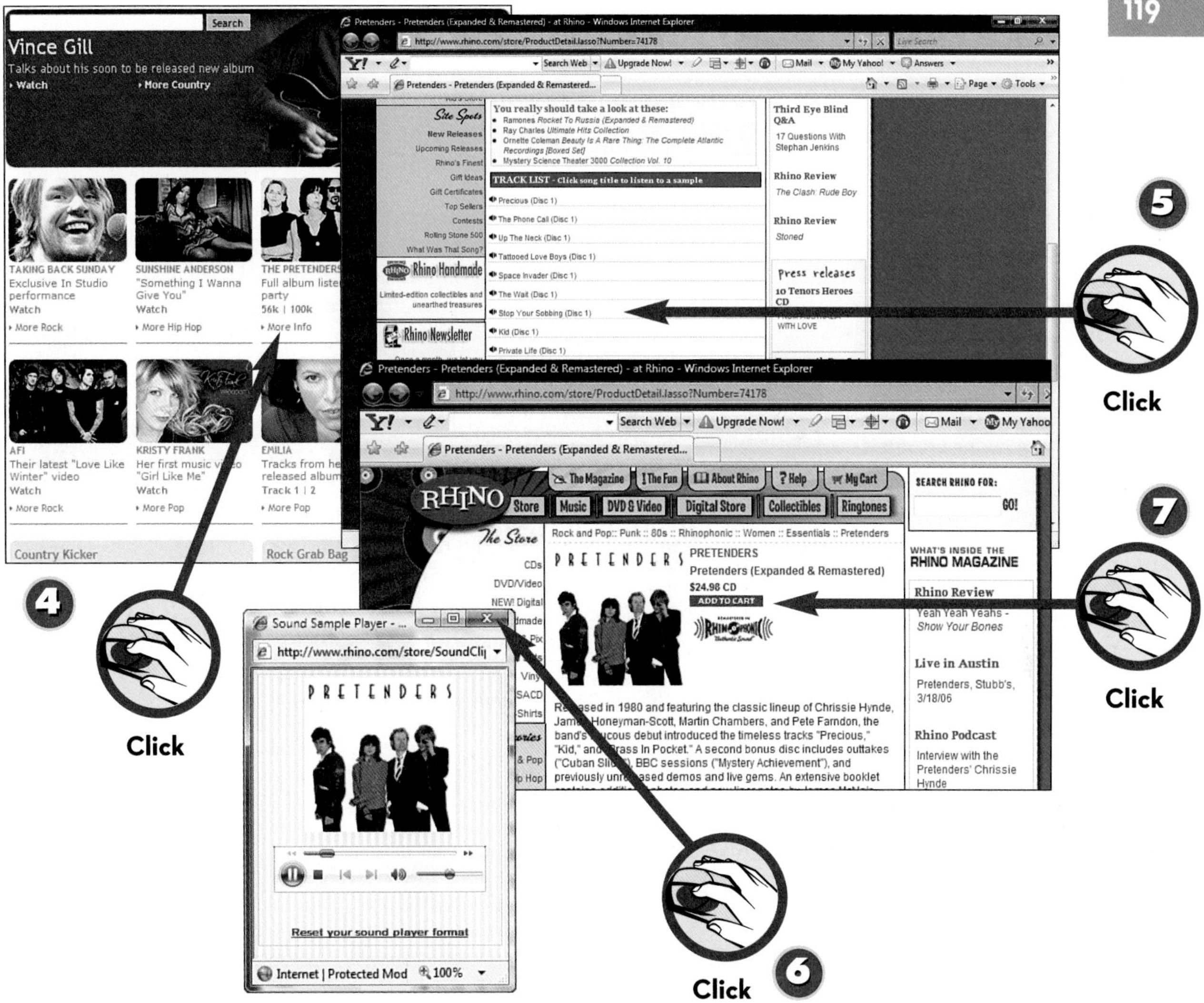

4. To view information about a listed album, click the **More Info** link.

5. Scroll down the page to view the available songs. The first song is played automatically. To play another song from the CD, click it.

6. The song sampling is played in its own little window. Click its **Close** button to close the window.

7. To purchase a song or CD, look for a purchase link. Click the appropriate link (here Add to Cart), and then follow the online instructions for checking out and buying music.

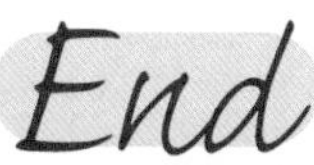

NOTE

Set Up an Account

To purchase music at many sites, you must first set up an account. This requires you to enter a username and password as well as credit card information. The first time you click a link to purchase a song or CD, you'll be prompted to set up an account. Simply follow the onscreen instructions.

TIP

Play the Purchased Files

You can access and play the songs or albums you purchased from the library.

CREATING A PLAYLIST

You can use the library to create a playlist of songs you have stored on your computer. You can then be your own DJ, playing songs in the order you select and from the artists you choose.

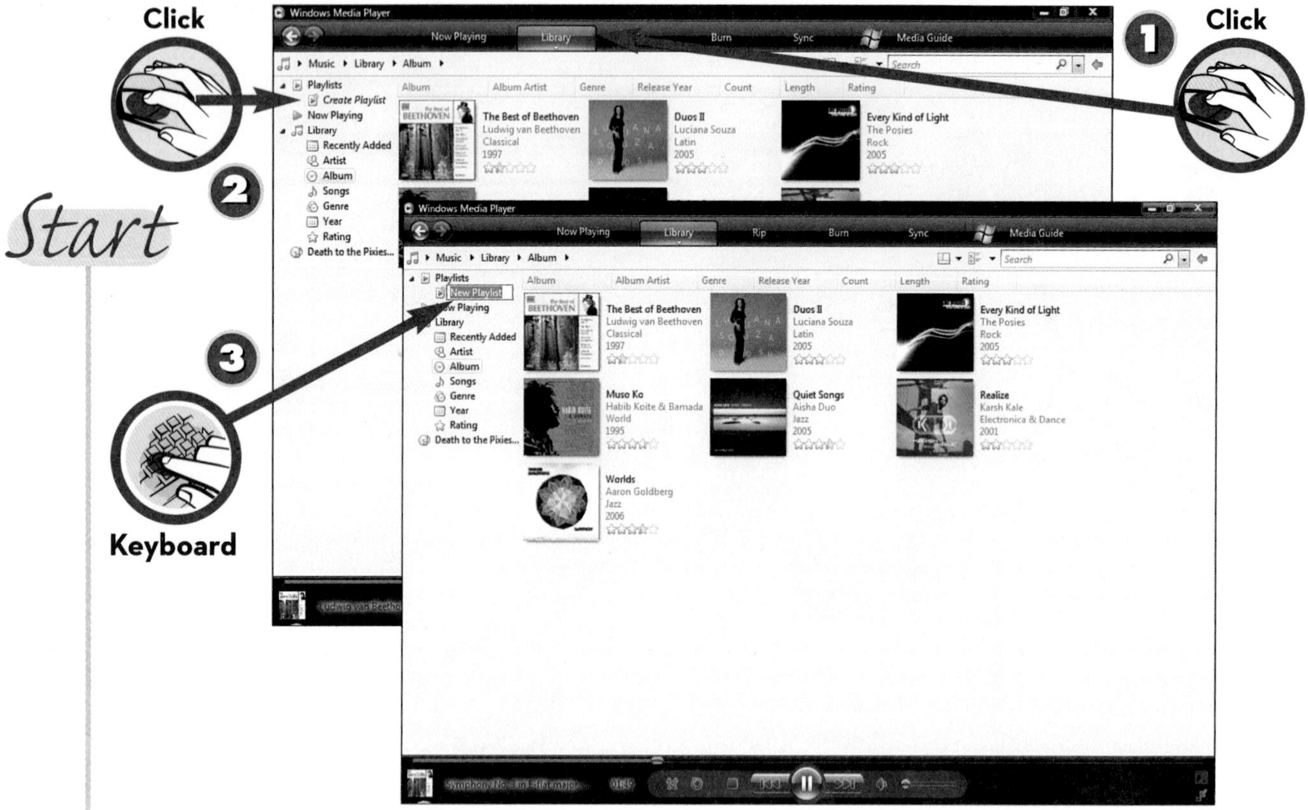

Start

1. Click the **Library** button in Windows Media Player.
2. Under Playlists, click the **Create Playlist** option.
3. The untitled playlist is highlighted; type a name for your playlist, and press **Enter**.

Continued

TIP

Copy Tracks

You can copy tracks from your own audio CDs and add them to your playlist. Refer to "Copying (Ripping) CD Tracks" later in this Part for more information.

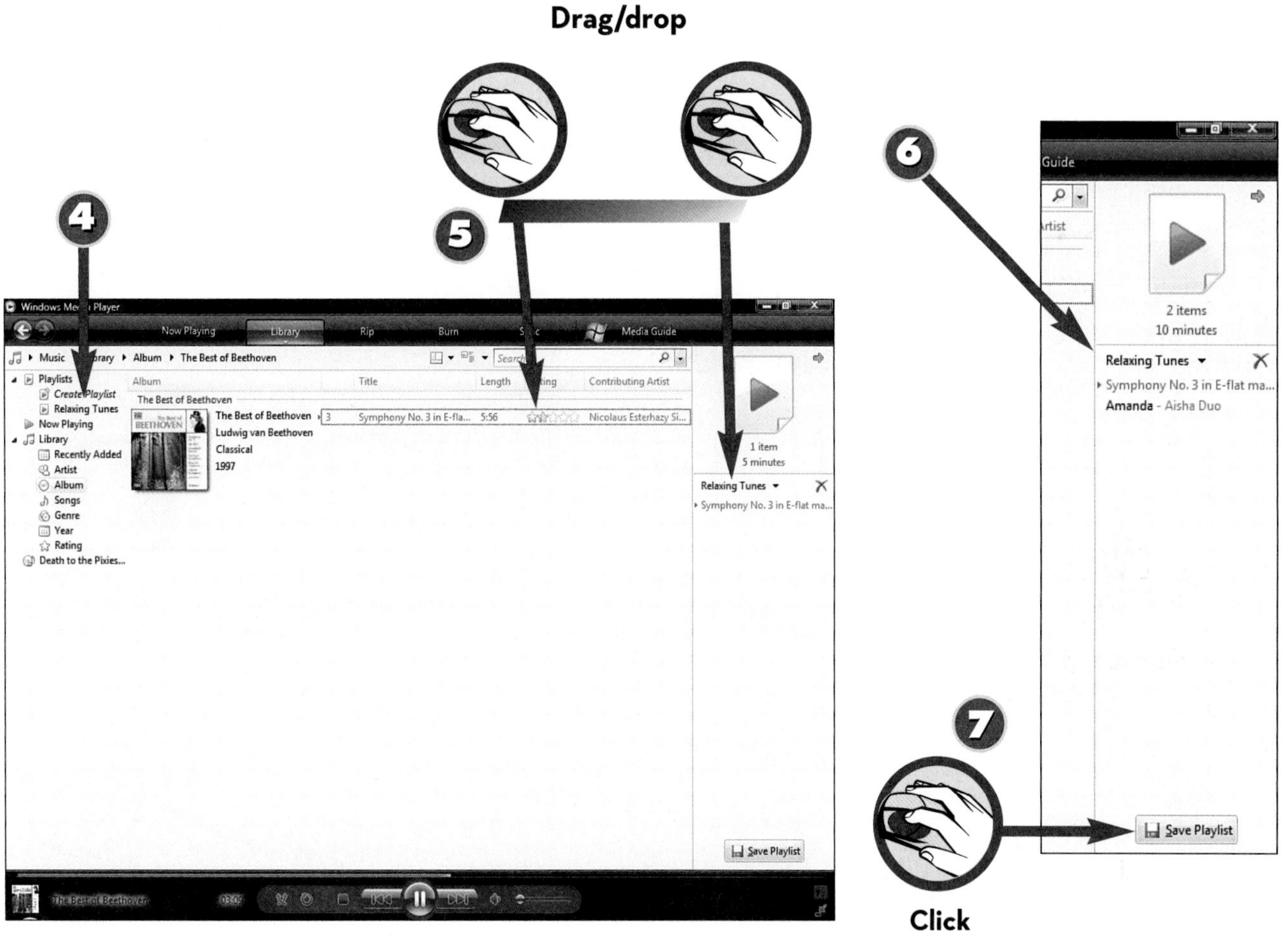

Drag/drop

Click

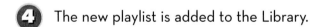

4 The new playlist is added to the Library.

5 Display the song you want to add to your playlist. Then drag it to the **Playlist** pane.

6 Continue dragging songs to the Playlist pane until you complete the playlist.

7 Click **Save Playlist**. The playlist is saved and listed in the Navigation pane.

End

TIP

Edit the Playlist

To edit the playlist, click it in the Navigation pane. To delete a song, click the song and press **Delete**. To rearrange the songs in the playlist, right-click the song and then click **Move Up** or **Move Down**.

TIP

Delete a Playlist

To delete a playlist, right-click it in the Navigation pane. Then click **Delete.** You can choose to delete the playlist from the Library or from the Library and your computer. (Usually you'll keep your songs on the computer, but simply delete them from the Library.)

COPYING (RIPPING) CD TRACKS

You can copy tracks from a CD to your computer. You can then add them to your playlists and play back the songs from the computer rather than the audio CD.

1. Insert the CD you want to copy tracks from, and then click the **Rip** button.
2. Check the tracks you want to copy.
3. Click the **Start Rip** button. You see the status as the tracks are ripped (copied).
4. Click the **Library** button, and use the Navigation pane to display the newly added songs.

TIP

Setting Rip Options

To set the audio format options, whether ripping/copying starts automatically, and other settings, click **Now Playing** and then click **More Options**. Click the **Rip Music** tab, make any changes, and click **OK**.

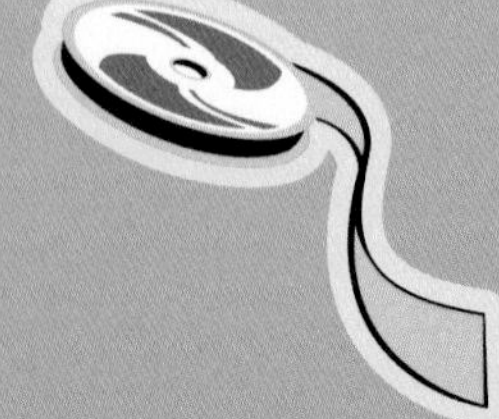

BURNING (CREATING) A CD

One of the benefits of copying your audio CDs to your computer is not only that you can play music from your computer, but you can also combine music from several different albums to create your own unique CD.

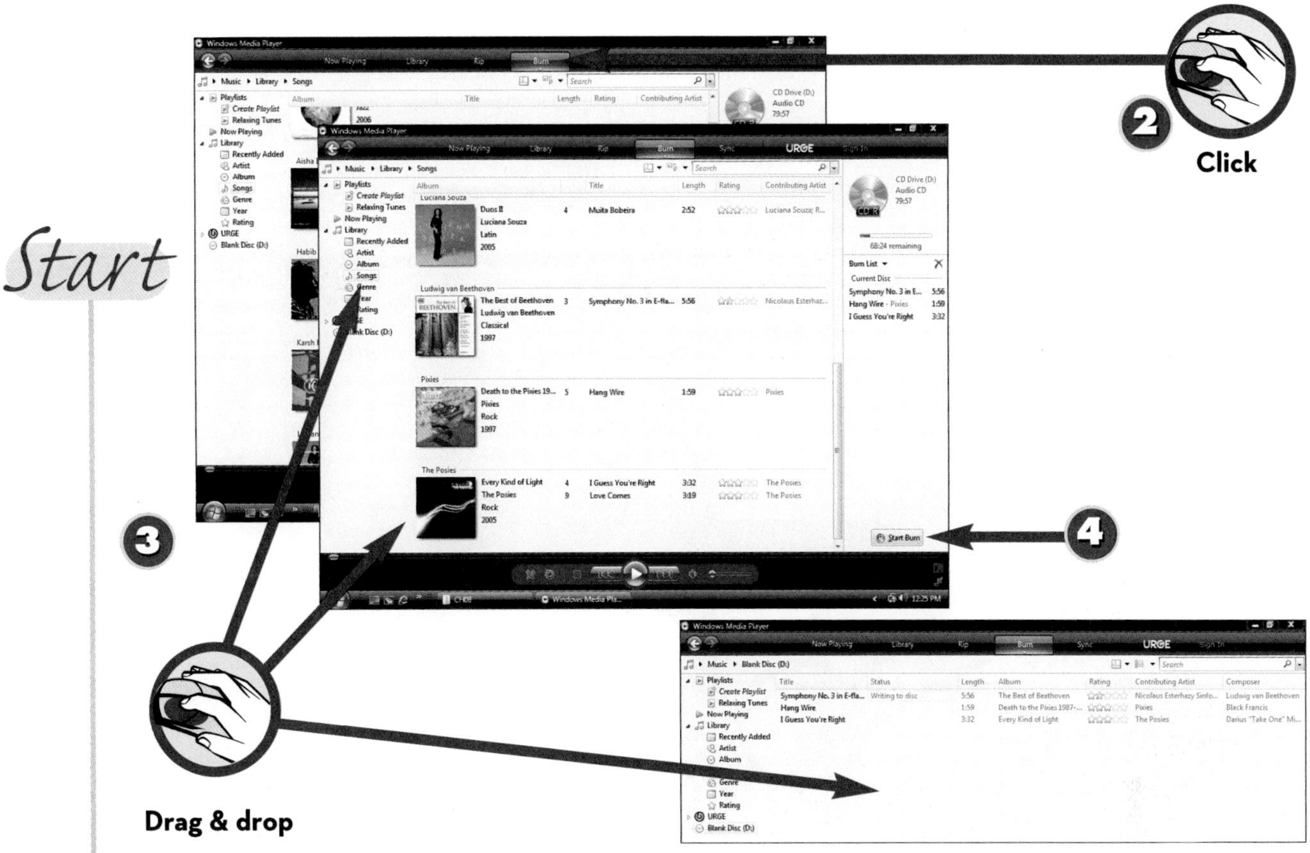

Start

Click

Drag & drop

1. Insert a burnable CD into your CD drive.
2. Click the **Burn** button in Windows Media Player.
3. Click **Songs** in the Navigation pane; the List area shows your albums and songs from your Library. Drag the songs from the List area to the Burn List.
4. When you've added all your tracks, click **Start Burn**. The tracks are burned to the CD. You can see the progress as the CD is created.

End

NOTE

Too Many Songs?

If you have more songs than will fit on the CD, you will be informed. You can then delete songs from the Burn List. Most CDs store roughly 80 minutes of music.

NOTE

Burn DVDs

If your computer has a DVD drive that can burn or copy DVDs, you can use it to make DVDs. For instance, you can make your own movie and then burn/copy it to a DVD. To make the copy, you need a DVD burning program. You can use Windows DVD Maker. Use online help to get instructions on how to use this program to burn a DVD.

PLAYING A VIDEO CLIP

In addition to playing music, you can use Windows Media Player to play videos. You can open any video file or select a file from the Media Library to play.

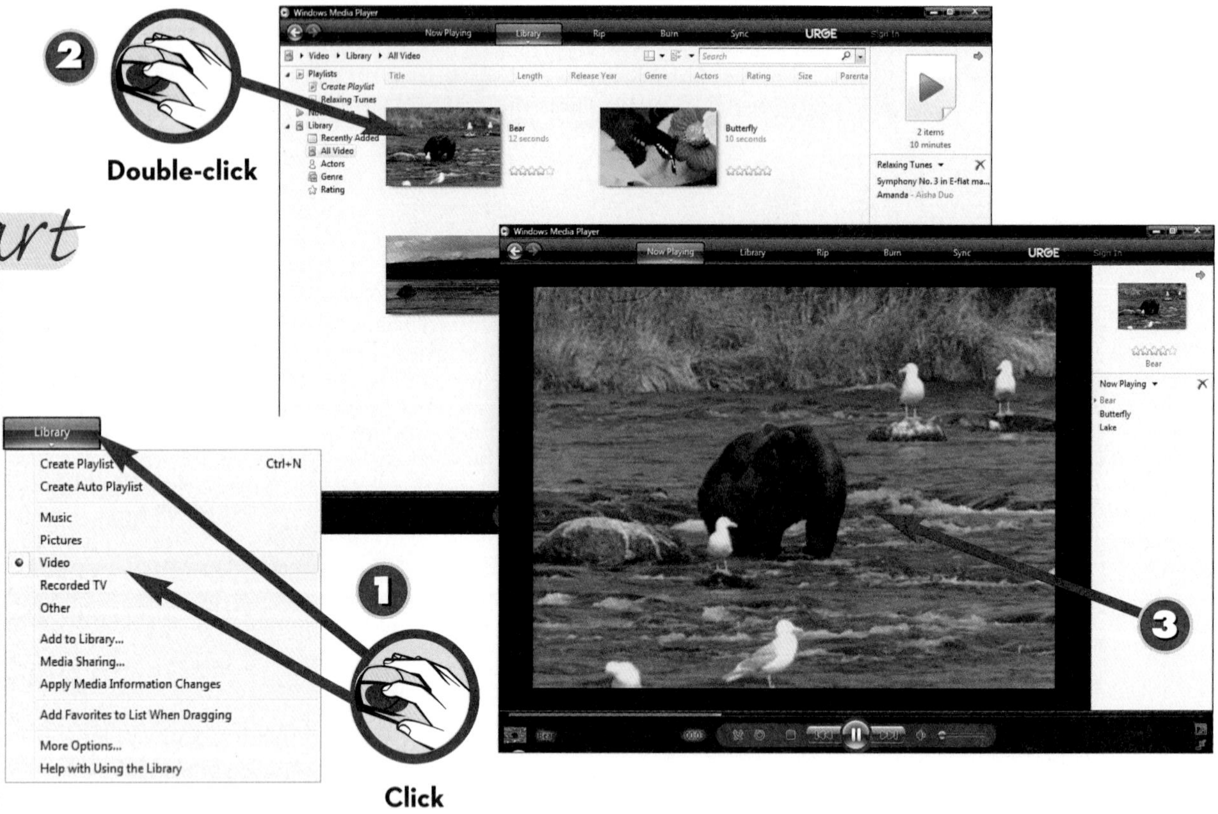

Double-click

Start

Click

1. Click the **Library** button, and then click **Video**.
2. Double-click the file you want to play.
3. The video clip begins playing in Media Player's Now Playing screen.

End

TIP

Playing a DVD

If you have a DVD drive, you can watch movies using Windows Media Center. Click **Start**, **All Programs**, **Windows Media Center**. Insert your DVD, and then click **play dvd**. You can also use any of the onscreen controls to pause, stop, and resume playback of the DVD.

PLAYING GAMES

Windows provides several games that you can play to break up your workday with a little entertainment. Playing games is also a good way to help you get the hang of using the mouse. For example, playing Solitaire can help you practice such mouse skills as clicking, dragging, and so on.

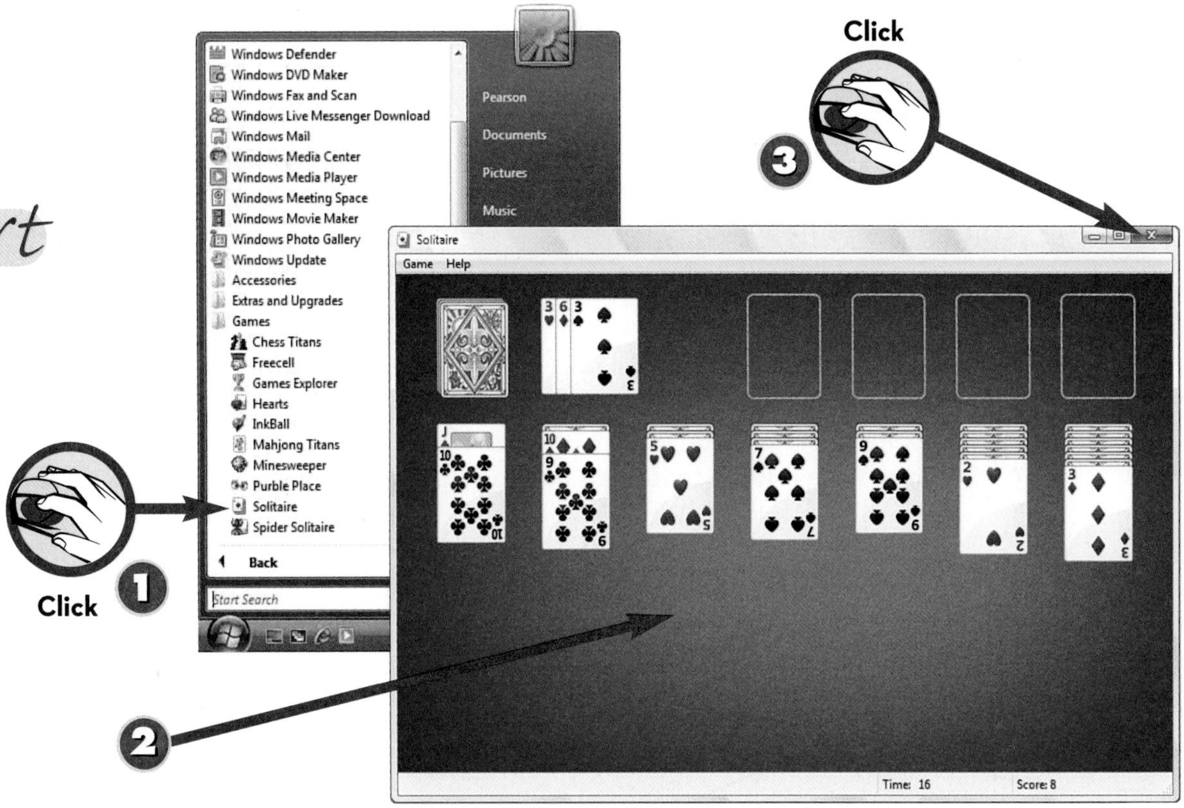

1. Click **Start**, **All Programs**, **Games**, and then click the name of the game you want to open (in this case, **Solitaire**).
2. Play the game.
3. When you are finished, click the **Close** button to exit.

TIP

Set Game Controllers

If you have gaming controllers, such as a joystick or other gaming devices, you can customize them using the Game Controllers control panel. Click **Start** and then **Control Panel**. In Classic View, double-click **Game Controllers**. Set up any new devices or make any modifications to existing devices, and then click **OK**.

TIP

Get Help

If you aren't sure how to play a game, get instructions using the online help. Open the **Help** menu and select the **Help** command.

SENDING EMAIL

One popular use of a computer is to communicate with others, most commonly through email. To send email, you need a modem and a connection to the Internet via an Internet service provider (ISP). You'll find different types of modems from dial-up, to cable, to DSL. Common ISPs are AOL and EarthLink, or you may use a local provider.

You also need a mail program. Your mail program gives you the tools to send and receive email, as well as organize and manage the messages you send and receive. Windows Vista includes Windows Mail (formerly known as Outlook Express). When you open Windows Mail, you'll see a pane on the left that shows the folders that are part of the program, such as the Inbox, Outbox, and Sent Items folders. When you click a folder, such as the Inbox, you see the contents of that folder (in this case, it would be email that you have received) in the right side of the window. Below the list of the folder contents, you'll see a preview of the currently selected message in the folder.

You can manage and organize your mail by creating new folders to save messages that you want to keep. You can set up options that will keep junk email (spam) from coming into your Inbox. You can also set up a Contacts list that stores all the contact information for people you want to send email to and receive email from.

All the details to get you started using Windows Mail to work with email are covered in the tasks in this Part.

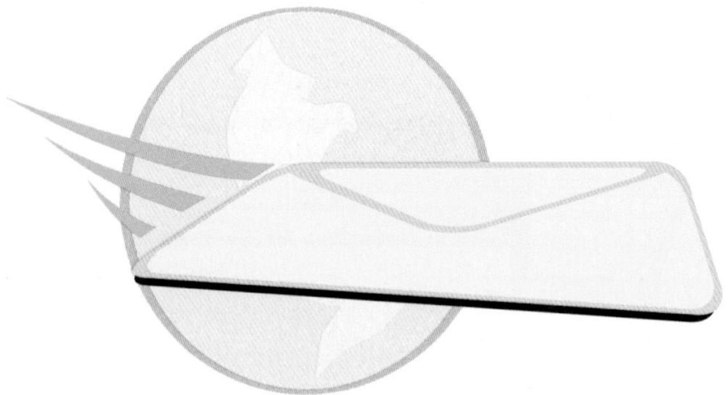

WINDOWS MAIL

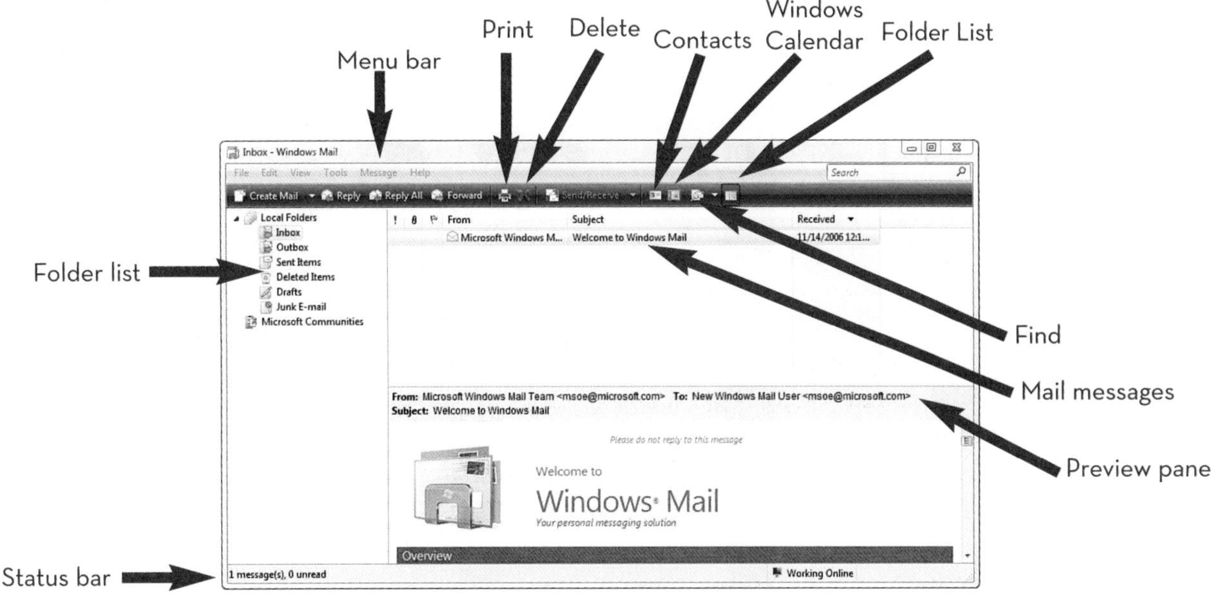

Name	Click To...
Create Mail	Create new mail messages.
Reply	Reply to a message you have received.
Reply All	If you have received a message that was sent to several people, click this button to send your reply to all original message recipients.
Forward	Send an existing message to a different recipient...
Print	Print a message...

Name	Click To...
Delete	Delete a message.
Send/Receive	Send and receive messages.
Contacts	Display your Contacts list so that you can select recipients, add contacts, or make other changes to your Contacts list.
Windows Calendar	Displays the Calendar.
Find	Search for a message.
Folder List	Hide or display the Folder List.

STARTING WINDOWS MAIL

After you set up a mail account with an ISP, you can use Windows Mail to create, send, and receive email over the Internet. To start, spend some time getting familiar with the Windows Mail window and its features.

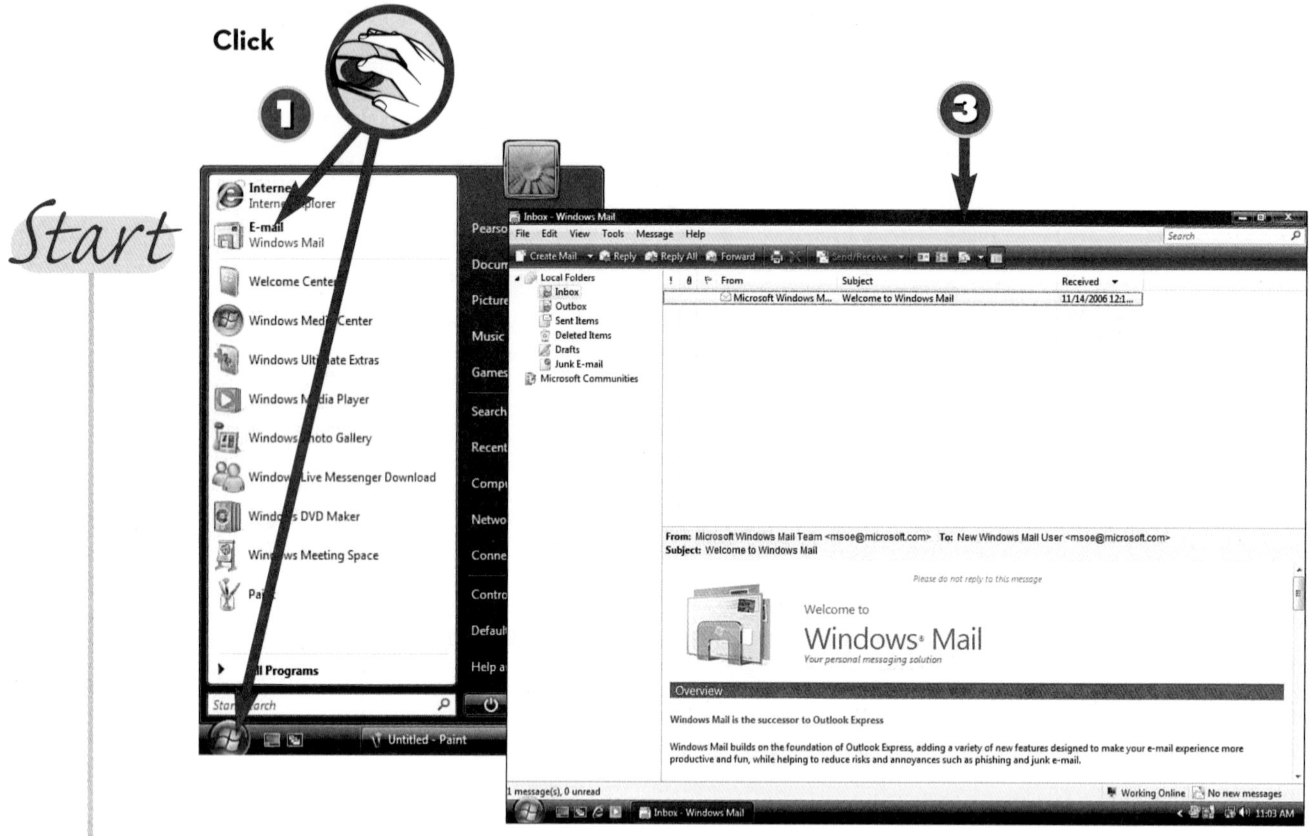

Click

Start

1. Click **Start**, and then click **E-mail (Windows Mail)**.
2. If prompted, connect to your ISP (not shown).
3. Windows Mail starts, and you see the various panes: the Folder List shows the mail folders, the Message Header pane displays key information about each message, and the Preview pane displays a preview of the currently selected message.

Continued

TIP

Logging On and Disconnecting

If you have a dial-up connection and connect through a regular phone line, you will most likely be prompted to log on to your ISP. You also need to be sure to log off when you are done reading your mail. To exit Windows Mail, click the **Close** button for the program window. If you are prompted to log off, select **Yes** or **Disconnect**. If you are not prompted, right-click the connec-

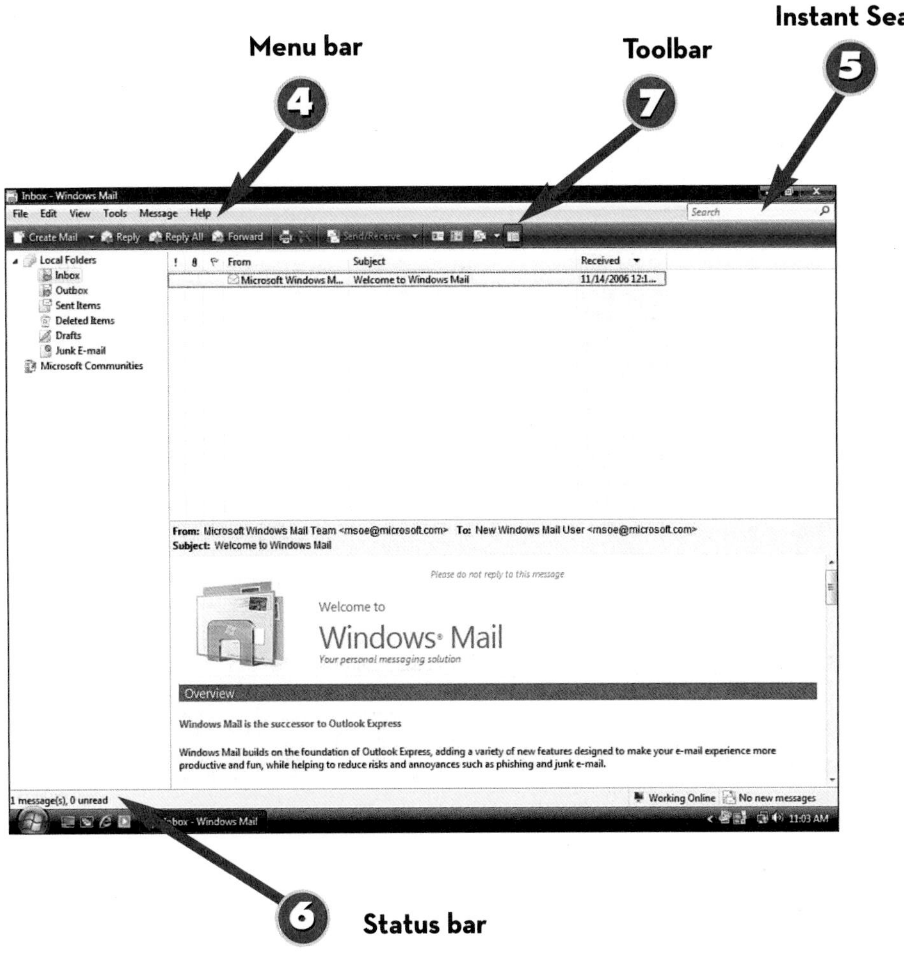

4. The menu bar lists menu commands.

5. Instant Search text box lets you search for messages.

6. The status bar displays the number of messages and the number of unread messages. It also lets you know if you are working on- or offline.

7. The toolbar displays buttons for working with messages. The table on page 127 describes the purpose for each of the toolbar buttons.

End

NOTE

Sending and Receiving Messages

You can set up Windows to automatically send and receive messages at a set interval. Or you can send and receive them manually by clicking the Send/Receive button. See "Setting E-mail Options" later in this Part.

TIP

Change Window Layout

You can change how the window appears. To do so, click **View** and then **Layout**. Check which items are displayed (Folder List, Toolbar, Status Bar, and other features). You can also select whether the Preview pane is displayed and if so, where it is positioned. Make your choices and click **OK**.

READING MAIL

When you start Windows Mail and connect with your ISP, your email messages are downloaded from your Internet mail server to your computer. The number of messages in your Inbox appears in parentheses next to the Inbox in the Folders list. The Message Header pane lists all messages. Messages appearing in bold have not yet been read. You can open and read any message in the message list.

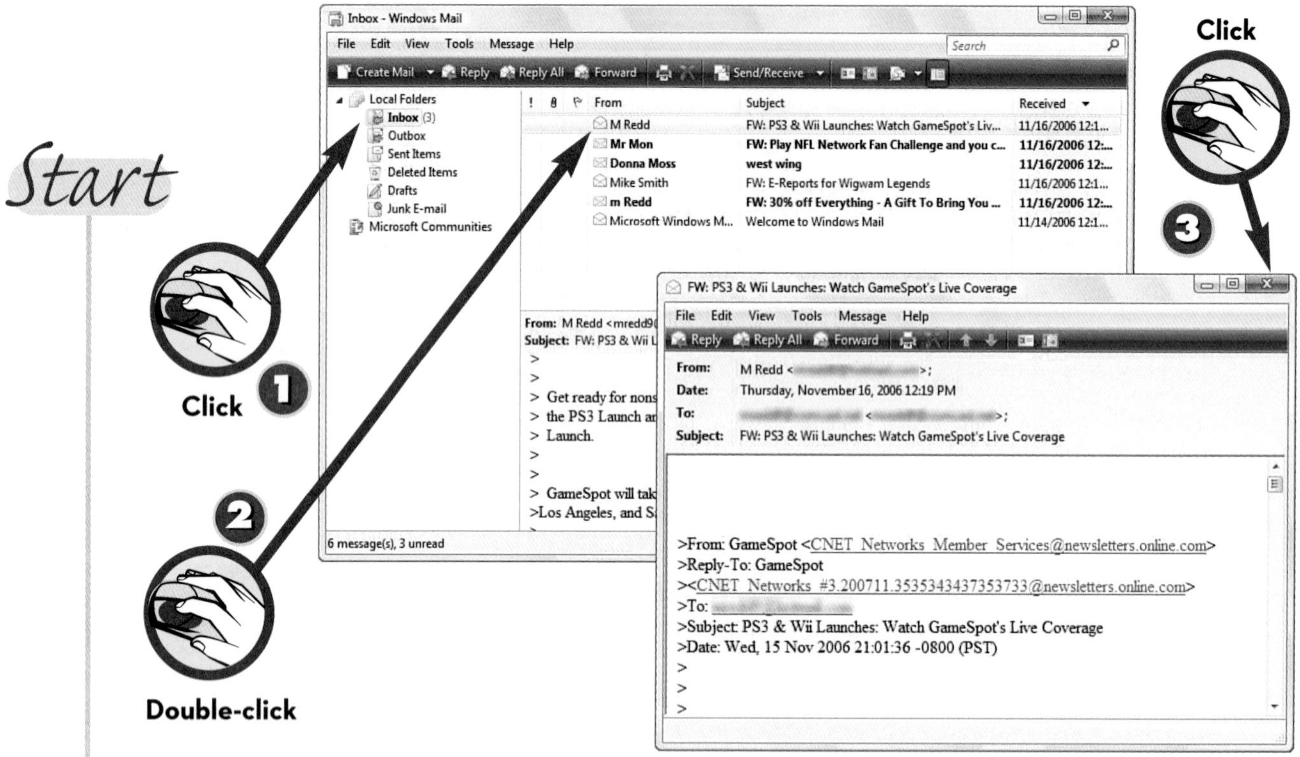

Start

Click 1

2 Double-click

Click 3

1. If necessary, click **Inbox** in the Folders List to display the email messages in the Message Header pane.
2. Double-click the message you want to read.
3. The message you selected is displayed in its own window. To close the message, click the **Close** button.

End

TIP

Display Other Messages

The toolbar in the opened email window is similar to the Windows Mail toolbar, but includes other buttons. For instance, you can use the **Previous** and **Next** buttons to display and the next (or previous) message in the list. You can also print a message by clicking the **Print** button.

TIP

Handling Spam or Junk Mail

You'll find that you get a lot of unsolicited email called spam (the email equivalent of junk mail). Windows includes filters that handle junk mail. You can find out more about filters (as well as phishing filters) in Part 11, "System Security and User Accounts."

REPLYING TO MAIL

You can easily respond to a message you've received. Windows Mail completes the address and subject lines for you; you can then simply type the response.

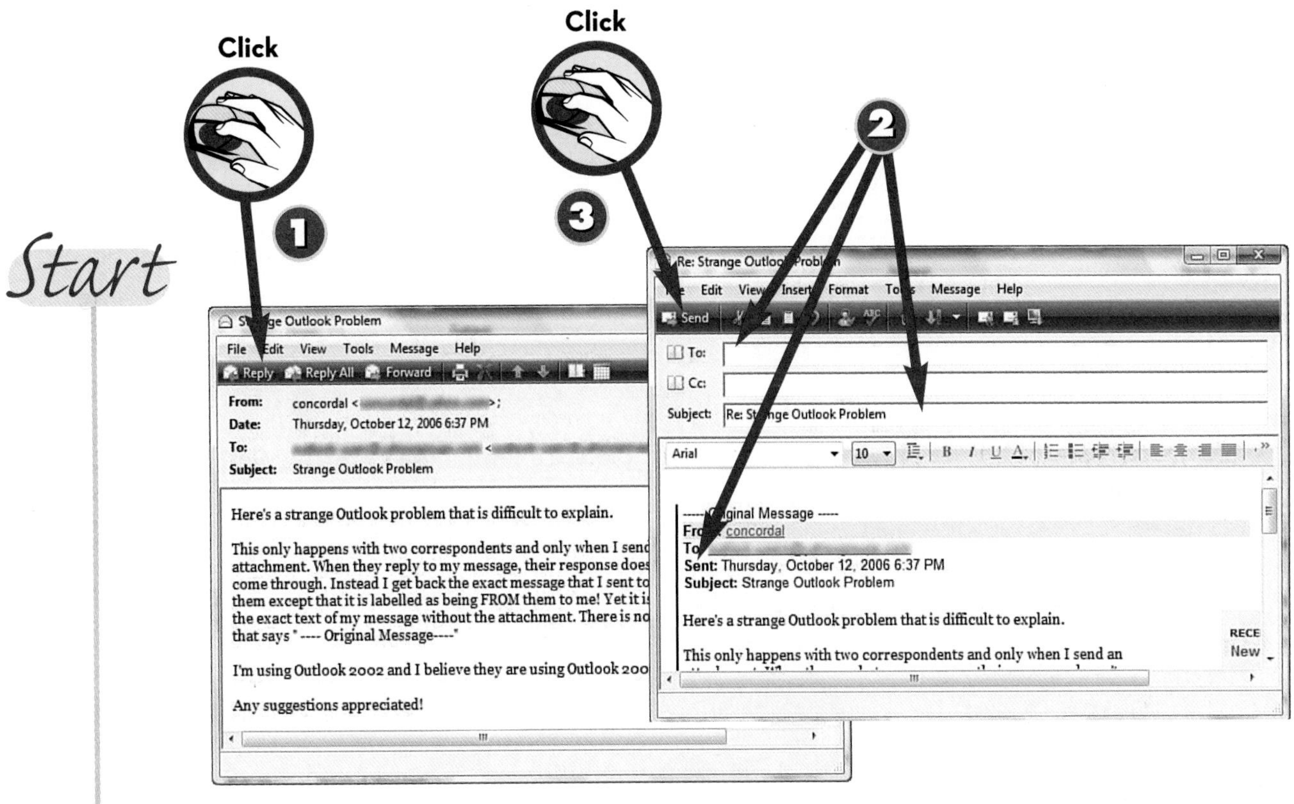

Start

1. Open the message to which you want to reply, and click the **Reply** button in the toolbar.
2. The address and subject lines are completed, and the text of the original message is appended to the bottom of the reply message.
3. Type the message (reply), and click the **Send** button.

End

TIP
Reply to All

If the message was sent to several people, you can reply to all the recipients. Click the **Reply All** button, type the message, and then click **Send**. If all recipients don't need to see the reply, you don't need to reply to all. You can simply reply to the sender.

TIP
Reply from Message Header Pane

You don't have to open a message to reply to it. You can select it in the Message Header pane and then click **Reply**, following the same steps covered in this task.

FORWARDING A MESSAGE

Sometimes you get a message you want to share with others. Jokes, for instance, are very popular forwarded messages (as are warnings about viruses and chain/good luck/friendship messages). In addition to forwarding these types of messages, you may also forward "legitimate messages" when you want to share an idea with someone or pass along something that was sent to you but really should have been sent to someone else.

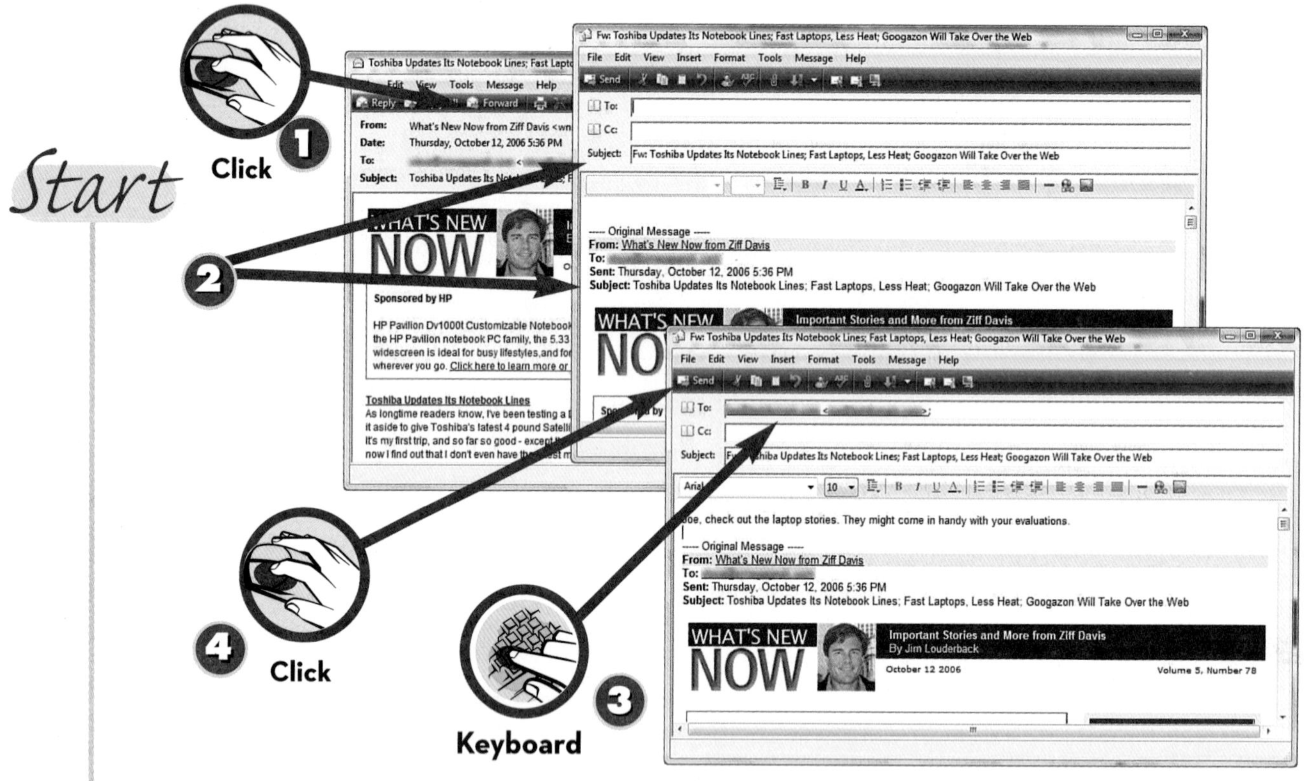

Start

Click

Click

Keyboard

1. Display the message you want to forward, and click the **Forward** button in the toolbar.
2. The subject line is completed, and the text of the original message is appended to the bottom of the reply message.
3. Enter the address for the recipient. Type any message you want to include with the forwarded message.
4. Click the **Send** button.

End

TIP

Cancel Message

If you decide you don't want to send a message, click the message window's **Close** button and then click **No** when asked whether you want to save changes to the message.

NOTE

When Messages Are Sent

Messages are either sent immediately or placed in the Outbox and then sent when you click **Send/Receive**. To change your send preferences, see "Setting Email Options" later in this Part.

SORTING MESSAGES

You'll be surprised how quickly your Inbox fills up with messages; you'll go from having 10 messages to having 300 or more in no time! Finding a particular message can be difficult. One way to find a message or work with a group of message is to sort them. You can sort messages by any of the message headers.

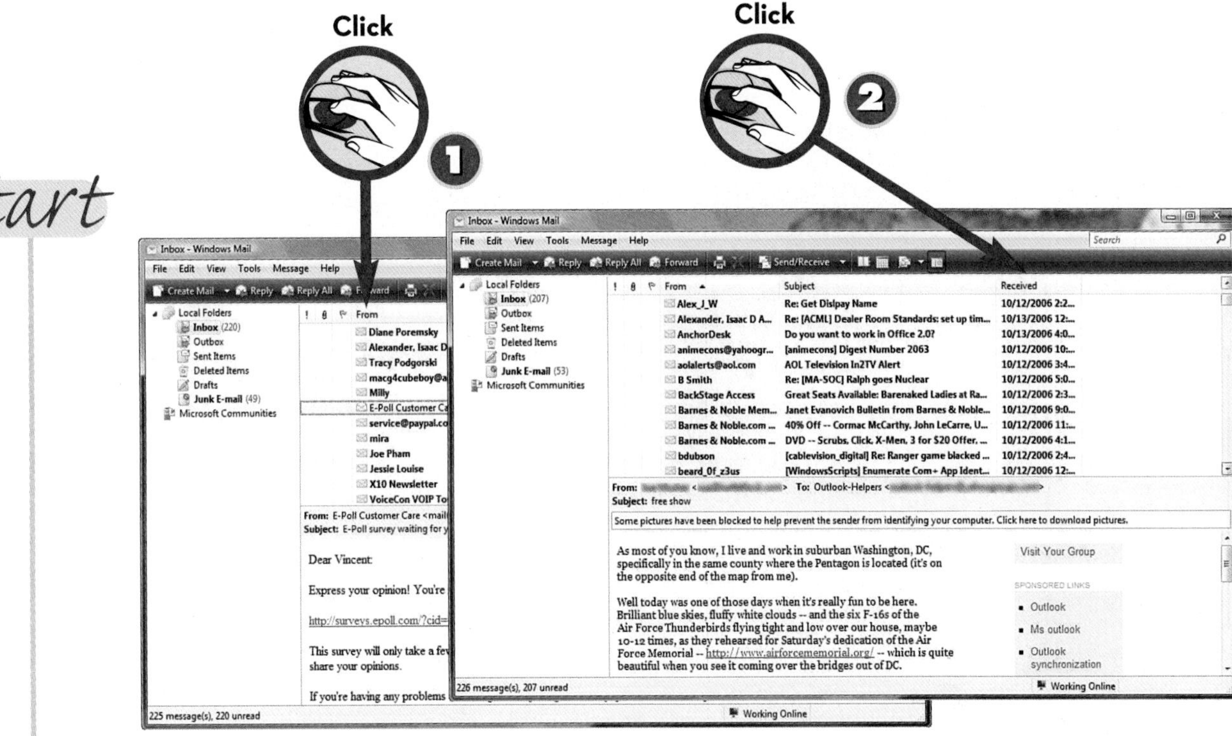

1. In the Windows Mail window, click the column header on which you want to sort. For instance, to sort by the name or email address of the sender, click the **From** column header.
2. The messages are sorted. Click another column header to sort by the content of that column.

End

TIP

Changing Order

You can click the same column header again to change the sort order. For instance, if you click the **Received** column header, you sort by received date (oldest to newest). To change from newest to oldest, click the column header again.

CREATING AND SENDING NEW MAIL

You can send a message to anyone who has an Internet email address. Simply type the recipient's email address, a subject, and the message. You can also send a carbon copy (CC) by entering an address for this field.

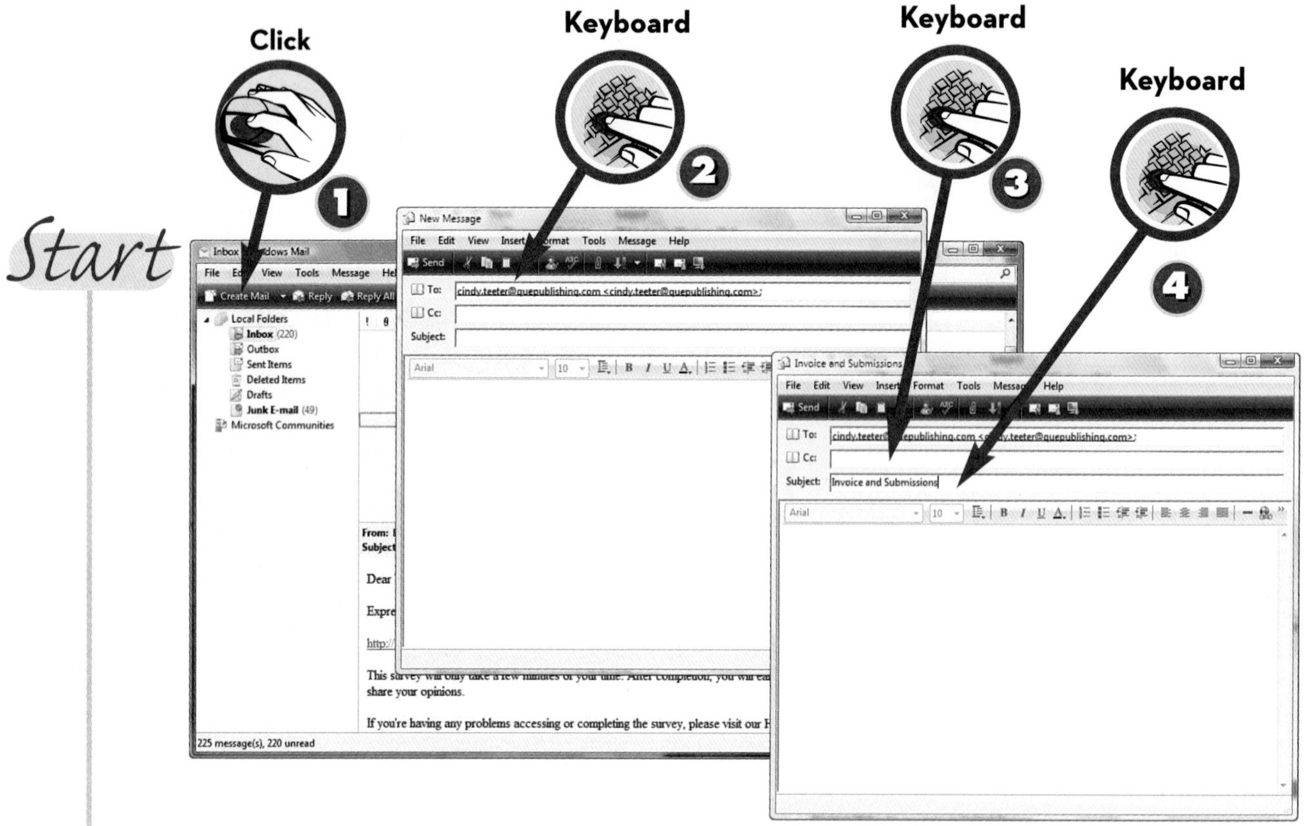

Start

Click

Keyboard

Keyboard

Keyboard

1. In the Windows Mail window, click the **Create Mail** button on the toolbar.
2. You see a blank mail message. Type the recipient's address. Addresses are in the format username@domainname.ext (for example, sohara@msn.com). Press **Tab**.
3. If needed, type an address for the CC (carbon copy), and press **Tab**.
4. Type a subject in the **Subject** text box, and then press **Tab**.

Continued

NOTE

Wrong Address?

If you enter an incorrect address and the message is not sent, you most likely will receive a Failure to Deliver notice. Try resending the message again after double-checking the address. Be sure to type the address in its proper format.

TIP

Select Name from Contacts List

Rather than type the address, you can select it from your Contacts list. To do so, click To and then select the name. See "Using Your Contacts list to Enter Names" later in this Part.

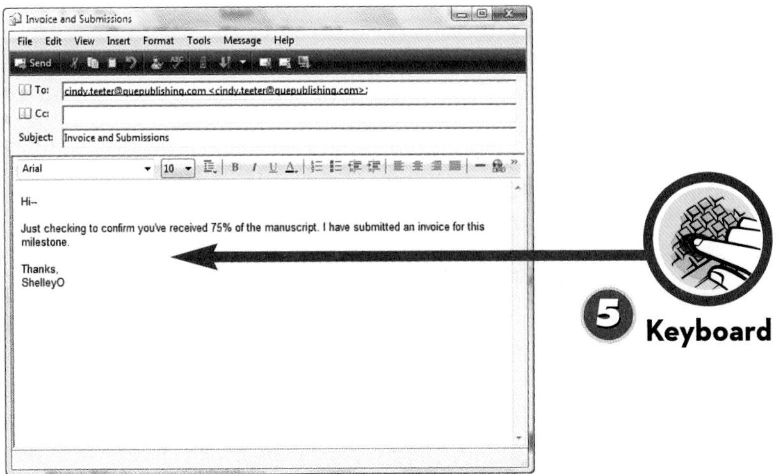

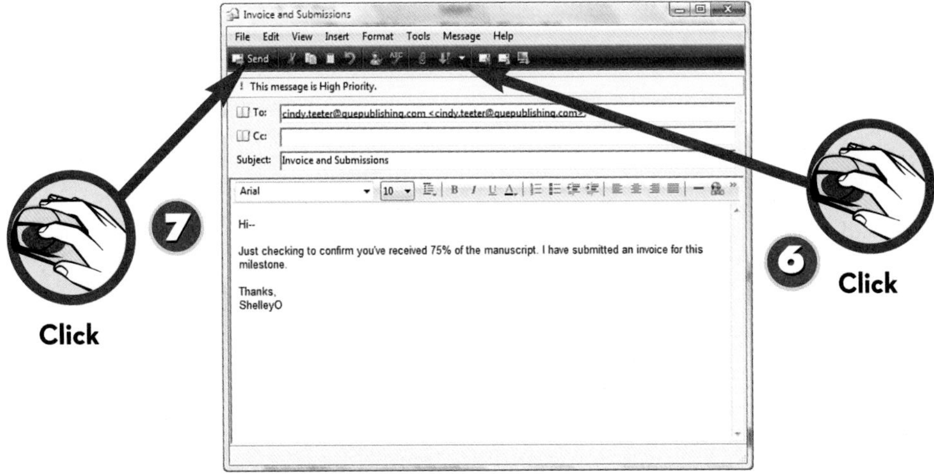

5. Type your message.
6. To change the priority level of the message, click the **Priority** button in the toolbar. You can select High, Low, or Normal. (Each time you click the button, it cycles through the choices.)
7. When you've completed the message, click the **Send** button.

End

NOTE

Check Sent Items

Windows Mail includes some default mail folders, including one for Sent Items. Windows Mail keeps a copy of all messages. To see these messages, click **Sent Items** in the folder list.

TIP

Sending a Blind Carbon Copy

You can send a blind carbon copy (BCC); the recipient receives the message, but does not know a copy was sent to the BCC recipient. Click **View** and then **All Headers**. This adds a text box for BCC. You can then type an address or use your Contacts to select a person.

ATTACHING A FILE

When you create a message, you can also attach a file to send with the message. You may send photographs, for instance, of your child. Or, if you work from home, you can attach documents such as a report or an expense worksheet. You can attach any type of file.

Keyboard

Click

Click

Click

Start

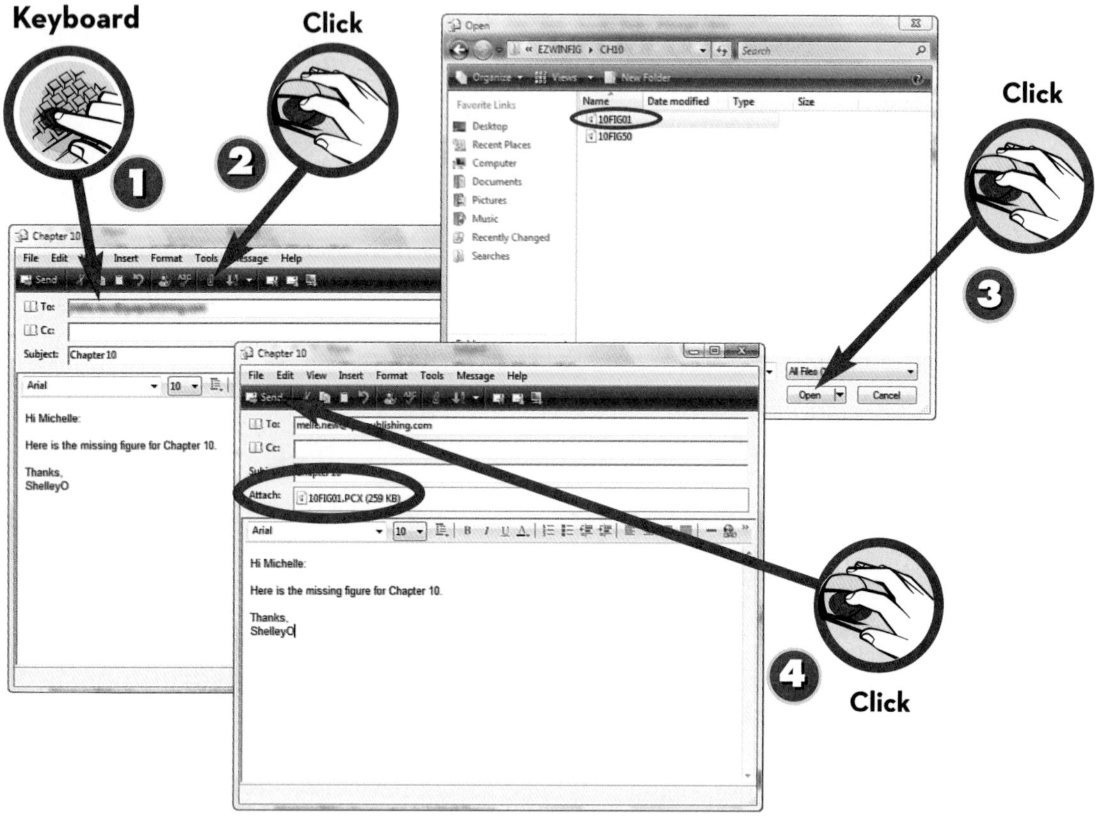

1. Create and address the new mail message.
2. Click the **Attach File to Message** button.
3. If necessary, navigate to the folder that contains the file you want to attach. Select the file to attach, and click the **Open** button.
4. The file attachment is listed in the Attach text box. Click the **Send** button to send the message and file attachment.

End

NOTE

File Sizes

Be careful when sending large files. The mail server or the mail recipient may have limits on the size of attachments. If you need to send a large file, use a compression program like WinZip to compress the file before sending.

OPENING A FILE ATTACHMENT

If someone sends you a file attachment, you can choose how to handle it. You can save it to your disk, or you can open it. To open the attachment, you must have a program that can open and display that particular type of file. For example, to open a file that was created in Microsoft Word (which usually has a .doc extension after the filename), you need to have Microsoft Word on your computer.

Start

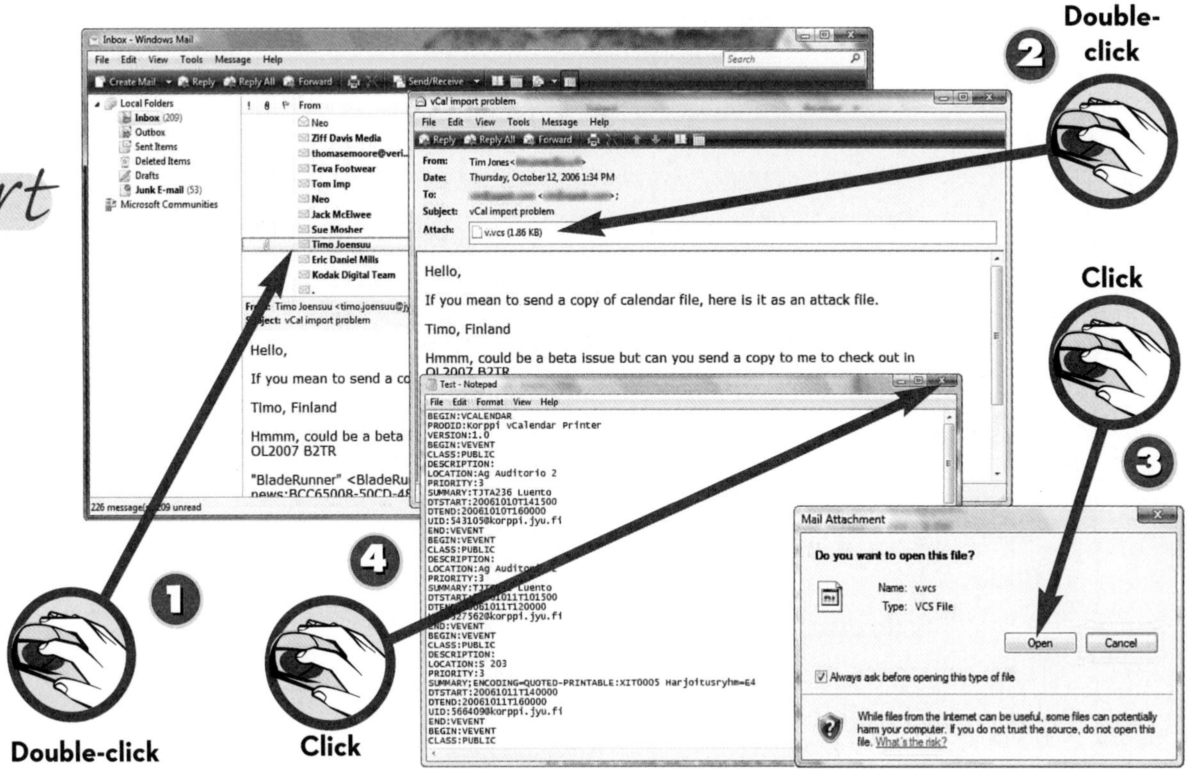

Double-click

Click

Double-click

Click

1. Messages with file attachments are indicated with a paper clip icon. Double-click the message to open it.
2. The file attachment(s) are listed in the Attach field in the opened email. Double-click the file attachment you want to open.
3. When prompted about whether you want to open the attachment, click **Open**. This is for security purposes so that you don't accidentally open a virus that is attached to an email.
4. The file is opened. Click the **Close** button to close the message.

End

TIP

Save an Attachment

You can also select to save an attachment. To save an attachment, right-click it and then click **Save As**. (If there are several files attached and you want to save them all, click the **Save All** button.) Select a folder in which to save the attachment, and click **Save**.

CAUTION

Checking Attachments

Be wary of opening attachments from senders you don't recognize because one way viruses spread is through email attachments. Part 11, "System Security and User Accounts," covers email security in more detail.

DELETING MESSAGES

To keep your Inbox uncluttered, you can delete messages you no longer want to keep. When you delete a message, it is not deleted but is moved to the Deleted Items folder. You can retrieve any messages if you accidentally delete them (unless you have emptied the Deleted Items folder).

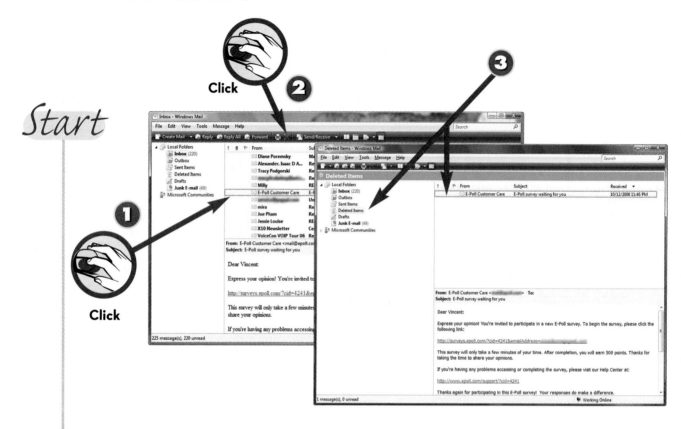

Start

Click

Click

1. In the Windows Mail window, select the message you want to delete.
2. Click the **Delete** button.
3. The message is removed from the Inbox and placed in the Deleted Items folder. You can open this folder by clicking it to confirm the deletion.

End

TIP

Undelete a Message

To undelete a message, open the Deleted Items folder, select the message, and then move it to another folder. See the task "Moving Messages" later in this Part for help on moving messages into other folders.

TIP

Delete from Mail Window

You can also delete a message after reading it, while the email window is open. To do so, click the **Delete** button in the email window.

CLEANING OUT THE DELETED ITEMS FOLDER

Deleted messages are stored in the Deleted Items folder. To save disk space or to totally delete a message, you can clean out this folder.

Start

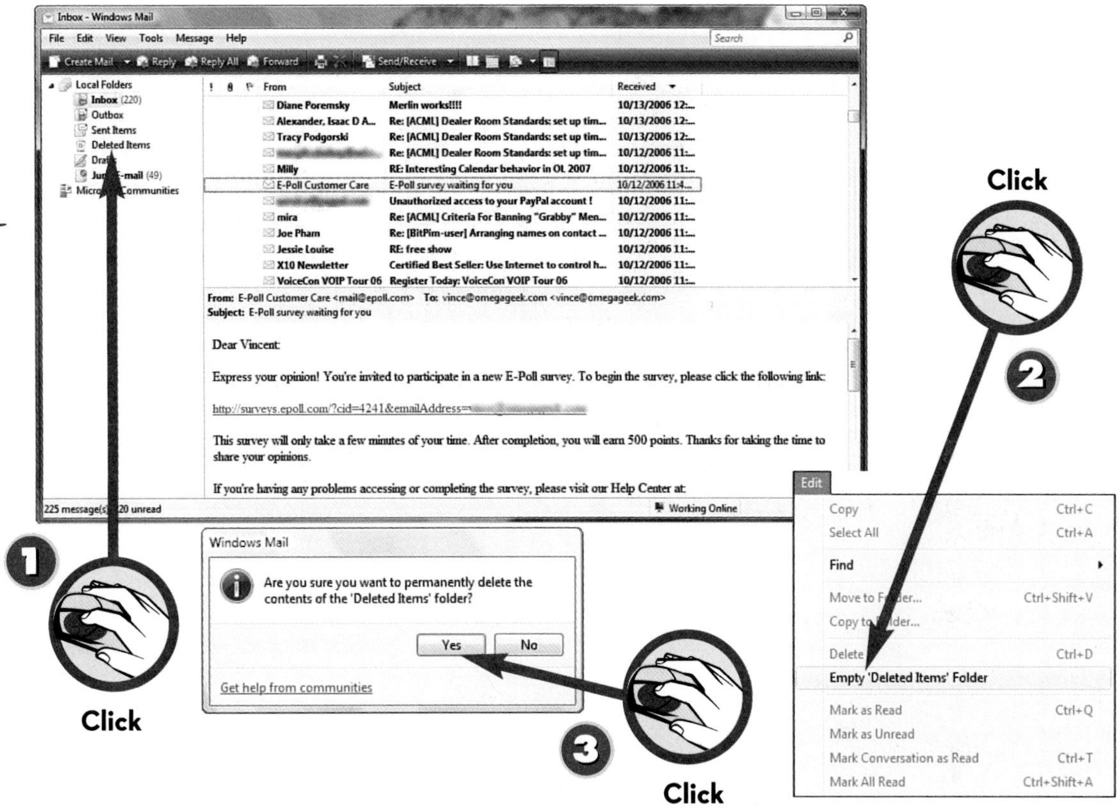

1. Click the **Deleted Items** folder in the Folder List, and make sure it does not contain any messages that you need.
2. Click **Edit** and click **Empty 'Deleted Items' Folder**.
3. Confirm the deletion by clicking **Yes**. The messages are permanently deleted.

End

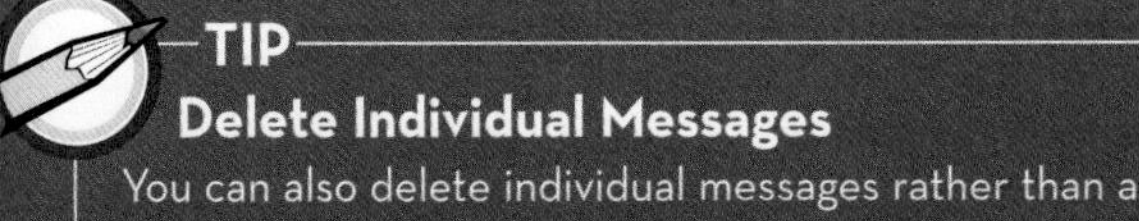

TIP
Delete Individual Messages

You can also delete individual messages rather than all the messages in the folder. To do so, open the folder, select the message(s) you want to delete, and click the **Delete** button. Confirm the deletion by clicking **Yes**.

SETTING EMAIL OPTIONS

Windows Mail uses certain defaults for how messages are handled when you create, send, and receive them. You can check out these settings and, if necessary, make changes.

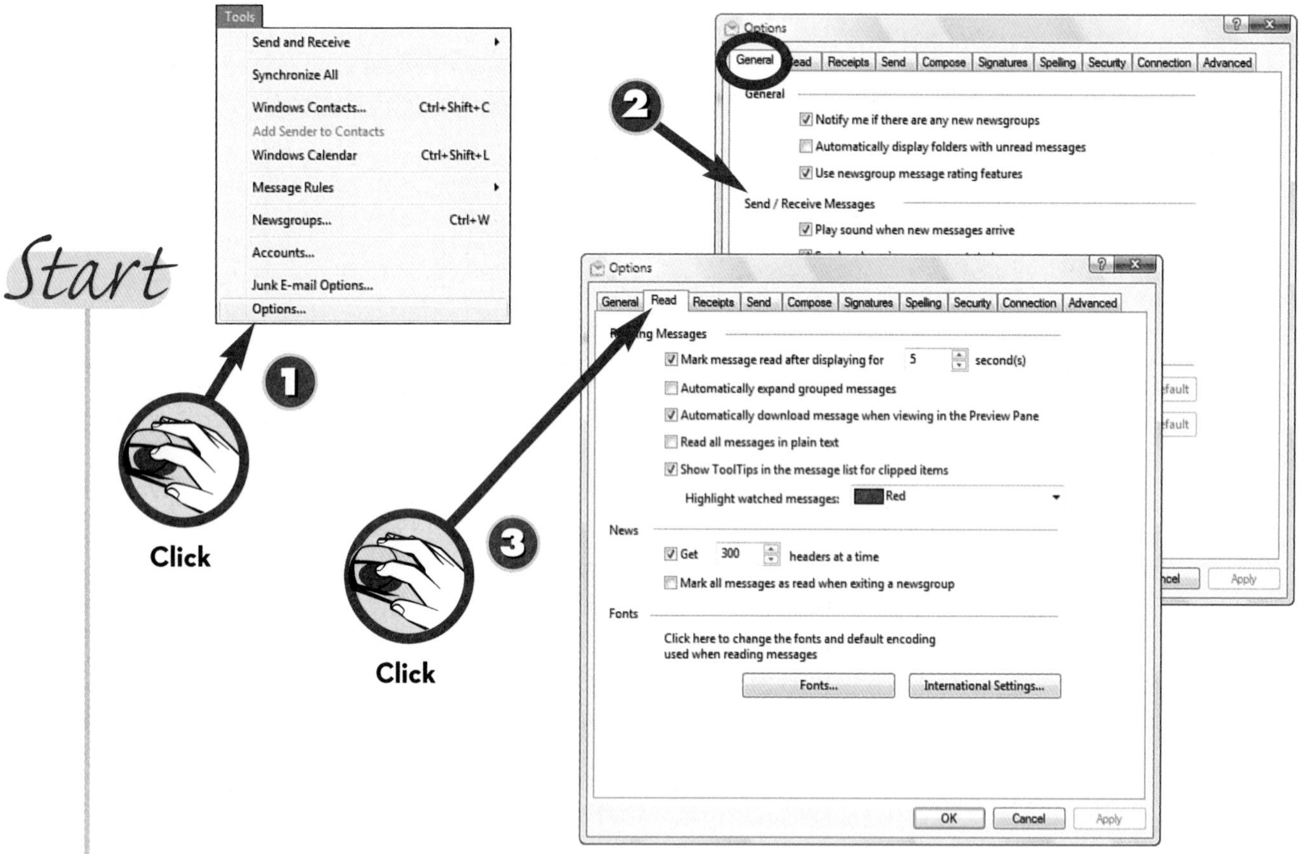

Start

Click

Click

1. In the Windows Mail window, click **Tools** and then click **Options**.
2. On the **General** tab, make changes to options, such as whether the Inbox is automatically displayed, how often messages are checked, and so on.
3. Click the **Read** tab, and make changes to how new messages are handled.

Continued

TIP

Not Sure About an Option?

To get help on options, look for a question mark icon in the upper-right corner of the dialog box. Click this icon to display help on these options.

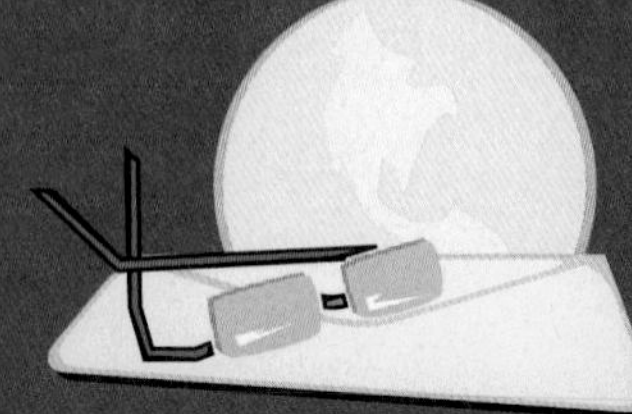

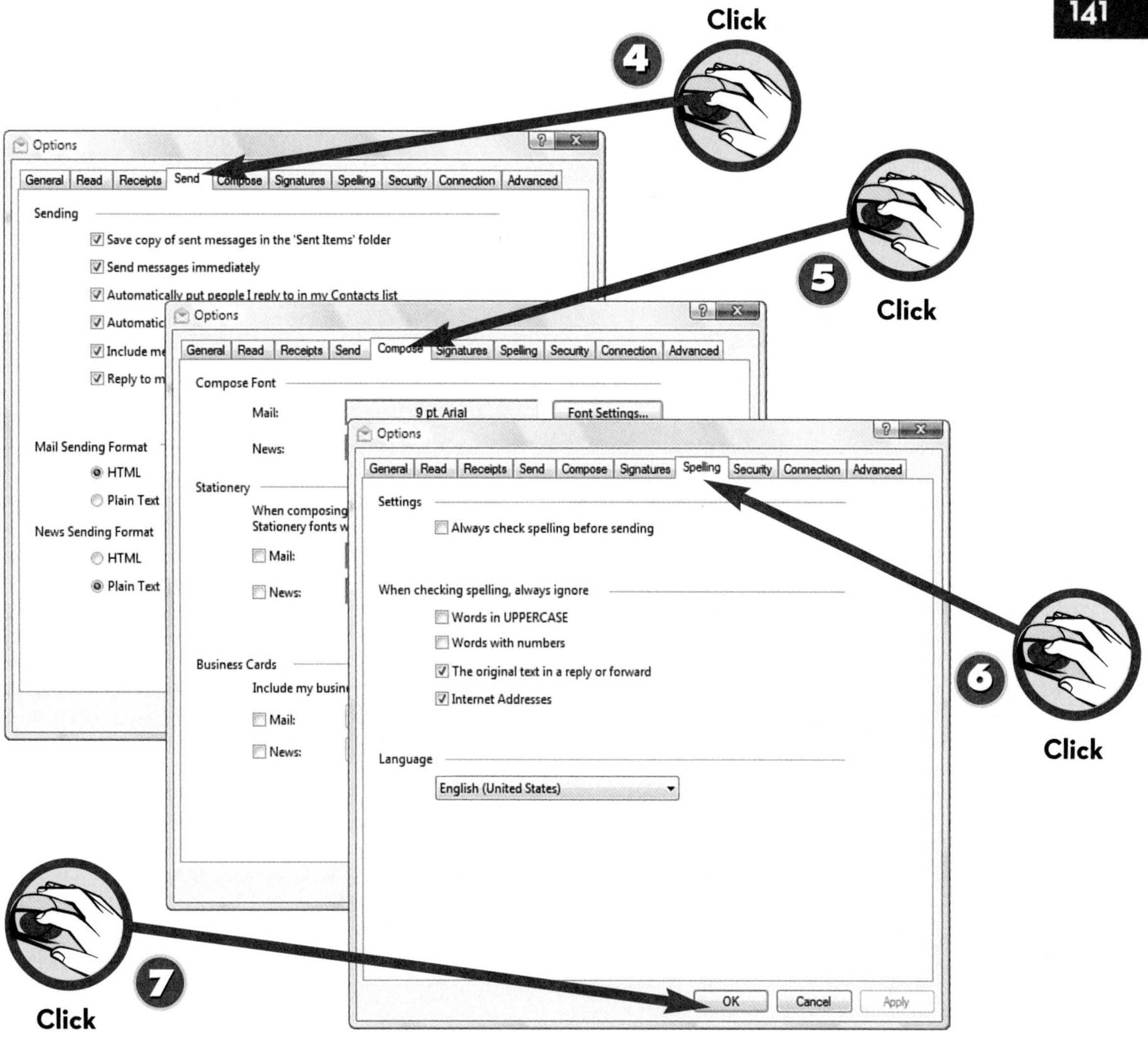

4. Click the **Send** tab, and make changes to how sent items are handled.
5. Click the **Compose** tab, and make changes to how the messages look, such as what font is used.
6. Click the **Spelling** tab to control whether spelling is checked and, if so, what options are ignored (such as Internet addresses).
7. When you're finished making changes, click the **OK** button.

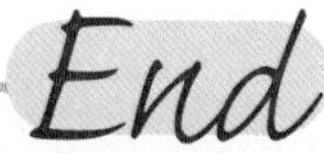

TIP

Checking Spelling

When you send a message, you can check the spelling to avoid embarassing spelling mistakes. To do so, click the **Spelling** button. Windows Mail will compare the words in your message to words in its dictionary and flag any words it can't find. You have options to select an alternative listed spelling, to edit and then change the misspelled word, to ignore the misspelling (sometimes words are spelled correctly but flagged anyway—for instance, names and technical terms), and select other spelling options.

ADDING ADDRESSES TO YOUR CONTACTS LIST

If you often send email to one person, you don't want to type the address each time. Instead, you can add the name to your Contacts list. Then you can quickly select this name and address when creating new messages or forwarding messages. The fastest way to add an address is to pick it up from an existing message.

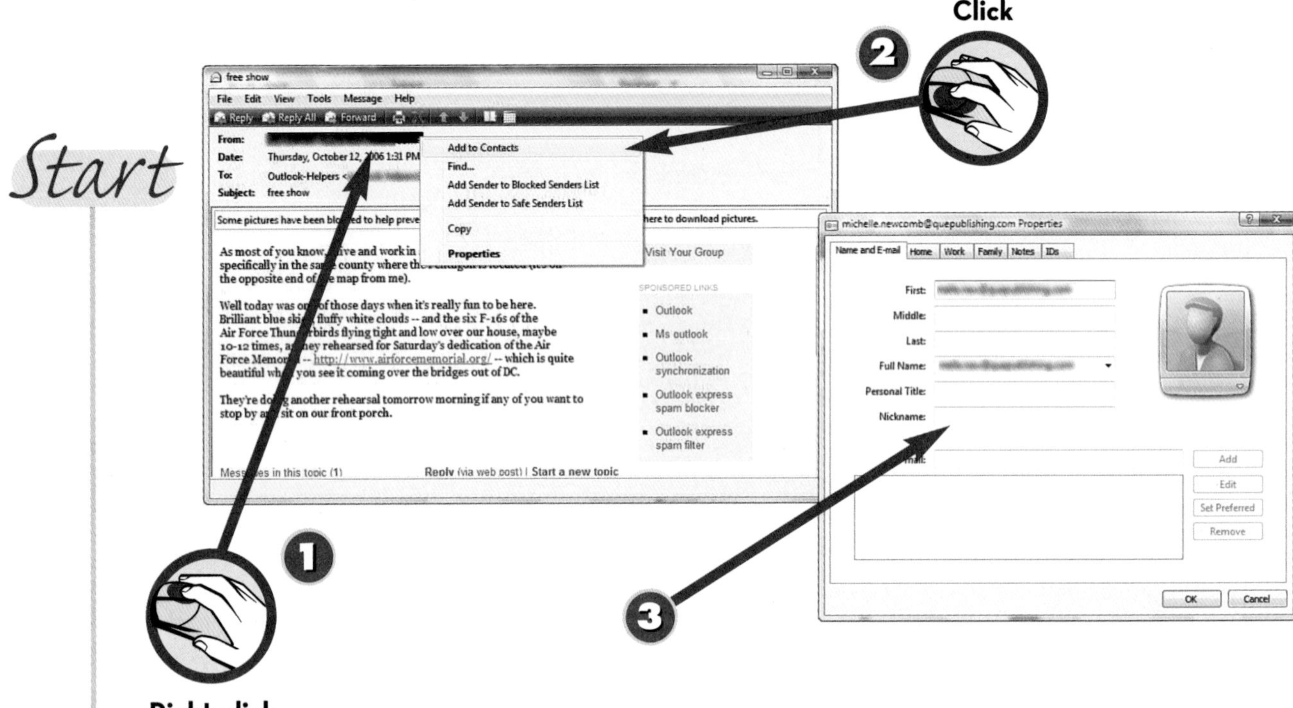

1. Open a message from the person you want to add, and right-click the email address.
2. In the menu that appears, click **Add to Contacts**.
3. The **Name and E-mail** tab displays the default name and email address.

Continued

TIP

Automatically Add Names

You can automatically add names to your Contacts list. To do so, click **Tools** and then **Options**. Click the **Send** tab. Check the **Automatically put people I reply to in my Contacts list**. See "Setting Email Options" earlier in this Part.

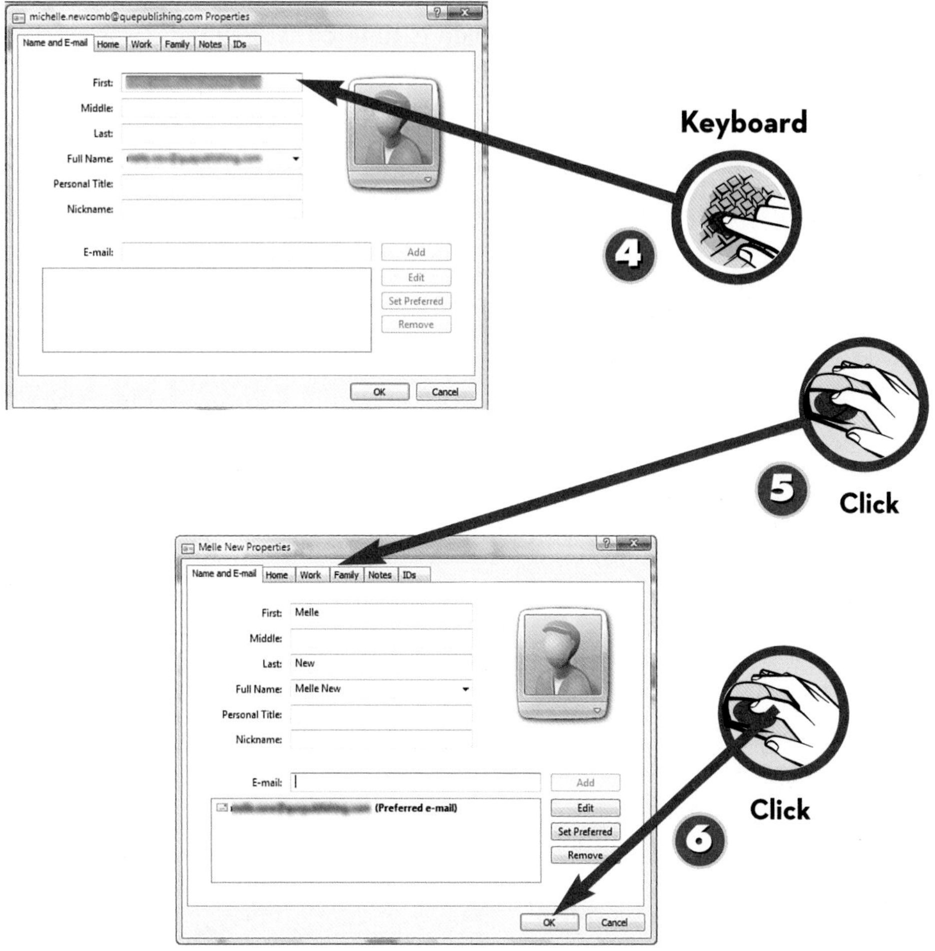

4. Make any changes to the display name (name that appears in the list).
5. Make changes to any of the other tabs.
6. Click **OK** to add the name.

End

TIP

More on Contacts

For all the details on using the Contacts list to enter and update information, see Part 15, "Using Windows Accessories."

USING YOUR CONTACTS LIST TO ENTER NAMES

Rather than type a long email address, which is time consuming and can easily result in a mistyped address, you can create a Contacts list of names and addresses. Then when you create a message, you can select the name from the Contacts list rather than type it.

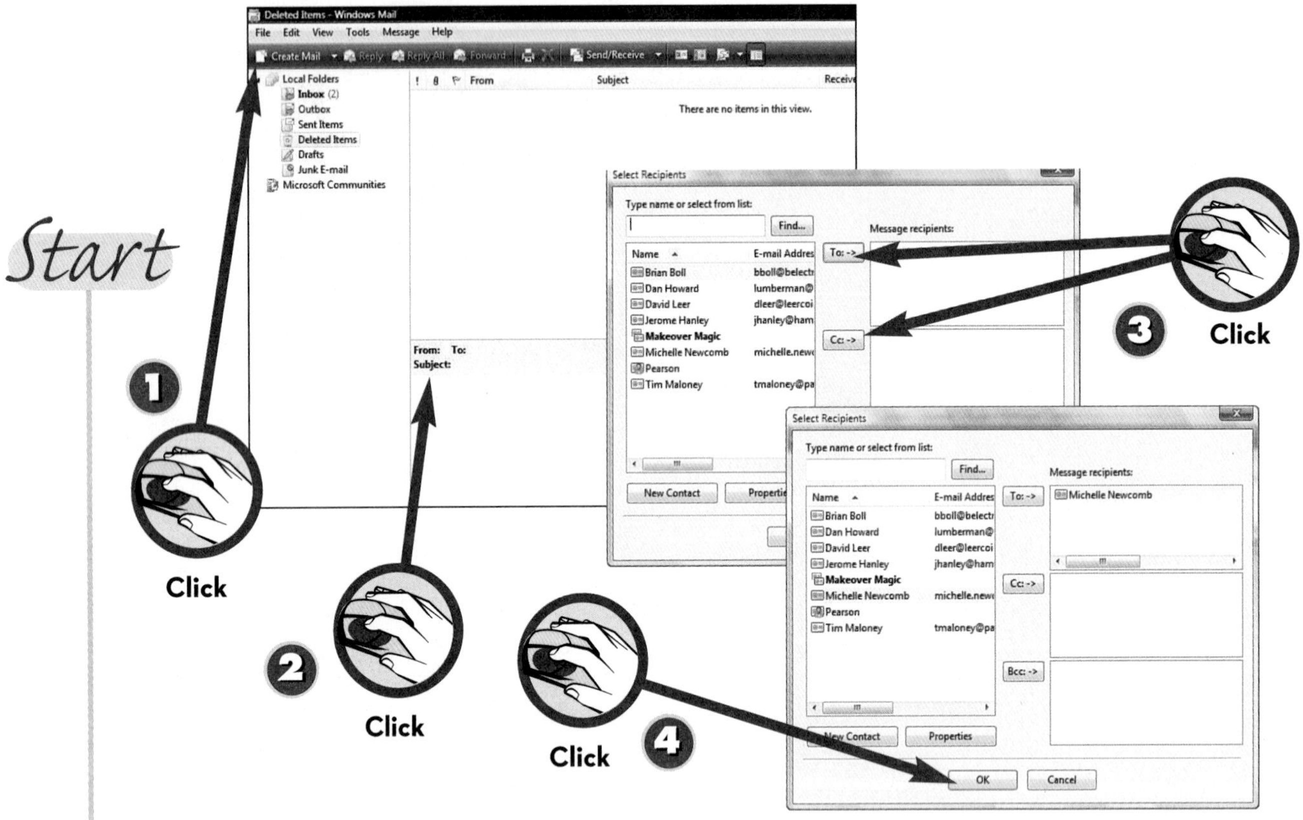

1. Click **Create Mail** to create a new mail message.
2. You see the Select Recipients dialog box listing contacts in your Contacts list. Select the person to add and click **To**.
3. Click **OK**. That person is entered as the recipient. Complete and send the message as you normally would.

TIP

Creating Messages

See the task "Creating and Sending New Mail" previously in this Part for help on creating and sending messages.

CREATING MAIL FOLDERS

To keep your messages organized, you should periodically clean out your Inbox so that is not cluttered. You can set up folders for important messages that you need to keep but don't want to keep in your Inbox.

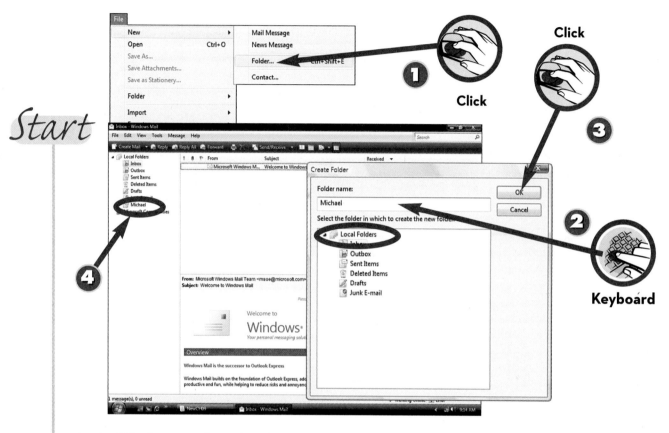

Start

1. In the Windows Mail window, be sure that one of the mail folders is selected. Then click **File**, **New**, and then click **Folder**.
2. Type a name for the folder.
3. Select **Local Folders** to place the folder at the same level as the default mail folders. Click **OK**.
4. The new mail folder is added.

NOTE

Default Folders

By default, Windows Mail includes your Inbox and Outbox as well as folders for Drafts, Sent Items, and Deleted Items. You can view the contents of any of these folders by clicking them in the Folders List.

TIP

Deleting Folders

If you find that you have folders you don't use, you can delete them. All messages inside the folder will also be deleted, so move any messages you want to keep to other folders. Select the folder, and then click **Delete**. Click **Yes** to confirm the deletion.

MOVING MESSAGES TO FOLDERS

If you have set up other mail folders, you can move messages you want to keep from your Inbox to these other folders. You can also move messages from any of the default mail folders to another folder.

Start

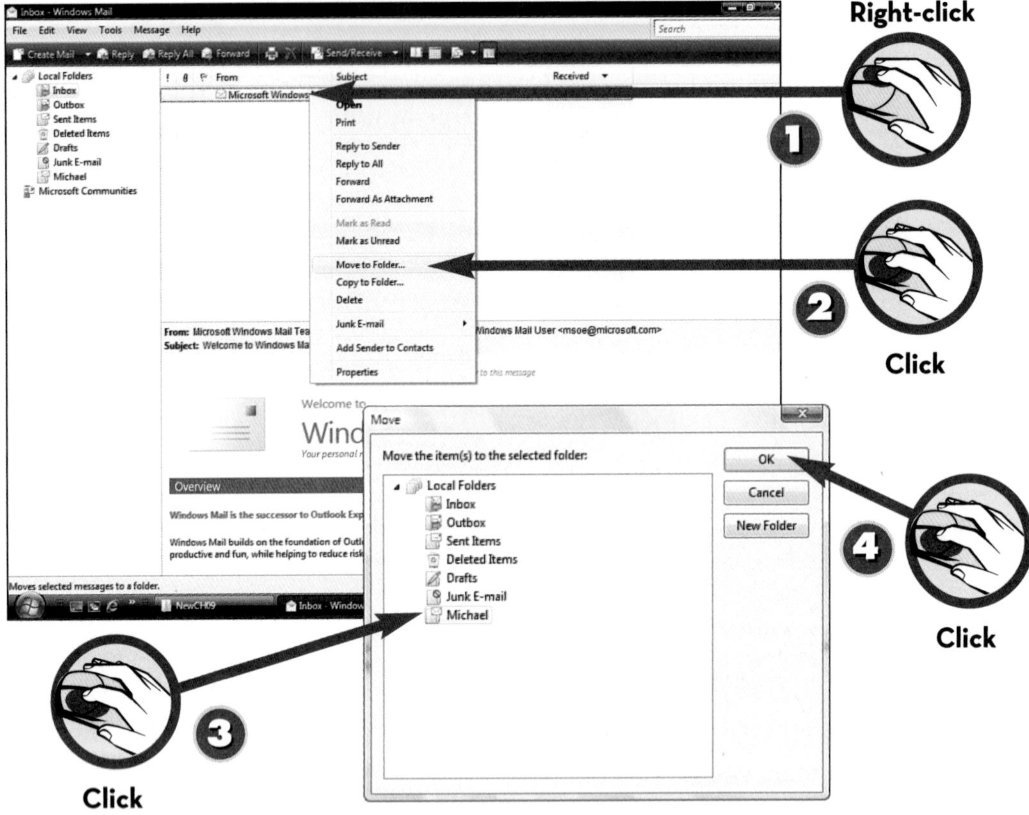

1. In the Windows Mail window, right-click the message you want to move.
2. Click **Move to Folder**.
3. Select the folder you want to move the message to.
4. Click **OK**; the message is moved.

End

TIP

Copying a Message

You can follow the same procedure to copy a message to another folder. From the shortcut menu, click **Copy to Folder**. Then select the folder. When you copy a message, it remains in its original location as well as in the folder in which you placed the copy.

SEARCHING FOR A MESSAGE

If you can't find a message by sorting, you can search for a message. You can search using a variety of criteria including sender, recipient, subject, message, and date or date range.

Start

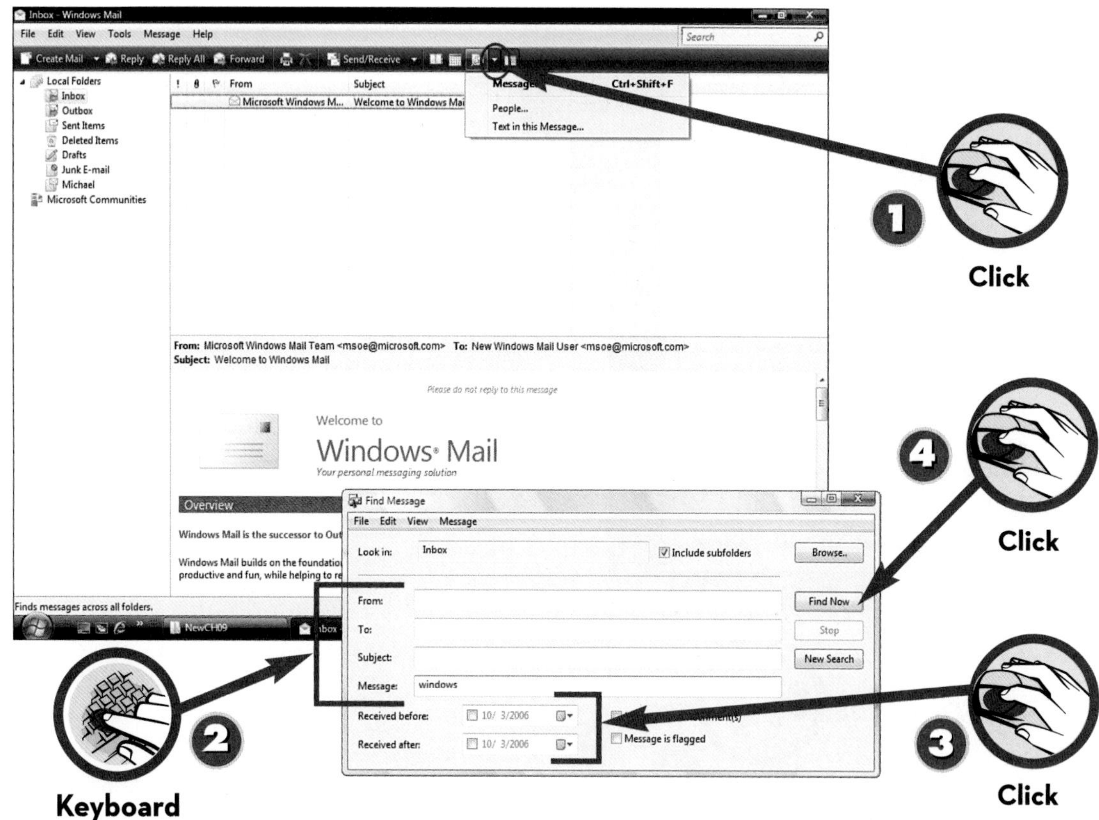

1. Click the down arrow next to the **Find** button, and click **Message**.
2. To search for a message using the **From**, **To**, **Subject**, or **Message** fields, type an entry in these fields.
3. To select a date range, display the drop-down arrows for **Received before** and **Received after**. From the calendar that appears, select the appropriate date.
4. Click the **Find Now** button.

End

TIP

Controlling What's Searched

To select another mail folder to search, click the **Browse** button, and then select the folder. Also, if you want to be sure that all subfolders are searched within the main folder, make sure that **Include subfolders** is checked.

TIP

Use Instant Search

You can also use Windows' new Instant Search. Type what you want to find in the **Search** text box. Part 5, "Working with Files," covers Instant Searching in more detail.

CONFIGURING YOUR FAX

Before you can use your fax modem to send and receive faxes, you must set it up in Windows, entering information about the fax phone number and fax device. To help you with this process, Windows Vista includes the Fax Configuration Wizard.

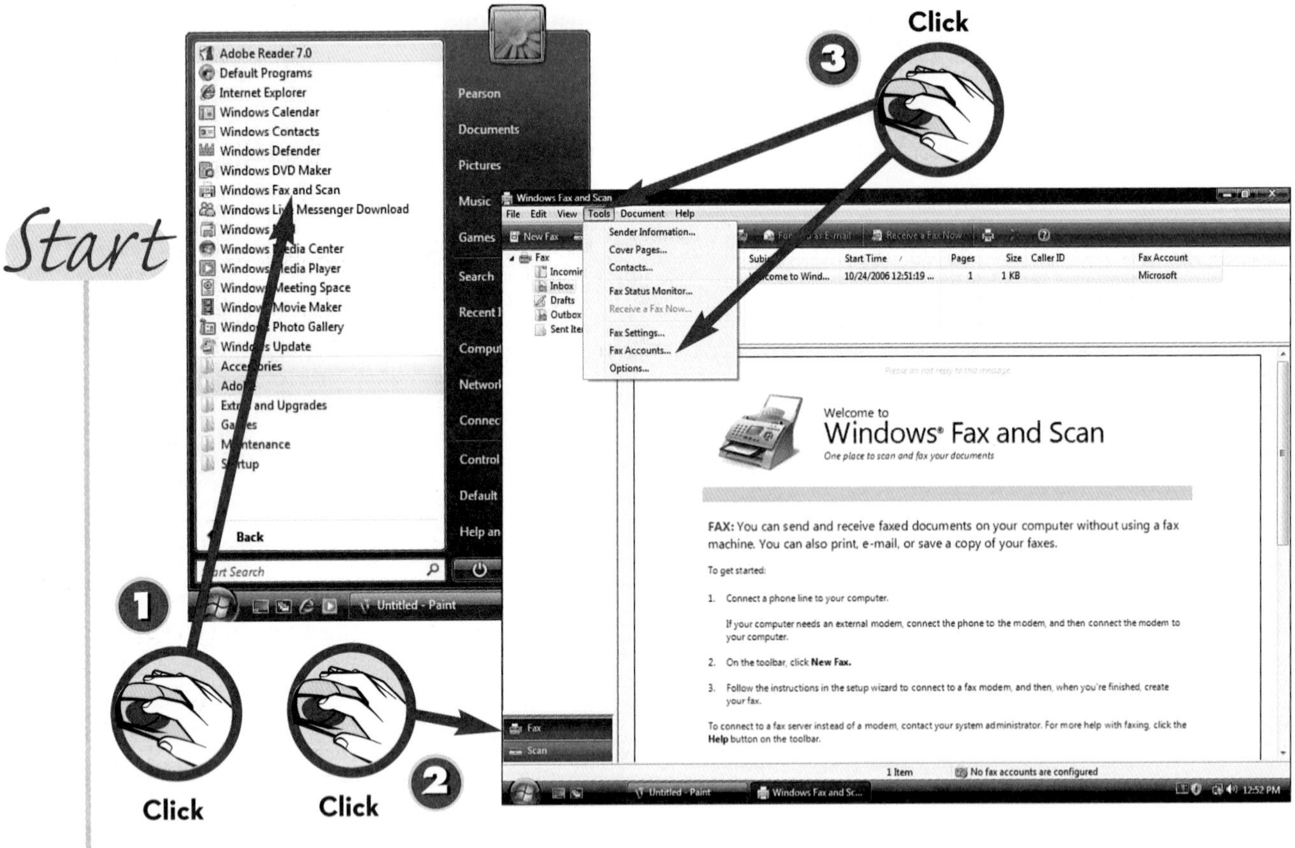

Start

Click

Click

Click

1. Click **Start**, **All Programs**, **Windows Fax and Scan**.
2. If necessary, change to fax view by clicking **Fax**.
3. Click **Tools**, and then click **Fax Accounts**. If you have any fax accounts set up already, they will be listed here.

Continued

TIP

Prompted for Protection

When you set up your fax, Windows will prompt you to confirm this action—to double-check this program is being added with your knowledge. Click **Continue** when these alerts appear.

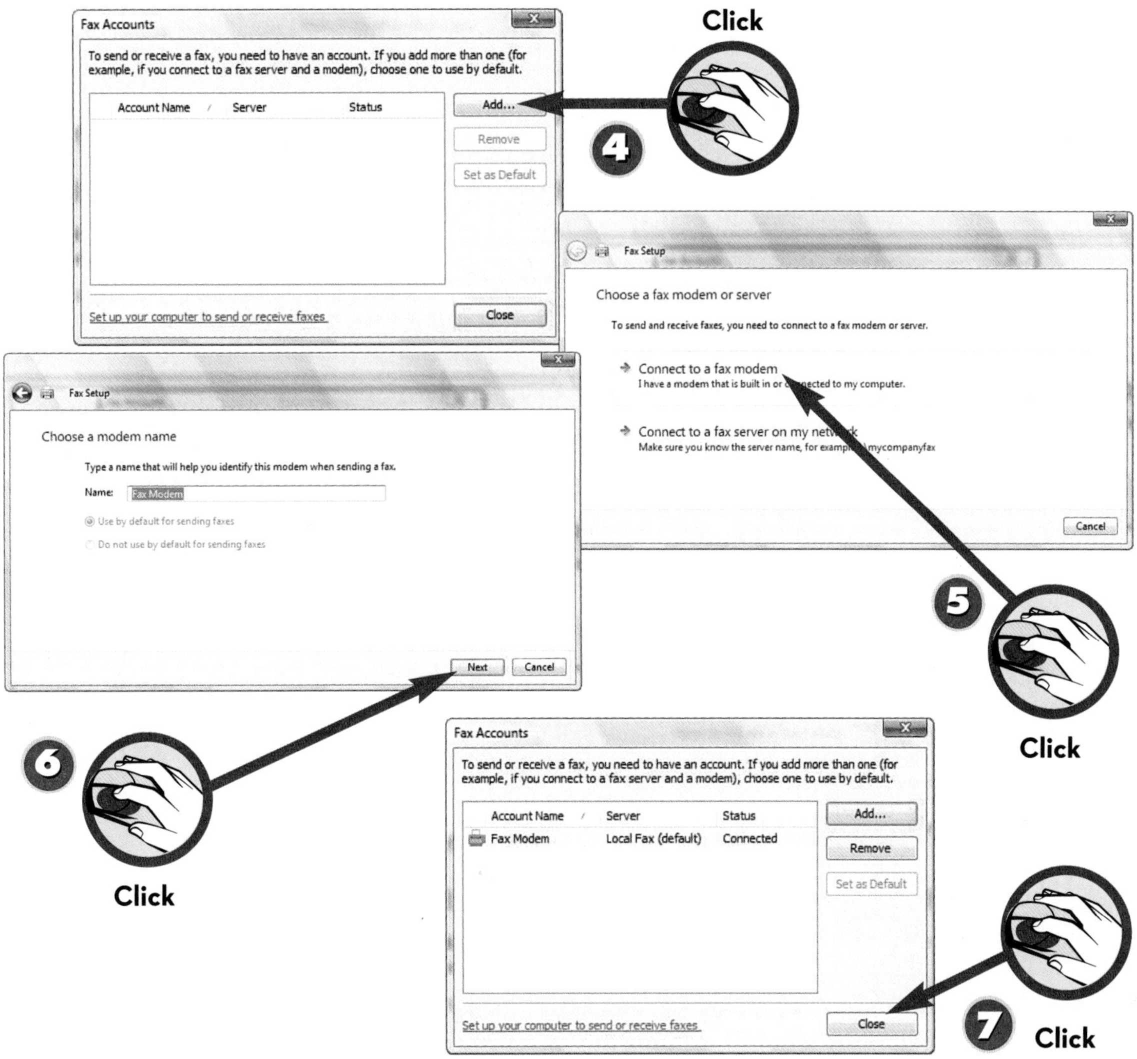

4. To add a new account, click **Add**.
5. Click **Connect to a fax modem**.
6. Follow the instructions to set up your connection to your fax modem. You will be prompted to enter a name and choose how to receive faxes. Click **Next**.
7. Once the setup is complete, click **Close** to close the Fax Accounts window.

End

TIP

Connecting to a Network Fax Server

If you are connecting to a fax server, click **Windows Fax Server Connection** for step 5, and then follow those instructions. You must have permission to use the fax server and know its network address. Check with your system administrator for help or questions with setting up this type of fax.

CREATING AND SENDING A FAX

You can send a fax to anyone; it might be someone with a standalone fax machine or a fax modem on his computer. To do so, you need to enter the recipient's name and fax number. You can choose to fax a document alone or with a cover sheet.

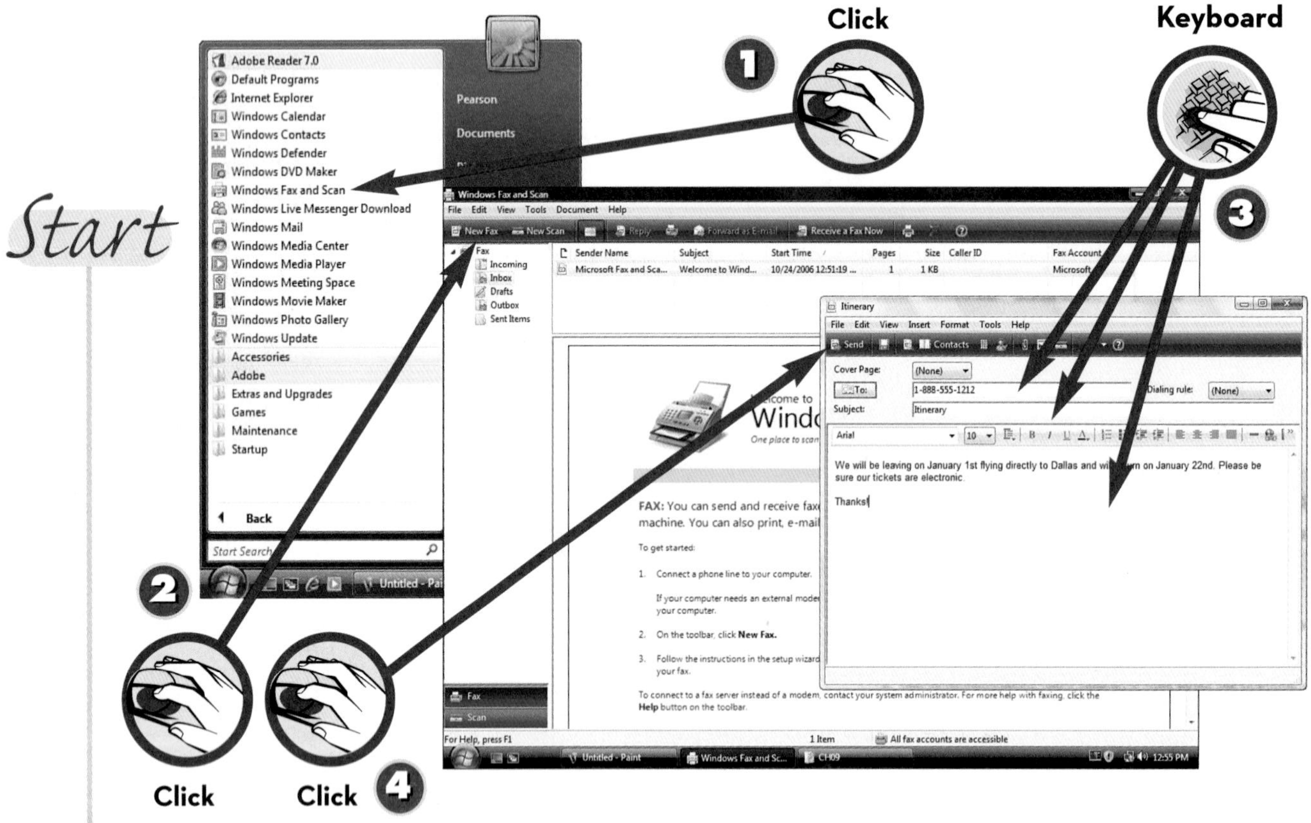

Start

1. Click **Start**, **All Programs**, **Windows Fax and Scan**.
2. Click **New Fax**.
3. Enter the fax number for the recipient, and type a subject and the message.
4. Click **Send**; the fax is sent.

End

NOTE

Use a Cover Page Template

You can display the Cover Page template drop-down list to select a template if you want to use a cover page. Also, use the Dialing Rule drop-down list to set any dialing rules, such as dialing 9 to get an outside line.

NOTE

Receiving a Fax

Your modem will receive any incoming faxes and handle them according to the option you selected when you set up the fax account. You can view and open the fax from the Windows and Fax Scan window (much like opening an email).

MANAGING JUNK MAIL (SPAM)

Windows Mail includes a built-in filter that checks incoming mail and flags junk mail (also called *spam*) when it is downloaded. The message is also placed in a special Junk Mail folder. You can select to open the folder and view the junk mail, set junk mail options (covered later), or close the warning box.

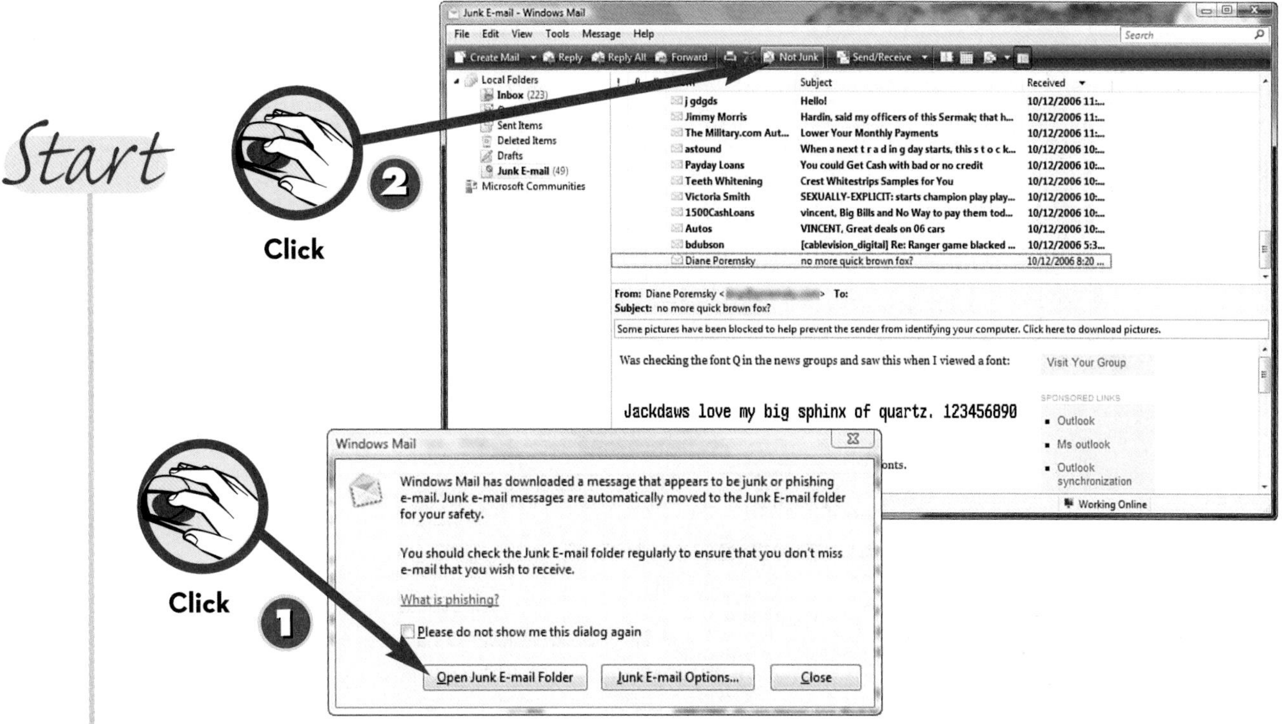

1. When Windows Mail thinks you have received a junk mail message, you see an alert. Click **Open Junk E-mail Folder**.
2. You see the (potential) junk mail messages in this folder. If an email message isn't junk mail, click the message to select it, and then click **Not Junk**.
3. The message is moved from the Junk E-mail folder to your Inbox.

End

TIP

Handling Junk Mail

You can work with the messages in the Junk E-mail folder just like any other messages. You can open them, delete them, reply to them, and so on.

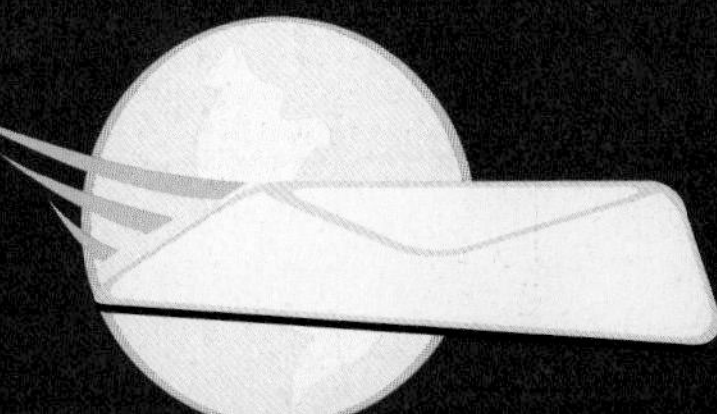

SETTING JUNK MAIL OPTIONS IN WINDOWS MAIL

You can control the level of screening as well as view blocked senders and safe senders by using the Junk E-mail options.

Start

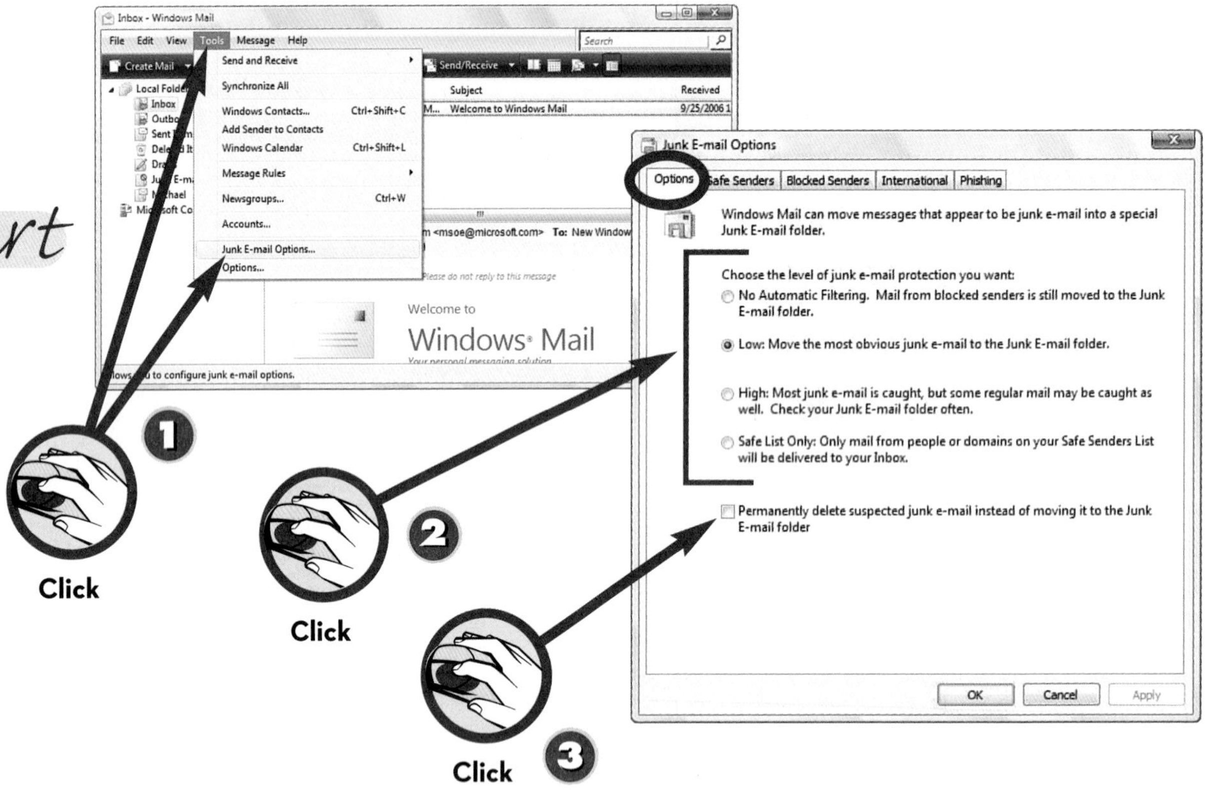

Click

Click

Click

1. In the Windows Mail window, click **Tools** and then **Junk E-mail Options**.
2. On the **Options** tab, choose the level of junk email protection you want.
3. If you would rather have Windows Mail delete the message instead of saving it in the special junk mail file, check **Permanently delete suspected junk e-mail instead of moving it to the Junk E-mail Folder**.

Continued

TIP

Blocked Senders

You can add or remove blocked senders from the list. To remove a sender, select the name, and then click the **Remove** button. To add a name, click the **Add** button, type the email address, and click **OK**.

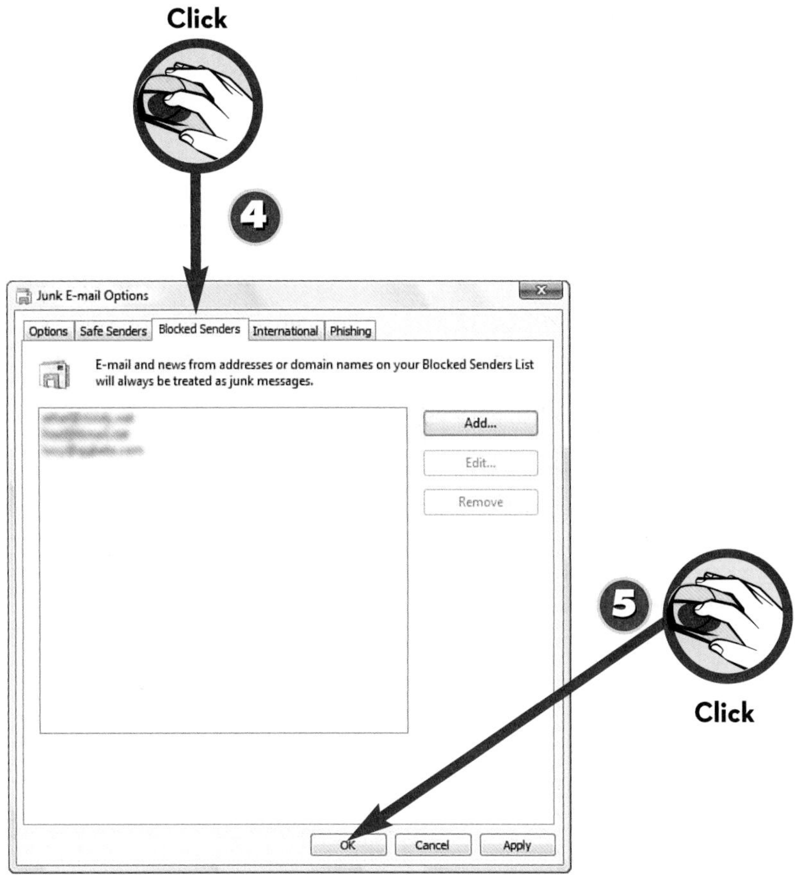

4 To view a list of blocked senders, click the **Blocked Senders** tab. You see a list of senders for which you've blocked incoming mail.

5 Click **OK**.

End

TIP

Adding Safe Senders

You can also set up a list of safe senders. To do so, click the **Safe Senders** tab. Click the **Add** button, type the email address, and click **OK** to add a safe sender.

10

BROWSING THE INTERNET

To explore the Internet, you must have a modem and an Internet connection. The modem can be inside your computer or, in the case of most cable modems, it can be an external piece of equipment that plugs into your computer's network card. The connection to the Internet is obtained through Internet service providers (ISPs) such as America Online, EarthLink, or MSN, or you can get connection through an independent local ISP. Your modem communicates with your ISP's computers, which in turn communicate with computers all over the world that make up the Internet, also known as the World Wide Web.

Before you can take advantage of all the benefits of the Internet, you must set up your Internet connection using the Internet Options Control Panel in Windows Vista. The specifics of setting up a connection depend on your type of connection (dial up, cable modem, or DSL, for example) and your ISP, so those details are not covered here. Follow the specific instructions you received from your ISP to set up your connection and your email account.

After you have a modem and have set up an account with an ISP, you can use Internet Explorer 7, the web browser included with Windows Vista, to explore the Internet. You can use Internet Explorer to view web pages, to search for specific topics, and to set privacy and security features to ensure safe browsing.

THE INTERNET EXPLORER 7 WINDOW

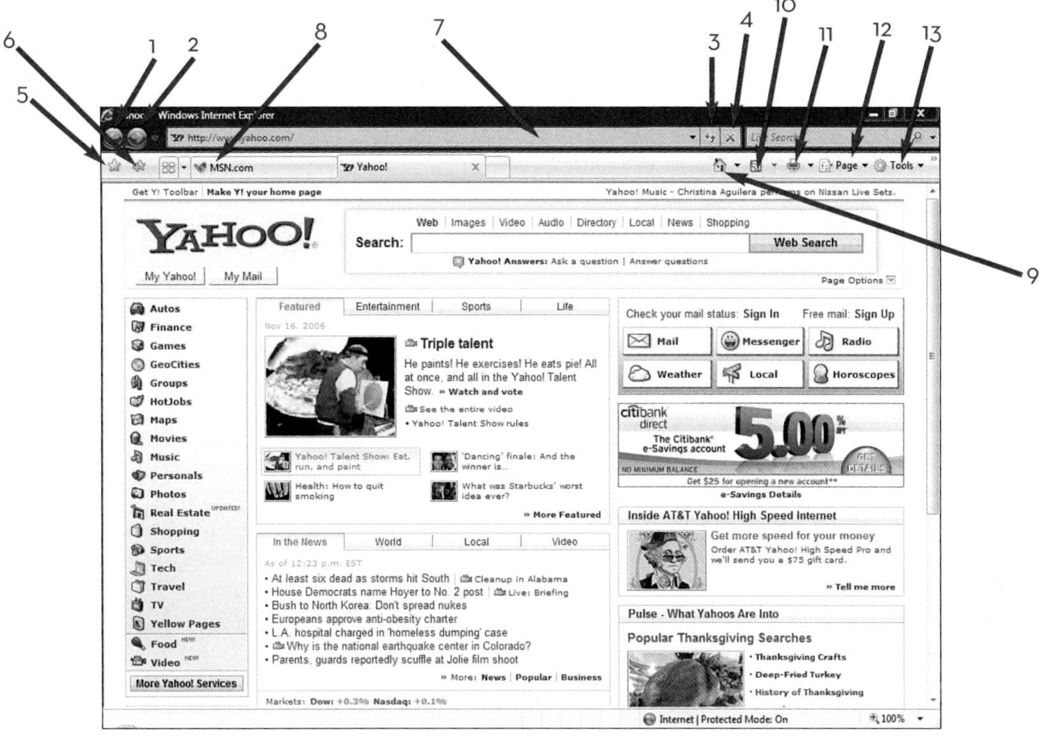

	Name	Click To...
1	Back	Go to the last page you visited.
2	Forward	Go forward a page, after going back.
3	Refresh Current Page	Redisplay the page, refreshing the data.
4	Stop	Stop the display of a page.
5	Favorites Center	Display a list of favorite sites. See "Adding a Site to Your Favorites Center" later in this Part.
6	Add to Favorites	Add the displayed page to your list of favorite sites.
7	Quick Tabs	Display thumbnail versions of all the tabs.
8	Tab	With Windows Vista, you can display links from a site on a separate tab within the same window. See "Viewing Tabs" later in this part.
9	Home	Return to your home page.
10	Feeds	Use to subscribe to RSS feeds of live Internet information.
11	Print	Print the current web page.
12	Page	Displays page options, such as opening a new window, sending a page, zooming the size of the window, and more.
13	Tools	Displays commands such for working offline, deleting your browsing history, displaying toolbars, and setting other Internet options.

STARTING INTERNET EXPLORER

After you've set up your Internet connection, you can start Internet Explorer. Before you start browsing the Web, take a look at the different tools within the Internet Explorer window. This task is an overview of the Internet Explorer window so that you can familiarize yourself with its features.

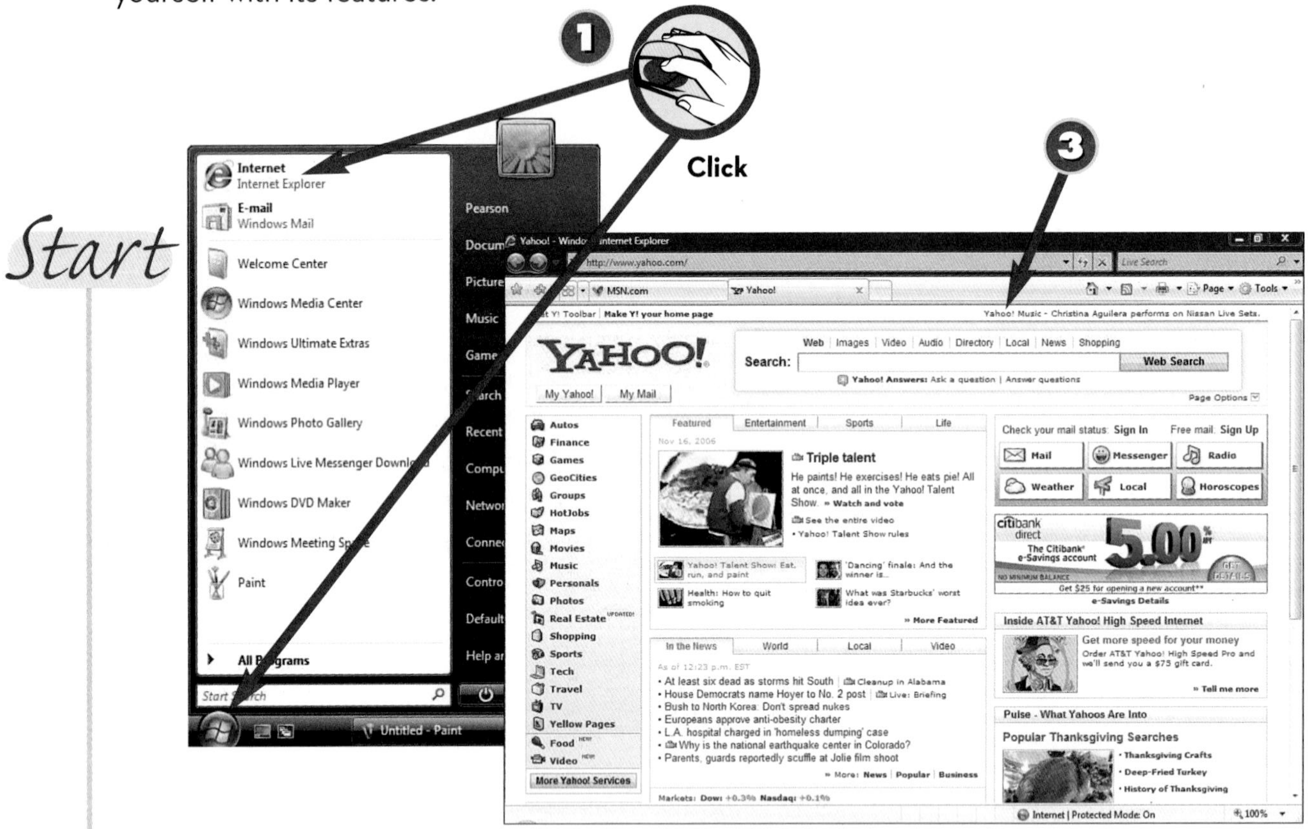

Start

1. Click **Start**, and then click **Internet**.
2. If prompted, enter your username and password (some information might have been completed for you), and then click the **Connect** button (not shown).
3. Windows connects to your ISP. The Internet Explorer window appears, and you see your home page.

Continued

TIP

Dial-Up versus Broadband Connections

Some Internet connections dial up and connect through your phone line; for these types of connections, you will usually be prompted to enter your password and username. Other connections connect through a different type of modem and connection, such as through your cable provider and a cable modem. (These connections are *much* faster than dial-up connections.) With this type of setup, you are connected 24/7, so you never need to log on after you set up your connection the first time.

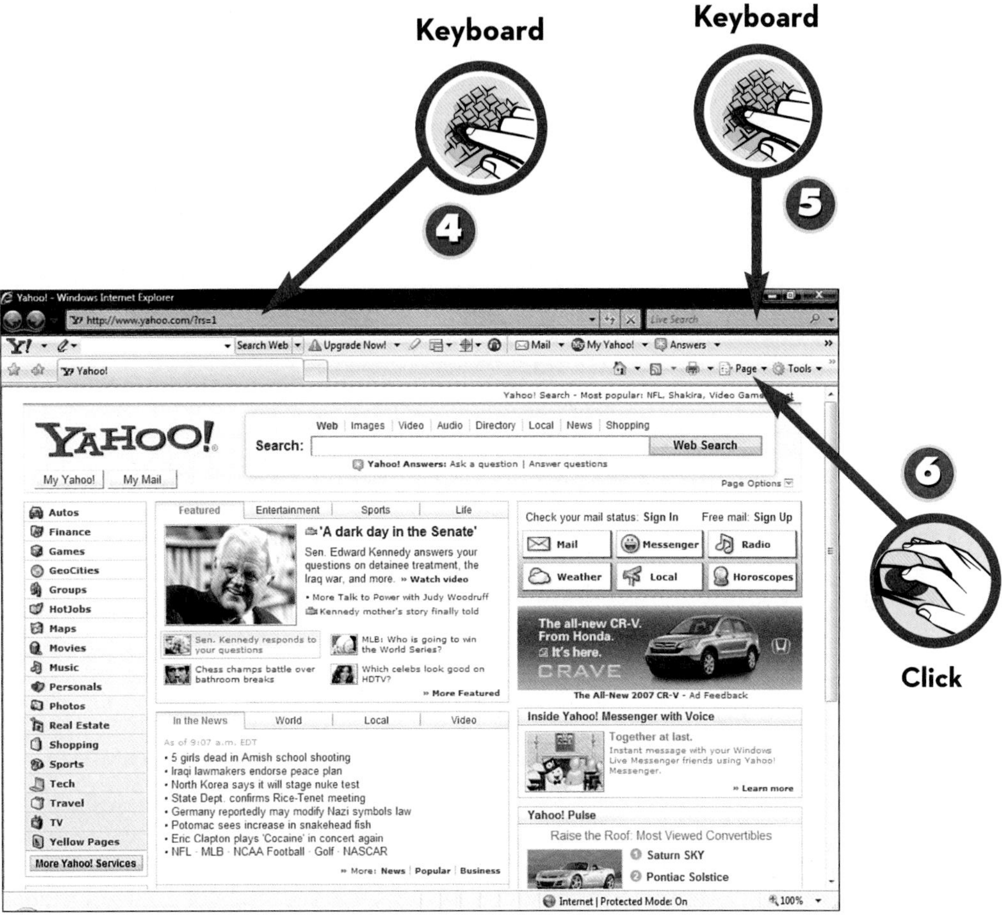

4 Type the address of the site you want to visit in the Address bar.

5 Type words or phrases in the Live Search text box to search the Internet for specific items.

6 Click toolbar buttons to navigate among pages and to access other features.

End

TIP

Log Off

When you exit Internet Explorer, you may be prompted to log off. If so, click **Yes** or **Disconnect Now**. If you are not prompted, be sure to log off. Right-click the connection icon in the status bar, and then select **Disconnect**.

TIP

Zooming

At the lower-right corner, you see a zoom icon. Click the down arrow, and select a zoom percentage. Or click the down arrow next to Page in the toolbar, click **Zoom**, and then select a zoom percentage.

BROWSING WITH LINKS

Information on the Internet is easy to browse because documents contain links to other pages, documents, and sites. Simply click a link to view the associated page. You can jump from link to link, exploring all types of topics and levels of information. Links are also called *hyperlinks* and usually appear underlined and sometimes in a different color.

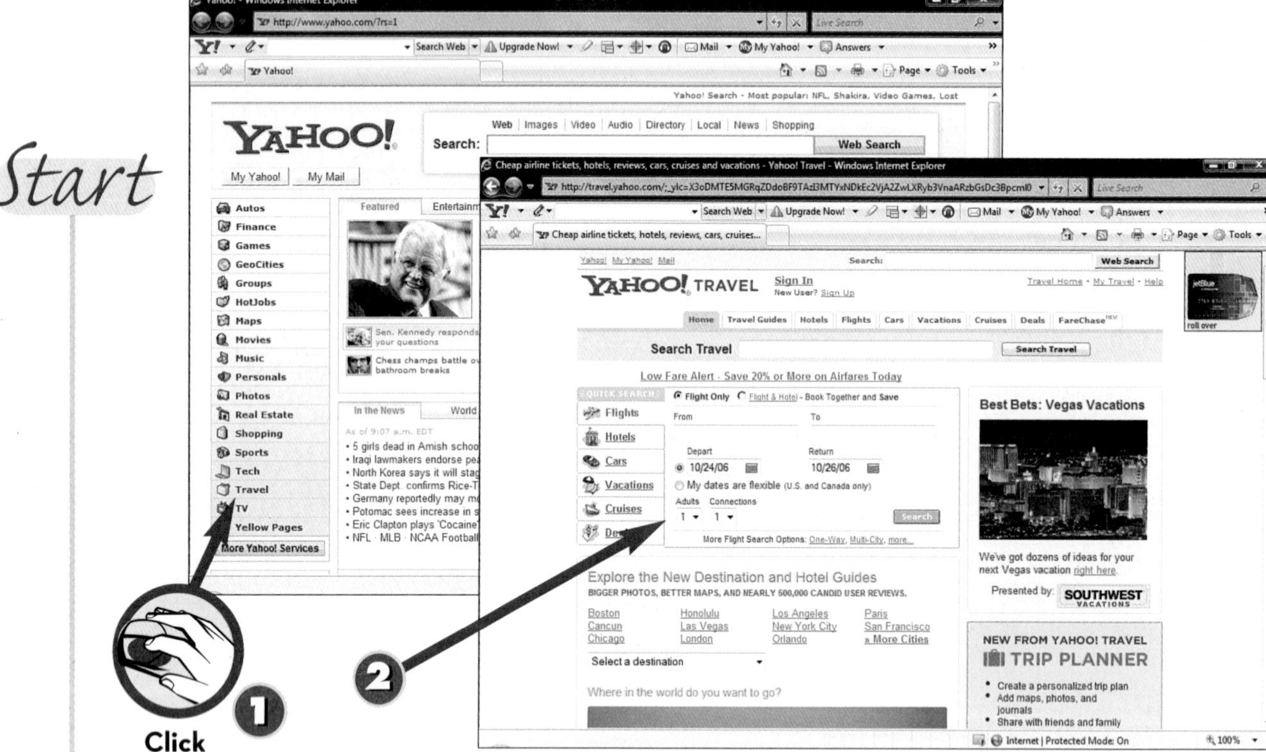

1. Click a link. From the Yahoo Start page, try clicking **Travel**.
2. The Yahoo page appears for Travel. Here you see options for booking travel arrangements.

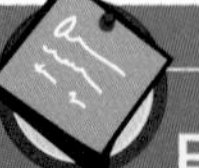

NOTE

Error?

If you see an error message when you click a link, it could indicate that the link is not accurate, is outdated, or that the server is too busy, or you have lost connection. Try again later.

TIP

Link to Link

When you click some links, you see pages that contain still more links, and you may have to click several links until you find the information you seek. Also note that sometimes images can be links.

TYPING AN ADDRESS

Typing a site's address is the one of the most direct ways to get to that site. An address, or uniform resource locator (URL), consists of the protocol (usually http://—you don't usually have to type this part) and the domain name (something like www.nba.com). The domain name might also include a path (a list of folders) to the document. The extension (usually .com, .net, .gov, .edu, or .mil) indicates the type of site (commercial, network resources, government, educational, or military, respectively).

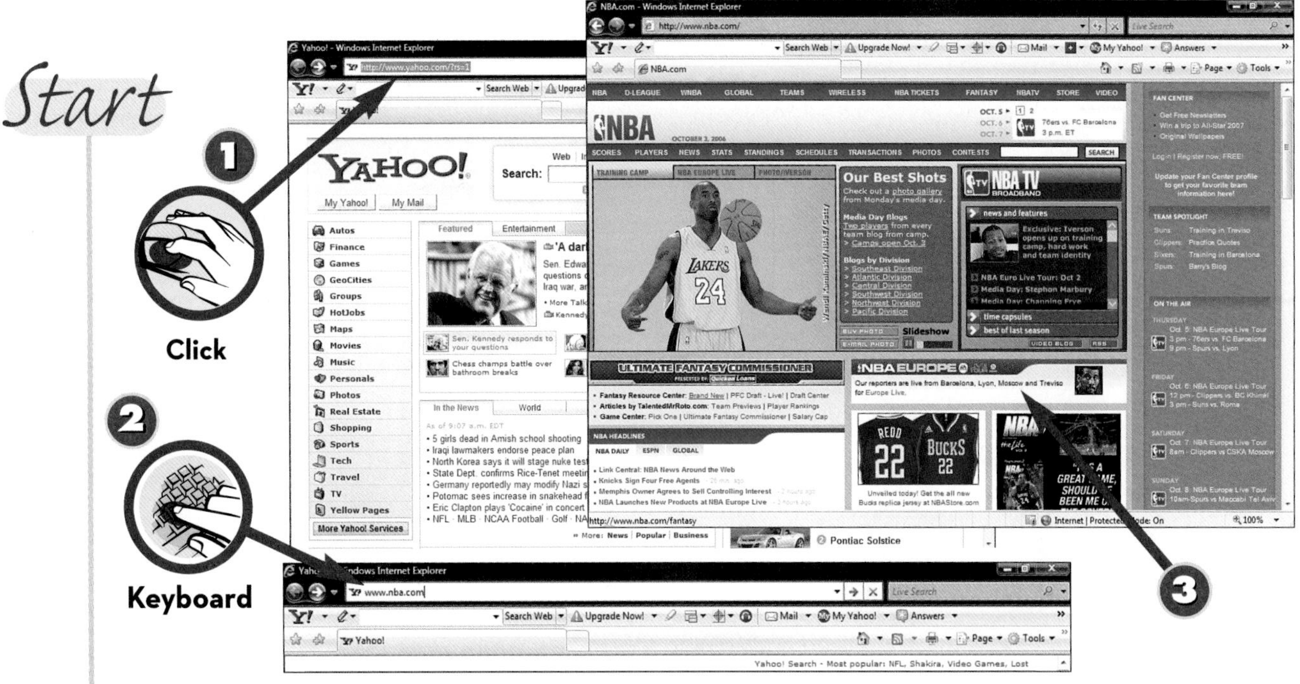

1. Click in the **Address** bar. The current address is highlighted.
2. Type the address of the site you want to visit.
3. Press **Enter**; Internet Explorer displays the page for that address.

End

TIP

Type the Address Correctly

Make sure you type the address correctly. You must type the periods, colons, slashes, and other characters in the exact order.

TIP

Try Guessing the Address

Often you can guess the name of a site because it's usually the company or organization name. For instance, the address for the NFL is www.nfl.com. Guessing doesn't hurt; if the address is incorrect, you see an error message. You can try again or try searching for the site using a search engine, such as Google.com.

VIEWING TABS

Often a page contains a lot of interesting links, and you'd like to look at several links rather than one link at a time on one page. With new tabbed viewing, you can display the contents of other links on tabs. You can then switch from tab to tab.

Start

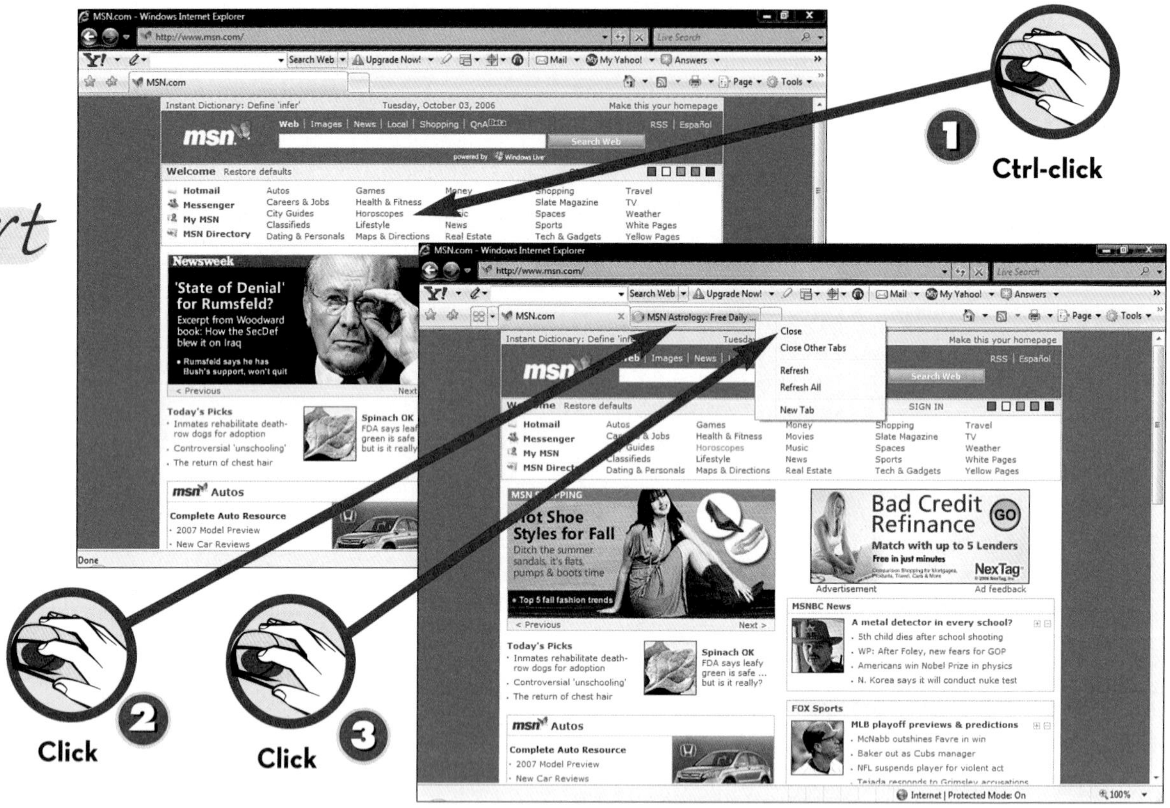

1 Ctrl-click

2 Click

3 Click

1. To display a link on a tab, hold down the **Ctrl** key and click the link. It is added to a tab.
2. You see a tab with the link you selected; click the tab to view the information (here on Horoscopes).
3. To close a tab, right-click the tab and click **Close** or click the tab's Close button.

End

NOTE

More Tabs

You can continue to Ctrl-click more links to display additional tabs.

SEARCHING THE INTERNET FROM MSN

The Internet includes many different sites. Looking for the site you want by browsing can be like looking for the proverbial needle in the haystack. Instead, you can search for a topic and find all sites related to that topic. Your home page likely includes a search text box; you can use that to start. You can also go to special sites designed exclusively for searching.

Start

1. In the search box (here on MSN's home page), type the topic. (Here I typed the name of an artist.)
2. Click the search button. (On MSN's home page, it's called **Search Web**.)
3. You see a list of matching sites. Click on any of these links to view the site.

End

TIP

Search for Specific Items

Using MSN Search, you can search for a specific type of information, such as news stories, images, or encyclopedia entries. To do so, click the option above the search bar.

NOTE

Searching for Text on a Page

Sometimes you visit a web page listed in your search's results but can't find where the matching word or phase appears on that page. You can search the web page to look for a particular word or phrase. To do so, while on the page, press **Ctrl+F** and then type the word or phrase into the Find box.

SEARCHING THE INTERNET USING A SEARCH ENGINE

In addition to built-in search tools on pages, you can use sites specifically set up to search. For instance, Google is a popular search tool. The more you use the Internet, you'll find that there are many other search tools, such as Ask.com. The search process is the same, but the results may vary.

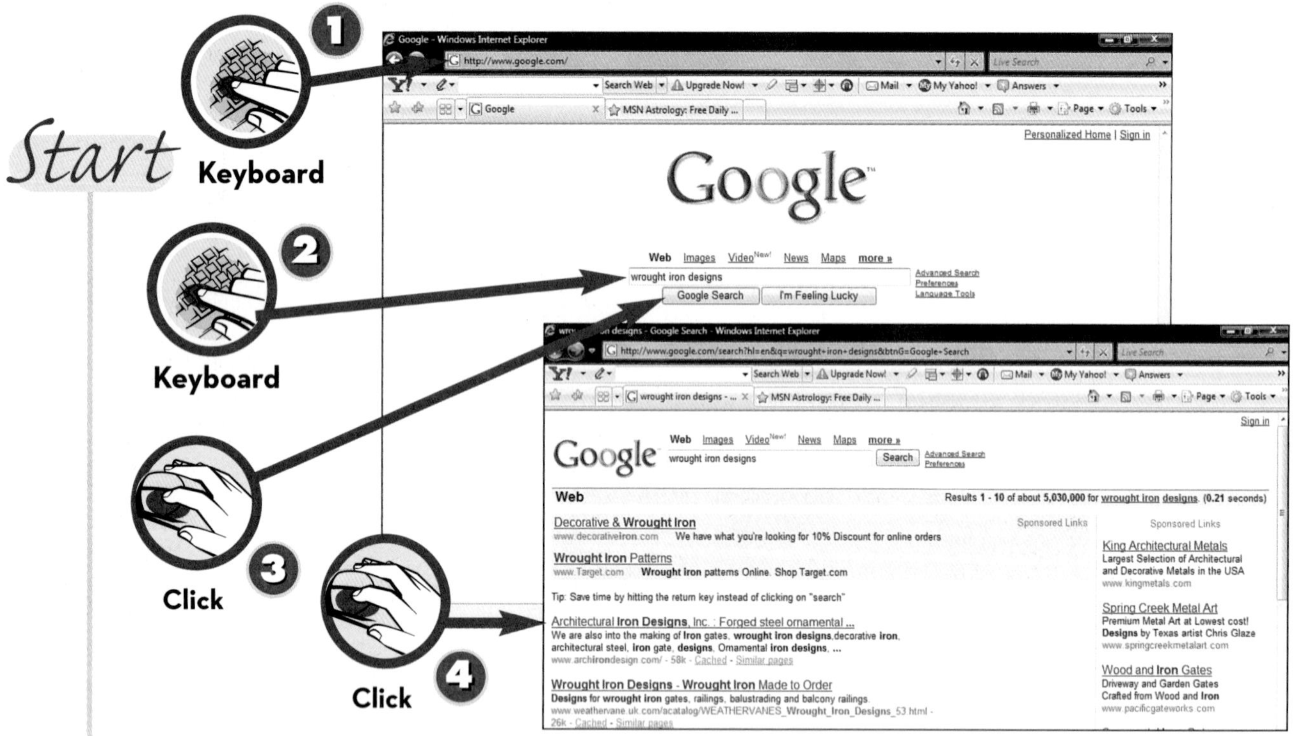

Start

1 Keyboard

2 Keyboard

3 Click

4 Click

1. Go to the search site you want to use. For instance, type **www.google.com** to use this search site.
2. Type the topic you seek in the **Search** field.
3. Click **Google Search** (or the appropriate button name for your site).
4. You see a list of matching sites. Click on any of these links to view the site.

End

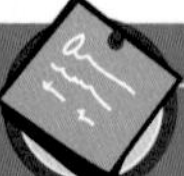

NOTE

Google Stats

Google includes statistics about the number of sites found in your search results list. It also doesn't allow advertising, but does provide for Sponsored Links, which get top billing along the top and right side of the results window.

TIP

View Other Matches

Often you find too many matches. You can scroll to the bottom of the screen to display the next set of matches. You can also look for and use advanced search options that will help limit the matches.

ADDING A SITE TO YOUR FAVORITES CENTER

When you find a site that you especially like, you might want a quick way to return to it without having to browse from link to link or having to remember the address. Fortunately, Internet Explorer enables you to build a list of favorite sites. You access those favorites by opening the Favorites Center and clicking a saved link.

Start

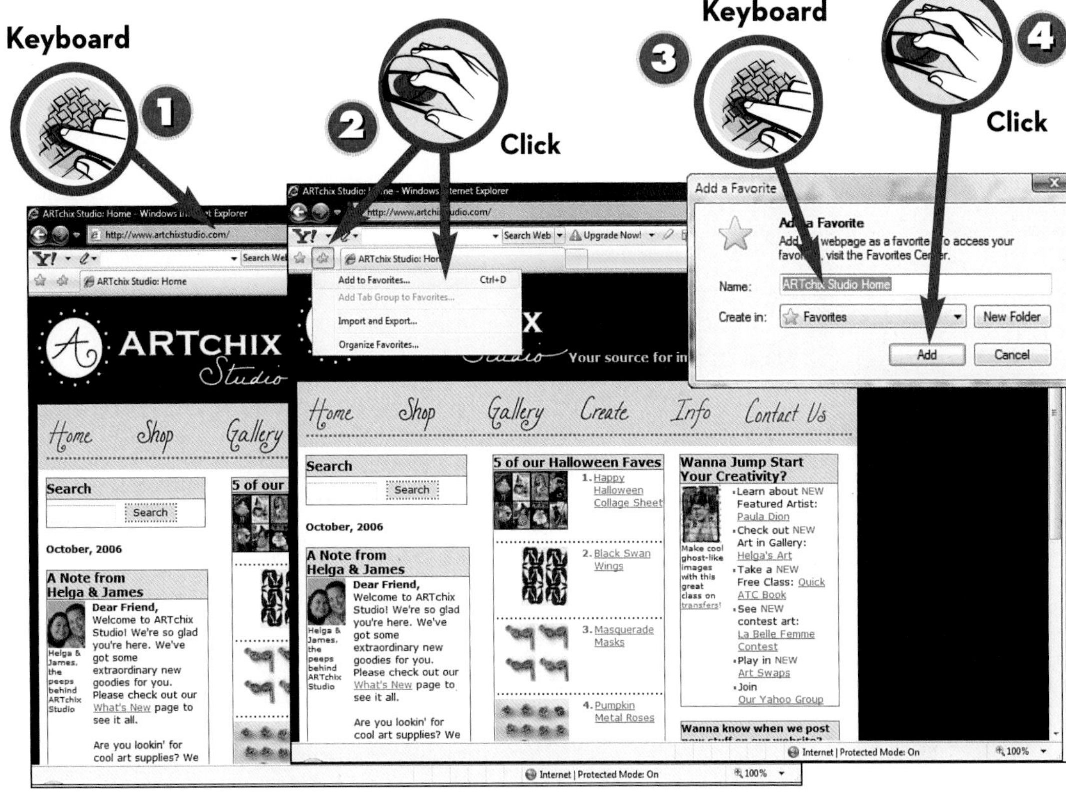

1. Go to the website that you want to add to your Favorites Center.
2. Click the **Add to Favorites** button in the toolbar and then click **Add to Favorites**.
3. Type a name for the page (if you're not satisfied with the default name that is provided).
4. Click **Add** to save the page in your **Favorites Center**.

End

TIP

Add to a Folder

You can add the site to a folder you have set up within the Favorites Center (covered in the task "Organizing Your Favorites Center" later in this Part). To do so, display the **Create in** drop-down list and select the folder.

ORGANIZING YOUR FAVORITES CENTER

If you add several sites to your Favorites Center, it might become difficult to use. You can organize the list by grouping similar sites together in a folder. You can add new folders and place sites in folders rather than in one long list.

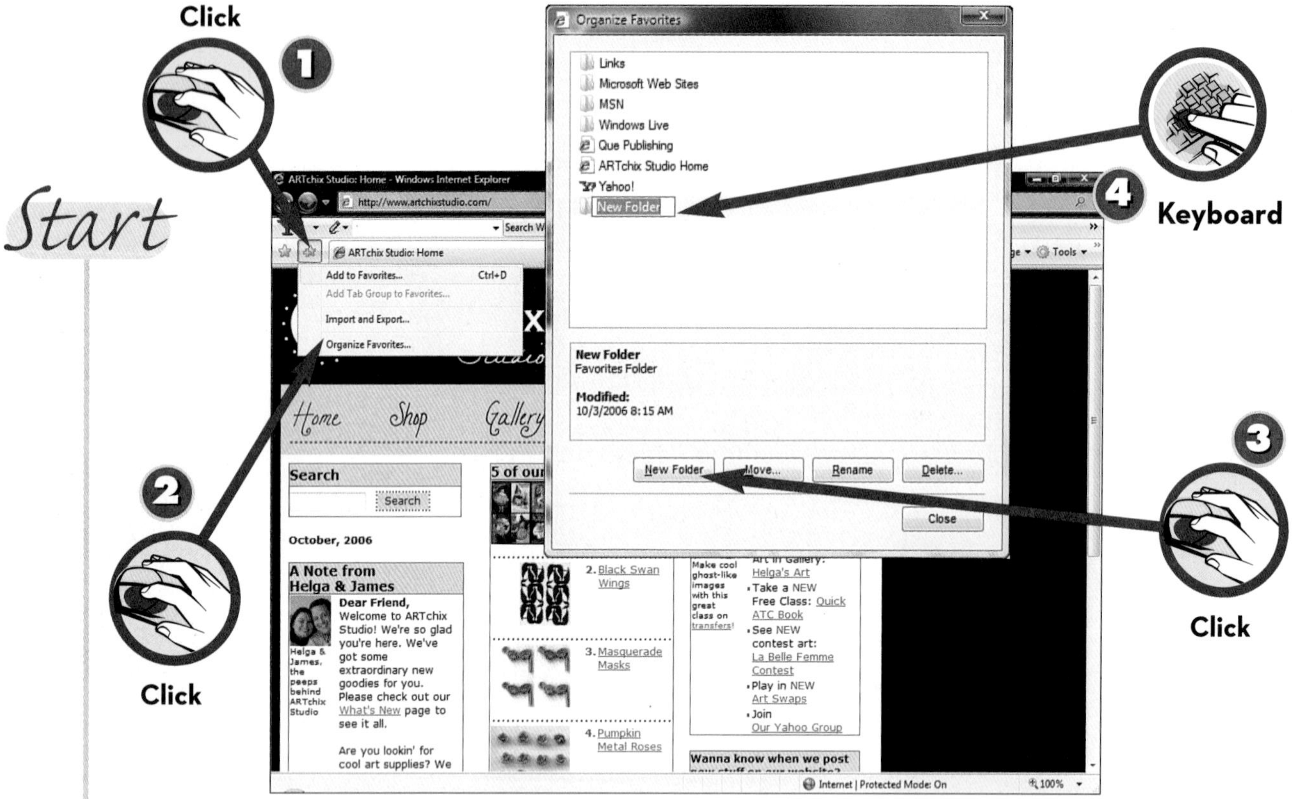

Start

Click

Click

Click

Keyboard

1. Click the **Add to Favorites** button on the toolbar.
2. Click **Organize Favorites**.
3. To create a new folder, click the **New Folder** button. The folder name is selected so that you can type a more descriptive name.
4. Type the folder name. The folder is added. Click **Close**.

End

TIP

Delete a Site

If your Favorites Center becomes clogged with sites you no longer visit or use, clean it out and delete these sites. To delete a site, select the site and click the **Delete** button in the Organize Favorites dialog box. Click **Yes** to confirm the deletion.

GOING TO A SITE IN YOUR FAVORITES CENTER

After you have added a site to your Favorites Center, you can easily reach that site by displaying the list and selecting the site.

Start

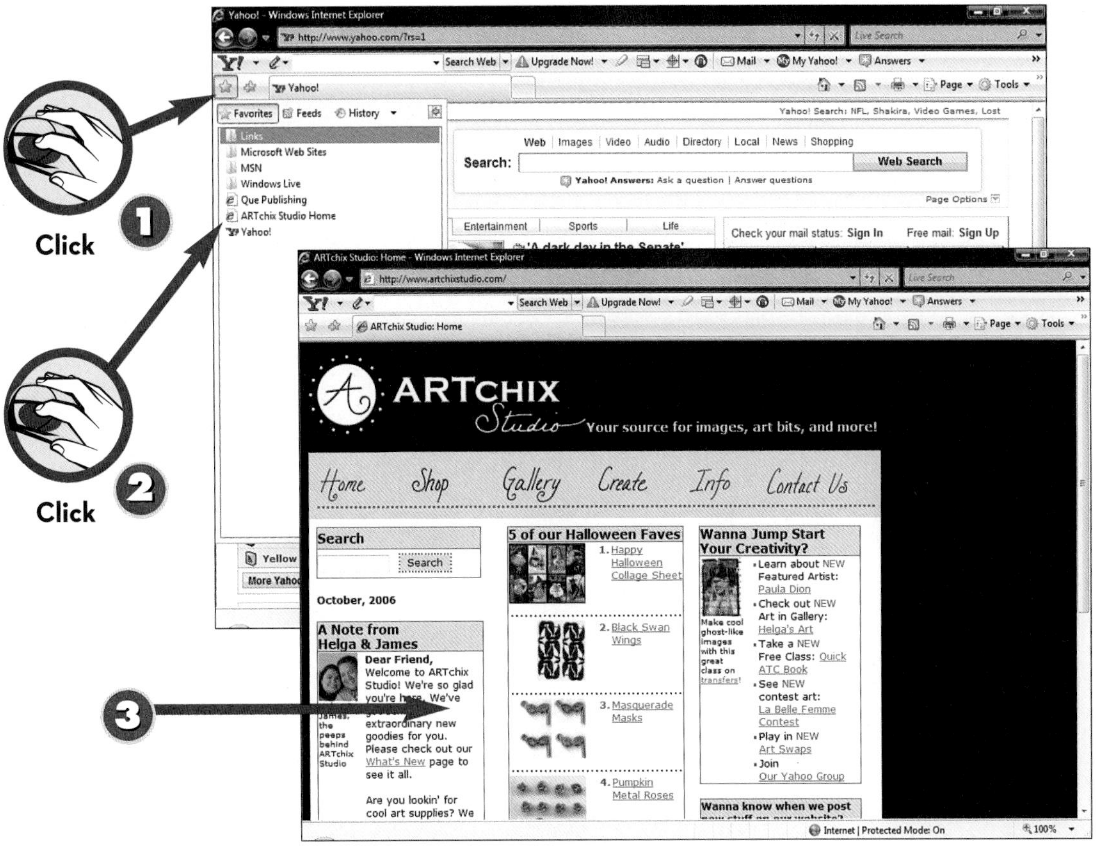

Click 1

Click 2

3

1. Click the **Favorites Center** button on the toolbar.
2. The Favorites Center is displayed in a window. Click the site you want to visit.
3. That site is displayed in your browser window, and the Favorites Center window is closed

End

TIP

Open Folders

If you have added a site to a folder within the Favorites Center, you need to click the folder first to open it, and then click the name of the site you want to visit.

REARRANGING YOUR FAVORITES CENTER

If you don't add folders before you add links to the Favorites Center, you can do so after. You can then reorganize a list of favorite links that may have become too long and unwieldy. Add a folder to the Favorites Center as described in the task "Organizing Your Favorite Center." You can then use the Move button to move sites to appropriate folders.

Start

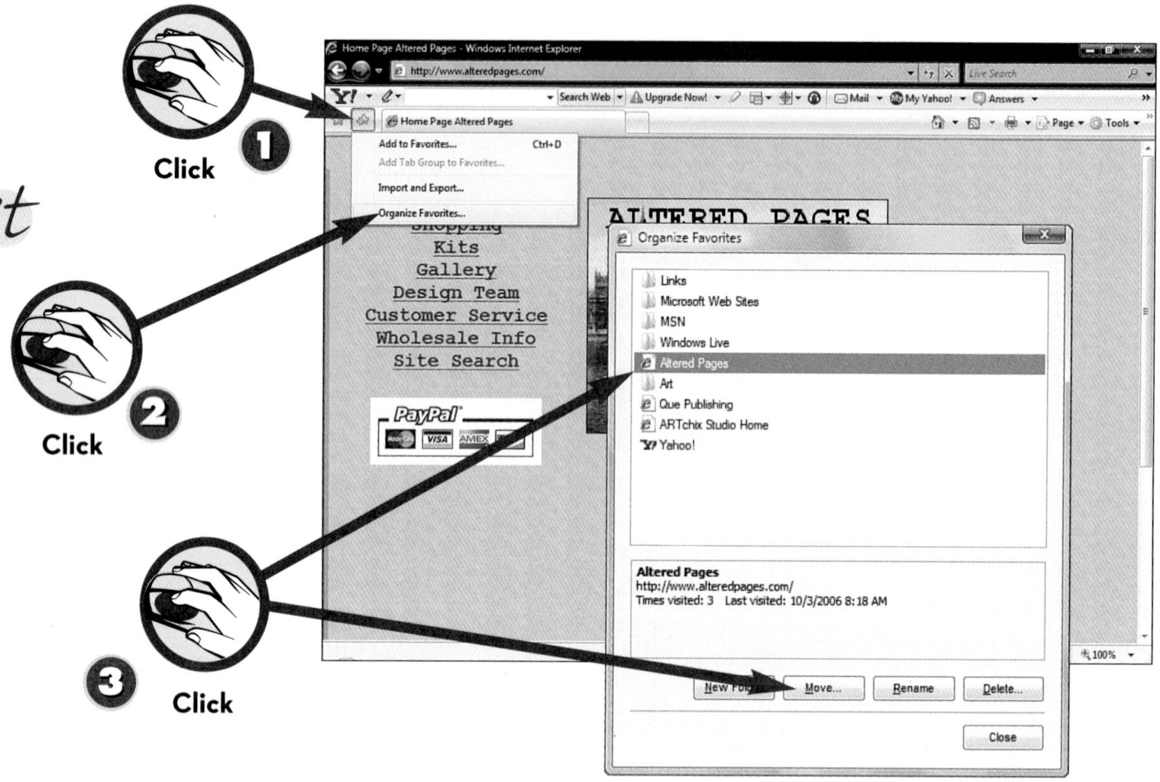

1. Click the **Add to Favorites** button on the toolbar.
2. Click **Organize Favorites**.
3. Select the site you want to move and then click the **Move** button.

Continued

NOTE

Make Several Moves at Once

When you are reorganizing, you can move as many sites as needed. Just follow the same procedure and click **Close** when you have made all your changes.

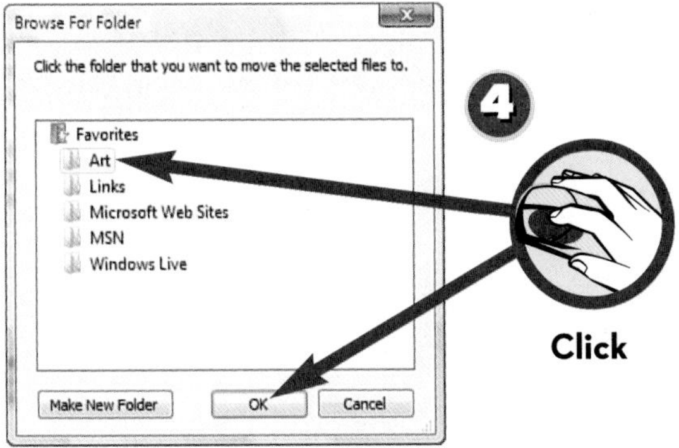

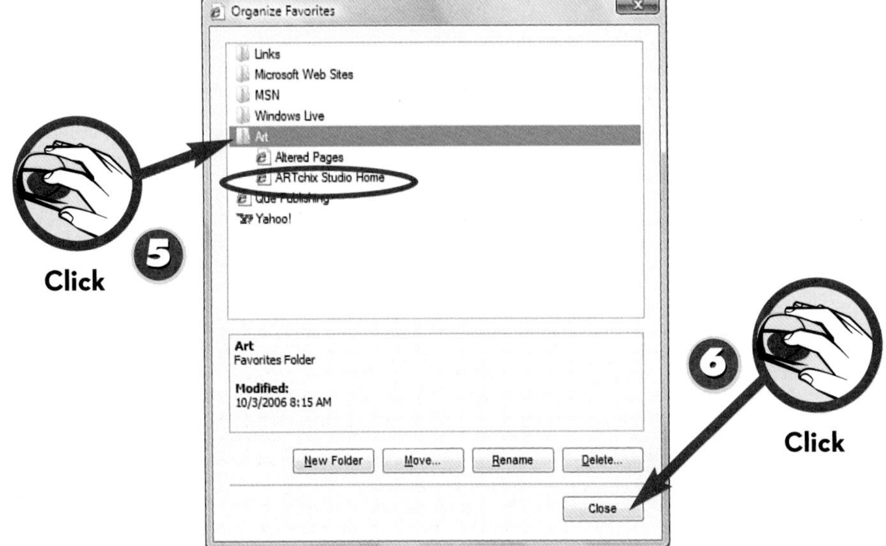

4. Select the folder to which you want to move the site, and click **OK**.
5. The site is moved to the new folder; click the folder to see the link.
6. Click **Close** to close the dialog box.

End

TIP

Drag Site

You can also drag a site from a list and drop it into a folder in the Favorites Center.

NOTE

Open Folder

To open a folder and view the sites you've moved or added to it, click the folder.

USING THE HISTORY LIST

As you browse from link to link, you might remember a site that you liked but not remember that site's name or address. You can easily return to sites you have visited by displaying the History list. From the list of visited sites, you can select the week and day you want to review the site you want to visit, and finally the specific page at that site.

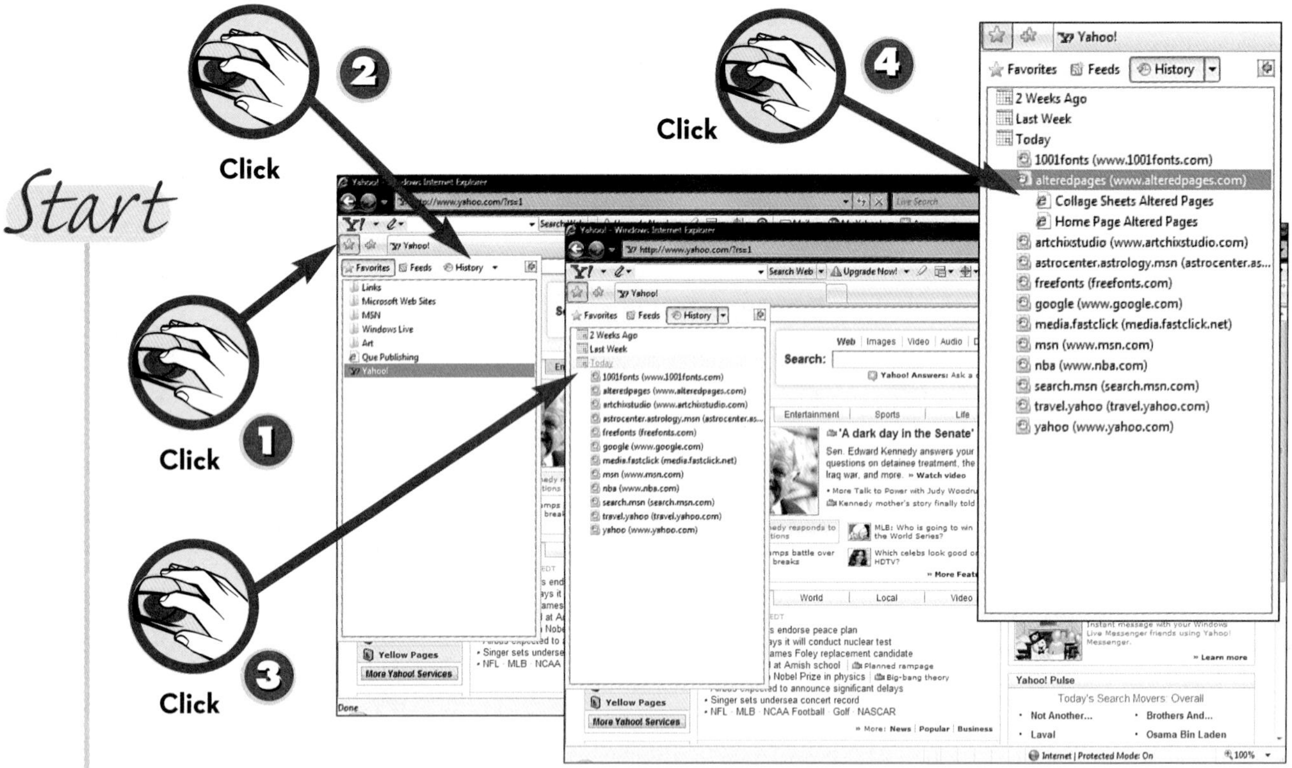

Start

Click

Click

Click

Click

1. Click the **Favorites Center** button on the toolbar.
2. Click the **History** button.
3. You see a schedule of dates from which you can select. Click the date heading to view the sites that you visited during that time period.
4. Click the site you visited; you see a list of pages visited at that site. Click the link to go to that page.

End

TIP

Select History View

To sort the History list, click the down arrow next to the **History** button. Then click the sort order (by date, by site, by most visited, or by order visited today).

CLEARING THE HISTORY LIST

To keep others from browsing through a list of sites you have visited, you can clear your History list. You might also do this to free up the disk space that Windows Vista uses to store this History list.

Start

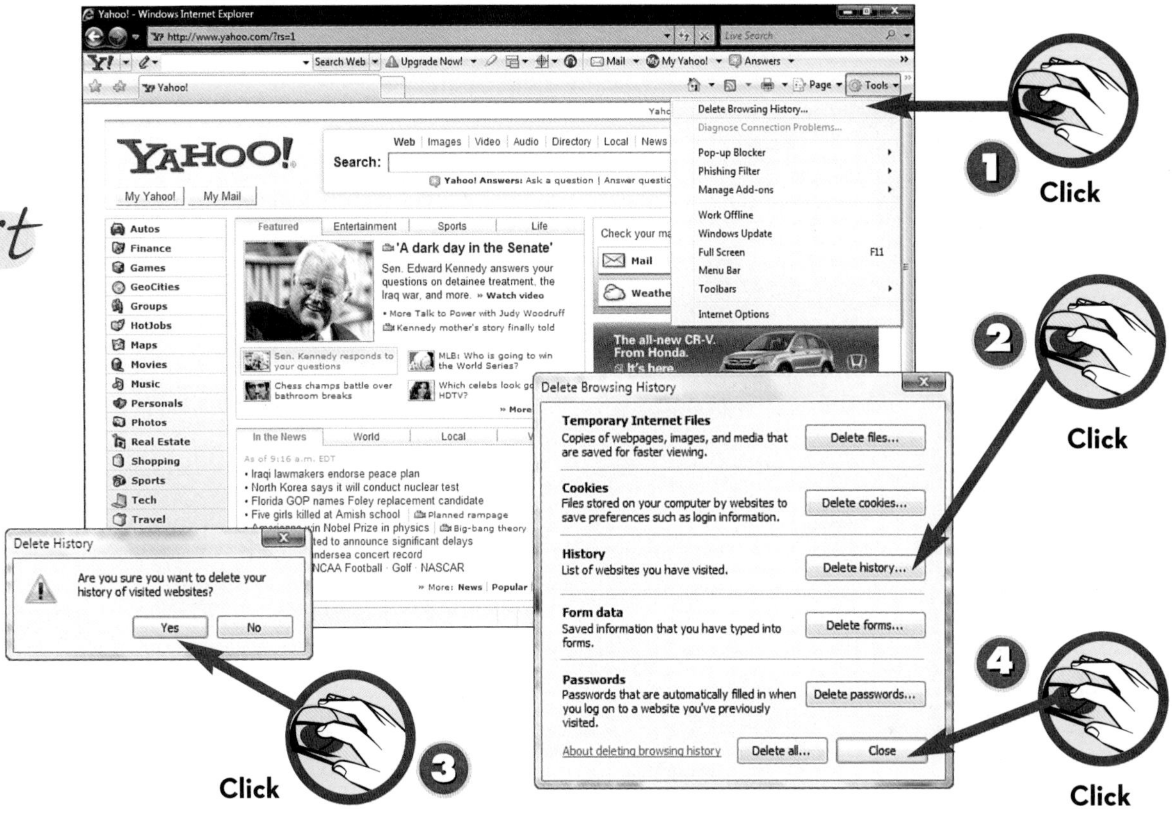

1. Click the down arrow next to **Tools** and then click **Delete Browsing History**.
2. Click the **Delete history** button.
3. Confirm the deletion by clicking **Yes**.
4. Click the **Close** button to close the dialog box.

End

NOTE

Deleting Other Files

You can get information about deleting temporary Internet files in Part 14, "Performance and Maintenance." Handling cookies and passwords is covered in Part 11, "System Security and User Accounts."

SETTING YOUR INTERNET EXPLORER HOME PAGE

When you click the Home button, Internet Explorer displays your home or start page. You don't have to use the page that is selected; you can use any wesite as your start page.

Start

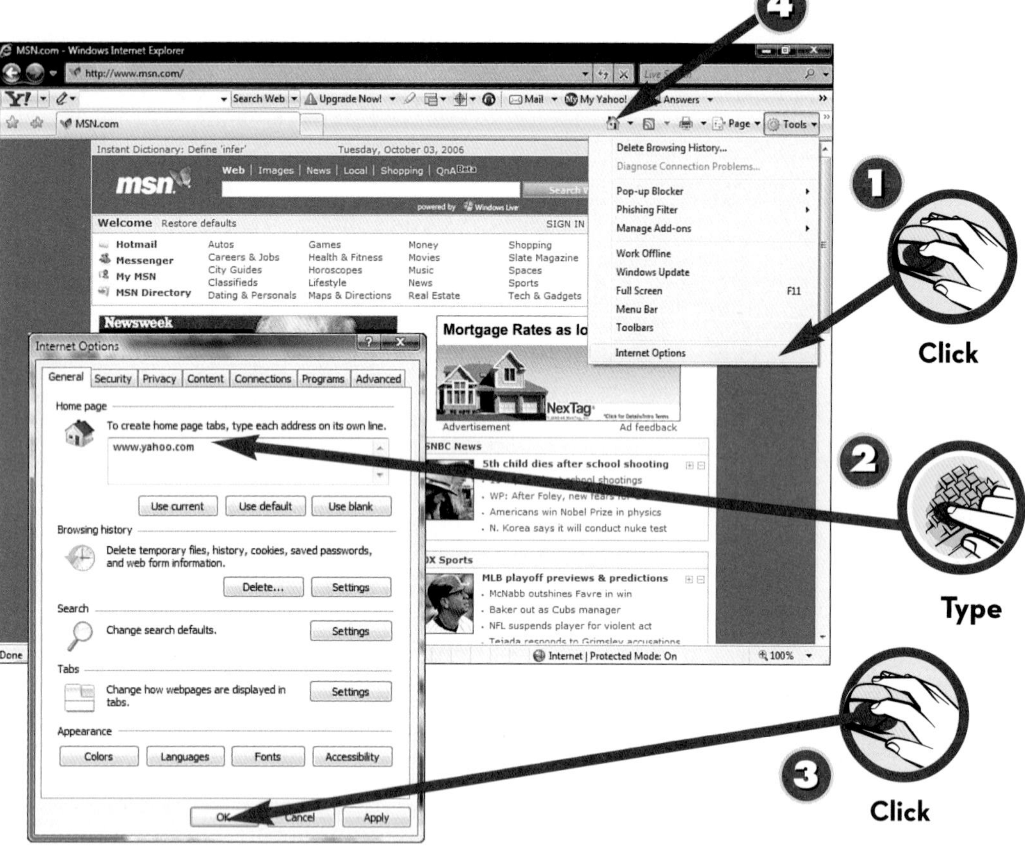

1. Click the down arrow next to **Tools**, and then click **Internet Options**.
2. Type the address for the page you want to use as the home page.
3. Click **OK**.
4. When you click the **Home** button on the Internet Explorer toolbar, the page you entered will be displayed.

End

TIP

Use the Default

To go back to the default page, follow the same steps, but click the **Use Default** button.

TIP

Use Current

Rather than type the address, you can display the page you want to use. Select **View**, **Internet Options**, and then click the **Use current** button.

EMAILING A PAGE OR LINK

If you find a page of interest and want to share it with someone, you can email the page or a link to that page from Internet Explorer. You can either type the recipient's address or select it from your list of Contacts.

Start

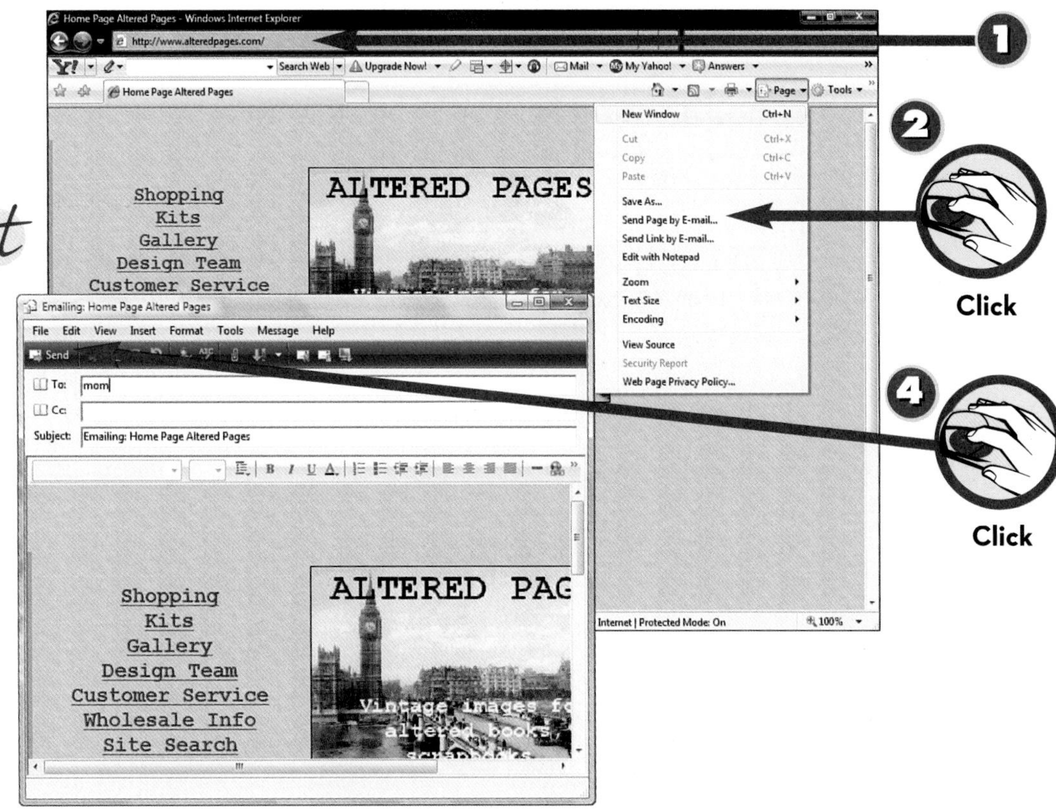

1. Display the page you want to send.
2. Click the down arrow next to the **Page** button and select the **Send Page by E-mail**, or **Send Link by E-mail**.
3. When prompted to allow this action, click **Allow** (not shown).
4. You see a mail window. Enter the recipient's address, type a subject, and click **Send**.

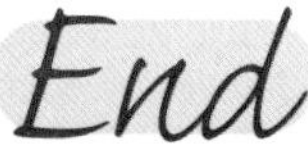

TIP

Sending Page vs. Link

If you send the page, it's like sending a picture of the page; you can't click or use any of the page features. If you send a link, you send a link to the page. The recipient can click the link to go to the page and then click any of the page linkis.

PREVIEWING AND PRINTING A WEB PAGE

If you want a hard copy of a web page, you can print one. You can also preview the page before printing (to see how it will look on the page and how it will fit).

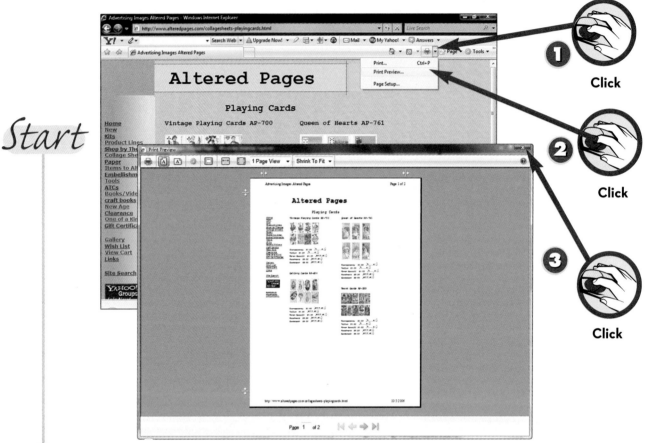

Start

Click

Click

Click

1. Click the down arrow next to the **Print** button.
2. Click **Print Preview**.
3. You see a preview of how the page will look when printed. When you are done viewing the page, click the **Close** button.

Continued

TIP

Full Width and Full Page

You can change the view. Click the **View Full Width** or **View Full Page** buttons to view how the pages look in these views. You can also select to view more than one page as well as shrink the page to fit on one page using the **Shrink To Fit** option.

TIP

Change the Orientation

If you want to change the orientation of the page, click the **Portrait** or **Landscape** buttons.

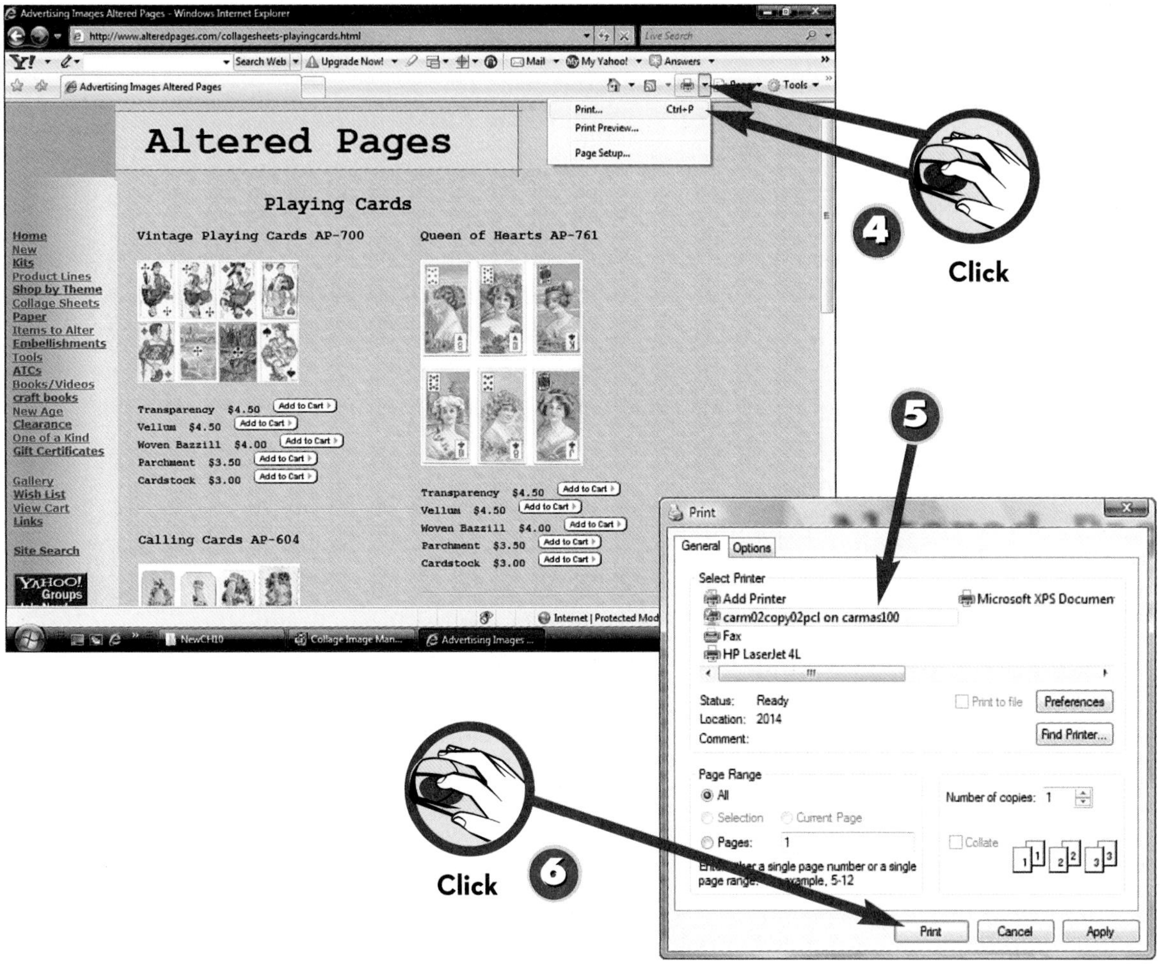

4. To print the page, click the down arrow next to the **Print** button and click **Print**.
5. Make any changes to the print options.
6. Click **Print**.

End

TIP

Print Options

When you print, you can select which printer to use, the number of copies, and the page range. For more information on printing, see Part 6, "Working with Printers."

TIP

Setting Up Page Options

You can set up page options, such as the paper, headers and footers, and margins. To do so, select **Page Setup** from the Print drop-down menu. Make your changes and click **OK**.

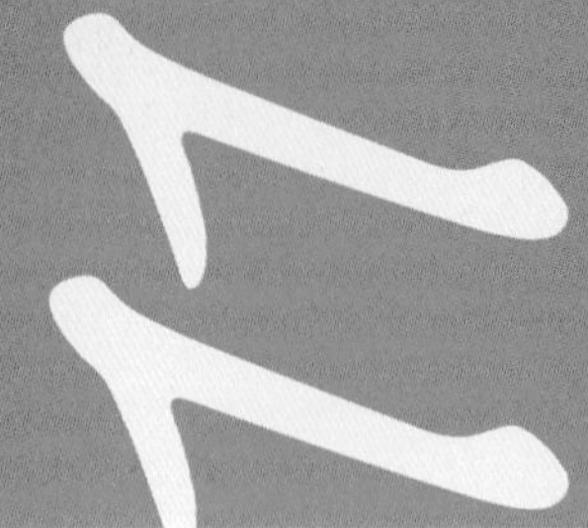

SYSTEM SECURITY AND USER ACCOUNTS

Using a computer provides many advantages, but as connectivity expands, so do the risks in using a computer. If you use the Internet or email, you need to provide security for your computer and its contents. People who seek to wreak havoc on others' computers run the gamut from playing harmless pranks to creating serious problems that can wipe out your entire hard drive and its contents.

Windows Vista adds Windows Defender, which provides one way to scan and check for malicious software. And Windows Security Center provides an overview of key security settings. In addition, Windows Mail has some built-in features for dealing with email-related problems, such as spam and "phishing" for information. All of these features are covered here.

This Part also covers user accounts, a feature that has new enhanced security options to help control who can install new programs and what types of changes can be made to the system.

WINDOWS SECURITY CENTER

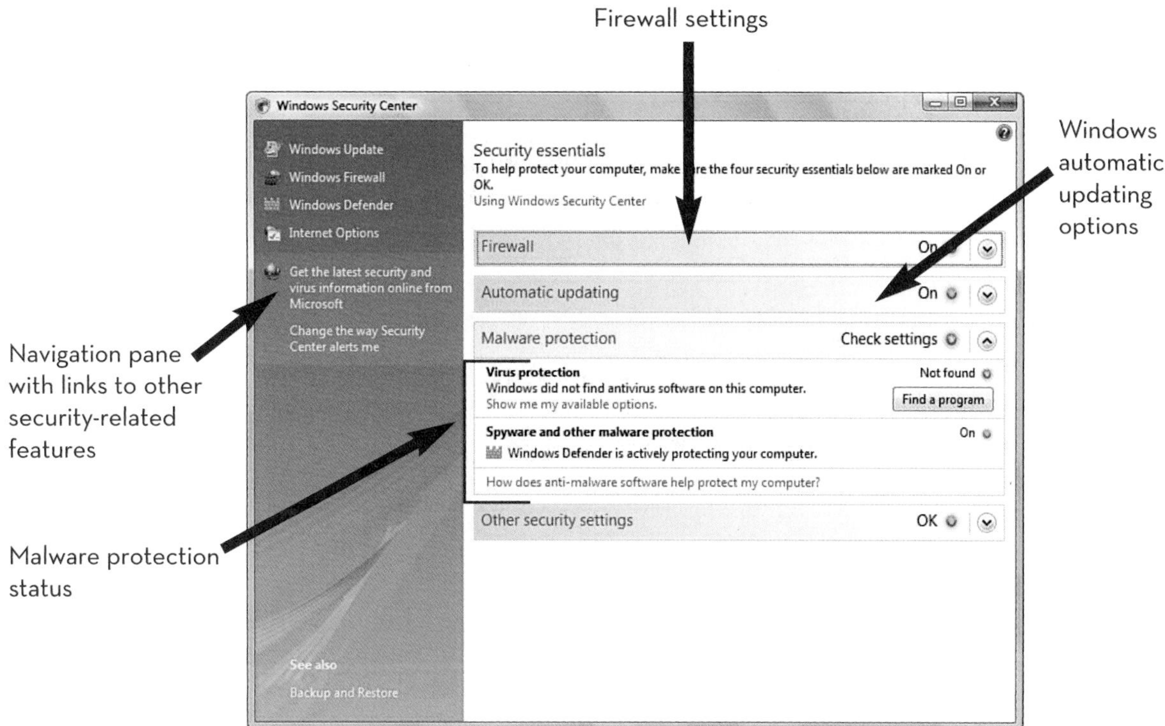

CHECKING SYSTEM SECURITY WITH WINDOWS SECURITY CENTER

The Windows Security Center provides an overview of the various protection features on your computer and whether they are on. This center, for instance, gives you the status of Window's firewall, virus, and malware protection. If you have other programs that provide these same security features, you may see those listed as well. For instance, you may have a virus protection program or a spyware-blocking program (separate from new built-in programs in Windows Vista). From the Security Center, you can also turn on and make changes to these features.

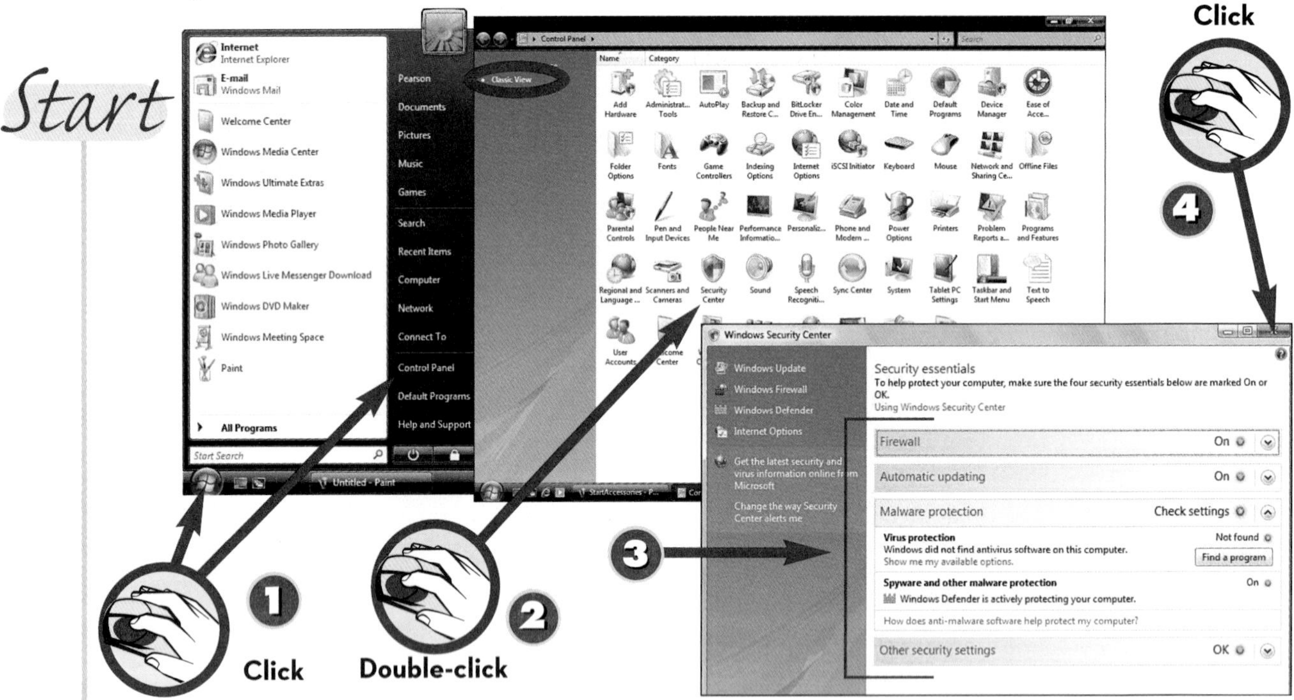

1. Click **Start** and then click **Control Panel**.
2. From Classic View, double-click the **Security Center** icon.
3. Review the default settings. For instance, you can see whether firewall protection is on, whether Windows is set up for automatic updating, and whether you are protected against viruses and malware.
4. Click the **Close** button to close the Security Center.

End

TIP

More Information

This task just explains how to view the Security Center. Later tasks cover using specific security features in more detail.

STARTING AND SCANNING WITH WINDOWS DEFENDER

Windows Vista includes Windows Defender, which helps protect against malware and *spyware* (software that is often installed without your knowledge when you visit a website or even from opening an email attachment). It tracks when a new program is installed and asks for your permission for this action to occur. You can also start Windows Defender to run a virus scan of your computer.

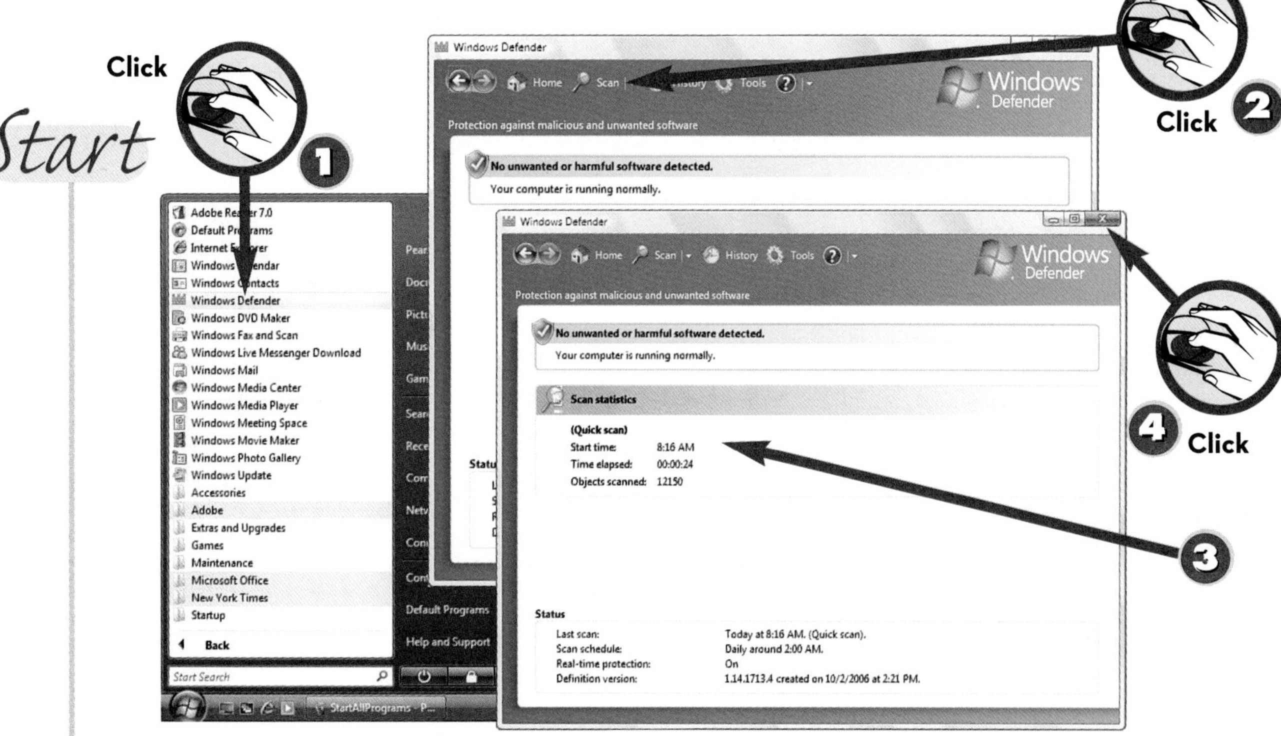

1. Click **Start**, **All Programs**, and then **Windows Defender**.
2. You see the current status of your system. To perform a scan of your system, click the **Scan** button.
3. Windows Defender scans your system for any suspicious programs. You see the results of the scan.
4. Click the **Close** button to close Windows Defender.

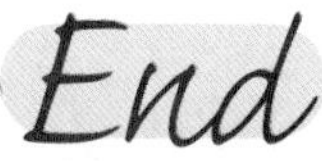

NOTE

Malware Protection

Malware includes viruses, worms, spyware, and other software that can steal personal information, track and relay to another site what sites you have visited on the Internet, and slow your system's performance.

TIP

Potentially Harmful Software

If a potentially harmful program is detected, Windows Defender flags it. You can choose to remove the program, review the program, or ignore the warning. You can safely ignore the warning if the software was something you intended to install.

SETTING WINDOWS DEFENDER OPTIONS

You can set options on how Windows Defender works. For instance, you can choose how often your computer is scanned as well as view and manage quarantined programs.

Start

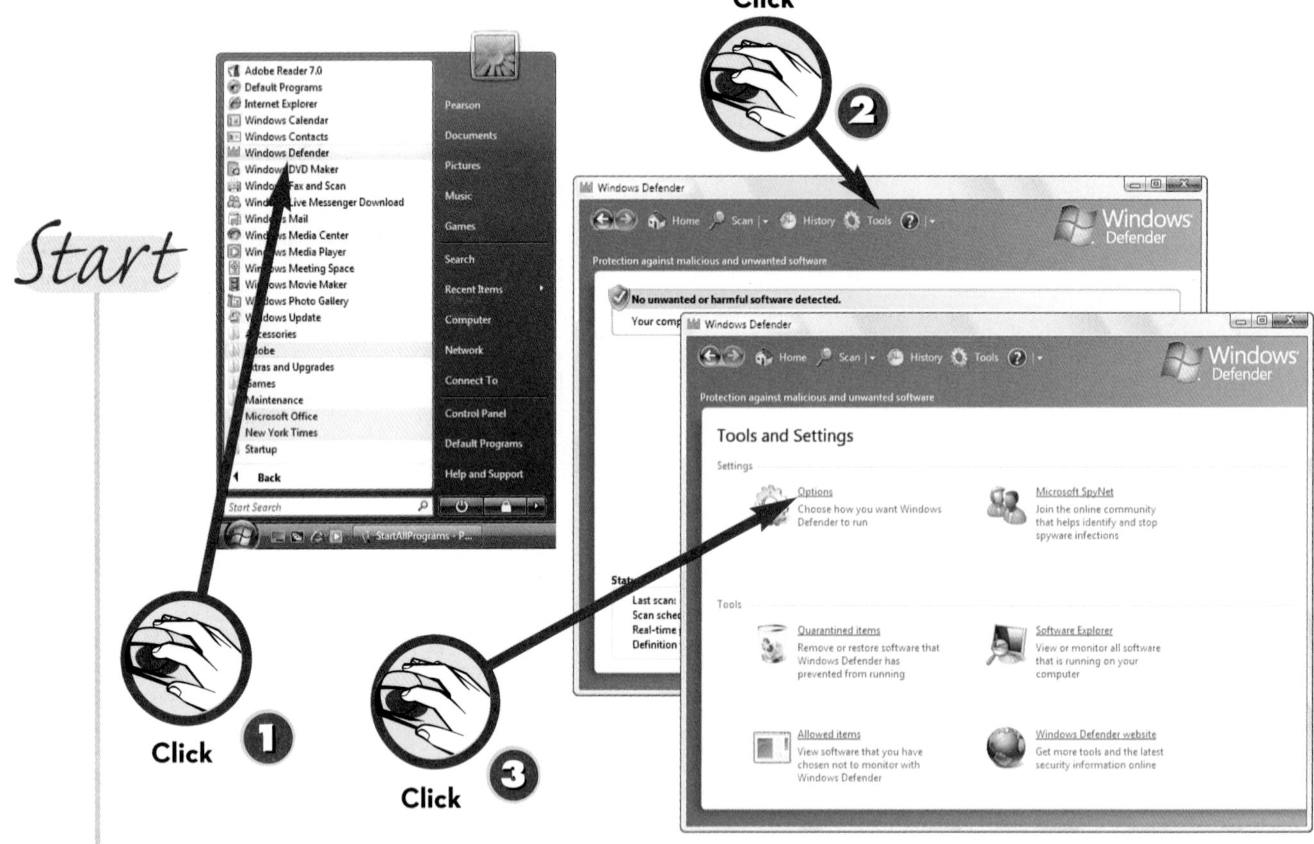

1. Click **Start**, **All Programs**, and then **Windows Defender**.
2. Click the **Tools** button.
3. In the panel of options, click **Options** in the Settings area.

Continued

TIP

Software Explorer

To view all software that is installed on your computer, in Windows Defender, click **Software Explorer** in the Tools and Options window. You can view which programs are allowed. You can also get program information and remove or disable programs from this list.

TIP

Quarantined Software

If Windows Defender finds a suspicious program, it may quarantine the program, letting you decide how to handle the program—whether to remove it from your computer or restore it (allow it to run). To view and handle quarantined programs, click the **Quarantined Items** option.

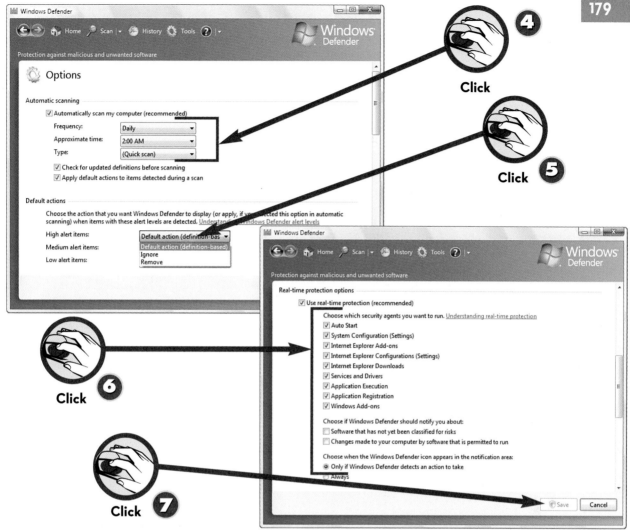

4. Make any changes to whether and how often Windows Defender scans your computer. You can select the frequency, time of day, and type of scan.
5. To change how the various alerted programs are handled, click the down arrow and select the option. You can choose from **Default action**, **Ignore**, or **Remove**.
6. In the **Real-time protection options** area, choose which security agents you want to run, select what you want to be alerted about, and choose when the Windows Defender icon appears in the notification area.
7. Click **Save** to save your changes.

End

CAUTION

Making Changes

For the most part, it's best to retain the default settings for Windows Defender. Let it run automatically and handle alerts with its alert messages. Make a change only if you have a specific reason or are directed to by technical support.

TIP

Viewing a History of Past Scans

To view a past history of scans and any flagged or troublesome programs, click the **History** button. You can see what programs were flagged and what actions were taken.

CHECKING THE VIRUS STATUS ON YOUR COMPUTER

Computer viruses range from simple, mischievous programs that might display a silly message to really dangerous ones that can wipe out all the data on a drive. To protect yourself, Windows Vista recommends you get and use a virus scan program. A virus protection program periodically checks your system for known viruses, scans incoming email messages and attachments, and provides warnings before any infected files are copied to your system.

Start

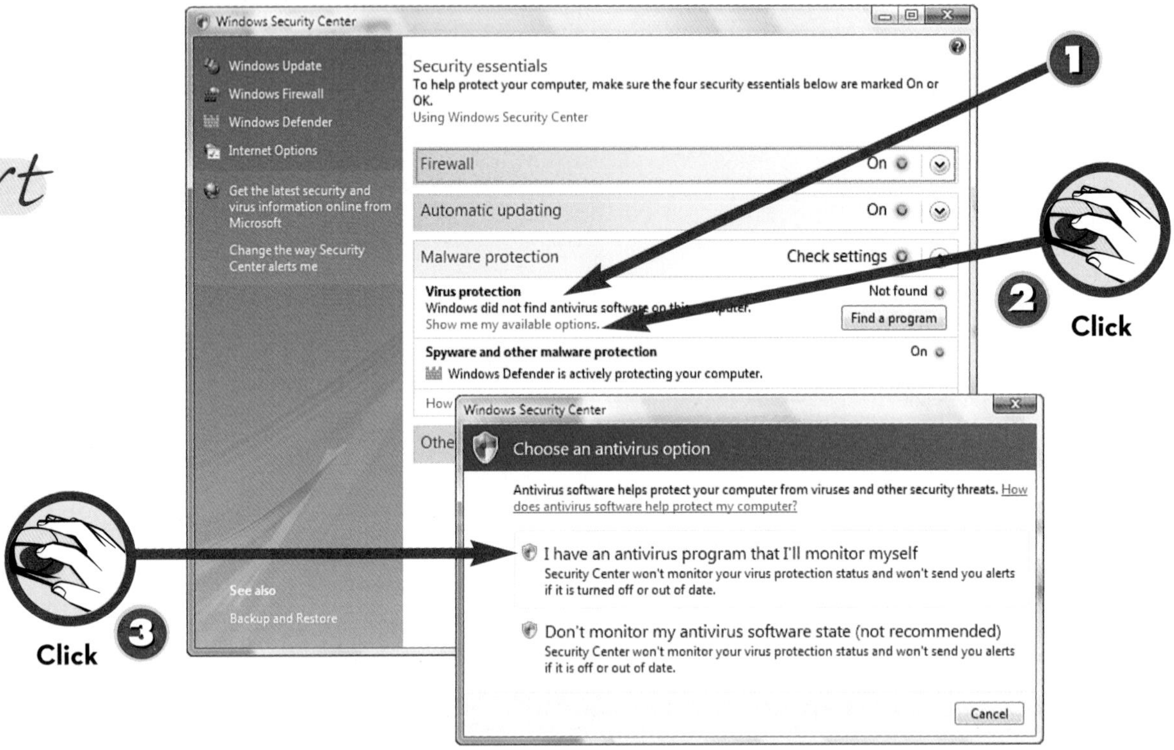

1. Open the Security Center. (See the earlier task "Checking System Security with Windows Security Center.") You see the status of your virus protection. (Here a virus program is not found on this system.)
2. If you have a program that's not listed, click **Show me my available options**.
3. If you have a virus program that is not recognized by Security Center, you can tell Windows that you have a program and will monitor it yourself. Select this option and then click **Continue** to confirm the action (when prompted).

Continued

TIP

Popular Virus Programs

Popular antivirus programs include Norton's AntiVirus (visit www.symantec.com for more information) and McAcfee VirusScan (visit www.mcafee.com for product information). In addition to purchasing the program, you often get a subscription plan to check for and download new virus updates. New viruses are created all the time, so if you don't have the latest upgrade, you can get a virus even if you are checking for viruses.

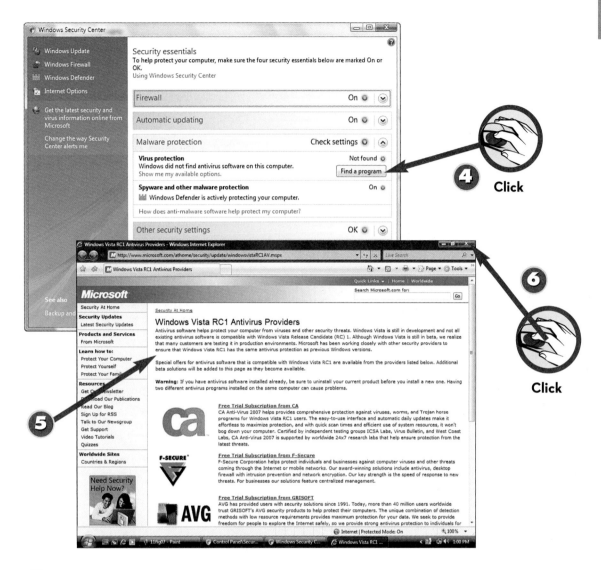

4 To have Windows find and recommend a program, click **Find a program**.

5 A website is displayed with virus program providers. Follow any onscreen instructions for selecting and installing a program.

6 If you simply want to review what's available, read the information and then click the **Close** button to close Internet Explorer.

End

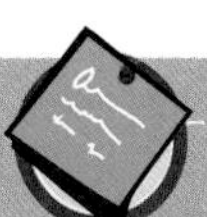

NOTE

How You Get a Virus

How does your PC become infected? Well, you can get a virus from any number of sources, including the Internet, email attachments, and opening a file that happens to be infected from a disk or other removable media (like a portable drive).

TURNING ON OR OFF FIREWALL PROTECTION

Many home users are selecting a different type of Internet connection than through a phone line. You may select, for instance, to use a cable connection or a special phone line (DSL is popular in homes). Because these types of connections are open 24/7, you need to protect your computer from outsiders gaining access to your system. You can check to be sure that firewall protection is on or turn it off (if you have another program that is providing firewall protection).

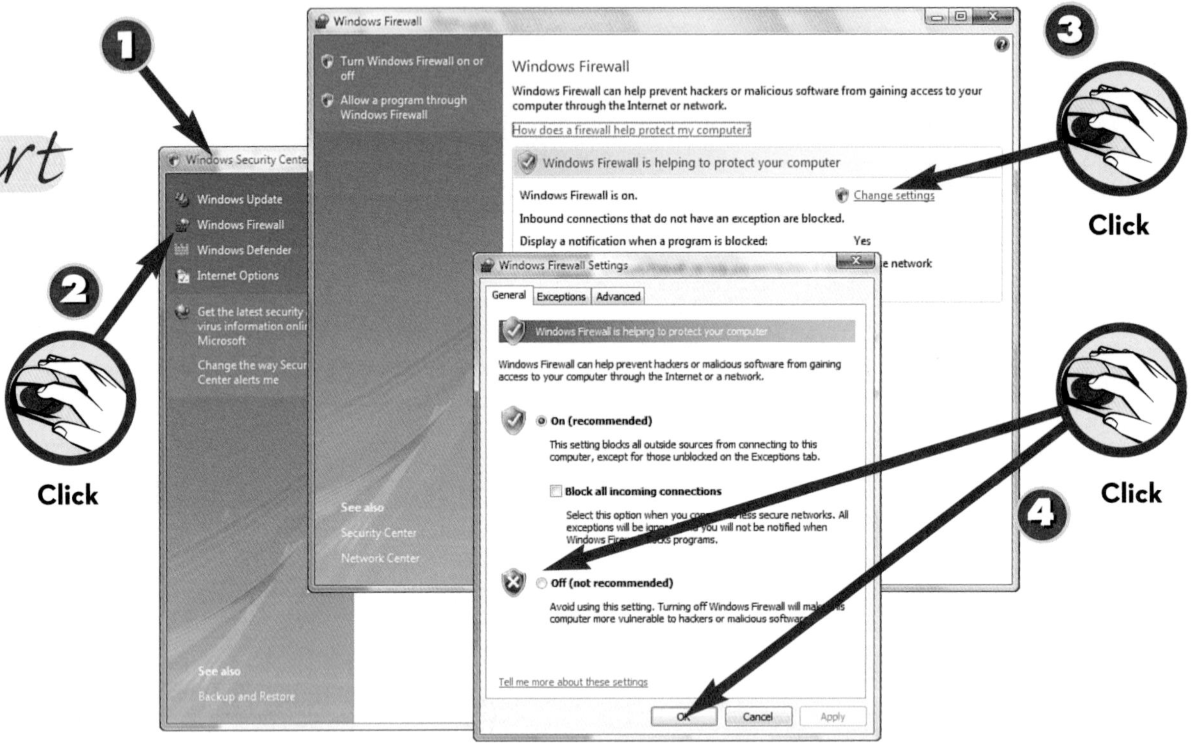

1. Open the Security Center. (See the earlier task "Checking System Security with Windows Security Center" if you need help with this step.) You see whether firewall protection is on.
2. To change the status of your firewall protection, click **Windows Firewall** in the Navigation pane.
3. To change settings, click **Change settings**, and click **Continue** when prompted.
4. If you want to turn off firewall protection, click **Off**. Then click **OK**.

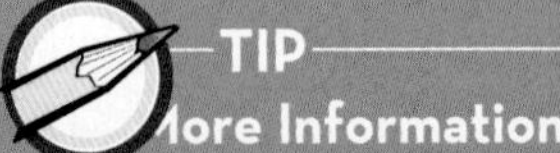

TIP

More Information

To display additional information on firewall protection, click the down arrow next to the **On** button. For more information on this type of protection, click the **How does a firewall help protect my computer?** link.

TIP

Firewalls and ISPs and Networks

Some networks or ISPs have firewalls already set up. Turning on Windows Firewall can then cause problems with your Internet connection. If this occurs, call your Internet Service Provider to get specific advice.

CHECKING A WEB SITE FOR PHISHING

Phishing is a term for when others attempt to get you to tell them personal information about you that they can then use. For instance, a wesite may ask you to register and then ask you for personal information, such as your social security number, password, or other key personal information. (You should never give this out online unless you are certain who you are dealing with!) You can check a site to see whether it is on a list that Microsoft keeps of phishing offenders.

Start

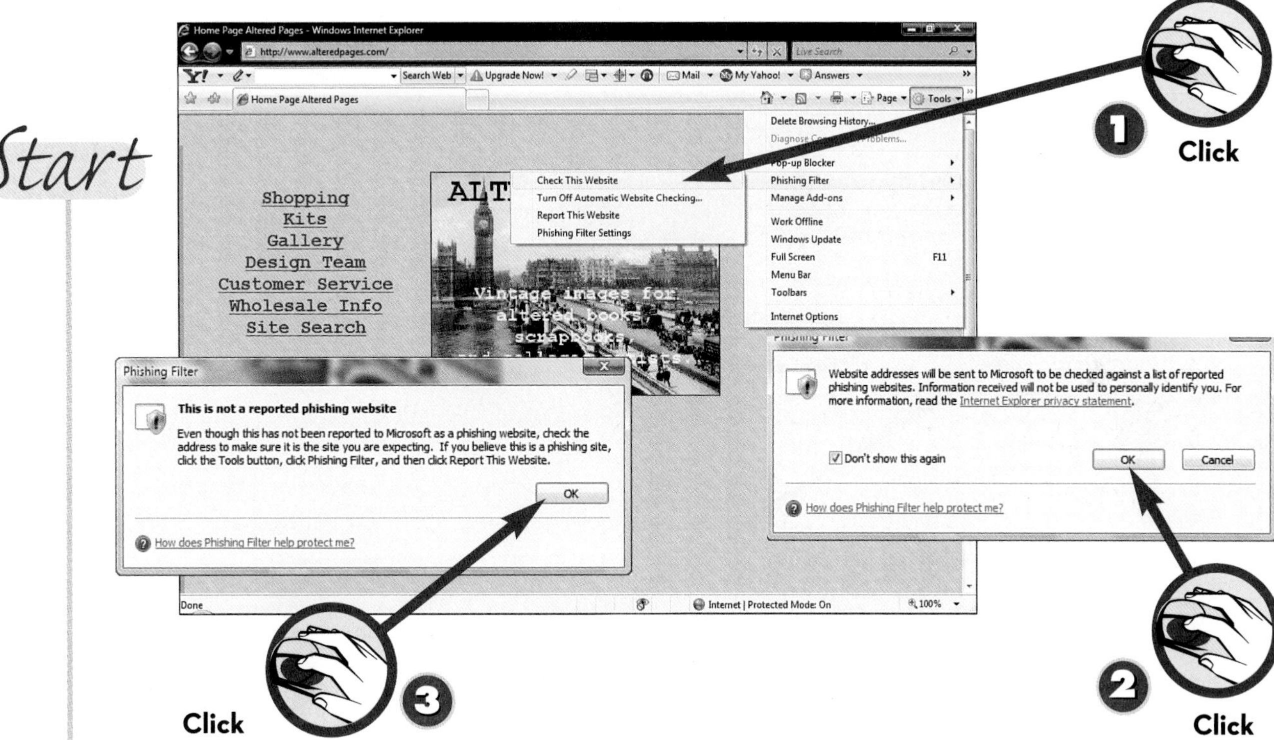

1. From within Internet Explorer, click **Tools**, **Phishing Filter**, and then **Check This website**.
2. You see an explanation of how the phishing check works. Click **OK**.
3. You see the results of the check (here there is no problem). Click **OK**.

End

CAUTION

Phishing Site?

If the site has been identified as a potential phishing site, you see a warning web page and a notification in the Address bar. You can continue or close the page. If the site seems as if it might be a phishing site (that is, has characteristics common to a phishing site), you are notified in the Address bar of this possibility. Click the notification for more information.

BLOCKING POP-UPS

A *pop-up* is an annoying window that pops up when you are browsing a website. Usually it's an advertisement. By default, Pop-up Blocker in Internet Explorer is turned on. You can turn it off (some sites won't display all the information if the blocker is on) as well as check Pop-up Blocker settings.

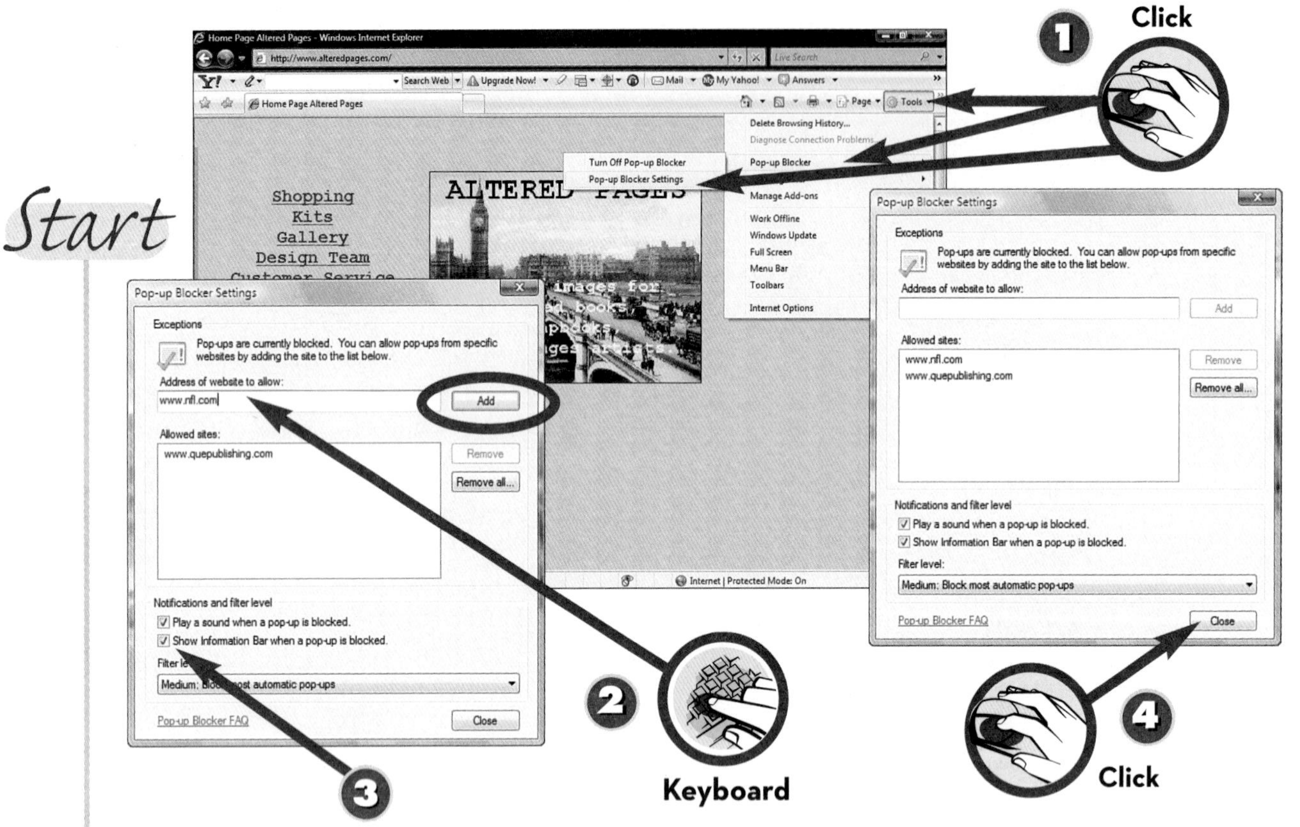

1. From within Internet Explorer, click **Tools**, **Pop-up Blocker**, **Pop-up Blocker Settings**.
2. If you want to allow pop-ups from certain sites, type the site's address and click **Add**.
3. To change pop-up options, such as whether a sound is played and whether an information bar appears, uncheck these options to turn them off.
4. Click **Close**.

TIP

Turning Off Pop-up Blocker

To turn off Pop-up Blocker, click **Tools**, **Pop-up Blocker**, **Turn Off Pop-up Blocker**, and then confirm this action by clicking **Yes**.

TIP

Display Pop-up

When a pop-up is blocked, you'll see a message in the Information Bar at the top of a Web page. You can choose to display the pop-up; you can also temporarily disable the pop-up blocker for that site by selecting the option (available from the Information Bar).

SETTING INTERNET PRIVACY LEVELS

You can assign various privacy levels for Internet sites. The privacy level controls such options as whether the site can use cookies (temporary files stored on you computer), whether the site has a privacy policy, and other options.

Start

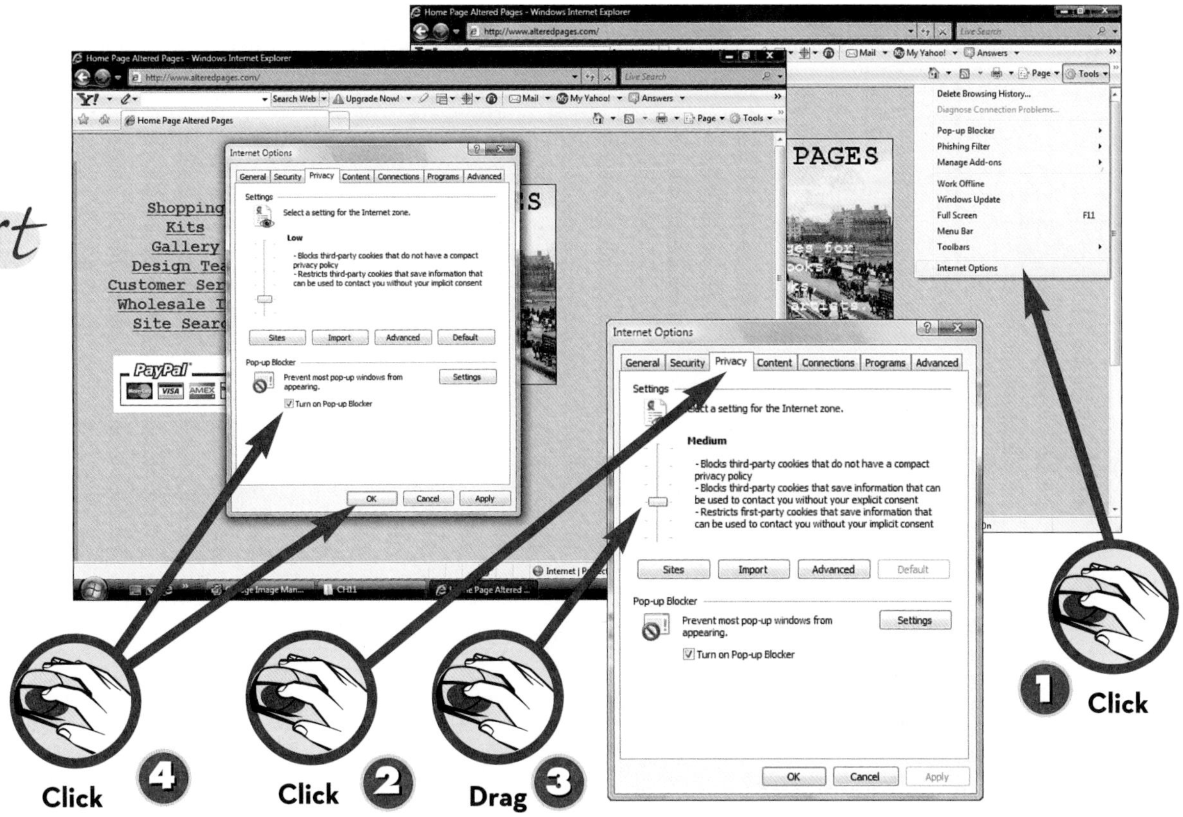

1. In Internet Explorer, click **Tools** and then choose **Internet Options**.
2. Click the **Privacy** tab.
3. To set the privacy level, drag the slider bar.
4. To block pop-ups, keep the **Turn on Pop-up Blocker** check box checked. Click **OK**.

TIP

Security

For more information on security, review the online help. Internet Explorer devotes an entire section of its help system to security issues. Click **Start** and then **Help and Support**. From the opening help screen, click **Security and Maintenance**, and then review that information.

NOTE

Pop-up Blockers

See the task “Blocking Pop-ups” for more information on this feature and its settings.

SETTING UP WINDOWS FOR MULTIPLE USERS

If more than one person uses your PC, you might want to set up user accounts. User accounts have also become more important in security as different users are allowed to perform only the allowed actions. In addition, you can personalize certain Windows settings for each person. For example, you can customize the desktop, Start menu, Favorites folder, Documents folder, and more.

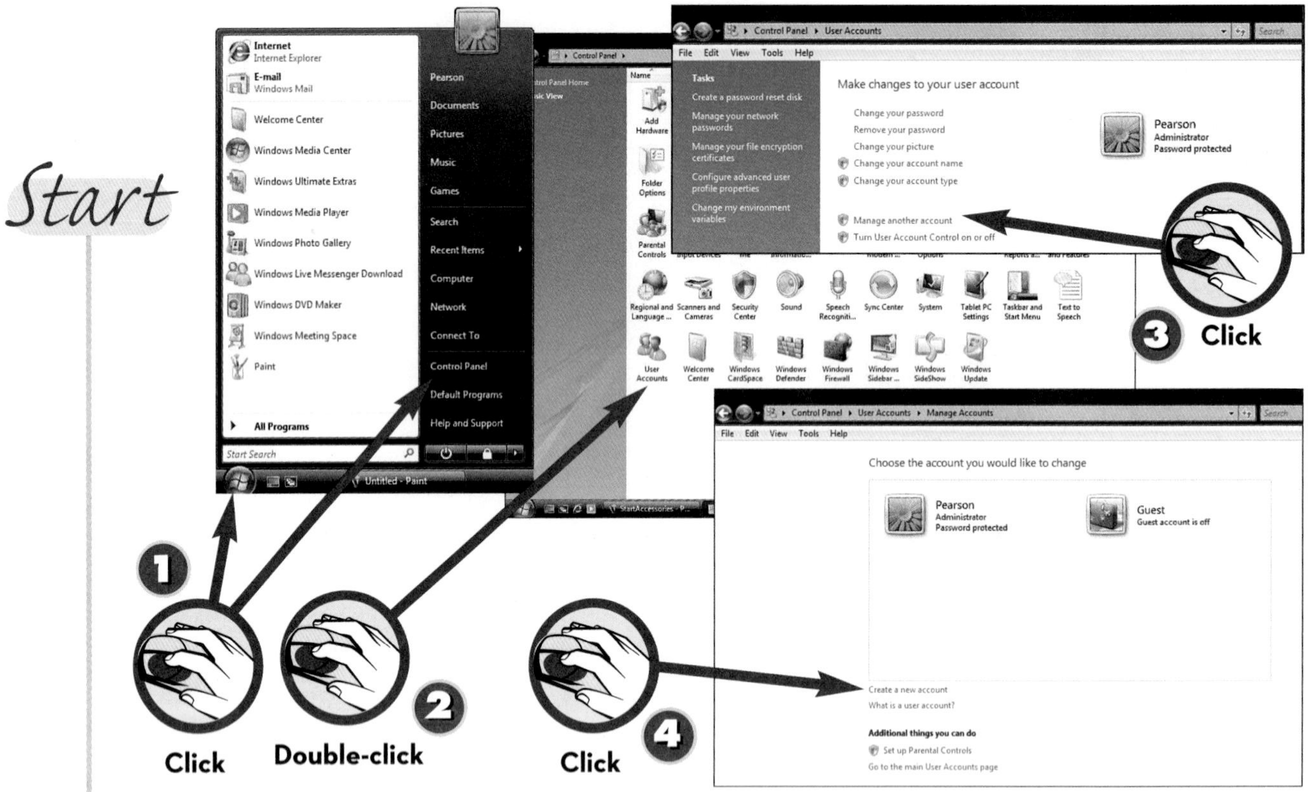

Start

1. Set up Windows the way you want. Then click **Start**, **Control Panel**.
2. In Classic View, scroll down (if needed) and double-click **User Accounts**.
3. Click **Manage another account** and if prompted, click **Continue**.
4. Click **Create a new account**.

Continued

NOTE

Modify the Account

You can modify the picture, add a password, change the account name, and more. See the other tasks in this Part.

NOTE

Delete the Account

Click **Delete the account**. You'll be asked whether you want to save the contents of the account's desktop and Documents folder; click the desired option, and the account will be deleted.

5. Type a name for this account.
6. Specify what type of account: Standard user or Administrator.
7. Click **Create Account**.
8. The new account is created.

NOTE

Administrator Versus Standard

Because security is tied to user account types in Windows Vista, consider having only one administrator account and making the other accounts standard. An administrator account can make most changes on the computer: install new programs, create and delete user accounts on the computer, and so on. A standard account is more limited, which provides another level of security, ensuring that others aren't installing programs without your knowledge.

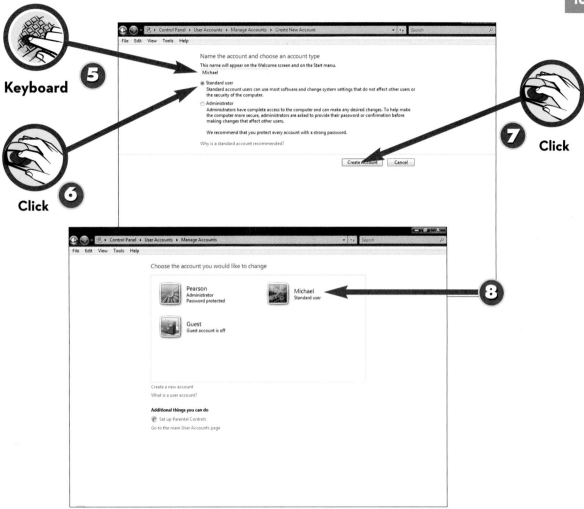

ADDING A PASSWORD TO THE USER ACCOUNT

To provide an additional level of security for your account, you can assign a password. To log on, you (or whoever else attempts to log on) must type the password.

Start

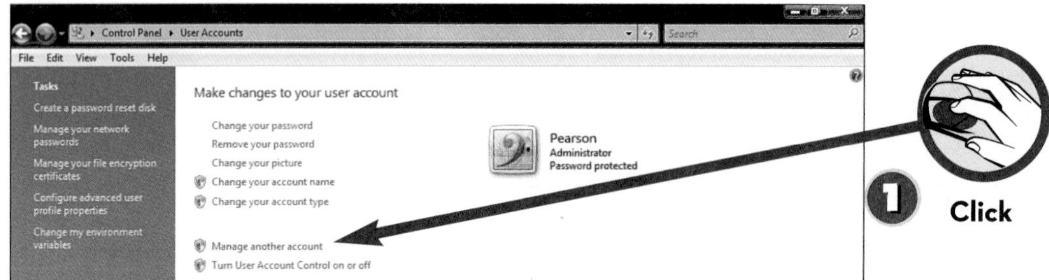

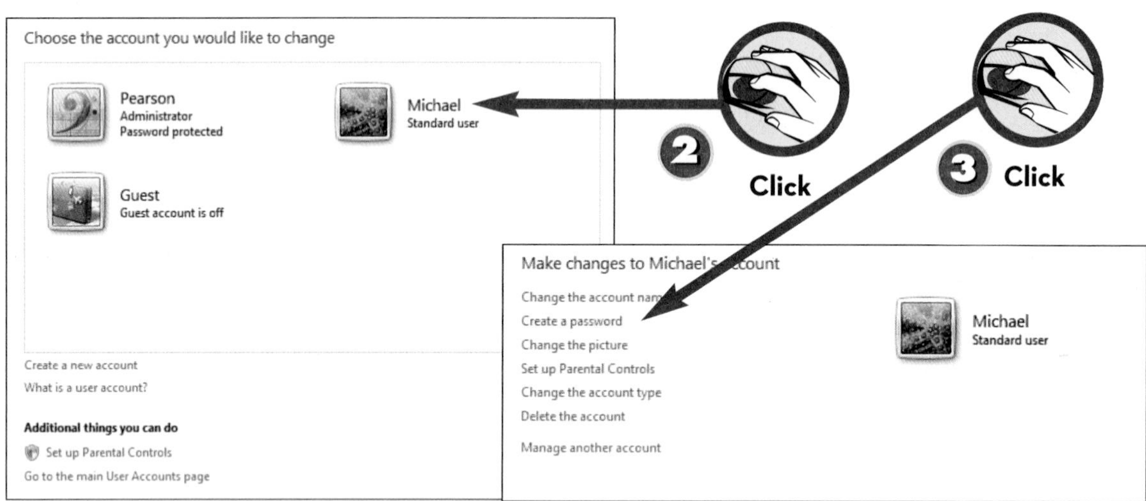

1. Open the User Accounts control panel and click **Manage another account**.
2. Select the account you want to modify.
3. To add a password, click **Create a password**.

Continued

TIP

Switch Account

To switch from one user account to another, click the **Start** button, and click the arrow button next to the lock. Click **Switch User** and then select the user account.

TIP

Change User Account Image

Open the User Accounts control panel; you see the account options for the person who is currently logged in. To change the picture, click **Change your picture**. Click the picture you want to use, and click **Change Picture**.

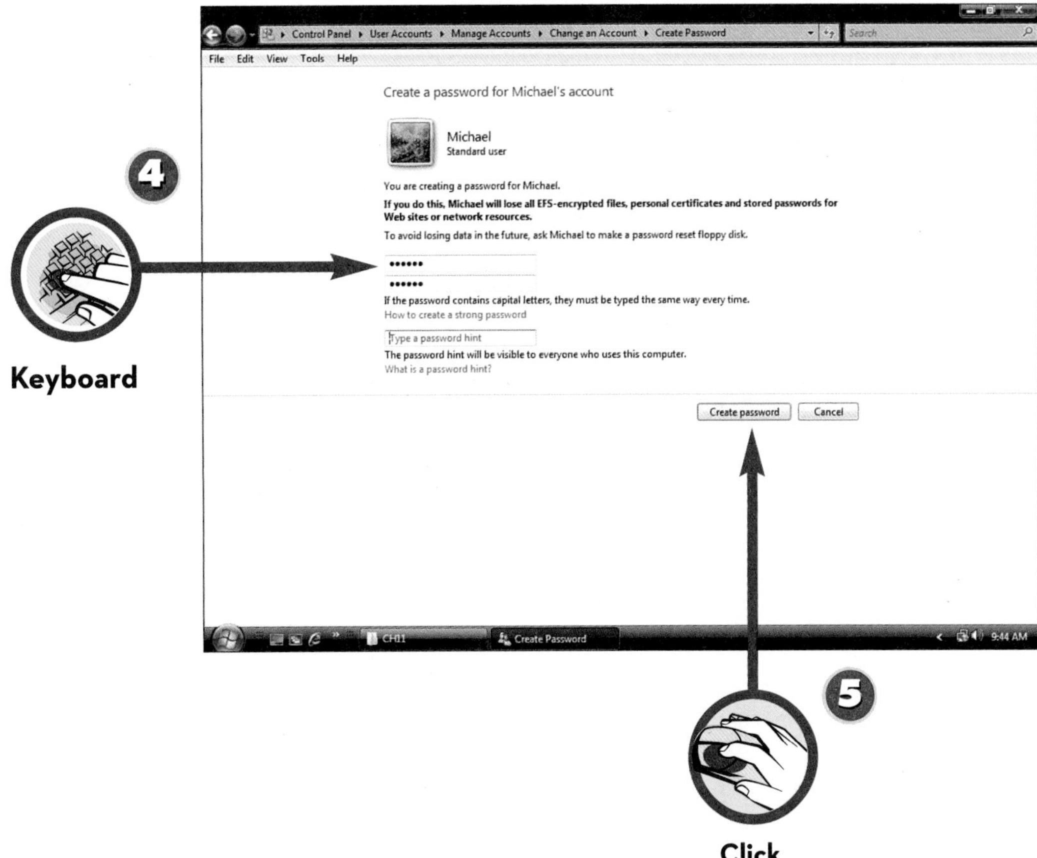

4 Type a password twice: once in the first password text box and then in the second one to confirm it. To add a hint in case you forget your password, type the hint.

5 Click **Create password**. The password is added.

End

TIP

Password Assigned

If you have already added a password, you don't have options for adding a password. Only options for changing or removing the password will appear in the User Accounts control panel.

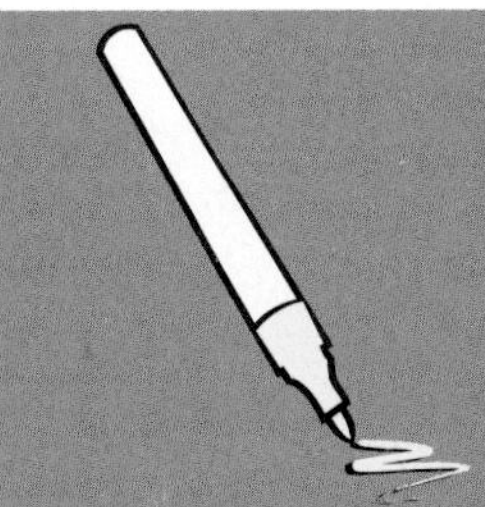

SETTING PARENTAL CONTROLS

If you set up user accounts, you can also use them to set controls for what actions that user can perform. This is especially important if you have children who use the computer. You can set parental controls on their accounts that control their access to programs and the Internet, as well as time spent on the computer.

Start

Click Double-click Click

1. Click **Start** and then **Control Panel**.
2. Double-click the icon for **Parental Controls**. If prompted, click **Continue**.
3. Select the account for which you want to set parental controls.

Continued

TIP

Access Parental Controls from User Accounts

You can also set up parental controls using the User Accounts control panel. In the control panel, select this option, click **Manage another account**, and then select the account to manage. At the bottom under Additional things you can do, you see a link **Set up Parental Controls**. You can click this link to access these features.

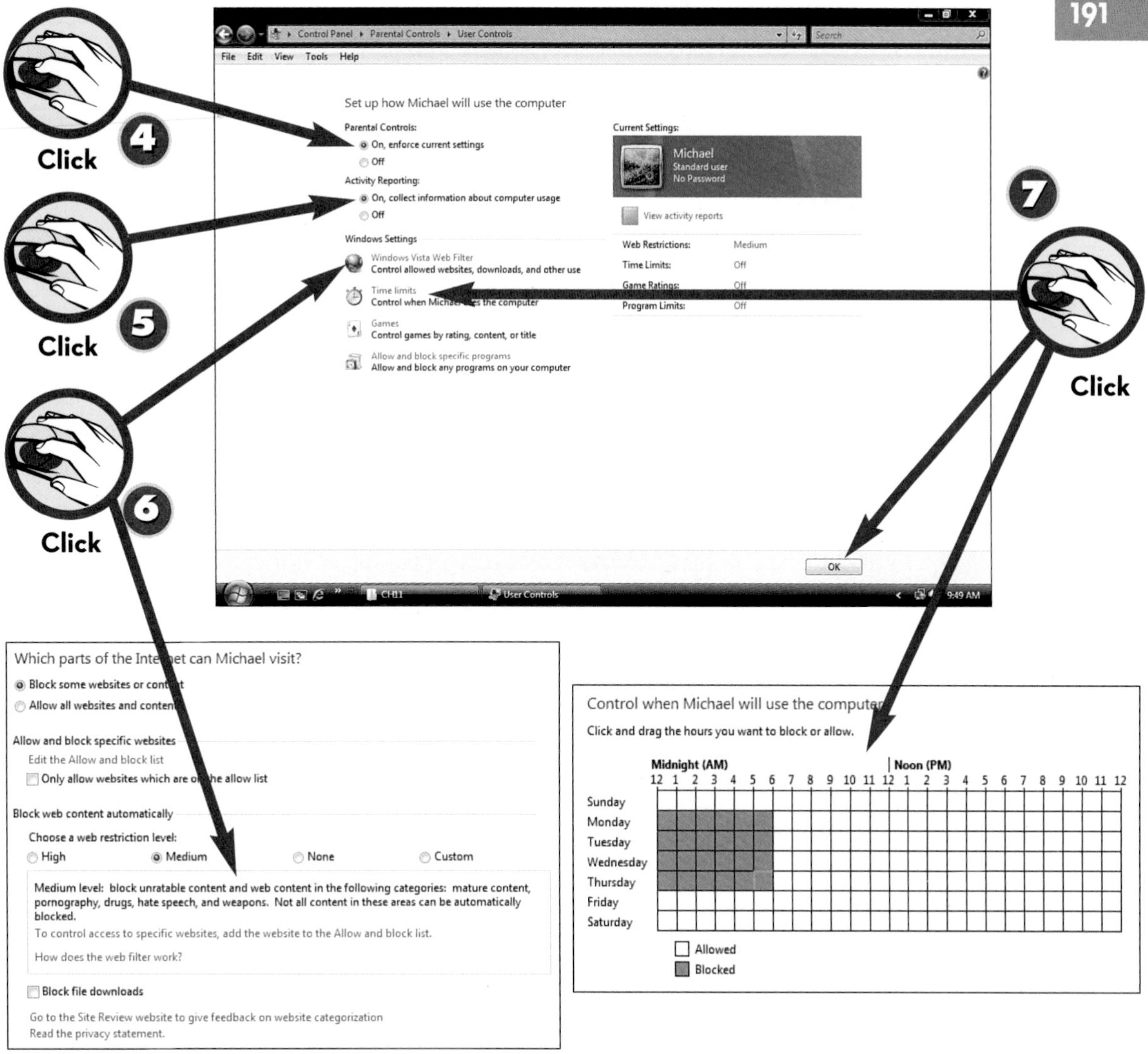

Click 4

Click 5

Click 6

Click 7

1. Click **On, enforce current settings** to turn on parental controls.
2. To get a report of the actions, click **On, collect information about computer usage**.
3. To control Internet access, click **Windows Vista Web Filter**. You can select whether you want to block some content. You can also block specific Web sites and choose a restriction level.
4. To set a time limit for computer usage, click **Time limits**. In the grid that appears, click any of the time periods you want to block access. Then click **OK**.

End

TIP

Games Access

To control access to games, click **Games**. Then select whether that user is allowed to play games, set the ratings for what games are allowed, and block (or allow) any games. Click **OK**.

TIP

Blocking Programs

To block certain programs from use, click **Allow and block specific programs**. Then check **[Name] can only use the programs I allow**. (The name will be that account's name.) Check any programs the user is allowed to use. Then Click **OK**.

12

PERSONALIZING WINDOWS

Windows Vista includes many options for setting up your work environment just the way you want. You can adjust the colors used for onscreen elements. You can also also add a background image or change the color of the desktop so that icons are easier to see. As another option, you can change the resolution or size of the images as they are displayed on your screen.

In addition, you have other ways to personalize Windows Vista. For example, you can change how the mouse works. This is particularly useful for left-handed users as well as those who have trouble timing the action of double-clicking. You can also customize when sounds are played (such as to alert you of some action) and which sounds are played.

This Part shows you how to customize Windows Vista so that options and features are more suitable to your style and preferences.

PERSONALIZATION CONTROL PANEL

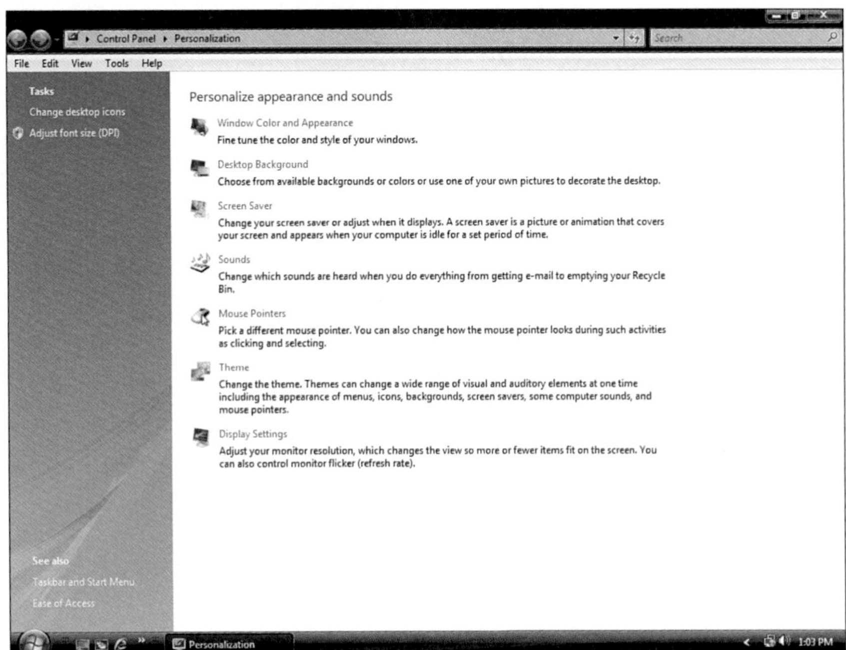

SELECTING A DESKTOP THEME

Windows Vista enables you to personalize your workspace by selecting a desktop theme. Desktop themes consist of a background, sounds, icons, and other elements. Windows Vista offers numerous color-coordinated themes to choose from; alternatively, you can create your own custom theme.

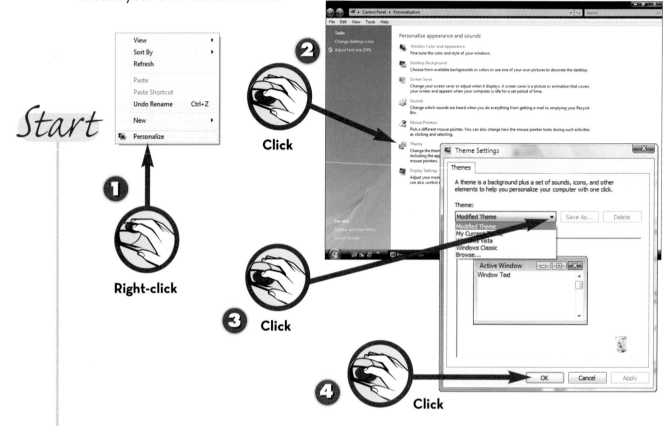

Start

Right-click

Click

Click

Click

1. On your desktop, right-click an empty spot, and select **Personalize** from the pop-up menu that appears.
2. In the Personalization control panel, click **Theme**.
3. In the Theme Settings dialog box, display the **Theme** drop-down list and select a theme. You see a preview of this theme.
4. Click **OK** to apply the theme.

End

TIP

Saving Your Changes

If you modify the chosen theme, you can save it as a new theme by clicking the **Save As** button. In the Save As dialog box, type a name, specify where you want to save the theme, and click the **Save** button. The theme is saved, and its name is added to the Themes drop-down list.

CHANGING THE COLOR SCHEME

Windows Vista enables you to change the sets of colors used for certain onscreen elements, such as the title bar and background. These sets of colors are called *schemes*, and you can select colors that work best for you and your monitor. Lighter colors might, for example, make working in some Windows applications easier on your eyes. On the other hand, you might prefer bright and lively colors.

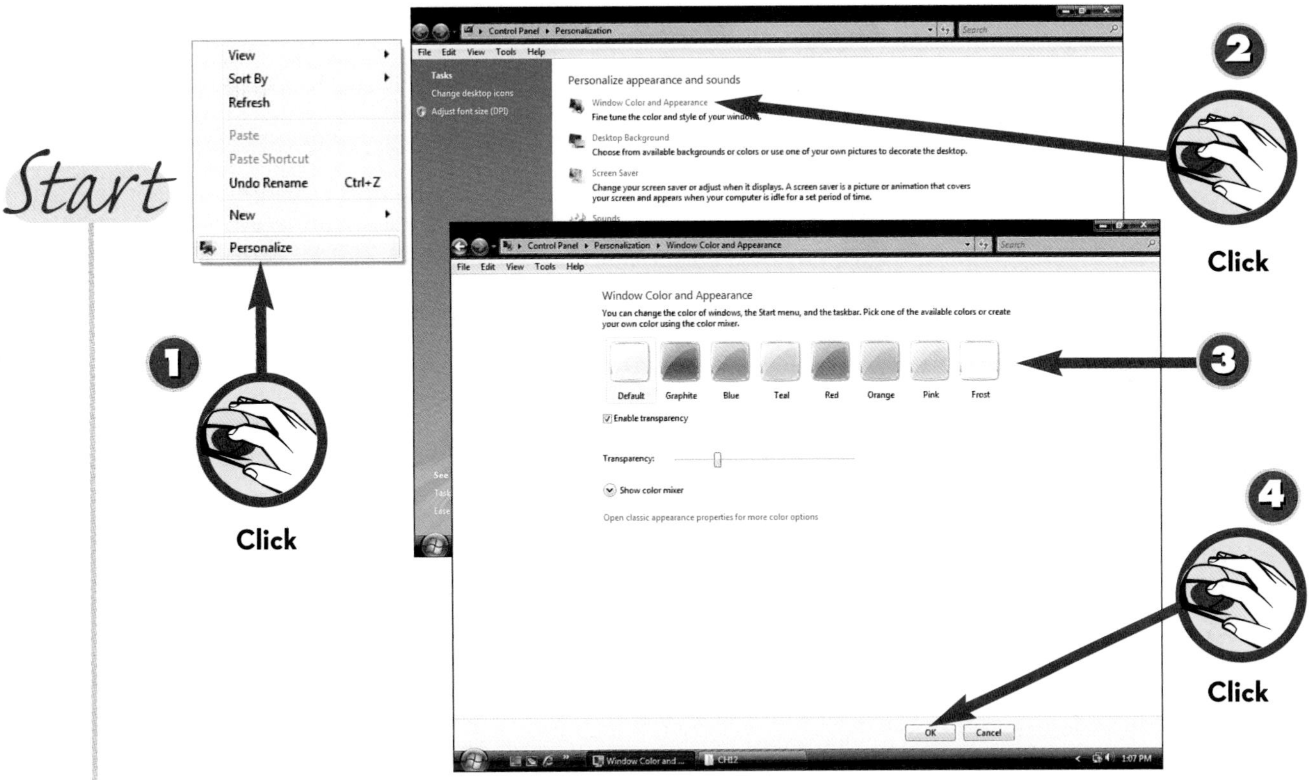

Start

Click

Click

Click

1. On your desktop, right-click an empty spot, and select **Personalize** from the pop-up menu that appears.
2. In the Personalization control panel, click **Window Color and Appearance**.
3. Select the color for windows, the Start menu, and the taskbar.
4. Click **OK** to apply the color theme.

End

TIP

Adjust Transparency

You can adjust the level of transparency by dragging the **Transparency** slider bar. Also, if you want to turn off the transparency effects, uncheck **Enable transparency**.

TIP

Select Own Unique Color

You can also select your own unique color by starting with one of the colors (the closest to the color you want). Then click the **Show color mixer** drop-down arrow. Use the slider bars to adjust the hue, saturation, and brightness of the color and then click **OK**.

APPLYING A BACKGROUND COLOR TO THE DESKTOP

You can personalize your desktop in Windows by applying a background color. You might choose a different color to make desktop items stand out, or you might choose a different color just because you like it.

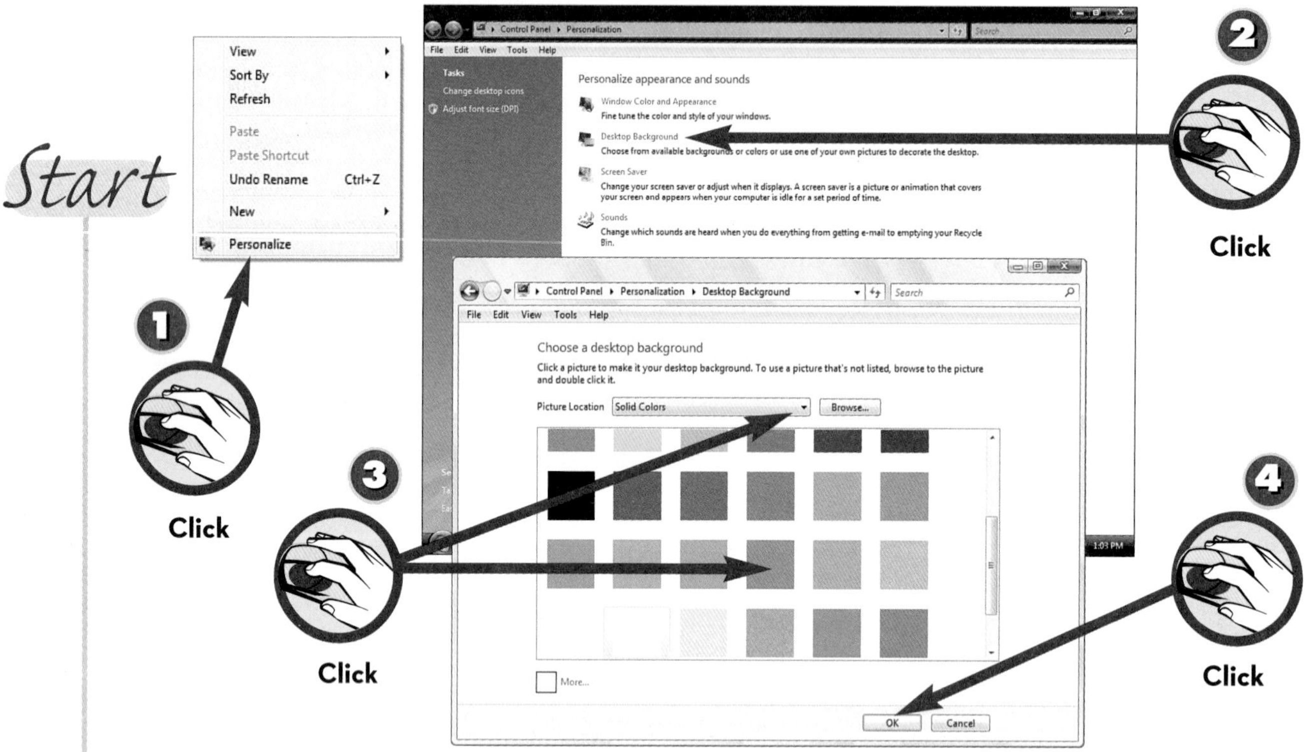

Start

Click

Click

Click

Click

1. On your desktop, right-click an empty spot, and select **Personalize** from the pop-up menu that appears.
2. In the Personalization control panel, click **Desktop Background**.
3. To select a solid color, make sure **Solid Colors** is chosen in the drop-down list, and then click a color in the palette. Be sure you can see desktop icons with the color you select.
4. Click **OK**.

End

NOTE

Background and Other Changes and Themes

If you make a change to the background color or other display options, it overrides any theme choices you have made. The theme will be listed as Modified on the theme tab. You can choose to save it. See the tip for the task "Selecting a Desktop Theme" for more information.

NOTE

Displaying an Image

See the next task, "Applying a Background Image to the Desktop," for other options available from this control panel, including textures, pictures, light auras, and more.

APPLYING A BACKGROUND IMAGE TO THE DESKTOP

You can personalize your desktop in Windows by applying a background image. Windows offers many colorful image options, including pictures, paintings, and textures.

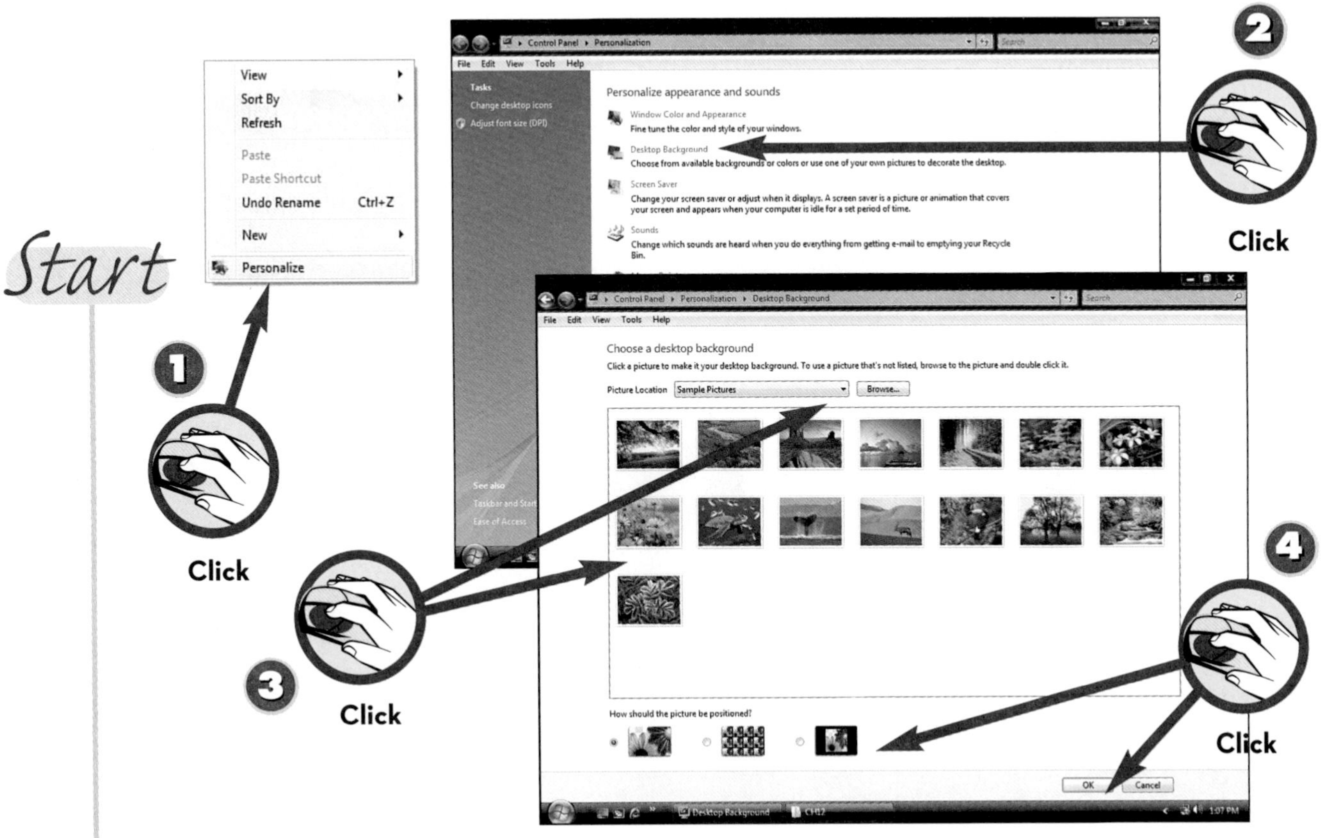

Start

Click

Click

Click

Click

1. On your desktop, right-click an empty spot, and select **Personalize** from the pop-up menu that appears.
2. In the Personalization control panel, click **Desktop Background**.
3. Display the drop-down list and select the item you want to use as your background. You can select from Windows wallpapers, pictures, sample pictures, or public pictures.
4. Select the image you want, and then click **OK**.

End

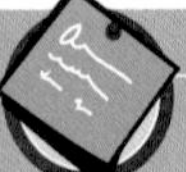

NOTE

Options Vary

Depending on what type of background you select, you'll see different options. You can select the one that suits your needs or likes. You can also experiment to see how each choice looks.

TIP

Display Your Own Photo

If you'd rather display one of your own digital photos, select **Pictures** from the drop-down list of background options, and then click the **Browse** button. Navigate to the folder that contains the image, select it, and click **Open**. Click the picture in the preview list, and click **OK**.

CHOOSING A SCREEN SAVER

In the past, screen savers helped prevent your monitor's screen from burn-in, in which a "ghost" of the Windows screen was still visible, even after you turned off your monitor. Screen savers helped protect monitors from burn-in by displaying a moving image whenever the computer was on but inactive. Although modern monitors do not suffer from burn-in, many people still use screen savers for fun.

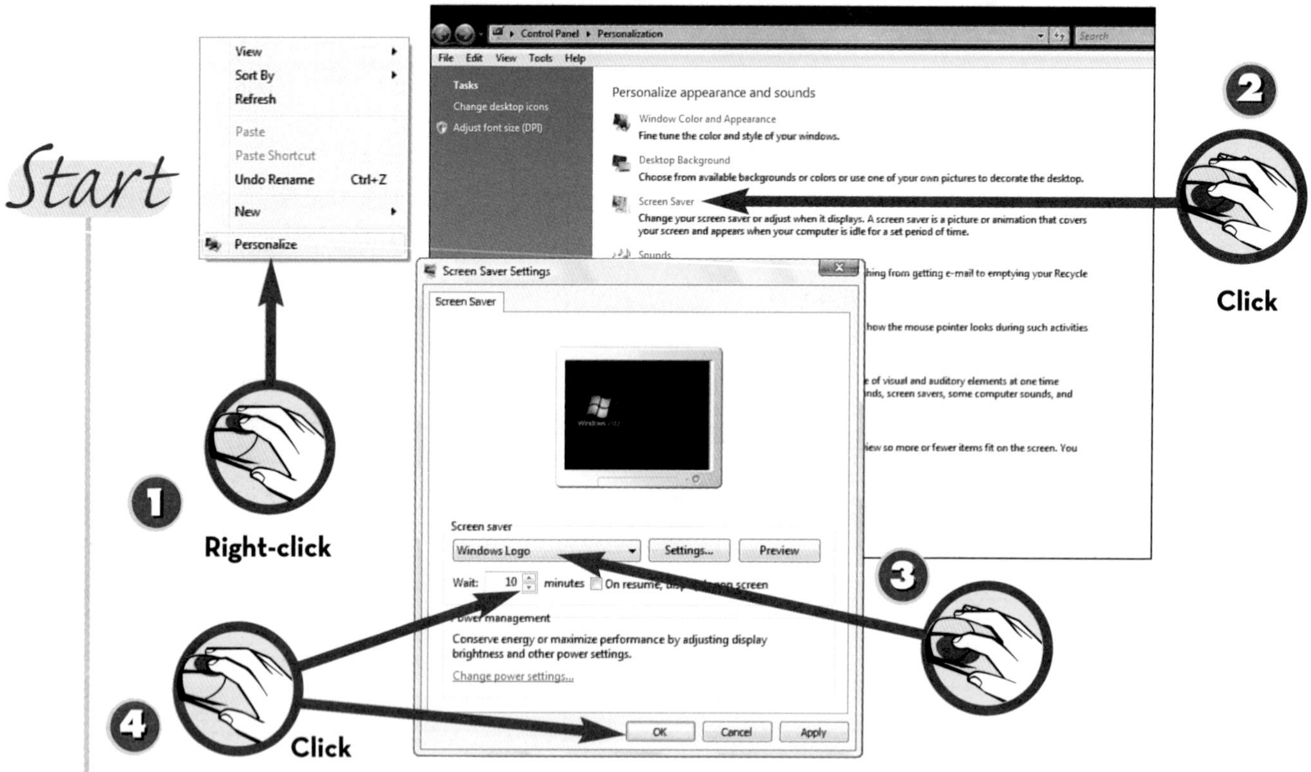

Start

Right-click

Click

Click

1. Right-click an empty spot on your desktop, and select **Personalize** from the pop-up menu that appears.
2. In the Personalization control panel, click **Screen Saver**.
3. Display the **Screen saver** drop-down list, and select the screen saver you want to use.
4. In the **Wait** box, click the up or down arrow button to choose the number of minutes of idle time that you want Windows to wait before it starts the screen saver. Click the **OK** button.

End

TIP

Preview Screen Saver

To see what the screen saver will look like when it is displayed on the full screen, click the **Preview** button. Click the mouse button or press the Spacebar to return to the Screen Saver settings dialog box.

TIP

Returning to the Regular Screen

When the screen saver is displayed, move the mouse or press the Spacebar to return to the normal view.

SETTING RESOLUTION AND COLOR QUALITY

Many monitors enable you to select certain options about how they operate, such as the number of colors they display or their resolution. In most cases, changing these options is not necessary. However, if you get a new monitor, want to update your monitor driver, or want to change how the monitor looks, you might need to change its display properties.

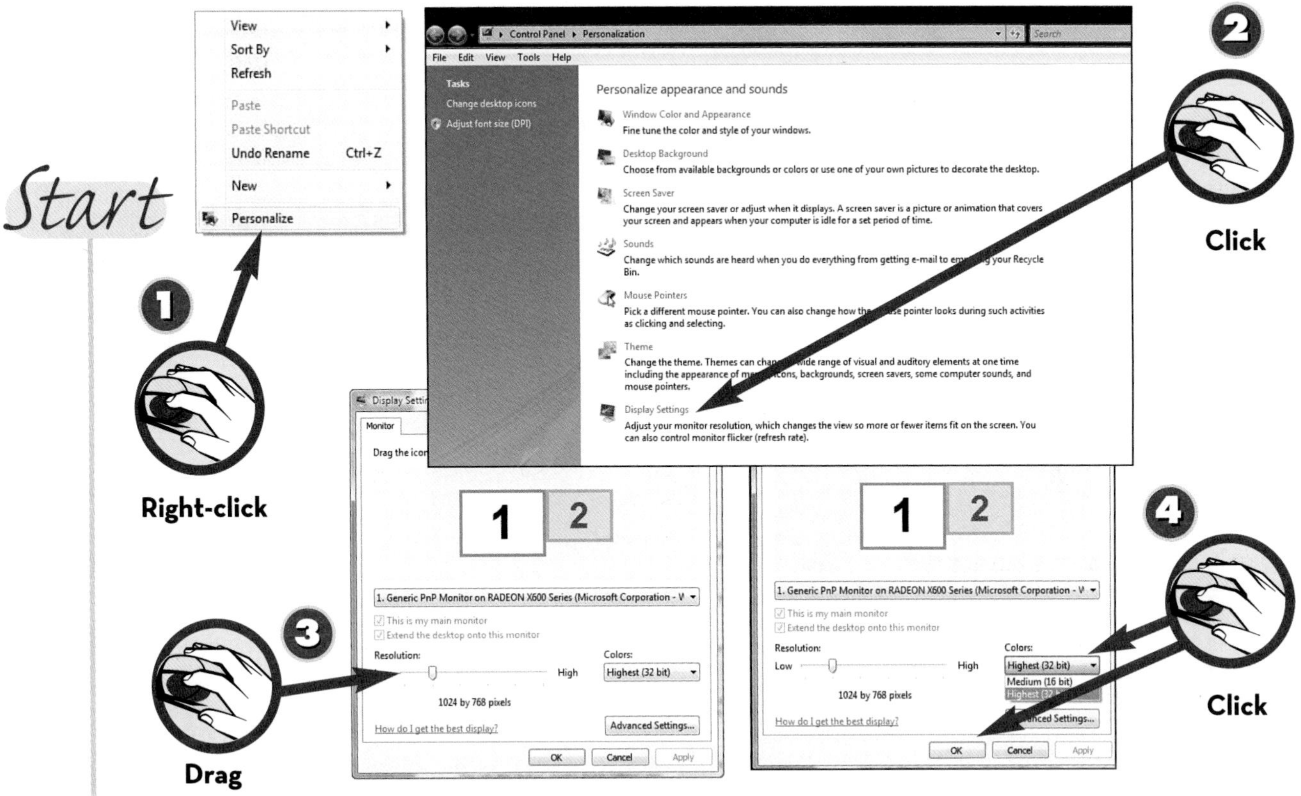

Start

Right-click

Click

Drag

Click

1. On your desktop, right-click an empty spot, and select **Personalize** from the pop-up menu that appears.
2. In the Personalization control panel, click **Display Settings**.
3. To change the size of the images onscreen, drag the resolution slider from low to high.
4. To change the number of colors used for the display, click the **Colors** drop-down list and choose the number you want. Click **OK**.

End

TIP

Resolution Defined

Resolution measures the number of pixels or picture elements displayed on the computer monitor. An example of a common resolution is 1024×768. The higher the number, the smaller the image is onscreen.

TIP

Additional Information and Settings

For additional information about your monitor, as well as more settings options, click the **Advanced Settings** button. This opens a dialog box containing information about your display adapter and your monitor, as well as settings for font size, compatibility, and more.

CHANGING HOW THE MOUSE WORKS

There are many ways you can adjust your mouse to make it work the way you want. If you are left-handed, you can switch the left-click mouse buttons. If you have trouble double-clicking, you can adjust the double-click speed. If you're not crazy about the way your mouse pointer looks onscreen, you can change it. In addition, you can slow your pointer speed to make it easier to see your mouse pointer when you move it onscreen.

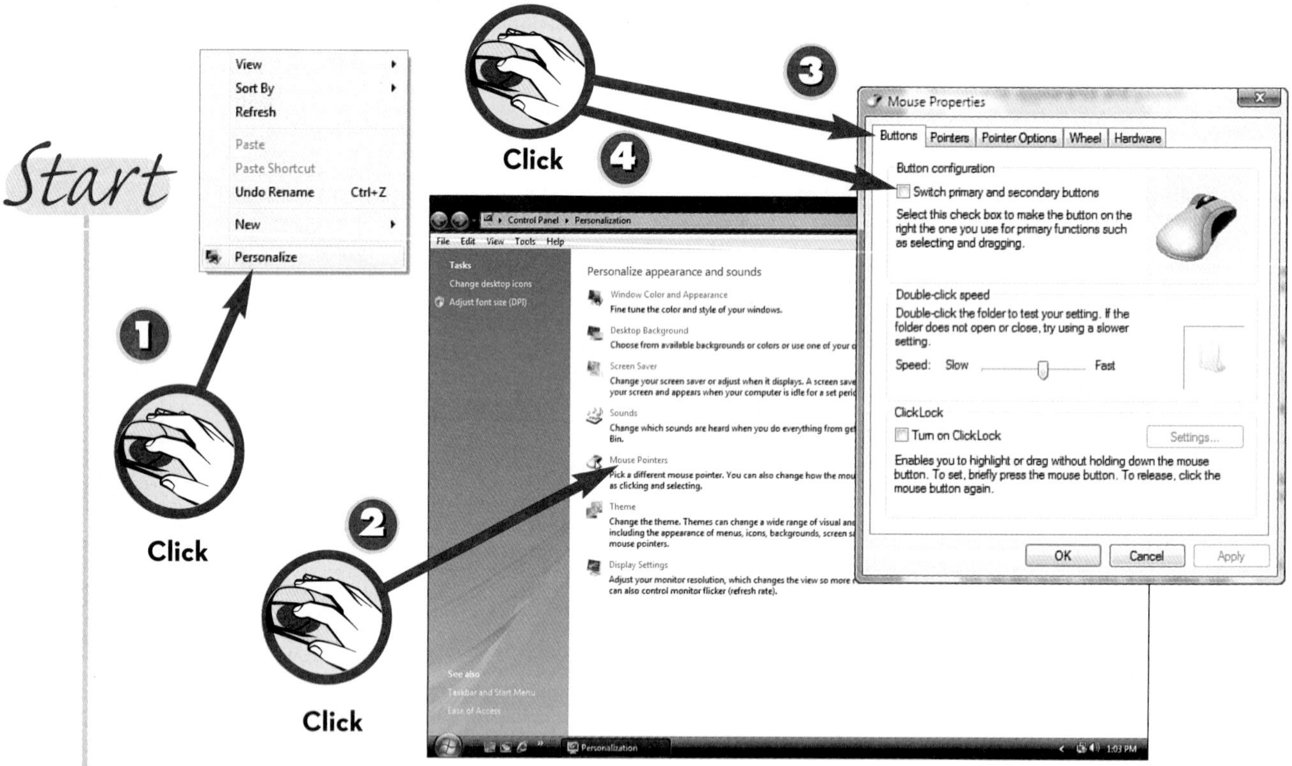

Start

Click

Click

Click

1. On your desktop, right-click an empty spot, and select **Personalize** from the pop-up menu that appears.
2. In the Personalization control panel, click **Mouse Pointers**.
3. Click the **Buttons** tab.
4. To switch from a right-handed mouse to a left-handed mouse, click **Switch primary and secondary buttons**.

Continued

NOTE

Other Options

If you have a mouse with a scroll wheel, you can use the Wheel tab to make adjustments. You can also view Hardware information about your mouse by clicking the Hardware tab.

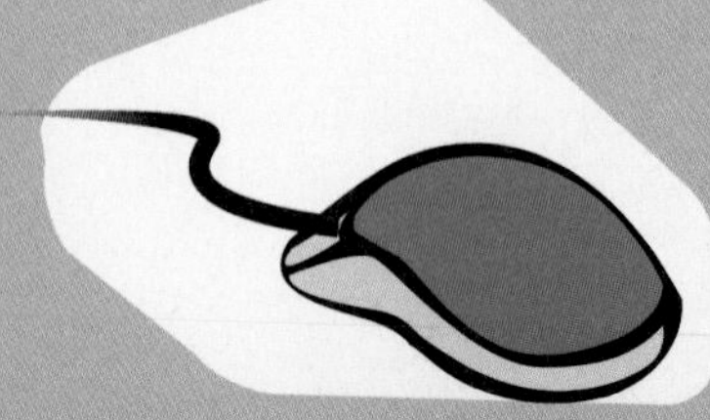

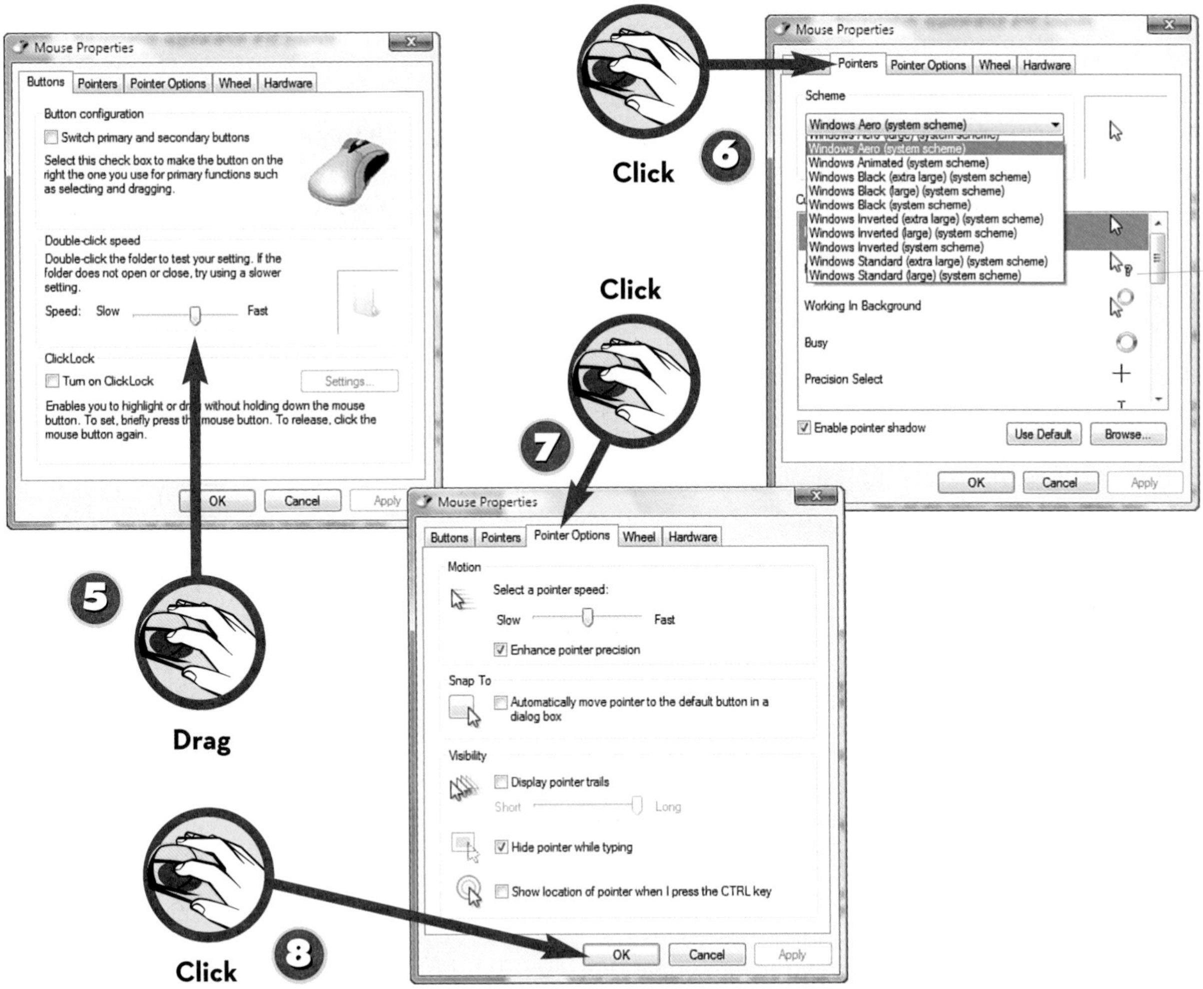

5 Drag the **Double-click speed** slider to make the double-click speed faster or slower, depending on your needs.

6 Click the **Pointers** tab. Then display the **Scheme** drop-down list and select a mouse pointer scheme.

7 On the **Pointer Options** tab, use the options to set a pointer speed (drag to make it faster or slower), to have Windows automatically snap the pointer to the default button, and to make visibility changes.

8 Click **OK** when you are done making changes.

End

TIP

Set Individual Pointers

You can select which pointer to use for each action. Simply select the action you want to change, click the **Browse** button, select the pointer you want to use, and click **Open**. Do this for each action you want to change, and then click the **OK** button.

TIP

Display Pointer Trail

To show a pointer trail, in the **Pointer Options** tab, check the **Display pointer trails** check box, and then select the length of the trail by dragging the Pointer trail slider between Short and Long.

CHANGING THE SOUND SCHEME

When you perform certain actions in Windows Vista, you might hear a sound. For example, you hear a sound when Windows Vista is started. You might also hear a sound when an alert box is displayed. You can stick with the default sounds, or you can select a different sound to use for each key Windows event.

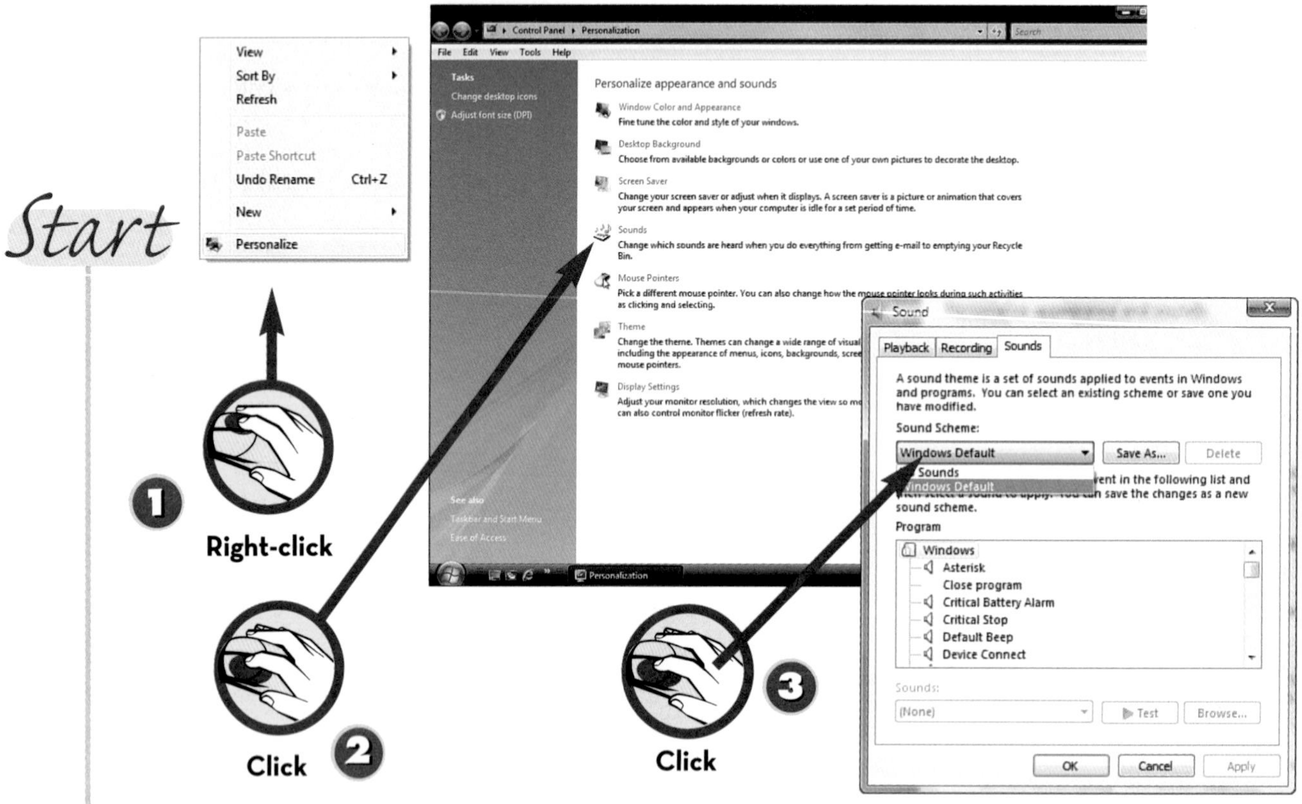

Start

1 Right-click

2 Click

3 Click

1. On your desktop, right-click an empty spot, and select **Personalize** from the pop-up menu that appears.
2. In the Personalization control panel, click **Sounds**.
3. To select a sound scheme, display the **Sound Scheme** drop-down list and select a scheme or set of sounds.

Continued

TIP

Build a Scheme

You can also build your own scheme of personalized sounds. Set each event sound, and then click **Save As** to save the new scheme.

NOTE

No Sound?

If you don't want a sound played for an event, select that event and then choose **(None)** from the **Sounds** list.

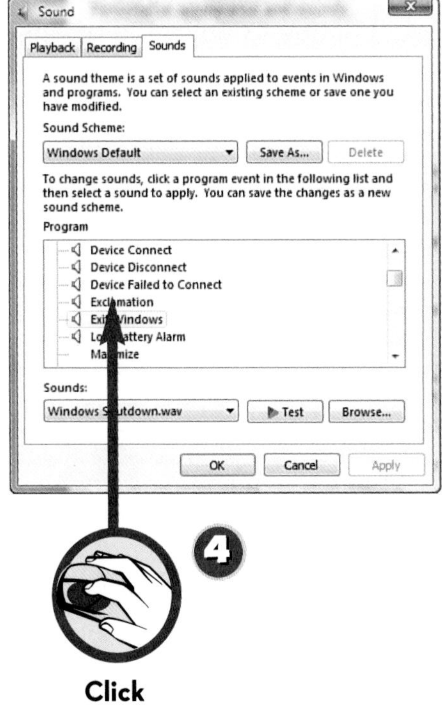

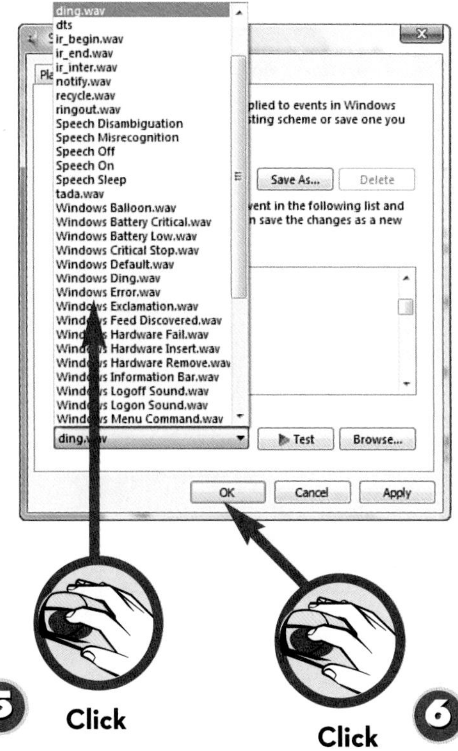

4 To change an individual sound, in the **Program** events list, click the sound event you want to change.

5 Display the **Sounds** drop-down list to select the sound that you want to assign to that event.

6 Click **OK**.

End

TIP

Preview the Selected Sound

To hear a preview of the sound, click the **Play** button to the right of the **Sounds** drop-down list.

TIP

Browse for Sounds

If the sound you want to use is not listed in the **Sounds** list, click the **Browse** button. A standard Browse dialog box opens, enabling you to locate the sound file you want to use.

CHANGING THE SYSTEM DATE AND TIME

You can place the pointer over the time in the taskbar to display the current date. If your system clock is wrong, you should correct it because Windows stamps the time and date on every file you save. You can make these changes using the Date and Time control panel.

Start

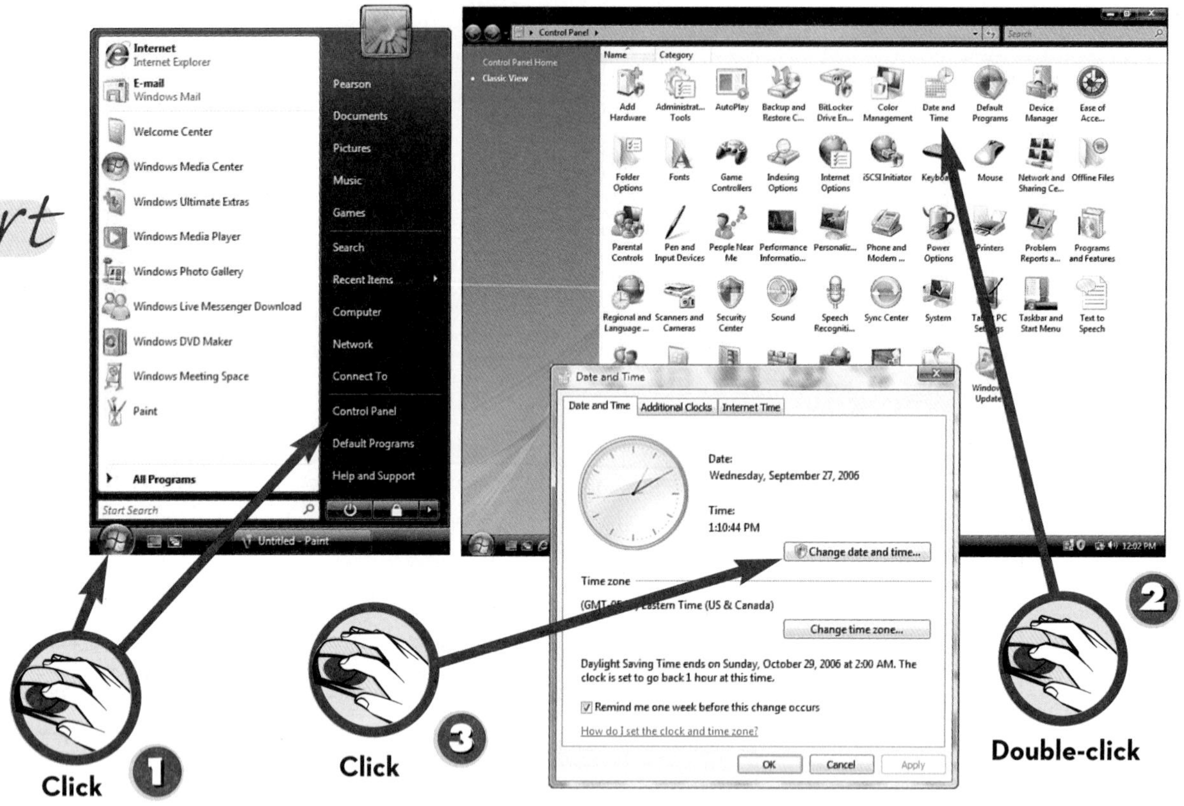

Click 1

Click 3

Double-click 2

1 Click **Start** and then **Control Panel**.

2 If needed, change to Classic View by clicking the link in the left pane. Then double-click the **Date and Time** icon in the Control Panel window.

3 Click **Change date and time**. If prompted, click **Continue** to authorize this change.

Continued

TIP

Shortcut

Display the Date and Time dialog box by double-clicking the time in the right corner of the taskbar.

NOTE

Date Wrong?

If the date is wrong, it could indicate that you have a dead battery. You must replace your computer's internal battery. (Check your system manual.) You may also have a virus; run your anti-virus program as well.

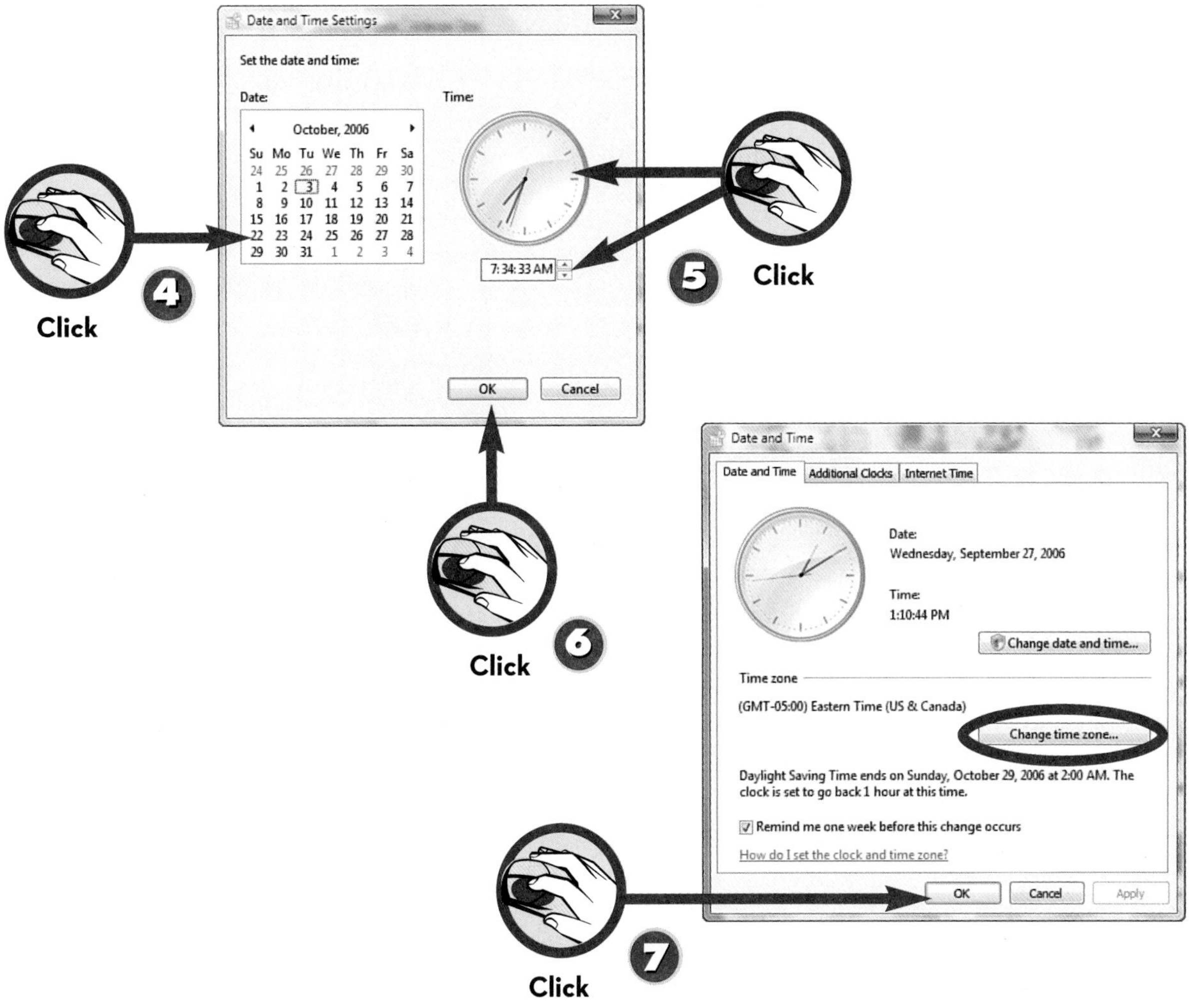

4. Click the correct date in the calendar.
5. Enter the correct time. You can click the correct time using the clock or use the time spin boxes to enter the correct time.
6. Click **OK**.
7. Click **OK** again to close the Date and Time dialog box.

End

TIP

Change Time Zone

To change the time zone, click the **Change time zone** button, and then select the appropriate time zone.

TIP

Internet Time

If you want your computer to automatically synchronize with a time clock on the Internet, click the **Internet Time** tab and click the **Change Settings** button to make changes. To sync your clock, for instance, check **Synchronize with an Internet time server**.

USING ACCESSIBILITY OPTIONS

Windows Vista offers programs that make it easier for those with disabilities to use the operating system. Magnifier enlarges the contents of your screen, Narrator reads the contents of your screen aloud, and On-Screen keyboard enables users who have limited mobility to type onscreen using a pointing device. You can manage all three of these programs using the Ease of Access Center.

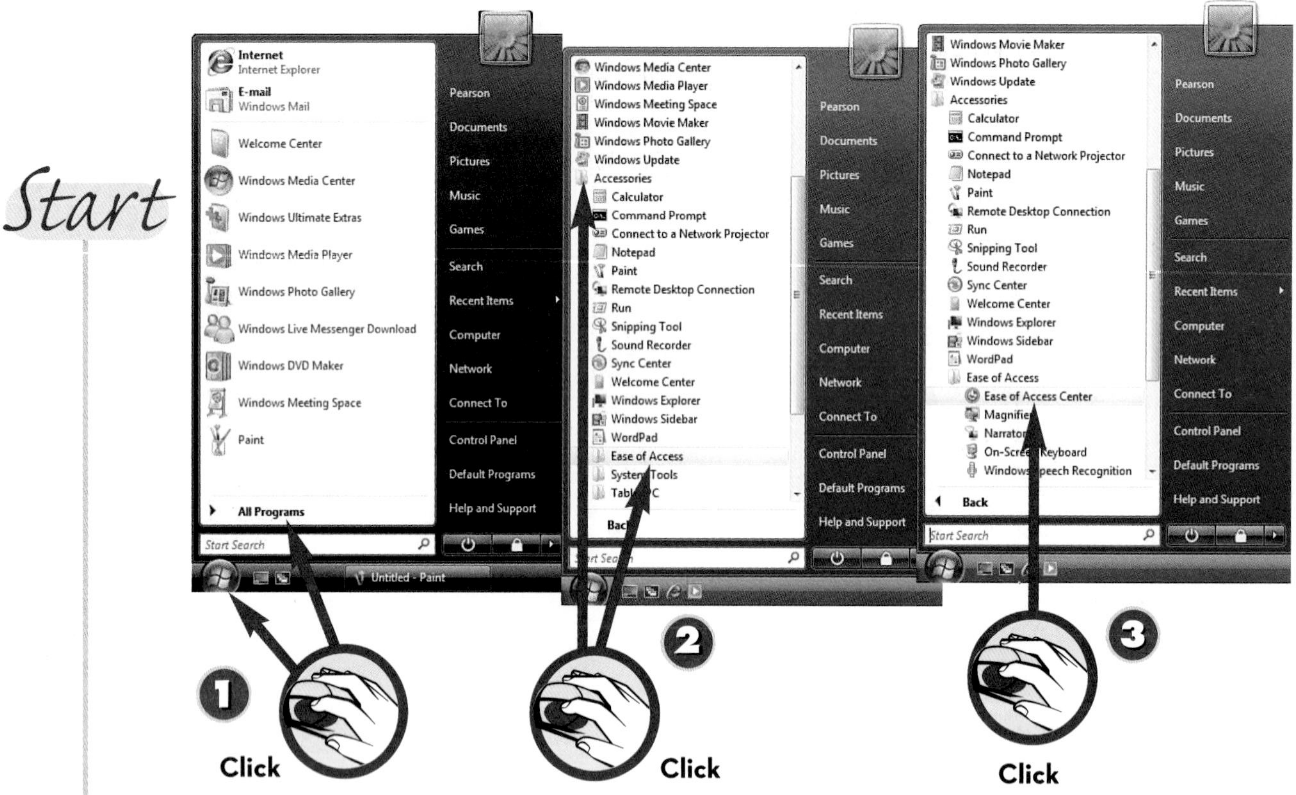

Start

Click

Click

Click

1. Click **Start** and then **All Programs**.
2. Click the **Accessories** folder and then the **Ease of Access** folder.
3. Click **Ease of Access Center**.

Continued

TIP

Not Sure Which Option Is Best for You?

To help you see what options are available and which might be of benefit to you, Windows includes a link **Get recommendations to make your computer easier to use**. Click this link and then answer the questions you are asked; Windows will use your answers to recommend what features and settings might be of use to you.

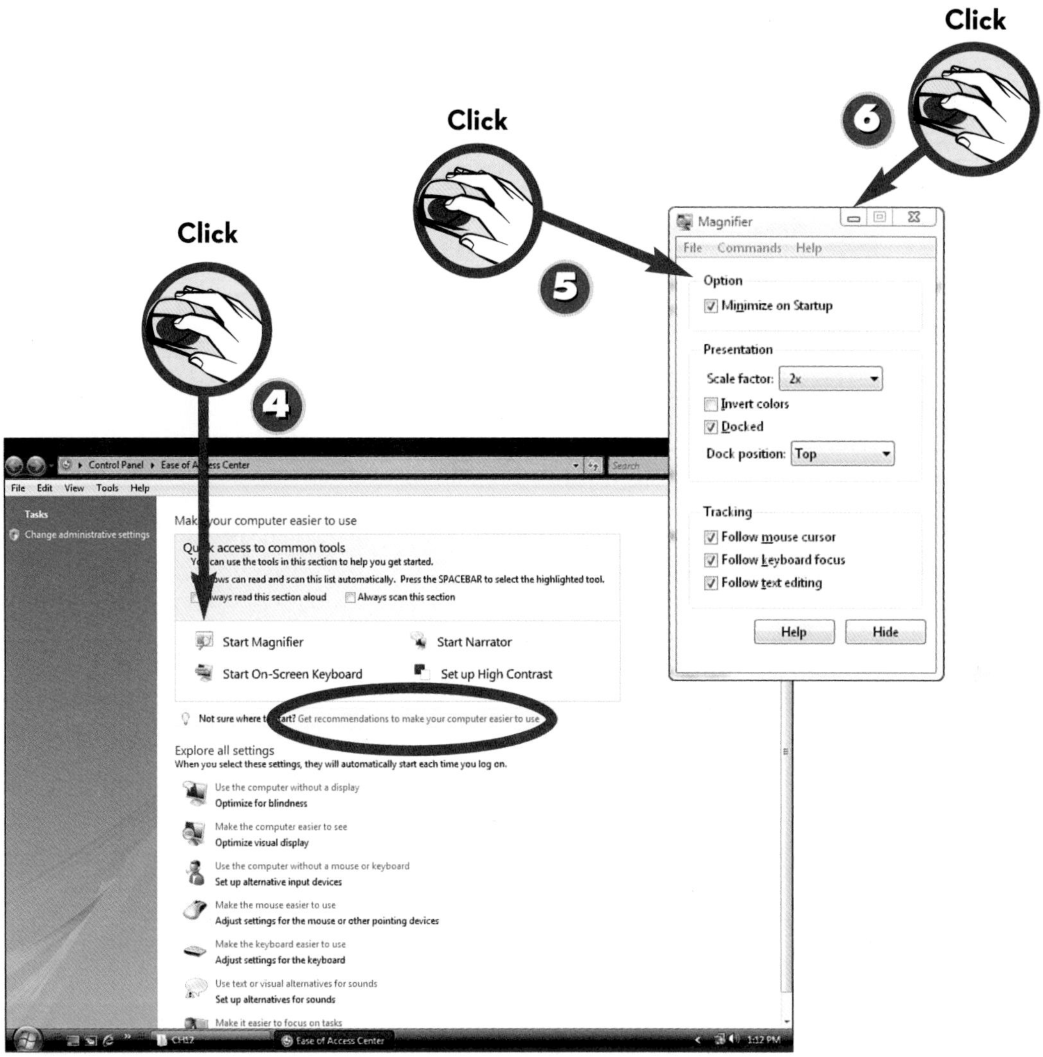

Click

Click

Click

4 You see the various options you can turn on. For instance, to turn on Magnifier, click **Start Magnifier**.

5 Select the various options for Magnifier, such as how it tracks the cursor location, how large it is (scale factor), and whether it is minimized on startup.

6 Click the **Minimize** button to keep the magnifier program running but close the dialog box.

Continued

TIP

Options Read Aloud

By default, Windows reads aloud and moves from option to option. To turn off this feature, uncheck **Always read this section aloud**. This task shows how to access features without narration (and with this option unchecked).

CAUTION

Exit Accessibility Programs

Clicking the **Exit** button on these ease of access programs actually closes the programs. To keep the program open but remove the dialog box from view, click the **Minimize** button in the top-right corner of the dialog box.

Start

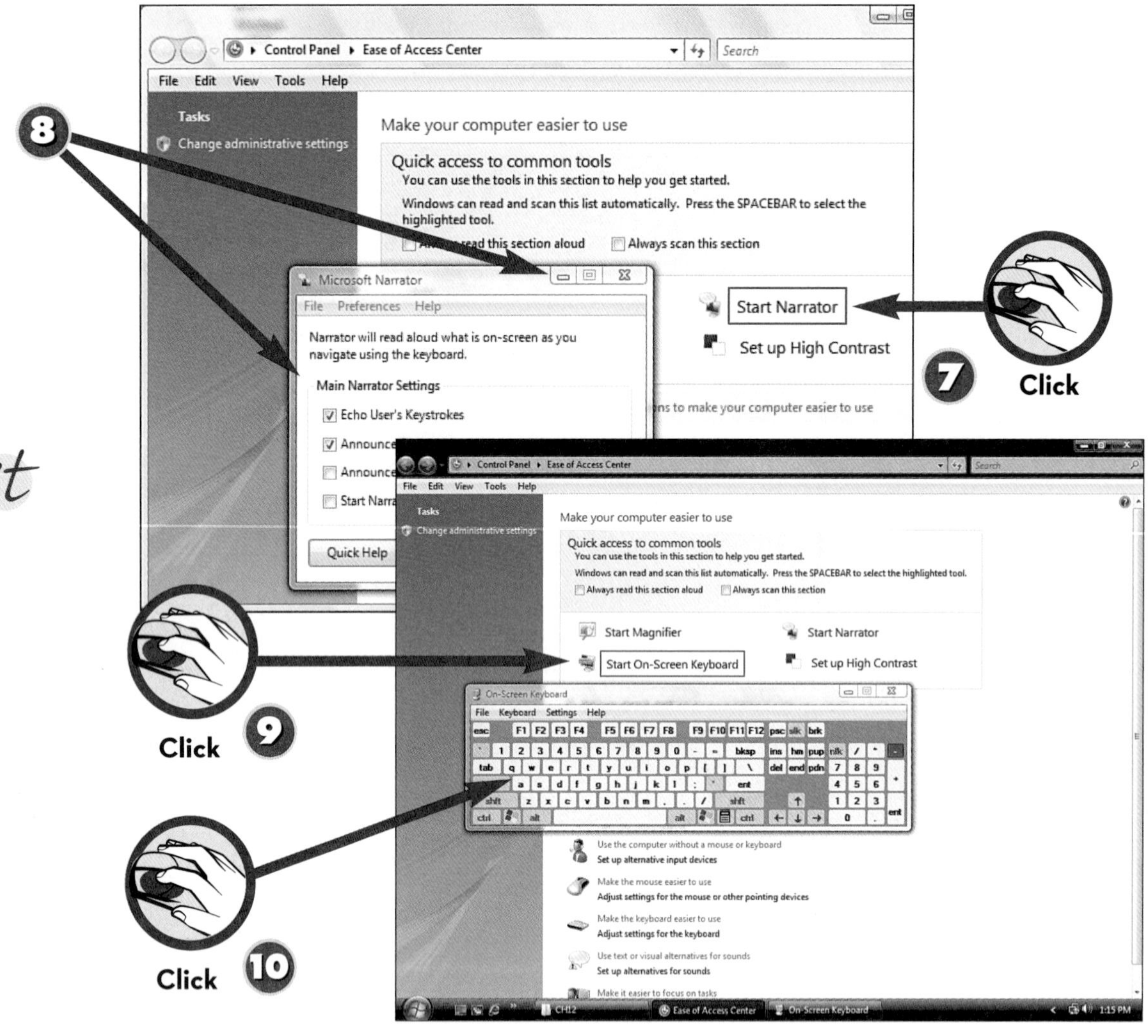

7 To turn on Narrator, click **Start Narrator**.

8 In the dialog box that appears, select the options for how Narrator works. For instance, you can have Narrator announce your keystrokes or announce system messages. Make your choices and then click the **Minimize** button.

9 To turn on the On-Screen Keyboard, click **Start On-Screen Keyboard**.

10 The keyboard appears. You can use it to type characters using the mouse.

Continued

TIP

Select a Narrator Voice

You can select a voice you want to use for Narrator, as well as the speed, volume, and pitch of that voice. To do so, click **Preferences** and then **Voice Settings** or click the **Voice Settings** button. Make your selections and click **OK**.

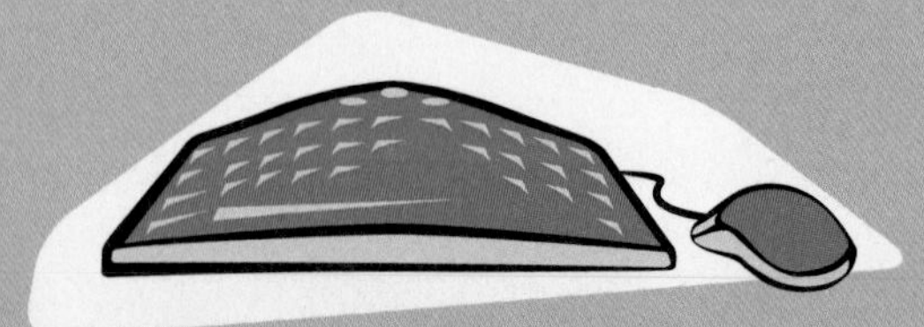

11 Click

12 Click

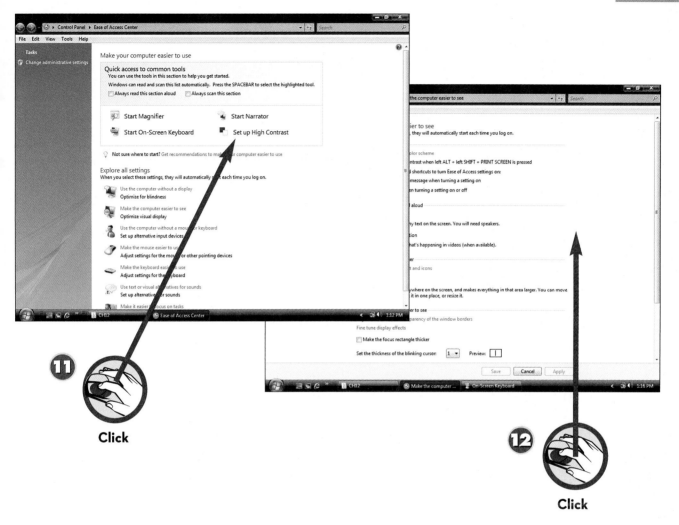

11 To turn on High Contrast, click **Set up High Contrast**.

12 Check to turn on a high contrast color scheme. Click **Save**.

End

NOTE

Type with On-Screen Keyboard

On-Screen Keyboard has three typing modes. In clicking mode, you click the onscreen keys with your mouse pointer to type text. In scanning mode, On-Screen Keyboard scans the keyboard, highlighting letters; you press a hotkey or use a switch-input device whenever On-Screen Keyboard highlights the character you want to type. In hovering mode, you use a mouse or joystick to hover the pointer over a key; then you type the selected character.

part 13

SETTING UP PROGRAMS

Most of the time you spend using your computer will be spent using some type of program. The first step is installing the program. Most programs today have an AutoPlay option and an automated installation routine that starts the installation automatically. You simply follow the onscreen prompts to install the program. This Part covers installing (and uninstalling programs).

To make it as easy as possible, Windows Vista enables you to set up several ways to start programs. You can create a shortcut to a program and place the shortcut on your desktop to make it more accessible. Rather than use the Start menu to start the program, you can then simply double-click the shortcut icon.

In addition to installing and providing other access to programs, you can make other customization changes. For instance, you can rearrange the programs on the Start menu so that they are more suited to how you work. Just keep in mind that there is no right or wrong way to set up your programs; you can select the style and organization that best suit you.

PROGRAMS AND FEATURES CONTROL PANEL

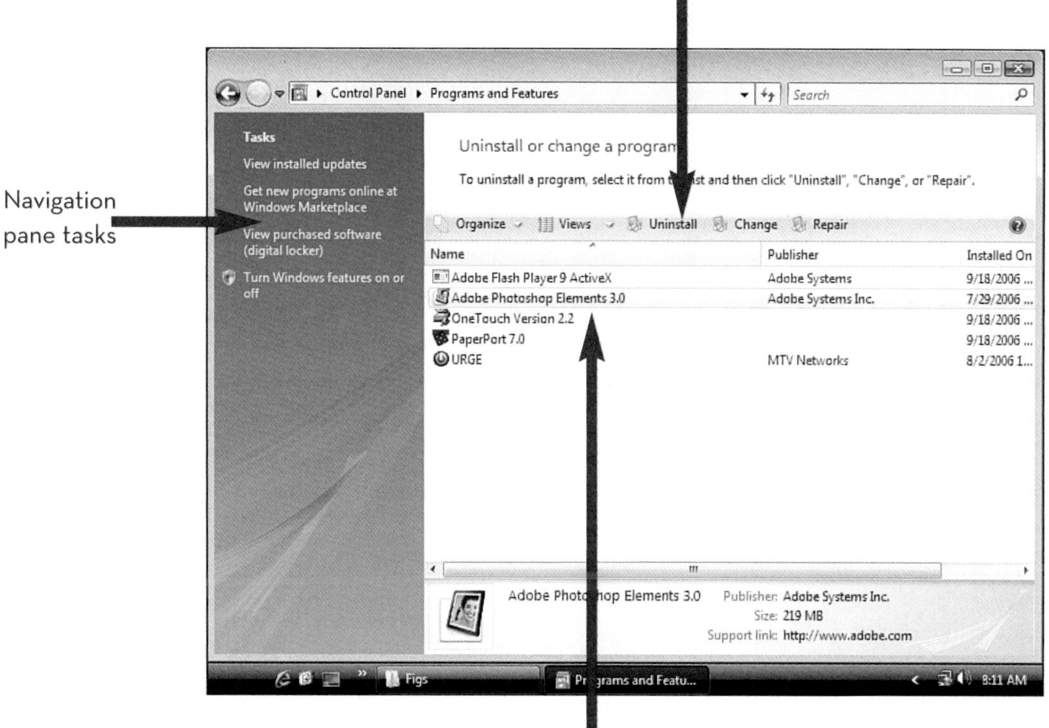

INSTALLING A NEW PROGRAM

Your computer came with some programs, such as Windows, already installed. When you purchase a new program, you must install it on your computer so that you can use it. You will either have a CD to install from, or if you purchase the program online, you will download a file to install from. If you install from CD, there is a feature in Vista called AutoPlay that will help you get the process started. Insert the CD and follow the steps in this task.

Start

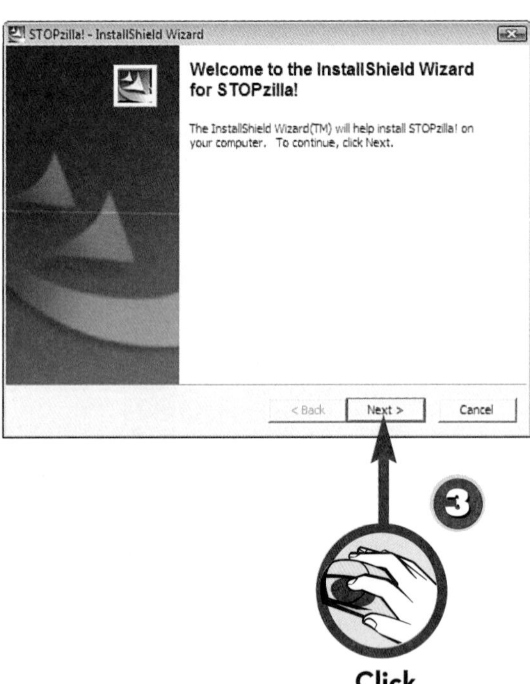

1 If AutoPlay is set up, after you insert the program installation CD, you see a dialog box with an option for installing the program. Click that option (here, **Run Setup.exe**.)

2 If prompted to confirm the installation, click **Allow** (not shown).

3 You are prompted with instructions on how to install the program. Follow the steps for your specific program and click **Next** as you proceed through the installation screens until you complete the installation.

End

NOTE

Add or Remove Programs

In previous versions of Windows, an Add or Remove Program Control Panel icon provided the steps for installing a program if it did not automatically install. Windows Vista does not include this; if the method described here does not work, check the documentation that came with your program and follow those instructions.

TIP

Installing from the Internet

You can often purchase and then download program files from the Internet. If you use this method for adding programs, follow the specific instructions given by that vendor for purchasing, downloading, and installing.

CREATING A PROGRAM SHORTCUT ICON

You can create shortcuts and place them on the desktop to provide quick access to programs. You can then double-click a shortcut to quickly start that program or open that file—without having to open menus and folders.

Start

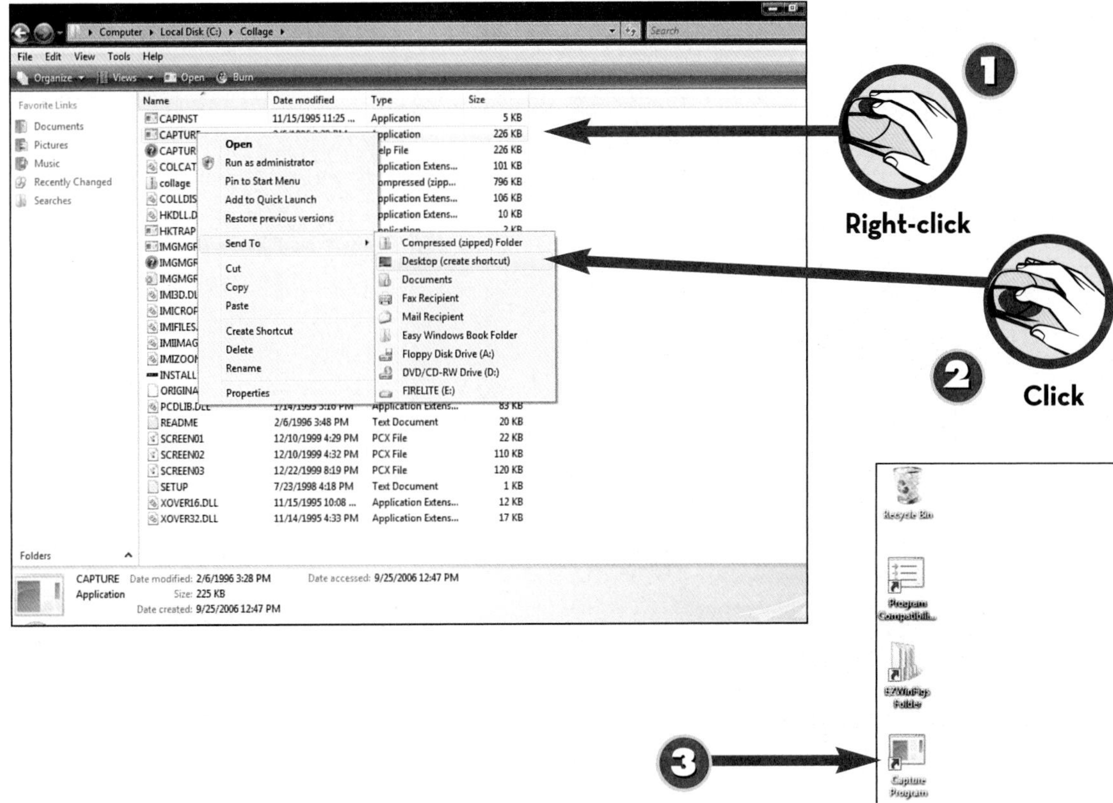

1. After you've located the program file for which you want to create a shortcut icon, right-click it.
2. In the menu that opens, choose **Send To**, and then select **Desktop (create shortcut)**.
3. Windows adds the shortcut to your desktop.

End

NOTE

Shortcuts to Files, Folders, or a Printer

In addition to creating shortcuts to programs, you can create them to files or folders or even to your printer.

TIP

Rename the Shortcut Icon

Windows Vista adds "Shortcut" to the name of the program icon when you create a shortcut. If you want to change the name, right-click it, click **Rename**, and type a new name. Then press **Enter**.

UNINSTALLING APPLICATIONS

When you want to get rid of a program and its files entirely, you must uninstall it. This removes the program and all its related files and folders from your hard drive. (You should move any data files from your program folders if, for example, you plan to use them in another program.) You should remove any programs you no longer use to free up disk space and make room for files and possibly other new programs.

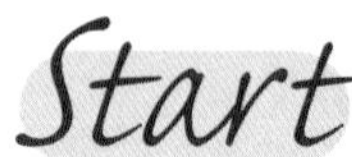

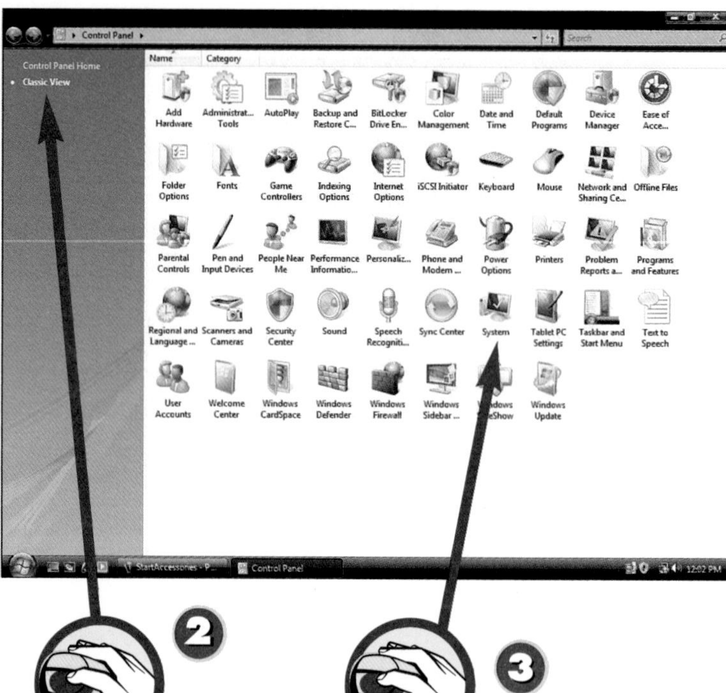

1. Click **Start** and then **Control Panel**.
2. If the Control Panel view is not set to Classic View, switch to it by clicking **Classic View** in the Navigation pane.
3. Double-click the Programs and Features icon. You see a list of currently installed programs.

Continued

CAUTION

The steps for uninstalling the program will vary from program to program. Simply follow the onscreen instructions.

NOTE

Windows Features

For information about installing or uninstalling certain Windows features, see Part 14, "Performance and Maintenance."

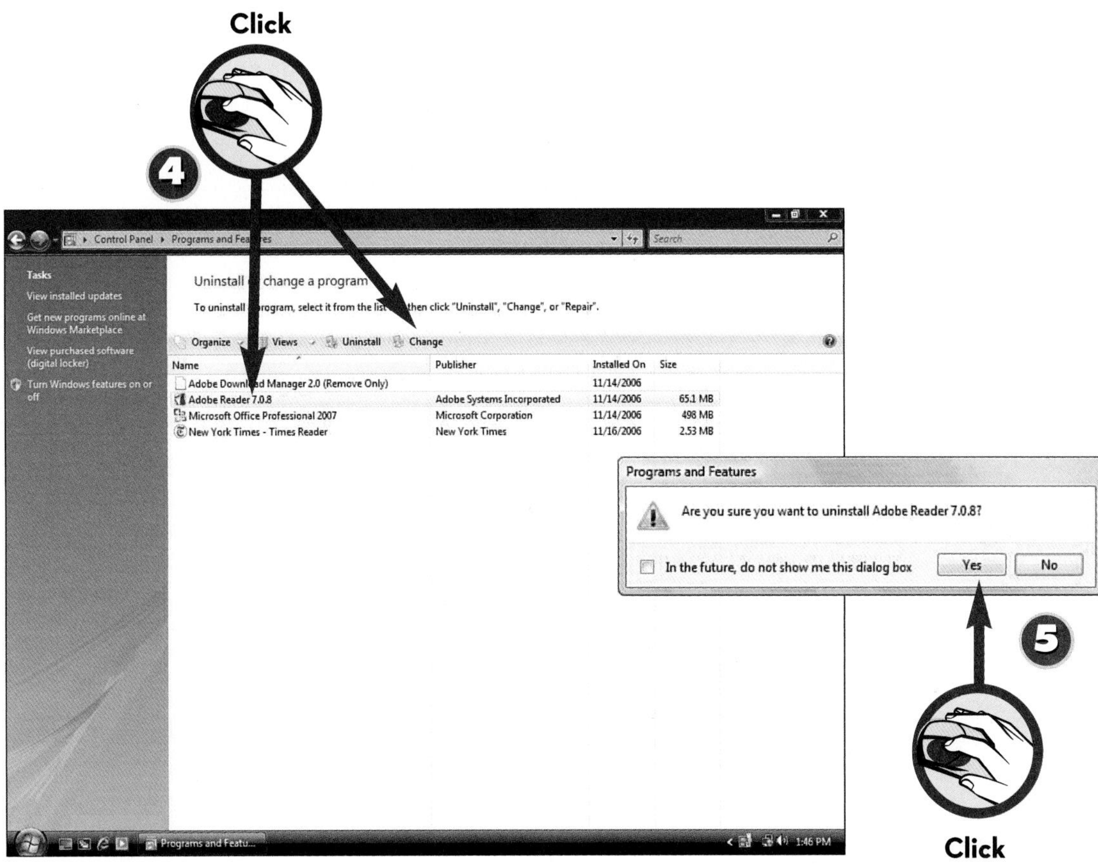

4 Click the program you want to remove and then click **Uninstall** or **Uninstall/Change** in the command bar. The command will vary depending on the program.

5 Some programs prompt you to confirm the uninstall. If prompted, click **Yes**. The program is removed.

End

TIP

Restart

You may be prompted to restart your computer to complete the process. If so, click **OK** to the restart immediately, or choose to restart your computer later.

NOTE

Uninstall Programs

You can purchase programs to keep track of what programs you have installed, where they are, and what changes they have made to your system such as Unstaller Plus or Advanced Uninstaller Pro.

DELETING A SHORTCUT ICON

At first, you may go a little crazy and add shortcut icons for all your programs, but then you'll quickly find that these clutter up your desktop. You should get rid of any shortcut icons you don't use.

Start

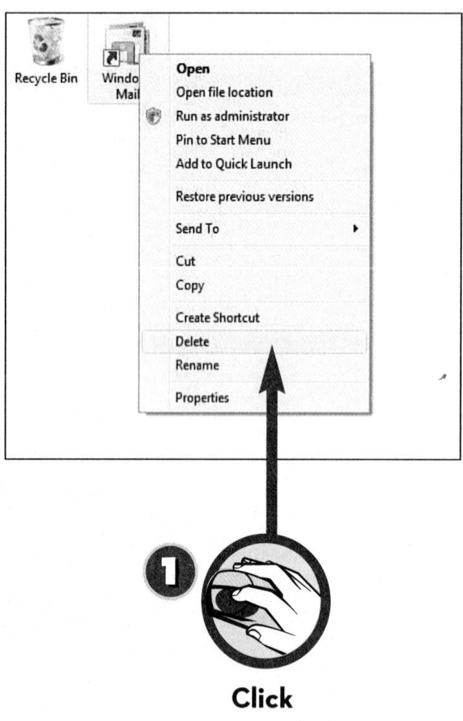

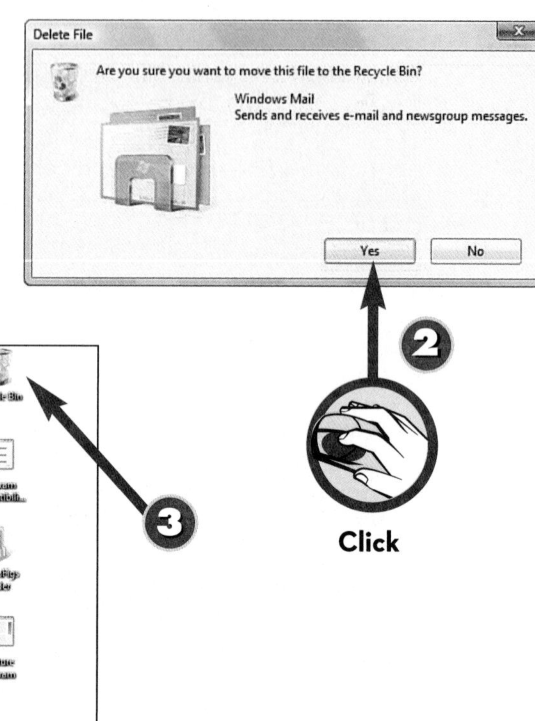

1. To delete a shortcut icon from your Desktop, right-click it, and choose **Delete** from the menu that appears.
2. In the Delete File dialog box, click **Yes** to delete the shortcut.
3. The shortcut is deleted from your desktop.

End

TIP

What Happens When You Delete?

Deleting a shortcut does not delete that program from your hard drive. To completely remove the program, you must uninstall it or delete the program and its related folders and files.

TIP

Change Your Mind?

You can restore items you've relegated to the Recycle Bin. To do so, double-click the **Recycle Bin** icon on the desktop. In the Recycle Bin window, right-click the item you want to restore, and choose **Restore**. The item returns to its original location.

PINNING A PROGRAM TO THE START MENU

At the top of the Start menu on the left side, Windows lists programs that you use often (such as your Internet and email programs). These programs are always displayed. You can choose to add other programs to this area so that they are always readily available. Doing so is calling "pinning" a program to the Start menu.

Start

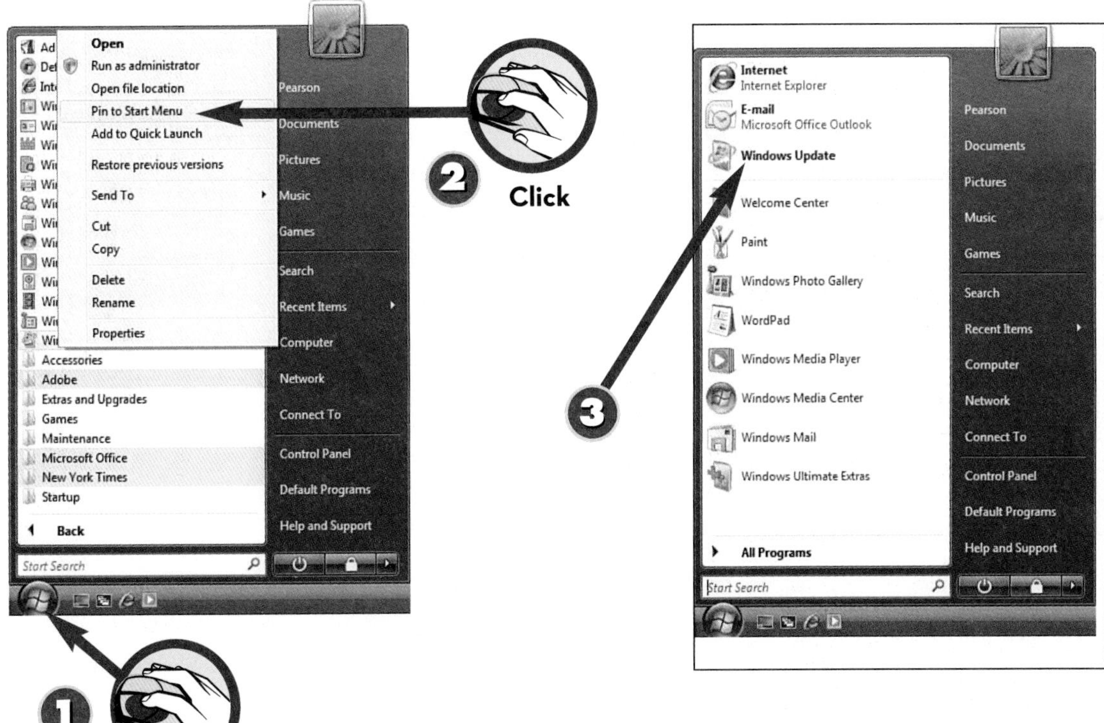

1. Click **Start**, **All Programs** to display the name of the program you want to pin to the menu.
2. Right-click the program icon, and choose **Pin to Start Menu**. Click outside the Start menu to close it.
3. Click **Start** to view the program; you can see it is now listed at the top-left pane.

End

NOTE

Unpin the Program

To unpin the program, right-click the program icon, and then click **Unpin from Start menu**.

CUSTOMIZING THE START MENU

You can customize the Start menu in several ways, such as selecting what items appear, choosing the size of the icons, and deciding whether items are listed as links or menus. You can also select how many recently used programs are listed on the Start menu.

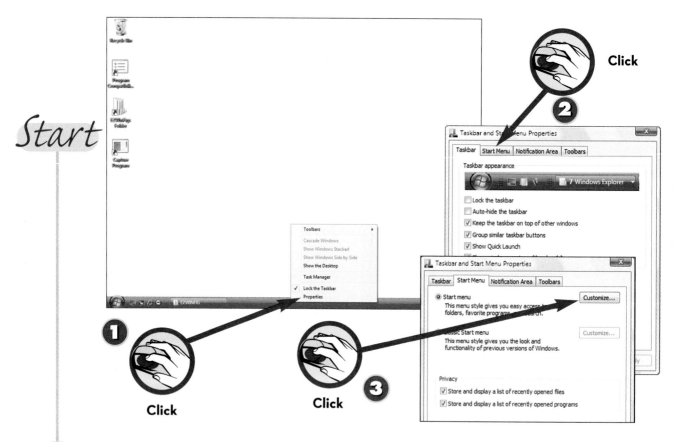

Start

Click

Click

Click

1. Right-click the taskbar and then click **Properties**.
2. Click the **Start Menu** tab.
3. Click the **Customize** button.

Continued

TIP

Display Documents

The Start menu lists recently opened programs. You can also choose to display recently opened documents. To do so, check the **Store and display a list of recently opened files** check box.

NOTE

Customize Classic Menu

The Classic Menu is a menu that looks like the Start menu from previous versions of Windows. You can elect to use this style of menu as well as customize it.

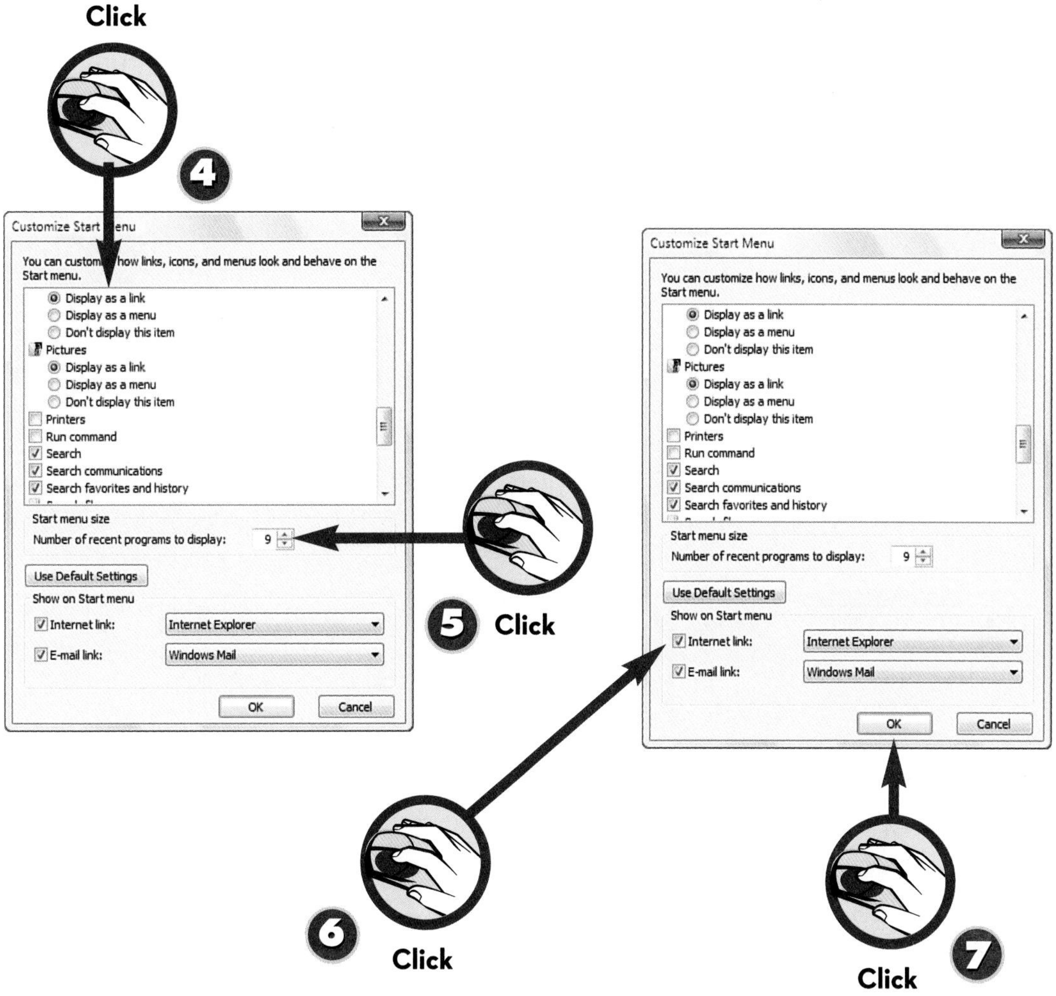

4. In the list of options, check and uncheck boxes to customize how the Start menu appears. For instance, you can check items that you want displayed, such as a Favorites menu or the Run command.
5. Use the spin arrows or type the number of recently used programs you want displayed on the Start menu.
6. Choose whether or not you want your Internet or email links to appear on the Start menu. You can also select which programs are used.
7. Click **OK**.

End

NOTE

Select Default Programs

For more information on selecting default programs, see the task "Selecting Default Programs" later in this Part.

TIP

Revert to Original Icons

To revert to the default Start menu options, click the **Use Default Settings** button.

CUSTOMIZING THE TASKBAR

In addition to customizing the Start menu, you can change options for the taskbar, such as what items appear on the bar. You can also move or resize it.

Start

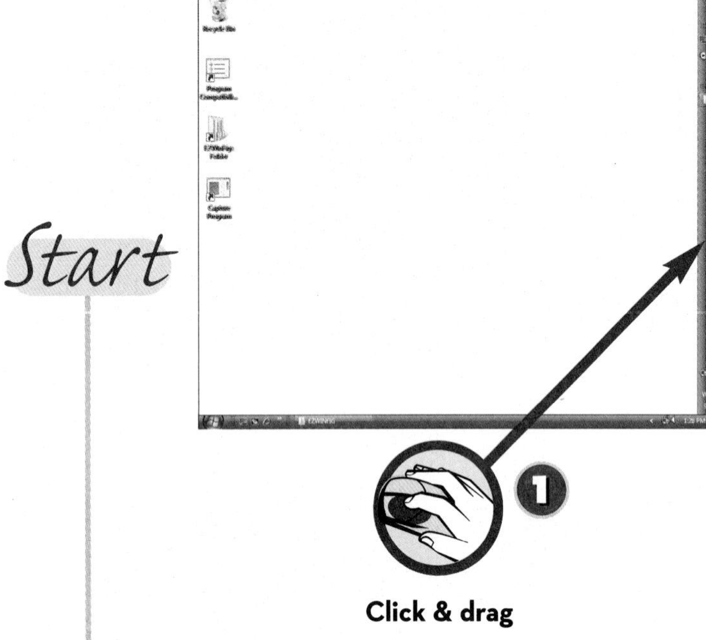

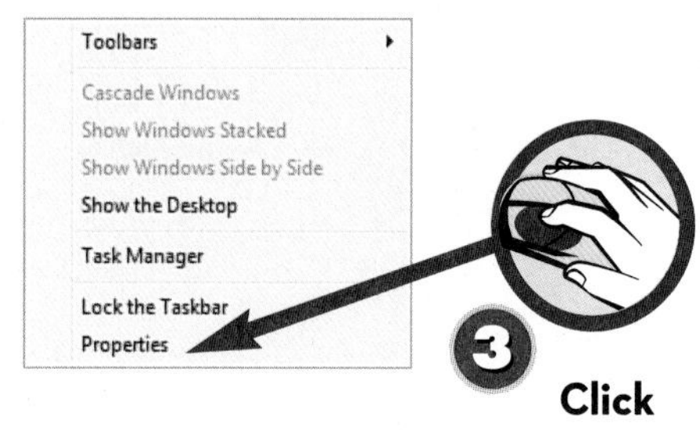

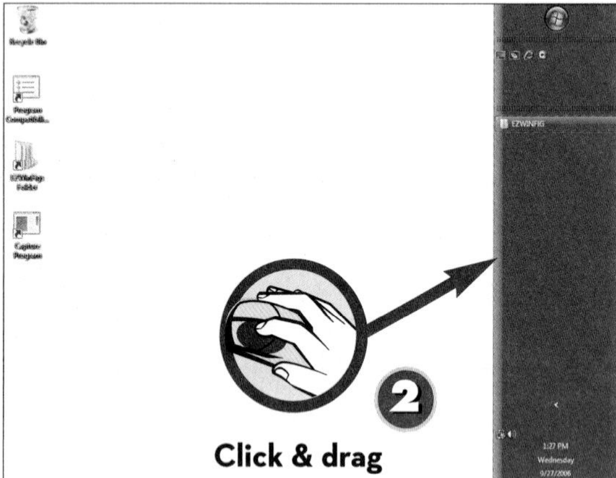

1. Place the mouse pointer anywhere on the taskbar except on a button or on the clock. Then press and hold the left mouse button and drag the taskbar to the location you want.
2. To resize the taskbar, position the mouse pointer on the taskbar's border. Drag the border until the taskbar is the desired size.
3. To customize the taskbar, right-click it and then click **Properties**.

Continued

TIP

Taskbar Won't Move?

If the taskbar won't move, it's probably locked into position. Right-click the taskbar and uncheck **Lock the taskbar**.

Click 4

Click 5

6 Hover

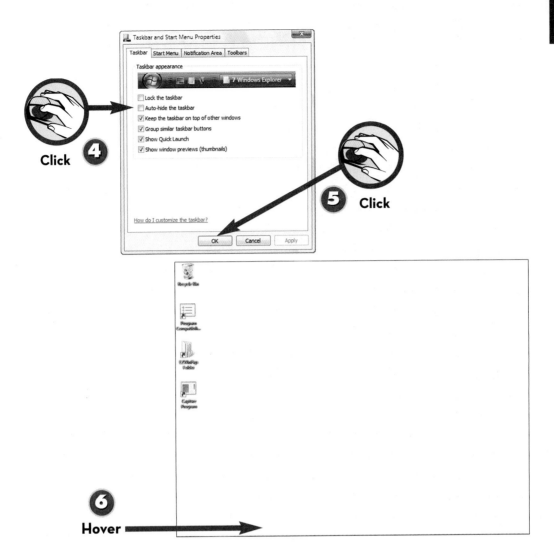

4 To hide the taskbar, click the **Auto-hide the taskbar** check box.

5 Click **OK**; the taskbar is hidden.

6 To redisplay the taskbar, hover the mouse pointer over the taskbar area, and the taskbar will reappear.

End

TIP

Undo the Change

If you don't want to hide the taskbar, turn it back on. Right-click the taskbar. Click the **Auto-hide the taskbar** option to remove the check mark. Then click **OK**.

NOTE

Other Changes

You can make other changes, such as lock the taskbar, keep the taskbar on top of open windows, group similar taskbar buttons together, or display the Quick Launch toolbar (or turn it off). To do so, make these changes and click **OK**.

CHANGING THE NOTIFICATION AREA

The *notification area* is the right end of the taskbar that displays icons for programs that are running in the background (like when a document is printing) and virus and security programs. It also displays the clock and volume control. You can modify the notification area to suit your preferences.

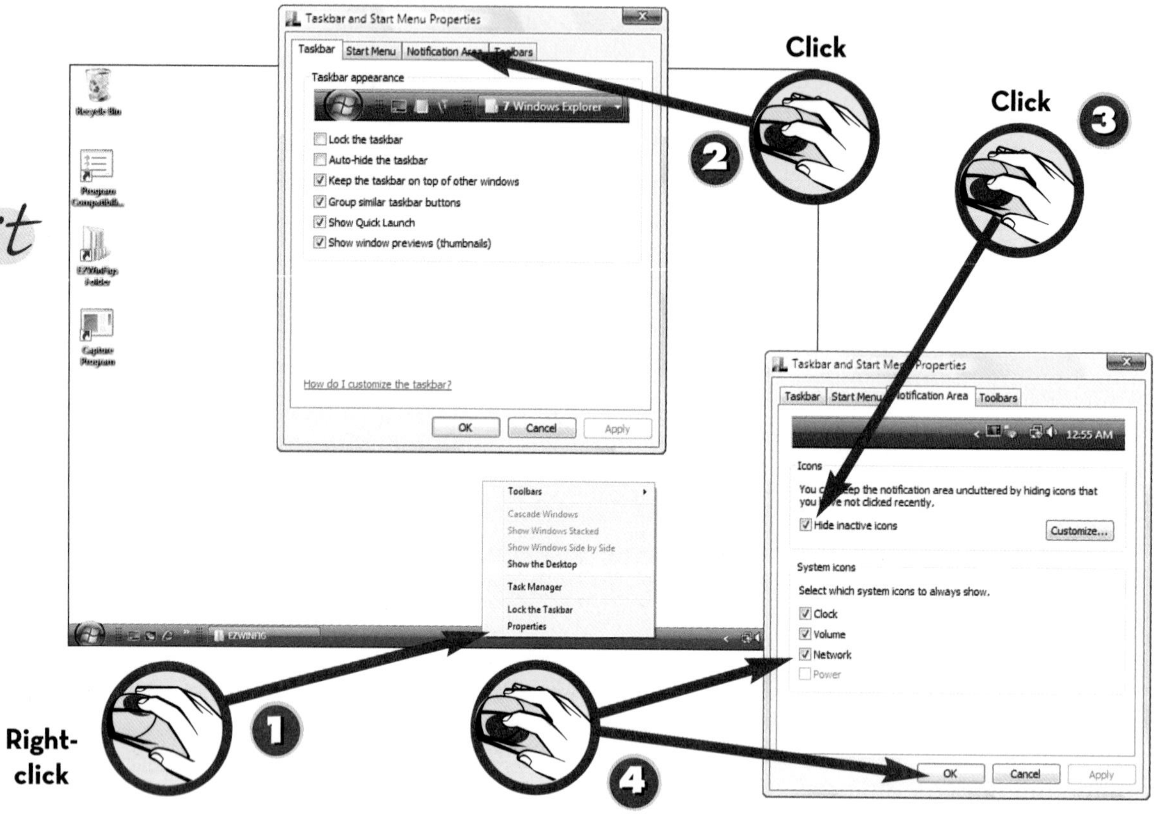

1. To customize the notification area, right-click the taskbar and then click **Properties**.
2. Click the **Notification Area** tab.
3. If you want all icons displayed, uncheck the **Hide inactive icons** check box. (Keep it checked if you want to keep inactive icons hidden.)
4. In the System icons area, check which icons you want displayed. Click **OK**.

End

TIP

Display Icons

When inactive icons are hidden or more icons can be displayed, you'll see an arrow next to the notification area. Click this arrow to display additional icons; click it again to hide these icons.

DISPLAYING OR HIDING TOOLBARS

You can display toolbars in the taskbar. For instance, the Quick Launch toolbar is displayed by default. (You can hide it if you want.) You can display toolbars for Windows Media Player, Desktop, and others.

Start

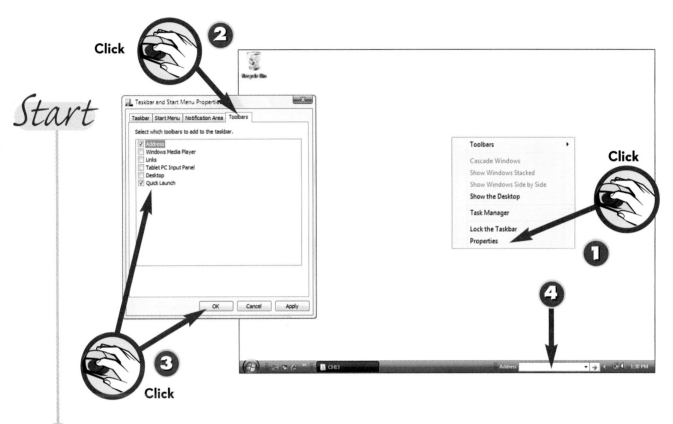

1. To customize the notification area, right-click the taskbar and then click **Properties**.
2. Click the **Toolbars** tab.
3. Check the toolbars you want displayed, and then click **OK**.
4. The toolbars you selected (here, the Address toolbar) are displayed.

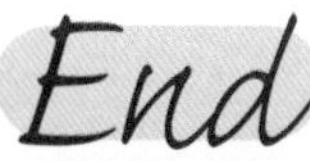

SETTING DEFAULT PROGRAMS

For some tasks, different programs are available. For instance, you can select which program you use to check your email or which program you use to browse the Internet. Windows Vista enables you to select the default program you prefer to use for these and other tasks.

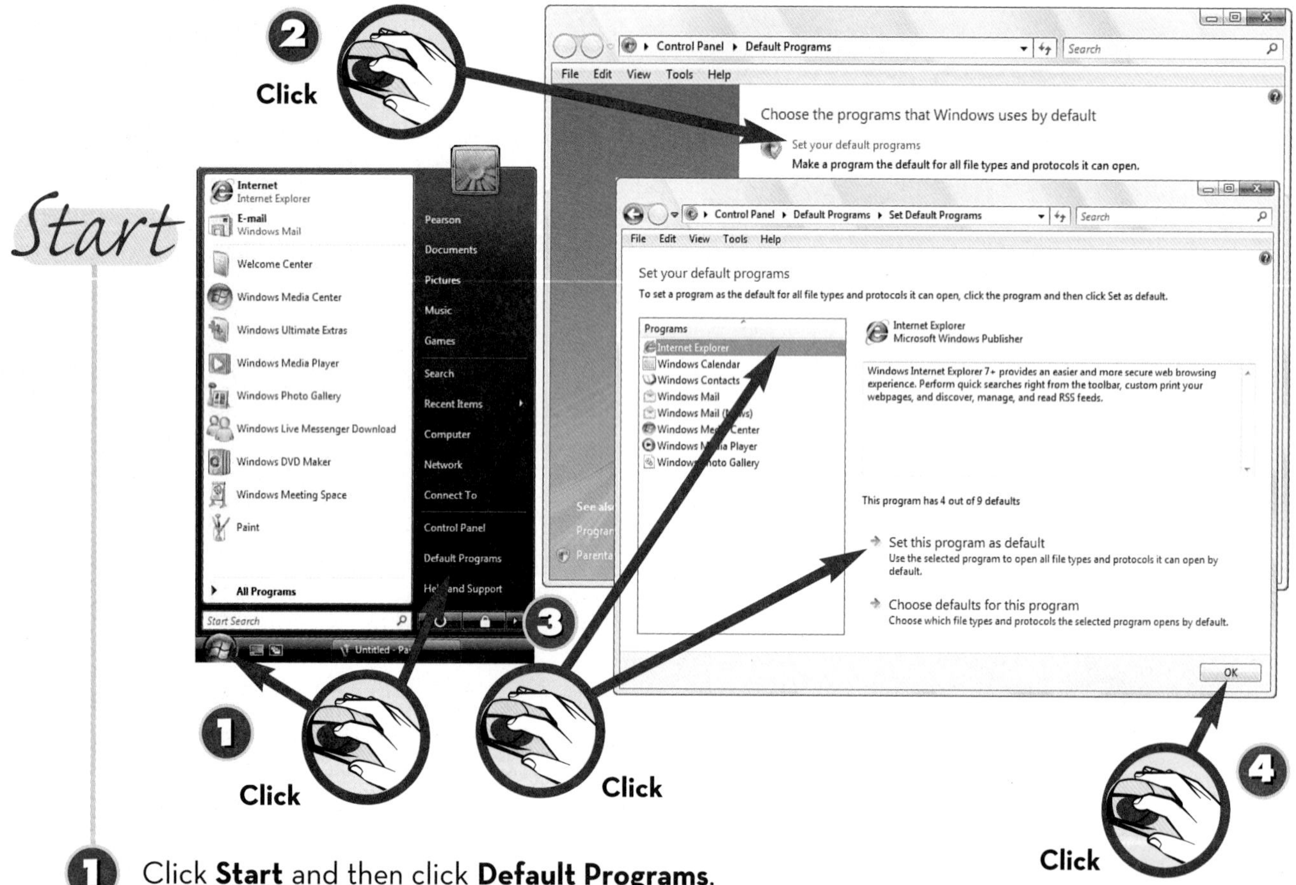

Start

1. Click **Start** and then click **Default Programs**.
2. Click **Set your default programs** in the Control Panel.
3. Select the program for which you want to set the default, and click **Set** this program **as default**.
4. Click **OK**.

TIP

Set as Default When Customizing Start Menu

You can also select your default Internet and email programs from the Customize Start Menu dialog box. Right-click the taskbar, click **Properties**, click the **Start Menu** tab, click **Customize**, and then select from the drop-down list the Internet

SETTING AUTOPLAY OPTIONS

When you insert a disc, Windows will use AutoPlay to figure out what you want to do with the contents of that disc. For instance, if you insert a blank disc, you are prompted whether you want to burn files to this disc. Rather than select an action when prompted, you can select what default actions occur when you insert an audio CD, a CD with pictures, a blank CD, a DVD, and other disc types.

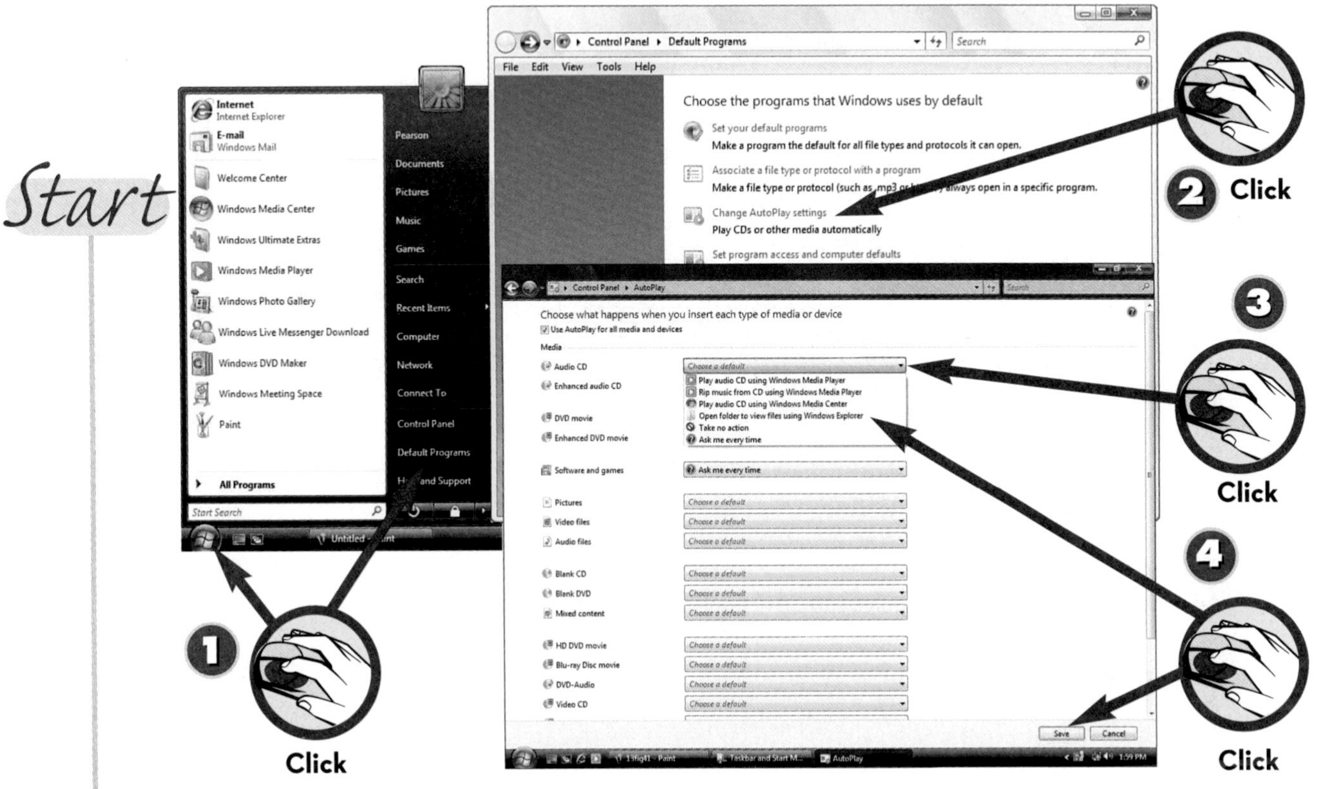

Start

1. Click **Start** and then click **Default Programs**.
2. Click **Change AutoPlay settings**.
3. Select the media for which you want to set the default, and then click the down arrow to display the drop-down list.
4. Select the action you want to perform for this media type, and then click **Save**.

End

TIP

Associate File Type with Program

You can use the **Associate a file type with a program** option to tell Windows which program to use for specific file types. Many programs already have a program associated with them, but you may want to change it. Or you can add associated programs to file types that don't have one. Click this option, select the file type, click the **Change program** button, and then select the program to use.

Part 4

PERFORMANCE AND MAINTENANCE

This Part introduces some techniques that are useful for keeping your system in shape and maintaining its performance: scanning a disk for corrupted files, restoring your system, troubleshooting hardware, and others. Use the techniques in this Part to solve problems with your system and to help keep problems from occurring.

You can help prevent system problems by using Windows Update, performing error-checking and disk defragmentation on a routine basis, removing unnecessary files, and understanding how to properly install new hardware.

To protect your system, create restore points for use with System Restore, and back up important files on a routine basis.

To find the cause of system problems, you can test your system's memory for errors, perform Windows Updates manually, and research your system's setup with System Information and Device Manager.

Although you don't have to do these tasks every day, you should be familiar with all of them and use them as recommended. You can automate many of them with Scheduled Tasks. Most of these tasks are performed through the Control Panel's System and Maintenance category (see figure on opposite page).

WINDOWS VISTA CONTROL PANEL'S SYSTEM AND MAINTENANCE CATEGORY

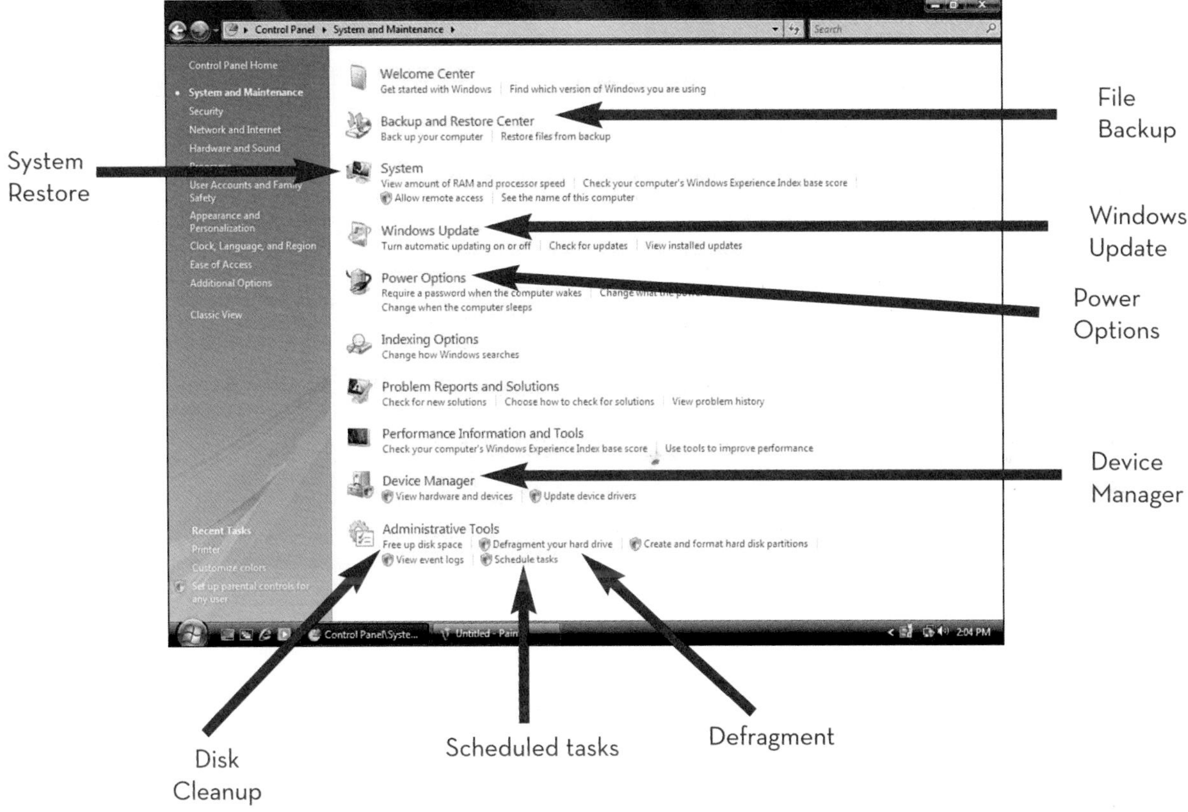

CONTROLLING WINDOWS UPDATES

Windows Vista is designed to automatically download updates to Windows from the Internet to enhance its security and features. However, if you are not always connected to the Internet or don't leave your computer running at all times, you may prefer to change when Windows Vista checks for updates.

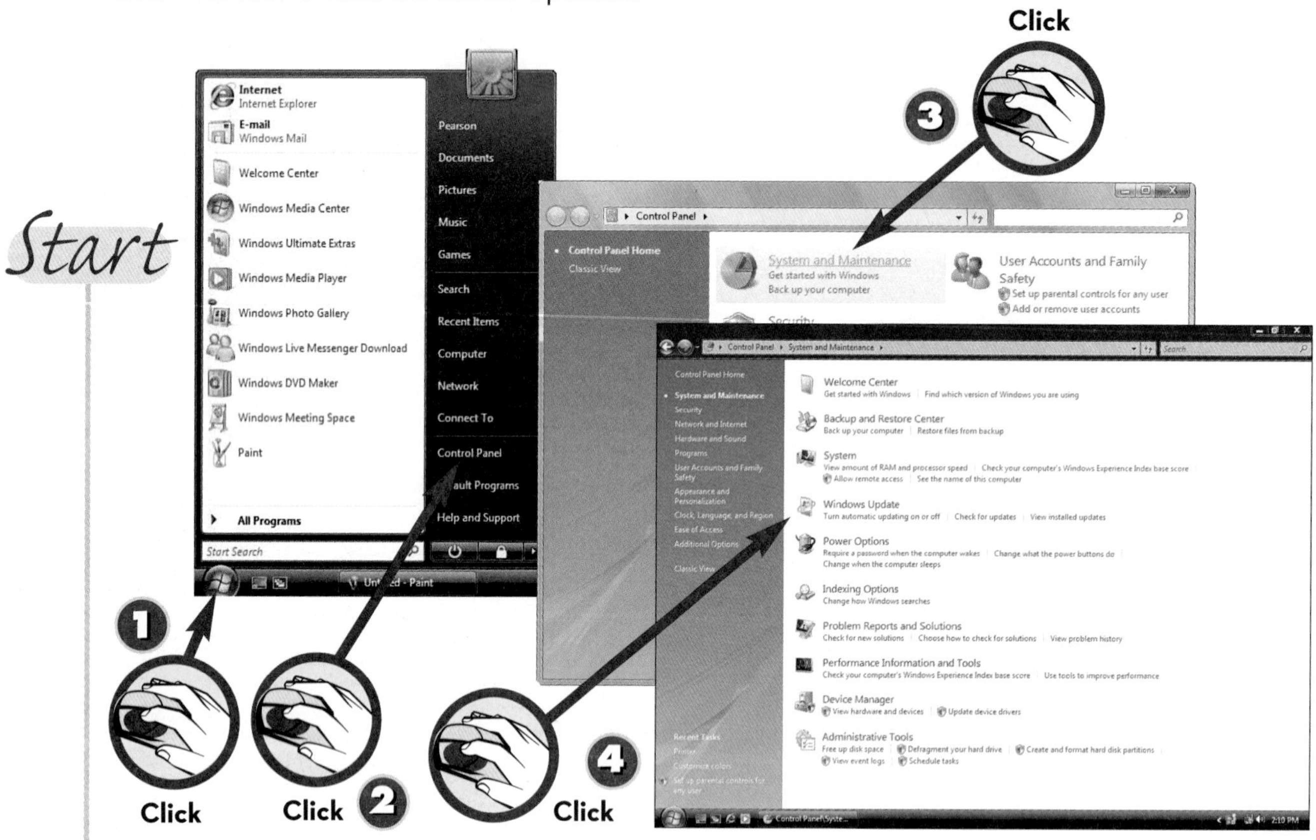

Start

1. Click **Start** to open the Windows Vista menu system.
2. Click **Control Panel**. If you don't see categories, click **Control Panel Home** before continuing.
3. Click **System and Maintenance** to open the System and Maintenance category.
4. Click **Windows Update** to continue. A status display appears, informing you of the last time Windows Update ran and the last time updates were installed.

Continued

NOTE

Recommended Updates

Recommended updates are those updates that Microsoft considers very important to the operation of your computer. Windows Update always notifies you of recommended updates unless you clear the checkbox. **Include recommended updates**.

TIP

The Best Day and Time

If you use a dial-up connection, choose a day and time when you normally don't use the telephone (late at night, for example), and make sure you leave the computer running so Vista can connect to the Internet and get updates.

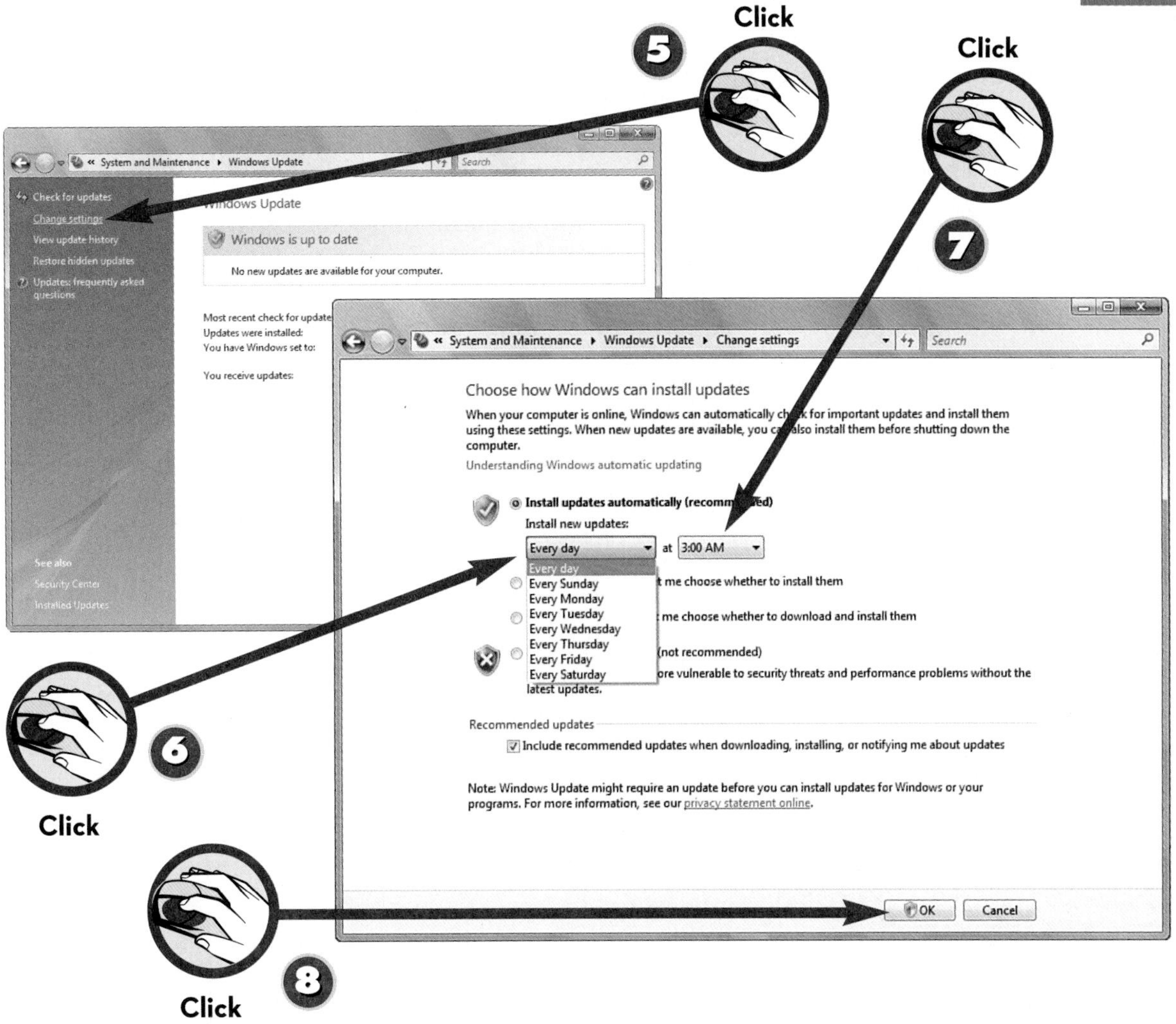

5. To change settings, click **Change settings** in the left pane.
6. To change how often Windows Update checks for updates, click **Every Day** and select a particular day of the week.
7. To change the time Windows Update checks for updates, click the Time button and select a time from the list when your computer is normally turned on.
8. After making the changes desired, click **OK** to close the dialog box. When the User Account Control dialog appears, click Continue to finish.

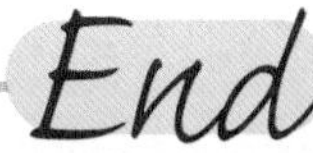

TIP

User Account Control

When you see the Windows security shield icon on a task or button, User Account Control will ask you to confirm the operation you are performing. A standard user must click **Continue** and enter an administrator's password to complete the operation.

CAUTION

Why Automatic Updates?

You can automatically download updates without installing them, or even choose to never check for updates automatically, but if you disable automatic updates, you are responsible for updating Windows. You're better off letting Vista update itself.

UPDATING WINDOWS MANUALLY

Although Windows Update automatically checks for updates and installs them for you, you can also check for updates manually. To manually run Windows Update, you must be connected to the Internet.

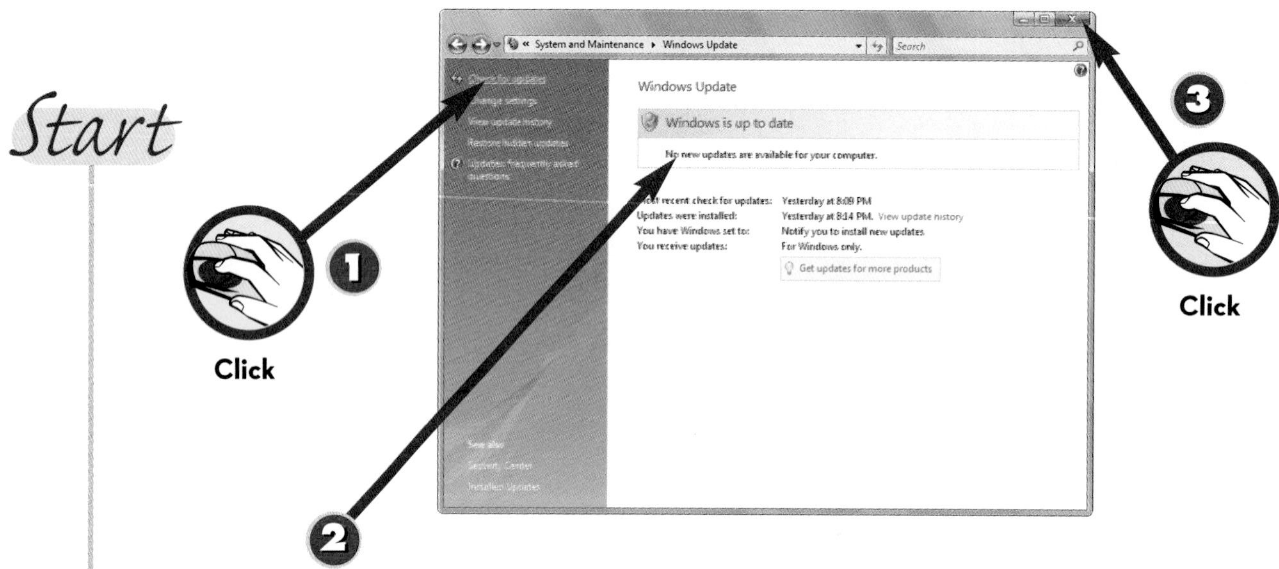

1. In the Windows Update control panel (see steps 1-3 of preceding task), click **Check for updates**. Windows Update checks to determine if updates are available.
2. If important updates are available, they are installed for you. Otherwise, you'll see a message indicating there are no new updates.
3. Click the **Close** (**X**) button to close the Windows Update dialog box.

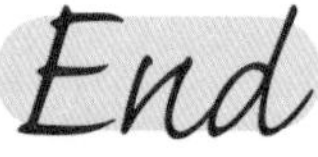

NOTE

Restart

You may be notified that your computer must be restarted for the new updates to be available. Close any open programs, and then click **Yes** to restart your computer.

NOTE

Optional Updates

You can also check for (and download) optional updates with this dialog box. An optional update can add new features but does not improve system security or stability.

SETTING POWER OPTIONS

Windows Vista provides power management for both desktop and laptop computers. Power management enables laptop computers to have longer run time on batteries and enables both types of computers to select the best balance of energy savings and performance. The Power Options dialog box in the Control Panel enables you to select the best power settings for your situation.

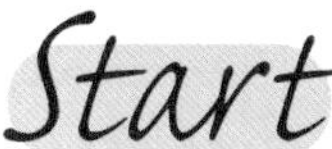

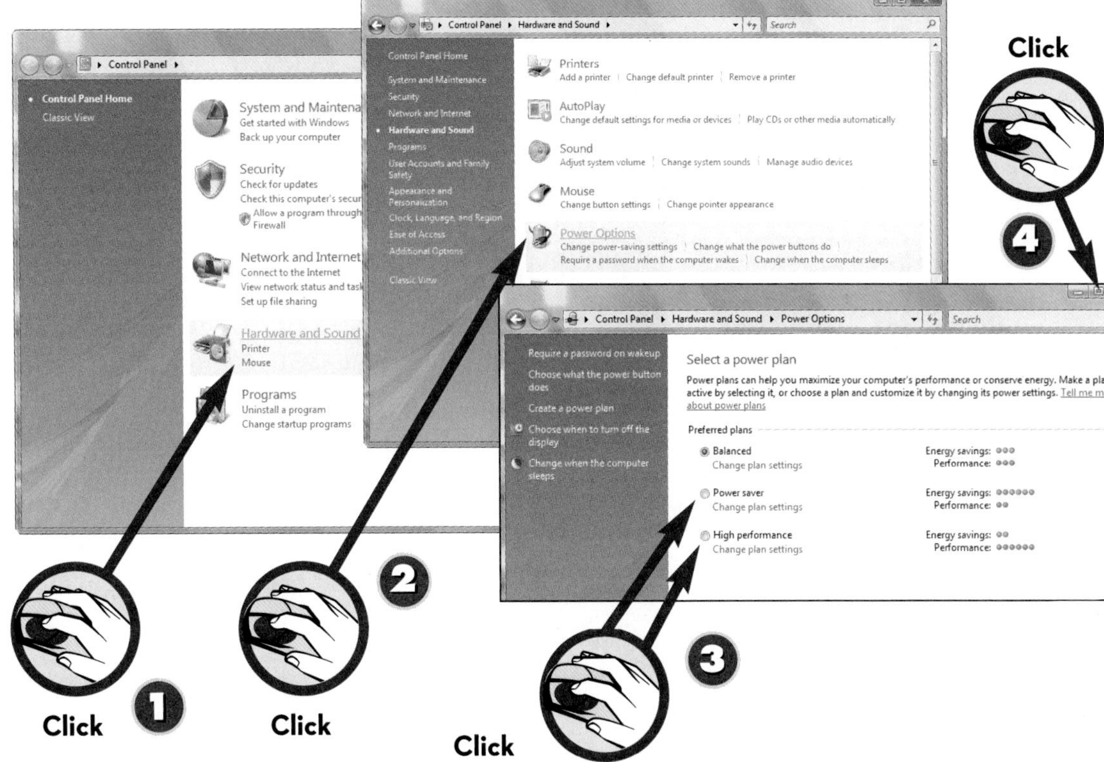

1. With the Control Panel open (see steps 1-3 of the first task in this Part), click **Hardware and Sound**.
2. Click **Power Options**.
3. By default, Windows Vista uses Balanced, which equalizes performance and power savings. To choose a different plan, click it.
4. Click **Close** (**X**) to close the Control Panel.

End

TIP

Best Power Plans

For the best performance on a desktop computer or a laptop computer running on AC power, select **High performance**. To improve battery life on a laptop, select **Power saver**. Power saver can also be used on desktop computers to save electricity, but it greatly reduces the performance of the computer.

DISPLAYING SYSTEM INFORMATION

When you are troubleshooting problems with your computer, you sometimes need to display detailed information about your system. Windows Vista displays all system information—including information about hardware configurations, computer components, and software—in one convenient spot: System Information.

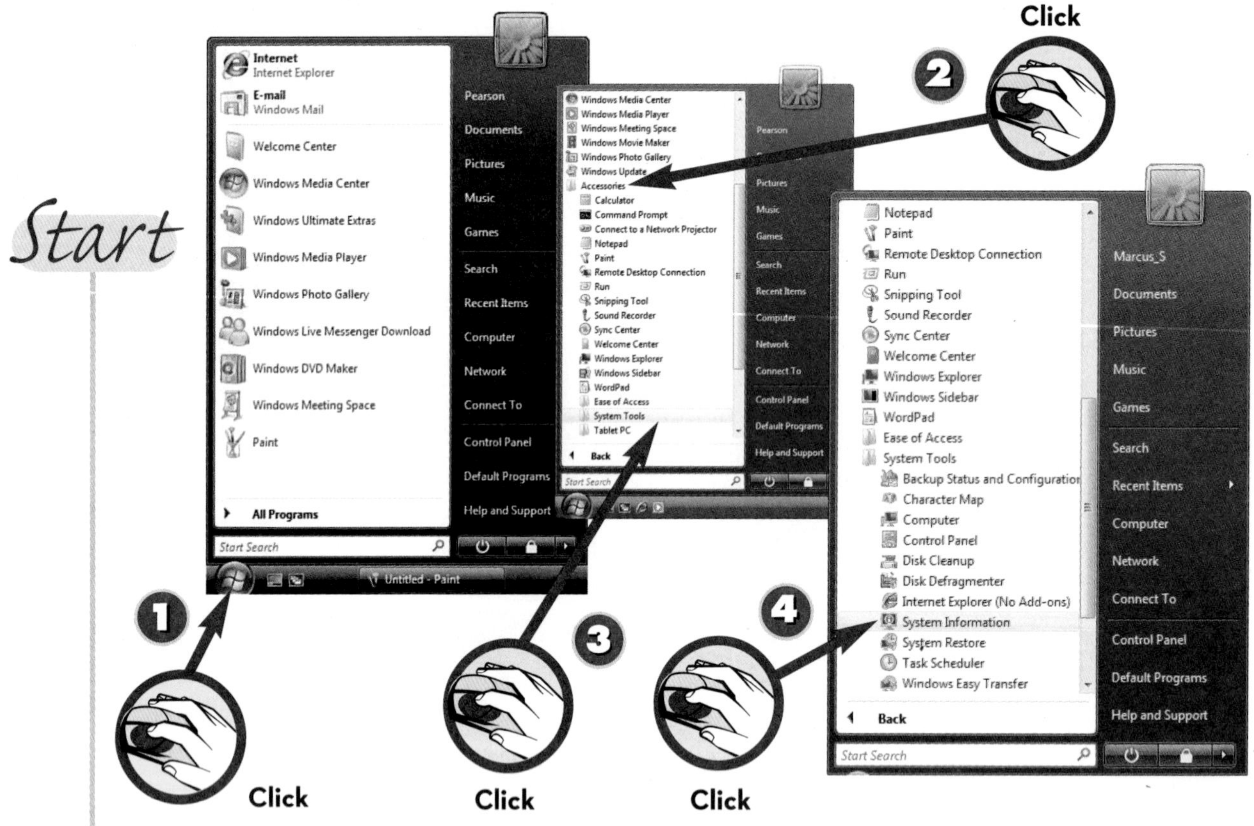

Start

1. Click the **Start** button and choose **All Programs**.
2. Click **Accessories**.
3. Click **System Tools**.
4. Click **System Information**.

Continued

TIP

Technical Information

Most of the device information in System Information is technical, and you will need to review or make changes only if you are having a problem. In that case, consider getting help from your technical support resource, who will lead you through the steps to make a change based on the hardware that is experiencing problems. It's usually not a good idea to experiment, especially with advanced settings.

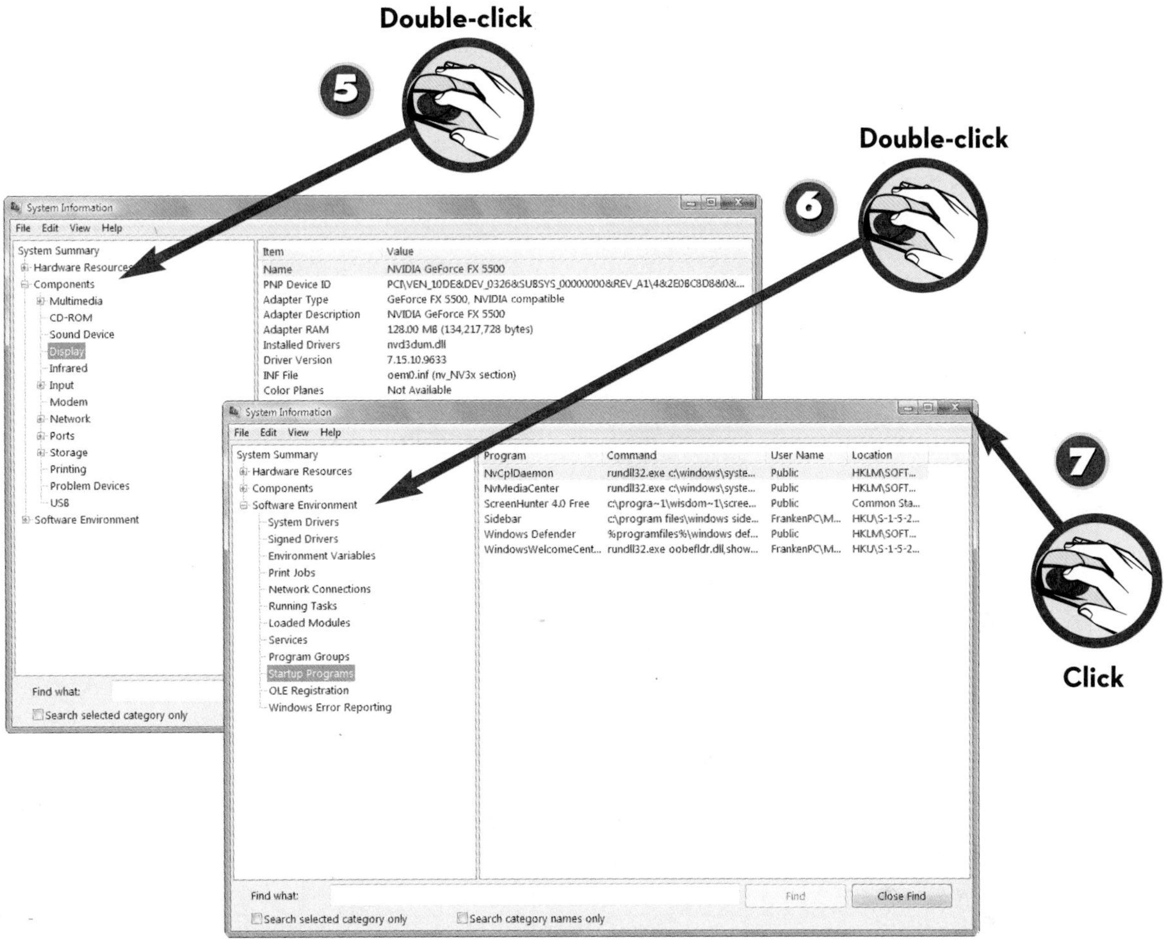

Double-click

Double-click

Click

5 Double-click the **Components** entry in the left-hand pane to open the **Components** folder, and then select one of the subcategories to view information.

6 Double-click the **Software Environment** entry in the left-hand pane to open the **Software Environment** folder, and then select one of the subcategories to view information.

7 Click **Close** to close the System Information window.

End

TIP

Find System Data

To quickly find the information you seek, type a word or words corresponding to the information you seek in the **Find what** text box at the bottom of the dialog box. (If this box is not visible, open the **Edit** menu, and uncheck the **Hide Find** entry.) Then select a search option (selected category, search category names only, or search all categories), and click the **Find** button.

TIP

Welcome Center

Open the Windows Vista Welcome Center in the Control Panel's System and Maintenance category to see a simple overview of system information.

DISPLAYING DISK INFORMATION

You can display information about your disks, such as the size, the amount of occupied space, and the amount of free space.

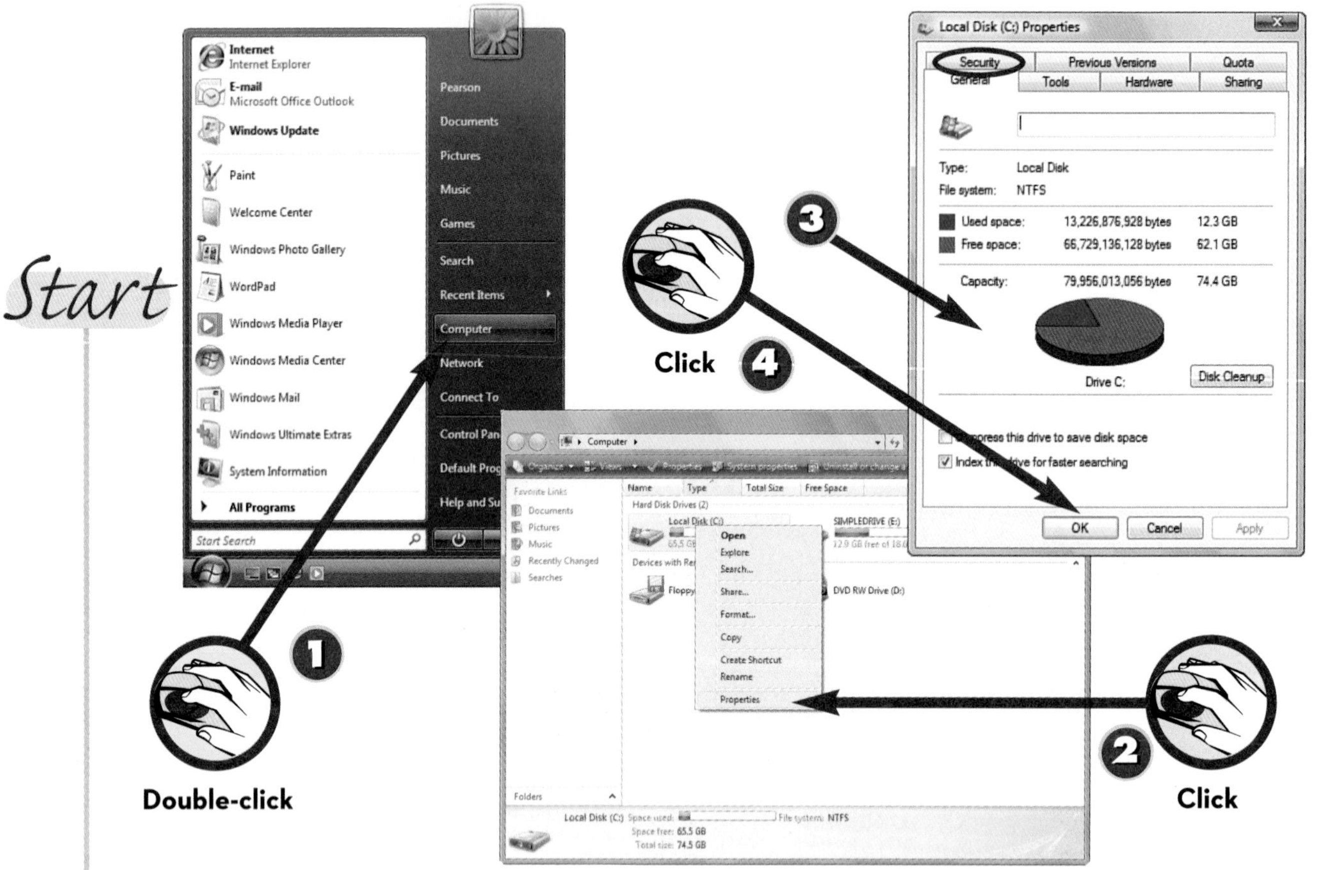

Start

1. Double-click the **My Computer** icon.
2. In the My Computer window, right-click the disk for which you want information, and choose **Properties** from the menu that appears.
3. The disk's Properties dialog box opens, with the General tab displayed. View information about used and free space.
4. Click the **OK** button to close the dialog box.

TIP

Add a Label

You can enter a label for a disk; this label is used in file windows to identify the disk. To do so, type a name for the disk in the text field at the top of the **General** tab of the Properties dialog box.

TIP

Use the Tools Tab

Use the **Tools** tab to select various programs for maintaining your system. This Part covers most of the tools found under this tab.

CLEANING UP UNNECESSARY FILES

On your system, unnecessary files might be hogging your disk space. For example, programs such as Internet Explorer store temporary files on your system that you can delete. The Recycle Bin also houses files that you have deleted but are still kept in case you need them. You can easily get rid of these files and gain some disk space by using Disk Cleanup.

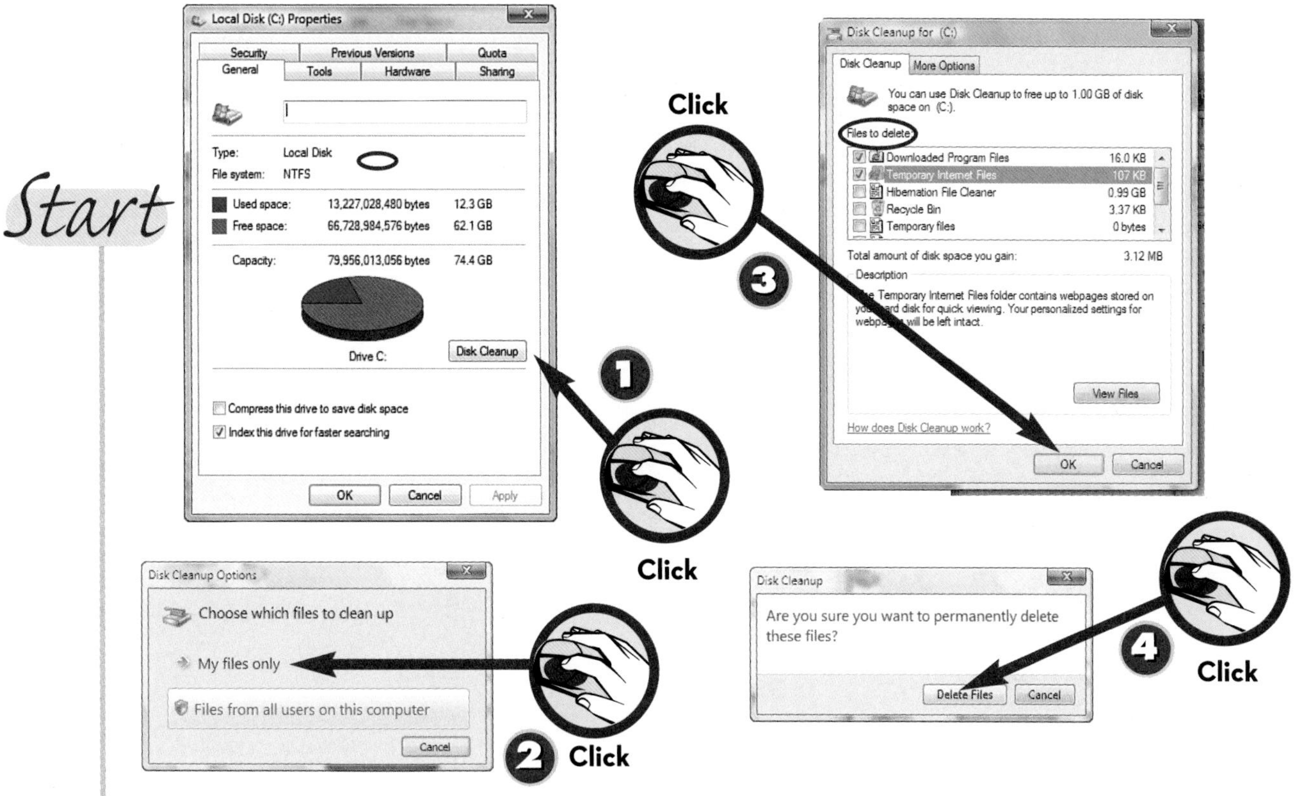

1. After you open the Properties dialog box for the disk you want to clean, click the **Disk Cleanup** button in the General tab. (Refer to the preceding task for help opening the Properties dialog box.)
2. To remove your unnecessary files, click My **Files Only**.
3. The Disk Cleanup dialog box opens. Check options in the **Files to delete** list to specify which files are deleted, and click the **OK** button.
4. When prompted to confirm the removal, click the **Delete Files** button.

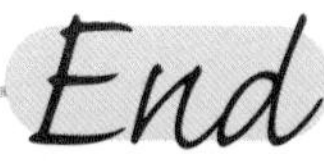

TIP

Review Files

You can view the files that are recommended for removal. Select the files you want to view, and then click the **View Files** button.

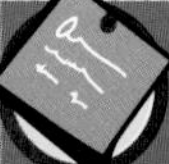

NOTE

More Options

Click the **More Options** tab in the Disk Cleanup dialog box for more space-saving options. From this tab, you can remove programs and features you don't use and remove all but the most recent restore point on your machine.

SAVING SPACE BY COMPRESSING FILES

If you store a lot of files on your system that you don't use very often, you can keep them available but reduce the amount of disk space they use by storing them in a compressed folder. A compressed folder, also known as a *Zip file*, can hold many files. It's also easier to email several files at one time by compressing them first and sending them as a single file attachment.

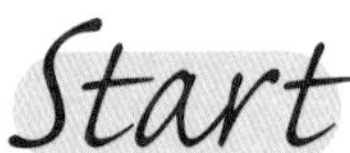

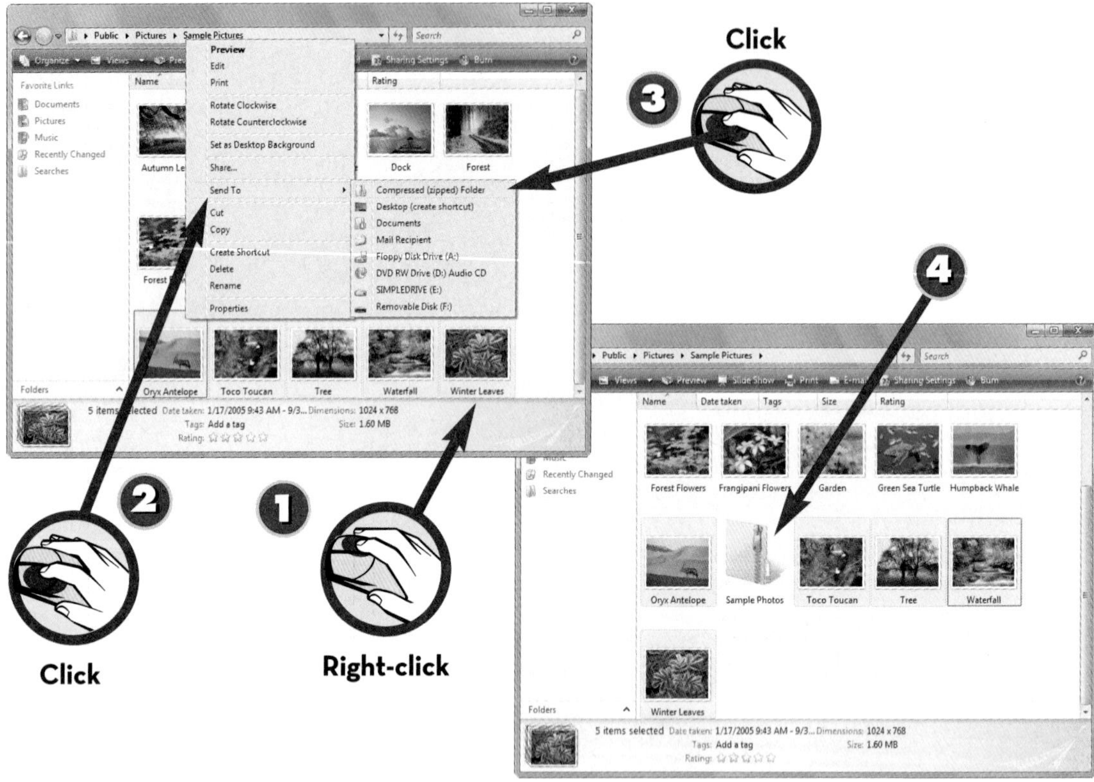

1. Right-click the file(s) or folder you want to compress.
2. Select the **Send To** command.
3. Select **Compressed (zipped) Folder**.
4. The files are stored in a compressed folder. (Note the zipper icon.)

Continued

TIP

Renaming the Compressed File

When you create a compressed file, it uses the same name as the file you right-clicked to start the process. To change the name, type over it when the compressed file first appears, or right-click the file and select **Rename**.

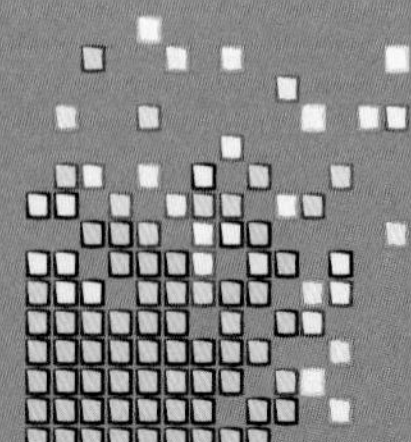

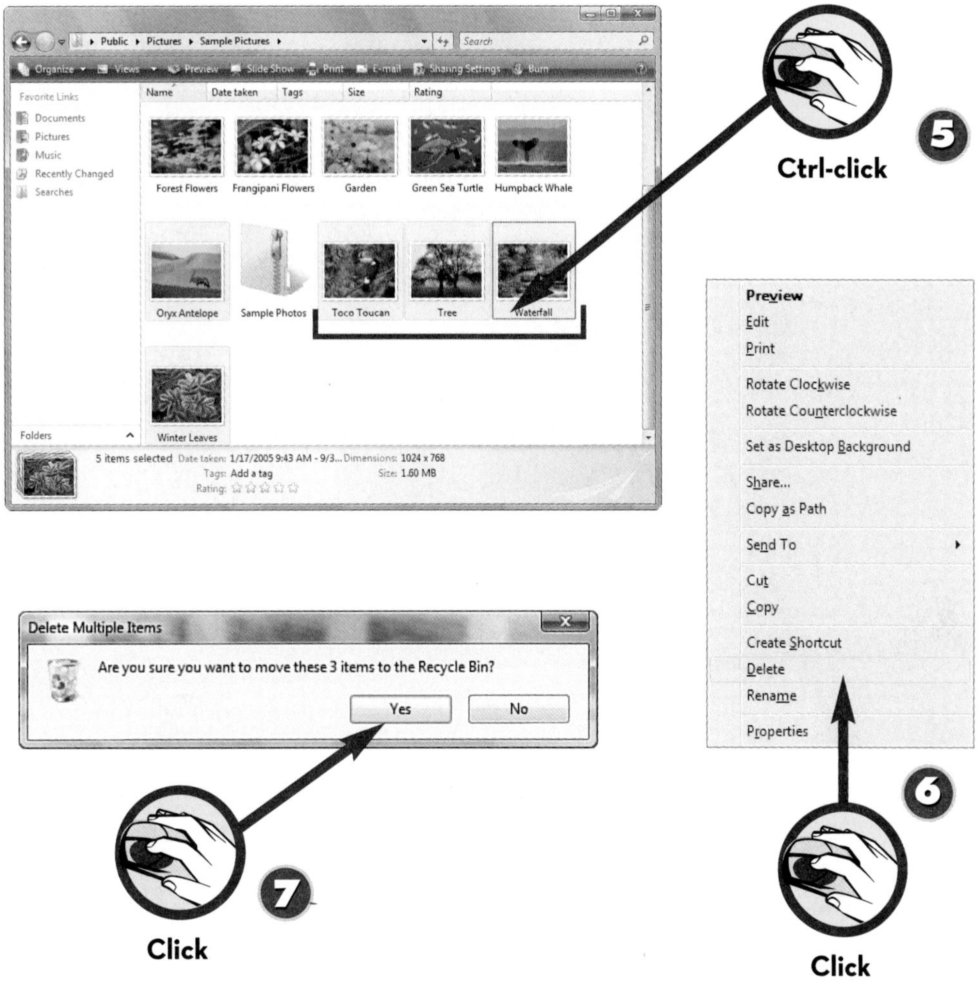

Ctrl-click

Click

Click

5 **Ctrl-click** the files that are now in the compressed file.

6 Right-click one of the selected files, hold down the **Shift** key, and then select **Delete** from the menu.

7 To delete the selected files, click **Yes**. The original files are removed, saving space on your system. The compressed file contains an exact copy of the deleted files for future use.

End

TIP

Adding Files to a Compressed File

To add one or more files to a compressed file, drag the files to the compressed file and drop them. They will be added automatically.

TIP

Selecting a Group of Files

To select more than one file, click the first file, and then hold down the **Ctrl** key on the keyboard. Continue to hold down the **Ctrl** key while you click the other files you want to select. Release the **Ctrl** key when finished.

USING COMPRESSED FILES

Before you can use files stored in a compressed file, you must expand them.

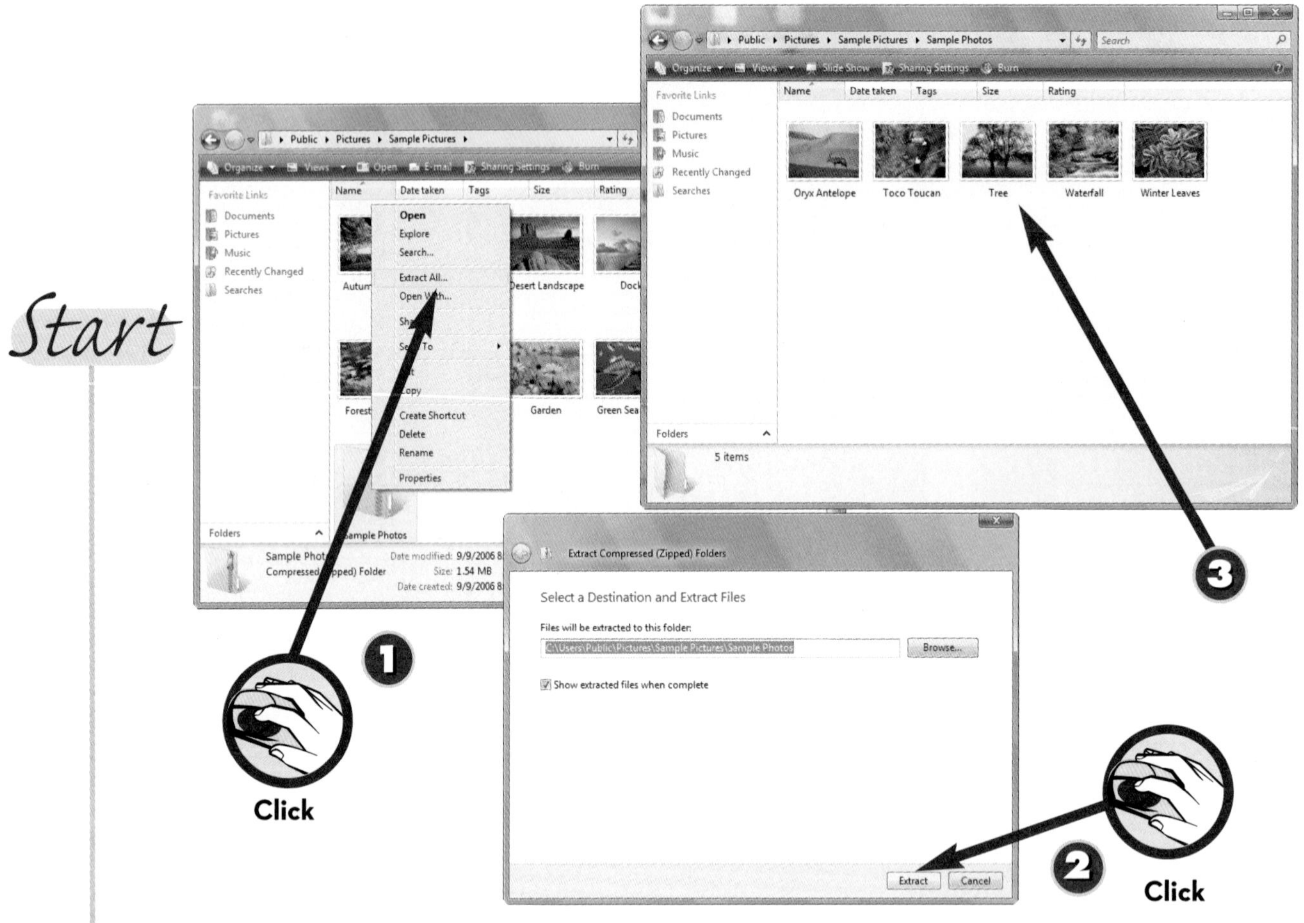

Start

Click

Click

1. Right-click the compressed file and select **Extract All**.
2. Click **Extract** to extract the files to the specified folder.
3. The files are displayed at the end of the process.

End

TIP

Extracting to Another Folder

The Extract Wizard extracts files to a folder with the same name as the original compressed file and in the same location. Use Browse in Step 2 to change where files are extracted. For example, you can browse to the folder Sample Pictures to place the photos compressed in the previous tutorial back in their original folder.

USING THE MEMORY DIAGNOSTIC TOOL

Windows Vista uses memory (RAM) for most of its operations. Consequently, problems with memory can cause your system to stop working correctly. To help track down memory problems, Windows Vista includes the new Memory Diagnostic Tool as one of the featured items in the Administrative Tools folder.

Start

Click

Click

Click

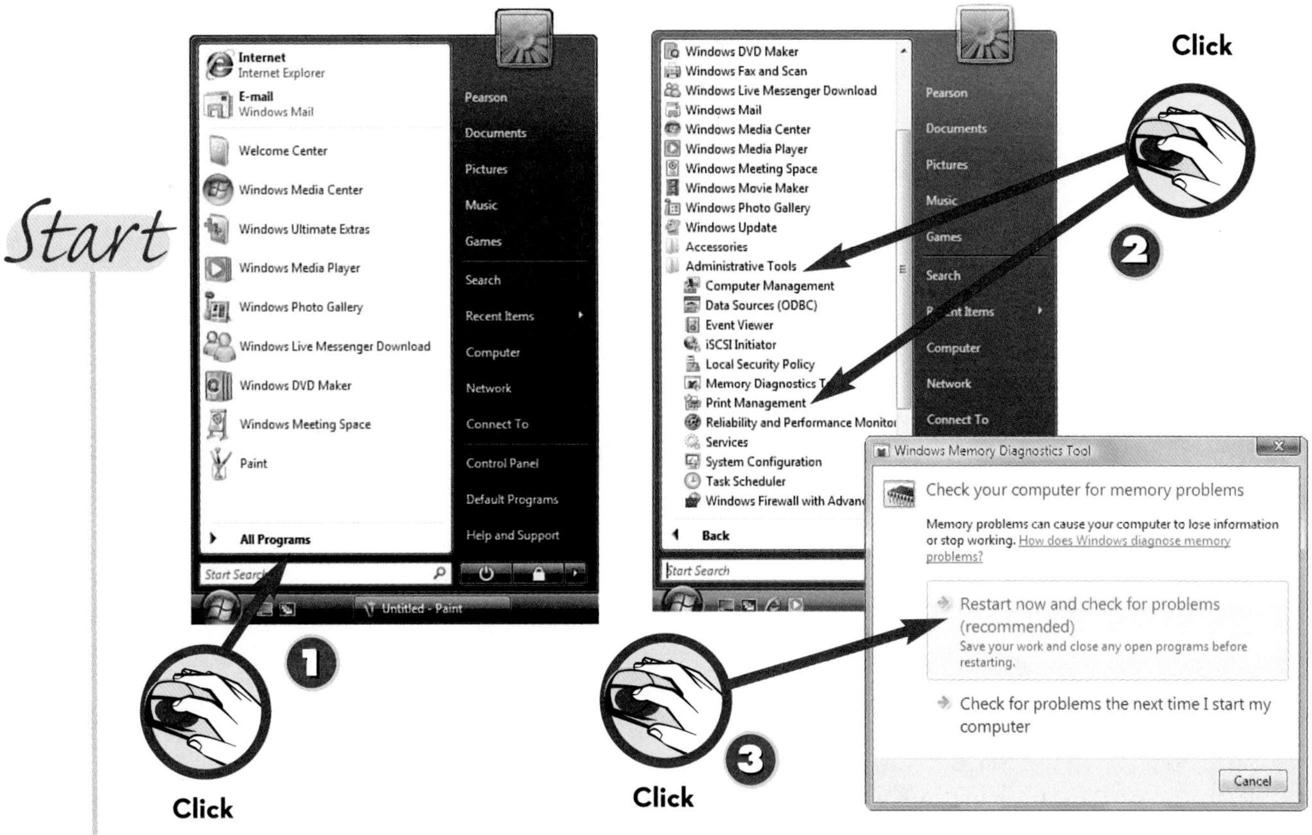

1. Click **Start** and then **All Programs**.
2. Click **Administrative Tool** and then **Memory Diagnostic Tool**.
3. Specify when to run the tool. If you select **Restart now and check for problems**, Windows Vista closes immediately and runs the tool before restarting Windows. The other option checks the memory the next time you start Windows.

End

NOTE

Reviewing Test Results

The Memory Diagnostic Tool runs before the Windows Vista desktop appears and displays errors after you log onto Windows. If it detects errors, you should have your system serviced.

TIP

Finding Memory Diagnostics

On some systems, the Administrative Tools folder might not be on the Start menu. To locate the Memory Diagnostics program, click the **Search** box on the Start menu and type **Memory Diagnostics**. The program will be listed at the top of the menu.

SCANNING YOUR DISK FOR ERRORS

Sometimes parts of your hard disk are unable to store information properly, and you might see an error message when you try to open or save a file. Alternatively, you might notice lost or disarrayed data in some of your files. You can scan the disk for damage using Windows's error-checking program (CHKDSK) to find and fix problems with your drive. You should do this periodically to help prevent problems.

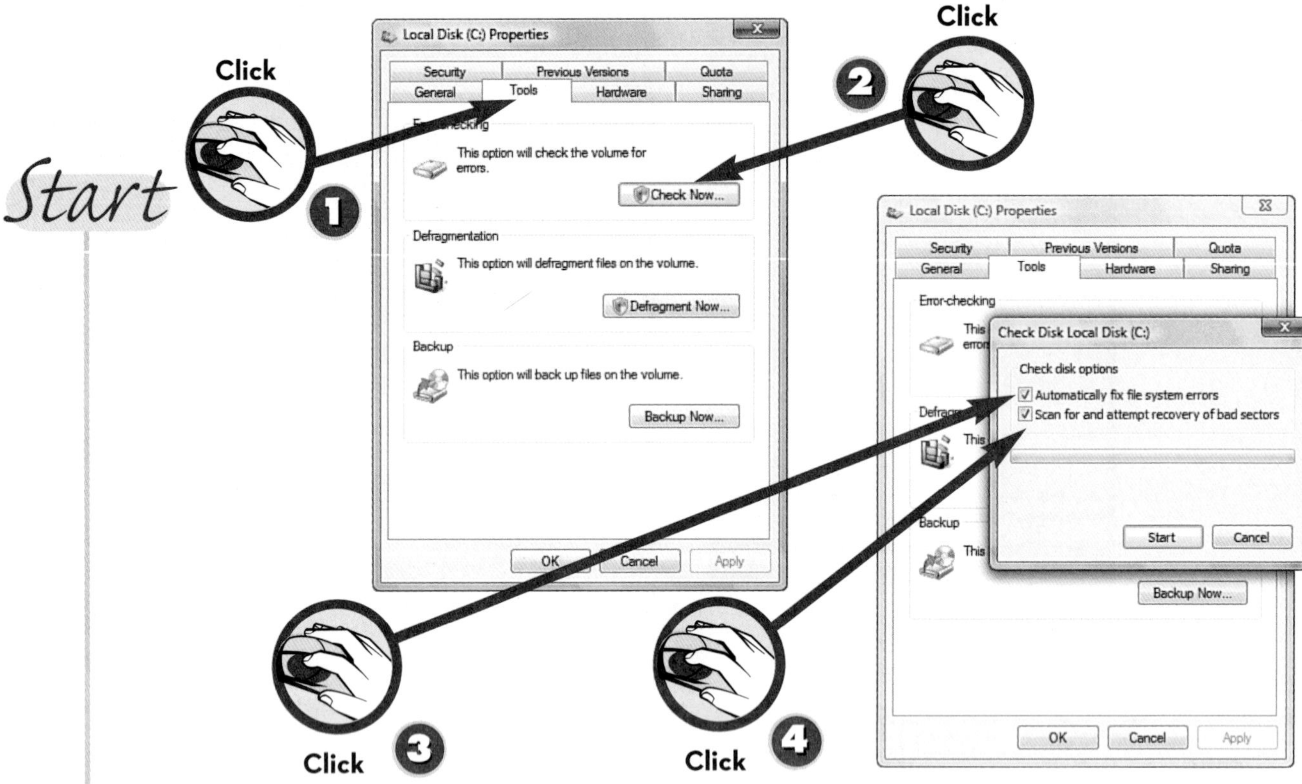

1. Click the **Tools** tab in the Properties dialog box for the disk you want to scan. (Refer to "Displaying Disk Information" earlier in this Part for help opening the **Properties** dialog box.)
2. Click the **Check Now** button in the tab's Error-checking area.
3. Click the **Automatically fix file system errors** check box.
4. Click the **Scan for and attempt recovery of bad sectors** check box.

Continued

TIP

Periodically Scan

It's a good idea to periodically run error-checking, even if you aren't having problems. Doing so helps keep your system running efficiently.

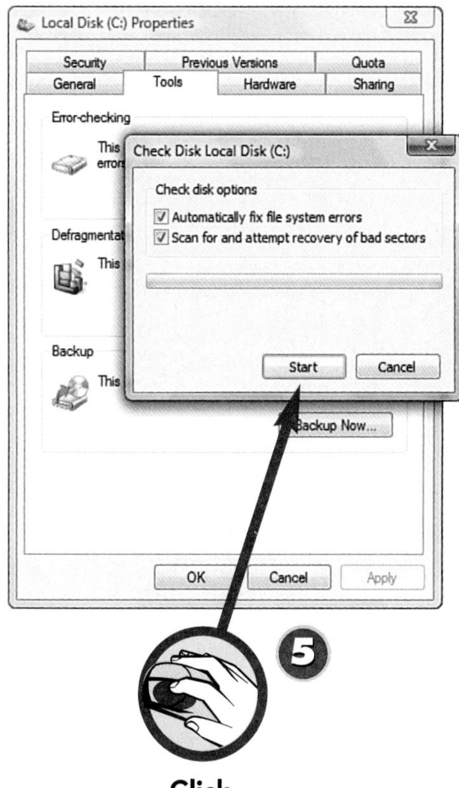

5 Click the **Start** button. If you are testing a drive other than the system (C) drive, the drive test starts immediately.

6 If you selected the system (C) drive, you will see a dialog box indicating the disk can't be checked now. Click **Schedule disk check** to check the drive on the next restart.

End

TIP

Errors Found?

If ScanDisk finds an error, a dialog box appears explaining the error. Read the error message and choose the option that best suits your needs. Click **OK** to continue. Do this for each message.

CONFIGURING THE DEFRAGMENT FEATURE

When a file is stored on your hard drive, Windows places as much of the file as possible in the first available section (called a *cluster*) and then goes to the next cluster to put the next part of the file. Initially, this process does not cause performance problems, but over time, your disk files become fragmented; you might find that it takes a long time to open a file or start a program. To speed access to files and to help prevent potential problems with fragmented files, Windows Vista automatically defragments your drive, and you can adjust how often or when this process occurs.

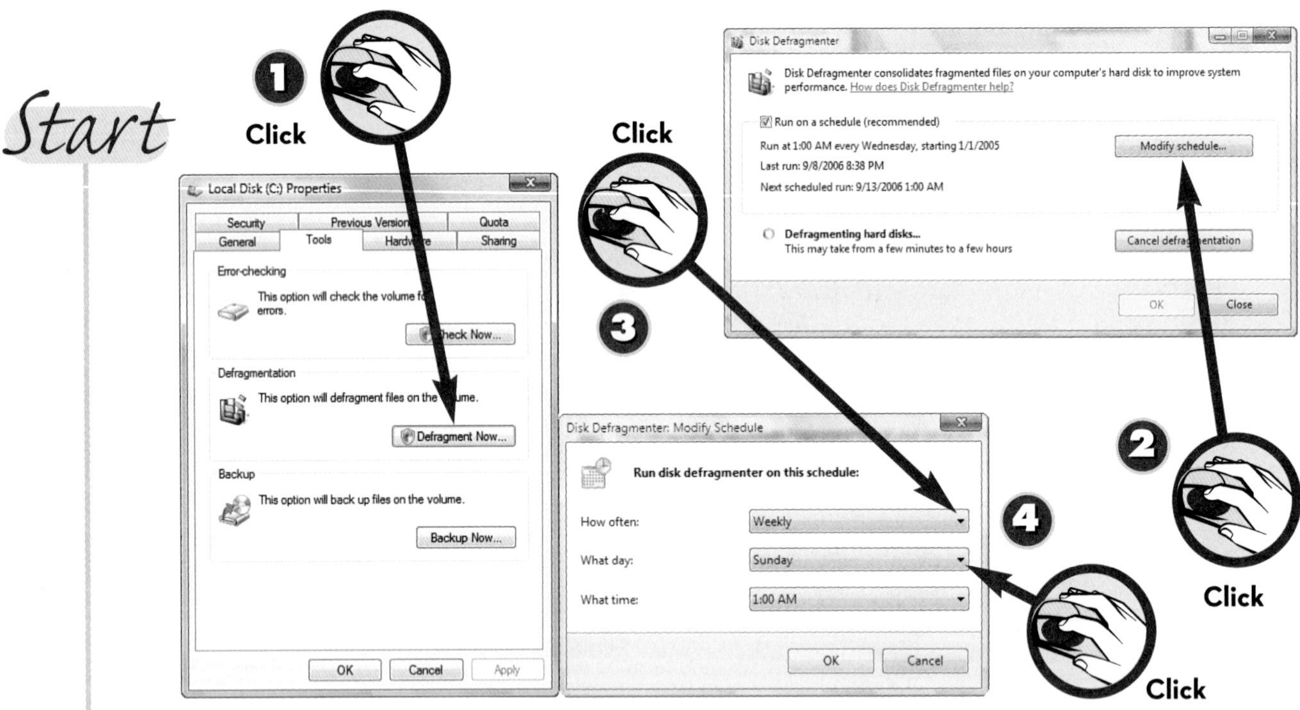

1. In the **Tools** tab of the Properties dialog box, click the **Defragment Now** button for the disk you want to scan.
2. To change when Windows Vista runs the defragment process, click **Modify schedule**.
3. Click the **How often** pull-down menu to change how often Defragment runs.
4. Click the **What day** pull-down menu to change the day of the week when Defragment runs.

Continued

NOTE

Error-Check, and Then Defragment

If you schedule error-checking to run automatically (see previous task), set up the schedule to check your drive a couple of hours before you schedule defragmentation. This helps ensure that the defragment process is storing data on a properly working hard disk.

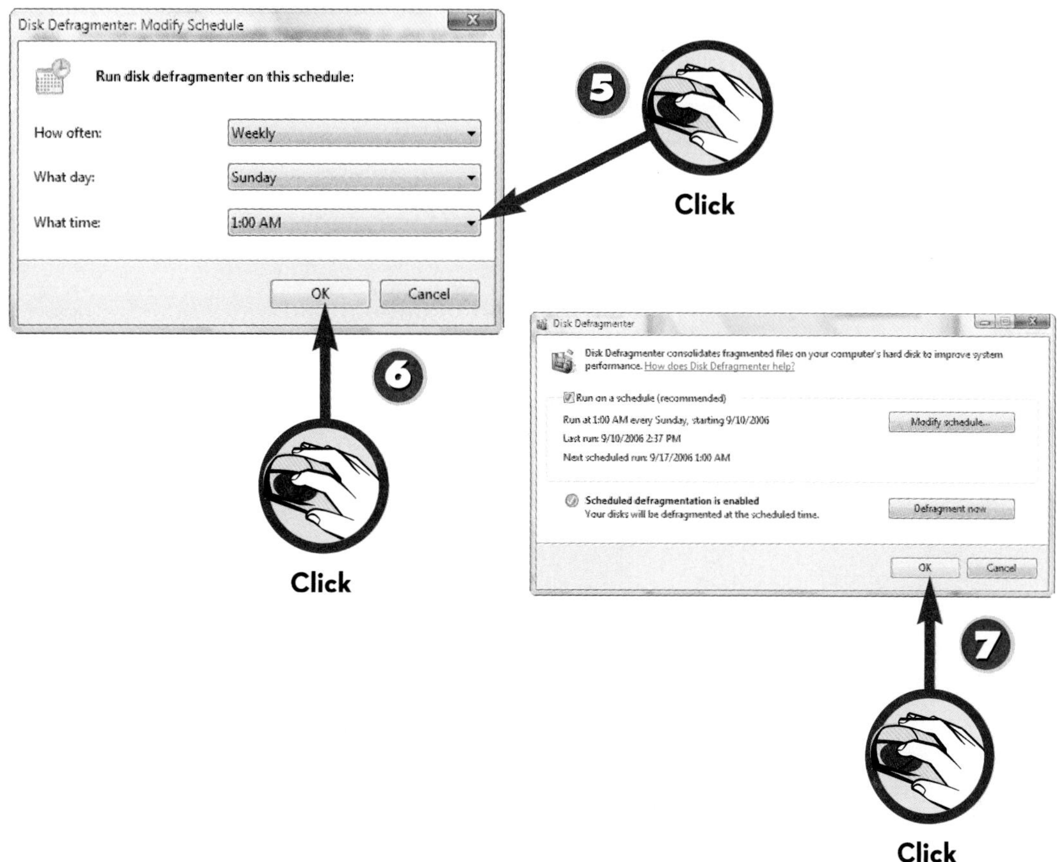

5. Click the **What time** pull-down menu to change the time when Defragment runs.
6. Click **OK** to close the dialog box.
7. The Disk Defragmenter dialog box reflects the changes. Click **OK** to close the dialog box.

End

TIP

Automatic Defragmentation

Windows Vista automatically defragments your system weekly if the **Run on a schedule** box is checked.

NOTE

Free Disk Space

For Disk Defragmenter to completely defragment your disk, the disk should have at least 15% free space. If the disk has less free space, it will be only partially defragmented.

SCHEDULING TASKS

If you perform the same tasks repeatedly, or if you often forget to perform routine maintenance tasks, you can set up a schedule that instructs Windows to perform these tasks automatically. In this example, we'll configure error-checking (chkdsk.exe) to run automatically on a weekly basis.

1. Open the Control Panel as discussed in the first task and click **System and Maintenance**.
2. From the System and Maintenance dialog box, click **Schedule tasks**. When the User Account Control dialog opens, click **Continue** (not shown).

Continued

TIP

User Account Control

When you see the Windows security shield icon on a task or button, User Account Control will ask you to confirm the operation you are performing. An administrator can click **Continue** to complete the operation, but a standard user must click **Continue** and enter an administrator's password to complete the operation.

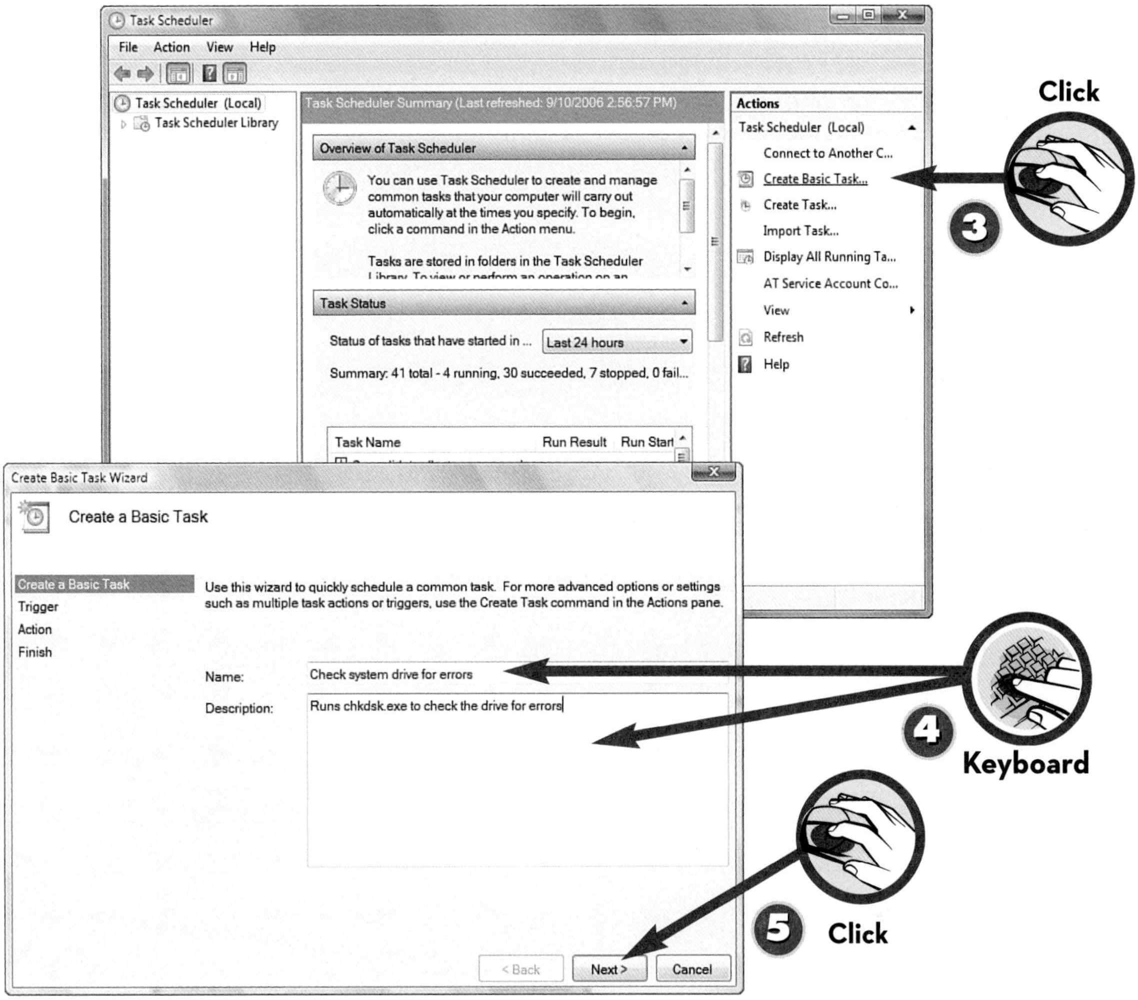

3. The Task Scheduler window opens. Click the **Create Basic Task** list item.

4. The Create Basic Task Wizard starts. Enter the name and a description of the task.

5. Click **Next** to continue.

Continued

TIP

Remove a Task

To remove a task from the list, display the **Task Scheduler** list of tasks. Right-click the item, and then choose **Delete**. Confirm the deletion by clicking the **Yes** button.

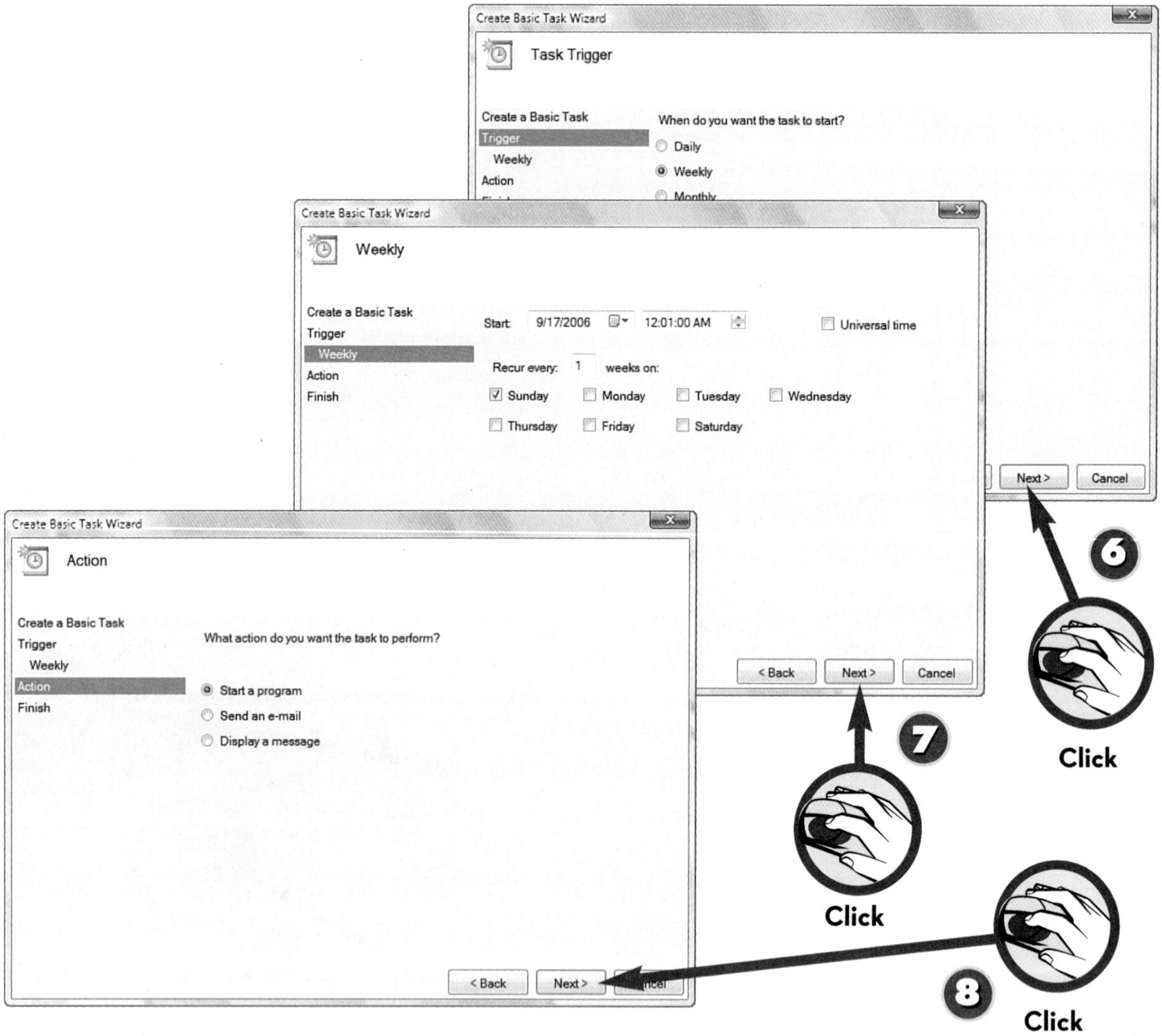

6 Select how often to perform this task. Click **Next**.

7 Specify other options needed, such as the first time to run the program and the day of the week. Click **Next**.

8 Select the type of action to perform. Click **Next**.

Continued

TIP

Change Settings

To change the settings for the task (the time, interval, name, and so on), display the **Task Scheduler** list. Right-click the item you want to modify, and then choose **Properties**. Make any changes to the tabs in the Properties dialog box, and then click **OK**.

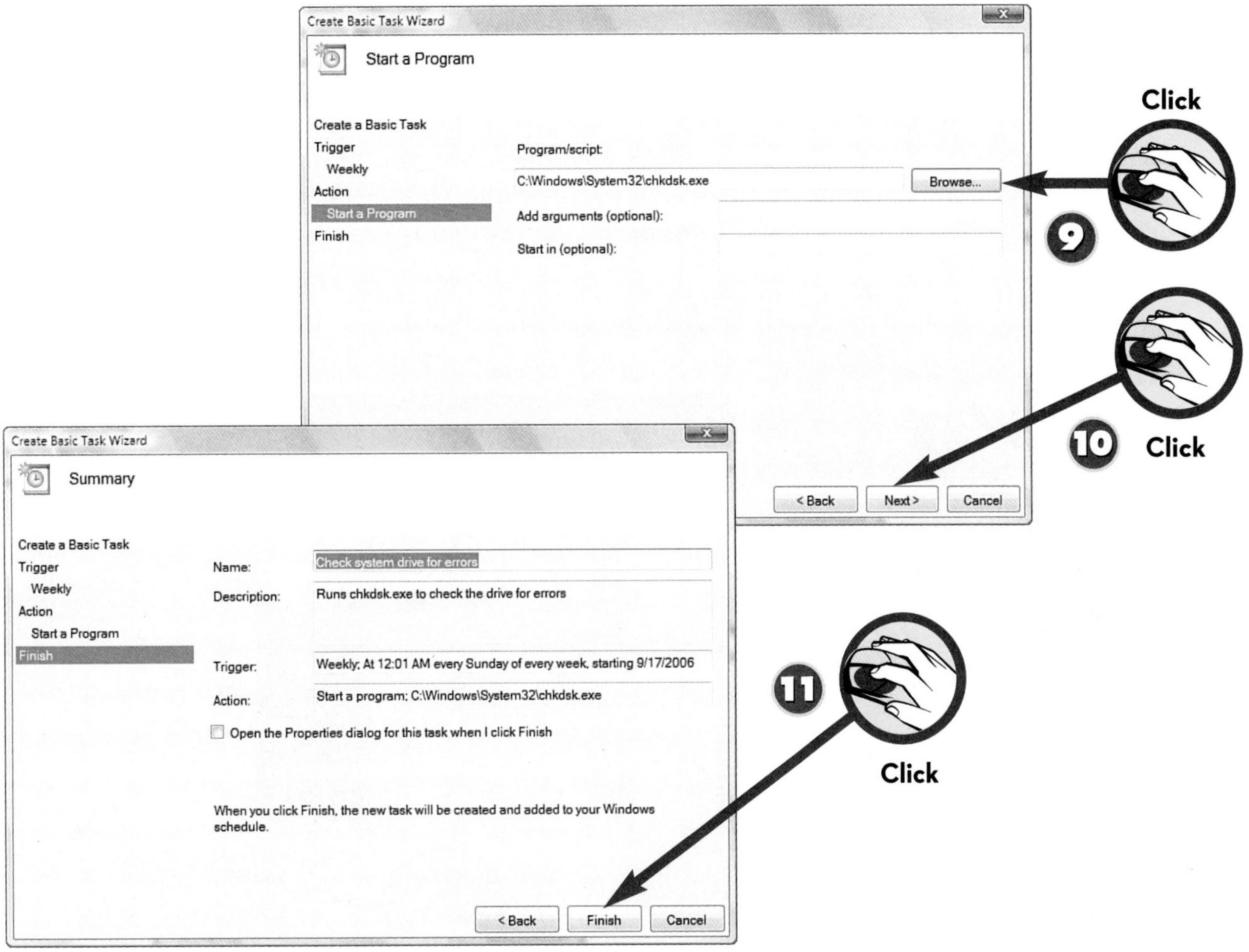

Create Basic Task Wizard

Start a Program

Create a Basic Task
Trigger
Weekly
Action
Start a Program
Finish

Program/script:
C:\Windows\System32\chkdsk.exe
Browse...
Add arguments (optional):
Start in (optional):

< Back Next > Cancel

Click
9
10 Click

Create Basic Task Wizard

Summary

Create a Basic Task
Trigger
Weekly
Action
Start a Program
Finish

Name: Check system drive for errors
Description: Runs chkdsk.exe to check the drive for errors
Trigger: Weekly; At 12:01 AM every Sunday of every week, starting 9/17/2006
Action: Start a program; C:\Windows\System32\chkdsk.exe

Open the Properties dialog for this task when I click Finish

When you click Finish, the new task will be created and added to your Windows schedule.

< Back Finish Cancel

11
Click

9. Click **Browse** to locate the program to run.

10. Click **Next**.

11. Review the task summary. Click **Finish** to complete the task.

End

TIP

Set Advanced Properties

Click the **Open the properties dialog for this task when I click Finish** check box to view more configuration options for the scheduled task.

TIP

View the Task

After you click the **Finish** button in step 11, the task is added to the Task Scheduler Library. Click it to see the task.

INSTALLING NEW HARDWARE MANUALLY

You can install a new printer, modem, or other hardware device, particularly those that plug into a USB port, quickly and easily by using Windows Vista's *Plug and Play* hardware detection. Plug and Play enables Vista to detect most types of hardware and install them automatically. However, if Vista does not detect your hardware, you can use the Add Hardware Wizard to manually install the hardware. In this example, we'll install an external dial-up modem that connects to a serial (COM) port.

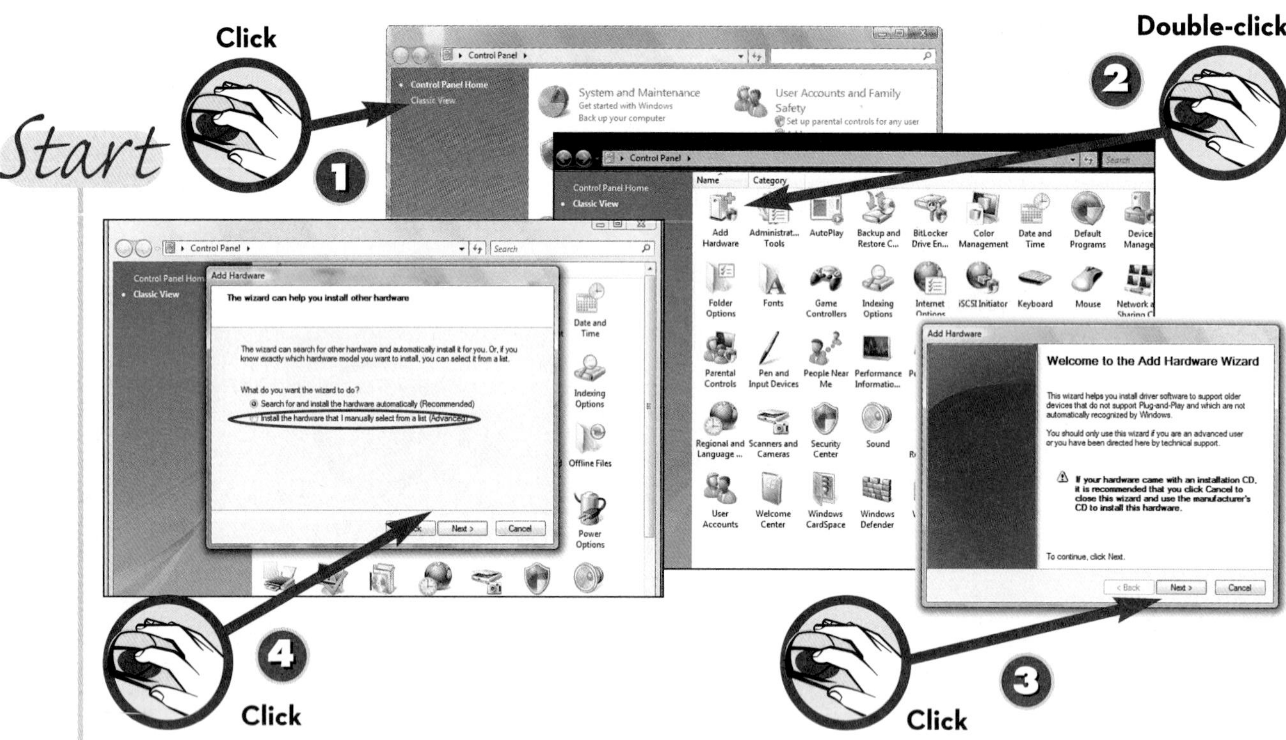

1. After you've connected the device to your computer (follow the instructions that came with the hardware device), click **Start**, **Control Panel** to open the Control Panel, and click **Classic View**.
2. Double-click the **Add Hardware** icon.
3. The Add Hardware Wizard starts, displaying its Welcome screen. Click the **Next** button to continue.
4. Click the **Search for and install the hardware automatically** radio button, and then click the **Next** button. Windows searches your machine for non-plug and play devices.

Continued

TIP

Automatic Setup

If Windows detects your hardware, it is set up automatically. You might be prompted to insert the appropriate software disks to set up the hardware. Follow the onscreen directions.

NOTE

Plug and Play

Most newer devices (especially those that plug into a USB or FireWire port) are plug and play, you likely won't need to go beyond step 4.

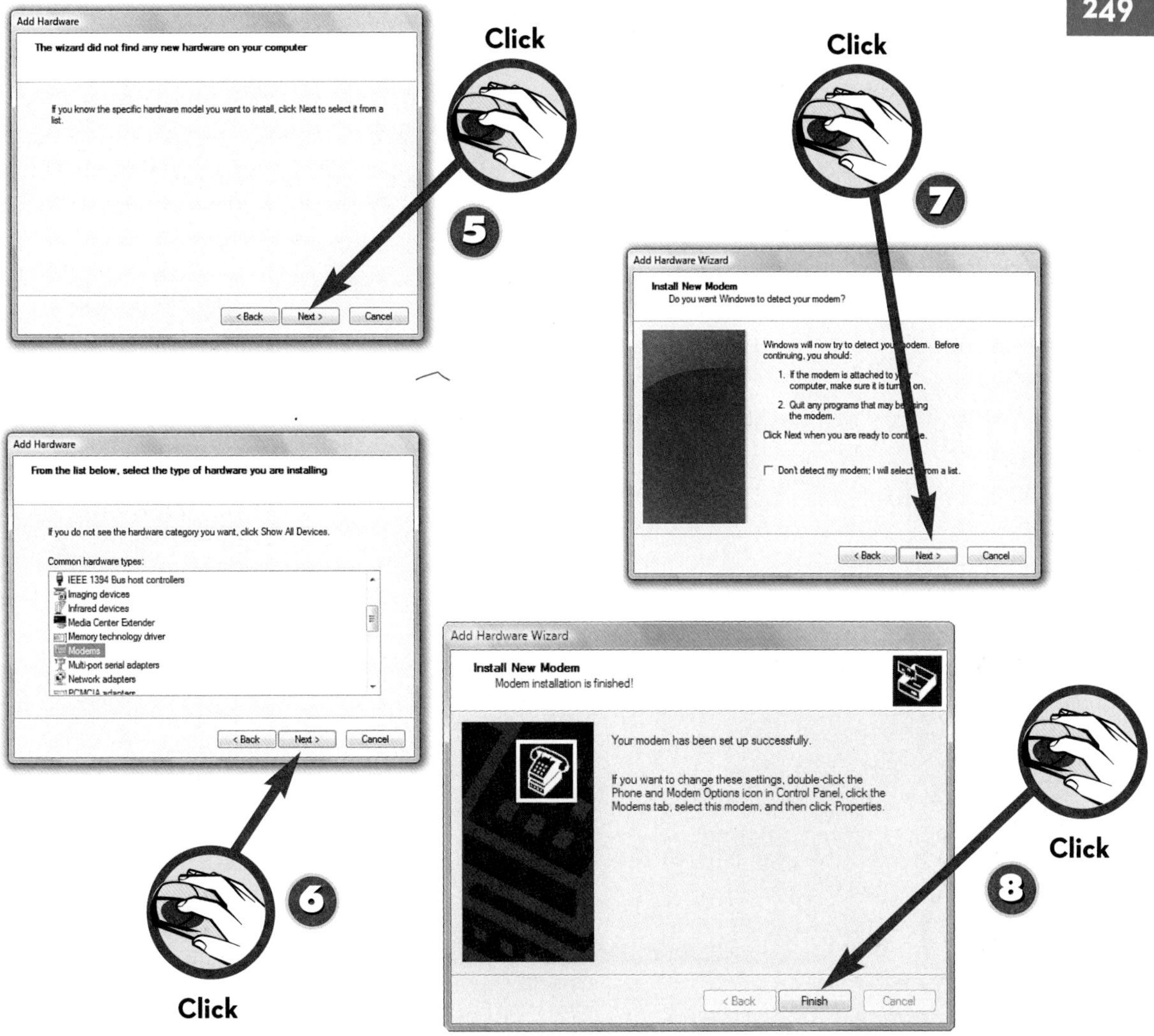

5 If a device is detected, Windows installs it automatically; click the **Finish** button to close the wizard. If no devices are found (as shown here), click the **Next** button to continue.

6 A list of common hardware types appears. Click the category that best describes the type of device you want to install, and then click the **Next** button.

7 You may be prompted to select a device manufacturer and model, or (as in this case) Windows may try to detect the device. Click **Next**.

8 What happens next depends on the hardware you're installing; follow the wizard's instructions to complete the process. Click **Finish** when prompted.

End

TIP

Using the Driver CD or Disk

If your hardware is provided with a driver CD or floppy disk, follow the vendor's instructions for use. In some cases, you may need to install the driver before connecting the device.

NOTE

Keeping Tabs on the Installation Process

During the installation process, you may see messages indicating that the device has been detected and that drivers are being installed. These messages appear in the notification area at the lower-right side of your screen.

VIEWING AND TROUBLESHOOTING INSTALLED HARDWARE

Windows Vista's Device Manager enables you to determine the status of installed hardware and helps you troubleshoot problems with hardware, such as missing drivers, conflicts, and disabled hardware.

Start

1. Open the Control Panel as described in the first task. Select **System and Maintenance** from the listed categories.
2. Click **Device Manager**.
3. Device Manager opens. Devices without drivers are displayed in the **Other devices** category.

Continued

TIP

Steps Vary

Depending on the type of device, the steps you follow will vary. Simply follow the solution wizard's instructions, clicking **Next** to go to the next step.

TIP

Reinstalling Drivers

The solution wizard may prompt you to search online or search your computer for driver software. If you have downloaded driver software, choose **Browse my computer**. Otherwise, select **Search automatically**. If Windows cannot find a suitable driver, visit the manufacturer's website.

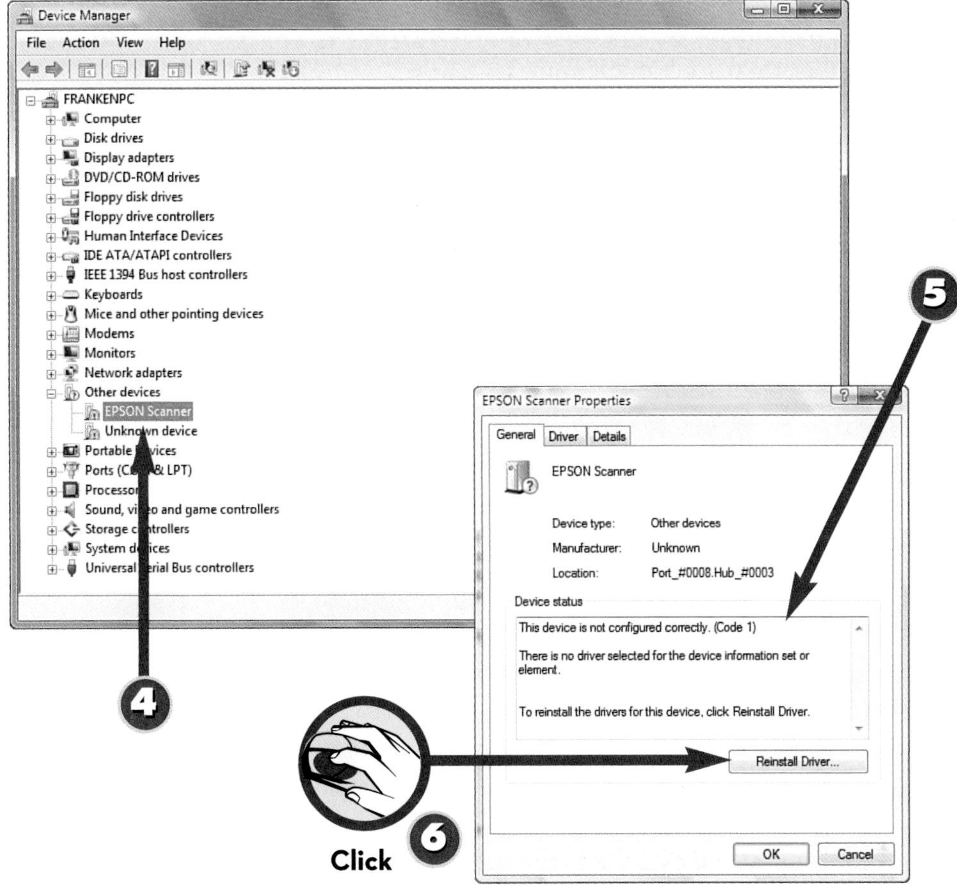

4 To determine the problem with a device, double-click the device to open its properties sheet.

5 The **Device Status** message on the General tab indicates the problem with the device.

6 To solve the problem, click the **Reinstall Driver** button and follow the prompts provided.

End

NOTE

Best Drivers and Substitutes

You should use a driver designed for Windows Vista for best results. However, if you cannot find a Vista driver, try a driver made for Windows XP. You can use the Device Manager to update the driver at a later time.

TIP

Alternative Paths to the Device Manager

You can also access the Device Manager by right-clicking **Computer**, selecting **Properties**, and selecting **Device Manager** from the System properties Tasks menu.

PROTECTING YOUR PC WITH SYSTEM RESTORE

After you add new programs or hardware, you might find that your system does not work properly. Trying to troubleshoot a problem such as this can be difficult. To help, Windows Vista includes System Restore, which you can use to return to a previous setup that did work. Using System Restore does not harm your documents, email messages, history lists, or favorites lists.

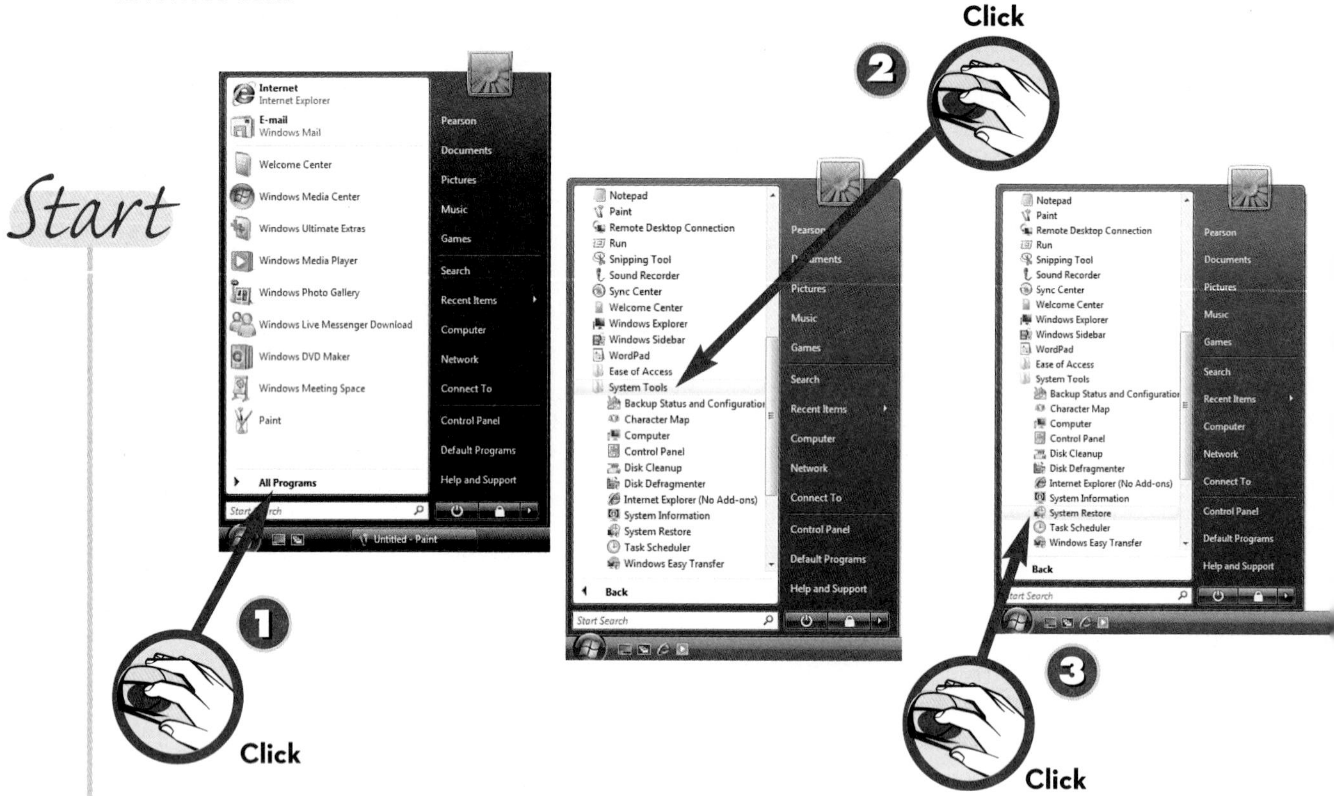

1. Click the **Start** button and select **All Programs**.
2. Click **Accessories**, and then click **System Tools**.
3. Select **System Restore**.

Continued

TIP

Undoing a Restore

To undo the last system restore, click **Undo System Restore**. Do this if using System Restore did not help your problem or made matters worse.

TIP

Cancel Restore

You can cancel the restore by clicking **Cancel** in any of the windows. Also, you can go back a step and make a change by clicking **Back**.

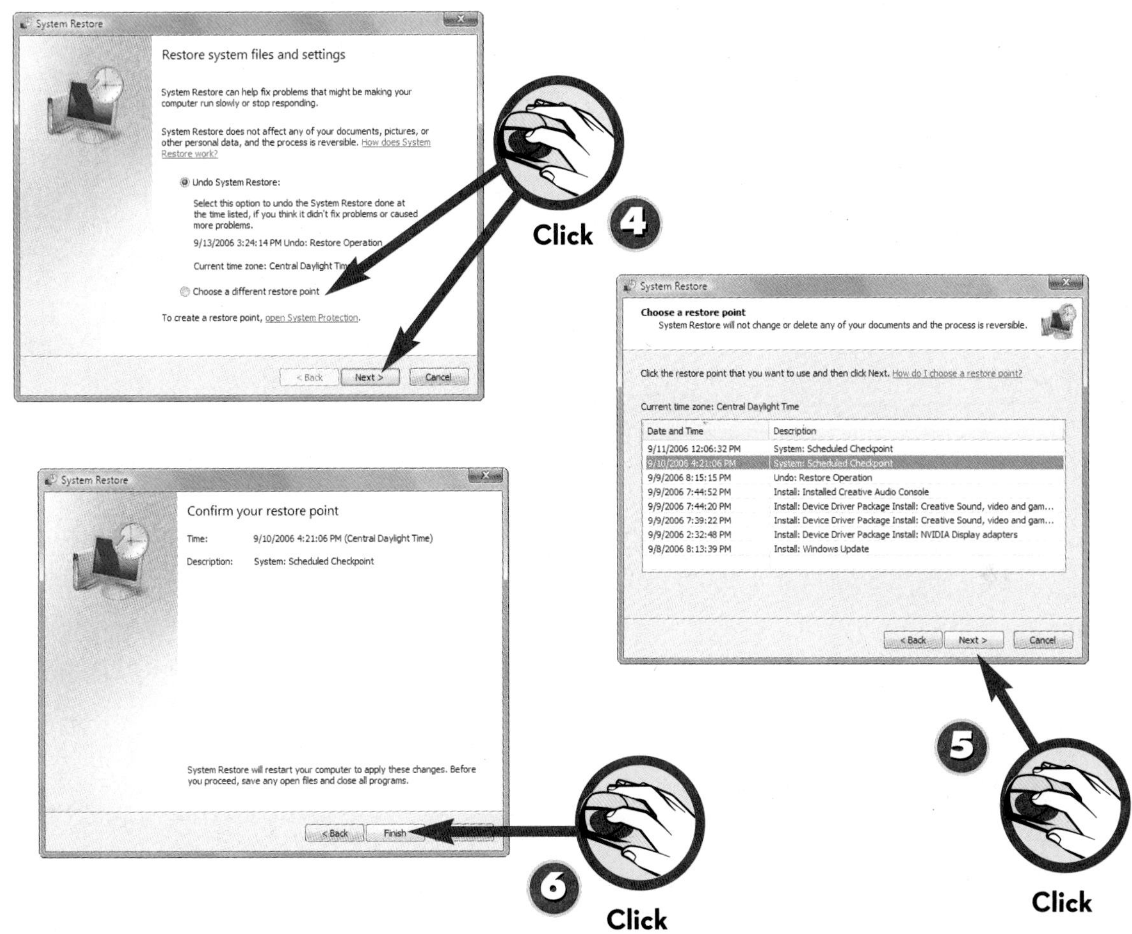

4 The System Restore window opens. Click the **Choose a different restore point** radio button, and then click **Next**.

5 Select a restore point from the list of restore points given, and click **Next**. Choose the most recent point at which your computer worked properly.

6 Review the restore point selected. Click **Finish** to start the restoration process. Windows restores and restarts your system.

End

NOTE

Restore Points

System Restore monitors changes to your system and creates *restore points* each day by default. System Restore also creates restore points when hardware or software is installed or when Windows updates are installed. If you have a problem immediately after a hardware or software installation or an update to Windows, choose a restore point immediately before that event.

BACKING UP FILES

Windows Vista includes the Backup and Restore Center control panel, which makes backups to popular devices, such as recordable and rewritable DVDs or external hard disks, very easy. After you make a file backup, Windows Vista continues to back up files on a set schedule for additional safety.

Start

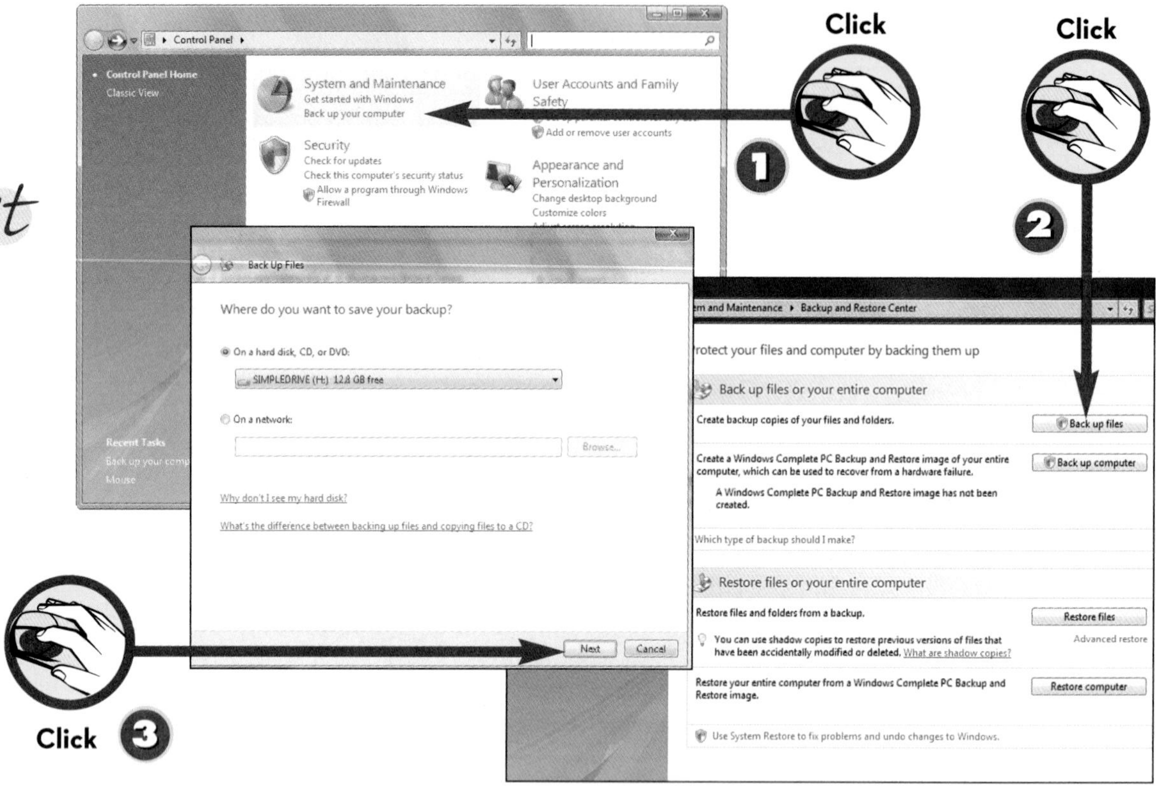

Click ❶ Click ❷ Click ❸

❶ Click **Start**, **Control Panel**, and then click **Back up your computer** in the System and Maintenance category.

❷ Click **Back up files**.

❸ You can use an external hard disk, a network folder, a CD, or a DVD for backup. Select the backup device, and click **Next** to continue.

Continued

TIP

Best Backup Drives

The easiest and most reliable device for backups is an external hard disk plugged into a USB port, such as the one shown in step 3. Although you can use CD or DVD media, each disk must be formatted, and such backups take longer and require you to swap media if you are backing up a lot of data.

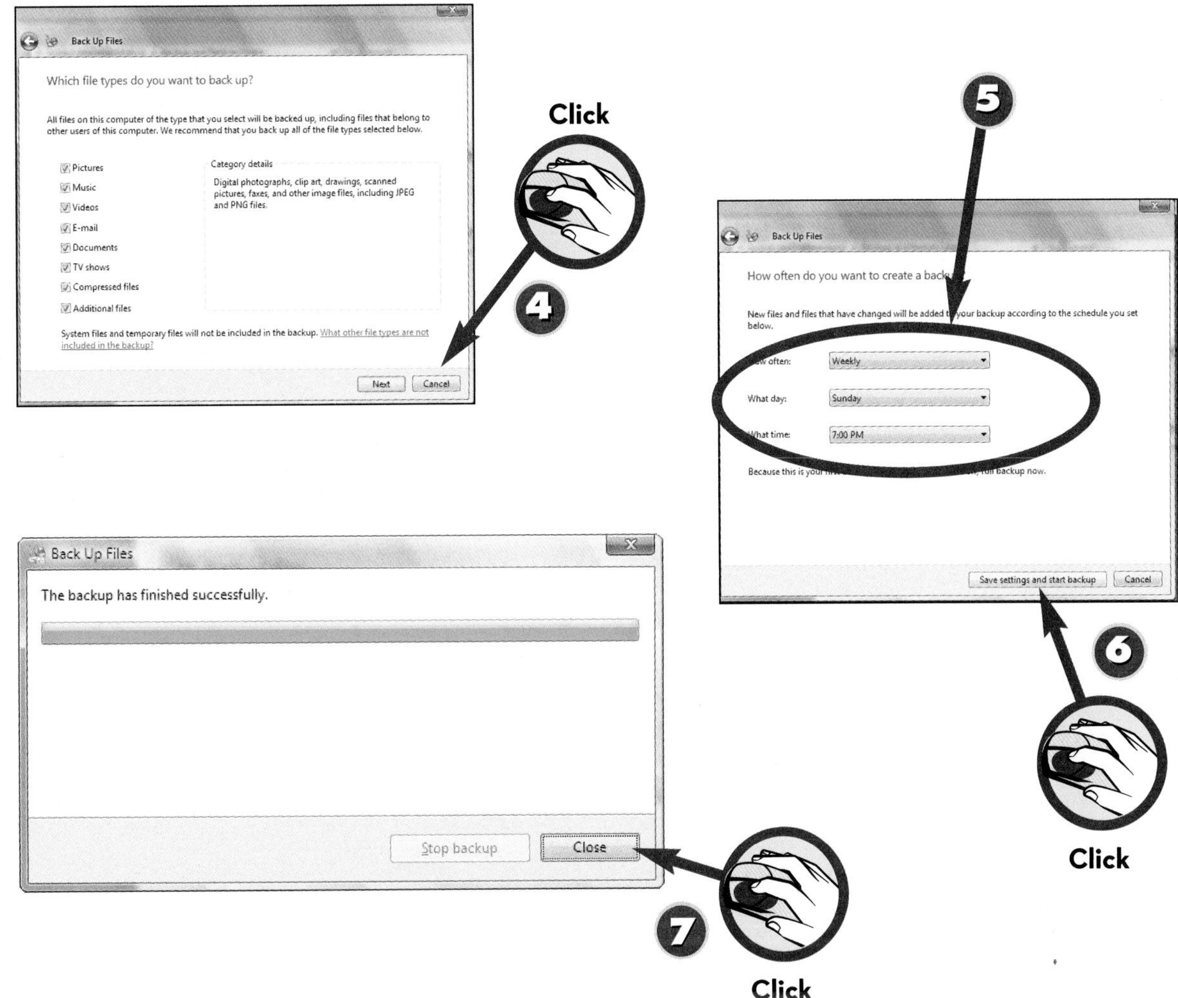

4 By default, all data files, email, and user settings (such as favorites) are selected for backup. Click **Next** to continue.

5 By default, backups are performed weekly on Sunday at 7 pm. To change settings, click the pull-down menus for how often, what day, and what time.

6 To start the backup process, click **Save settings and start backup**.

7 At the end of the backup process, click **Close**.

End

NOTE

Full Backup for Files Only

Although file backup includes all user files the first time you run it (see step 5), the backup process in Vista Home Premium does not back up your Windows installation. Windows Vista Ultimate features a Complete PC Backup that does back up Windows as well as user files, enabling you to restore your entire system in case of a system failure.

RESTORING BACKUP FILES

If you accidentally delete a file, multiple files, or even entire folders, you can restore them using Windows Vista's Restore Files feature in the Backup and Restore Center.

Start

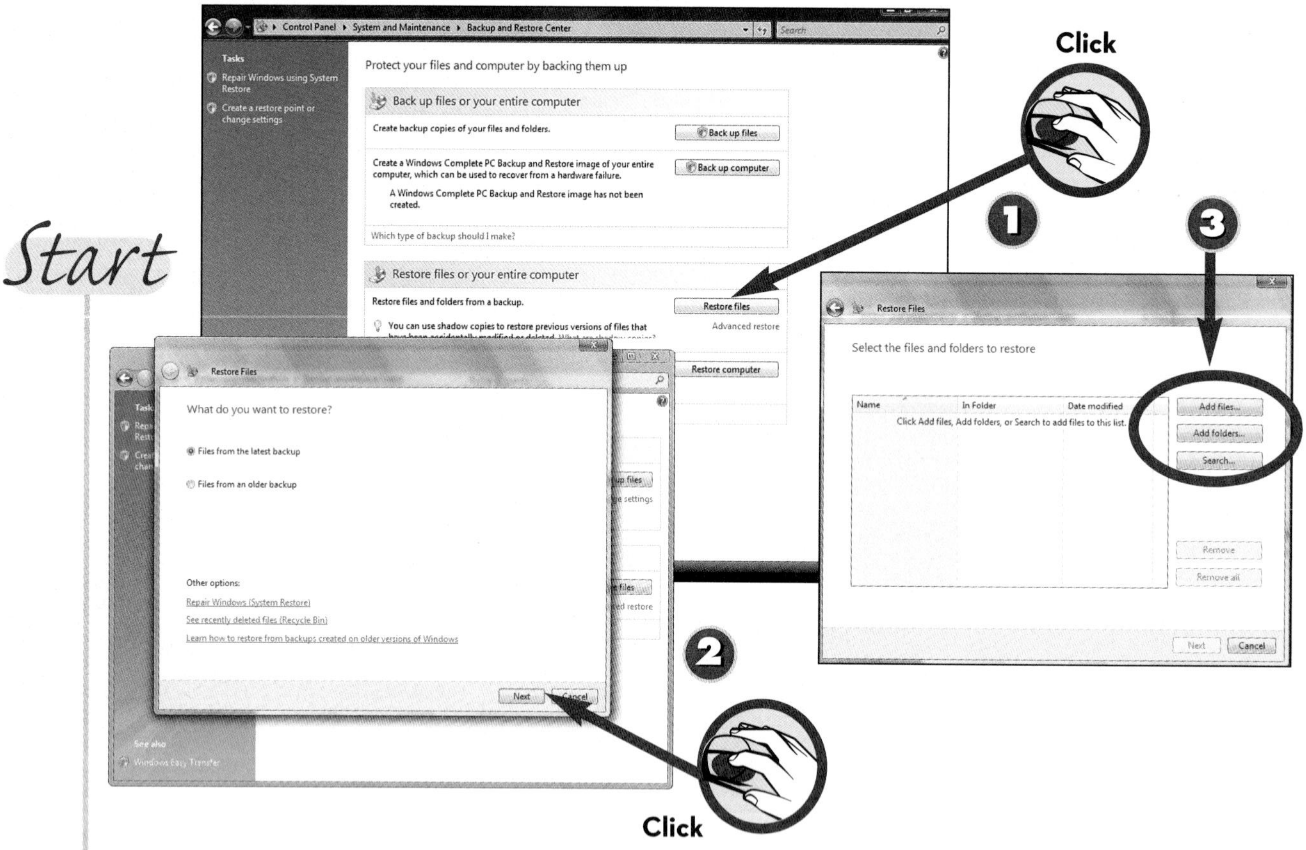

1. From the Backup and Restore Center (refer to the previous task to learn how to open it), click **Restore files**.
2. Click **Next** to restore files from the latest backup. You can also select the option to choose from older backups. Connect your drive, or insert the last disk of the backup set.
3. To restore a particular file, click **Add files**. To restore a particular folder, click **Add folders**. Click **Search** to look for files or folders matching search terms.

Continued

TIP

Restoring from CD or DVD

If you are restoring from CD or DVD, insert the last disk in the backup set into the system, even if the file or folder you want to restore is on an earlier disk. Windows Vista will tell you when to swap disks.

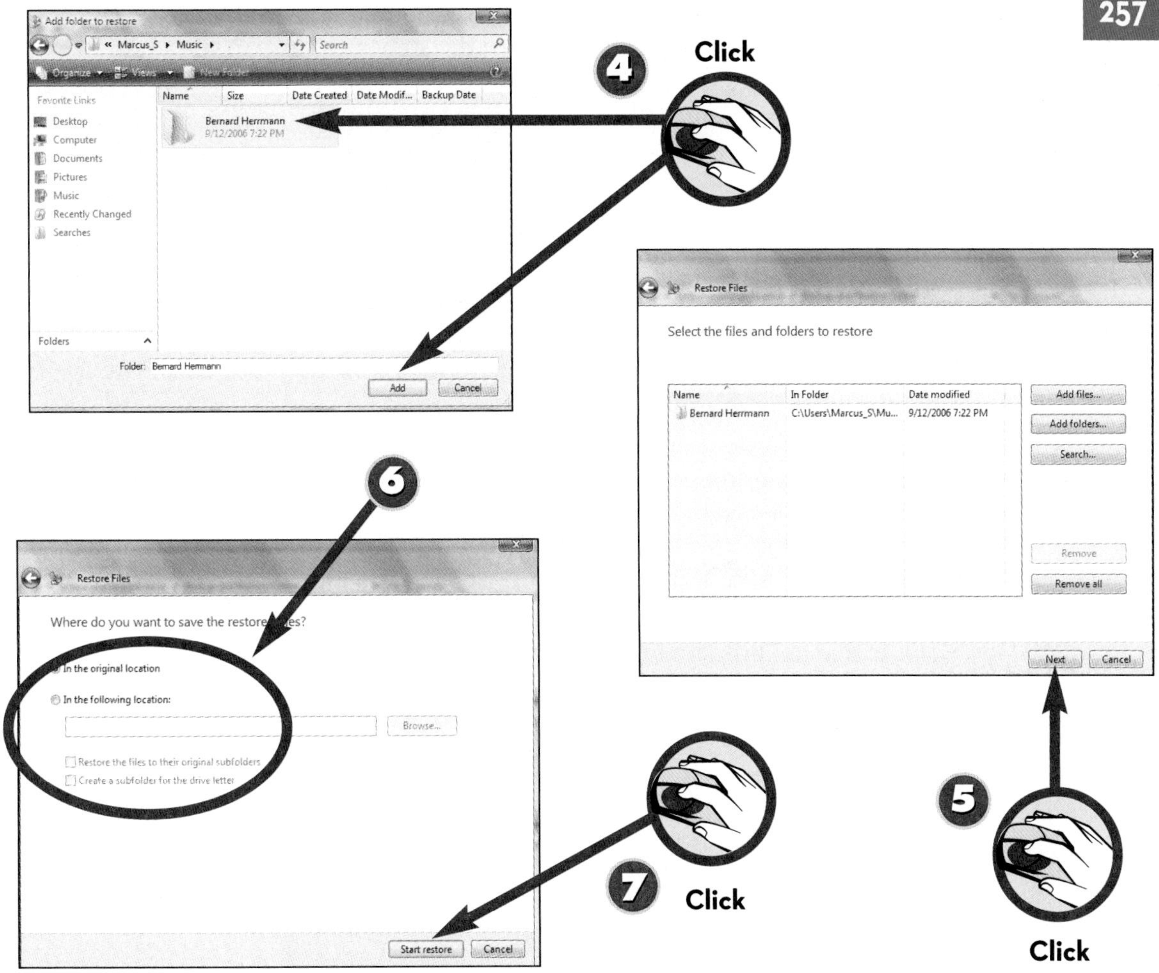

4 Highlight the file or folder you want to restore, and click **Add**.

5 Repeat steps 3 and 4 until you have selected all the files or folders you want to restore. Click **Next** to continue.

6 Windows Vista will restore the folders or files to their original locations unless you select other options.

7 Click **Start restore** to restore files or folders. A progress window appears. At the end of the process, click **Finish** (not shown).

End

TIP

Testing Your Backup

You can use the option to restore to another location to test a backup. Create a folder called "Test," and restore some files from a backup you made to that folder. If you can restore your files, you know your backup works.

USING WINDOWS ACCESSORIES

Windows Vista provides several accessories, or *applications*, that you can use to help you in your work. These accessories are not full-featured programs, but they are useful for specific jobs in the Windows environment. Accessories include a Calendar, contact manager, calculator, painting program, word processor (WordPad), text editor (Notepad), games, and other programs.

Note that in addition to programs included in the Accessories folder, Windows has other programs, and these programs are covered in detail in other Parts. For instance, entertainment programs are covered in Part 8, "Entertainment," Windows Mail in Part 9, "Sending Email," and Internet Explorer in Part 10, "Browsing the Internet."

USING ACCESSORIES

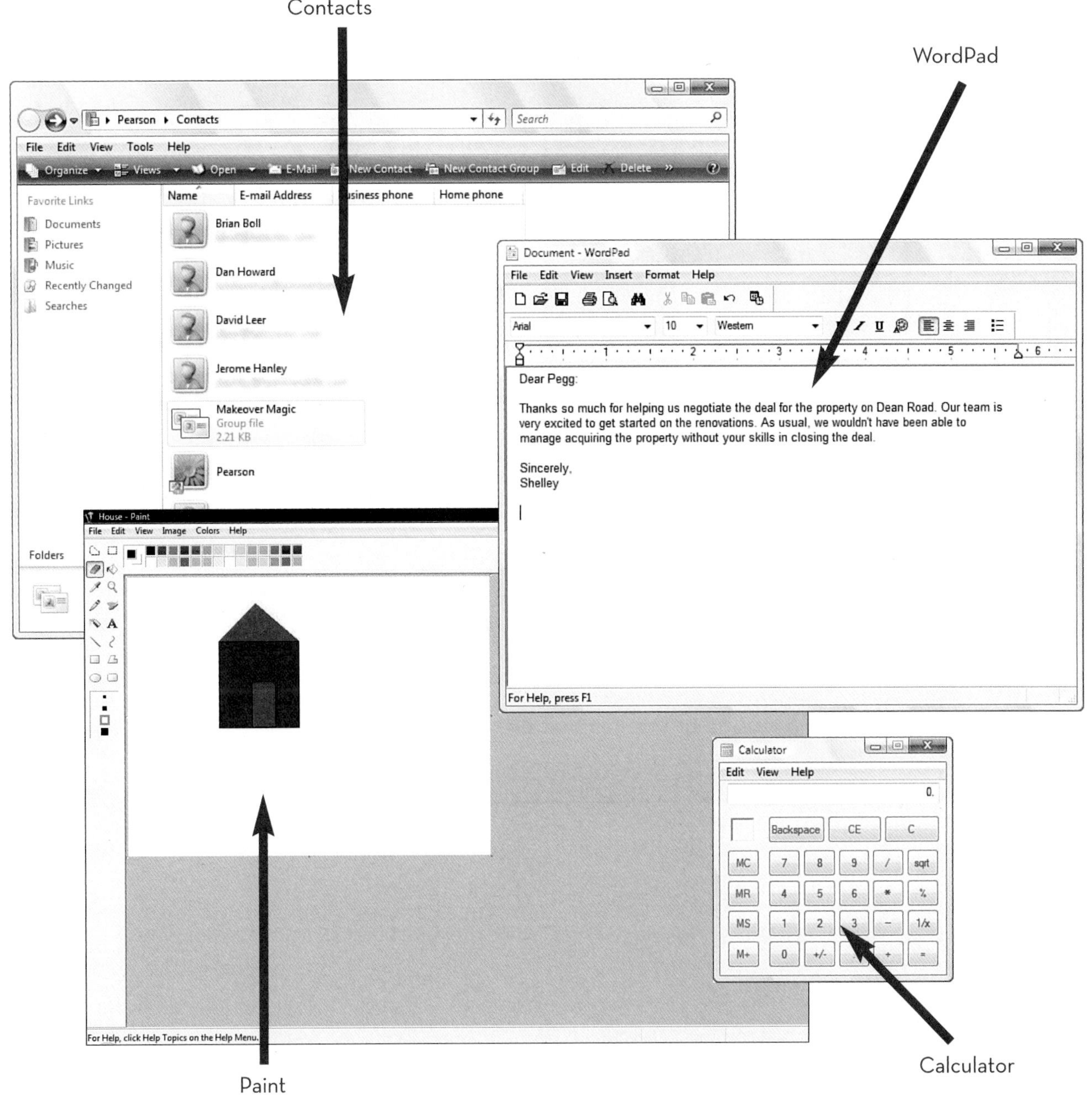

USING THE CALCULATOR

If you need to perform a quick calculation, use the Calculator program included with Windows Vista. You can add, subtract, multiply, divide, figure percentages, and more with this handy tool.

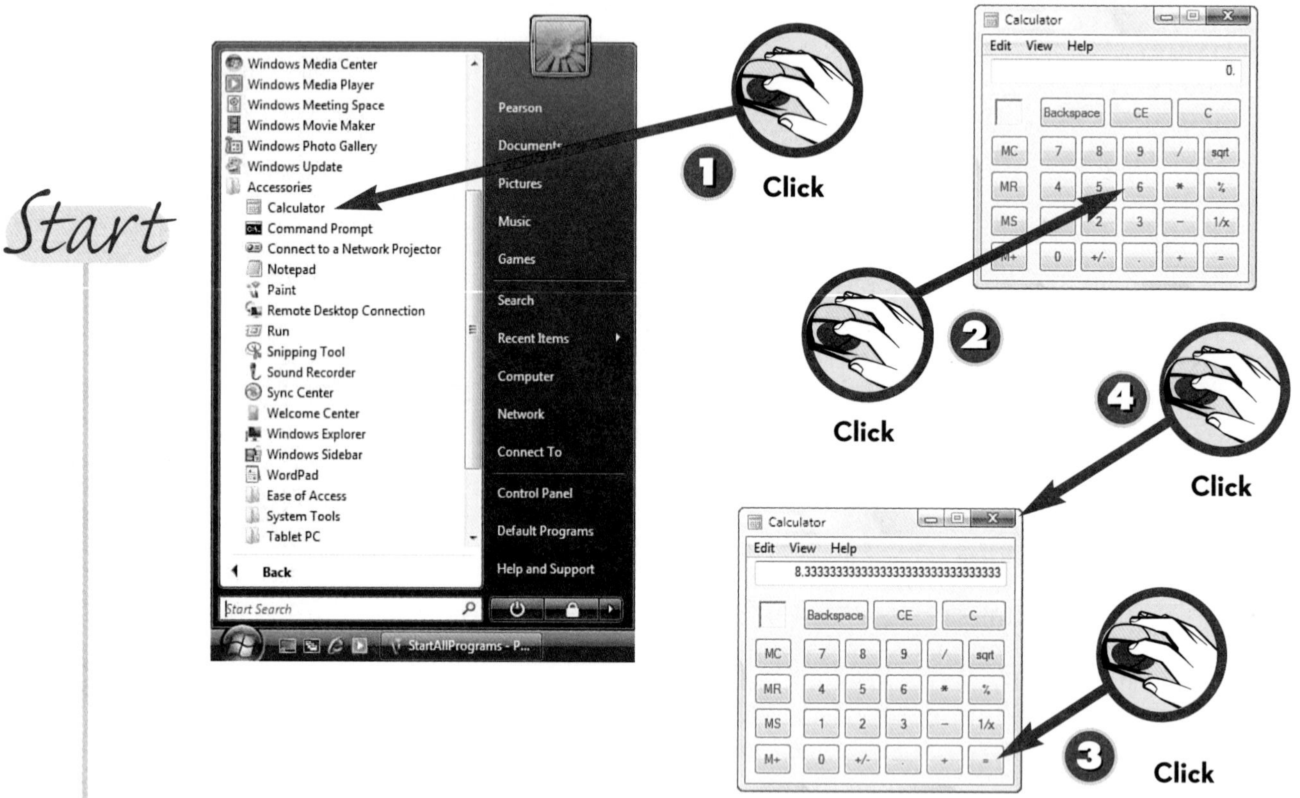

Start

1 Click

2 Click

3 Click

4 Click

1. Click **Start**, **All Programs**, **Accessories**, and then click **Calculator**.
2. Click the buttons on the calculator to enter an equation.
3. Click **=** to see the results of the calculation.
4. Click the **Close** (X) button to close the Calculator window.

End

TIP

Scientific Calculator

To use a more complex scientific calculator, click the calculator's **View** menu, and then click **Scientific**.

TIP

Copy Results to a Document

You can copy the results of a calculation into a document. To do so, select the results, click **Edit**, and then choose **Copy**. Then move to the document where you want to paste the results, click **Edit**, and choose **Paste**.

ADDING NEW CONTACTS

Often you use your computer to keep in touch with others using email, the telephone, or regular mail. In previous versions of Windows, you used the Address Book to keep track of contact information. Windows Vista includes a new type of address book called Contacts. You can use it to keep track of as much or as little information as you'd like about friends, family, co-workers, and clients. This task describes how to add a new contact to the Contacts list.

Start

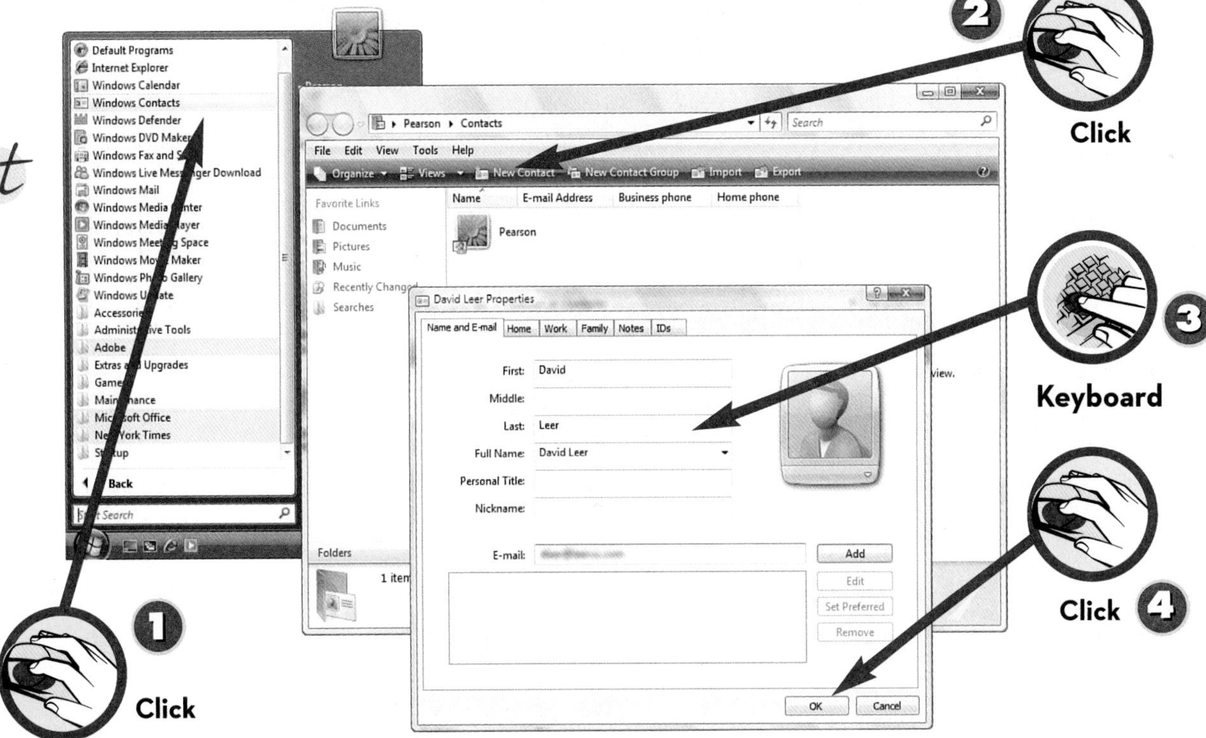

1. Click **Start**, **All Programs**, and then **Windows Contacts**.
2. To add a new contact, click **New Contact** in the command bar.
3. For each of the fields, enter the appropriate information.
4. Click **OK** to add the contact.

End

NOTE

Home and Work

Use the Home and Work tabs to enter home and work contact information; you can use Windows Contacts to keep track of as little or as much information as you require. (Many people, for instance, simply keep track of email addresses.)

TIP

Family Information

If you want to keep up-to-date information on your clients, you can also track family information, such as spouses' and children's names, birthdays, and other dates.

EDITING CONTACT INFORMATION

Contact information frequently changes; people move, change jobs, and get new cell phone numbers or email addresses. To keep your contacts up-to-date, you can edit a contact's information.

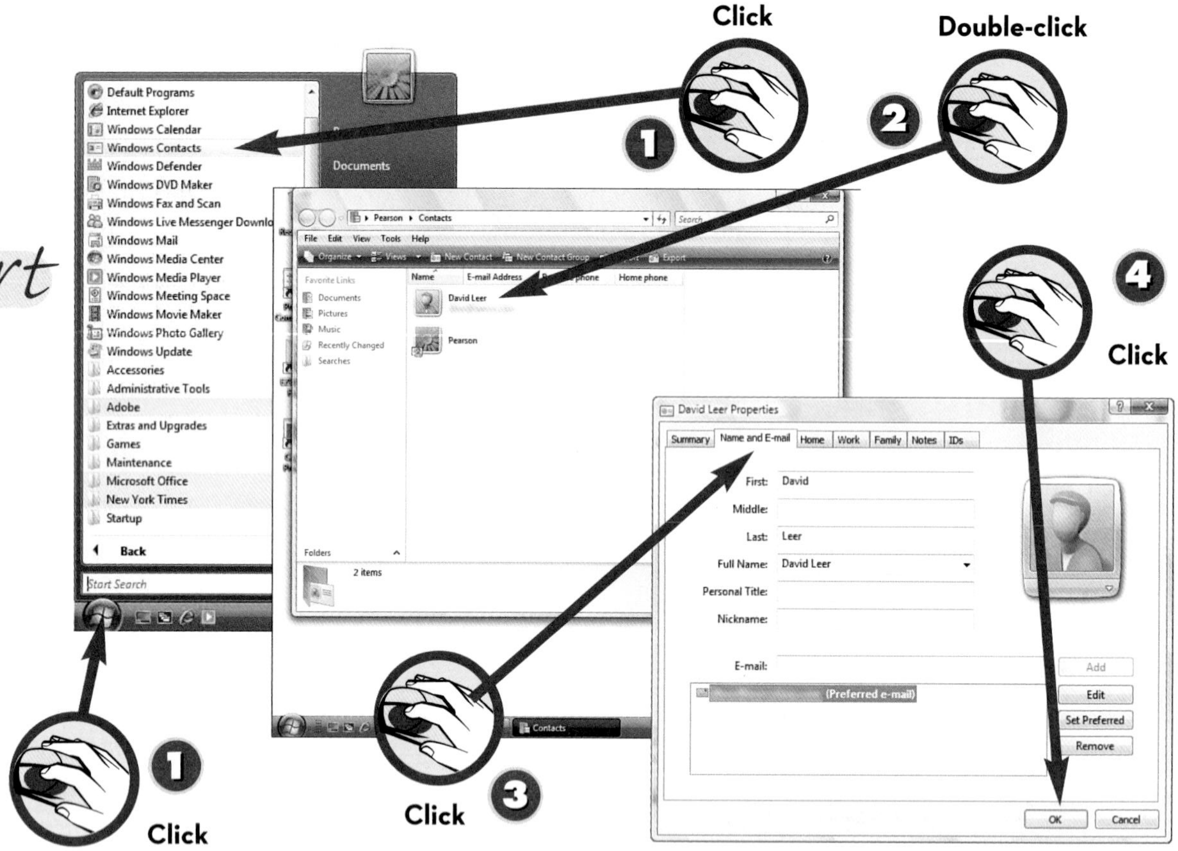

1. Click the **Start** button, and then click **All Programs**, **Windows Contacts** to open Windows Contacts.
2. Double-click the contact you want to edit.
3. Click the appropriate tab, and then make any changes. For instance, click the **Name and E-mail** tab to make changes to office information.
4. Click **OK** to save the changes.

TIP

Send an Email

When you select a contact, you see options in the command bar for working with that contact. For instance, you can click the **New E-mail Message** button to send an email message.

FINDING A CONTACT

Windows Vista has greatly enhanced its search capabilities. You can use Instant Search from the Contact Explorer to quickly locate a contact.

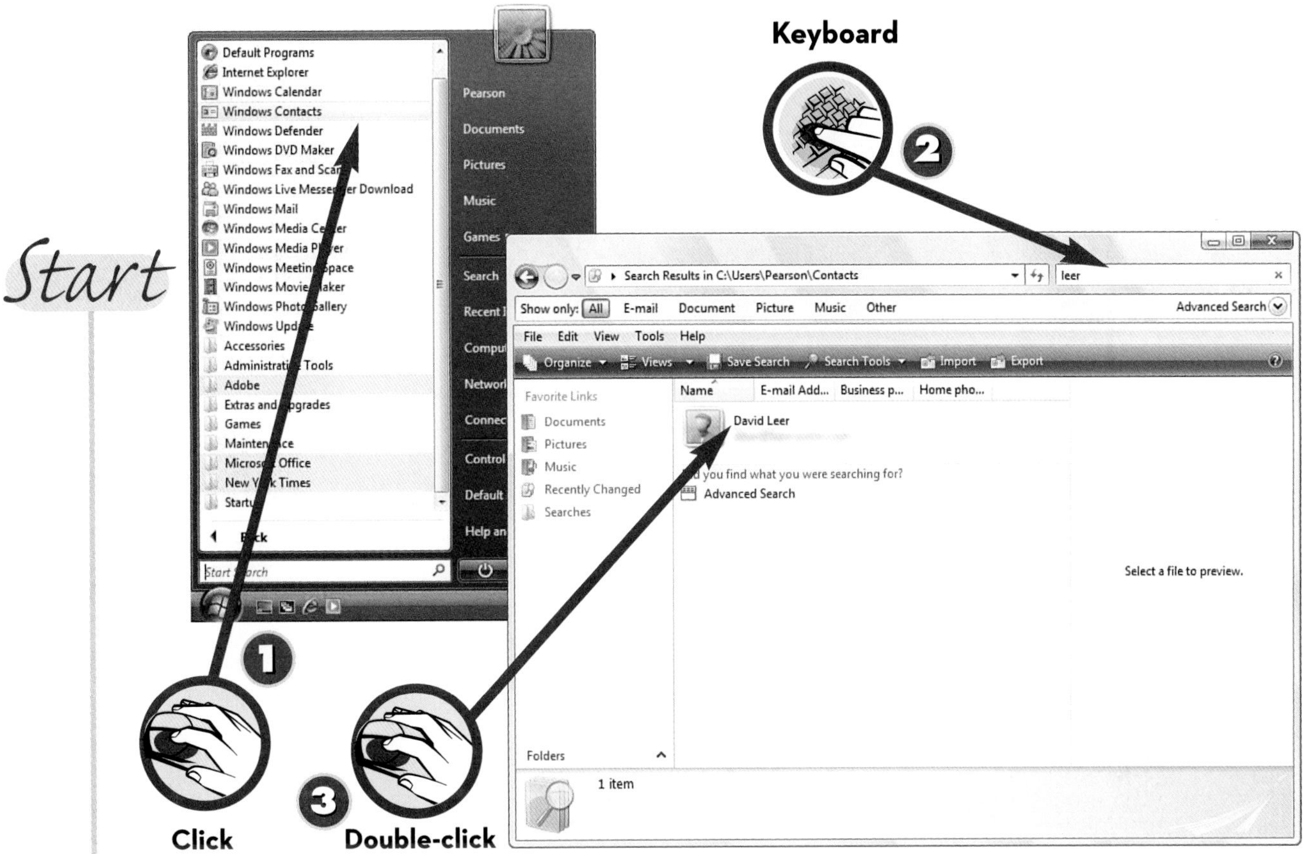

Keyboard

Start

Click

Double-click

1. Click the **Start** button, and then click **All Programs**, **Windows Contacts**.
2. In the search text box, type any identifying information, such as the person's name or company information.
3. Matching entries are displayed. You can double-click an entry to open the contact information.

End

NOTE

Properties

New in Windows Vista is the Preview pane; here you can view properties about the selected item. For instance, if you select a contact, the pane shows key dates about the contact.

TIP

Changing Views

You can also change the views of how the contacts are listed by selecting from the **View** drop-down list on the toolbar. A different view many help you locate the contact you seek.

GROUPING CONTACTS

If you have a group of people you send email to regularly, you can create a contact group to avoid having to add each person to the email individually. After setting up a contact group, you can type one contact name, such as "School PTO," and all members assigned to that group will receive the email.

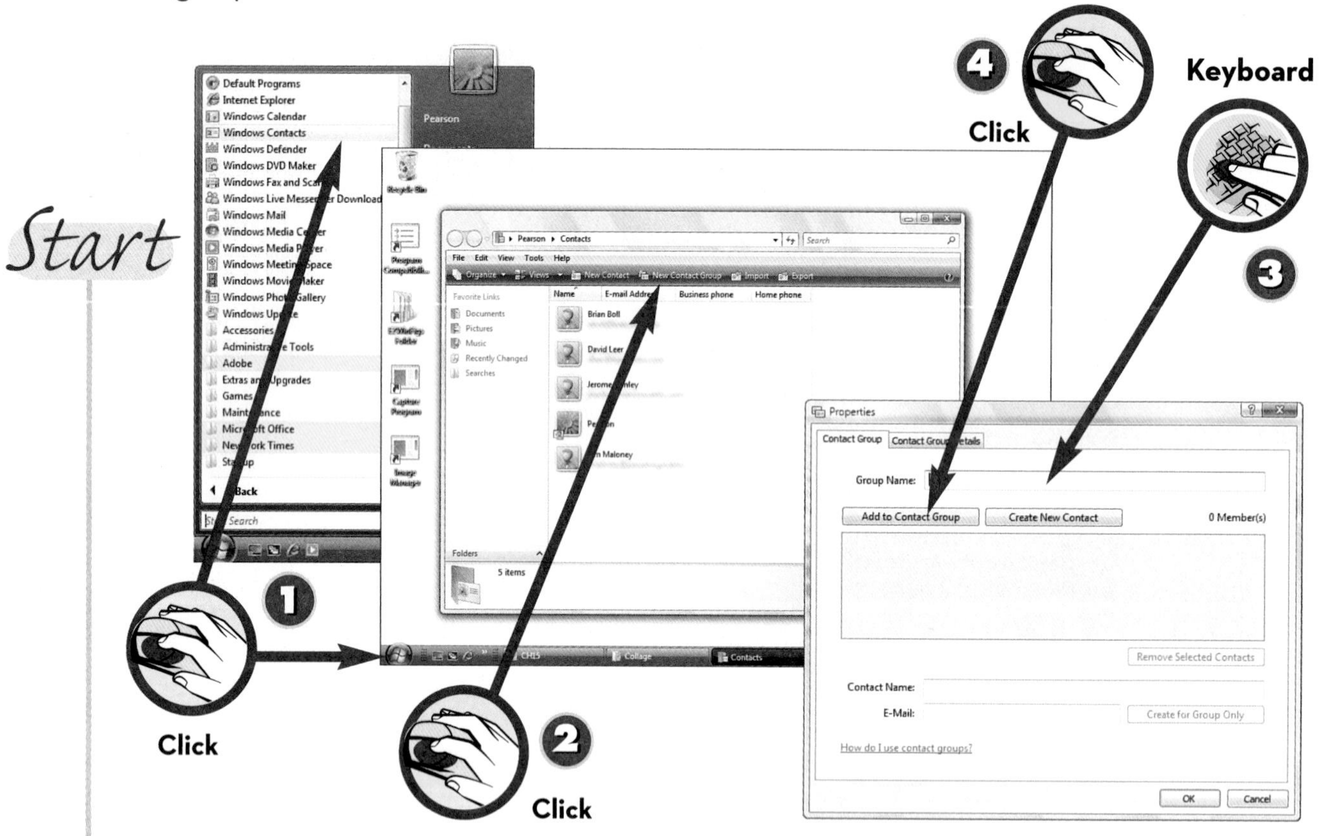

Start

1. Click the **Start** button, and then click **All Programs**, **Windows Contacts**.
2. Click **New Contact Group**.
3. Type a name for the group.
4. Click **Add to Contact Group**.

Continued

TIP

Adding Members to a Group

When you click the **Add to Contact Group** button, you are able to select existing contacts to add to the group. Or you can add new contacts on the fly. To add new contacts, click the **Create New Contact** button when setting up the group. New contacts are automatically added as members of the group when they are added to your contact list.

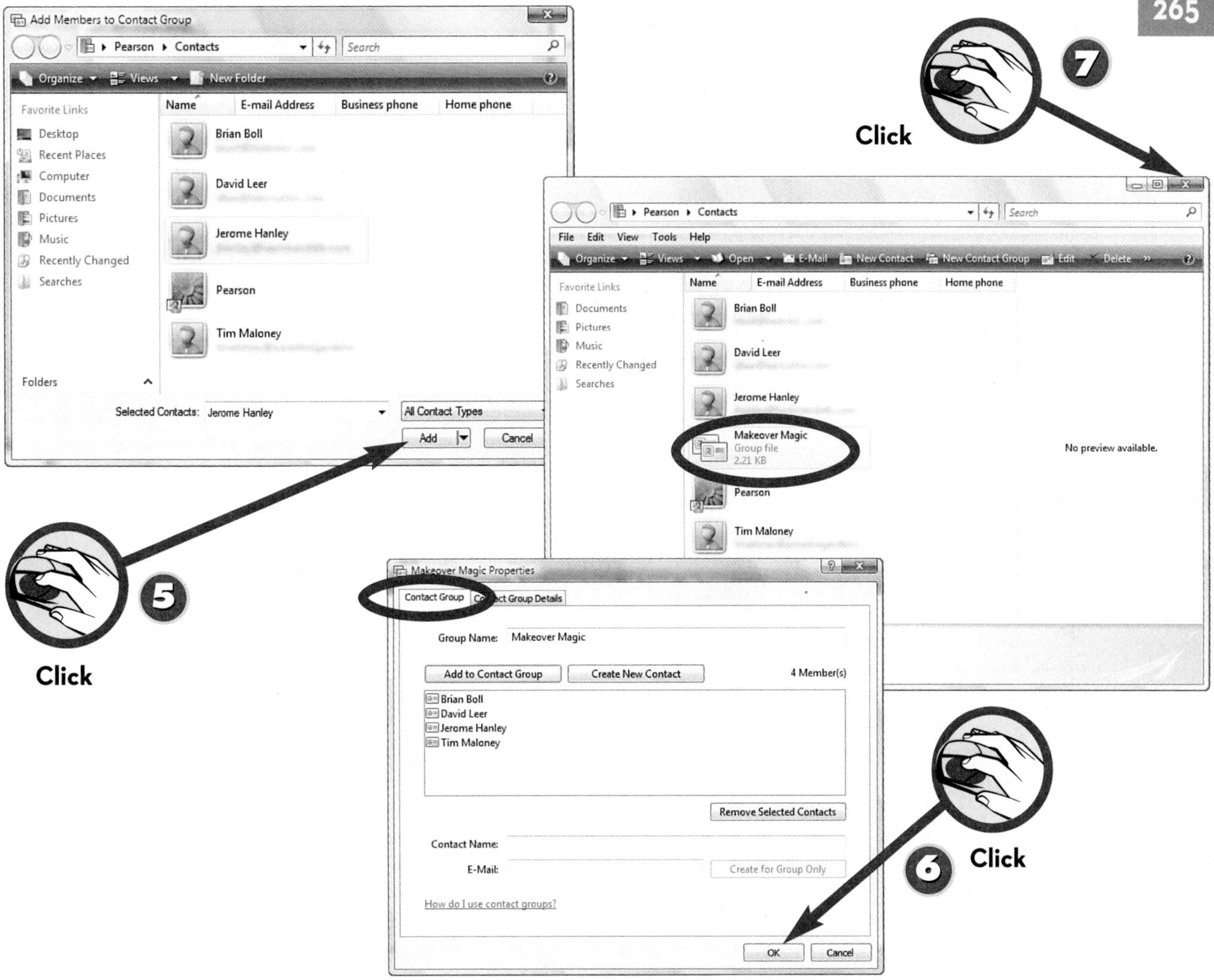

5 Click

6 Click

7 Click

5 You see your list of contacts. To add a contact to the group, select it in the list and then click the **Add** button.

6 The contact is added to the group list, and you are returned to the Contact Group tab. Continue following steps 4 and 5 until the group is complete. When all the members are added, click **OK**.

7 The group is listed in the Contact list. If you want to close the list, click the **Close** (X) button.

End

TIP

Updating the List

If you edit an individual entry for a member, the list is updated automatically. Add a new member using the **Add to Contact Group** button and follow the process. Or select the contact to delete and click the **Remove Selected Contacts** button.

TIP

Removing a Group Entirely

To delete the entire group, right-click it in the Contacts window, click **Delete**, and then confirm the deletion by clicking **Yes**.

DELETING A CONTACT

If you no longer communicate with a contact, it's best to delete that person from your Contacts list. You'll be surprised how quickly your Contacts list fills up if you don't manage that person. Including people you no longer keep in contact with just clogs up the list and makes finding the contact you seek more difficult.

Start

1 Click

2 Right-click

3 Click

4 Click

1. Click the **Start** button, and then click **All Programs**, **Windows Contacts**.
2. Right-click the contact you want to delete.
3. From the shortcut menu that appears, click **Delete**.
4. Click **Yes** to confirm the deletion.

End

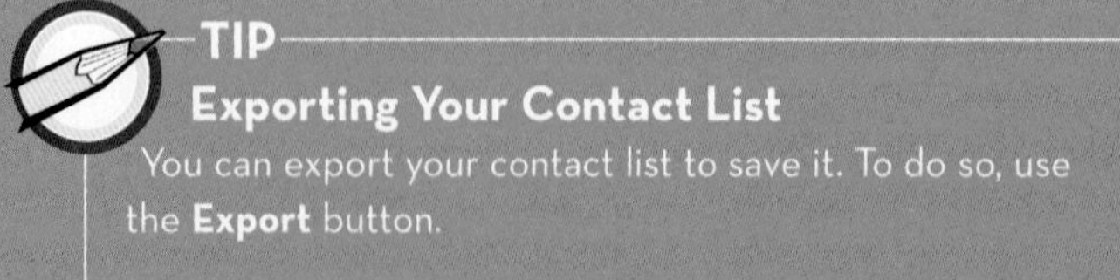

TIP

Exporting Your Contact List

You can export your contact list to save it. To do so, use the **Export** button.

VIEWING YOUR CALENDAR

The Windows Calendar has also gotten an overhaul. You can use it to schedule events, appointments, and meetings. You can also share your Calendar with others so that they can see your availability. Some users even post their calendars on the Internet.

Start

1. Click **Start**, **All Programs**, and then **Windows Calendar**.
2. You see that date's calendar of events.

End

TIP

Scrolling to Other Months or Years

To view another month, click the scroll button next to the month name. You can scroll backward or forward through the months.

SCHEDULING AN APPOINTMENT

You can use your Calendar to schedule a variety of events, including appointments, meetings, and events. Some appointments are one-time events; others may be reoccurring, such as your weekly board meeting. Calendar makes it easy to schedule appointments, including details such as start time, duration, location, and more.

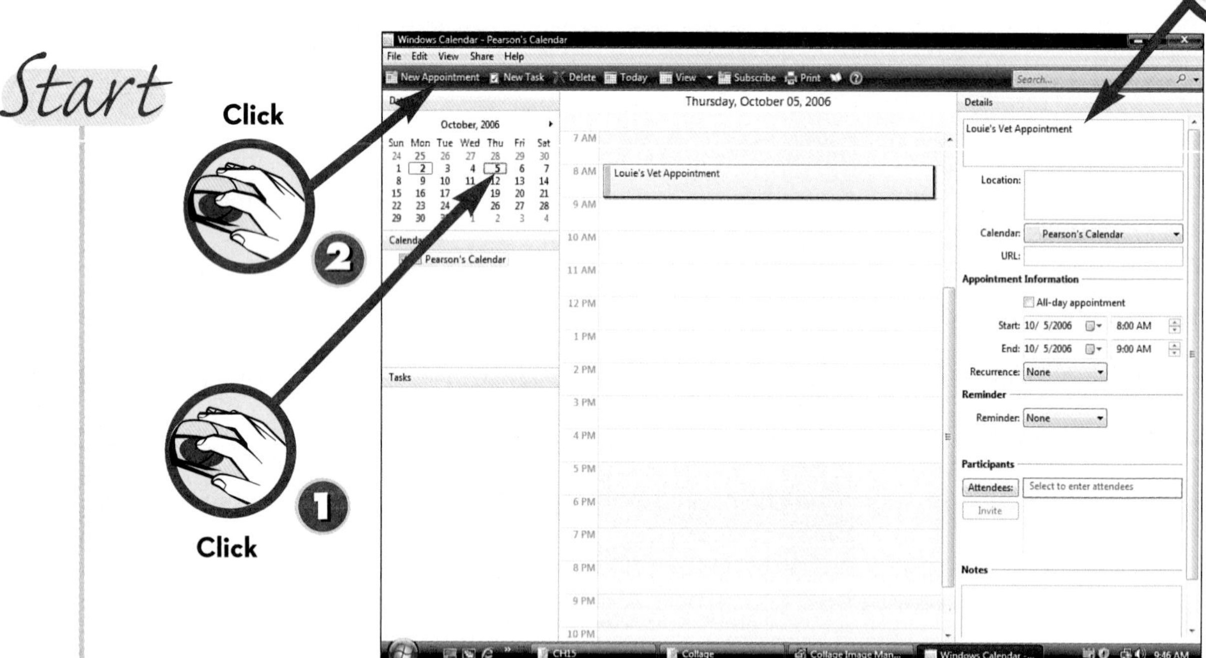

1. In Windows Calendar, click the day for which you want to set up an appointment.
2. Click **New Appointment** in the command bar.
3. In the **Details** area, type a name for the appointment. The name appears on the calendar as you type.

Continued

TIP

Going to a Date

You can click on the calendar to select a date or use the **View**, **Go to Date** command to go to a specific date.

TIP

Listing Participants

If you want to invite participants, they must be listed in your Contacts list. They will receive a reminder. To do so, click **Attendees**, select the contact from your Contacts list, and click **To**. Do this for each contact you want to invite. Then click **OK**. To set up an email reminder, click **Invite** and complete the email message.

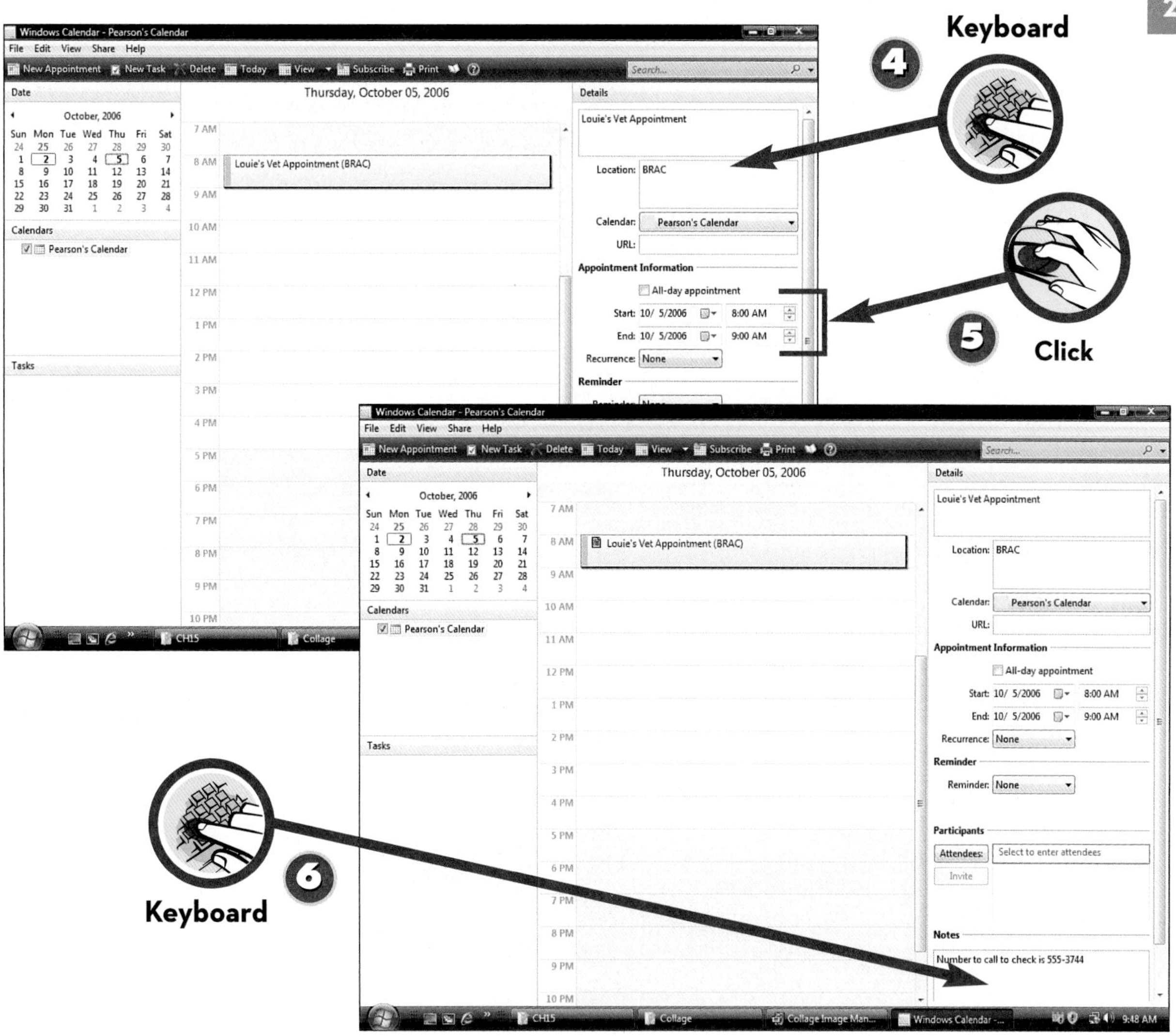

4 Type a location.

5 Use the drop-down arrow or spin boxes to select a start and end time.

6 If needed, scroll down through the Details pane and type any notes, such as reminders for the appointment, in the **Notes** field. The appointment is then saved to your calendar.

End

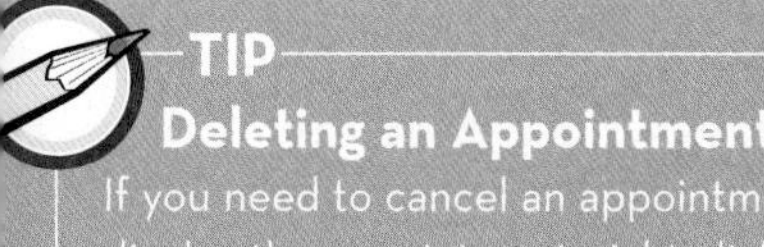

TIP

Deleting an Appointment

If you need to cancel an appointment, display the appointment, right-click it, and then click **Delete**. Click **Yes** to confirm the deletion.

TIP

Setting a Reminder

To remind yourself of an upcoming appointment, display the **Reminder** drop-down list and then select the amount of time before the appointment that you want the reminder sound to ring. You can select from 0 minutes to 2 weeks, or a particular date.

CHANGING CALENDAR VIEWS

Depending on what you need to find in your Calendar, you can change views to make your job easier. Want to know what's scheduled for a particular day? Change to a day view. Want to look a little farther into the future? You can view a week's list of events. You can also view several months out.

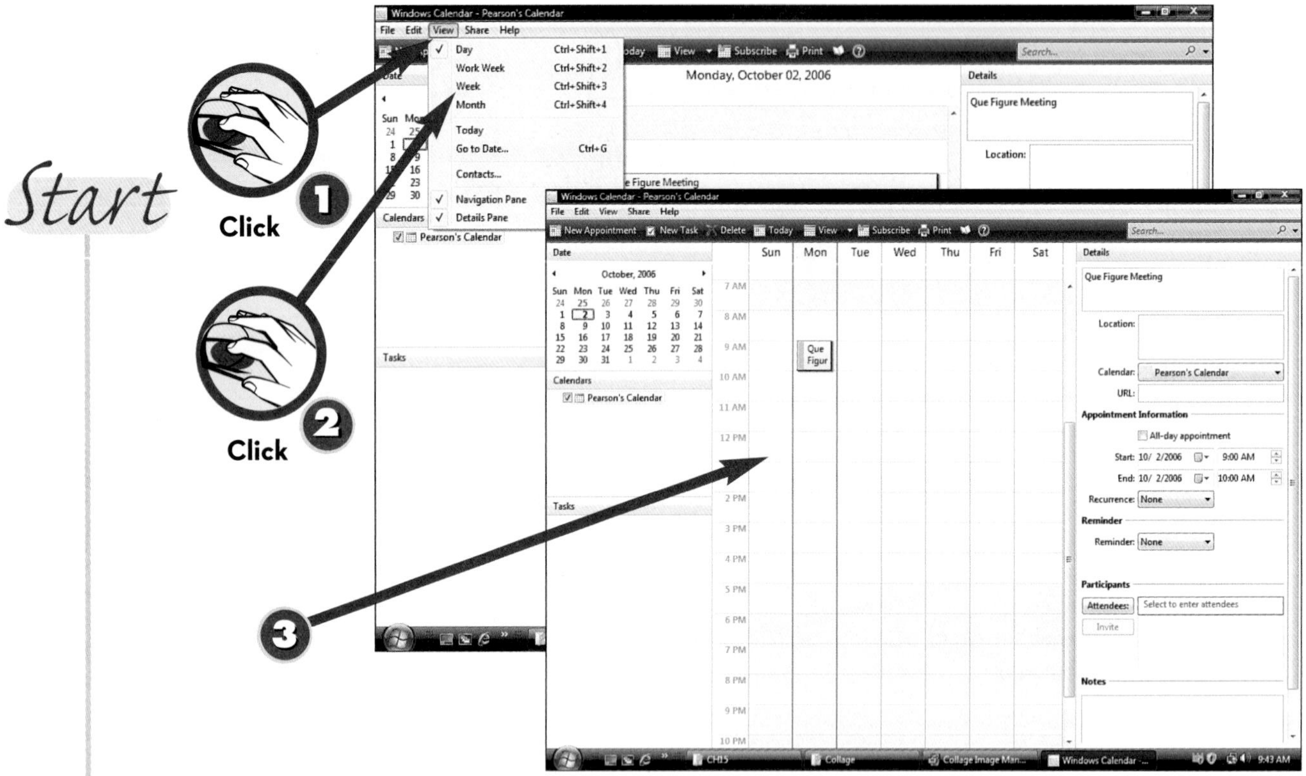

Start

Click 1

Click 2

3

1. From Windows Calendar, click **View**. You see a list of the available views.
2. Click the view you want to see.
3. Here you see Week view.

End

TIP

More Room

To make more room to display the calendar and its details, you can hide certain Calendar panes. For instance, you can hide the Navigation pane or the Details pane. To do so, click **View** and then uncheck these options to turn them off.

ENTERING A TASK

In addition to appointments, you can schedule tasks on your calendar. Doing so helps you keep track of what you need (or hope!) to accomplish during a day or other period.

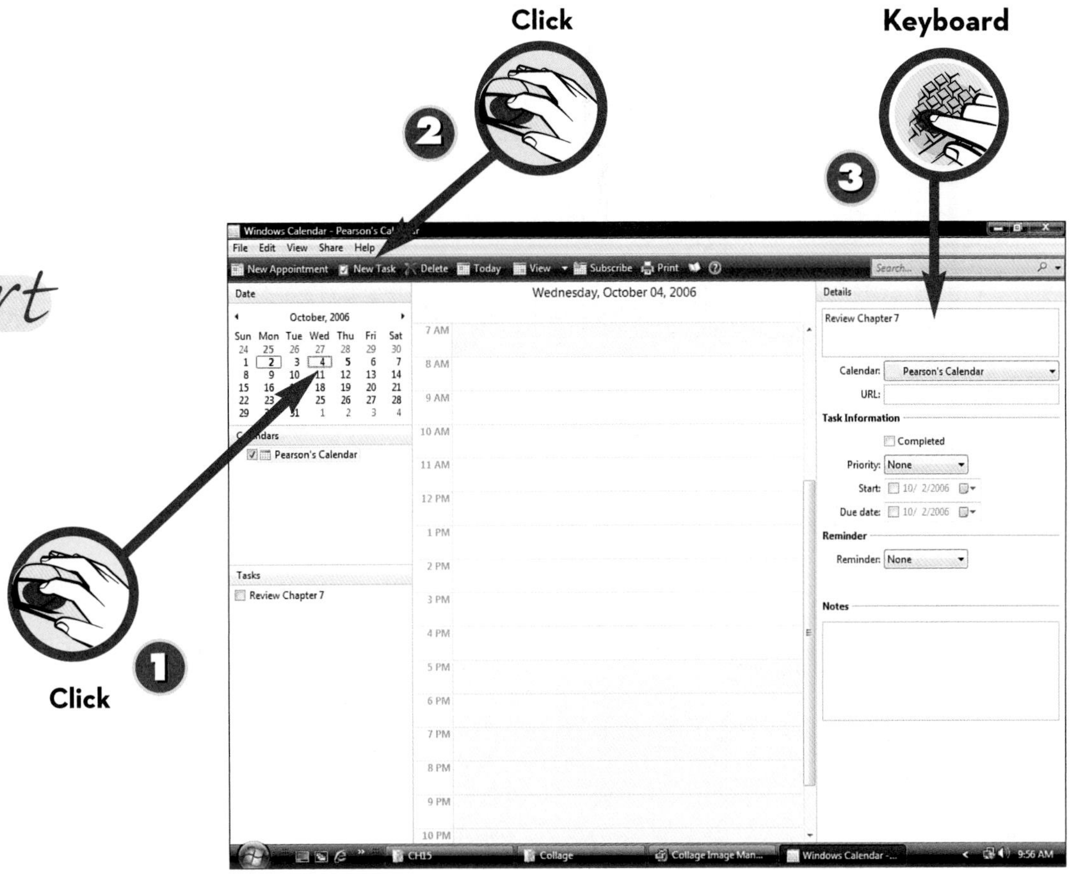

Start

1. In Windows Calendar, display the day that you want to complete the task.
2. Click the **New Task** button. A new task item is added to the Tasks list in the lower-left corner of the Calendar window.
3. Type a name for the task. The task is added to your calendar.

End

TIP

Deleting a Task

To delete a task, right-click it, click **Delete**, and then click **Yes** to confirm the deletion.

TIP

Setting a Task Reminder

Just as you can for appointments, you can set a reminder alert to tell you when a task deadline is approaching. Display the **Reminder** drop-down list and select **On** date. You will be reminded on the task due date.

USING WORDPAD

WordPad can be used as a simple word processing program. You can use it to edit text files or to create simple documents, such as notes, memos, and fax sheets.

Start

Click

Click

Click

Click

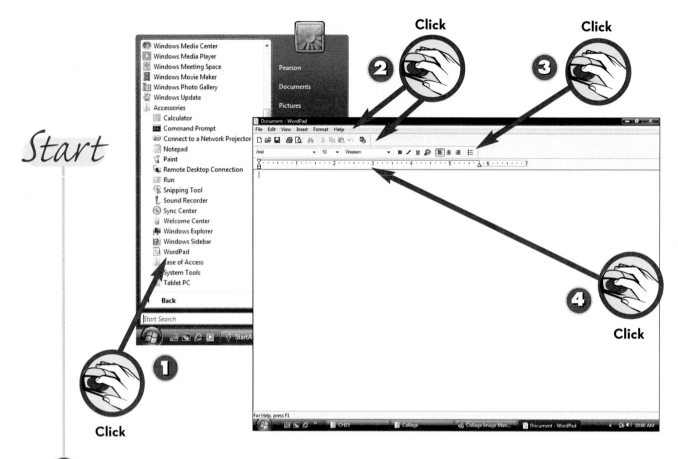

1. Click the **Start** button, and then click **All Programs**, **Accessories**, **WordPad**.
2. Use the **menu bar** to change the view, edit the text, insert image files, and so on. Use the **toolbar** to select buttons for frequently used commands.
3. Use the **format bar** to make changes to the appearance of the text.
4. Use the **ruler** to set tabs and indents.

End

TIP

Hide a Toolbar

To hide any of the screen elements in WordPad, open the **View** menu and click the tool you want to hide. A check mark indicates that the tool is showing; no check mark indicates that it is hidden.

NOTE

WordPad's File Format

WordPad saves files in a format called rich text format (or RTF), which most other word processing programs can open; this format retains most of the formatting. You can also save the file as a simple text (TXT) file; in this case, formatting is sometimes lost.

TYPING TEXT

One of the great things about word processing programs is how simple they are to use. To add text to a new document, you simply type the text you want to include. A word processor, even a simple one like WordPad, enables you to easily change what you've typed.

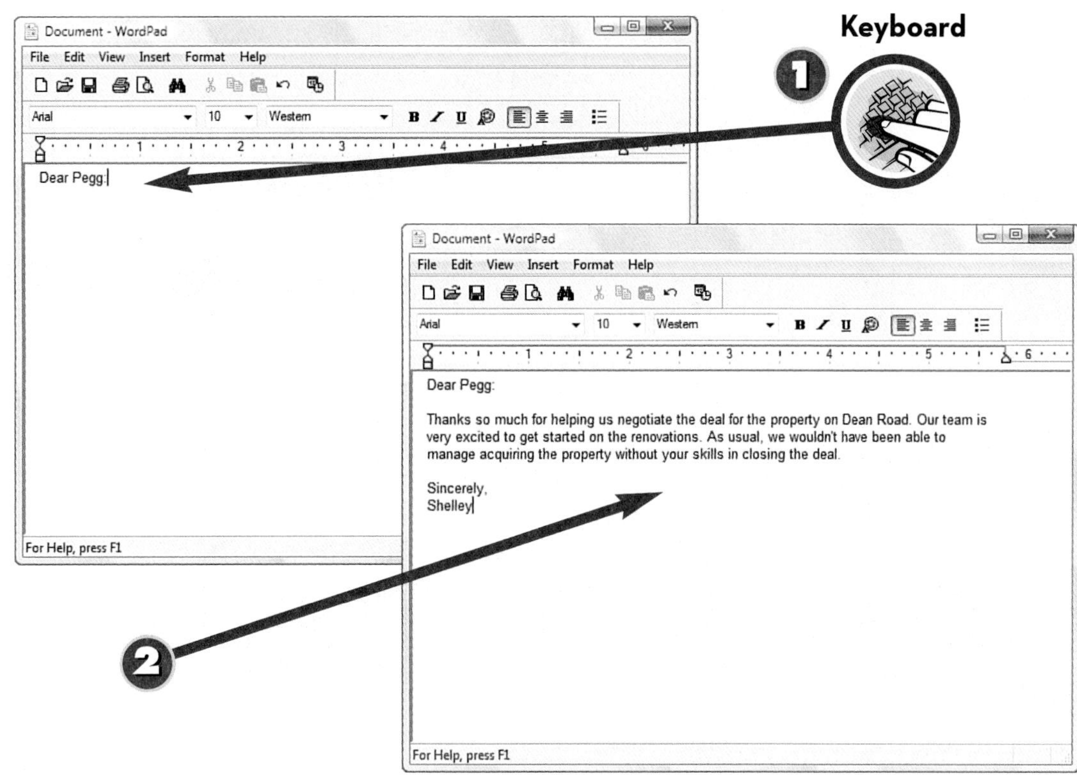

1. Type text. To end a paragraph and start a new one, press **Enter**. The insertion point moves to the next line.
2. Continue typing to add to and complete the document. For paragraphs, you don't need to press **Enter** at the end of each line; WordPad automatically wraps the lines within a paragraph.

End

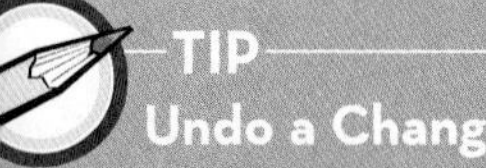

TIP

Undo a Change

If you make a mistake, you can undo the last action by clicking the **Edit** menu and choosing **Undo**.

TIP

Save Your Document

Be sure to save your document as you continue to work on it. Click **File** and choose **Save** (or click the **Save** button on the toolbar) to save your work. For more information, refer to the task "Saving a Document" in Part 3, "Working with Programs."

SELECTING TEXT IN A WORDPAD DOCUMENT

Knowing how to select data in a document (text, graphics, and so on) is important when using WordPad, as well as many other programs. For example, you can select text and then delete it, move it, copy it, change its appearance, and more. You'll use this skill (selecting text and graphics) in many programs.

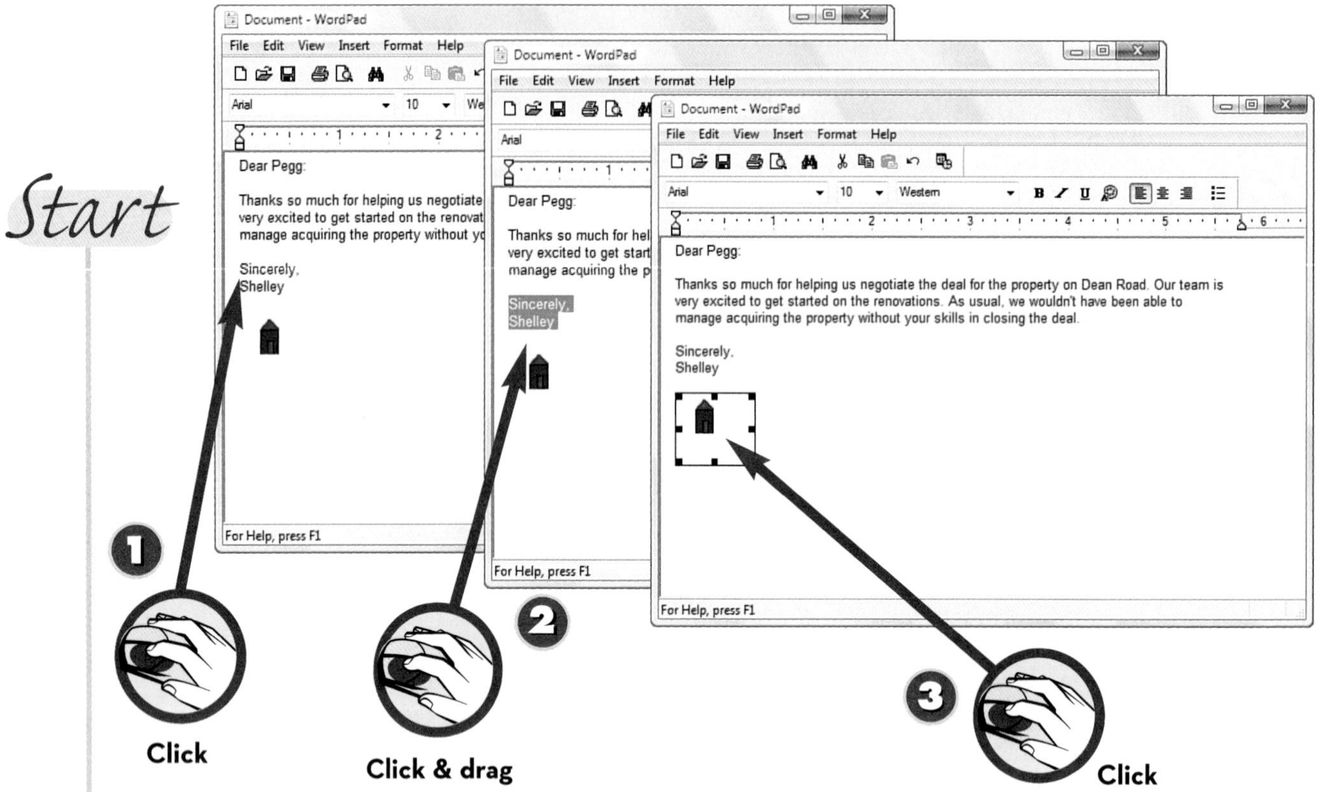

Start

Click

Click & drag

Click

1. Click at the beginning of the text you want to select.
2. Hold down the mouse button and drag across the text; then release the mouse button. The selected text appears highlighted.
3. To select an image, click it. You see selection handles around the image.

End

TIP

Making Changes to Selected Text

After you select text, you can make edits to the entire selection at once, such as cutting, copying, or adding formatting (bold, italic, and so on).

TIP

Use the Keyboard

If you prefer to use the keyboard to select text, hold down the **Shift** key and use the arrow keys to highlight the text you want to select.

DELETING TEXT

Just as you can add text, you can easily delete it. You can delete characters, words, paragraphs, pages, or even all the text in a document.

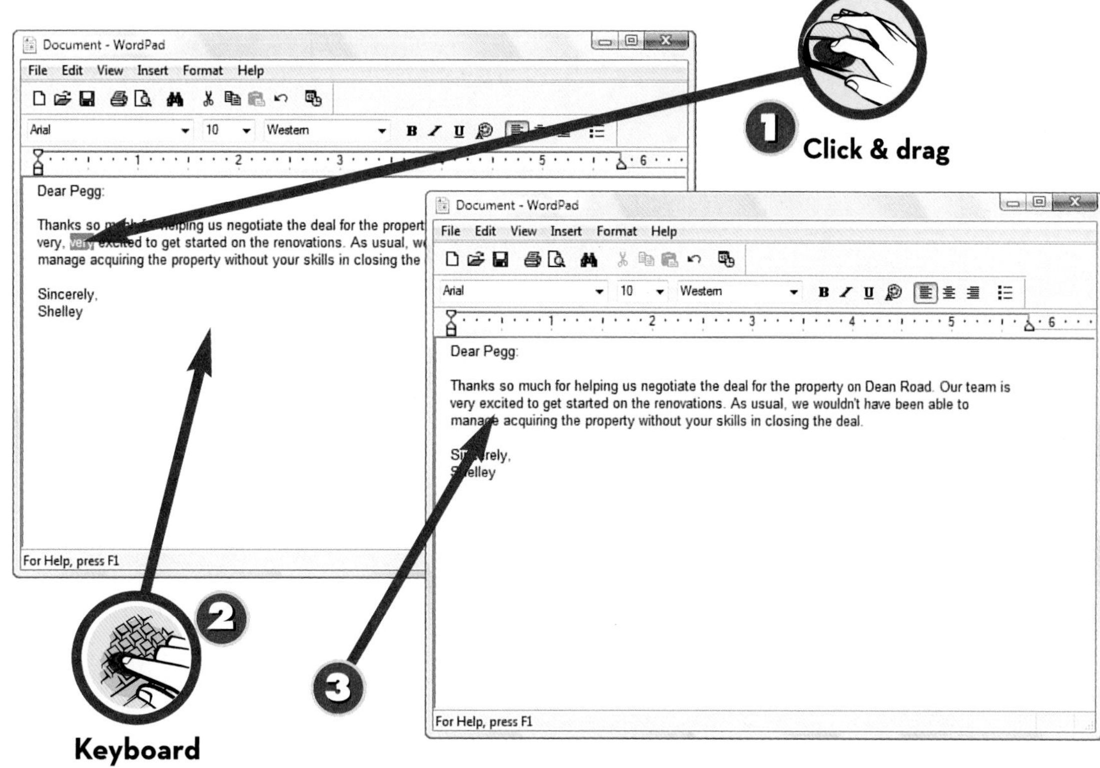

1. Click and drag over the text you want to delete to select it.
2. Press the **Delete** or **Backspace** key on your keyboard.
3. The text is deleted.

End

TIP

Undo Deletion

To undo the deletion, click the **Undo** button in the toolbar, or choose **Edit**, **Undo**.

TIP

Select All

To select all the text in a document, press **Ctrl+A** on the keyboard, or choose **Edit**, **Select All**. You can now cut, copy, or reformat the entire document at one time.

COPYING TEXT

One of the most common editing tasks is copying text. You can copy text and then paste it into the current document or into another document. You can also copy text to reuse it. For example, if you want something similar to what you've already typed, you can copy and paste, and then edit the text rather than typing it from scratch.

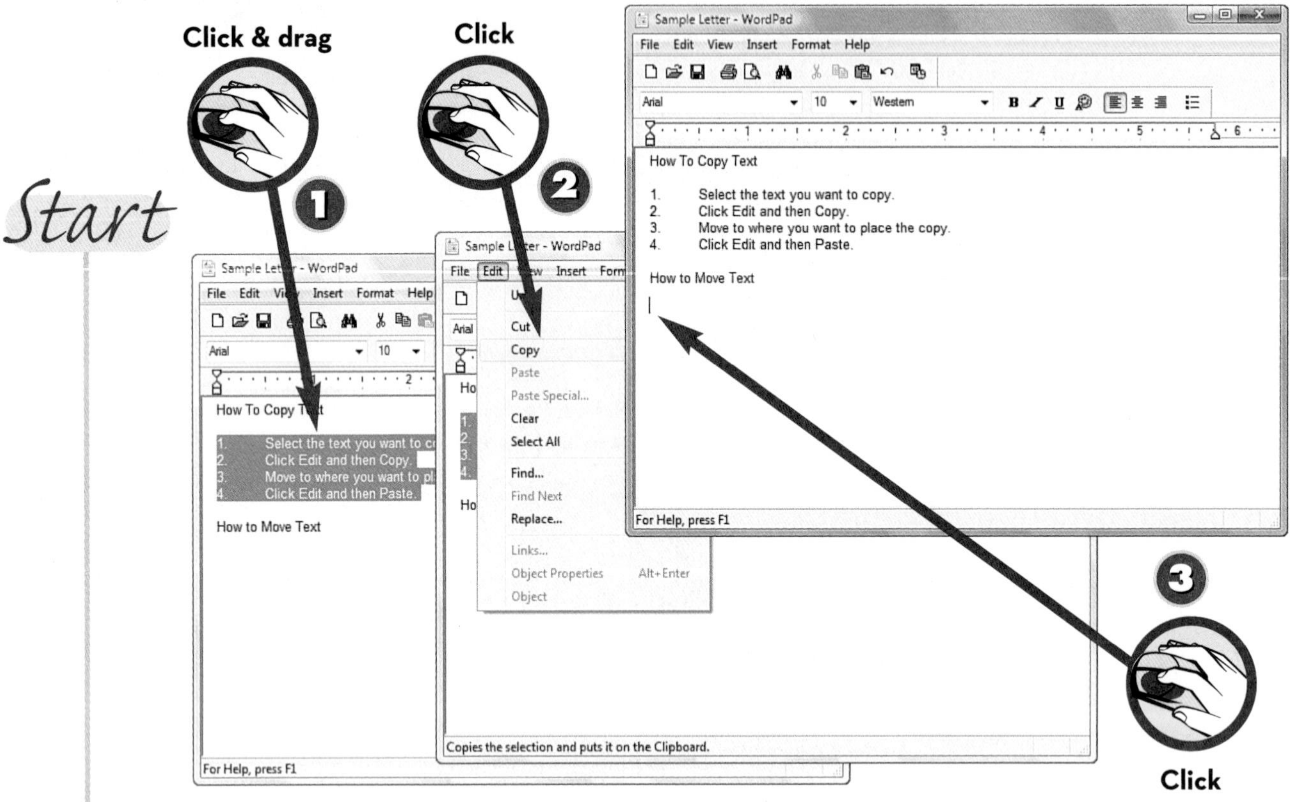

1. Click and drag over the text you want to copy to select it.
2. Click **Edit**, and then select the **Copy** command. Windows copies the data from the document and places it in the Clipboard, a hidden temporary holding spot.
3. Click the spot in the document where you want to put the copied data.

Continued

TIP

Can't Paste?

If the **Paste** command is grayed out, it means you have not copied anything. Be sure to click **Edit** and then select the **Copy** command before you try to paste the text.

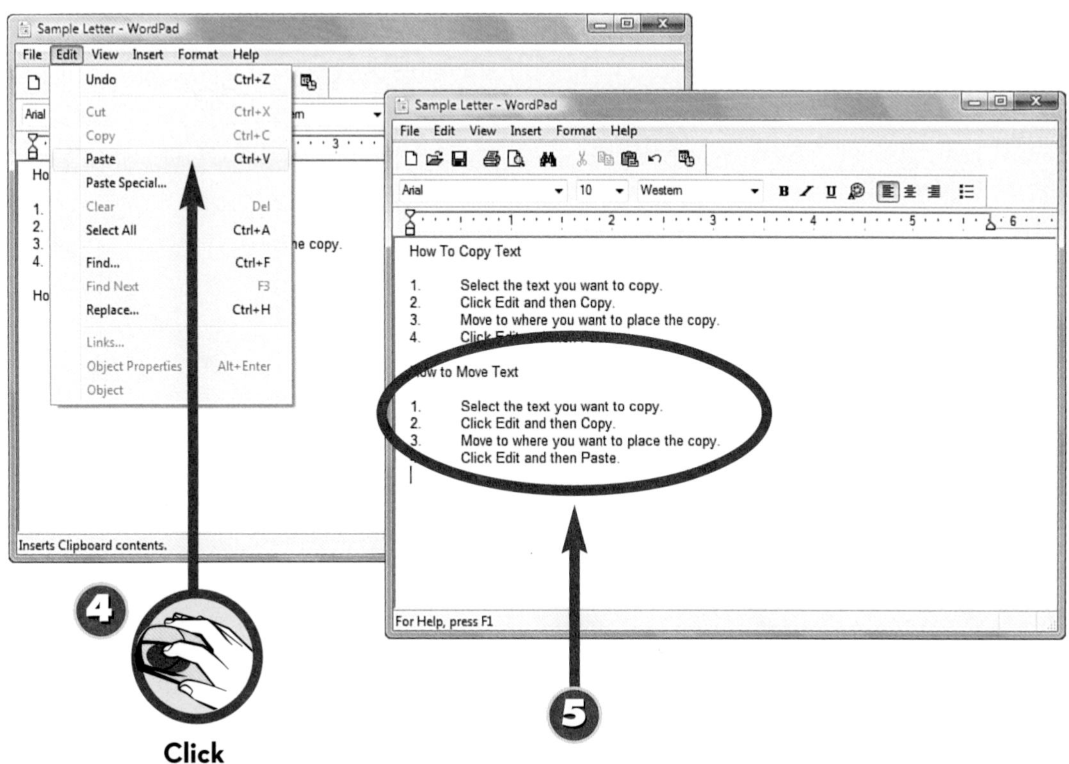

4. Click **Edit**, and then select the **Paste** command.
5. The copied data is pasted. Here you can then edit the steps to explain how to move since moving and copying text are very similar.

End

TIP

Use Keyboard Shortcuts

You can also use keyboard shortcuts: **Ctrl+X** for the Cut command, **Ctrl+C** for the Copy command, and **Ctrl+V** for the Paste command.

MOVING TEXT

Just as you can copy text, you can move it from one location to another in the same document. You can also move text from one document to another. When you rewrite or edit a document, you often want to make organizational changes, such as moving text to a different location. Moving text is similar to copying text, except that when you move something, it is deleted from its original location.

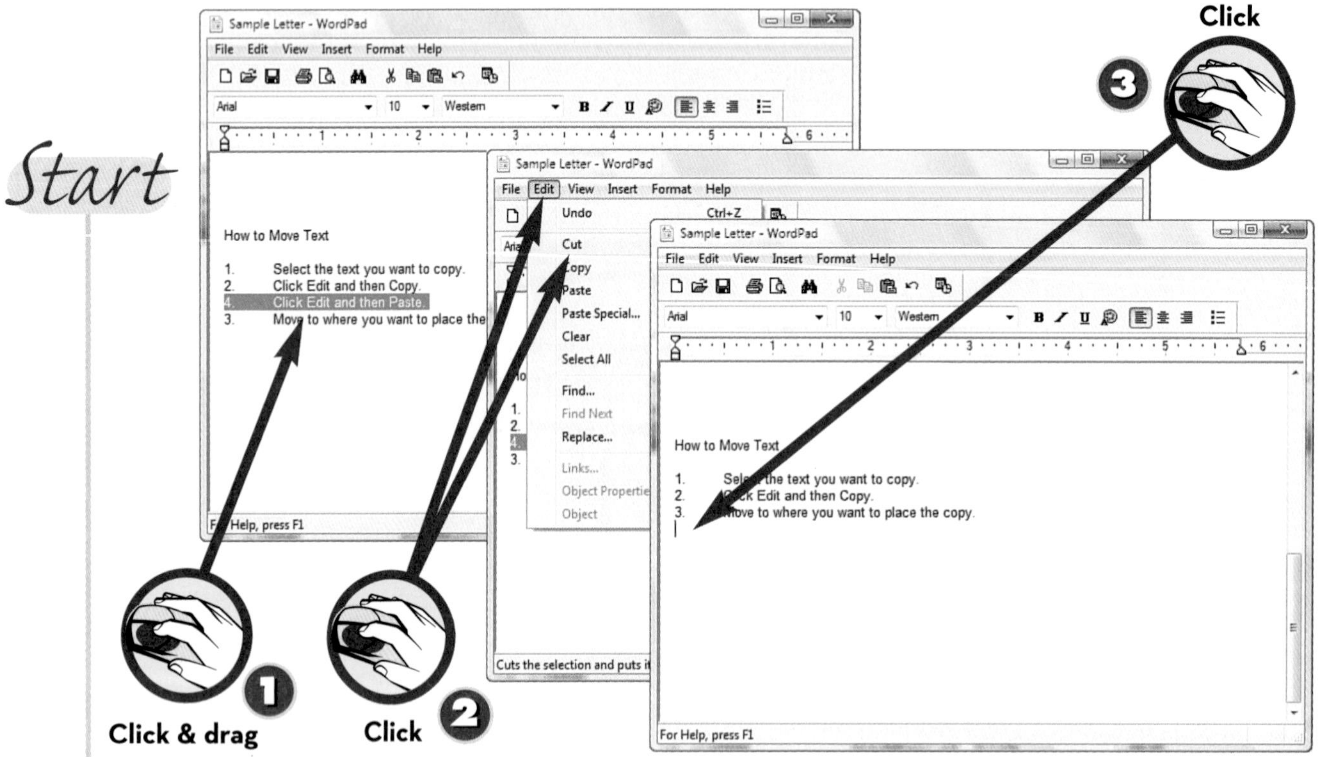

Start

Click & drag ❶ Click ❷ Click ❸

1. Click and drag over the text you want to move to select it.
2. Click **Edit**, and then click the **Cut** command. Windows deletes the data from the document and places it in the Clipboard.
3. Click in the document where you want to place the text.

Continued

TIP

Move Text to Another Application

To move cut or copied text from WordPad to another application, simply switch to the desired application, click the spot where you want the text to be placed, open the **Edit** menu, and select **Paste**.

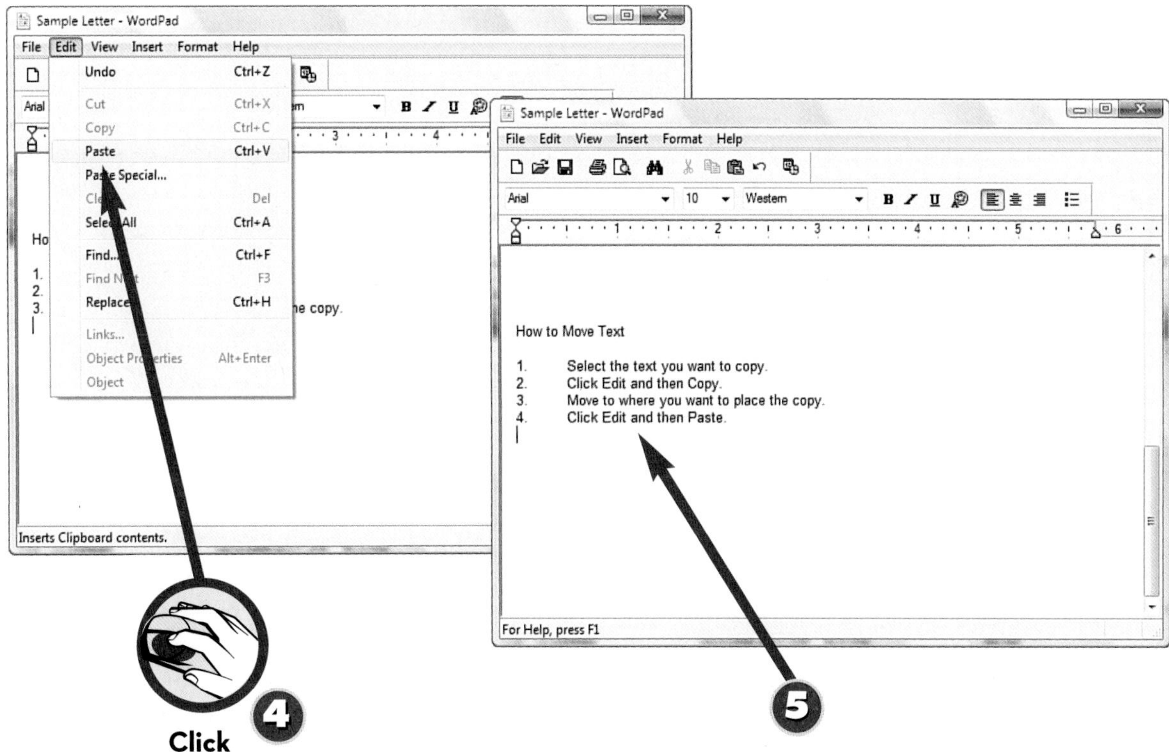

4. Click **Edit**, and then select the **Paste** command.

5. The text is pasted into the new location.

End

TIP

Undo a Move

You can undo a paste operation if you change your mind after performing the action. Simply click **Edit**, and then select the **Undo Paste** command to remove the text you just pasted.

NOTE

Shortcuts

WordPad and many other programs include toolbar buttons and keyboard shortcuts for Cut, Copy, and Paste operations. The keyboard shortcuts are **Ctrl+X** (Cut), **Ctrl+C** (Copy), and **Ctrl+V** (Paste).

FORMATTING TEXT

You can easily make simple changes to the appearance of text. For example, you can change the font or font size, and you can make text bold, italic, or underlined. This task touches on just a few of the formatting changes you can make in WordPad. Experiment and try out some of the other available formatting features by selecting other options in the Format menu.

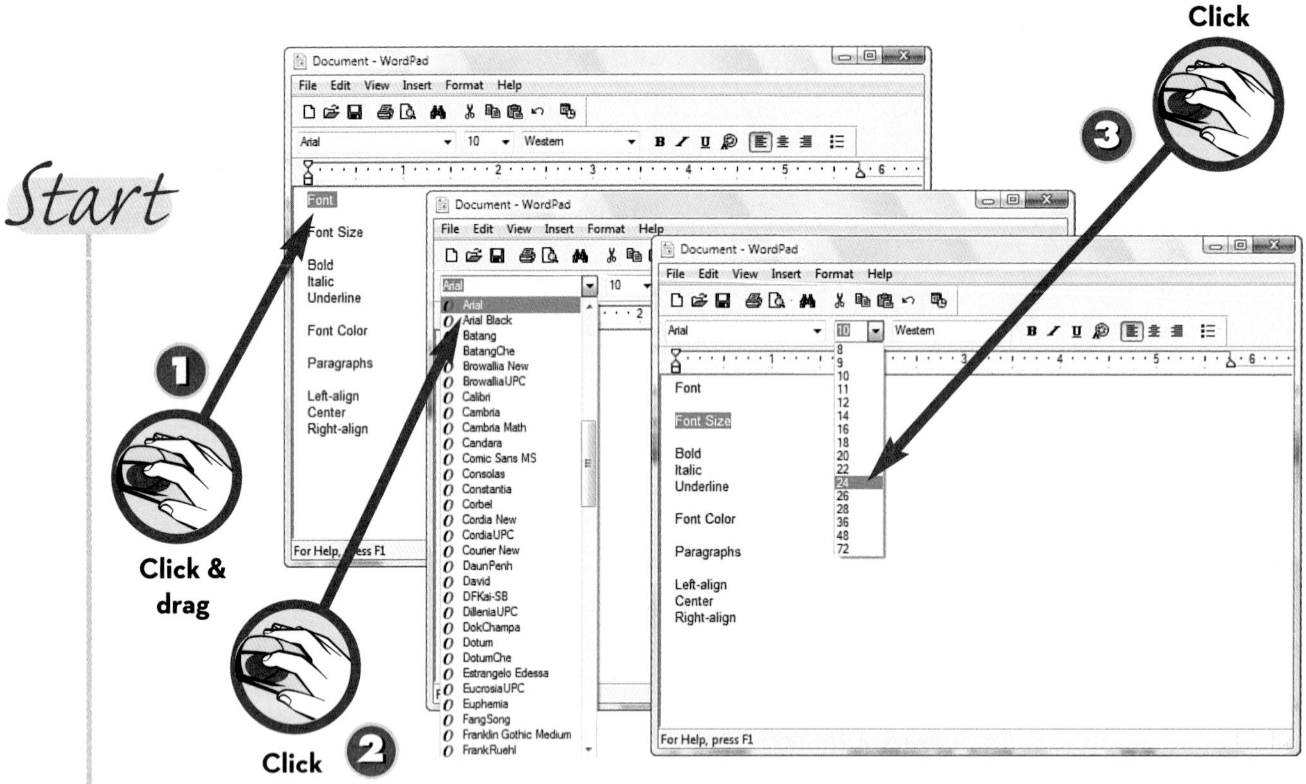

Start

1. Click and drag over the text you want to change to select it.
2. To use a different font, click the drop-down arrow next to the **Font** field and click the name of the font you want to use.
3. To use a different font size, select the text you want to change, click the drop-down arrow next to the **Font Size** field, and click the size you want to use.

Continued

NOTE

Document Formats

Formatting options are available only if you have created and are working in a rich text format file (RTF); this is the default file format in WordPad, so you should not have problems.

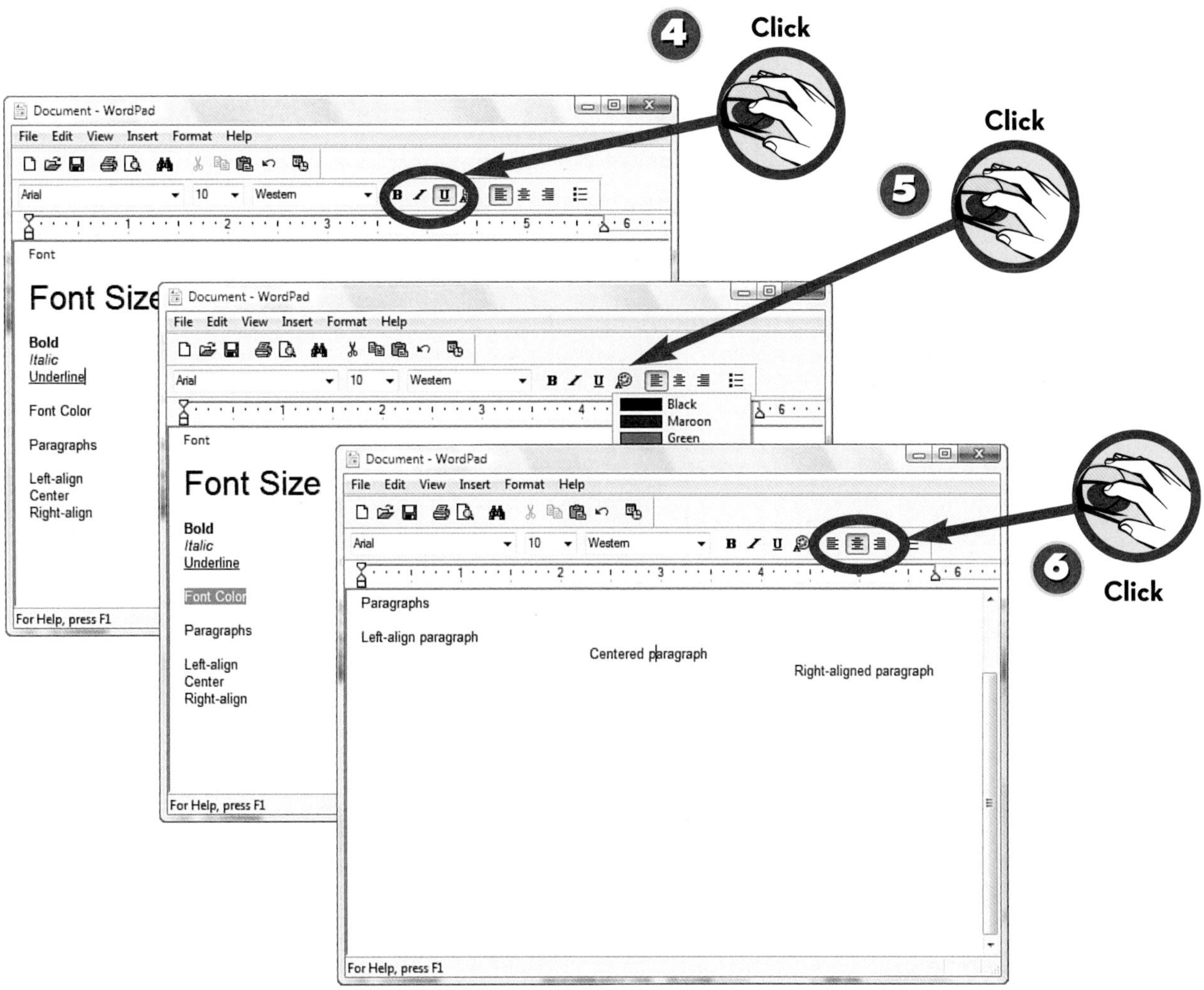

4 Click

5 Click

6 Click

4. To make text bold, italic, or underlined, select it, and then click the appropriate button in the **format** bar.
5. To change the font color, select the text you want to change, and then click the **Font Color** button. Select the color you want from the drop-down list that appears.
6. Change the alignment of a paragraph by selecting it and clicking any of the **Alignment** buttons on the toolbar (Align Left, Center, or Align Right).

End

TIP

Undoing a Change

To undo a change, click the **Undo** button on the toolbar. The Undo button is the one with a curved arrow pointing to the left.

TIP

Using the Format Menu

In WordPad, you can use the commands in the Format menu to change the appearance of your document. Included on the Format menu are commands to set the font, the bullet style, the paragraph style (centered, left-justified, or right-justified), and the tabs.

USING NOTEPAD

While most documents are more sophisticated than the simple text file, the text file is the most common type of file. It's a common denominator among programs because almost all programs on any operating system platform can open and display a text file. You can find instructions on a CD about how to install a program, and other information in text files. To edit and work with this type of file, you can use Notepad, a simple text editor provided with Windows Vista.

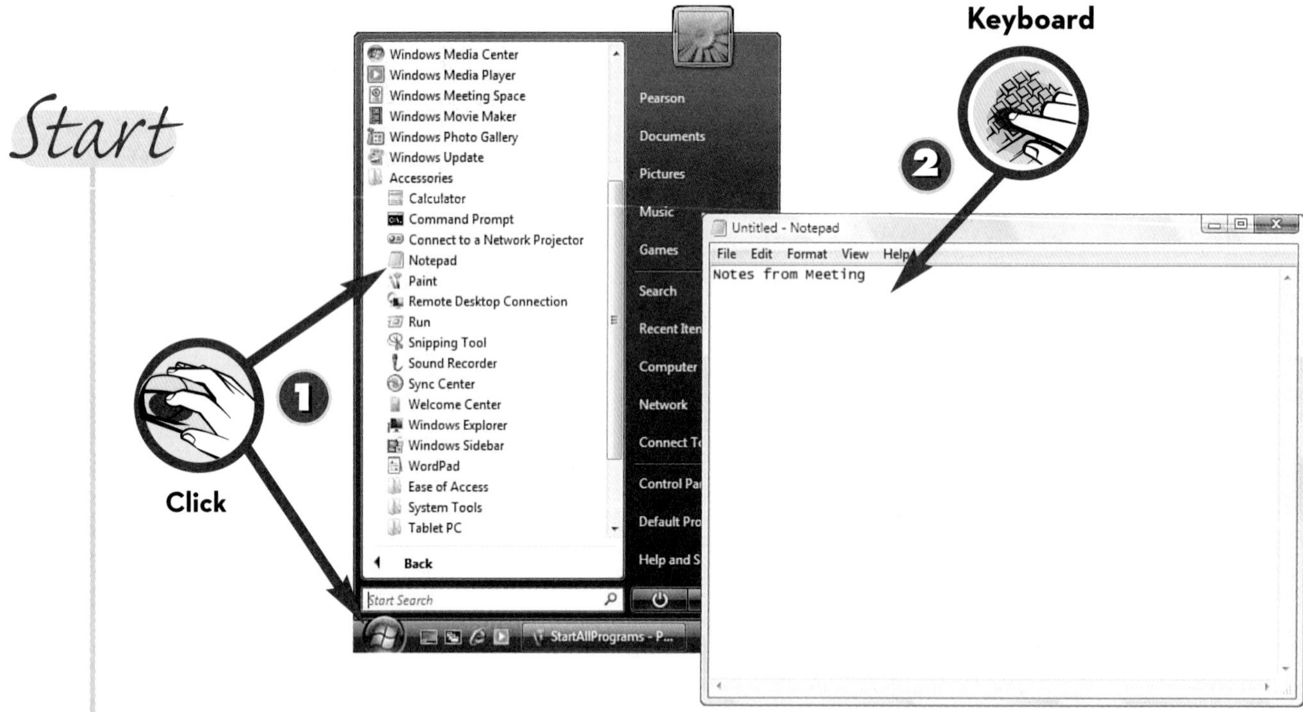

1. Click the **Start** button, choose **All Programs**, **Accessories**, and then click **Notepad**.
2. To type a document, type in the window (exactly like you did in the previous tasks on using WordPad).

End

NOTE

Notepad Versus WordPad

Notepad is similar to WordPad in that both are text-editing programs. WordPad, however, is more full-featured than Notepad, supporting more formatting options and other features.

TIP

Open and Saving a Text File

To open a file in Notepad, click **File**, and then click **Open**. Navigate to the folder, and then double-click the file to open it. If you make changes to the file, save them by opening the **File** menu and choosing **Save**.

USING PAINT

Paint is a program you can use to create simple drawings and use them in creative projects, such as invitations or crafts. (Kids especially like to play with Paint.) Use Paint to create art and to edit graphics such as clip art, scanned art, and art files from other programs. You can add lines, shapes, and colors, as well as alter the original components. The best way to learn how to use Paint is to experiment, like scribbling on a piece of paper.

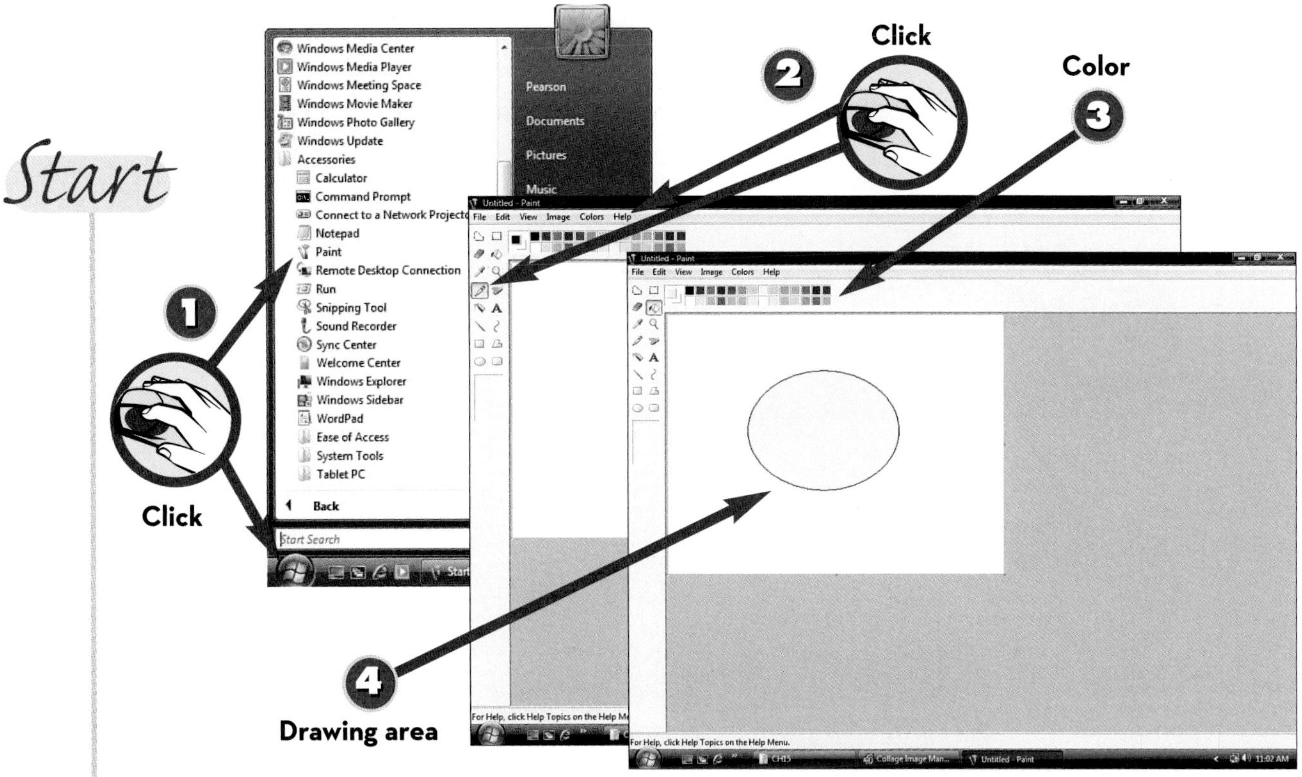

Start

Click

Click

Color

Drawing area

1. Click **Start**, **All Programs**, **Accessories**, and click **Paint**.
2. Use the menus to select commands. Use the toolbox to select the drawing tools.
3. Use the color box to select colors for the lines and fills of the objects.
4. Draw in the drawing area.

End

TIP

Zoom In

You can zoom in on your drawing using the **Magnifier** tool. Click the tool and then click the area to magnify. Or click **View**, **Zoom**, **Custom**, and select a zoom percentage.

NOTE

Flip, Rotate, and Other Options

For more options on editing the image, use the **Image** menu. You can select here, for instance, to flip or rotate the image. You can also resize, invert the colors, and make other changes.

DRAWING A SHAPE WITH PAINT

Using Paint, you can create many different types of shapes, including lines, curves, rectangles, polygons, ovals, circles, and rounded rectangles.

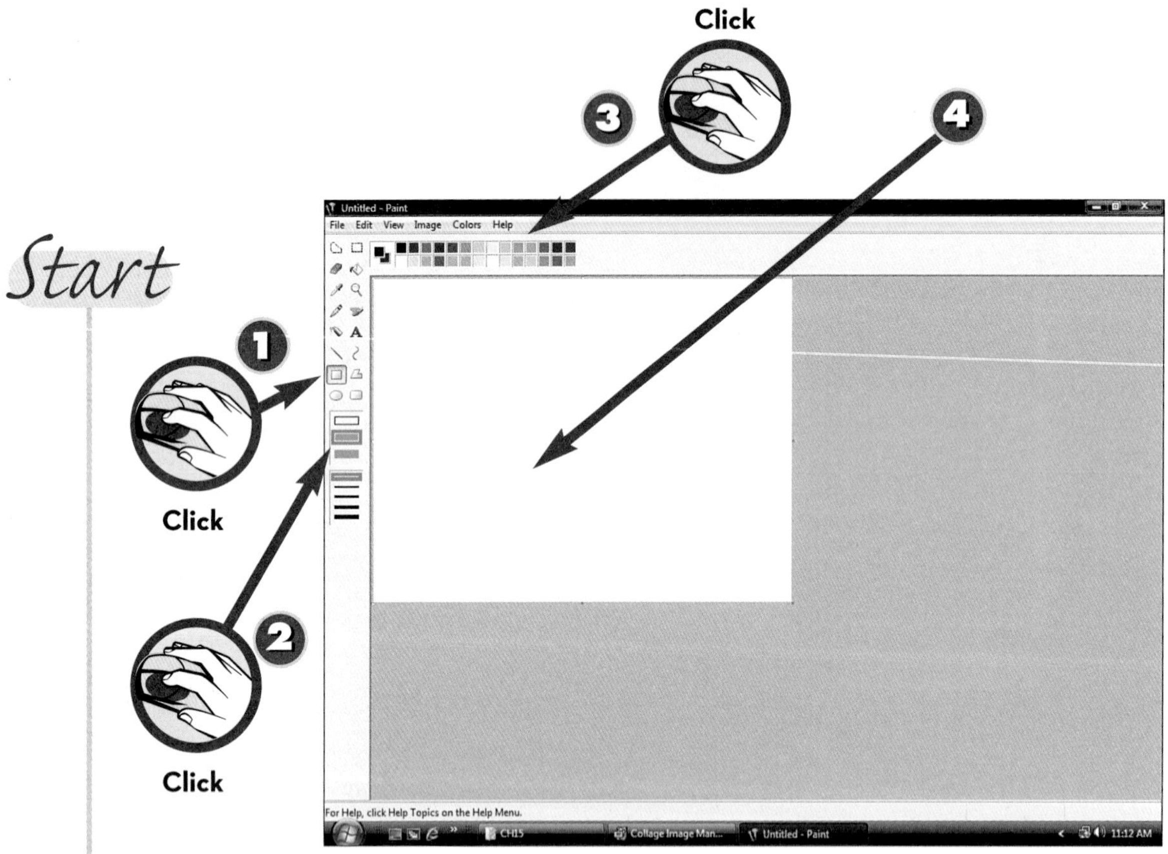

Start

1. Click the tool you want to draw with (in this case, the **Rectangle** tool).
2. Options for the Rectangle tool are displayed. Choose whether you want to draw an empty rectangle, a filled rectangle with a border, or a filled rectangle without a border.
3. To change the colors used, click the color to use for the border of the drawing. Right-click the color to use if you are drawing a filled object.
4. Move the pointer into the drawing area. Click and drag in the white canvas area to draw.

End

TIP

Draw Perfect Shapes

To draw a circle, square, or straight line, hold down the **Shift** key as you use the **Ellipse**, **Rectangle**, or **Line** tool to draw the object.

TIP

Drawing Shapes Freehand

In addition to using the Rectangle and Ellipse tools, you can draw freehand shapes, as you would with a pencil or pen. Simply click the **Pencil** tool, move the pointer into the drawing area, and drag the pencil icon to draw.

ADDING TEXT TO A DRAWING

You can include text as part of your drawing. To do so, draw a text box, and then type the text you want to include. By combining drawings with text, you can create invitations, maps, flyers, and other simple publications.

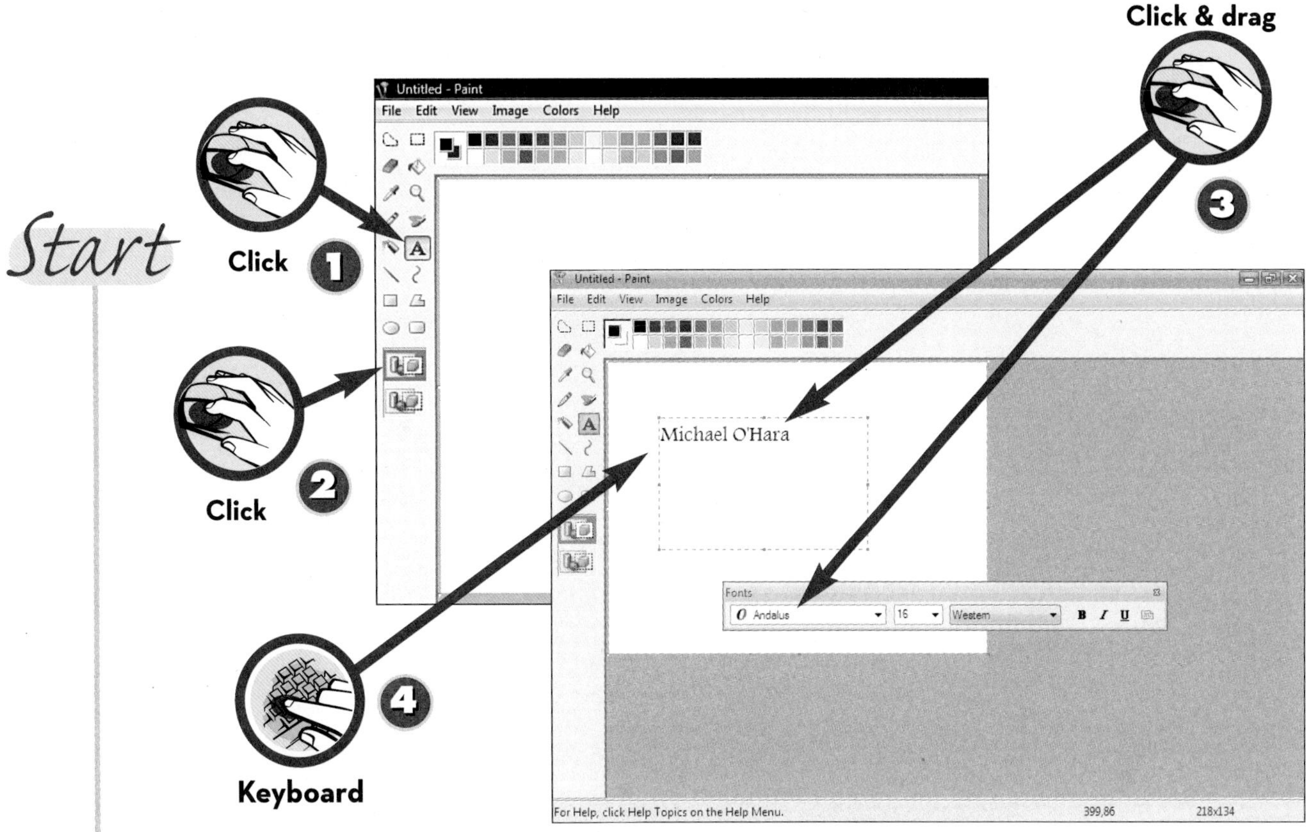

1. Click the **Text** tool.
2. Options for the **Text** tool are displayed. Choose whether you want to draw a text box that obscures the image beneath it or one that enables the image beneath it to be seen.
3. Move the pointer into the drawing area. Click and drag to draw a text box.
4. Type the text you want to add. The text is added to the text box.

End

TIP

Font Change

You can use the **Fonts** toolbar to select the font, size, and style of the text.

TIP

Undo

If at any time you do not like what you've drawn, open the **Edit** menu and choose **Undo** to undo the last action (or press **Ctrl+Z**).

ADDING COLOR TO A DRAWING

There are several ways to add color to a drawing. One way is to use the Brush tool to add paintbrush-style strokes to your image (covered here). You can also use the Airbrush tool to spray-paint on color or use the Paint Bucket tool to fill an object with color (see the tips on this page for using these tools).

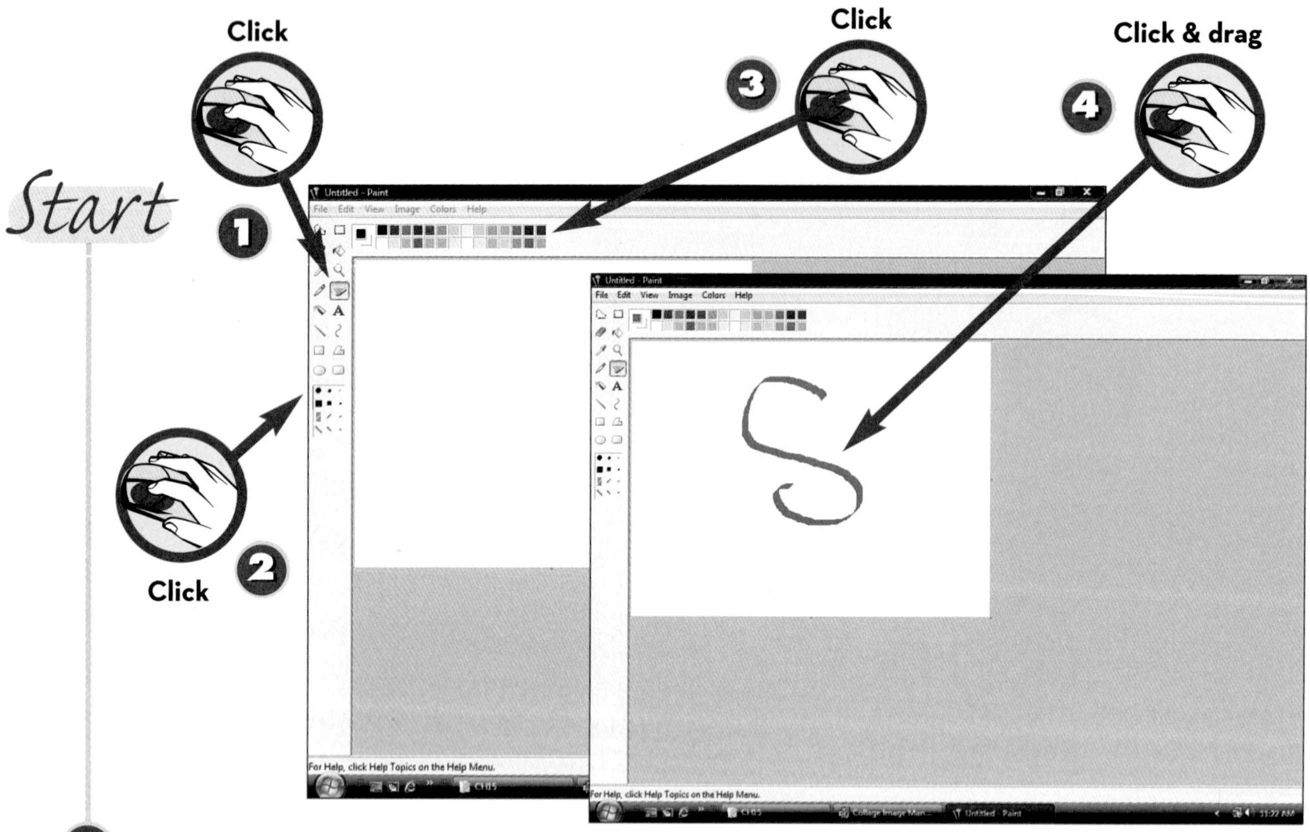

Start

1. Click the **Brush** tool.
2. Click the brush size and shape.
3. Click the color to use for the brush.
4. Click and drag across the page to "paint" with the brush.

Continued

TIP

Fill with Color

To fill a drawn object with color, click the Paint Bucket tool and then click the color to use as the fill. Click the tip of the Paint Bucket tool inside the object to fill it with the selected color.

TIP

Spray-Paint

To get a spray-paint effect on the drawing area, use the **Airbrush** tool.

ERASING PART OF A DRAWING

If you make a mistake in a drawing and want to get rid of something you have added, you can use the Eraser tool. You can erase part of the drawing; you can also erase the entire canvas and start again.

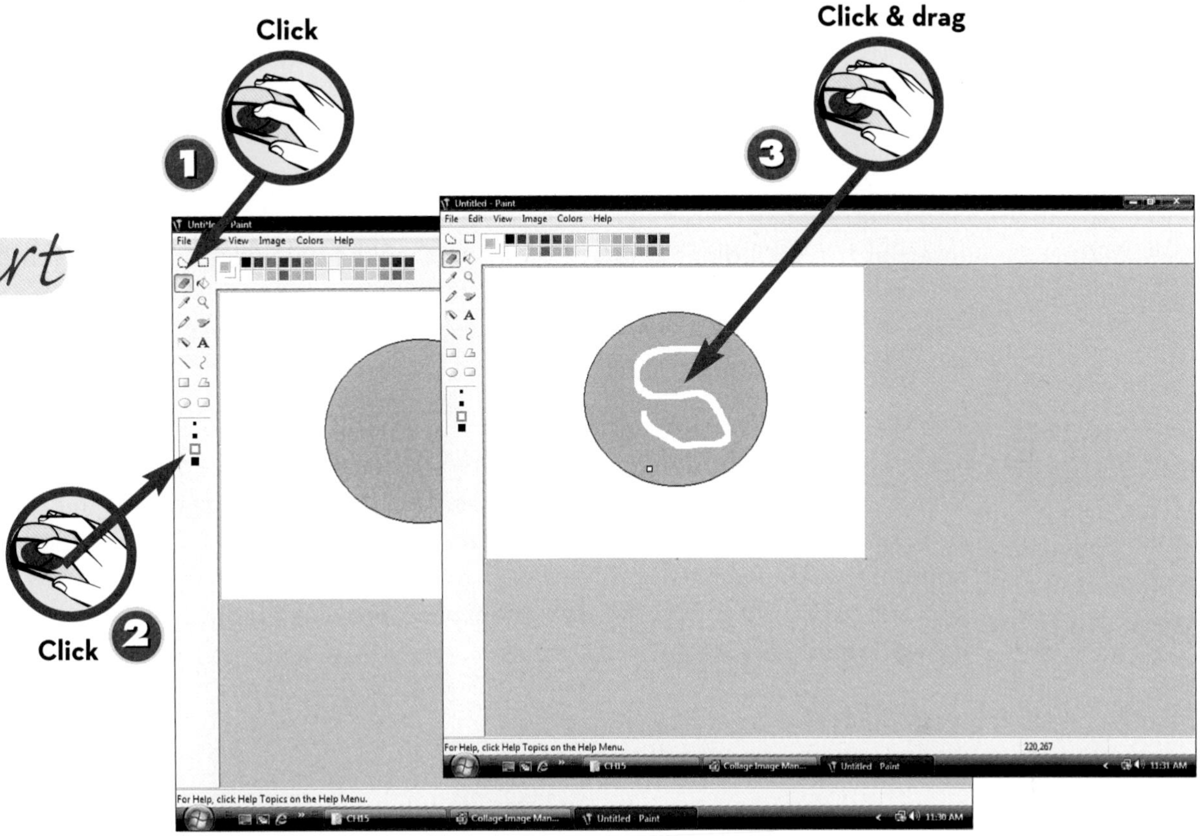

Start

Click

Click & drag

Click

1. Click the **Eraser** tool.
2. Click in the options area to choose the size you want the eraser to be.
3. Click and drag across the part you want to erase.

End

TIP

Erase Selected Area

To erase a selected part of a drawing, click the **Select** tool (the top-right button on the toolbar) and drag the mouse across part of your drawing. Press the **Delete** key to remove the selected part of the drawing.

TIP

Clear the Whole Page

To clear everything on the page, open the **Image** menu, and then choose **Clear Image**.

HOME NETWORKING BASICS

Home networking enables you to share a single Internet connection, printer, and drive folder between two or more PCs, enabling you to save time, money, and frustration. It also helps everyone to enjoy the wide world of network and Internet fun, including surfing the Internet, online gaming, multimedia content, and much more. With a home network, computers running Windows Vista can share printers and information with computers running older versions of Windows or other operating systems.

There are three steps necessary to having a home network: planning the network, installing and configuring the network hardware, and configuring Windows Vista's network setup features. This Part concentrates on the third step: helping you to use Windows Vista's networking features. To learn more about network planning and hardware configuration, use Windows Vista's Help and Support Center and the documentation provided by the vendors of your network hardware.

USING THE NETWORK MAP FEATURE TO CREATE A DIAGRAM OF YOUR NETWORK

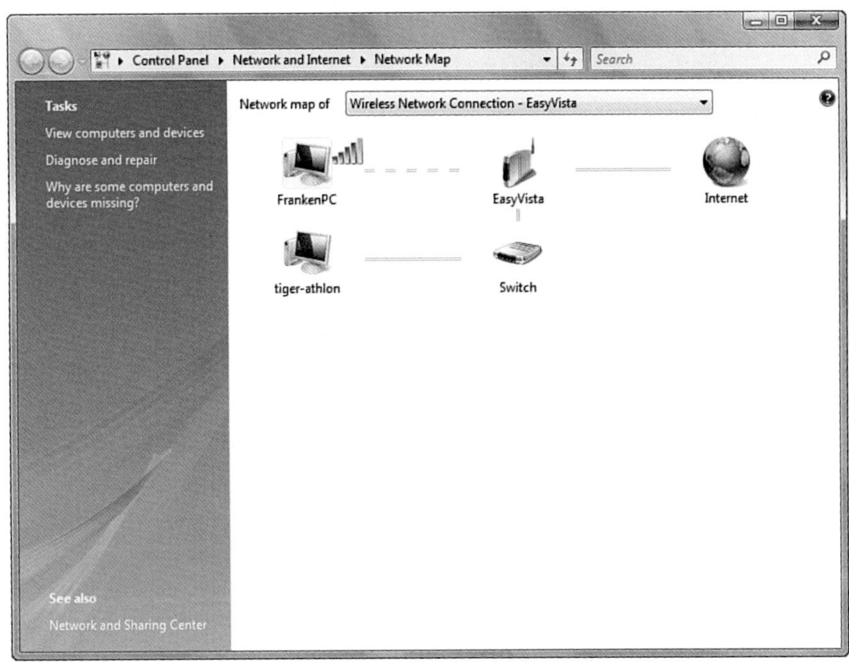

SETTING UP A WIRELESS NETWORK CLIENT

Before you can perform any network tasks, you must set up your network. The most popular type of home network today is a wireless network. A typical wireless network includes a cable or DSL modem for the Internet connection, a wireless router, and wireless adapters for each PC on the network. Some PCs, especially laptops, have a wireless adapter built in.

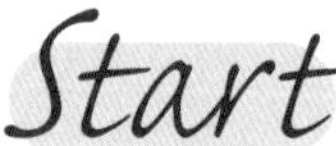

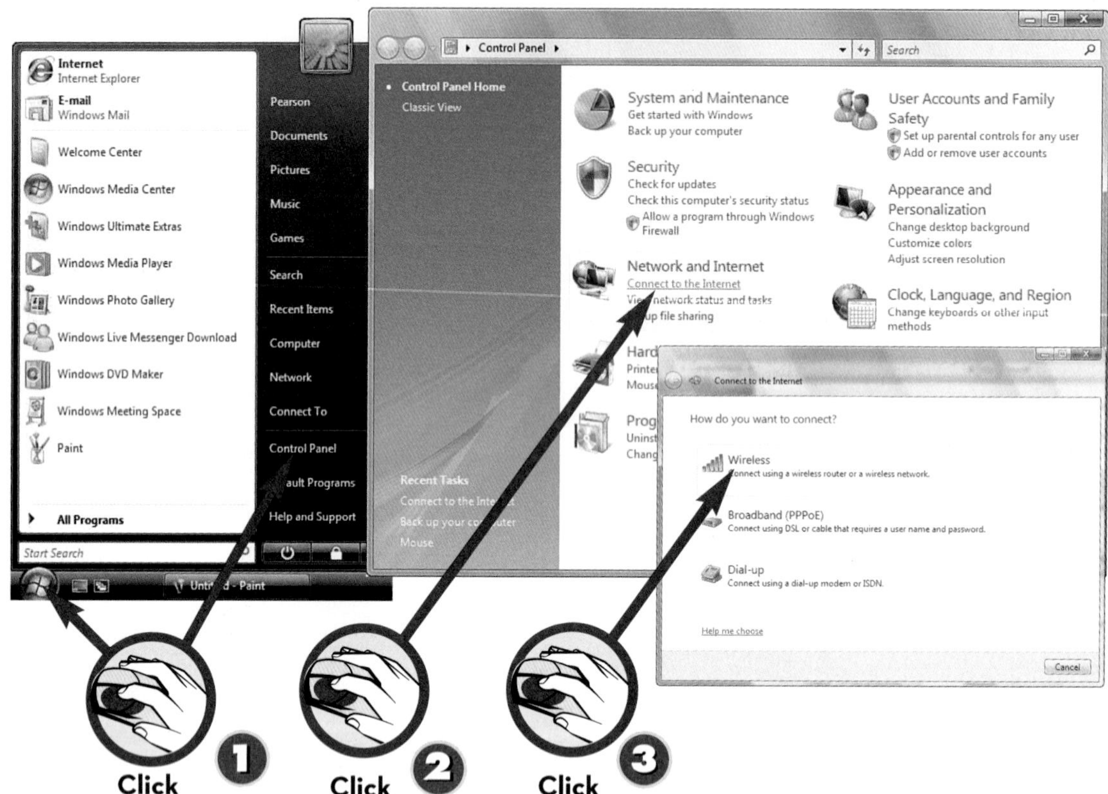

1. Click **Start**, **Control Panel**.
2. Click **Connect to the Internet**.
3. Select **Wireless** from the list of choices.

Continued

NOTE

What You Need to Know

When you install your wireless router, make sure you note the following: the SSID (the name of the wireless network), the type of security (WEP, WPA, WPA2), and the encryption key used. You must provide this information to each computer on your network, either through a USB keychain drive or by entering the information manually into each system's configuration. For more information about wireless security, see the book *Absolute Beginner's Guide to Home Networking*, by Mark Edward Soper.

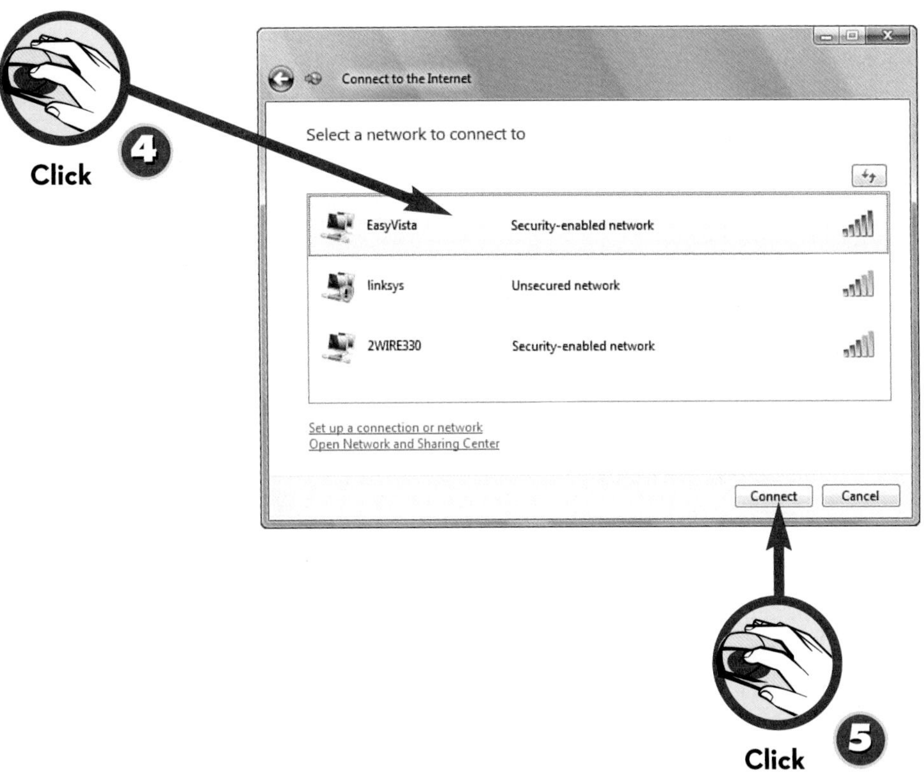

4 You may see more than one wireless network. Select your network from the list. If you do not see your network name, but you see an "unnamed network," select it.

5 Click **Connect**.

End

TIP

"Unnamed" Networks

For additional security, you may have disabled broadcast of your wireless router's SSID. If you selected this option when you set up your router, your network shows up as an "Unnamed Network." When you connect to an "Unnamed Network," you must provide the SSID, which is the name of your wireless network.

TIP

Getting More Help

To access dozens of articles on networking, click **Start**, **Help and Support**, and enter **network setup** into the search window. You can also contact the provider of your networking hardware.

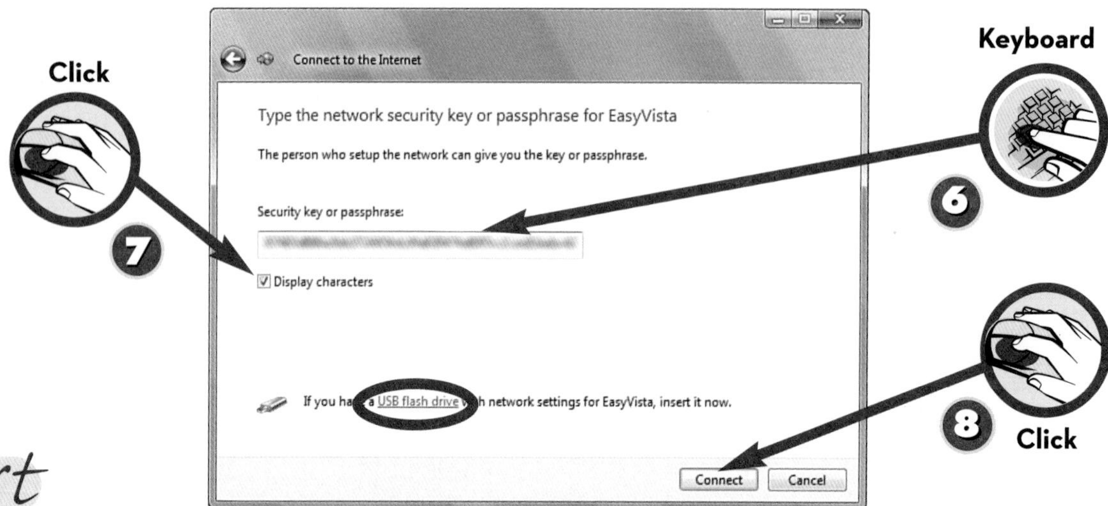

Start

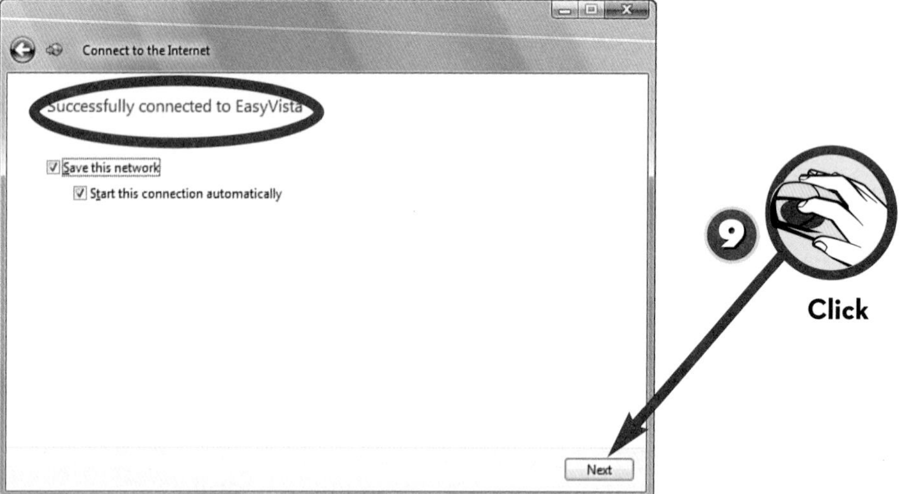

6 On a secured network, you will need to enter the network security key or passphrase. Type it in when prompted, or insert a USB flash drive that contains the settings (if your router saved them to a flash drive when you set it up).

7 To see the characters as you enter them, click the **Display characters** check box.

8 Click **Connect**.

9 Windows indicates you have made a successful connection. Click **Next** to continue.

Continued

TIP

Creating a Strong Network Security Key

A strong network security key needs to use randomized alphanumeric text. To automatically generate a strong network security key you can use with your wireless network, go to www.kurtm.net/wpa-pskgen/ and select Maximum WPA Security (63 characters). Click **Generate**. Follow the instructions on the website to copy the key to your wireless router setup and to each wireless client. You can save the key to a text file on a USB drive to make it easy to move around.

10 Windows tests your Internet connection.

11 After the testing is complete, click **Browse the Internet now** to open Internet Explorer in a separate window.

12 Note the instructions to start your Internet connection the next time.

13 To close the connection wizard, click **Close**.

End

TIP

Repeat This Process for Each PC

You must repeat this process for each computer on your wireless network.

TIP

Connecting a Network Printer

See the task "Setting Up a Network Printer," later in this Part, for the steps necessary to configure a printer to work with your network.

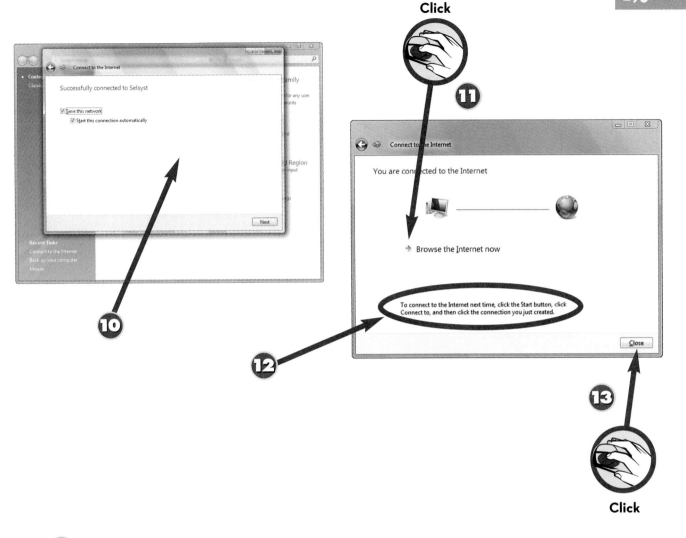

SETTING SHARING OPTIONS

After you set up each station on the network to use the Internet, the next step is to set up sharing options. Sharing is configured through the Network and Sharing Center.

Start

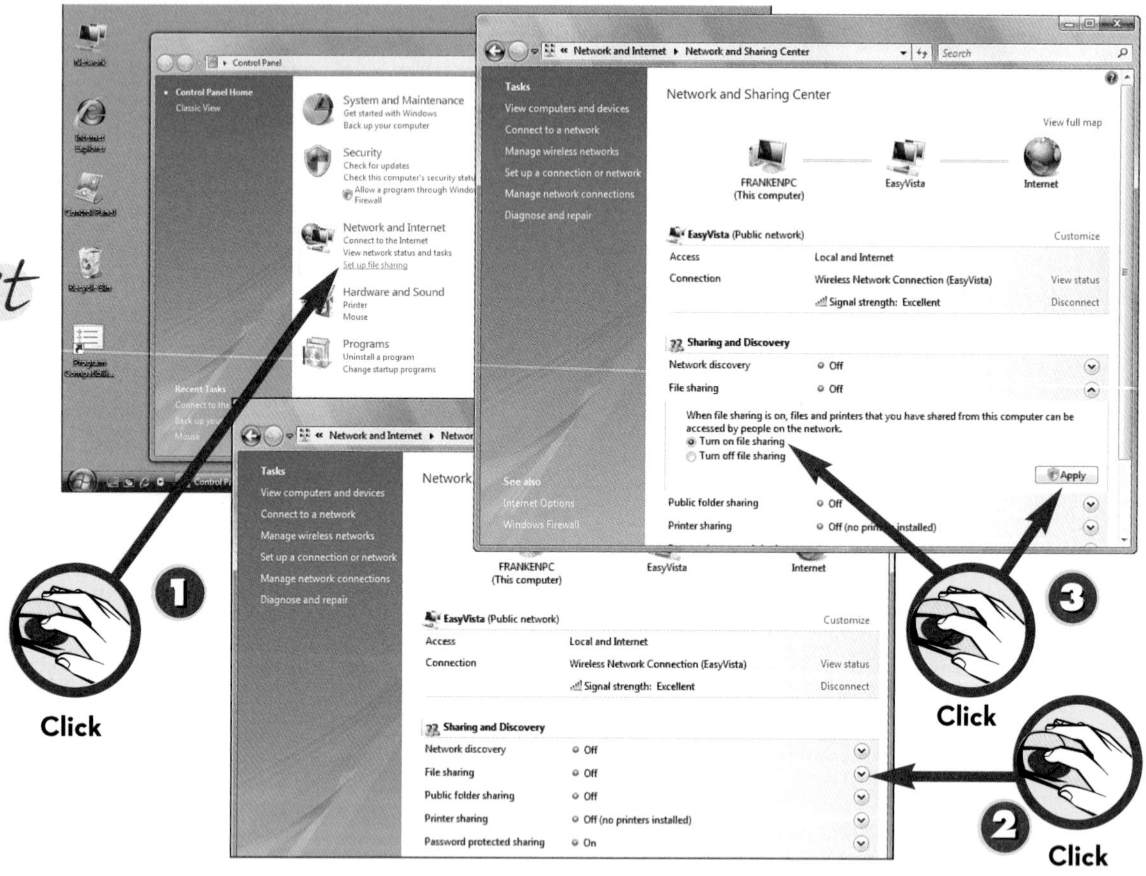

Click

Click

Click

1. Click **Start**, **Control Panel**, and then click **Set up file sharing** from within the Network and Internet category.
2. Click the arrow next to **File sharing**.
3. Select **Turn on File Sharing** and click **Apply**.

Continued

TIP

Working with User Account Control

Some steps in this and other tutorials may bring up a User Account Control dialog box. Click **Continue** to finish the step. If you are using a standard account, you will also be prompted to provide a password from an administrator account.

TIP

Public Folder Sharing

To prevent other network users from changing the files you store in the Public folder, select the first **Turn on sharing** option listed in step 7. To enable other users to change your files, select the second **Turn on sharing** option listed in step 7.

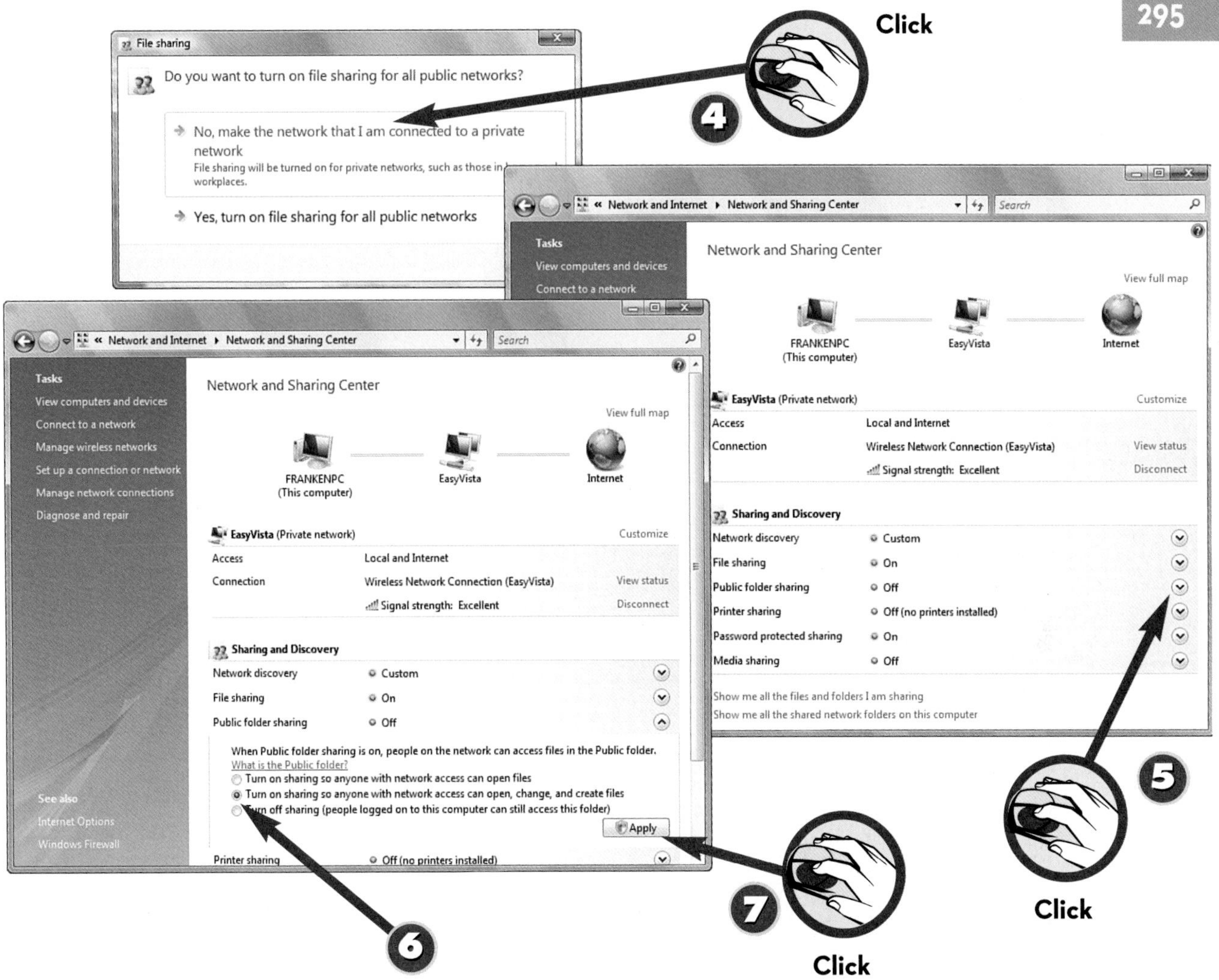

4 A pop-up File Sharing dialog box appears. Click **No, make the network that I am connected to a private network** to make your network a private one. A private network is more secure than a public network.

5 Click the arrow next to **Public folder sharing**.

6 Select a sharing option.

7 Click **Apply**.

End

TIP

Setting Up Multiple Users

By default, Windows Vista uses password protection on shared folders to prevent unauthorized users from getting into network shared folders. To enable other users, including users on other computers, to access the shared folders on your system, you must add their usernames and passwords to your computer's list of users. To learn more, see "Setting Up Windows for Multiple Users" in Part 11, "System Security and User Accounts." It is possible to disable password-protected sharing through the Network and Sharing Center, but for greatest security, you should set up additional users and passwords instead.

VIEWING NETWORK STATUS

After you have set up your network, you may need to check its status if things aren't working properly. To help you determine the status of your network, you can use the Network and Sharing Center and the Network Map features of Windows Vista.

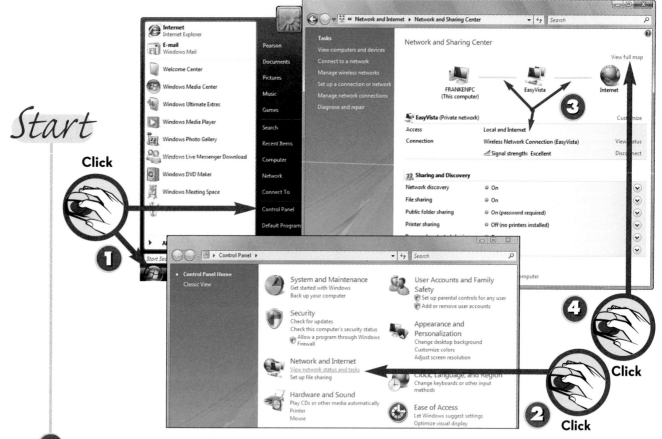

1. Click **Start**, **Control Panel**.
2. Under Network and Internet, click **View network status and tasks**.
3. The Network and Sharing Center opens and displays a visual representation of your network.
4. To determine if other computers on the network are connecting properly, click **View full map**.

Continued

TIP

Fixing Connection Problems

Click **Connect to a Network** in the Tasks pane, select your network, and then click **Connect**. If this doesn't work, unplug your network adapter or cable, wait a few seconds, and then plug it in again. If you are using wireless networking with security enabled, make sure you have correctly entered the security key and other settings. Make sure the wireless router or network switch is plugged in and working.

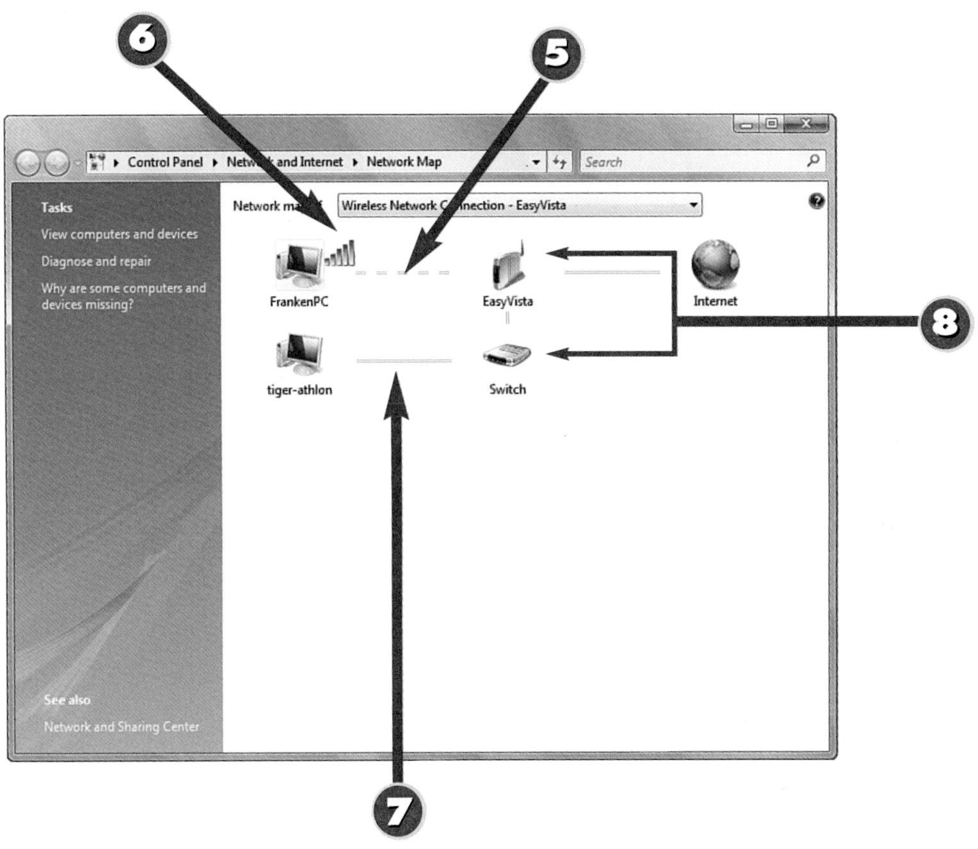

5 Dotted lines indicate wireless connections between computers and a wireless router.

6 If your computer uses a wireless connection, the number of bars indicates the signal strength of the connection.

7 Solid lines indicate wired connections between devices.

8 Although a wireless router and switch are listed as separate devices on the net, they may be built into a single physical unit.

End

TIP

Signal Strength

Generally, the closer your computer is to the wireless router, the stronger the signal. Steel, brick, or concrete walls can absorb signals, making your connection slower. To improve signal strength, you can add high-gain antennas to some wireless routers, or, if you have a USB wireless adapter on a cable, move the adapter around. You may also want to try different channels in your wireless router setup. 1, 6, and 11 are the best channels to use. Read *Absolute Beginner's Guide to Home Networking* for more information.

VIEWING NETWORK FOLDERS AND FILES

Use Network view to see the folders and printers that are being shared by other computers on the network and the folders and printers you are sharing.

Start

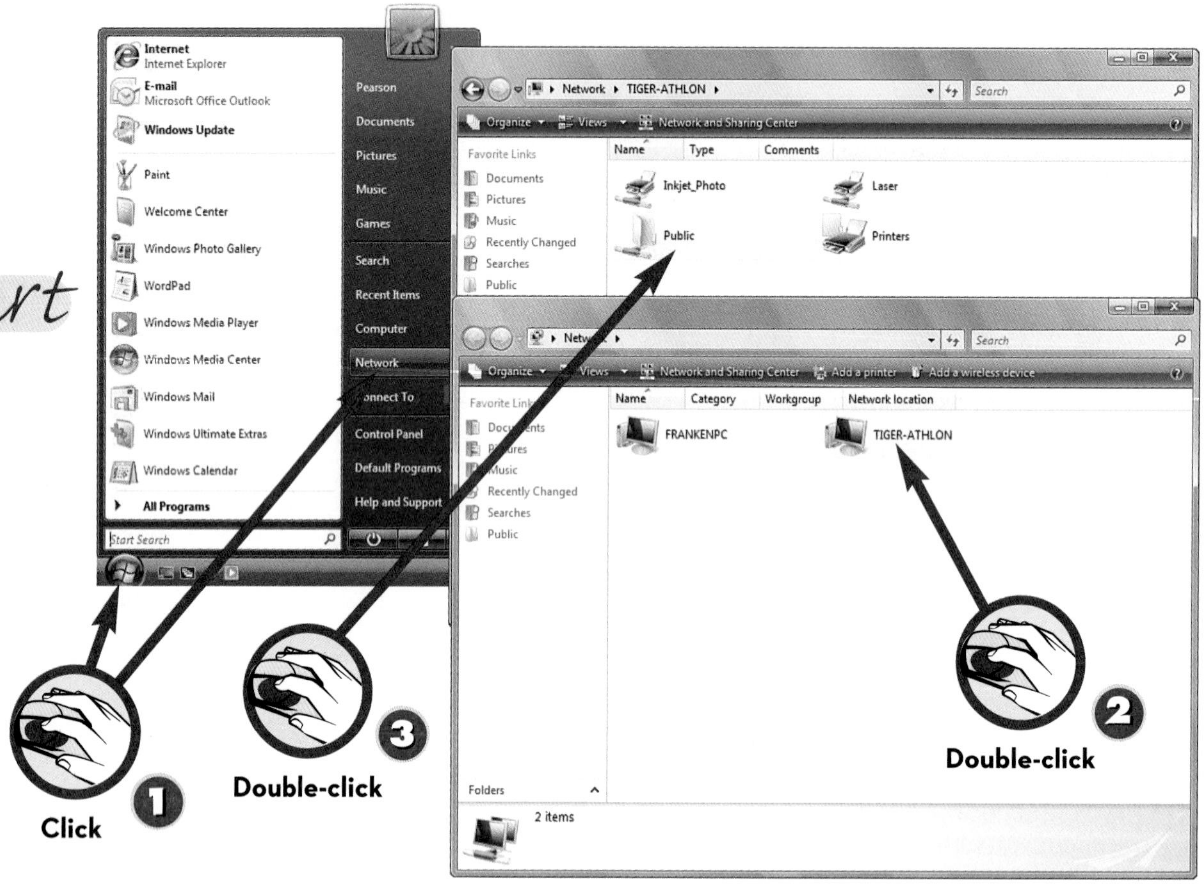

Click 1

Double-click 3

Double-click 2

1. Click **Start**, **Network**.
2. The Network view opens. To see the available folders and printers on another computer, double-click that computer's icon.
3. To view the files in a particular folder, double-click a folder, such as the **Public** folder.

Continued

NOTE

Windows XP and Vista Network Differences

If you are unable to view another computer in Network view, it might have a different workgroup name. All computers that share folders and printers must use the same workgroup name. Windows Vista uses the default name WORKGROUP. The default workgroup name in Windows XP is MSHOME. To learn how to view and change the workgroup name, open Help and Support, enter **workgroup name** as a search term, and follow the links given to join or create a workgroup.

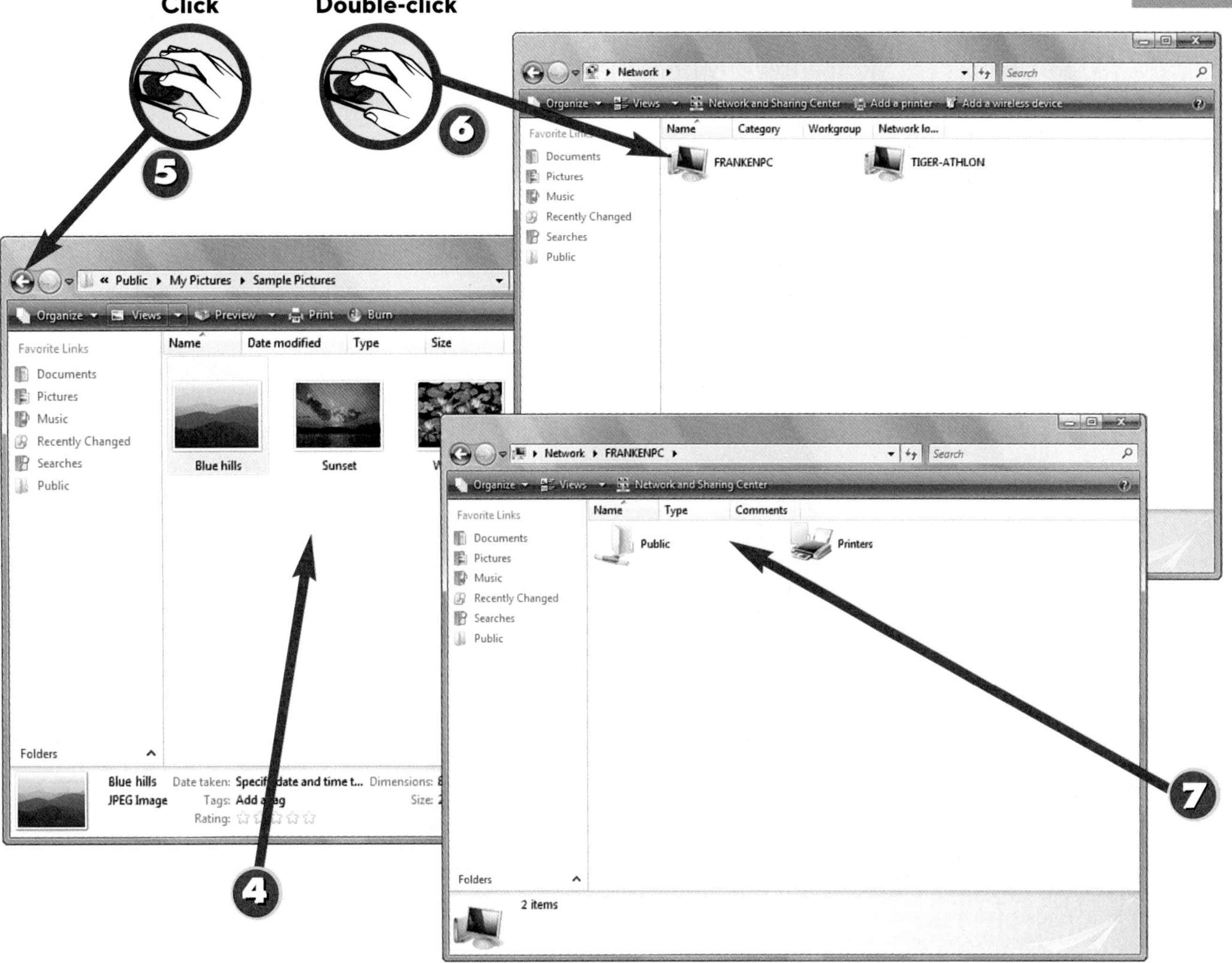

4. Navigate through the subfolders until you see the files you are looking for.
5. To redisplay the computers on your network, click the back arrow until they are visible.
6. Double-click your computer.
7. The shared folders and printers on your system are displayed.

End

TIP

Sharing More Folders

To share another folder, use the Folders view that opens on the left side of the Network view. Right-click a folder and select **Share**. Select the users you want to grant access. If the user is absent, click **Create a new user**, and enter the username and password. To permit read-only access, select **Reader** for the permission level. To permit a user to add or change files he or she saves, select **Contributor**. To permit a user to add, change, or delete files in the folder, select **Co-owner**. Click **Share** to complete the sharing process.

SETTING UP A NETWORK PRINTER

When you enable file sharing, any printers already connected to your system are automatically shared with other users. However, if you add or change printers later, new printers are not automatically shared. This tutorial shows you how to set up a newly installed printer as a network printer.

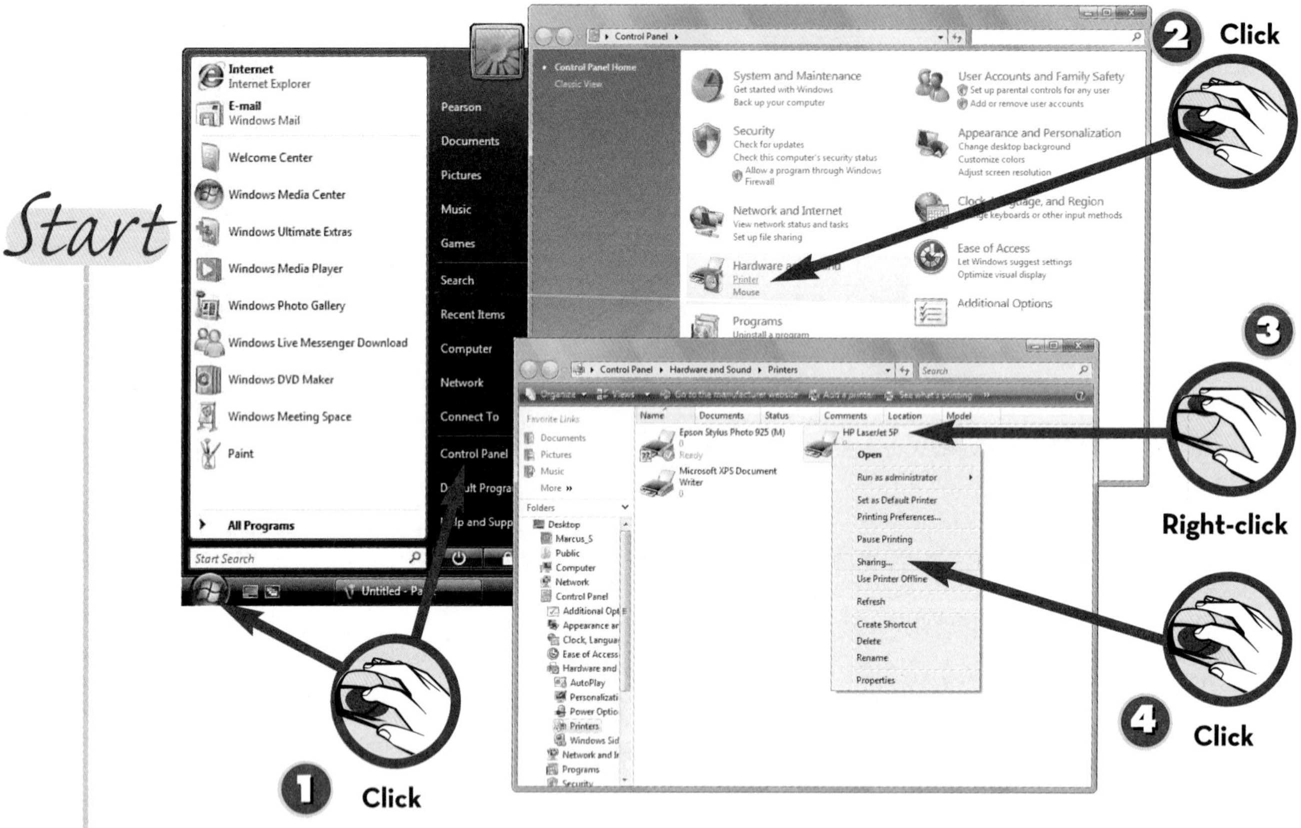

Start

1. Click **Start**, **Control Panel**.
2. Select **Printer** from the Hardware and Sound category.
3. Right-click the printer you want to share.
4. Select **Sharing** from the contextual menu.

Continued

5. Click **Change sharing options**.
6. Click **Share this printer**.
7. Click **OK**.

End

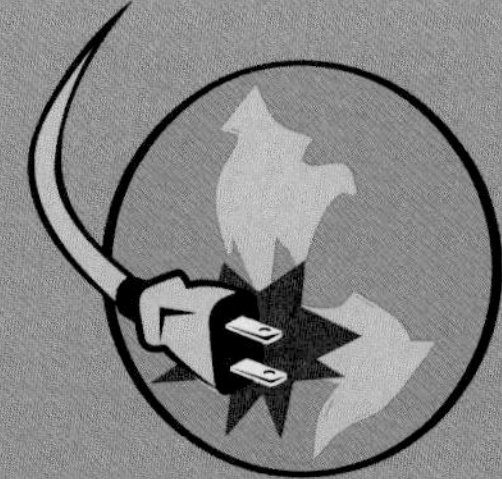

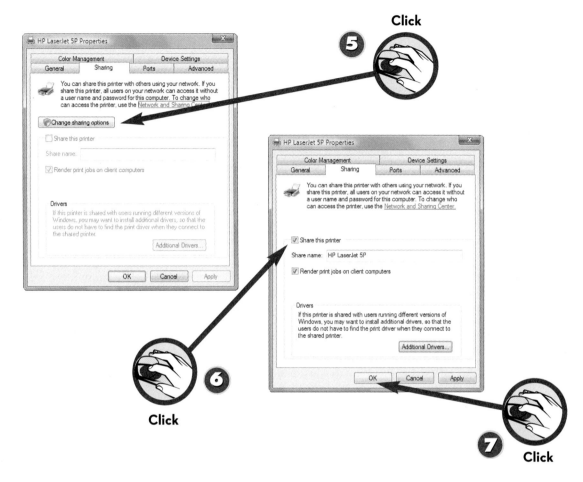

SELECTING A SHARED PRINTER

After you set up a network printer, other users on the network must configure their systems to use it. This task shows you how to select a network printer from another computer on the network. After the printer is selected, you can use it just like a local printer.

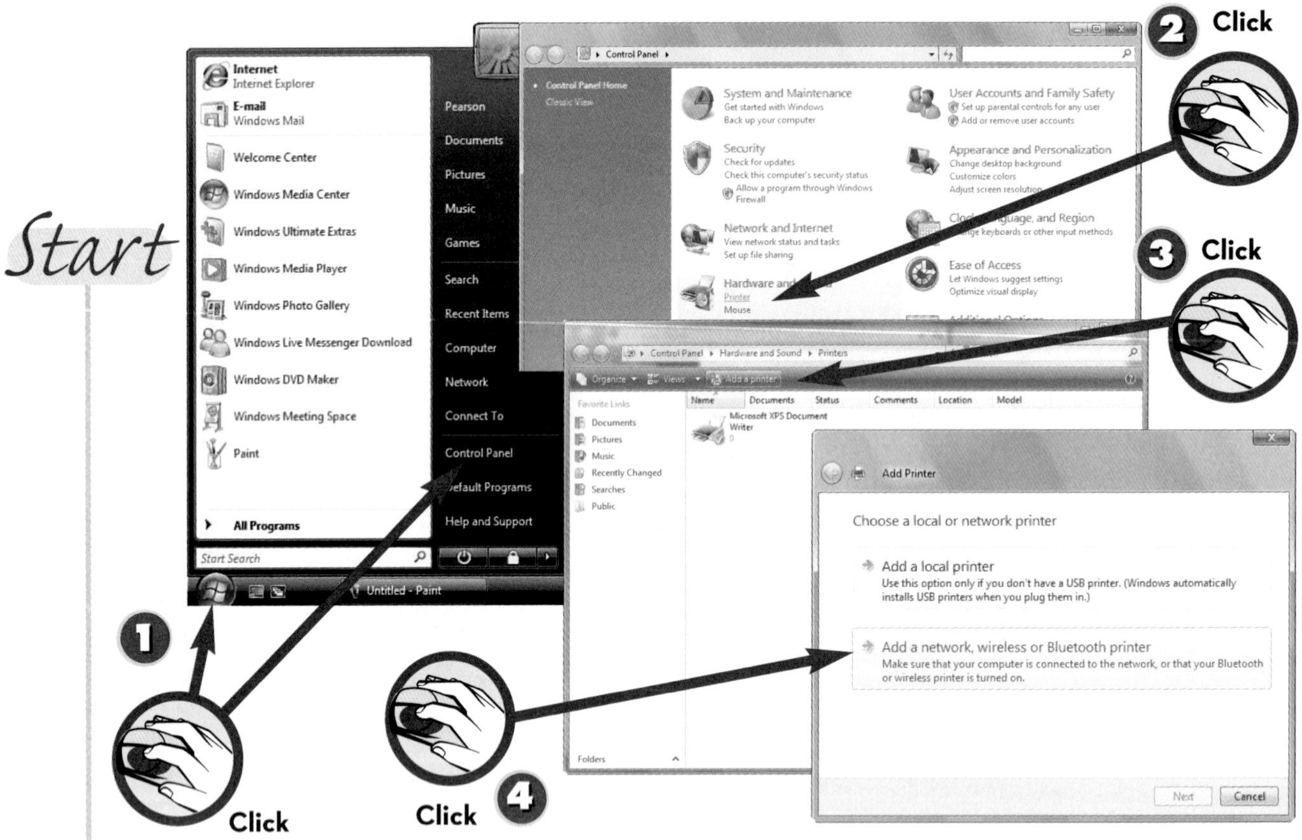

Start

1. Click **Start**, **Control Panel**.
2. Click **Printer** in the Hardware and Sound section of the Control Panel.
3. Click **Add a Printer**.
4. Select **Add a network, wireless or Bluetooth printer**.

Continued

TIP
Setting Up Other Types of Printers

If you want to install a local printer (a printer that connects directly to your computer using a cable), connect it to the computer and turn it on. If Vista recognizes the printer, it will set it up for you automatically. You will need to install drivers only if Vista does not recognize the printer.

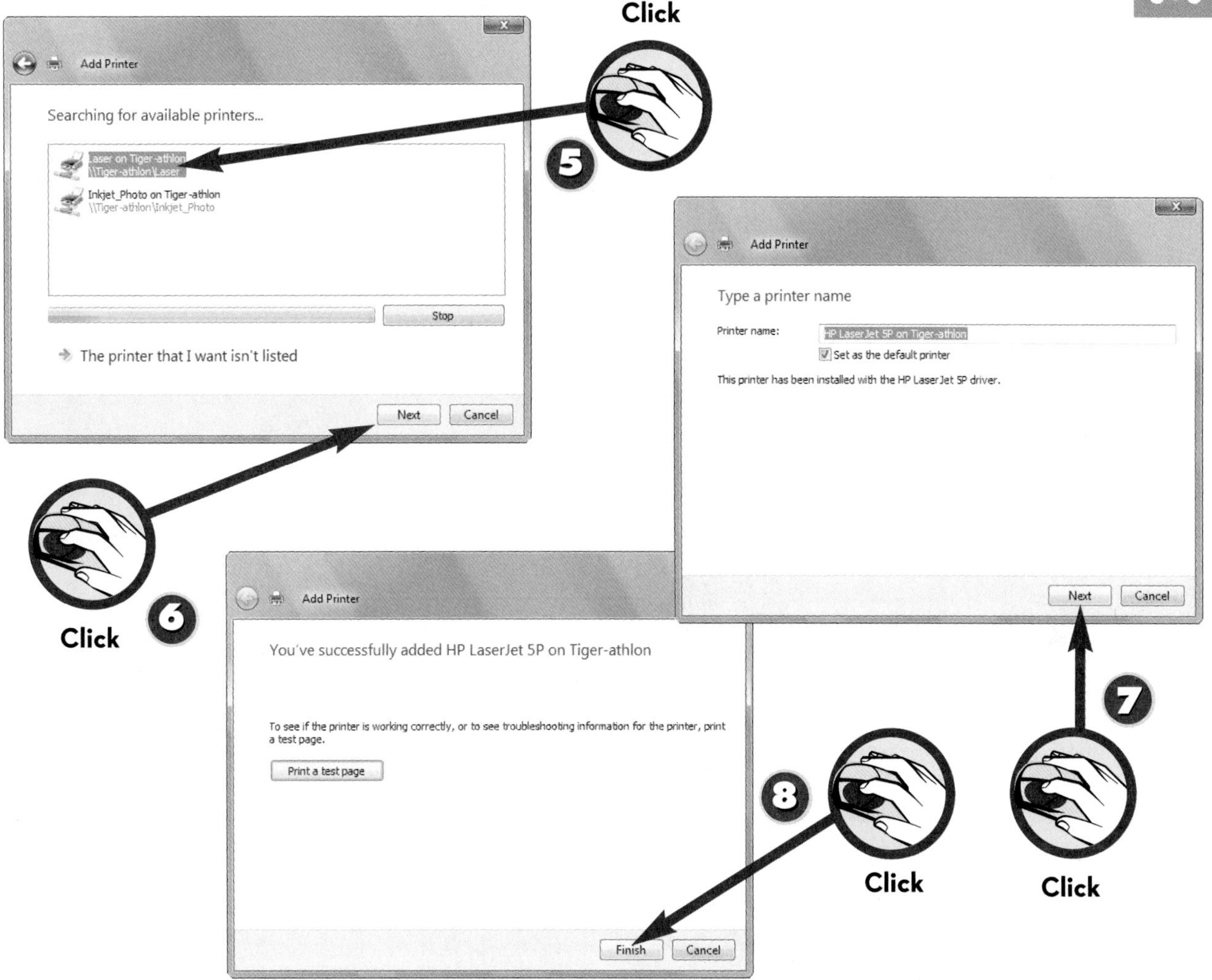

5. Select a printer from the list of shared printers.
6. Click **Next**. The computer connects to the shared printer.
7. To keep the default printer name, click **Next**.
8. Click **Finish** to complete printer setup.

TIP

Testing the Printer

To make sure you can print over the network, in step 8, click **Print a test page** before clicking **Finish**. If the test page looks okay, you can use the network printer. If not, make sure the printer works properly when used by its host computer. See Part 6, "Working with Printers," for more information about printers.

TRANSFERRING FILES AND SETTINGS FROM ANOTHER PC

If you're now using a new PC with Windows Vista but don't want to leave your existing files, favorites, and other settings behind, use Windows Easy Transfer to move your information from your old computer using Windows XP to your new computer. Windows Easy Transfer can also transfer files (but not program settings) from a computer running Windows 2000. In this tutorial, we'll use Windows Easy Transfer to perform a transfer from a system using Windows XP to your new system over a network connection.

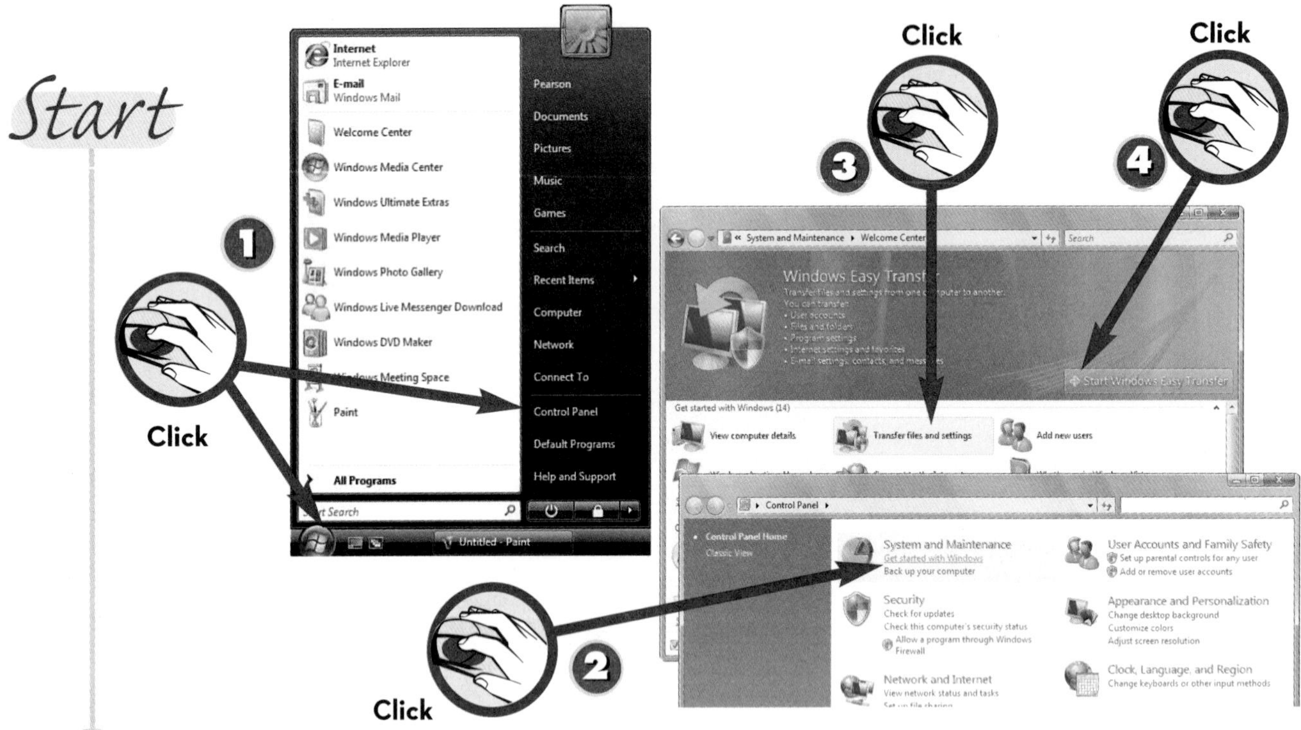

1. Click **Start**, **Control Panel**.
2. Click **Get Started with Windows** in the System and Maintenance section of the Control Panel.
3. From the Welcome Center dialog box, click **Transfer files and settings**.
4. Click **Start Windows Easy Transfer**.

Continued

NOTE

Settings You Can Transfer with Easy Transfer

Easy Transfer copies user accounts, files and folders, program settings, Internet settings and favorites, email settings, contacts, and messages from a Vista or Windows XP system to another Vista system.

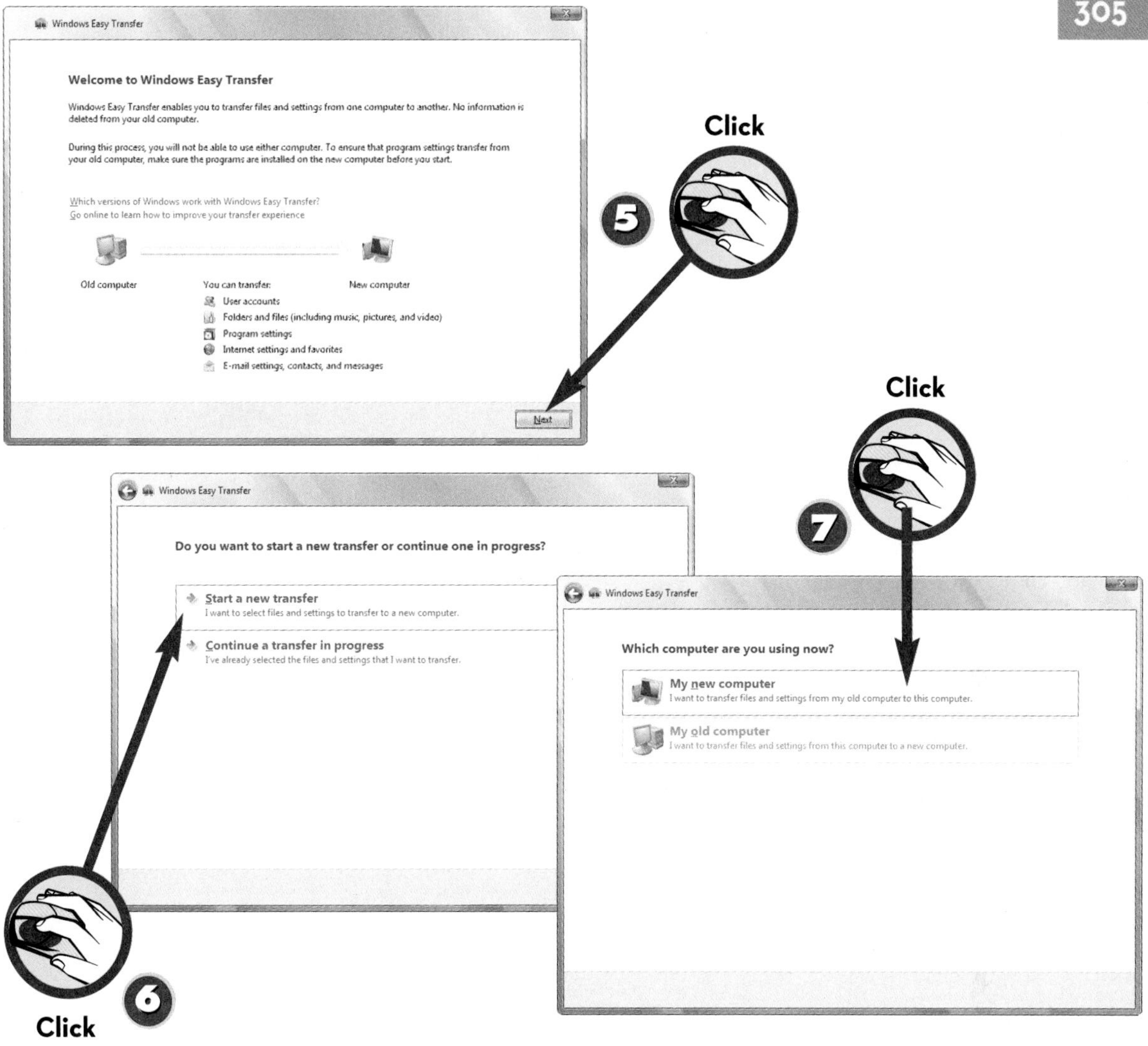

Click

Click

Click

5 Click **Next** to continue.

6 Click **Start a new transfer**.

7 Click **My new computer**.

End

NOTE

Transfer Methods

This task uses a network connection to transfer files, but you can also use CD or DVD media or an external hard disk or network folder to perform transfers.

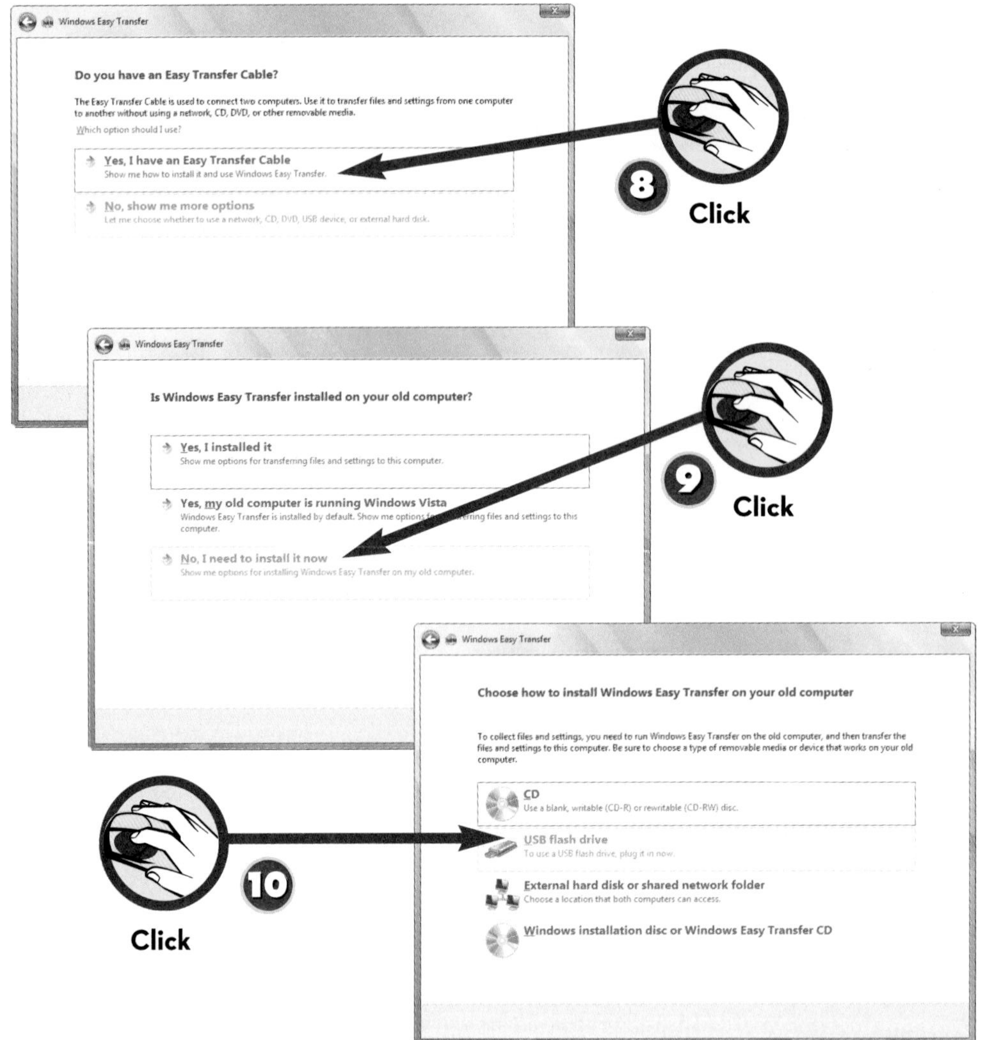

8. If you have an Easy Transfer Cable (a special USB cable made for file transfers), click **Yes, I have an Easy Transfer Cable**. Otherwise, click **No, show me more options**.
9. When asked if Windows Easy Transfer is installed on your old computer, click **No, I need to install it now**.
10. To use a USB flash drive to install Windows Easy Transfer, insert the drive and click **USB flash drive**.

Continued

NOTE

Inserting the Flash Drive

If both computers have USB ports, a USB flash drive is the easiest way to install Windows Easy Transfer. Insert it when prompted.

CAUTION

Not Transferring Files and Settings Yet

When you connect the USB drive in step 12, you are preparing it to install the program on the other computer. The transfer of files and settings from the old system to the new system does not occur until after the USB drive is connected to your old computer and the transfer software is installed on that computer.

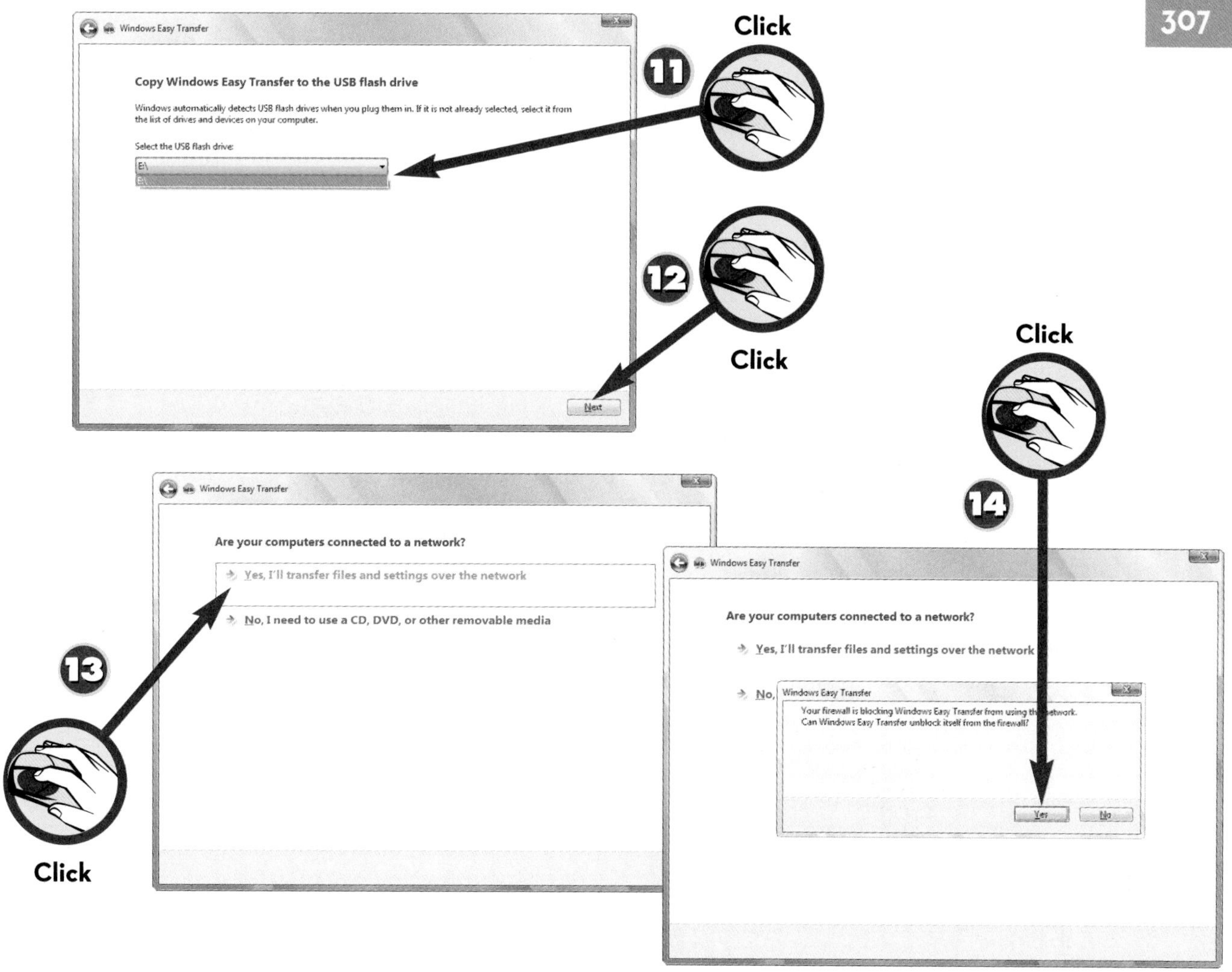

1. Select the drive letter used by the USB flash or other drive.
2. Click **Next**. The Easy Transfer software is copied to the drive.
3. To use your network for the transfer, click **Yes, I'll transfer files and settings over the network**.
4. If you use a firewall, it may block the transfer when it takes place. Click **Yes** to unblock the transfer.

Continued

TIP

Windows Firewall

The warning shown in step 14 might not appear on your system. If it does not appear, your computer's Windows Firewall is already configured to permit the transfer. Continue to step 15.

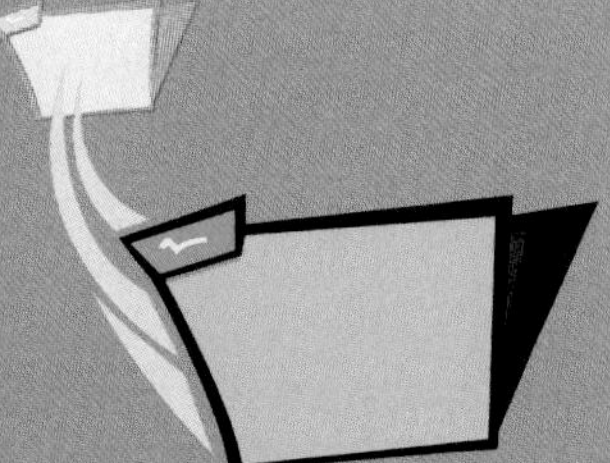

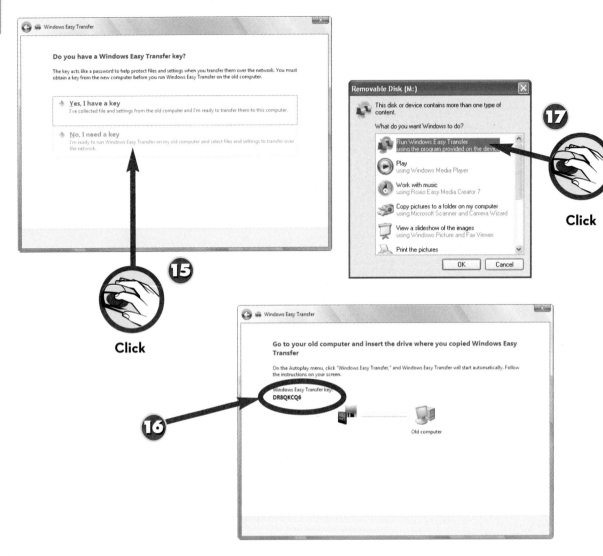

15 When the "Do you have a Windows Easy Transfer key?" screen appears, click **No, I need a key**.

16 Write down the Windows Easy Transfer key when it is displayed. Remove the USB flash drive from your new computer and plug it into your old computer.

17 Double-click **Run Windows Easy Transfer** when your old computer displays the Autoplay menu.

Continued

TIP

Open Programs? Close Them First

Before starting Windows Easy Transfer on your old computer, make sure you have closed all running programs and saved your data.

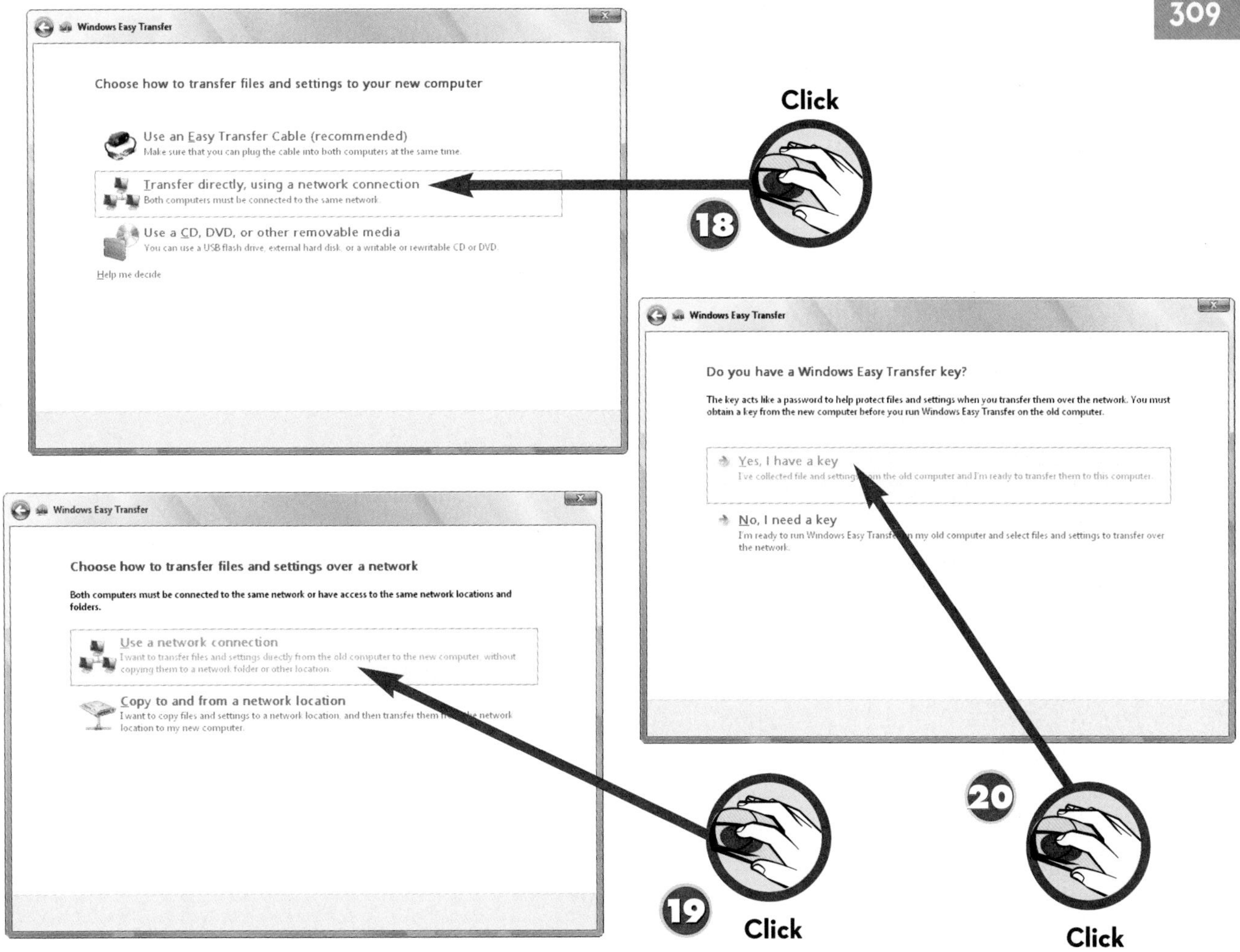

18 Select **Transfer directly, using a network connection**.

19 Click **Use a network connection**.

20 Click **Yes, I have a key**.

Continued

NOTE

Are You Connected?

When you do a network transfer, after you start Windows Easy Transfer on your old computer, your new computer displays a message: Your computers are now connected. If you don't see this message, your network may not be working properly.

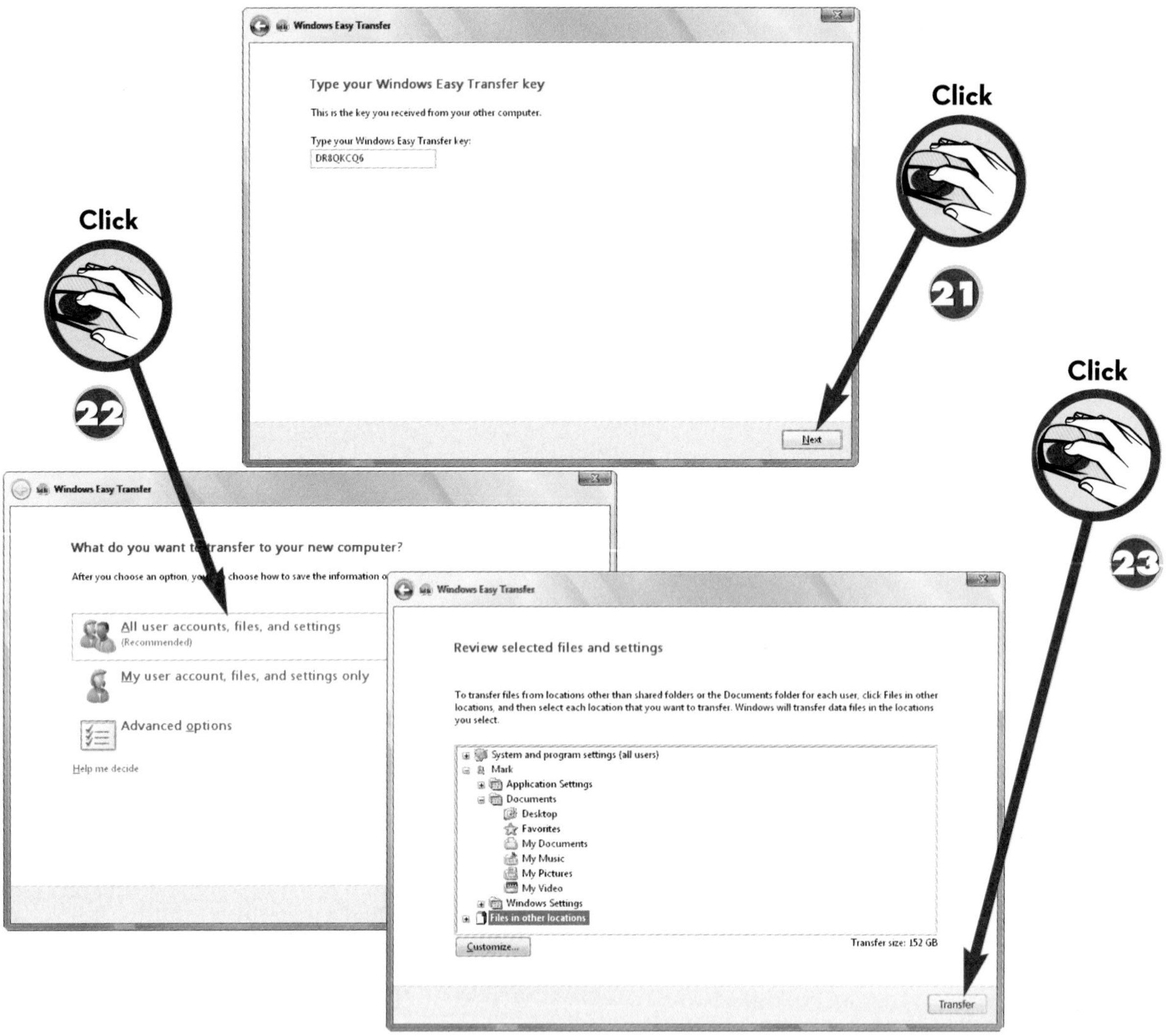

21 Verify that the key shown is the correct key, and click **Next**.

22 Click **All user accounts, files, and settings**.

23 To transfer all items, click **Transfer**. The files are transferred to your new computer.

Continued

TIP
Customizing the Transfer

To transfer only certain items, click **Customize** on the Transfer menu (step 23) and clear check marks for items you do not want to transfer, or add check marks for items you can transfer but that are not already checked. Click **Transfer** when you're finished.

NOTE
Transfer Time

The transfer may take up to an hour or more, depending upon the speed of your connection and the amount of information to be transferred. An animated progress bar is displayed during the transfer.

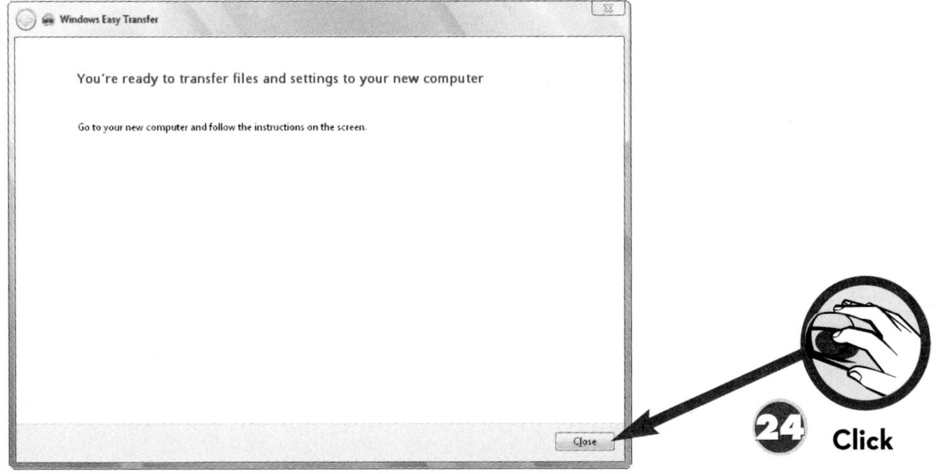

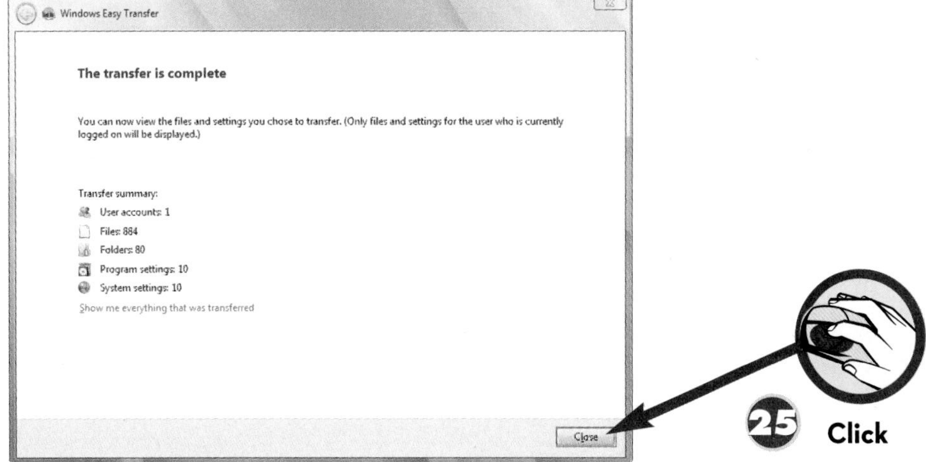

 After the transfer is complete, click **Close**. Return to your new computer.

 At your new computer, a summary of the transferred information is displayed. Click **Close**.

End

TIP
When Does the Transfer Take Place?

If you use CD or DVD media or a network folder to hold your information, the transfer isn't done until you follow instructions on the other computer. But when you use a direct USB or network connection, it's done when you are prompted to click **Close** on your old computer (step 24).

TIP
Seeing Transfer Details

To see a detailed list of what was transferred, click **Show me everything that was transferred** on the "The transfer is complete" dialog box shown in step 25.

A

accessory A mini-application that comes free with Windows Vista. Examples include WordPad, Paint, and Calculator.

active window The window you're currently using or working in.

Aero A new Windows Vista interface; it has the appearance of translucent glass.

application Software that accomplishes a specific practical task such as typing text (word processor), editing photographs (Photoshop), and others. Also called a program.

application window A window that contains a running application, such as Paint or WordPad.

B

boot To start your computer. The term *booting* comes from the phrase "pulling oneself up by one's own bootstraps," which refers to the fact that your computer can load everything it needs to operate properly without help from you.

bps Bits per second. The rate at which a modem or other communications device sends data through a phone line or cable.

browser A program used to view sites on the World Wide Web. The browser that comes with Windows is called Internet Explorer.

byte A single character of information.

C

cable modem A modem that enables you to connect to the Internet through your cable company. Cable modems provide much faster connection speeds than dial-up accounts.

cascade menu A group of additional commands that appear under certain menu commands found in pull-down menus.

CD drive A special computer disk drive that's designed to handle CD discs, which resemble audio CDs. CDs have enormous capacity (about 500 times that of a typical floppy disk), so they're most often used to hold large applications, graphics libraries, software, and huge collections of shareware programs.

character formatting Changing the look of text characters by altering their font, size, style, and more.

check box A square-shaped switch that toggles a dialog box option on or off. The option is toggled on when a check mark appears in the box and off when it is empty.

click To quickly press and release a mouse button.

Clipboard An area of memory that temporarily holds data during cut-and-paste operations.

command bar In Explorers, a toolbar that displays tasks relevant to the files displayed in that window. For instance, a window that contained photos would include commands for working with photos in the command bar.

command button A rectangular "button" (usually found in dialog boxes) that, when clicked, runs whatever command is spelled out on it.

commands The options you see in a pull-down menu. You use these commands to tell the application what you want it to do next.

D

data files The files used by you or your programs. See also *program files*.

desktop The screen that you see when Windows starts. Starting a Windows application is similar to putting a folder full of papers (the application window) on your desk. To do some work, you pull some papers out of the folder (the document windows) and place them on the desktop.

Details Pane Rather than view file properties using the Properties dialog box (as in past Windows versions), you can use the Preview Pane to view file properties.

device driver A small program that controls the way a device (such as a mouse or printer) works with your system.

dialog boxes Windows that pop up on the screen to ask you for information or to seek confirmation of a requested action.

digital camera A special camera that saves pictures using digital storage (such as a memory card) instead of film. You can transfer pictures from your camera to your PC.

directory See *folder*.

diskette See *floppy disk*.

document window A window opened in an application. Document windows hold whatever you're working on in the application.

double-click To quickly press and release a mouse button twice in succession.

double-click speed The maximum amount of time Windows allows between the mouse clicks of a double-click.

drag To press and hold down the mouse button on an object and then move the mouse.

drag-and-drop A technique you use to run commands or move things around; you use your mouse to drag files or icons to strategic screen areas and drop them there.

drop-down list box A list box that normally shows only a single item but, when selected, displays a list of options.

DSL Digital Subscriber Line. A special type of phone line that provides faster Internet connection speed.

DVD Digital Video Disc. A type of storage medium similar to a CD but with better sound, graphics, video quality, and greater storage capacity. Some computers now come with a DVD drive rather than a CD drive. You can find movies and programs on DVDs. You can also use standard data and audio CDs in a DVD drive. One of the newest additions to computer capabilities is the ability to burn a DVD.

E–F

Explorer bar The left pane of a folder window. You can choose to display different lists in this area, including a Folders list, a History list, or a Favorites list.

Explorers A view that shows the content of windows and, unlike other past versions of Windows, Windows Vista Explorers have a single, consistent interface. They are the primary tools for finding and viewing documents.

Family Safety Settings New parental controls that help track and handle children's computer use.

Favorites A list of folders, files, or Web sites. You can add items to the Favorites list and then quickly access the item.

file An organized unit of information inside your computer. Documents, images, spreadsheets, and any other items you can create and save on your computer are generically called files.

floppy disk A portable storage medium that consists of a flexible magnetic disk protected by a plastic case. Floppy disks are available in a variety of sizes and capacities.

folder A storage location on your hard disk in which you keep related files together.

Folder list A list of the drives and folders on your system. In folder windows, you can display the Folder list by clicking the Folders button.

font A character set of a specific typeface, type style, and type size.

format bar A series of text boxes and buttons that enable you to format the characters in your document in WordPad. The format bar typically appears under the toolbar.

formatting The process of setting up a disk so that a drive can read its information and write information to it. Not to be confused with character formatting.

fragmented When a single file is chopped up and stored in separate chunks scattered around a hard disk. You can fix this by running the Windows Disk Defragmenter program.

G–H

gadgets Mini-applications that you can run in Windows. Some uses include displaying weather information, news updates, and traffic maps. They aren't limited to just information delivery; they can also include games, sticky notes, calculators, and other programs.

gigabyte 1,024 megabytes. Usually abbreviated as GB when writing and as gig when speaking. See also *byte*, *kilobyte*, and *megabyte*.

hard disk A storage medium that consists of several metallic disks stacked on top of each other, usually protected by a metal outer case. Hard disks are available in a variety of sizes and capacities and are usually the main storage area inside your computer. The main hard drive is housed inside the system unit, but you can also purchase additional external drives that connect to your computer.

History list A list of folders, files, or Web sites you have opened recently. You can display the History list and then select to view any of the items in the list.

hover To place the mouse pointer over an object for a few seconds. In most Windows applications, for example, if you hover the mouse over a toolbar button, a small banner pops up that tells you the name of the button.

I–J

icons The little pictures that Windows uses to represent programs and files.

infrared port A communications port, usually found on notebook computers and some printers. Infrared ports enable two devices to communicate by using infrared light waves instead of cables.

insertion point The blinking vertical bar you see inside a text box or in a word-processing application, such as WordPad. It indicates where the next character you type will appear.

Instant Search A new Windows Vista feature that provides fast access to searching from the Start menu and Explorer windows. You can search for documents, music, programs, pictures, email messages, contacts, and more.

Internet A network of networks that extends around the world. You can access this network by setting up an account with an Internet service provider. See also *ISP*.

intranet The implementation of Internet technologies for use within a corporate organization rather than for connection to the Internet as a whole.

IR Short for infrared. See also *infrared port*.

ISP Stands for Internet Service Provider. The company that provides access to the Internet. Depending on your setup, you may dial and connect to this network, or you may get access through your cable or phone company. When connected to your ISP, you have access to the entire Internet.

K

Kbps One thousand bits per second (bps). A measure of the speed of how fast a modem can transmit data.

keyboard delay The amount of time it takes for a second character to appear when you press and hold down a key.

keyword See *tag*.

kilobyte 1,024 bytes. This is often abbreviated K or KB. See also *megabyte* and *gigabyte*.

L

list box A small window that displays a list of items, such as filenames or folders.

local area network (LAN) A network in which all the computers occupy a relatively small geographical area, such as a department, an office, a home, or a building. All the connections between computers are made via network cables.

LPT port See *port*.

M

Malicious Software Removal Tool (MSRT) A Windows feature that looks for and removes viruses and malware.

malware Malicious programs, such as viruses, worms, spyware, and other problems. Microsoft Windows Vista contains many security features to protect your computer from malware.

maximize To increase the size of a window to its largest extent. A maximized application window fills the entire screen except for the taskbar. A maximized document window fills the entire application window.

Mbps One million bits per second (bps).

megabyte 1,024 kilobytes, or 1,048,576 bytes. This is often abbreviated in writing to M or MB and pronounced meg. See also *gigabyte*.

menu bar The horizontal bar usually on the second line of an application window. The menu bar contains the application's pull-down menus.

metadata See *tag*.

minimize To remove a program from the desktop without closing it. A minimized program appears as a button on the taskbar.

modem An electronic device that enables two computers to exchange data over phone, cable, or DSL lines.

multitasking The capability to run several programs at the same time.

N–O

Navigation pane A pane that appears in Explorers windows that provide access to commonly used folders.

network A collection of computers connected using special cables or other network media (such as Ethernet ports or wireless communication devices) to share files, folders, disks, peripherals, and applications. See also *local area network (LAN)*.

Network Explorer A Vista Explorer that lets you browse content on networked PCs, including documents and printers.

Network Map A graphical representation of the contents of your network.

newsgroup An Internet discussion group devoted to a single topic. These discussions progress by "posting" messages to the group.

option buttons See *radio buttons*.

P–Q

phishing A computer fraud used by others to get personal information from you and then steal your identity or use your information for their own purposes (such as your credit card numbers and Social Security number).

point To place the mouse pointer so that it rests on a specific screen location.

port The connection into which you plug the cable from a device, such as a mouse or printer. Your computer has several types of ports, including an LPT port (usually used to connect a printer), a serial port (also used for a printer or scanner or other devices), and USB ports (used for printers, scanners, digital cameras, and other devices).

program files The files that run your programs. See also *data files*.

R

radio buttons Dialog box options that appear as small circles in groups of two or more. Only one option from a group can be chosen. These are also called *option buttons*.

RAM Stands for Random Access Memory. The physical memory in your computer that Windows uses to run your programs.

Really Simple Syndication (RSS) Technology that sends information to you (versus your looking for and finding that information). You subscribe to the information you want to receive.

Remote Assistance With your permission, Remote Assistance enables someone at a remote location to view and troubleshoot problems on your computer.

repeat rate After the initial delay, the rate at which characters appear when you press and hold down a key.

right-click To click the right mouse button instead of the usual left mouse button. Right-clicking something usually pops up a contextual menu.

S

scrollbar A bar that appears at the bottom or on the right side of a window when the window is too small to display all its contents.

Search Folders A special type of folder that stores searches that you have run. You can open the folder and run these searches again at any time, without having to rearrange files that you have run and saved.

serial port See *port*.

shortcut A special file that points to a program or file. Double-clicking the shortcut starts the program or opens the file.

shortcut menu A menu that contains a few commands related to an item (such as the desktop or the taskbar). You display the shortcut menu by right-clicking the object.

sleep A new power state (formerly known as Hibernate) that saves current information to memory and the hard drive so that you can quickly restart the computer, plus have the added protection from the saved information on the hard disk.

system resources Memory areas that Windows uses to keep track of things such as the position and size of open windows, dialog boxes, and your desktop configuration (such as wallpaper).

T

tag A keyword or property that you can attach to a document. Doing so helps you more easily find that document. You can also use tags to group and view similar documents.

taskbar The horizontal strip across the bottom of the Windows screen. Each running application is given its own taskbar button, and you can switch to a running application by clicking its taskbar button.

text box A screen area in which you type text, such as a description or a filename.

text editor A program that lets you edit files that contain only text. The Windows Vista text editor is called Notepad.

title bar The area on the top line of a window that displays the window's title.

toolbar A series of buttons that typically appear beneath the menu bar. These buttons provide access to commonly used commands.

tracking speed The speed at which the mouse pointer moves across the screen when you move the mouse on its pad. You can adjust the speed if needed.

TrueType A font-management program that enables you to add fonts to your system.

type size A measurement of the height of a font. Type size is measured in points; there are 72 points in an inch.

type style Character attributes, such as regular, bold, and italic. Other type styles (often called type effects) are underline and strikethrough.

typeface A distinctive graphics design of letters, numbers, and other symbols.

U-Y

URGE A new digital music service from MTV and integrated in Windows Media Player.

USB port See *port*.

User Account Control A revamped set of controls for setting up and controlling user accounts.

Volume Shadow Copy A data protection feature that lets you retrieve files you have deleted.

window A rectangular screen area in which Windows displays applications and documents.

Windows Backup A new, revamped backup program that provides more options for backing up your data. You can choose to back up to a CD or DVD, a hard drive on your PC, or via a cable or through a network.

Windows Calendar A revamped accessory for keeping track of your appointments and to-do lists. You can also share your calendars and post them on the Internet.

Windows Contacts The new term used to describe the Address Book.

Windows Defender A Windows feature that protects your system from spyware and other unwanted software.

Windows Flip and Flip 3D A new way to flip through and view multiple open windows. In previous versions, when Alt+Tab was pressed, you saw a generic icon. With Windows Flip, you see live thumbnails of the open windows. With Windows Flip 3D (available in the Aero interface of Windows Vista), you see a three-dimensional stack of open windows.

Windows Media Center A new Windows Vista feature that enables you to find, play, organize, and manage your digital media.

Windows Meeting Space A way to collaborate with groups in sessions (in the same room).

Windows Photo Gallery A new Windows Vista feature that enables you to view, organize, and share your photos more easily.

Windows ReadyBoost A new method for adding memory to your computer and improving system performance.

Windows SuperFetch A new Windows Vista technology enhancement that loads applications and files much faster than previous Windows versions.

Z

Zip drive A special disk drive that uses portable disks that hold hundreds of megabytes of data.

Index

A

Absolute Beginner's Guide to Home Networking, 290
accessibility options, 206-209
accessories
  calculator, 260
  Calendar
    changing views, 270
    entering tasks, 271
    scheduling appointments, 268-269
    viewing, 267
  Contacts
    adding, 261
    deleting, 266
    editing, 262
    grouping, 264-265
    searching, 263
  new and improved, 8
  Notepad, 282
  Paint, 283
    adding text, 285
    color, 286
    drawing shape, 284
    erasing part of drawing, 287
  WordPad, text, 272
    copying, 276-277
    deleting, 275
    formatting, 280-281
    moving, 278-279
    selecting, 274
    typing, 273
accounts
  administrator *versus* standard, 187
  computer
    log off, 26
    logon, 14
    switching users, 26
  deleting, 186
  multiple user set up, 186-187
  music purchase, 119
  parent control setting, 190-191
  password assignment, 188-189
address books, Contacts
  adding, 261
  deleting, 266
  editing, 262
  grouping, 264-265
  searching, 263
addresses, Web sites, 159
administrators, user types, 187
Aero Glass, 4
All Programs list, 31
antivirus programs, 180
applications. *See also* programs; software
  calculator, 260
  Calendar
    changing views, 270
    entering tasks, 271
    scheduling appointments, 268-269
    viewing, 267
  Contacts
    adding, 261
    deleting, 266
    editing, 262
    grouping, 264-265
    searching, 263
  Notepad, 282
  Paint, 283
    adding text, 285
    color, 286
    drawing shape, 284
    erasing part of drawing, 287
  versus programs and software, 30
  WordPad, text, 272
    copying, 276-277
    deleting, 275
    formatting, 280-281
    moving, 278-279
    selecting, 274
    typing, 273
appointments, scheduling, 268-269
arranging windows, 23
associations, files, setting, 69
Attach File to Message button, 136
attachments, email
  adding to message, 136
  opening, 137
audio CDs
  burning, 123
  playing, 110
  ripping tracks, 122

shuffling tracks, 113
visualizations, 115
volume options, 114

automatic installations, digital cameras and scanners, 100

AutoPlay, setting options, 225

B

Back buttons, 24

back ups, file restoration, 256-257

backgrounds, desktop, 15
changing, 15
colors, 196

Backup and Restore Center, 254-255

BCC (blind carbon copy), email messages, 135

blocked senders, 152

blocking pop-ups, 184

broadband connections *versus* dial-up, 156

browsing Internet, hyperlinks, 158

Brush tool, 286

C

calculators, 260

Calendar, 8
changing views, 270
entering tasks, 271
scheduling appointments, 268-269
viewing, 267

calendars, sharing, 8

CD-ROMs, copying files, 65

CDs
audio
playing, 110
shuffling tracks, 113
visualizations, 115
volume options, 114
copying pictures to, 103

Classic Menu, customizing, 218

Classic View, Control Panel, 78, 82

Close command, 19

closing windows, 22

colors
adding to drawing, 286
desktop background, 196
schemes, customizing Vista, 195
selecting unique, 195

compressed files
extracting, 238
saving space, 236-237

Computer menu, computer system drives, 42

Computer window, sorting content, 50

computers
back up file restoration, 256-257
Backup and Restore Center, 254-255
disk
cleanup, 235
compressing files, 236-238
defragmentation, 242-243
information, 234
Memory Diagnostic Tool, 239
scanning for errors, 240-241
hardware installation
manually, 248-249
troubleshooting, 250-251
power management, 231
restarting, 27
scheduling tasks, 244-247
shutting down, 27
System Information, 232-233
System Restore, 252-253
viewing drives, 42
Windows Updates
automatic, 228-229
manually, 230

configuration, faxes, 148-149

connections
Internet, hardware requirements, 154
troubleshooting network, 296

Contacts
adding, 261
deleting, 266
editing, 262
grouping, 264-265
searching, 263

contacts, email
adding addresses, 142-143
using to enter names, 144

Contacts List, 8, 134
Control Panel, 17
  different views, 78
  System and Maintenance category, 226
    back up file restoration, 256-257
    Backup and Restore Center, 254-255
    compressing files, 236-238
    defragmentation, 242-243
    disk cleanup, 235
    disk information, 234
    hardware installation, 248-251
    Memory Diagnostic Tool, 239
    power management, 231
    scanning disk for errors, 240-241
    scheduling tasks, 244-247
    System Information, 232-233
    System Restore, 252-253
    Windows Updates, 228-230
Control Panel Home view, 78
controllers, games, 125
controls, Windows Media Player, 112
copying
  files, 64-65
  folders, 54
Cover Page template, 150
Create Mail button, 134
customizing Start menu, 218-219
customizing taskbars, 220-221
customizing Vista
  accessibility options, , 206-209
  color schemes, 195
  desktop
    applying image, 197
    backgroups, 196
    theme, 194
  monitors, resolution setting, 199
  mouse movements, 200-201
  screen saver selection, 198
  sound scheme, 202-203
  system date and time, 204-205

D

dates, system change, 204-205
defaults
  audio CDs, 110
  file
    programs, 69
    searches, 73
  printers, 80, 83
  programs, 224
  Windows Defender, 179
  Windows Mail, 145
defragmentation, disks, 242-243
Delete File dialog box, 216
Delete Files button, 235
Delete Items folder, cleanup, 139
deleting
  Contacts, 266
  email folders, 145
  Favorites Center sites, 164
  file tags, 74
  files, 66-67
  folders, 53, 57
  printers, 83
deselecting files, 60
desktops, 4, 12
  applying image, 197
  backgrounds, 15
    changing, 15
    colors, 196
  color schemes, 195
  computer
    logging off, 26
    logon, 14
    restarting, 27
    shutting down, 27
    switching users, 26
  Help command, 24-25
  icons, 15
  main elements, 15
  selecting themes, 194
  Start menu, 16-17
  windows
    arrangement, 23
    closing, 22

maximizing, 18-19
minimizing, 19
moving, 20
resizing, 18, 21

Details pane, 61

Device Manager, 251

Device Settings tab, 86

dial-up *versus* broadband connection, 156

digital cameras, 96
- deleting images, 99
- setup
  - automatically, 98
  - manual, 100-101
- transferring images from, 99
- Windows Photo Gallery
  - copying pictures to CD or DVD, 103
  - fixing photos, 104-105
  - organizing pictures, 102
  - printing photos, 106-107

Disk Cleanup dialog box, 235

Disk Defragmenter dialog box, 243

disks
- cleanup, 235
- compressed files
  - extracting, 238
  - saving space, 236-237
- defragmentation, 242-243
- information, 234
- labels, 234
- Memory Diagnostic Tool, 239
- scanning for errors, 240-241

displaying toolbars, 223

documents
- printing
  - cancel job, 91
  - previewing, 87
  - steps, 88-89
- saving, 36

Documents folders, 43

downloads, visualizations, 115

drag-and-drop copying, folders, 54

dragging files
- copying, 64
- moving, 63

drawings
- adding text, 285
- color, 286
- erasing part, 287
- shapes, 284

drivers
- best substitutes, 251
- reinstallation, 250

drives
- Explorer Window, basics, 44-45
- locating files, 38
- viewing system contents, 42

DVDs
- burning, 123
- copying pictures to, 103
- playing, 124

E

Ease of Access Center, 206-209

email
- contacts
  - adding addresses, 142-143
  - using to enter names, 144
- files, 70
- junk mail
  - filtering, 151
  - setting options, 152-153
- mail folders
  - creating, 145
  - moving messages, 146
  - searching for messages, 147
- pictures, 106
- sending, 126, 262
- Windows Mail
  - attaching file to message, 136
  - Delete Items folder cleanup, 139
  - deleting messages, 138
  - email options setting, 140-141
  - forwarding messages, 132
  - opening file attachment, 137
  - reading mail, 130
  - responding to mail, 131
  - sending new mail, 134-135
  - sorting messages, 133
  - starting, 128-129

entertainment, media management, 7
Eraser tool, 287
error messages, hyperlinks, 158
exiting programs, 32
Explorer, 2, 5
  files
    opening, 68
    printing, 70
Explorer Window
  changing folder view, 49
  customizing layout, 51
  grouping content, 52
  opening folders, 44-45
  sorting content, 50
extracting compressed files, 238

F

Failure to Deliver notices, 134
favorite links, 39
Favorites Center
  adding site, 163
  organizing, 164
  rearranging, 166-167
  selecting site, 165
faxes
  configuring, 148-149
  receiving, 150
  sending, 150
files
  associations, setting, 69
  back up restoration, 256-257
  changing views, 61
  compressed
    extracting, 238
    saving space, 236-237
  copying, 64-65
  deleting, 66-67
  deselecting, 60
  disk cleanup, 235
  email sizes, 136
  emailing, 70
  Explorer
    opening, 68
    printing, 70
  grouping content, 52
  keywords, 6
  locating, 6, 38
    Instant Search, 71
    running saved searches, 73
    saving searches, 72
  moving, 63
  opening, 38-39
  preset folders, 43
  properties, adding, 75
  refreshing list, 46
  renaming, 62
  selecting, 60
  tags, 6, 74
  viewing details, 61
  viewing on home network, 298-299
  Windows Easy Transfer, 304-311
filters, junk mail, 151
firewalls
  Windows Easy Transfer, 307
  Windows Security Center, 182
flash drives, Windows Easy Transfer, 306
folders, 40
  copying, 54
  creating, 53
  deleting, 53, 57
  email
    creating, 145
    deleting, 145
    moving messages, 146
    searching for messages, 147
  Explorer Window
    basics, 44-45
    changing view, 49
    customizing layout, 51
    grouping content, 52
    sorting content, 50
  files
    copying, 64-65
    deleting, 66-67
    locating, 38
    moving, 63
  hierarchical lists, 45
  instant search, 46
  moving, 55
  naming, 53
  navigation, 46-47

- opening, 44
- presets, 43
- renaming, 56
- selection, 48
- sharing, 299
- viewing computer drives, 42
- viewing on home network, 298-299

fonts
- printers
  - installing new on computer, 94-95
  - viewing, 92-93
- printing sample list, 93
- sources, 92

G

Gadgets, 8

games
- controllers, 125
- controlling access, 191
- Windows Media Player, 125

Games folder, 2, 7

Google, search statistics, 162

Graphic Equalizer settings, 115

groups, 52

H

hard drives
- cleanup, 235
- compressed files
  - extracting, 238
  - saving space, 236-237
- defragmentation, 242-243
- disk information, 234
- Explorer Window, basics, 44-45
- Memory Diagnostic Tool, 239
- scanning for errors, 240-241
- viewing system contents, 42

hardware
- installation
  - manually, 248-249
  - troubleshooting, 250-251
- Internet requirements, 154

Help command, 24-25

Hibernate option, 26

hiding toolbars, 223

history, Windows Defender scans, 179

History List
- clearing, 169
- viewing, 168

Home buttons, 25

home networking
- printer
  - selecting shared, 302-303
  - set up, 300-301
- sharing options, 294-295
- viewing folders and files, 298-299
- viewing status, 296-297
- Windows Easy Transfer, 304-311
- wireless client set up, 290-293

home pages, Internet Explorer, 170

hyperlinks, browsing Internet, 158

I

icons
- creating for programs, 213
- deleting, 216
- desktop, adding, 15

images
- deleting from camera, 99
- displaying to desktop, 196-197
- transferring from digital camera, 99

input devices, volume options, 114

installation
- fonts on computer, 94-95
- hardware, manually, 248-249
- new programs, 212

installed printers, displaying, 82

Instant Search
- bar, 46
- feature, 6
- field, 10
- locating files, 71

interface, 4

Internet
- access from online services, 154
- emailing links, 171
- enhanced features, 9

Favorites Center
adding a site, 163
organizing, 164
rearranging, 166-167
selecting site, 165
firewalls protection, 182
hardware requirements, connecting, 154
History List
clearing, 169
viewing, 168
hyperlinks, 158
ISP accounts, 154
music purchase, 118-119
ordering photos, 107
printing Web page, 172-173
privacy levels, 185
search engines
basics, 162
searching text on page, 161
site built-in tools, 161
tabbed viewing, 160
time, 205
typing URL addresses, 159

Internet Explorer
emailing link, 171
launching, 156-157
setting home page, 170

Internet service providers. *See* ISPs

ISPs (Internet service providers), 154
connecting to Internet, 154
firewalls, 182
logging on and off, 128

J-L

junk mail, 130
filtering, 151
setting options, 152-153

keypads, 260

keywords, adding to files, 6, 74

labels, disks, 234

launching Internet Explorer, 156-157

layouts, windows, 129

Library, Windows Media Player, 113, 116, 120-121

links
emailing from Internet Explorer, 171
favorites, 39

List pane, hiding, 111

locating files
Instant Search, 71
running saved searches, 73
saving searches, 72

logoffs
computer account, 26
ISPs, 128

logons
computer account, 14
ISPs, 128

LPT ports, printers, 79

M

Magnifier tool, 283

mail
attaching file to messages, 136
Delete Items folder cleanup, 139
deleting messages, 138
email options setup, 140-141
forwarding, 132
opening file attachment, 137
reading, 130
responding to, 131
sending new, 134-135
sorting, 133

maintenance
back up file restoration, 256-257
Backup and Restore Center, 254-255
disks
cleanup, 235
compressing files, 236-238
defragmentation, 242-243
information, 234
Memory Diagnostic Tool, 239
scanning for errors, 240-241
hardware installation
manually, 248-249
troubleshooting, 250-251
power management, 231
scheduling tasks, 244-247
System Information, 232-233

System Restore, 252-253
Windows Updates
automatic, 228-229
manually, 230
malware, Windows Defender, 177-179
maximizing windows, 18-19
McAcfee VirusScan, 180
media, management, 7
Media Center, 2
Media Library, 7
Memory Diagnostic Tool, 239
Message Header pane, 131
messages
attaching file, 136
canceling before sending, 132
Delete Items folder cleanup, 139
deleting, 138-139
email options setting, 140-141
forwarding, 132
junk mail
filtering, 151
setting options, 152-153
locating, 147
moving to folders, 146
opening attachment, 137
receiving, 129
sending, 129
sending new, 134-135
sort order, 133
sorting, 133
spell check, 141
Minimize command, 19
minimizing windows, 19
modems, 126
monitors, resolution setting, 199
mouse, movement settings, 200-201
Move command, 19
movies, media management, 7
moving
files, 63
folders, 55
windows, 20
MSHOME default workgroups, 298
MSN, searching Internet, 161
multiple users
public folder sharing, 295
set up, 186-187
music
setting options, 113
Windows Media Player
burning CDs, 123
creating playlist, 120-121
online purchase, 118-119
ripping CD tracks, 122
searching, 117
Music folders, 43

N

naming
folders, 53, 56
renaming files, 62
navigation folders, 46-47
Navigation pane, 5, 63
folder hierarchical list, 45
opening folders, 44
Network and Sharing Center, 11, 294-295
Network Awareness, 11
Network Diagnostics, 11
Network Explorer, 11
networks
expanded features, 11
fax server connection, 149
firewalls, 182
printer
selecting shared, 302-303
set up, 300-301
sharing options, 294-295
viewing folders and files, 298-299
viewing status, 296-297
Windows Easy Transfer, 304-311
wireless client set up, 290-293
Norton AntiVirus, 180
Notepad, 282
notification areas, changing, 222
Num Lock button, 260

Index

O-P

opening files, 38-39, 68
optional updates, 230
Organize Favorites dialog box, 164
output devices, volume options, 114

Paint, 283
adding text, 285
color, 286
drawing shape, 284
erasing part of drawing, 287
paper sources, printer, 85
parental controls, setting for user accounts, 190-191
passwords
adding to account, 14
adding to accounts, 188-189
pausing printers, 91
performance
back up file restoration, 256-257
Backup and Restore Center, 254-255
disks
cleanup, 235
compressing files, 236-238
defragmentation, 242-243
information, 234
Memory Diagnostic Tool, 239
scanning for errors, 240-241
hardware installation
manually, 248-249
troubleshooting, 250-251
power management, 231
scheduling tasks, 244-247
System Information, 232-233
System Restore, 252-253
Windows Updates
automatic, 228-229
manually, 230
Personalization Control panel
accessibility options, 206-209
color schemes, 195
desktop
applying image, 197
backgrounds, 196
theme, 194
monitors, resolution setting, 199
mouse movements, 200-201
screen saver selection, 198
sound scheme, 202-203
system date and time, 204-205
phishing scams
checking Web sites, 183
defined, 10
Photo Gallery, 7
photos
copying to CD or DVD, 103
editing, 104-105
emailing, 106
media management, 7
ordering prints online, 107
organizing, 102
printing, 106-107
pictures
copying to CD or DVD, 103
deleting, 104
editing, 104-105
emailing, 106
ordering prints online, 107
organizing, 102
printing, 106-107
saving edited, 105
Pictures folders, 43, 101
Play Slide Show button, 102
playlists
audio CDs, 121
Windows Media Player, creating, 120-121
Plug and Play hardware detection, 248
pointers, mouse movement settings, 201
pop-ups, 184
ports, printers, 79
Ports tab, 86
power management, 231
Power Options dialog box, 231
preferences, setting for printer, 84-85
presets, folders, 43
Preview pane, 5, 129
previewing Web page, 172-173
Print buttons, 25, 88

Printer icons, displaying print queue, 90
printers
  adding, 78-81
  canceling print job, 91
  defaults, 80
  deleting, 83
  disk, 81
  displaying installed, 82
  documents
    preview, 87
    steps, 88-89
  fonts
    installing new on computer, 94-95
    viewing, 92-93
  multiple print copies, 89
  networks
    selecting shared, 302-303
    set up, 300-301
  paper sources, 85
  pausing, 91
  ports, 79
  preference selection, 84-85
  print ranges, 89
  setting default, 83
  setup, 70
  testing, 303
  viewing
    properties, 86
    queue, 90
Printers control panel, 70
printing
  files from Explorer, 70
  help topics, 25
  Web pages, 172-173
privacy, Internet security levels, 185
programs, 28. *See also* applications; software
  blocking access, 191
  documents, saving, 36
  exiting, 32
  installation, new, 212
  opening files, 38-39, 69
  pinning to Start menu, 217
  setting defaults, 224
  shortcut icon
    creating, 213
    deleting, 216
  starting from shortcut icon, 33
  starting from Start menu, 30-31
  switching between
    taskbar buttons, 34
    Windows Flip 3D, 35
  uninstalling, 214-215
  versus applications and software, 30
properties
  adding to files, 75
  viewing for printer, 86
Properties dialog box, 61, 234
public folders
  multiple user set up, 295
  sharing options, 294

Q-R

quarantined software, 178
queues, printers, 90

RAM (random access memory), 34, 239
Reading Pane, 5
recommended updates, 228
Rectangle tool, 284
Recycle Bin, 67
refreshing file lists, 46
reminders
  tasks, 271
  text, 75
renaming
  files, 62
  folders, 56
Reply All button, 131
resizing windows, 18, 21
resolution, monitors, 199
restarting computer, 27
restarts, computer updates, 230
restoration
  back up file restoration, 256-257
  Backup and Restore Center, 254-255
  System Restore, 252-253
Restore command, 19

S

safe senders, 153
Save As dialog box, 194
Save Search button, 72
saved searches, running, 73
saving
  documents, 36
  email attachments, 137
ScanDisk utility, 241
scanners, 96
  document scan, 100
  setup
    automatically, 98
    manual, 100-101
scans, Windows Defender, 179
scheduling tasks, 244-247
schemes, colors, 195
scientific calculators, 260
screen savers, selection, 198
scrollbars, 21
search engines
  basics, 162
  searching text on page, 161
  site built-in tools, 161
Search Folders, 6
searching files
  Instant Search, 71
  running saved searches, 73
  saving searches, 72
security
  account passwords, 14
  blocking pop-ups, 184
  email attachments, 137
  Internet privacy levels, 185
  users
    multiple user set up, 186-187
    parental controls, 190-191
    password assignment, 188-189
  Web site phishing, 183
  Windows Defender, 177-179
  Windows Security Center, 176
    checking virus status, 180-181
    firewall protection, 182
Security Center, 174, 176
  checking virus status, 180-181
  firewall protection, 182
  icon, 176
selecting
  files, 60
  folders, 48
Send To command, copying files, 65
senders
  blocking, 152
  safe, 153
sending
  email
    messages, 129
    system requirements, 126
  faxes, 150
Sent Items folders, 135
serial ports, printer connection, 79
settings, Windows Easy Transfer, 304
shapes, drawing, 284
sharing
  home networks, 294-295
  folders, 299
Sharing tab, 86
Sharing Wizard, 11
shortcut icons
  creating, 33
  creating for programs, 213
  deleting, 216
  starting programs, 33
shortcuts, Print button, 88
shutting down computer, 27
signal strengths, wireless networks, 297
Size command, 19
slide shows, 102
software. *See also* applications; programs
  versus programs and applications, 30
  quarantine, 178
  viewing installed programs, 178
Software Explorer, 178
Soper, Mark Edward, *Absolute Beginner's Guide to Home Networking*, 290
sound, scheme change, 202-203

spam, 130
  filtering, 151
  setting options, 152-153
speakers, volume control, 114
spell checking, email messages, 141
Spelling button, 141
spooling, 86
spyware, Windows Defender, 177-179
standard folders, Windows presets, 43
standard users, user types, 187
Start button, desktop, 15
Start menu
  customizing, 218-219
  desktop, 16-17
  pinning program, 217
  starting programs, 30-31
switching users, 188
System and Maintenance category, 226
  back up file restoration, 256-257
  Backup and Restore Center, 254-255
  disks
    cleanup, 235
    compressing files, 236-238
    defragmentation, 242-243
    information, 234
    Memory Diagnostic Tool, 239
    scanning for errors, 240-241
  hardware installation
    manually, 248-249
    troubleshooting, 250-251
  power management, 231
  scheduling tasks, 244-247
  System Information, 232-233
  System Restore, 252-253
  Windows Updates
    automatic, 228-229
    manually, 230
System Information, 232-233
System Restore, 252-253
system security, Windows Security Center, 176

T

tabbed viewing, Internet, 160
tags
  adding to files, 74
  adding to pictures, 104
  assigning to pictures, 103
  deleting, 74
  files, 6
taskbar buttons
  switch between programs, 34
  windows movements, 22
taskbars
  changing notification area, 222
  customizing, 220-221
  desktops, 15
tasks
  entering on Calendar, 271
  scheduling, 244-247
technical information, 232
testing printers, 303
text, WordPad
  copying, 276-277
  deleting, 275
  formatting, 280-281
  moving, 278-279
  selecting, 274
  typing, 273
Text tool, 285
Theme Settings dialog box, 194
themes, desktops, 194
time, system change, 204-205
time zones, changing, 205
toolbars, displaying or hiding, 223
Tools tab, 234
tracks
  audio CDs
    copying, 120
    shuffling, 113
  ripping audio CDs, 122
transparency, adjustment, 195

troubleshooting
- back up file restoration, 256-257
- Backup and Restore Center, 254-255
- hardware installation, 250-251
- Help commands, 24-25
- System Information, 232-233
- System Restore, 252-253

U

UAC (User Account Protection), 9

uniform resource locator (URLs), 159

unique colors, 195

unnamed networks, 291

updates
- optional, 230
- recommended, 228
- Windows Updates
  - automatic, 228-229
  - manually, 230

URGE, 7

URLs (uniform resource locator), 159

USB flash drives, Windows Easy Transfer, 306

USBs, printer connection, 79

Use Default Settings button, 219

User Account Control, 229

User Account Control dialog box, 229, 294

User Account Protection (UAC), 9

users
- multiple user set up, 186-187
- parental controls, 190-191
- password assignment, 188-189
- switching, 26, 188

V

video, Windows Media Player, 124

View Files button, 235

views, files, 61

viruses
- available antivirus programs, 180
- infecting computers, 181
- Windows Defender, 177-179
- Windows Security Center, checking status, 180-181

Visualizations, 115

volume, audio CDs, 114

W-Z

Web
- Favorites Center
  - adding a site, 163
  - organizing, 164
  - rearranging, 166-167
  - selecting site, 165
- History List
  - clearing, 169
  - viewing, 168
- hyperlinks, 158
- printing page, 172-173
- search engines
  - basics, 162
  - searching text on page, 161
  - site built-in tools, 161
- tabbed viewing, 160
- URLs defined, 159

Web sites, checking for phishing, 183

Welcome Center, 14, 233

Window Vista Web Filter, 191

windows
- arrangement, 23
- closing, 22
- layout change, 129
- maximizing, 18-19
- minimizing, 19
- moving, 20
- resizing, 18, 21
- scrollbars, 21

Windows Calendar, 8

Windows Defender, 174, 177-179

Windows Easy Transfer, 304-311

Windows Explorer, displaying, 47

Windows Flip 3D, switch between programs, 35

Windows Mail, 127
- attaching file to message, 136
- contacts
  - adding addresses, 142-143
  - using to enter names, 144
- Delete Items folder cleanup, 139
- deleting messages, 138
- email options setting, 140-141
- folders
  - creating, 145
  - moving messages, 146
  - searching for messages, 147
- forwarding messages, 132
- junk mail
  - filtering, 151
  - setting options, 152-153
- opening file attachment, 137
- reading mail, 130
- redesign, 10
- responding to mail, 131
- sending new mail, 134-135
- sorting messages, 133
- starting, 128-129

Windows Media Player, 108
- audio CD
  - playing, 110
  - shuffling tracks, 113
  - visualizations, 115
  - volume options, 114
- burning CDs, 123
- controls, 112
- games, 125
- Library, 113, 116, 120-121
- music
  - online purchase, 118-119
  - searching, 117
- playing video clips, 124
- ripping CD tracks, 122
- window basics, 111

Windows Photo Gallery, 2, 7
- camera
  - copying pictures to CD or DVD, 103
  - manual setup, 100-101
  - organizing pictures, 102
- digital camera
  - automatic setup, 98
  - transferring images from, 99
- photographs
  - fixing, 104-105
  - printing, 106-107
- scanner
  - automatic setup, 98
  - manual setup, 100-101

Windows Security Center. *See* Security Center

Windows Update dialog box, 230

Windows Updates
- automatic, 228-229
- manually, 230

Windows Vista, updates
- accessories, 8
- Explorers, 5
- finding files, 6
- interface, 4
- Internet features, 9
- media management, 7
- network feature expansion, 11
- Windows Mail redesign, 10

WinZip, compressing email files, 136

wireless networks, client set up, 290-293

wizards
- adding printers, 78-81
- dialog box Back button, 78

WordPad, text, 272
- copying, 276-277
- deleting, 275
- formatting, 280-281
- moving, 278-279
- selecting, 274
- typing, 273

WORKGROUP default workgroups, 298

workgroup names, 298

worms, Windows Defender, 177-179

zooming, 283